Striving in the Path of God

Asma Afsaruddin is Professor of Islamic Studies and Chairperson of the Department of Near Eastern Languages and Cultures at Indiana University, Bloomington. She is the author of *The First Muslims: History and Memory* (2008) and *Excellence and Precedence: Medieval Islamic Discourse on Legitimate Leadership* (2002).

Striving in the Path of God

Jihād *and Martyrdom in Islamic Thought*

ASMA AFSARUDDIN

OXFORD
UNIVERSITY PRESS

OXFORD
UNIVERSITY PRESS

Oxford University Press is a department of the University of Oxford.
It furthers the University's objective of excellence in research, scholarship,
and education by publishing worldwide.

Oxford New York
Auckland Cape Town Dar es Salaam Hong Kong Karachi
Kuala Lumpur Madrid Melbourne Mexico City Nairobi
New Delhi Shanghai Taipei Toronto

With offices in
Argentina Austria Brazil Chile Czech Republic France Greece
Guatemala Hungary Italy Japan Poland Portugal Singapore
South Korea Switzerland Thailand Turkey Ukraine Vietnam

Published in the United States of America by
Oxford University Press
198 Madison Avenue, New York, NY 10016

First issued as an Oxford University Press paperback, 2024

Library of Congress Cataloging-in-Publication Data
Afsaruddin, Asma, 1958-
Striving in the path of God : jihād and martyrdom in Islamic thought / Asma Afsaruddin.
p. cm.
Includes bibliographical references and index.
ISBN 978–0–19–973093–3 (hardcover : alk. paper) | ISBN 978–0–19–778709–0 (paperback)
1. Jihad. 2. Religious life – Islam. 3. Martyrdom – Islam. I. Title.
BP182.A34 2013
297.7'2 – dc23
2012037220
ISBN 978–0–19–973093–3

Paperback printed by Marquis Book Printing, Canada

MIX
Paper | Supporting responsible forestry
FSC® C103567

To my mother, Maleka Khatun, for all that I owe her

Contents

Preface

SINCE THE PUBLICATION of *Striving in the Path of God: Jihād and Martyrdom in Islamic Thought* in 2013, interest in the term *jihād* and its meanings has not abated, either inside or outside the Western academy. Despite the polyvalence of the term *jihād*, it continues to be deployed, particularly in many Western media outlets, as primarily one that should evoke fear on the part of Western populations. *Jihād*, these outlets routinely inform us, exclusively connotes violent ideological warfare to be waged relentlessly by Muslims *in toto* against Westerners *in toto*, because the former are religiously required to subdue or even annihilate the latter (never mind that there are Western Muslims as well). *Jihād* is thus inevitably violent in nature and constitutes "holy war"—often conceived along the lines of the medieval European crusades launched against Muslim southwest Asian lands.

A recent development in some sectors of the American media and in American politics has been to use *jihād* as a term of opprobrium to describe the activities of groups or individuals one disagrees with and dislikes. On his show that aired on Fox Business Network on July 30, 2018, the media personality Lou Dobbs described Robert Mueller, then Special Counsel in the US Department of Justice, as being "on a *jihād* of some sort" against former President Trump for undertaking an investigation into possible Russian interference during the 2016 US presidential elections. Through this cavalier use of the term *jihād*, Dobbs meant to impress upon his audience that Mueller's investigation was illegitimate, motivated only by ideological, partisan reasons, the undertaking of which threatened to sabotage an orderly way of life. In a similar vein, Colorado Representative Lauren Boebert described Minnesota Representative Ilhan Omar as a member of a "jihād squad," who could be credibly suspected of carrying a bomb into the elevator of the US congressional building, solely because she is Muslim. Apparently, *jihād*, in contemporary American shorthand, may carry the imputation of extremism to the beliefs and conduct of those one regards with disdain, even, or perhaps especially, in the highest political circles.

Not too long after the book's appearance in 2013, new terror groups, most notably ISIS, purporting to carry out *jihād*, gained prominence on the world stage. Prior to their appearance, al-Qaeda had seemed deadly enough; ISIS by comparison was over the top, reveling in a no-holds-barred violence particularly directed at civilians and performing acts that in their own words amounted to "savagery."[1] Their brutal actions commanded global attention, reviving debates over what constitutes the legitimate parameters of a military *jihād*. The overall objectives of *Striving in the Path of God* thus remain just as relevant in 2023 as they did a decade ago: to "seek to retrieve early multivalent connotations of the terms *jihād* and *shahīd* in the formative period and to contextualize the competing discourses that crystallized around these terms through the centuries."[2] Such a longue-durée approach helps us understand the various meanings assigned to *jihād* by various actors in specific socio-historical and political circumstances and the way they became manifest in response to these specific circumstances. Such an approach helps us avoid falling into an essentialist and reductive mode of thinking.

ISIS's usurpation of the term *jihād* to describe its campaign of terror did not go uncontested. In September 2014, 122 prominent Muslim scholars, jurists, and community leaders came together to issue a stinging denunciation of ISIS and its scorched-earth tactics in what was called the "Letter to al-Baghdadi," addressed to the self-styled ISIS caliph, Abu Bakr al-Baghdadi (d. 2019). The document provided a detailed theological and legal refutation of ISIS's views on the military *jihād*, emphasizing how far they had veered from mainstream scholarly understandings of the same. Above all, the document stressed that Islamic law forbids the killing of innocent civilians and that a legitimate military *jihād* can only be defensive. Torture of prisoners of war and mutilation of corpses are morally unconscionable and constitute a grave violation of fundamental Islamic ethical and legal principles.

Many of the points stressed in the "Letter to al-Baghdadi" find reflection in *Striving in the Path of God*. These points are extrapolated from a close, holistic reading of the Qur'an, comprehensive surveys of exegeses of relevant Qur'ānic verses, scrutiny of relevant prophetic and non-prophetic reports culled from the voluminous hadith literature, and literary treatises in praise of both non-combative and combative dimensions of *jihād*. In this holistic vein, the book highlights the Qur'ānic position that Muslims may resort to fighting only when attacked by the enemy first. Peaceful people, regardless of their religion, are to be left alone and treated kindly. Given this defensive nature of the military *jihād* outlined in the Qur'ān, it is not surprising that early Qur'ān exegeses and early hadith compilations record the dismay of many pious Muslims from the first and second centuries of Islam over the launching of offensive military campaigns under the rubric of *jihād* by the Umayyads and, later, the Abbasids. These sources frequently document the reluctance of piety-minded individuals to enlist in the imperial armies and their growing concern over attempts in political and legal circles to aggrandize the importance of armed combat and military martyrdom.

The sources further reveal a regional divide between Hijazi and Syrian scholars during the Umayyad period, with many among the former continuing to uphold the Qur'ānic position of fighting only in self-defense while many among the latter came to endorse offensive military activity. There was also a substantial contingent of Muslims in the early period who robustly maintained that fighting was a religious obligation imposed on the Companions only during the time of the Prophet against the aggressive pagan Meccans who had attacked them, and that this obligation had lapsed after Muhammad's death, basing their position on interpretations of Qur'ān 2:216. This diversity of views in the early period is significant because it undermines the position that jihad is unremittingly aggressive in nature and that this was the consensual view among Muslims already in the first century of Islam.

Another finding that emerges from a close and holistic reading of the Qur'ān and a diachronic survey of the exegetical literature is that Muslims in the early centuries of Islam did not accord a superior status to the military martyr over the pious individual who dies of natural causes. The Qur'ān does not even have a term that refers exclusively to the military martyr; in its Qur'ānic usage, the term *shahīd* (as well as its cognate *shāhid*) refers only to an eye-witness and/or a legal witness. The later meaning of martyr attached to the term *shahīd* took a while to develop under the influence of extraneous sources. The view that the cult of martyrdom is inherent in the Islamic tradition is then readily belied by these Qur'anic perspectives. Militant groups, however, have no patience with, or time for, perspectives that contradict their own. They thumb their noses at evidence-based scholarly perspectives that undermine their violent worldview, even if they can be credibly attributed to the "pious forebears" (*al-salaf al-ṣāliḥ*), whose positions they claim to revere and replicate.[3] The scholarly consensus expressed in the "Letter to al-Baghdadi" expressing condemnation of ISIS's militancy based on such perspectives firmly places these groups outside of the Islamic mainstream.

Unlike most academic writings on *jihād*, *Striving in the Path of God* additionally emphasizes the non-combative and peaceful dimensions of *jihād* encapsulated by the Qur'ānic term *ṣabr* (which I translate as patient forbearance) and its derivatives. Given the conditional and limited nature of the military *jihād* as described in the Qur'ān, the practice of patient forbearance by the faithful during their quotidian internal and physical struggles is accorded far greater importance in the Qur'ān. Muslim scholars have always recognized the importance of this trait; some of them wrote treatises in praise of *ṣabr* as the unconditional, enduring aspect of *jihād* undertaken by Muslims in the course of their daily lives in order to enjoin what is good and to prevent and resist wrongdoing with a variety of means. The famous scholar Fakhr al-Dīn al-Rāzī (d. 606/1210), for example, emphasized the practice of *musābara* (a word derived from *sabr* that means "showing patient forbearance with others") as an integral, mundane dimension of *jihād* which prompts believers to be continuously engaged in counseling one another to behave righteously and to curb their own base desires.[4]

These variegated perspectives on the multiple aspects of *jihād* get lost if we only focus on the legal genre of *siyar*, which, by virtue of its raison d'être, developed as a result of early juridical concern for crafting international law that governs relations with external polities. Within this circumscribed world, the military *jihād* played an essential role in ensuring the security and defense of Muslim realms and of the lives of all those, Muslim and non-Muslim, who resided there. To restrict academic discussions of *jihād* to the legal realm only and ignore various non-legal genres that also deal with this critical concept is to miss the big picture. Since this tendency still remains the norm, the multiple inflections of the term *jihād* have become all but occluded in the Western academy, so much so that certain academics in the West can still get away in the contemporary period with asserting that *jihād* refers primarily to violent military activity that can be carried out by Muslims willy-nilly against non-Muslims without provocation and just cause and that modern Muslims are dissembling when they ascribe a Qur'anic pedigree to the concept of spiritual *jihād*.

In contrast to this Western Orientalist tradition of deprecating any attribution of a peaceful dimension to the concept of *jihād*, *Striving in the Path of God* establishes a clear and direct genealogical connection between *ṣabr* as the constant, predominant dimension of *jihād* in the Qur'ān and the later evolution of the concept of *jihād al-nafs* ("spiritual struggle") or *al-jihād al-akbar* ("the greater struggle") through discussion of relevant sources. As I point out, when al-Ghazālī (d. 505/1111) and Ibn Qayyim al-Jawziyya (d. 751/1350) discuss the spiritual and moral aspects of *jihād*, they use the term *ṣabr*, providing us with valuable textual evidence for the direct derivation of the notion of spiritual struggle from the Qur'ān itself. This genealogical connection allows us to move beyond arid conversations fixated on proclaiming the lateness and unreliable status of the much-cited *ḥadīth*: "We have returned from the lesser *jihād* to the greater *jihād*"—as if that by itself can provide "ammunition" (so to speak) for the position that *jihād* refers only to violent military activity. Instead, by breaking with Western academic tradition in this case and canvassing a broader range of relevant non-legal genres, the book engages in a much richer and more rewarding discussion of how the intrinsically spiritual and moral dimensions of the Qur'ānic *jihād* continued to inform Muslim perspectives from the very beginning of Islam on how to strive to live purposeful, meaningful lives amid the vicissitudes of human earthly existence. My hope remains that the book's discussion of the spiritual and moral aspects of *jihād* will continue to contribute to the awareness that terminologies can change as they evolve in response to changing socio-historical circumstances and crystallize around certain concepts and ideas. The careful scholar does not lose sight of this basic fact when consulting primary sources.

By reading in the nooks and crannies of religious and literary texts, I was also able to exhume certain voices from the earliest centuries of Islam that questioned and decried the increasing militarization of Muslim societies from the late first/seventh century onward. Such voices were critical of the tendency of Umayyad and Abbasid rulers to place the project of empire-building under the rubric of *jihād* and the exaggerated importance given to the military *jihād* in such an enterprise. These voices and perspectives can be retrieved from the copious hadith and exegetical literature, and from certain edifying literary works, such as *al-Sabr wa al-thawab 'alayhi* composed by the third/ninth century scholar Ibn Abī 'l-Dunyā (d. 281/894).

This pre-modern strand of moral and ethical thinking on *jihād* has enjoyed a resurgence in the modern period. In 2022, Jawdat Said and Wahiduddin Khan, two prominent proponents of the peacemaking and non-violent aspects of *jihād*, whose thought I discuss in the book, passed away. However, the importance of their thought and the impact of their writings have not faded. In recent times, attention on such peacemaking efforts within the Islamic milieu which draw their inspiration from Islamic texts and historical precedents has only grown.[5]

It is to be hoped that the issuance of this more affordably-priced paperback edition of *Striving in the Path of God* will allow nuanced and informed conversations on *jihād* to continue to grow among both a specialist and non-specialist readership in the United States and elsewhere. Moving forward, if such conversations help to strip public discussions of this vital topic of the sensationalism and uninformed hysteria that unfortunately often accompanies them, I will consider the book to have achieved one of its principal objectives.

Acknowledgments

FIRST AND FOREMOST, I acknowledge with gratitude the research grant awarded to me by the Harry Frank Guggenheim Foundation that allowed me to go on sabbatical leave during 2003–2004, when I began the initial research for this monograph. Profound gratitude is also owed in particular to the Carnegie Corporation of New York for a very generous grant that funded another sabbatical year (2006–2007), during which period the research for this project was completed and the bulk of the writing accomplished. I also thank the Institute for Scholarship in the Liberal Arts and the Joan B. Kroc Institute for International Peace Studies, both at the University of Notre Dame, for awarding me grants in the summers of 2003 and 2008 to carry out additional research for this project.

The comments and feedback provided by several colleagues at various stages have been invaluable. I gratefully acknowledge their generosity with their time and am indebted to the following (in alphabetical order) for their careful reading of all or parts of the manuscript: Jonathan Brockopp, Wael Hallaq, Louise Marlow, and David Marshall. Over the years, I have benefited from my conversations on *jihād* and related matters with a number of friends and colleagues: Harifyyah ʻAbd al-Haleem, Muhammad Abu Nimer, Waleed al-Ansary, Mahmoud Ayoub, Karim Crow, Maria Dakake, Sohail Hashmi, Qamar-ul Huda, James Turner Johnson, Ibrahim Kalin, John Kelsay, Muqtedar Khan, Joseph Lumbard, Stephen Sizer, James Sterba, and Brian Wicker. Portions of this manuscript at various stages were presented at various colloquia and invited lectures. My thanks to all those who provided feedback and comments at these gatherings sponsored by the University of Edinburgh, Mt. Holyoke College, George Mason University, Georgetown University, the United States Institute of Peace, the United Nations Peacekeeping Forces, the Carnegie Corporation, Columbia University, Indiana University, Lund University, Sweden; Birkbeck College, London; Goettingen University, Germany; School of Oriental and African Studies, London; University of Leeds, England; and Blackfriars Hall, Oxford University.

My thanks are further due to two of my former undergraduate research assistants at the University of Notre Dame, Laura Meyer and Kendall Hannon, who helped me compile the bibliography for this book. I also owe a considerable debt of gratitude to my current graduate research assistant at Indiana University, Michael Bevers, who meticulously proofread the entire manuscript and painstakingly prepared the index. My thanks also go to the library staff at the University of Notre Dame, Indiana University, the Chester Beatty Library in Dublin, Ireland, the Bibliothèque Nationale de France in Paris, and the Bodleian Libraries at Oxford University for helping me gain access to necessary materials, both published and unpublished.

The editor at Oxford University Press, Cynthia Read, was an expert and cheerful guide from start to finish, and her efficient staff members were most helpful during the production stage. It was a delight to work with them, and I remain most grateful for their gracious assistance throughout the complex process of finalizing the manuscript for publication.

I would be gravely remiss if I did not acknowledge all the students in my class "War and Peace in the Islamic Tradition," which was taught at Indiana University in fall 2010 and fall 2011. Their lively engagement with the near-final version of the manuscript prompted me to clarify and fine-tune some of the material. I thank the following graduate students in particular for useful discussions beyond the classroom during the last three years: Christopher Anzalone, Michael Bevers, and Kevin Arif Meskill.

I would also be remiss if I did not acknowledge the moral support of my family—especially my mother, Maleka Khatun, whose love for learning and commitment to integrity at all levels have considerably shaped my own worldview. I dedicate this book to her in profound acknowledgment of her influence in my life. My sisters, Najma Hasib and Salma Hassan, constantly egged me on toward the finishing line.

Finally, as always, I remain indebted to my husband, Steve Vinson, without whose unflagging championship and constant encouragement this project could not have been accomplished. Despite his own hectic schedule, he took the time to read through the manuscript and saved me from a number of infelicities. Needless to say, any remaining mistakes are mine alone.

Striving in the Path of God

Introduction

MODERN ACADEMIC TREATMENTS of *jihād* almost invariably focus on the legal dimensions of this concept and hence emphasize its military signification. Such discussions mostly draw upon the extensive pre-modern Islamic juridical literature for explicating the semantic and legal parameters of the term.[1] Comprehensive surveys of broader, multiple inflections of the concept in other non-legal genres and corpora are far less common.[2] In both popular and scholarly literature, *jihād* is primarily assumed to be a monovalent concept referring to "military/armed combat," as became the predominant meaning in juridical and administrative literature by the second/eighth century. This assumption facilitates the discussion of *jihād* as a term with a nearly fixed, universal meaning divorced from the varying sociopolitical contexts in which it has been deployed through time. Recent scholarship has continued to replicate these discussions, but now usually with an added study of the violent movements that invoke *jihād* in the contemporary period.

In contradistinction to this approach, this monograph seeks to study in a more holistic manner the changing significations of *jihād* from the earliest formative period of Islam to the contemporary period, against the background of specific historical and political circumstances that have mediated the meanings of this critical term. This larger objective has entailed canvassing a more varied genre of texts—a discussion of which occurs below—to recreate a more multifaceted understanding of *jihād* as a dynamic discursive term throughout time.

Linked to *jihād* is the socio-legal concept of "martyrdom." Martyrdom, in particularly its military sense, came to be signified by the Arabic term *shahāda* by the second/eighth century. The plurality of meanings associated with *jihād* in early and especially non-legal literature is complemented by early multiple conceptualizations of martyrdom. Both concepts would subsequently become considerably circumscribed in meaning. To retrieve the semantic trajectory of these two concepts, particularly from the first three centuries of Islam, we have to consult diverse relevant sources. First on the list of these sources, of course, is the Qur'ān and early commentaries on it, followed by early *ḥadīth* compilations predating the better-known authoritative *ḥadīth* collections from the third/ninth century on and early treatises on the excellences of *jihād*.

The Qur'ān—the earliest recorded text we have dating from the first century of Islam—is the point of departure for the treatment of the first diverse inflections of the concepts of *jihād* and martyrdom in the Islamic milieu.[3] The Qur'ān preserves in particular a semantic spectrum for the term *jihād* and its derivatives that progressively came to be either downplayed or elided in much of the later literature. In the Qur'ān, derivatives from the root *jhd* (usually occurring as verbal forms) have the basic signification of "struggling," "striving," and "exertion." The lexeme *jihād* occurs only twice in the Qur'ān. In extra-Qur'anic literature, *jihād,* usually with the definite article *al-* is frequently conjoined to the phrase "*fī sabīl allāh*" (lit. "in the path of God"); the full locution in Arabic—*al-jihād fī sabīl allāh*—then yields the meaning of "struggling/striving for the sake of God." This translation points to the polysemy of the term *jihād* and the potentially different meanings that may be ascribed to it in different contexts, because the phrase "in the path of/for the sake of God" allows for human striving to be accomplished in multiple ways.

Two other Qur'anic terms are of relevance here: *Qitāl* is the term used in the Qur'ān to specifically refer to "fighting" or "armed combat" and is a component of *jihād* in specific situations. *Ḥarb* is the Arabic word for "war" in general. The Qur'ān employs this last term four times: to refer to illegitimate wars fought by those who wish to spread corruption on earth (5:64); to the thick of battle between believers and nonbelievers (8:57; 47:4); and, in one instance, to the possibility of war waged by God and His prophet against those who would continue to practice usury (2:279).[4] This term is never used with the phrase "in the path of God" and has no bearing on the concept of *jihād*.[5]

There is yet a fourth Qur'anic term that I argue has a direct bearing on *jihād,* although it has not received due attention as such in most academic literature. This term is *ṣabr,* referring to the attributes of "patience," "forbearance," and "steadfastness," and which we, for the most part, translate as "patient forbearance." In Qur'anic discourse, *ṣabr* is a stable component and manifestation of the striving of the righteous; quietist and activist resistance to wrongdoing is equally valorized in a number of verses. For example, one Qur'anic verse (16:110) states: "As for those who after persecution fled their homes and strove actively (*jāhadū*) and were patient (*ṣabarū*) to the last, your Lord will be forgiving and merciful to them on the day when every soul will come pleading for itself." Another (Qur'ān 47:31) states: "We shall put you to the test until We know the active strivers (*al-mujāhidīn*) and the quietly forbearing (*al-ṣābirīn*) among you."

The Qur'anic conjoining of derivatives from *jhd* and *ṣbr* in several verses is highly significant but has barely been noted in most modern, particularly Western, academic treatments of *jihād*. The principal reason for this is that most modern discussions of this concept have typically focused on Muslim juridical discussions of *jihād* as an important duty within the context of state security and international relations, mainly in the Arabic legal genre known as *siyar*. As a consequence, the reduction by jurists of *jihād* to primarily one, albeit important, component of it—*qitāl* or fighting—receives undue emphasis in these modern academic works.[6] In contradistinction to this approach, pre-modern Muslim edifying literature concerned with "striving in the path of God" in various aspects of life beyond the arena of international politics often dealt with *ṣabr* as an essential ingredient of *jihād*, broadly understood as the overall human struggle on earth. A number of modern and contemporary works (twentieth century to the present time) have started to place a renewed, greater emphasis on *ṣabr* as the most important Qur'anic component of *jihād* that particularly conduces to principled nonviolence, as we discuss in chapter 9.

The progressive juridical—as well as exegetical—conflation of *jihād* with *qitāl* that occurred in the pre-modern period (and continued into the modern period)[7] is reflected in the way martyrdom also came to be progressively understood in similar contexts as essentially dying on the battlefield. The Qur'ān, early *ḥadīth* works, and early exegetical literature provide important correctives to this later, reductive view. It is highly significant that the Qur'ān does not have a single word for "martyr" or "martyrdom"—two concepts that are assumed to be intrinsically linked to the concept of *jihād* as armed combat against external enemies. The common Arabic word for martyr became *shahīd*. It is telling that nowhere in the Qur'ān is this lexeme used for a martyr; rather it is only used, interchangeably with *shāhid*, to refer to a legal witness or an eyewitness. Its plural *shuhadā'* is similarly used in reference to legal or eyewitnesses. Only in later extra-Qur'anic sources does *shahīd* (and its plural *shuhadā'*) acquire the specific meaning of "one who bears witness for the faith," particularly by laying down his (or her) life.

The Qur'ān, however, does express a high regard for those among the faithful who die in the service of Islam, particularly in its military defense. One of the Qur'anic verses (3:169—cf. also 47:4; 2:154) that has been construed to refer to the special status of the military martyr states: "Do not think that those who were slain in the path of God are dead. Rather they are alive and well provided for by their Lord." Early exegetical and *ḥadīth* works make clear, however, that the phrase "slain in the path of God" was not understood as an exclusive reference to those who fall in battle only, but could be glossed in several ways. For example, the early *ḥadīth* work *al-Muṣannaf* of ʿAbd al-Razzāq (d. 211/827), which was compiled earlier than the authoritative *ḥadīth* collection of al-Bukhārī (d. 256/870), contains a number of reports that relate multiple combative and non-combative definitions of martyrdom that are not always reproduced in later compilations.[8]

The comparison and interrogation of a larger variety of sources—the Qur'ān, early and later *ḥadīth* compilations, and exegetical and ethical/edifying literature—lead to the conclusion that the progressive formulation of fairly monolithic classical juridical views of *jihād* and martyrdom owes considerable impetus to the rise and consolidation of the imperial Umayyad and ʿAbbasid states and the establishment of a strong military during these periods. This is reflected in the way that some jurists working in the heartlands of Syria and Iraq, such as Makḥūl al-Dimashqī (d. between 112/730–119/737) in the second/eighth century and al-Shāfiʿī (d. 204/820) in the third/ninth century, were often willing to defer to *Realpolitik* and interpret the military purview of *jihād* in ways that were at times downright contradictory to Qur'anic injunctions—for example, in their endorsement of the military *jihād* as an obligatory duty for all and as offensive combat. Arguably, support for statist policies of territorial expansion provided the impetus, at least partially, for this interpretive and legal proclivity. Other authorities, like Abū Salāma b. ʿAbd al-Raḥmān (d. between 94/712–104/722), and Sufyān al-Thawrī (d. 161/777), not known to be close to the ruling elites of their time, would endorse only a defensive *jihad* in response to a prior act of aggression by enemy forces and did not regard the combative *jihād* to be a religious obligation. The nexus between the rise of the Umayyad and ʿAbbasid states and their imperial objectives, the consolidation of a powerful class of religious scholars, and the classical narratives of *jihād* as military combat are among the intriguing issues that we attempt to explore in this study.

Without doubt, the historical reality was complex; master narratives woven together by official chroniclers and men of religion were contested and sometimes rewritten, usually on the margins of society. Counterposed to the predominant and better-known juridical and statist narratives of *jihād* was also what I call the "dissenting literature," produced by amorphous groups that appear to have challenged the exclusively militarist interpretations of *jihād* and martyrdom. As some sources indicate, these alternate voices belonged to certain pietist individuals and groups in the early period, who appear to express their dismay in these narratives at the perceived self-aggrandizing, materialistic motivations for *jihād* on the part of the administrative-military establishment. These alternate voices are occasionally embedded in early *ḥadīth* works, such as the aforementioned *al-Musannaf* of 'Abd al-Razzāq al-Ṣan'ānī, and in didactic/edifying/hortatory works written in praise of patient forbearance (Ar *faḍā'il al- ṣabr*), as part of the prolific *faḍā'il* literary genre, such as the one by Ibn Abī 'l-Dunyā (d. 281/894) discussed in chapter 7. A number of reports included in such early works clearly contest reports in later *ḥadīth* collections that assign the highest merit to military martyrs. Taken together, the existence of these two parallel strands in the *ḥadīth* and edifying literature testify to competing discourses on modalities of piety and the construction of moral excellence, particularly in the early centuries of Islam. Proceeding from this premise, part of this study goes on to contextualize the evolution of this didactic and hortatory literature: to explore why and when these particular types of *faḍā'il* works were being produced and to attempt to identify the probable external influences shaping the broader contours of this discourse.[9]

Thesis and Plan

The main thesis of this study is that the conceptualizations of *jihād* as *primarily* armed combat and of *shahāda* as *primarily* military martyrdom are relatively late and contested ones, and deviate considerably from the Qur'anic significations of these terms. A comprehensive interrogation of variegated early and late sources belonging to the genres identified above allows valuable evidence to be adduced in favor of early and competing multiple definitions of "striving in the path of God." By diachronically tracing the discourse on *jihād* through a close examination of the contents of these primary sources, this work aims to conclusively establish the change in the trajectory of meanings assigned to this term and its correlate *shahīd* over time, linking the narrowing of the semantic purview of these terms to specific sociopolitical circumstances—insofar as it is possible for us to reconstruct them. This linkage will occasionally be further anchored through a critical examination of the chains of transmission (*isnād*) of frequently cited reports in the earlier and later exegetical and *ḥadīth*, including *faḍā'il*, works pertaining to *jihād* and martyrdom. Close scrutiny of the chains of transmission of certain significant reports occurring in these literatures allows us to focus on the principal and recurrent narrators of such reports and to reflect on what that might tell us about the possible provenance of these statements, the probable time of their propagation, and the likely ideological motivations of the narrators. Through the diachronic study of the different sources identified above, we seek to retrieve early multivalent connotations of the terms *jihād* and *shahīd* in the formative period and to contextualize the competing discourses that crystallized around these terms through the centuries.

This book consists of nine chapters in addition to this introduction, followed by a conclusion. Chapter 1 discusses the non-combative dimensions of the Qur'anic concepts of *jihād* and *ṣabr* from the middle-Meccan to the early Medinan period through the prism of selected pre-modern Sunnī, Shīʿī, and Ibāḍī exegetical works from the Umayyad through the Mamluk periods. Modern exegetical discussions of *jihād* are deferred to later chapters.

Chapters 2 and 3 discuss the Qur'anic imperative of *qitāl* (fighting) introduced in the Medinan period as an important component of *jihād* in specific circumstances and subject to certain conditions. The focus in these chapters, as in chapter 1, is on the retrieval of multiple and contested understandings of this conditional religious obligation through a diachronic survey of exegeses of key, relevant verses. Chapter 4 discusses the concept of martyrdom in the Qur'ān as primarily adumbrated in the ambiguous and multivalent phrase *man qutila fī sabīl allāh* ("those who are slain in the path of God") and its variants, once again through a diachronic survey of the exegeses of key verses containing a version of this locution. One verse (Qur'ān 4:74) that refers to bartering one's life in this world for life in the next is also discussed. Chapter 5 scrutinizes the *faḍā'il al-jihād* reports contained in the early *ḥadīth* works, including the early *Muṣannaf* works of the previously mentioned ʿAbd al-Razzāq (d. 211/827) and Ibn Abī Shayba (d. 235/849) and the six authoritative Sunni *ḥadīth* compilations. Chapter 6 discusses and compares early *faḍā'il al-jihād* treatises, such as the *Kitāb al- jihād* of ʿAbd Allāh Ibn al-Mubārak (d. 181/797) with later *faḍa'il al-jihād* works (roughly after the fourth/tenth century), such as the *Mashāriʿ al-ashwāq ilā maṣāriʿ al-ʿushshāq* of Ibn al-Naḥḥās (d. 814/1411). An extensive comparison of these treatises enables us to map the semantic landscape forming around *jihād* and related terms, as reflected in this primarily *ḥadīth*-based discourse, and permits the establishment of a repertoire of meanings assigned to these terms and their sociopolitical/legal implications in different historical contexts. In both chapters 5 and 6, the chains of transmission of a number of critical reports are scrutinized in order to single out their most prolific narrators and dwell on their status as *ḥadīth* transmitters, thereby allowing us in some cases to speculate on the probable motivations for the propagation of these reports and assess their reliability. Chapter 7 focuses on literature that extols the merits of patient forbearance (*ṣabr*), which includes mainly Qur'ān commentaries and individual treatises on this topic. To what extent this emphasis on the inculcation of *ṣabr* mitigates and challenges the predominantly statist/military conceptualizations of *jihād* is explored. Once again, we resort to selective scrutiny of the chains of transmission of a number of these reports in praise of *ṣabr* to determine their probable provenance and the possible ideological motivations of their transmitters.

Chapter 8 discusses modern and contemporary discourses on *jihād* by some of the better-known proponents of political Islam in the nineteenth and twentieth centuries. It also analyzes the discourses of radical militants, especially after September 11, 2001, some of whom have adopted suicide bombing as a manifestation of (in their view) legitimate martyrdom. We examine the Islamicizing rhetoric of these militants and discuss how they use and misuse classical and later sources to grant religious legitimacy to their violent enterprises. Chapter 9 focuses on the views of a different set of modern and contemporary religious scholars and intellectuals on the topics of *jihād* and martyrdom, who typically emphasize the historical polysemy of these concepts. These scholars have been adamantly critical of militant projects and the application of the term *jihād* to them. Needless to say, such criticism has intensified in certain quarters after September 11, and a number of key works composed after this period are discussed. The conclusion provides a summary of our findings and assesses how, and why scholars in the classical and medieval periods—particularly exegetes and *ḥadīth* specialists—increasingly chose to privilege a monovalent, combative understanding of *jihād* roughly from the late second/eighth century on, instigating counter-narratives from a pietist segment that foregrounded and praised its non-militant aspects. The historical and political motivations propelling these developments are reconstructed as far as the literature allows us and how this approach broadens and nuances current perspectives on *jihād* and martyrdom is indicated.

The Significance of a Diachronic Survey of Qur'ān Commentaries and Other Texts

As should have become evident from the discussion of sources above, Qur'ān commentaries form an important and integral part of the sources consulted for our project of reconstruction and analysis of construals of *jihād* through the centuries. The historian of Islam Roy Mottahedeh has pointed to the invaluable nature of *tafsīr* works in reconstructing the major theological, intellectual, social, and political concerns of the pre-modern Islamic past.[10] As he rightly emphasizes, the continuous nature of this genre from the earliest centuries of Islam through some of the most productive and tumultuous periods of Islamic history render it an unparalleled repository of formative ideas and perspectives, some of which were either attenuated or completely lost in later centuries. This is certainly borne out in our study of exegetical works in reference to key Qur'anic verses dealing with *jihād* and its derivatives.

At the risk of being repetitive, we decided to provide the relevant views of individual commentators on specific verses, often in great detail. Because the emphasis in this work is on diachronic shifts in the formulations of *jihād* at the level of micro-discourses, staying as close as possible to the reported views of the exegetes allows us to more vigilantly monitor subtle changes in nuance and semantics over time. The reader may find that this occasionally makes for dense reading, but given the importance of the textual evidence, this detailed attention at the micro-level to the specific vocabulary and perspectives of influential commentators was deemed important and necessary.

We also decided not to provide lengthy conclusory paragraphs for each chapter, but rather to postpone the summation and analysis of the textual material presented to the final concluding chapter. This further allows the conclusion to be read as a stand-alone section providing a detailed overview of the major points that emerged in the preceding chapters.

In regard to Qur'anic verses, we have adopted the common and conventional periodization of the life of the Prophet Muḥammad, particularly the broad temporal division of the Meccan and Medinan periods, as occurs in the usual historical and biographical sources. This periodization was adopted by the early biographers Ibn Isḥāq (d. 150/767) and Ibn Hishām (d. 218/833) in their famous *sīra* of the Prophet and by al-Ṭabarī (d. 310/923) in his magisterial universal history *Ta'rīkh al-rusul wa-'l-mulūk*, among others, and remains the conventional historical chronology adopted in modern works. With regard to the classification of Qur'anic chapters as Meccan and Medinan, we have also followed the traditional dating of the *sūras*, as followed by the editors of the standard 1924 Cairo edition of the Qur'ān. The traditional dating remains the one generally adopted in modern scholarship.[11]

The comparison of early and late sources and texts is *the* key feature of our study, which seeks to thereby chart both the constancies and changes in the spectrum of meanings and repertoire of activities included under the term *jihād* and the broad rubric of martyrdom. In addition to Qur'ān exegeses, this study compares and contrasts early and late works of *ḥadīth* and the excellences of *jihād* literature. One major genre not covered here is the juridical one—precisely because we wish to emphasize the more diverse, non-legal significations of *jihād* and martyrdom that emerge in other literary corpora. Historical chronicles are also not much in evidence here. Both the legal and historical literatures have received ample scholarly attention in relation to *jihād*. The focus on exegetical works, early *ḥadīth*, and edifying literature in this study is meant to compensate for the scant attention they have received to date in discussions of *jihād* and martyrdom. The diachronic survey of early and later texts belonging to these diverse genres allows us to credibly exhume a repertoire of meanings assigned to *jihād* and martyrdom that were far more variegated, fluid, and contested in the early formative period (comprised roughly of the first three centuries of Islam) when compared with later centuries. The subsequent predominance of the legal/military dimensions of these terms attests to the eventual ascendancy of the scholarly juridical class and a powerful administrative/military bureaucracy, leading to the marginalization of important early perspectives.[12] This kind of historically-anchored diachronic survey disabuses us of essentialism when it comes to the study of key historical terms and concepts associated with Muslim-majority societies, as remains far too common in both academic and popular discourses. The semantic mutability and discursive malleability of the terms *jihād* and *shahīd* as deployed through time in variegated contexts have important implications for us today, a subject that we explore further at the conclusion of this study.

1

Striving "for," "in," and "in the Path of" God

QUR'ANIC IMPERATIVES IN THE MIDDLE MECCAN–EARLY MEDINAN PERIOD

JURISTS, USUALLY IN contradistinction to Qur'ān exegetes, *ḥadīth* scholars, and ethicists, primarily dealt with *jihād* as one of the obligations of the Muslim ruler and his Muslim subjects, mainly in the context of external relations with non-Muslim polities. The law of nations or international law (*siyar*) as an integral part of classical Islamic law developed early due to this pragmatic juridical concern for the intricacies of political relations with the broader non-Muslim world, as well as with religious minorities within Islamic realms. Allowing for a degree of oversimplification, we can basically agree with Majid Khadduri's statement that the Islamic law of nations "was essentially a law governing the conduct of war and the division of booty."[1] Within legal/administrative contexts, *jihād* is primarily military in nature.

Jihād in the Qur'ān, however, is a polyvalent concept, as we noted already in the Introduction, and is by no means reducible to only a combative dimension. Early Arabic lexicographers conveyed the meaning of the basic verb *jahada* as "He strove, laboured, or toiled; exerted himself or his power or efforts or endeavours or ability. . . ." The intransitive variant verb *jahida* implied that "It (a state of life) was, or became, hard, difficult, strait, or distressful." Other verbal forms and nouns imply human exertion in encounters with particularly difficult circumstances, difficult problems, and difficult people.[2]

Various lexical derivatives from the productive Arabic root *jhd* occur in several verses in the Qur'ān with multiple inflections, grounded as they often are in specific historical contexts. These contexts are cryptically indicated for us occasionally by the Qur'anic narrative itself, but more expansively and commonly by the commentaries produced to explain the "occasions of revelation" (*asbāb al-nuzūl*) of these verses. Forty-one verses containing derivatives from *jhd*, mostly as verbal forms, occur in the Qur'anic text. In addition to these derivatives, the related Qur'anic terms *qitāl* ("fighting") and *ṣabr* ("patience," "forbearance") and their derivatives occur in several verses in variegated contexts as components of what became termed in the extra-Qur'anic literature as "striving in the path of God" (*al-jihād fi sabīl allāh*).[3] These related terms also have to be taken into account for an adequately comprehensive and holistic understanding of the broad Qur'anic imperative to strive in the path of God.[4] An exhaustive study of all these verses within the restricted parameters of this monograph is, of course, not possible. We are therefore selectively studying the exegeses of a number of these verses with two primary objectives in mind: (1) to obtain a wide sampling of a range of meanings, combative and non-combative, nestled within these verses revealed during various historical circumstances, as may be reconstructed through a diachronic study of key exegetical works; and (2) to thereby derive a sense of both historical continuity and change in the semantic trajectory of these various lexemes.

Bearing in mind these objectives, the following specific verses have been selected for closer scrutiny and clustered according to the dimension(s) of *jihād* that they signify:

1. *Jāhidū fī 'llāh* and *jāhidū fīnā* (Qur'ān 22:78; 29:69)
2. *Jāhidhum bihi jihādan kabīran* (Qur'ān 25:52)
3. *Ṣabr* and its derivatives (Qur'ān 3:200)
4. *Qitāl* and its derivatives (Qur'ān 22:39–40; 2:190–194; 9:12–13; 2:216; 9:5; 9:29; and 4:95)
5. Verses referring to abstention from and termination of hostilities (Qur'ān 60:7–9; 9:6; and 8:61)
6. *Jāhadū/yajhadūn fī sabīl allāh bi-amwālihim wa-anfusihim* (Qur'ān 4:95)
7. The phrase *qutiltum fī sabīl allāh* and its variants (Qur'ān 3:157–158; 4:74; 22:58; 2:154; and 3:169)
8. Reference to *shuhadā'* (Qur'ān 4:69)
9. Heavenly compensation for the practice of *ṣabr* (Qur'ān 39:10)
10. Derivates of *jhd* and *ṣbr* together (Qur'ān 16:110; 3:142)

This chapter deals mainly with the first three categories of verses (1–3), which span the late Meccan and early Medinan periods and encode primarily non-combative meanings of *jihād*. The discussion of verses from the other categories occurs in subsequent chapters.

The *tafsīr* works consulted in this study include the early commentaries composed during the Umayyad period by Mujāhid b. Jabr (d. ca. 104/722) and Muqātil b. Sulaymān (d. 150/767); the commentaries of 'Abd al-Razzāq al-Ṣan'ānī (d. 211/827), al-Ṭabarī (d. 310/923), and al-Wāḥidī (d. 468/1076) from the 'Abbasid period; the commentary of the Ibāḍī exegete Hūd b. Muḥakkam al-Huwwārī (d. ca. 290/903); the early Shī'ī commentaries of al-Qummī (d. after 307/919), al- 'Ayyāshī (d. ca. 320/932), and Furāt b. Ibrāhīm (fl. second half of third/ninth century) from the pre-Buwayhid period; the commentaries of al-Zamakhsharī (d. ca. 538/1144) and Fakhr al-Din al-Rāzī (d. 606/1210) from the Saljuq period; and the Andalusian exegete al-Qurṭubī (d. 671/1273) in the seventh/thirteenth century, corresponding to the waning of Muslim rule in Spain and to the Mamlūk period in the Islamic East. This array of *tafsīr* works allows us to obtain representative samplings of views from some of the most influential exegetes from a variety of eras. The exegesis of the popular commentator from the Mamluk period—Ibn Kathīr (d. 774/1373)—has not been consulted in any detailed manner in this section, although references to it occur sometimes in the text and/or in the notes. We also discuss his separate treatise on *jihād* in chapter 6, which provides us with sufficient insight into his influential perspectives on this topic. Additionally, when relevant, we have referred in the notes to the early exegetical works of 'Abd Allāh b. Wahb (d. 197/812) and Abū 'Ubayd al-Qāsim b. Sallām (d. ca. 224/838).

A brief discussion of the biographies of the principal exegetes consulted in this study now follows in order to anchor their perspectives and writings in their historical circumstances and to indicate briefly some of their doctrinal proclivities, when relevant, that potentially colored their exegeses. In chronological order, they are:

Tafsīr of Mujāhid b. Jabr: The Umayyad commentator Mujāhid b. Jabr was born in Mecca in 21/642. The extant published *Tafsīr*, first edited by 'Abd al-Raḥmān al-Ṭāhir b. Muḥammad al-Suratī, is fragmentary and incomplete and based on a later redaction of this important work.[5] It is, however, the oldest published work of exegesis available to us. Mujāhid was one of the most prominent students of the celebrated Companion Ibn 'Abbās and is said to have faithfully transmitted the latter's commentary on the Qur'ān.[6] Mujāhid displays rationalist tendencies in his exegesis and often resorted to *ra'y* (personal opinion), for which he was criticized by some scholars.[7] However, other scholars praised his scholarship; Yaḥyā al-Qattān (d. 198/813), for example, maintained that "the [Muslim] community was agreed upon the [religious] leadership of Mujāhid" after his death in 104/722.[8]

The edition of Mujāhid's *Tafsīr* used in this study is the one by Abū Muḥammad al-Asyūṭī. The editor does not include any information about the manuscripts consulted in the preparation of this recension. However, based on internal textual evidence, we are able with a large degree of confidence to state that the views expressed in the published work at our disposal appear to be credibly those of Mujāhid himself. His comments on select verses as recorded in the al-Asyūṭī edition are transmitted practically verbatim by exegetes after him, such as al-Ṭabarī—this will become evident in the instances we record in several chapters in this book.[9] This high degree of congruence in the views attributed to Mujāhid as attested in multiple exegetical works after him permits us to invoke these perspectives as authentically representative of the early period (mid-first/seventh to early second/eighth century), against which later understandings of a number of critical issues can be juxtaposed for comparison and contrast.[10]

***Tafsīr* of Muqātil b. Sulaymān** (d. 150/767): Another Umayyad commentator, Muqātil b. Sulaymān b. Bashīr al-Azdī al-Balkhī, lived in Basra and then in Baghdad, where he achieved renown as a Qur'ān commentator and a *mutakallim* (scholastic theologian). Like Mujāhid, he too is said to have often relied on *ra'y* in his commentary and to have made use of the *isrā'īliyyāt* (Israelite tales) attributed to Jewish and Christian sources. He was accused by some of anthropomorphism and of displaying Murji'ī and Zaydī leanings. He died in Basra at an advanced age.[11]

Muqātil made generous use of earlier commentaries often without attribution, providing us with a valuable window into early layers of exegeses from the first and second centuries of Islam.[12] As in the case of Mujāhid, cross-referencing Muqātil's comments as recorded in his published *Tafsīr*[13] with those reported by later exegetes, especially al-Ṭabarī, on select verses reveals, once again, an overwhelming degree of congruence, allowing us to credibly attribute these views to Muqātil himself in his early Umayyad milieu.[14]

***Tafsīr* of 'Abd al-Razzāq b. Ḥammām b. Nāfi' al-Ṣan'ānī** (d. 211/827): From the generation after Muqātil, this relatively early 'Abbasid *tafsīr* work contains important perspectives on many significant issues pertaining to *jihād* and martyrdom that have not always been preserved in later works. Its author was an important Yemeni scholar, who studied with some of the most prominent scholars of his time, initially in Ṣan'a and then later during trips to Syria and the Ḥijāz. These scholars included Ma'mar b. Rashīd (d. 153/770) in Ṣan'a, the Meccans Ibn Jurayj (d. 150/767) and Sufyān b. 'Uyayna (d. 198/813–14); the Kufan Sufyān al-Thawrī (d. 161/778), the Syrian al-Awzā'ī (d. 157/774), and the Medinan Mālik b. Anas (d. 179/795), all of whom had distinctive views on *jihād* preserved by our exegete. 'Abd al-Razzāq's *tafsīr*, which is based on an earlier exegesis by his teacher Ma'mar, as well as his *Muṣannaf*, therefore remain highly valuable repositories of information, particularly about early second/eighth century scholarship in Mecca, Medina, and Basra, and "provide access to some of the earliest compilations of legal and exegetical traditions not preserved as original sources."[15]

Tanwīr al-miqbās: The early *tafsīr* work with the title *Tanwīr al-miqbās min tafsīr Ibn 'Abbās*, purporting to contain the exegesis of the Companion Ibn 'Abbās (d. ca. 68/687), has been generally attributed to the later exegete and genealogist Muḥammad b. al-Sā'ib al-Kalbī (d. 146/763). This attribution to Ibn 'Abbās via al-Kalbī remains open to debate, however, among modern scholars. Some editions of the commentary have also attributed the work to the much later scholar al-Firūzabādī (d. 817/1414).[16] Because the tone and content of much of the exegetical material contained in this work often tend to agree with that of other certifiably early works, suggesting the genuinely early provenance of many of the views recorded in this work, the *Tanwīr al-miqbās* is treated here as an early work (roughly before the end of the third/ninth century), but of undetermined date and authorship.[17]

The commentary of third/ninth century Ibāḍī commentator Hūd b. Muḥakkam al-Huwwārī (d. ca. 290/903), titled *Tafsīr kitāb allāh al-'azīz*, was recently edited by Balḥāj b. Sa'īd Sharifī and published in Beirut in 1990. Not much is known about this Maghribi exegete; his father served as a judge for the Ibāḍī Imām 'Abd al-Wahhāb b. 'Abd al-Raḥmān b. Rustam (ruled 171-208/788-824).[18] Ibn Muḥakkam's *tafsīr* is the oldest extant Ibāḍ ī Qur'ān commentary available to us.

***Tafsīr* of al-Qummī** (d. after 307/919): 'Alī b. Ibrāhīm al-Qummī was an early Shī'ī commentator from the critical period between the period of the Lesser and Greater Occultation (260/874–329/941) when the Imāmī Shī'ī doctrine had not been fully formed. As became common after him, al-Qummī engages in allegorical interpretation of the Qur'anic text, which is assumed to contain esoteric references to the family of the Prophet and to the special status of 'Alī. Al-Qummī frequently records the exegetical opinions particularly of the fifth and the sixth Imams, Muḥammad al-Bāqir (d. ca. 114/732) and Ja'far al-Ṣādiq (d. 148/765), unlike later Shī'ī exegetes.

***Tafsīr* al-'Ayyāshī** (d. ca. 320/932): Abū 'l-Naṣr Muḥammad b. Mas'ūd b. Muḥammad al-'Ayyāshī was originally from Samarqand and converted to Shi'ism from Sunnī Islam in his youth. He was said to have been a prolific scholar, having composed over 200 works. Among his students were Muḥammad b. 'Umar al-Kashshī (d. ca. early fourth/tenth century), author of a famous Shī'ī *rijāl* work. Although al- 'Ayyāshī was regarded as narrating weak traditions, he is frequently cited by later authors. Like al-Qummī before him, he interprets many Qur'anic verses as containing direct references to the *ahl al-bayt*, generally on the authority of the fifth and sixth Imams.[19]

***Tafsīr* of Furāt b. Ibrāhīm** (fl. second half of third/ninth century): Very little is known about Furāt b. Ibrāhīm b. Furāt al-Kūfī, including his precise birth and date years. Fuat Sezgin's suggested death date of circa 310/922 is certainly plausible. Furāt was clearly affiliated in some way with Kufa, as his *nisba* suggests, and we know that he transmitted from al-Ḥusayn b. Saʿīd al-Kūfī (d. ca. 300/912). Abū 'l-Ḥasan ʿAlī b. Bābawayh (d. 329/940), father of the more famous Muḥammad b. ʿAlī b. Bābawayh (d. 381/991), transmitted traditions from Furāt. He is also quoted extensively by later Shīʿī scholars like al-Ḥurr al- ʿĀmilī (d. 1104/1693) and al-Majlisī (d. between 1110/1699–1111/1700).[20]

***Tafsīr* of al-Ṭabarī** (d. 310/923): The celebrated exegete Abū Jaʿfar Muḥammad b. Jarīr, originally from Ṭabaristān, is the author of probably the most widely consulted work of Islamic exegesis, the *Jāmiʿ al-bayān fī tafsīr al-qur'ān*, more simply known as *Tafsīr al-Ṭabarī*.[21] Along with the magisterial work of history that he compiled, this work showcases al-Ṭabarī's encyclopedic knowledge of the various Islamic sciences. The *Tafsīr* is notable for its emphasis on *ijtihād* or independent reasoning; besides religious dogma and law, al-Ṭabarī also plays close attention to grammar and lexicography in this work. Al-Ṭabarī's pro-ʿAbbasid bias—he had worked for the ʿAbbasid government in various capacities—is frequently quite apparent in his *Tafsīr* as it is in his *Ta'rīkh*, and sometimes explains the overall cast of his interpretations.[22]

***Tafsīr* of al-Wāḥidī** (d. 468/1076): ʿAlī b. Aḥmad b. Muḥammad al-Wāḥidī al-Nīsābūrī is the author of several exegetical works, including the *Tafsīr al-wāsiṭ*, the work used in this study.[23] In Nīsābūr, he studied with the well-known Qur'ān scholar Abū Isḥāq al-Thaʿlabī (d. 427/1035) and studied *ḥadīth* and Shāfiʿī law with Abū 'l- ʿAbbās al-Aṣamm (d. 265/878). Al-Wāḥidī is said to have completed the *Wāsiṭ* around 461/1069, having started it five decades earlier. In comparison with the popular and shorter commentary *Asbāb al-nuzūl*, the *Wāsiṭ* is more extensive in its scope.[24] As will become evident below, al-Wāḥidī emphasizes in his commentary the close philological study of the Qur'ān and often offers fresh perspectives, particularly as he is said to have often discounted the views of other exegetes for what he deemed to be their imperfect, non-philological understanding of the Qur'anic text.[25]

***Tafsīr* of al-Zamakhsharī** (d. 538/1144): Abū 'l-Qāsim Maḥmūd b. ʿUmar al-Zamakhsharī, from Zamakhshar in Persia, was an accomplished grammarian, philologist, theologian, exegete, litterateur, and author of a highly regarded Qur'ān commentary.[26] He lived for a long time in Mecca, where he studied grammar, theology, and *tafsīr*. His Muʿtazilī (rationalist) affiliation is evident in this work of exegesis, which has a strong linguistic focus and contains very little *ḥadīth* (the Mu'tazila in general being skeptical of the probative value of *ḥadīth*), in comparison with other exegetical works of a similar period.[27]

***Tafsīr* of al-Rāzī** (d. 606/1210): Muḥammad b. ʿUmar b. al-Ḥusayn Fakhr al-Dīn al-Rāzī, as indicated by his last name, was from Rayy in Persia, where he was educated in grammar, philosophy, *kalām* (scholastic theology), and jurisprudence. He later went to Khwārazm, where he is said to have relentlessly debated the Mu'tazila, who eventually forced him to leave. After meeting the same fate in Transoxania, he returned to Rayy. By way of other towns, he finally settled down in Herat, where he acquired a great reputation as a formidable scholar with numerous disciples, earning the title *shaykh al-islām*. Al-Rāzī was an ardent Sunnī and, besides the Mu'tazila, he also dueled with the Karrāmiya, who were proponents of anthropomorphism. But he was also selectively critical of Ash'arism while yet a proponent of it; he rejected, for example, al-Ash'arī's doctrine of divine attributes and his atomism. His *tafsīr* thus pays considerable attention to issues of *kalām* and philosophy and attempts to justify his own theological and philosophical reasoning on the basis of specific Qur'anic verses.[28]

It should be noted that during the lifetime of this Seljuq scholar, the Third and the Fourth Crusades (1189–1192 and 1198–1207 CE respectively) were launched, which fact seems on occasion to have directly impacted al-Rāzī's conceptualizations of the military *jihād*, as will become evident in our subsequent discussion.

Tafsīr of al-Qurṭubī: Muḥammad b. Aḥmad b. Abī Bakr al-Qurṭubī (d. 671/1273), the well-known Andalusian scholar of Qur'ān and *ḥadīth*, is the author of the exegetical work *al-Jāmi' li-aḥkām al-qur'ān*. An adherent of the Mālikī school of law, al-Qurṭubī was known equally for his prodigious scholarship and personal piety. The *Jāmi'* makes considerable use of *ḥadīth* and has a strong legal focus, while also paying close attention to the philological and rhetorical aspects of the Qur'anic language. Compared with a number of his predecessors, al-Qurṭubī is sparing in his use of the *isrā'iliyyāt* in his commentary.[29] Written during the time of the Spanish Reconquista, this *tafsīr* work evinces the anxieties and concerns of Andalusian Muslims of the period, and shapes al-Qurṭubī's perspectives on the parameters of the military *jihād*.

We now proceed to the exegeses of a selection of critical verses from the first three categories under the following broad rubrics.

Jihād in the Middle–Late Meccan Period (ca. 617 – 622 CE)

"Do not obey the unbelievers and strive against them mightily with it" (Qur'ān 25:52)

This verse, believed to have been revealed in the middle Meccan period (ca. 617–619 CE), contains an important injunction derived from *jhd* to connote a specific type of striving against unbelievers. In Arabic, the verse runs: *Fa- lā tuṭiʿ al-kāfirīn wa-jāhidhum bihi jihādan kabīran.*

The second/eighth century exegete **Muqātil b. Sulaymān** briefly states that he understands the enclitic pronoun in *bihi* to refer to the Qur'ān,[30] as does **Hūd b. Muḥakkam.** The latter exegete further states that *jihādan kabīran* in the verse means to strive intensely (*shadīdan*). This kind of *jihād* refers to *jihād* of the tongue (*wa-hādha al-jihād innamā huwa bi-'l-lisān*) in the Meccan period before fighting was permitted.[31] The *Tanwīr al-miqbās* understands both the Qur'ān and the sword to be indicated in this verse.[32]

Muḥammad b. Jarīr al-Ṭabarī in the early fourth/tenth century understands this verse to warn the Prophet: "Do not obey the unbelievers in regard to their summons to worship their gods for then we will cause you to taste the weakness of [this] life and of death. Instead, strive against them mightily with this Qur'ān so that they may be led to believe in what is contained within it of God's commandments, to comply with it [sc. the Qur'ān], and implement its injunctions, willingly or unwillingly." Among those who subscribed to this view was Ibn ʿAbbās, while Ibn Zayd was of the opinion that it was "Islam" with which one should strive.[33]

Al-Wāḥidī dwells briefly on this verse and explains it as follows: "When he [sc. Muḥammad] is summoned to the religion of his fathers, he should strive against them with the Qur'ān, comprehensively and firmly."[34]

Al-Zamakhsharī regards the enclitic pronoun in *bihi* to refer to either the Qur'ān or the avoidance of obedience to unbelievers. In the case of the latter, the intent of the verse would be to exhort the Prophet to exert his utmost to counter the relentless efforts of the unbelievers to sabotage his mission. These exertions on the part of the Prophet are deemed "a mighty striving" because of the great hardships they entailed. It is also possible, al-Zamakhsharī states, that the enclitic pronoun encodes a reference to the previous verse, which states, "If we had so willed, we would have sent a warner to every city (*qarya*)." Because Muḥammad is to be considered as a warner to all cities, he also combines in himself the efforts of each individual warner sent to each city. These combined efforts on his part constitute the great striving referred to in this verse.[35]

Al-Rāzī relates that some believed that the verse referred to the effort expended in implementing [the laws of God] and inviting to Islam, whereas others believed that it referred to fighting; yet others said that it referred to both. He says that the first strand of interpretation is the most plausible because the chapter is Meccan and the command to fight was given after the migration to Medina. Like al-Zamakhsharī, he considers *jihādan kabīran* to refer to the herculean efforts expended by the Prophet in his role as the warner to all cities.[36]

Al-Qurṭubī lists the referent for *bihi* as the Qur'ān, according to Ibn 'Abbās; Islam, according to Ibn Zayd; and the sword, according to unnamed others. Al-Qurṭubī, like al-Rāzī, discounts the third possibility as the chapter containing this verse is Meccan and was revealed before the command to fight was given.[37]

In summary, a majority of the exegetes, including al-Ṭabarī, understood the enclitic pronoun in *bihi* to be a reference to the Qur'ān, primarily on the authority of Ibn 'Abbās. Ibn Zayd is the source of the alternate view that it referred to Islam. The minority view that it referred to "the sword" or fighting against the polytheists is recorded in the *Tanwīr al-miqbās*. Both al-Rāzī and al-Qurṭubī reject this interpretation as ahistorical, because the verse is universally deemed to be Meccan, and the command to fight was not given until the Medinan period. It should also be added here that "a great striving" mentioned in this verse prefigures the well-known distinction between the greater and lesser *jihād* articulated in a later prophetic report.

"As for those who struggle in regard to Us, we will surely guide them to Our paths. Indeed God is with those who do good" (Qur'ān 29:69)

In Arabic, this verse states: *Walladhīna jāhadū fīnā la-nahdiyannahum subulanā wa-inna allāh la-ma'a 'l-muḥsinīn*. The twenty-ninth chapter (Sūrat al-'Ankabūt) is generally regarded as a late Meccan revelation.

Muqātil explains this verse as referring to those who do good deeds for the sake of God (*'amilū bi -'l-khayr li-llāh*) and cross-references Qur'ān 22:78 here. "We will guide them to our paths" means that they will be guided to "our religion" (*ya'ni dīnanā*) and that God provides help (*al-'awn*) for those who do good.[38]

The **Tanwīr al-Miqbās** glosses "those who struggle in regard to Us" as [those who struggle] to obey us. According to Ibn 'Abbās, "We will guide them to Our paths" means that "those who act according to what they know, we will grant them success in what they do not know." Others say it means that "we will guide them to our paths in order to raise them to an honorable status in regard to their nature (*bi-'l-ṭab'*), obedience (*wa-'l-ṭaw'*), and sweetness [of disposition] (*al-ḥalāwa*)." Yet others say the verse means that "we will guide them to our paths in order to grant them success for obeying us." "God is with those who do good" means that "He helps those who do good through speech and deed by granting them success and impeccability" (*al-'iṣma*).[39]

Hūd b. Muḥakkam very briefly glosses *walladhīna jāhadū fīnā* as a reference to those who "act for us" (*'amalū lanā*). "Our paths" in the verse refers to "the path of guidance," which refers to "the road to heaven" (*al-ṭarīq ilā 'l-janna*). The verse was revealed, he continues, before the military *jihād* was commanded in Medina. The *muḥsinīn* are the believers (*al-mu'minīn*).[40]

In his very brief commentary on this verse, **Furāt b. Ibrāhīm** records that Abū Ja'far (sc. Muḥammad al-Bāqir, the fifth Imām) had understood this verse as having been revealed "concerning us, the *ahl al-bayt*."[41]

Al-Qummī understands "those who struggle in regard to us" as describing those "who are patient (*ṣabarū*) and strive with the Messenger of God," without offering any further details on the nature of this striving. Characteristically, he sees a reference to the family of Muḥammad and their partisans (*li ashyā'ihim*) in this verse, on the authority of Abū 'l-Jārūd and Abū Ja'far.[42] Of great significance is al-Qummī's coupling of *jihād* and *ṣabr* in his exegesis of this verse.

In comparison with these early exegetical perspectives, we note a sharp semantic and exegetical shift in **al-Ṭabarī**'s commentary. Al-Ṭabarī says that the verse refers to "those who fought (*qātalū*) the unbelievers from the Quraysh for the lies that they fabricate against God," and "for having denied the truth which came to them concerning us." The believers fight to establish the superiority of their claims and ensure "[divine] help for our religion," he says. "We guide them to our paths" means "we grant them success in attaining the straight paths" (*al-ṭuruq al-mustaqīma*). This is to be understood as "the attainment of the religion of God, which is Islam, with which God sent Muḥammad, peace and blessings be upon him," continues al-Ṭabarī. The last part of the verse means that God helps those who are of good character (*aḥsana min khalqihi*) and who fight the polytheists for His sake, affirming the truth of the divine message proclaimed by His messenger. Al-Ṭabarī states in general that other exegetes have commented similarly on this verse, but specifically mentions only Ibn Zayd (d. 182/798)[43] who had glossed *jāhadū fīnā* as *qātalū fīnā*.[44] Ibn Zayd's explicit collapsing of the two verbs *jāhadū* and *qātalū* clearly meets with al-Ṭabarī's approval, indicating to us that in his time (late third/ninth–early fourth/tenth century), the equation *jihād* = *qitāl* had already gained ground and become predominant in influential circles during the 'Abbasid period. Al-Ṭabarī does not refer to other scholars who may have understood this verse to refer to non-combative striving.

In the following century, **al-Wāḥidī** similarly takes note of Ibn Zayd's exegesis of Qur'ān 29:69 as referring to fighting the polytheists,[45] but expresses strong reservations about its validity. Instead, he expresses a preference for Ibn 'Abbās's interpretation that the verse referred to the *Muhājirūn* (Meccan Emigrants) and the *Anṣār* (the Medinan Helpers) in general, with no implicit or explicit connotation of fighting against the Quraysh.[46]

In his brief commentary, **al-Zamakhsharī** stresses that the word "striving" (*al-mujāhada*) as it occurs in this verse is used in a general sense and is not in reference to any specific individual, group, or object. Thus "striving" here can be directed against the carnal self that inclines to evil, to Satan, and to the enemies of religion. *Fīnā* variously means "in regard to our rights" (*fī ḥaqqinā*), "for our sake" (*min ajlinā*), and "exclusively for our selves" (*li-wajhinā khāli*[an]). "We will guide them to our paths" means that we will increase them in guidance to "the paths of goodness" (*ilā subul al-khayr*) and success, as is indicated in Qur'ān 47:17.[47]

Al-Rāzī says that after the unbelievers are rebuked for their unbelief in Qur'ān 29:68, the following verse offers consolation to the believers by assuring them that whoever strives in obedience will be guided to the paths of paradise. "God is with those who do good" is understood in relation to Qur'ān 10:26, where it is stated, "For those who do good, there is goodness (*al-ḥusnā*) and more." The last part of the verse signifies companionship and closeness to God, which augments the reward of the one who does good.[48]

The verse may also be understood to endorse the epistemic value of critical investigation of the truth, continues al-Rāzī. Thus "those who strove in regard to us" may refer to "those who have critically examined our proofs" (*alladhīna naẓarū fī dalā'ilina*) so that "they may attain knowledge concerning Us," he states. Al-Rāzī refers approvingly to his Mu'tazilī colleagues, who understood this verse as suggesting that God is the guide for the righteous who guard against absolutism and obstinacy (*yattaqūna al-ta'aṣṣub wa-'l-'inād*) and resort to critical examination (*al-naẓar*) of divine proofs.[49] Like al-Wāḥidī and al-Zamakhsharī immediately before him and all the pre-Ṭabarī commentators we looked at, al-Rāzī discerns a general injunction in this verse to obey God to the best of one's ability and, additionally, on the basis of Mu'tazilī exegeses, a command to critically and strenuously examine divine proofs from which the Truth may be deduced.

Al-Qurṭubī glosses "Those who strove in regard to us" broadly as "[those who] strove against the unbelievers in regard to us; that is, in seeking our satisfaction." Striving against the unbelievers in this verse thus refers primarily to non-combative acts of piety and resistance to wrongdoing. Al-Qurṭubī next proceeds to record an impressive range of interpretations that ascribe primarily spiritual and intellectualmeanings to *jihād* as occurs in this verse, according to several early authorities. Thus he observes that the well-known early Kufan exegete al-Suddī (d. 128/745)[50] and other commentators had noted that this verse had been revealed before the imposition of fighting as a religious duty. The fourth/tenth century exegete Ibn 'Aṭiyya (d. 383/993)[51] had also affirmed that the verse came down before "the conventional [sc. military] *jihād*" (*al-jihād* *al-'urfi*) was sanctioned, and that the *jihād* referred to in this verse is to be understood as "a general striving for the religion of God and the seeking of His satisfaction." Al-Hasan b. Abī 'l-Hasan[52] had commented that the verse refers to pious worshipers in general (*al-āya fi-'l-'ubbād*). Additionally, Ibn 'Abbās, the Umayyad caliph 'Umar b. 'Abd al- 'Azīz (d. 101/720), 'Abd Allāh b. al-Zubayr, and Ibrāhīm b. Adham (d. ca. 163/779) had understood this verse to refer to nonviolent striving.[53] Combative meanings are assigned to *jihād* in this verse by al-Qurṭubī on the authority of a far smaller number of scholars, specifically Sufyān b. 'Uyayna (d. 196/811) and Sulaymān al-Dārānī (d. ca. 205/820), who regarded fighting as part of the overall human striving in this world. This survey notably reveals that post-al-Ṭabarī commentators continued to preserve and emphasize the non-combative dimensions of *jihād* that were prominent in commentaries attributed to early exegetes before al-Ṭabarī.[54]

Jihād in the Late Meccan–Early Medinan Period (ca. 619 CE -2/624)

"Strive in regard to God a true striving as is His due"[55]

In Arabic: Wa-jāhidū fī 'llāh ḥaqqa jihādihi (Qur'ān 22:78)

The Arabic locution *fī'llāh* ("in regard to God") in this precise formulation occurs only once in the Qur'ān and tends to be overlooked in most discussions of the term *jihād*. This variant formulation, along with *fīnā* in Qur'ān 29:69 discussed above, of what became the more common locution [*al-jihād*] *fī sabil allāh* are worthy of closer attention. There is debate among the exegetes as to whether the entire chapter (Sūrat al-Ḥajj) from which this verse is derived is Meccan or Medinan—a critical distinction after all in understanding the meaning of *jihād* in this verse. Based on the exegetical discussion below, we are treating it as a "transition" verse, so to speak, straddling the late Meccan–early Medinan period, and encapsulating a broad array of semantic possibilities in relation to *jihād* and its derivatives.

Muqātil b. Sulaymān understands *wa-jāhidu fī 'llāh* to mean "He commands them to act" (*ya'muruhum bi-'l-'amal*) and *ḥaqqa jihādihi* to mean "Do good deeds for God as is His due" (*a'milū li-'llāh bi-'l-khayr ḥaqqa 'amalihi*). In his understanding, *jāhidū* in this verse establishes the imperative to excel in the performance of good deeds in general to earn divine approbation.[56] A similar meaning can be found in the *Tanwīr al-miqbās*, where *wa-jāhidū fī 'llāh ḥaqqa jihādihi* is glossed as "Work for God as is His due" (*wa-'malū li-'llāh ḥaqqa 'amalihi*).[57] This verse thus enjoins, according to the *Tanwīr*, that humans should strive to act for the sake of God as is appropriately due Him.

Hūd b. Muḥakkam simply remarks that this verse was considered to have been abrogated by Qur'ān 64:16 (which states, "Revere God to the extent that you are able").[58] Furāt b. Ibrāhīm and al-Qummī also have only the briefest remarks preserved in their extant commentaries on Qur'ān 22:78, the former affirming on the authority of Muḥammad al-Bāqir that the Shī'ī imams were the referent in this case,[59] and the latter stating that it is a specific reference to the family of Muḥammad (Āl Muḥammad).[60]

By the time we get to **al-Ṭabarī**, a significant shift, once again, appears to have occurred in the primary meaning assigned to the phrase *jāhidu fī-'llāh* in comparison with these earlier views. Al-Ṭabarī admits that there are differences of opinion among exegetes regarding the meaning of this verse, but the meaning he privileges on the authority of some of these unnamed exegetes (*fa-qāla ba'ḍuhum*) is "Struggle against the polytheists (*wa-jāhidū 'l-mushrikīn*) in the path of God as is rightly due Him." In al-Ṭabarī's *tafsīr*, therefore, the prepositional phrase *fī 'llāh* is now deemed to be the equivalent of *fī sabīl allāh*, an equation we did not find in the extant versions of earlier commentaries referred to above. Furthermore, *jāhidū* in this context is understood by al-Ṭabarī to connote struggling—with the implication of fighting—against associationists, again a connotation not encountered in the earlier works referenced above. This meaning is further anchored by the invocation of an additional authority—'Umar b. al-Khaṭṭāb—who is said to have understood the report as counseling fighting against the two Qurayshī tribes of Makhzūm and 'Abd Shams.[61]

The main authority al-Ṭabarī cites in support of this changed meaning is, interestingly, Ibn 'Abbās, who, according to a chain of transmission ending with Yūnus,[62] is said to have understood *jāhidū fī 'llāh ḥaqqa jihādihi* as "struggle against them as [you did] the first time" (*kamā jāhadtum awwal marra*). Ibn 'Abbās is also quoted, via a different *isnād* culminating in al-Qāsim,[63] as understanding this phrase to mean "For the sake of God, do not be afraid of the censure of those who censure" (*la takhāfu fī 'llāh lawmat lā'im*).[64] Two divergent strands of meaning—one potentially combative, the other not—are thus attributed by different narrators to the same prominent Companion.

After listing these glosses, al-Ṭabarī refers to unnamed others (*ākharūn*) who were of the opinion that *jāhidū fī 'llāh ḥaqqa jihādihi* means "Perform a deed appropriately as is due Him" (*a'milū bi-'l-haqq ḥaqqa 'amalihi*). This commentary was transmitted on the authority of al-Ḍaḥḥāk by some "whose narration was regarded with suspicion,"[65] cautions al-Ṭabarī. He then goes on to express his preference (*wa-'l-ṣawāb min al-qawl*) for the school of thought that held *jāhidū fī 'llāh ḥaqqa jihādihi* means "fighting in the path of God" (*al-jihād fī sabīl allāh*), as that had become by his time the established meaning of *jihād*. This school of thought, he asserts, is more prevalent than the one that interprets this phrase to mean exerting oneself to the utmost in the performance of an action for the sake of God.[66] It is worthy of note that al-Ṭabarī's main reason for privileging the meaning of this verse as referring to "fighting in the path of God" is not because Ibn 'Abbās in his opinion is the more reliable transmitter in this case, but because this meaning had become by his time the predominant one—an assertion that is remarkable for its circular reasoning.

In contradistinction to al-Ṭabarī, **al-Wāḥidī** (d. 468/1076)[67] privileges the non-combative meanings of *jāhidū fī 'llāh* in his exegesis. He states that a majority of the commentators have understood the meaning of *jihād* in this context to apply to "all acts of obedience" (*jāmi' a'māl al-ṭā'a*), and the phrase *ḥaqqa 'l-jihād* refers to the performance of such acts in sincere dedication to God (*ṣādiqat*[an] *khāliṣat*[an] *li-'llāh ta'ālā*). According to the early exegete Muqātil b. Ḥayyān (d. ca. 150/767),[68] *ḥaqqa 'l-jihād* refers to "striving diligently in [one's] deeds (*yajtahidū fī 'l-'amal*)."[69] Al-Wāḥidi further refers to 'Abd Allāh b. al-Mubārak (d. 181/797)[70] who understood this verse as referring to "striving against one's desires and the [carnal] self."[71]

By the sixth/twelfth century, it is clear that both the combative and non-combative strands of meaning in relation to Qur'ān 22:78 had become widely accepted by the exegetes. Thus **al-Zamakhsharī** understands *wa-jāhidū* in this verse to command both "fighting" (*amara bi-'l-ghazw*) and striving against one's carnal self and desires (*wa-bi-mujāhadat al-nafs wa-'l-hawā*). The latter constitutes "the greater *jihād*." This is so, al-Zamakhsharī says, because it is known that when the Prophet returned from one of his military campaigns, he remarked, "We have returned from the lesser *jihād* to the greater *jihād*." *Fī 'llāh* means "exclusively for the sake of God."[72]

Al-Rāzī in the late sixth/twelfth century begins by referencing al-Zamakhsharī's views[73] and similarly states that this verse emphasizes above all that one undertake *jihād* only and absolutely for the sake of God (*fī dhāt allāh wa-min ajlihi*). And what is the nature of this *jihād*? Al-Rāzi explains that what is specifically intended here is fighting the unbelievers (*anna 'l-murād qitāl al-kuffār khāṣṣat*[an]). *Ḥaqqa jihādihi* means, first, that one should not carry out *jihād* "except as an act of worship, desiring neither renown nor riches in the world," and second, that Muslims should fight in latter times as robustly as they had fought in the early period, especially during the battle of Badr. This is referenced by a report from Ibn 'Abbās in which he states, "Strive/fight in regard to God a true striving as is His due just as you strove/fought the first time" (as also recorded by al-Ṭabarī above). Al-Rāzī also refers to 'Umar's exegesis of the verse as counseling fighting against the Makhzūm and 'Abd Shams.[74]

Other early authorities cited by al-Rāzi, however, contradictorily impute non-combative meanings to *jihād* in this verse. Thus, according to Ibn 'Abbās, *ḥaqqa jihādihi* means that one should not fear the censure of other people for the sake of God, while al-Ḍaḥḥāk believed that it means that one should act for the sake of God as is His due; views that were also recorded by earlier commentators as we saw. Another possible meaning, continues al-Rāzī, is that one should exert one's utmost to revive the religion of God and establish His rights through waging war with one's hands, tongue, and whatever else one can muster, and to ward off base desires and inclinations. Like al-Ṭabarī, al-Rāzī references 'Abd Allāh b. al-Mubārak, who had explained *ḥaqqa jihādihi* as striving against one's self and desires (*mujāhadat al-nafs wa-'l-hawā*). Al-Rāzī further mentions that when Muḥammad returned from the campaign to Tabūk (in 9/630), he commented, "We have returned from the lesser *jihād* to the greater *jihād*." It is therefore more appropriate to believe, he says, that this phrase applies to all kinds of obligations (*'alā kull al-takālīf*), for the effort to fulfill God's positive commandments and avoid what is prohibited is *jihād*, properly speaking. As for the opinion expressed by Muqātil and al-Kalbī that Qur'ān 22:78 was abrogated by Qur'ān 64:16, it is dismissed by al-Rāzī as untenable, because God does not ordain anything that is beyond human ability.[75]

Al-Qurṭubī in the seventh/thirteenth century relates that, according to some, this verse refers to fighting against the unbelievers (*jihād al-kuffār*), whereas, according to others, the verse refers in general to the observance of all the commandments of God and refraining from everything He has proscribed. The latter includes struggling against the following four sources of temptation and disorder: (1) against one's carnal self in order to obey God and restrain it from following base desires; (2) against Satan in order to repel his evil insinuations (*waswasatahu*); (3) against oppressors to ward off their oppression; and (4) against unbelievers to refute their unbelief. *Jihād* here is to be understood, continues al-Qurṭubī, to refer to the human internal struggle [against one's carnal self], as is indicated by the *ḥadīth* narrated by Ḥayāt b. Shurayḥ, who quoted the Prophet as saying, "The striver (*al-mujāhid*) is one who strives against his self for the sake of God, the Mighty, the Exalted." *Jihād* is furthermore the duty to always speak a word of truth, he affirms, as becomes evident in another *ḥadīth* narrated by Abū Umāma, in which a man asked the Prophet, "Which is the best *jihād*?" After a period of silence, he received the reply, "[The best *jihād* is] a word of justice to a tyrannical ruler."[76]

The trajectory of shifting meanings and emphases over time in connection with *jihād*—as becomes apparent in the exegeses of the verses discussed above—is highly revealing of the emergence of competing paradigms of piety linked to a growing communal identity on the part of early Muslims. The contested nature of the parameters of this identity as it was coalescing in the formative period becomes encoded in these discourses of moral excellence that seek to decipher the best way to strive—at both the individual and communal levels—for the sake of God.

Patient Forbearance as a Component of Striving in the Path of God

We now move on to a treatment of patient forbearance as a nonviolent component of *jihād* in Qur'anic discourse. As we noted before, *ṣabr*, commonly and variously translated into English as "patience," "forbearance," and "steadfastness," is typically not described as a component of *al-jihād fī sabīl allāh* in legal and other works. And yet the Qur'ān often singles out *ṣabr* as an essential trait of the believers in their striving to fulfill the religious duties incumbent upon them—which is *jihād* broadly understood in the Qur'anic context, as our previous discussion of relevant verses established. The Qur'ān also occasionally couples *jihād* and its derivatives with *ṣabr* and its derivatives. The *mujāhid* (the striver) and the *ṣābir* (the patient/steadfast) together are often extolled as the most morally excellent among humankind, a coupling that became more common during the Medinan period when the combative *jihād* became permissible after the *hijra*. In this chapter, we focus specifically on a particular verse (Qur'ān 3:200), regarded as an early Medinan revelation, that over time through semantic and hermeneutic manipulation became anachronistically associated with *ribāṭ*—the post-prophetic military activity of guarding the *thughūr* (frontiers). A comparison of the exegeses of early and late commentators on this verse is highly revealing of the contested nature of this martial interpretation and points to critical transformations in the conceptualizations of *jihād* and its relation to the vital attribute of *ṣabr* over time.

Qur'ān 3:200: *Ṣabr* and Its Derivatives

Qur'ān 3:200 states, "O those who believe, be patient and forbearing (iṣbirū), outdo others in forbearance (ṣābirū), be firm (rābiṭū), and revere God so that you may succeed"

In his brief commentary on this early Medinan verse,[77] the early Meccan exegete **Mujāhid b. Jabr al-Makkī** (d. 104/722) attributes to his contemporary al-Hasan al-Baṣrī (d. 110/728) the comment that the verse counsels believers to be steadfast in their religion, to bear patiently with the unbelievers until they despair of their religion, and to be firm against the polytheists.[78]

About a generation later, **Muqātil b. Sulaymān** comments that the verse exhorts believers to be steadfast in carrying out the commands and duties imposed by God, forbearing with the Prophet wherever he is, and firm against the enemy in the path of God (*wa-rābiṭū 'l-'aduw fī sabīl allāh*) "until they forsake their religion for yours."[79] Despite the invocation of *fī sabīl allāh*, there does not appear to be any hint of military combat in engaging the adversary in this manner.

In his very brief exegesis of this verse, the early third/ninth century Yemeni exegete **'Abd al-Razzāq al-Ṣan'ānī** (d. 211/827)[80] records a report from Ma'mar relating from Qatāda that this verse counsels believers to bear patiently with the polytheists (*ṣābirū al-mushrikīn*) and hold fast in the path of God (*rābiṭū fī sabīl allāh*).[81] Once again we note the conjoining of *fī sabīl allāh* with *ribāṭ* without the overt implication of military activity.

In the second half of the third/ninth century, **Hūd b. Muḥakkam** cites unnamed exegetes who interpreted this verse as counseling "patient perseverance in obeying God, forbearance with the people of error (*ahl al-ḍalāla*), and remaining firm in the path of God." Others said that it means "Persevere in [carrying out] the religious obligations, and be firm with the enemy." Ibn Muḥakkam also makes no explicit association between *rābiṭū fī sabīl allāh/ rābiṭū al-'aduw* and fighting.[82]

Our early Shī'ī exegetes from the second half of the third/ninth century understand this verse as generally counseling patience and perseverance in observing one's religious duties. Thus **Furāt b. Ibrāhīm** comments that *aṣbirū* in the verse counsels believers to be patient with "yourselves" (*anfusakum*); *ṣābirū* means to be forbearing with your enemies; and *rābiṭū* means to be steadfast in the path of God (*fī sabīl allāh*). The verse, he says, was revealed in reference to Muḥammad, 'Alī, and Hamza b. 'Abd al-Muṭṭalib.[83]

Both **al-Qummī** and **al-'Ayyāshī** (d. ca. 320/932)[84] quote the sixth Shī'ī Imam Ja'far al-Ṣādiq as counseling in explanation of this verse, "Be patient during your tribulations (*al-maṣā'ib*), steadfast during the [performance of] religious duties (*al-farā'iḍ*), and adhere to the Imāms."[85] The eighth Imām 'Alī al-Riḍā (d. 202/818) is said to have described the *ṣābirūn* as those who had patiently carried out their religious obligations and the *mutaṣabbirūn* as those who had been steadfast in avoiding what has been prohibited.[86] In a more sectarian vein in a slightly later period, al-'Ayyāshī records that according to Abū 'l-Ṭufayl, the fifth Imam Muḥammad al-Bāqir had said that the [true] *murābiṭ* would be "from among our offspring."[87]

Al-Ṭabarī as usual offers us a much more variegated and detailed exegesis emanating from different sources that nicely encapsulate for us the contested meanings of this verse by the late third/ninth century. A number of exegetes, as he documents, understood the verse to mean "Remain steadfast in your faith and bear patiently the unbelievers[' harm] and be firm with them."

Among this group of exegetes were the Successors al-Ḥasan al-Baṣrī, Qatāda b. Di'āma (d. 118/736),[88] Ibn Jurayj (d. 150/767),[89] and al-Ḍaḥḥāk.[90] Another group of exegetes, which included Muḥammad b. Ka'b al-Quraẓī (d. 118/736),[91] maintained that the verse means "Remain steadfast in your faith, and wait patiently for My promise to you regarding your obedience to Me, and be firm against your enemies."[92] In these two exegetical clusters, it is noteworthy that the term *jihād* does not occur, and fighting the enemy is not indicated.

In a third cluster of comments, *jihād* is explicitly mentioned by a group of exegetes who explained this verse as "Be patient in *jihād* [here implying fighting] and steadfast against your enemies and be firm against them." Among this group was Zayd b. Aslam (d. 136/753),[93] who said that the verse counsels believers to be patient during the military *jihād*, and to remain steadfast and firm against their enemies. Another report from Zayd b. Aslam states in connection with this verse that Abū 'Ubayda b. al-Jarrāḥ (d. 18/639) wrote to 'Umar b. al-Khaṭṭāb and referred to the mobilization of a large number of Byzantine troops and the fear they had induced in Muslims. 'Umar wrote back remarking that whenever hardship befalls a pious believer, God confers joyous relief (*faraj*) on him afterward, and that this verse had been revealed to convey this assurance.[94] This report references 'Umar's deployment of this verse in a specific military context, signaling the addition of this new semantic dimension in the post-prophetic period.

Yet other commentators offered an altogether different and noteworthy meaning of *rābiṭū*, namely to "Observe your prayers," literally "wait for them [the prayers] one after another." Thus, according to one report, Abū Salama b. 'Abd al-Raḥmān (d. between 94–104/712–722)[95] once asked his nephew, "Do you know what this verse was revealed about?" When the boy answered in the negative, Abū Salama said, "My nephew, there were no campaigns (*ghazw*) during the time of the Prophet which required guarding the frontiers (*yurābaṭ fīhi*). It rather means to be vigilant concerning the [performance of the] prayers, one after the other." Another report on the authority of Shuraḥbīl [b. Sa'īd] (d. ca. 123/740)[96] relates that 'Alī had remarked that the Prophet once asked, "Shall I not indicate to you what will cause God to blot out your sins and lapses? The performance of the full ablution in difficult circumstances and anticipation of the prayers, one after another—that is *al-ribāṭ*."[97]

At this point, al-Ṭabarī weighs in and begins to sort through these reports and evaluate them. He establishes first of all that the verse addresses those who believe in God and His messenger and counsels them—*iṣbirū*—to be steadfast in their religion and in obedience to their Lord.[98] *Wa-ṣābirū*, al-Ṭabarī continues, means "Be steadfast with your enemies from among the polytheists." This is the preferred understanding, he maintains, because the third verbal form in Arabic, as is well-known, usually requires that there be two or more actors implied in the verb. Therefore, the believers are counseled here to be more patient or steadfast than their enemies, until God grants the former victory over the latter and His word is paramount and their enemies are disgraced.[99] *Rābiṭū* means "Be firm in the path of God with your enemies and the enemies of your religion from among the polytheists." Al-Ṭabarī considers the verbal noun *ribāṭ* in this verse to be already a reference to the deployment of horses to secure the frontiers against enemy cavalry forces.[100] In this highly significant exegesis of this important verse, al-Ṭabarī makes clear that by his time, *ribāṭ* had acquired a predominantly military inflection, for which he shows a clear preference, superseding what was clearly the earlier common understanding of this term as mainly indicating vigilance and steadfastness in daily prayers. Al-Ṭabarī offers no explanation as to why the Qur'ān would be referring to a practice—*ribāṭ* as guarding the frontiers—that had developed after the death of the Prophet, a point that had been noted by a number of his predecessors and had caused them to dismiss this possible construal.

Al-Wāḥidī says that this verse, according to al-Ḥasan [al-Baṣrī], means "[Be steadfast] in your religion and do not forsake it on account of hardship." Zayd b. Aslam, however, was of the opinion that *iṣbirū* means to be steadfast in fighting (*'alā 'l-jihād*); *ṣābirū* meant to outdo one's enemies in steadfastness/forbearance ["so that the enemy is not more steadfast than you"], and *rābiṭū* meant that they should undertake to fight their enemies in battle. After considering these exegeses, al-Wāḥidī, like al-Ṭabarī, expresses his opinion that *ribāṭ* here refers to the deployment of horses against enemies at certain frontiers. The duty of *jihād*, he says, consequently acquired the name of *ribāṭ* and *murābaṭa*; he indicates that many exegetes by his time subscribed to this view. Other unnamed exegetes, al-Wāḥidī is careful to point out, subscribed to a different understanding, however.[101]

Al-Wāḥidī also records the opinion of the previously mentioned Successor Abū Salama b. 'Abd al-Raḥmān, who had affirmed to his nephew that there was no military campaign at the time of the Prophet during which people guarded the frontiers; *rābiṭū* must rather mean "waiting steadily for the prayers one after another." Further corroboration is provided by al-Ḥākim Abū 'Abd Allāh (sc. al-Ḥākim al-Nīsābūrī, d. 404/1014),[102] who transmitted this report in his *Ṣaḥīḥ*. There is also a sound *ḥadīth* from Abū Hurayra in which he related as follows:

> The Messenger of God, peace and blessings be upon him, said, "Shall I not indicate to you that on account of which God blots out sins and elevates the status [of people]?" They [Companions] replied, "Yes indeed, O Messenger of God." He said, "Ablution in difficult circumstances,

going frequently to the mosque and waiting for the prayers one after another—that is *ribāṭ* for you, that is *ribāṭ* for you, that is *ribāṭ* for you."[103]

Muslim [b. Ḥajjāj] is also said to have related this *ḥadīth* from Ismā'īl b. Ja'far (d. 180/796),[104] affirming that waiting for the prayers was called *ribāṭ*, for all those who are steadfast in carrying out a command is said to have "devoted [lit. "attached"] his heart to it" (*rabaṭa qalbahu 'alayhi*) and "girded himself" (*rabaṭa nafsahu*) for that purpose.[105]

Despite these proof-texts conscientiously recorded by al-Wāḥidī that stress primarily devotional meanings for *ribāṭ* and its derivatives, this prominent exegete in the fifth/eleventh century understands all three imperatives in Qur'ān 3:200 to refer essentially to steadfastness in battle. His preference clearly establishes for us, once again, the predominance of combative meanings assigned in his day to the lexemes *rābiṭū* and *ribāṭ*.

In the following century, **al-Zamakhsharī** says that the verse exhorts believers to be steadfast in their religion and its obligations and to be firm with the enemies of God in *jihād*—that is, to surpass them in steadfastness during the trials of battle and to be at least the equal of them in displaying patience and endurance. *Al-muṣābara*, the verbal noun derived from *ṣābara*, is a type of patience/steadfastness that goes beyond ordinary patience, comments al-Zamakhsharī, indicating steadfastness in the face of unusual hardship and severity. *Wa-rābiṭū* means to stand guard on the frontiers on horseback, ever-vigilant and prepared for a military foray (*ghazw*). In corroboration of this understanding, al-Zamakhsharī quotes the verse, "Muster against them all you can of force and tethered horses (*ribāṭ al-khayl*), so as to cast fear upon the enemies of God and of you" (Qur'ān 8:60) and the *ḥadīth*: "Whoever stands guard at the frontier a day and a night in the path of God earns the equivalent of fasting for a month and staying up for prayer at night [during the month], not breaking fast nor desisting from supererogatory prayer except to attend to necessities."[106] Worthy of note is that al-Zamakhsharī is the first commentator to connect Qur'ān 3:200 to Qur'ān 8:60, allowing him to specifically equate *rābiṭu* in the former verse with *ribāṭ al-khayl* in the second, and thus impart a combative meaning to the former. We recollect that even though al-Ṭabari expressed a preference for the opinion that *rābiṭu* referred to the activity of *ribāṭ* (guarding the frontiers), he did not attempt to impose this meaning on this verse by yoking it to Qur'ān 8:60. By al-Zamakhsharī's time in the sixth/twelfth century, the parallel invocation of these two verses is revealing of an exegetical attempt to elide earlier non-combative understandings of *rābiṭū* in Qur'an 3:200 and to explicitly impute military activity to it .

In his interpretation of Qur'ān 3:200, **al-Rāzī** painstakingly describes the various inflections of patience, necessitated by the fact that human existence is comprised of two spheres: one that has to do with the individual only, and the second that is shared with others. In the first sphere, humans must practice patience and steadfastness (*al-ṣabr*) [in relation to themselves and their duties], whereas in the second, they must practice forbearance (*al-muṣābara*) vis-à-vis others. Patience (*ṣabr*) is of various kinds, continues al-Rāzī. For example, one must have patience in learning the complexities of proofs when acquiring knowledge of God's unity, justice, prophecy, and resurrection, and in undertaking the difficulties inherent in carrying out religious obligations. These various manifestations of patience are subsumed under His command *aṣbirū*.[107]

As for *muṣābara*, it refers to forbearance during unpleasant occurrences between oneself and others. This includes showing forbearance toward members of one's family, neighbors, and relatives when they behave badly. *Muṣābara* also includes refraining from taking revenge on those who cause you harm, as counseled in Qur'ān 7:199: "Turn away from the ignorant." Further included in *muṣābara* is showing a preference and love for the other over oneself, as mentioned in Qur'an 59:9: "They prefer [others] over themselves even when reaping poverty." Thus *muṣābara* also consists of forgiving those who wrong or oppress you (*al-'afu 'amman ẓalamaka*); al-Rāzi references Qur'ān 2:237 here, which states, "Forgiveness is closer to God-conscious piety" (*li-'l-taqwā*). Moreover, *muṣābara* includes commanding good and preventing wrong.[108] Because the one undertaking this duty may face harm, it includes fighting (*al-jihād*) in self-defense. It also involves showing forbearance with the foolish in trying to assuage their doubts and dispel their inclinations toward falsehood. Therefore, *aṣbirū* has to do with the individual, whereas *ṣābirū* deals with interactions between the individual and others.[109]

Al-Rāzī warns, however, that even when practicing patience and forbearance, humans are still subject to the baser aspects of their natures, such as carnal desires, anger, and covetousness, which cause them to lose patience and sacrifice forbearance—hence they are counseled to hold firm (*wa-rābiṭū*). To summarize this rather lengthy section, al-Rāzī says *al-murābaṭa* refers to the effort expended in controlling and suppressing all manner of evil propensities (*al-quwa*) within the human self, and *al-falāḥ* (success) is the end result for those who thereby prefer to please God out of reverence for Him over submission to their base desires.[110]

As for His saying *wa-rābiṭū*, al-Rāzī says that there are two principal ways of understanding it. First, it could be understood as referring to the tethering of horses on the frontier just as the enemy forces do, each prepared to fight the other. Al-Rāzī references Qur'ān 8:60 here and the *ḥadīth* in which the Prophet compares spending a day and night on the frontier to fasting and supererogatory prayers for a month. Second, the meaning of *murābaṭa* is to wait for prayer one after another, which exegesis is supported by the previously-mentioned *ḥadīth* from Abū Salama 'Abd al-Raḥmān in which he said there were no military raids (*ghazw*) requiring *ribāṭ* during the time of the Prophet, and by the *ḥadīth* from Abū Hurayra in which Muḥammad affirms three times that *ribāṭ* means waiting for the prayers in sequence.[111]

Al-Rāzī allows that both of these exegeses are semantically plausible. *Al-ribāṭ* is derived from *al-rabṭ*, which implies firmness (*al-shidd*). Whoever abides by a commandment in patience has resolved his (or her) heart upon it. Others say that *ribāṭ* refers to adherence to something and endurance (*al-luzūm wa-'l-thabāt*), which meanings may be supported by his previous discussion of *ṣabr* and self-control (*rabṭ al-nafs*). Moreover, this kind of steadfastness and endurance may be displayed during both fighting (*'alā 'l-jihād*) and prayer—"and God knows best!"[112]

Like al-Rāzī, **al-Qurṭubī** affirms that Qur'ān 3:200 encompasses within it much counsel concerning a range of issues—from how to present oneself in this world to the enemy to attaining the felicity of the next world. It urges believers to be steadfast in their obligations and in fighting their base desires, for *ṣabr* is self-restraint. As for *muṣābara*, some said its meaning is to be firm with the enemy, as maintained by Zayd b. Aslam, whereas al-Ḥasan al-Baṣrī said it means steadfastness in observing the five prayers. Others said it means to persist in acting contrary to the incitements of one's carnal self, "for it beckons and he resists." According to the early scholar Atā' [b. Abī Rabāḥ] (d. 115/733) and the previously mentioned al-Quraẓī, it means to wait patiently for the fulfillment of the promise made to humans [by God] and to not despair subsequently, waiting instead for deliverance and relief (*al-faraj*) [after their hardship]. Abū 'Umar[113] would say, "Waiting for deliverance with patience is an act of worship."[114]

Al-Qurṭubī cites the well-known commentary of Abū Salama that the verb *rābiṭū* refers to waiting for the daily prayers, since the practice of manning the frontiers did not exist during the Prophet's time. Like al-Ṭabarī and other exegetes, al-Qurṭubī notes that Abū Salama had also related the *ḥadīth* in which Muḥammad repeats three times that *ribāṭ* meant waiting for the prayers one after another, and that acts associated with prayer, like ablution under difficult circumstances and going frequently to the mosque, wipe out one's sins.[115]

In contrast to these views, Ibn 'Aṭiyya had asserted that *ribāṭ* primarily means "adhering to the path of God" (*al-mulāzama fī sabīl allāh*) because it is derived from "tethering one's horse" (*min ribāṭ al-khayl*); thus the one who manned the frontiers of Islam was called a *murābiṭ*, whether on horseback or on foot. The Prophet's statement in reference to prayer, "And that is *ribāṭ* for you," is similar to *ribāṭ* in the path of God, he declared. The grammarian Khalīl b. Aḥmad (d. 175/791), "one of the greatest masters and experts of language," continues al-Qurṭubī, had commented that *ribāṭ* refers to manning the frontiers, as well as to the diligent observance of prayers. Upon weighing the evidence, our exegete concludes that *ribāṭ* in the sense of waiting for prayers is to be regarded as the basic linguistic derivation, as affirmed by the Prophet. The common understanding of *murābaṭa* is "to fasten something/tie a knot on something" so that it does not remain loose. This harks back to the idea of steadfastly refraining from something and restraining one's heart through good intentions and one's body in order to perform acts of obedience. Among the greatest and most important of such acts is the tying of the horse in the path of God, as commanded in Qur'ān 8:60, and devoting oneself to prayers, as stated by Muḥammad and related by Abū Hurayra, Jābir, 'Alī, and countless others.[116] Through this line of reasoning, al-Qurṭubī harmonizes the two predominant strands of interpretation concerning this critical verse, without privileging one over the other.[117]

Concluding Remarks

It is clear from our survey that Qur'ān 3:200 is a highly critical verse that allowed commentators from roughly the third/ninth century on to begin to yoke the attributes of patience and forbearance, as encapsulated in *ṣabr* and its derivatives, to *jihād* and its multiple, particularly combative, significations. Early exegetes from the first three centuries of Islam uniformly emphasized that *ṣabr* and its derivatives referred to patience and forbearance in the carrying out of general religious duties, particularly under adverse conditions; and that the Qur'anic *rābiṭū* counseled the faithful to exhibit firmness under such conditions, particularly in unwavering observance of the daily prayers. It is in al-Ṭabarī's commentary, not surprisingly, that we first observe that both *ṣabr* and *ribāṭ*, while retaining these early connotations, become conjoined to the combative *jihād* and specifically to military vigilance on the frontiers. The source of this interpretation was the Medinan Zayd b. Aslam, whose pro-Umayyad sympathies are well-known and who frequently served as advisor to the Umayyad Caliph al-Walīd b. Yazīd on legal matters.[118] Like his son Ibn Zayd, he often expressed belligerent views on *jihād* and was regarded as a very weak (*ḍa'īf jiddan*) transmitter by Ibn Sa'd, for example.[119] It is here that we may well detect the impetus—in the context of belligerent Umayyad-Byzantine relations—for the importation of the verb *rābiṭu* into the Umayyad military lexicon to describe armed vigilance on the frontiers. Equating the patient anticipation of the daily prayers with stoic vigilance against the enemy at the borders conferred the much-needed veneer of a religiously mandated activity upon the latter. As our survey reveals, other Ḥijāzī authorities like Abū Salama b. 'Abd al-Raḥmān not known to have harbored strong affection for the Umayyads resolutely upheld the non-combative significations of *rbṭ* and its derivatives.[120] It is noteworthy that al-Rāzī in the late sixth/twelfth century and al-Qurṭubī in the seventh/thirteenth century re-emphasized the non-combative pious and spiritual significations of the derivatives of *rbṭ* and expounded more expansively on their merits, while acknowledging that *ribāṭ* had also come to mean the manning of frontiers on horseback.[121] We cannot therefore assume a steady linear progression from non-combative to combative meanings for these two terms from the first century of Islam to the sixth; instead, we observe a frequent shifting in their valences.

To continue our delineation of the expanding semantic landscape of *jihād*, we must now turn our attention to the combative component (*qitāl*) that came to be included within the umbrella term *jihād*. The questions we must ask are when, where, why, and how did *qitāl* become a required component of striving in the path of God, according to the Qur'ān and its interpreters? In the following chapter, we take a close look at the exegeses of critical verses that deal with the necessity of fighting under certain conditions as a religious duty imposed upon believers.

II

Fighting in the Path of God

A RELIGIOUS AND MORAL OBLIGATION

WHEREAS STRIVING IN the path of God in myriad, quotidian ways without resorting to physical combat was a general Qur'anic injunction laid upon Muslims in the Meccan and early Medinan periods, as we noted, a new, specific aspect of *jihād—qitāl* (fighting)—was introduced shortly thereafter. The Qur'ān (2:216) informs us that the divine commandment to fight the pagan Meccans was not universally welcomed by the Muslims. Consequently, it adopts trenchant language to impress upon the faithful that in response to certain conditions, *qitāl* was an essential component of *jihād*, and that believers should not shrink from carrying out this religious and moral obligation when commanded to do so by God and His prophet. The taking of human life that armed combat entails in such specific situations is acknowledged in the Qur'ān as an act of enormity. Several verses enumerate the conditions under which *qitāl* becomes necessary, and they outline the limits of justified military combat that should not be contravened by the faithful. Such verses would become the object of further reflection by jurists, theologians, and ethicists in the classical and medieval periods.

There are fifty-four Qur'anic verses containing various lexemes from the third verbal form of the root *qtl*. Once again, we are able to discuss at length only a select number of these verses. The verses below have been chosen primarily because of their frequency of occurrence in discussions of *jihād* as armed combat and because they help us map to a considerable extent an exegetical landscape of shifting and contested meanings for both *jihād* and *qitāl*—and the relationship between them—over time. A number of the verses in the Qur'ān dealing with *qitāl* are concerned with a priori reasons for engaging in justified armed combat (*jus ad bellum*) and the kind of people against whom fighting under certain conditions is not only justified but required. Some of these verses also prompted a vigorous discussion among the exegetes of what kind of people must *not* be fought against by Muslims out of consideration of humane conduct (*jus in bello*) during the waging of a legitimate *jihād*, as is evident from the bulk of the exegeses presented.

In this chapter, we focus on Qur'ān 22:39–40 and 2:190–94, widely believed to be the earliest verses giving the command to fight in the Medinan period. In chapter 3, we discuss another cluster of verses that deal with the obligatory nature of fighting and the rules of conduct during and after the hostilities.

Reasons for Recourse to Fighting

Exegeses of Qur'ān 22:39–40

These verses state, "Permission is given to **those who are fought against/against whom fighting has been initiated** (*yuqātalūna*)[1] because they have been wronged/oppressed (*ẓulimū*), and God is able to help them. These are they who have been wrongfully expelled from their homes merely for saying 'God is our Lord.' If God had not restrained some people by means of others, monasteries, churches, synagogues, and mosques in which God's name is mentioned frequently would have been destroyed. Indeed God comes to the aid of those who come to His aid; verily He is powerful and mighty."

According to a majority of the exegetes we surveyed, Qur'ān 22:39 was the first verse revealed permitting Muslims to engage in armed combat against the pagan Meccans.[2] The reasons for sanctioning fighting at this stage are primarily twofold: (1) because Muslims had been physically harmed by the pagan Meccans and expelled from their homes; and (2) because such persecution was visited upon the Muslims merely because of their monotheistic belief and not because of any wrongdoing on their part. *Qitāl* in this verse is thus in response to prior aggression by the Meccans and unambiguously defensive, according to all the exegetes surveyed. The right to profess belief in the one God and to defend this right when violently encroached upon is clearly stressed in all the exegeses consulted here.

Thus the late first/seventh century exegete **Mujāhid b. Jabr** (d. ca. 104/722) comments that the verse refers to the believers who emigrated from Mecca to Medina, pursued by the unbelievers from the Quraysh. Consequently, God gave the believers permission to fight through the revelation of this verse, and they subsequently fought the unbelievers.[3] As for the part of the verse that states, "If God had not restrained some of the people by means of others," Mujāhid comments that it means that God had restrained some of them through others "in regard to bearing witness and with regard to truth" (*fī 'l-shahāda wa-fī 'l-ḥaqq*). If this were not the case, then monasteries and all other houses of worship would have been destroyed. The verse refers to the *ṣawāmi'*, which are the monasteries or cells of the Christian monks (*al-ruhbān*), as well as to all the other places of worship "belonging to the People of the Book and to Muslims" (*li-ahl al-kitāb wa-ahl al-islām*).[4]

The late Umayyad exegete **Muqātil b. Sulaymān** (d. 150/767) explains this verse as follows: Permission was given to those who fight in the path of God because the unbelievers of Mecca (*kuffār makka*) oppressed them and God helped them against these unbelievers after the prohibition [sc. against fighting]. Oppression consisted of being driven from their homes because of the physical torture and verbal abuse to which many Muslims had been subjected. The pagan Meccans expelled the believers from their homes only because the latter acknowledged God and affirmed His oneness. If God had not constrained the polytheists through the agency of the Muslims, then the former would have prevailed and killed the latter. Subsequently, the monasteries of the monks, the churches of the Christians, the synagogues of the Jews, and the mosques of the Muslims would all have been destroyed. All these religious groups (*al-milal*) mention the name of God profusely in their places of worship, and God defends these places of worship through the Muslims.[5]

According to the ***Tanwīr al-miqbās***, this verse permitted the believers to fight against the unbelievers of Mecca because of the latter's oppressive behavior: They had evicted the Muslims from their homes without due cause or any wrongdoing on the part of the Muslims (*bi-lā ḥaqq wa-lā jurm*), except that they attested to the oneness of God and bore witness that Muhammad is His messenger. If God had not restrained the following groups of people by others: believers by means of the prophets, the unbelievers by the believers, and the sitters-at-home without a legitimate excuse (*al-qāʿidīn bi-ghayr ʿudhr*) by those who fight (*bi-'l-mujāhidīn*), then the monasteries (*ṣawāmiʿ*) of the monks, the synagogues (*biyaʿ*) of the Jews, and the fire-temples of the Magians—and all of these are entrusted for their protection to Muslims (*li-anna kulla hāʾulāʾī fī maʾman al-muslimīn*)—as well as the mosques of the Muslims in which God is much exalted and glorified, would have been destroyed. God aids the one who aids Him and His prophet against his enemy, concludes the *Tanwīr*.[6]

In his commentary, the early third/ninth century exegete **ʿAbd al-Razzāq** (reporting from Maʿmar from Qatāda[7]) comments that this was the first verse revealed about fighting (*al-qitāl*), granting permission to the Muslims to engage in combat.[8] Like his predecessors, he similarly engages in a discussion of the various houses of worship mentioned in this verse and relates in this context another Qur'anic verse (22:17), which states, "Those who believe, and those who are Jews, Sabians, Christians, and Magians, and those who are polytheists," as a reference to religious communities whose existence is recognized in the Qur'ān. The religions are six in number; however, "five are for Satan and one is for the Merciful One (*al-Rahmān*)!" proclaims 'Abd al-Razzāq.[9]

In the second half of the third/ninth century, **Hūd b. Muḥakkam** comments that this verse is a reference to the persecution of a certain group of Muslims and eviction from their homes by the pagan Meccans; al-Hasan al-Baṣrī is cited as a source for this interpretation. When these Muslims set out to emigrate to Medina, the pagan Meccans attempted to prevent them; thereupon, they were given permission to fight. Some [unnamed] exegetes were of the [minority] opinion that it referred to an earlier group of Muslims who were given permission to fight after they had been driven from their homes by the polytheists and subsequently emigrated to Abyssinia.[10]

With regard to the houses of worship, Ibn Muḥakkam references Mujāhid's gloss on *ṣawāmi'* as the cells of monks, and agrees that the *biya'* refer to Christian churches, *ṣalawāt* to the Jews, and *masājid* to the Muslims. However, in a remarkable departure from the views of the earliest exegetes (Mujāhid and Muqātil) in this survey, Ibn Muḥakkam asserts that the phrase "in which God's name is much praised" applies only to mosques (*ya'nī fī 'l-masājid*).[11]

In the first quarter of the third/ninth century, **Ibrāhīm al-Qummī** understands Qur'ān 22:39 in a particularist, Shī'ī vein and reads into it an exclusive reference to 'Alī, Ja'far, and Hamza. The following verse (22:40) is understood by him to refer not to events in the Muslim community during the time of the Prophet, but rather to al-Ḥusayn and his confrontation with Yazīd, the Umayyad caliph, and the former's subsequent death in Kufa.[12] Similarly, Furāt b. Ibrāhīm (fl. second half of third/ninth century) discerns in Qur'ān 22:40 on the authority of Abū 'Abd Allāh (cf. Ja'far al-Ṣādiq) a reference to 'Alī, al-Ḥasan, al-Ḥusayn, Ja'far and Hamza, from after the time of the Prophet.[13]

Al-Ṭabarī (d. 310/923) has an extensive commentary on these two verses, recording a variety of views on their significations. First of all, unlike his predecessors referred to here, he discusses the variant readings of 22:39—*udhina* versus *adhina*, but more importantly, *yuqātalūna* versus *yuqātilūna*. Al-Ṭabarī avers—somewhat disingenuously—that there is very little difference in meaning between the passive form *yuqātalūna* and the active form *yuqātilūna*, for, he says, when someone fights another person, each is equally a "combatant" (*muqātil*).[14] The larger ramifications of the passive form of this critical verb for underscoring the defensive function of the military *jihād* are ignored by him.

Al-Ṭabarī affirms that this verse was the first revelation that permitted fighting, ending the prohibition against it for the preceding ten years; Ibn Zayd, Ibn Jurayj and Qatāda are cited as the sources for this interpretation. Al-Ṭabarī documents the differences of opinion regarding the identity of those who were specifically granted permission in this verse to engage in fighting. Those who said it referred to only the Prophet and his Companions included Ibn 'Abbās and Sa'īd b. Jubayr (d. 95/714).[15] Other commentators maintained that the verse referred to a group of Muslims who wished to leave enemy territory and emigrate to Medina, but who were prevented from doing so. Among those who subscribed to this view were Ibn Abī Najīḥ, Mujāhid, Ibn Jurayj, Qatāda, and others.[16]

With regard to Qur'ān 22:40, al-Ṭabarī says that it refers to the believers who were evicted from their homes and subjected to physical torture and verbal abuse by the pagan Meccans for affirming their faith in God and His messenger that forced them to emigrate. The pagans had no right to resort to such actions, remarks al-Ṭabarī, as they were clearly the wrongdoers.[17]

As for the phrase, "If God had not restrained some of the people by means of others," there are differences of opinion regarding its referent. Some exegetes, such as Ibn Jurayj, said that it meant "If God had not constrained the polytheists through the Muslims." Others, such as Ibn Zayd, said that it meant "were it not for fighting and *jihād* in the path of God" (*wa-law-lā 'l-qitāl wa-'l-jihād fī sabīl allāh*). Yet others said that its meaning is "If God had not defended the Successors (*al-tābi'īn*) who followed by means of the Companions of the Messenger of God, peace and blessings be upon him."[18] Another group of exegetes, which included Ibn Abī Najīḥ and Mujāhid, were of the opinion that the verse had a much broader application and that it referred generally to those who are trustworthy witnesses in matters concerning the rights of some people over others, and who prevent others who are not similarly trustworthy from committing wrongful acts, such as shedding blood, for example.[19]

At this point, al-Ṭabarī makes his preference known and says that it is most appropriate to understand this verse to mean that, if God did not restrain some people by means of others, then the mention of His name, for example, would cease; the polytheists were thereby prevented from doing that by the Muslims. The ruler who prevents his subjects from oppressing one another, and the trustworthy individual who prevents the abuse of someone's rights through his or her truthful testimony also serve as examples of this kind of divine restraining of one group of people by another. Without this system of checks and balances, people would wrong one another (*taẓālamū*), "and the victors would destroy the monasteries and churches of the vanquished," as well as the other places mentioned by God. Such a general interpretation is established not through transmitted reports, but through reasoning and the obvious meaning of the words of this verse, asserts al-Ṭabarī.[20]

Like his predecessors, al-Ṭabarī also focuses on the identification of the specific places of worship mentioned in the verse and similarly refers to the variant interpretations advanced by various authorities, which need not be detailed here.[21]

Al-Wāḥidī (d. 468/1076) in his *Tafsīr* comments that permission to fight was granted for the first time in this verse because the Muslims had been subjected to persecution and aggression by the pagan Meccans, which resulted in physical harm for the Muslims and expulsion from their homes. Al-Wāḥidī confirms the passive reading *yuqātalūna*, but he does not dwell on its significance.[22] He also proceeds to identify the various places of worship mentioned in the verse as belonging to four monotheistic communities—Christian, Sabian, Jewish, and Muslim. In this context, the verse is understood to mean "If God had not restrained some people by means of others through fighting (*'an al-qitāl*), then the places of worship associated with the revealed law (*sharī'a*) of every prophet would be destroyed."[23]

Like his predecessors, **al-Zamakhsharī** (d. 538/1144) says that the verse specifically granted the Companions of Muḥammad permission to fight because they were subjected to severe persecution (*adhan shadīdan*) at the hands of the Meccan polytheists. After the emigration to Medina, this verse was revealed, allowing fighting for the first time, after more than seventy verses had previously prohibited it.[24] He notes that the passive verbs *udhina* and *yuqātalūna* have been read as active by some unnamed exegetes. With regard to "If God had not restrained some people by others," al-Zamakhsharī says that it means that He fortified the Muslims against the unbelievers through [armed] struggle (*bi-'l-mujāhada*). If that were not so, then the polytheists would have gained control over the people of various religious communities (*'alā ahl al-milal al-mukhtalifa*) and their places of worship and destroyed them. Thus they would not have left standing the churches of Christians, the monasteries of the monks, the synagogues of the Jews, and the mosques of the Muslims. The verse may also be read as referring to the polytheists specifically during the time of Muḥammad, who would have [otherwise] triumphed over the Muslims and over the People of the Book in the protection of the Muslims and destroyed their various houses of worship.[25]

Al-Rāzī (d. 606/1210) notes that the people of Medina and 'Āṣim preferred the reading *yuqātalūna*, whereas Ibn Kathīr, Ḥamza, and al-Kisā'ī read the verb as *yuqātilūna*, but he does not indicate a personal preference. He also agrees that this verse was the first allowing Muslims to engage in fighting after more than seventy verses had prohibited it. Divine permission to fight was based on the fact that the Muslims had been persecuted in two ways: (1) They were expelled from their homes; and (2) their expulsion was because of their affirmation of the oneness of God. Both of them constituted acts of great persecution, as indicated by the phrase *min ghayr ḥaqq* ("without just cause/wrongfully") in the verse.[26]

What is the nature of this restraining? It consists of allowing the people of His religion to fight the unbelievers, continues al-Rāzī. Were this not so-that is, if the polytheists were not reined in by the believers by granting the latter permission to fight the former and aiding the believers against their enemies—then the polytheists would be allowed the upper hand over the people of various religions (*ahl al-adyān*) and their places of worship would be destroyed. Permission is thus granted to believers to fight the enemies of religion so that the people of religion may be free to worship and construct their houses [of worship] (*li-yatafarragha ahl al-dīn li-'l-'ibāda wa-binā' al-buyūt lahā*). It is in this context that the monasteries, churches, and synagogues are mentioned, even though they belong to non-Muslims (*li-ghayr ahl al-islām*); they are not after all "houses for the worship of idols;" and during the time of the Prophet were founded "on the Truth before corruption and supersession [of the Jewish and Christian scriptures set in]."[27]

Like a number of other exegetes we have already discussed, al-Rāzī indicates a variety of opinions regarding the identification of the specific houses of worship mentioned in this verse that need not be reproduced here.[28] He next deals with the question of whether the clause "in which God's name is much mentioned" refers to mosques specifically or to all houses of worship. According to al-Kalbī and Muqātil, the clause is a reference to all of them, for God is mentioned frequently in these places. But, al-Rāzī says, it is more appropriate to understand the verse as referring only to mosques "in special recognition of them" (*tashrīfan lahā*), for the profuse mention of God's name occurs in them [alone],[29] a view we encountered for the first time in Ibn Muḥakkam's commentary. In a similar vein, another question may be posed about why the other houses of worship are mentioned before mosques. The answer, according to al-Rāzī, is because they were established earlier in time. Chronology, however, has nothing to do with greater moral excellence, for, after all, "the messenger of God, peace and blessings be upon him, is the best among the messengers and his community is the best of communities, despite the fact that they are the last of them." This is also the true import of another *ḥadīth*, which states, "We are the last, [yet] we precede" (*naḥnu al-ākhirūn al-sābiqūn*).[30] This is a new concern—establishing the greater moral excellence of Muslims vis-à-vis the People of the Book metonymically through mosques—that we observe for the first time in our survey.

The verse continues with God's promise of aid and support for those who support Him and His religion by undertaking *jihād*, according to al-Rāzī. He acknowledges that others have commented that the verse refers to those who carry out religious obligations in general, and not to *jihād* specifically, but he deems it more appropriate to understand this verse as containing the divine promise that God will help His servant by strengthening him against his enemies and granting him [military] victory.[31] Al-Rāzī's assertion indicates to us that the combative *jihād* by his time is being promoted in certain circles as the most important way to serve and defend Islam and Islam alone, undermining the ecumenism suggested by Qur'ān 22:40 and recognized as such by earlier interpreters.

In his exegesis of Qur'ān 22:39, **al-Qurṭubī** (d. 671/1273) comments that it was the first verse to permit fighting revealed after the emigration to Medina. According to "our scholars," he continues, the Prophet was not given permission before the pledge of 'Aqaba to wage war (*al-ḥarb*) or to shed blood. Rather, he was commanded to pray to God, show forbearance in the face of injury, and to forgive the ignorant for ten years, "so as to establish God's proof against them" (as indicated in Qur'ān 17:15, which states, "We did not punish until we had sent a messenger"). Al-Qurṭubī notes the two possible readings, *yuqātalūna* versus *yuqātilūna*, and demarcates the differences in meaning between them—the first reading conveys that it is the polytheists who fight the believers, whereas the second indicates that the believers fight their enemies. Although he does not explicitly state a preference, our exegete seems to suggest that the first reading is more appropriate, because the verse continues with another passive verb, *ẓulimū*, in reference to the believers who had been driven from their homes.[32]

Significantly, al-Qurṭubī introduces a new element into the discussion of this verse that we have not previously encountered—the concept of *naskh*.[33] He declares that subsequently this verse abrogated all the other verses in the Qur'ān that advocate turning away from one's enemies and forgiving them. The abrogating status (*nāsikh*) of Qur'ān 22:39 was not advanced by the earlier exegetes consulted here, but it is clearly a position that has great resonance in al-Qurṭubī's Andalusian context. As Muslim rulers continued to retreat before advancing Christian armies in al-Qurṭubī's time, the military *jihād* against a hostile enemy is clearly being promoted by our exegete to be urgently undertaken by Muslims in his own milieu in emulation of the early battles of Islam fought against equally deadly enemies.[34] Thus, continues al-Qurṭubī, if God had not commanded His prophets and the believers to fight their enemies, then the polytheists would have gained the upper hand and destroyed the places of worship for the various religions. Fighting was therefore commanded to repel the polytheists and to allow the people of religion to worship freely – which serves as a cautionary tale for Muslim in al-Andalus in the seventh/thirteenth century.[35]

Al-Qurṭubī then engages in an extended description of the various houses of worship (and the possible etymologies of their names) mentioned in this verse that is very similar to the one offered by al-Rāzī, for example, and does not need to be reproduced here in detail. Worthy of note are Ibn ʿAṭiyya's views, as recorded by al-Qurṭubī, that these names for various houses of worship were shared by many of these religious communities and refer only to those religious groups that had a revealed scripture (*lahā kitāb*). They therefore do not include the Zoroastrians (*al-mājūs*) or the polytheists "because they do not possess what must be protected, and the mention of God is not made except among the people of the revealed laws" (*ʿinda ahli ʾl-sharāʾiʿ*).[36] Like al-Rāzī before him, al-Qurṭubī is exercised by the question of why mention of the other houses of worship precedes that of mosques in Qur'ān 22:40. Like al-Rāzī, he says simply that this is so because the non-Muslim places of worship came into existence earlier. Others said it was because they were closer to the occurrence of the word "destruction" in the verse, whereas "mosques" were closest to "the mentioning [of God's name]." Those who morally precede (*al-sābiq*), reminds al-Qurṭubī, may be mentioned last, as is evidenced also in Qur'ān 35:32.[37] Interestingly, al-Qurṭubī appears to simultaneously subscribe to two rather dissonant perspectives: On the one hand, he upholds the importance of Muslims protecting the right of the People of the Book to worship freely, but on the other hand, he is anxious to assert the superiority of Muslim houses of worship over all others—a telling commentary perhaps on his own historical period, characterized as it was by alternately conciliatory and belligerent relations with different groups of scriptuaries.

To briefly summarize this section, the fighting commanded in these verses is clearly defensive in nature and ensues in response to prior persecution and aggression by the enemy, according to all the exegetes surveyed. The right to profess belief in the one God and to resort to armed combat to defend this right when violently encroached upon by a relentlessly hostile enemy is stressed in all the exegeses consulted. The defensive nature of the military *jihād* is underscored by the passive verbs *yuqātalūna* and *ẓulimū* that occur in the verse, but scant attention is paid to them by our exegetes, early and late. Al-Ṭabarī is even dismissive of the potentially divergent meanings that would ensue if one were to give preference to the passive *yuqātalūna* over the active *yuqātilūna* and vice versa. Close attention however was paid by exegetes to the specific wording of Qur'ān 22:39–40 in relation to other religious communities, particularly their houses of worship, because of their broader legal and theological implications for Muslim relations with non-Muslims. In comparison with most of their predecessors, al-Rāzī's and al-Qurṭubī's perspectives clearly appear more exclusionary vis-à-vis the People of the Book and considerably attenuate the ecumenical potential of Qur'an 22:39–40. Their commentaries establish that, by the Seljuq and Mamluk periods in the wake of the Crusades, the

Mongol invasions, and, in the case of al-Qurṭubī, by the time of the Spanish Reconquista, Muslims were increasingly fearful and on the defensive against non-Muslims.[38] Such changing circumstances clearly affected Muslim sensibilities, causing at least some influential Muslim scholars to re-imagine their relationships with other religious communities in less tolerant ways and find sanction for them in readings of their holiest text.

Exegeses of Qur'ān 2:190–194

> Fight in the way of God those who fight you and do not commit aggression (*wa lā ta'tadū*), for God does not love aggressors. Slay them where you find them and expel them from where they expelled you, for *fitna* is worse than killing. Do not fight them near the Sacred Mosque until they fight you in it. If they fight you then slay them, for that is the recompense of the unbelievers. If they desist, then God is forgiving and merciful. And fight them until there is no more discord and religion is for God. If they cease, then there is no more aggression except for those who are wrong-doers. The forbidden month is for the forbidden month and forbidden things are [subject to] retaliation [in equal measure]. Whoever attacks you attack him to the extent of his attack. Fear God and know that God is with the God-fearing.
> Qur'ān 2:190–194

Our exegetes directed quite a bit of attention to these critical verses that provided the nucleus for classical juridical discussions about the ethics of war and peace in the Qur'ān. Because a full and detailed discussion of every point raised by our exegetes in connection with each of these verses would be rather lengthy and repetitive in parts, an extensive summary of the highlights of their exegeses is provided below.

All our exegetes are in agreement that these verses refer to the events at al-Ḥudaybiyya in 8/628. In that year, the Muslims were granted divine permission to defend themselves in the hallowed precincts of the Ka'ba in the event of an attack upon them by the pagan Meccans during one of the pre-Islamic sacred months, something they were previously forbidden to do. Our earliest exegetes understand the interdiction in Qur'ān 2:190, "Do not commit aggression for God does not love aggressors," as a clear and general prohibition against initiating hostilities under any circumstance. Thus **Mujāhid** comments that, according to this verse, one should not fight until the other side commences fighting.[39] According to **Muqātil b. Sulaymān**, this verse is specifically a denunciation of the Meccans who had commenced hostilities at al-Hudaybiyya, leading to a repeal of the prohibition imposed upon Muslims against fighting near the Ka'ba. "Do not commit aggression" and "God does not love aggressors" is an indictment, he asserts, against the Meccans who began to fight during the sacred month in the sacred sanctuary, a clear act of aggression (*fa-innahu 'udwān*). The verse then gives permission to believers to slay the polytheists wherever one may find them as a consequence of their aggression and expel them from Mecca from where the Muslims were expelled, for *fitna*, glossed by Muqātil as "polytheism," is a greater offense in the sight of God (*a'ẓam 'inda allāh 'azza wa-jalla jarm*[an]) than killing, as affirmed also in Qur'ān 9:49. Permission to engage the pagan Meccans in fighting was clearly contingent, according to Muqātil, upon their having initiated hostilities, which abrogates the earlier prohibition against fighting in the Sanctuary. "If they desist" means that, if they should cease fighting and acknowledge the oneness of God, then God will forgive their previous adherence to polytheism and show mercy toward them "in Islam." A parallel to this verse is found in Qur'ān 9:39.[40] Qur'ān 2:192 specifically concerns the "Arab polytheists" (*mushrikī 'l-'arab*), continues Muqātil, and exhorts the believers to keep fighting them until there is no more polytheism among them and they affirm the oneness of God and worship no other.[41]

The ***Tanwīr al-miqbās*** similarly understands this command as prohibiting Muslims from initiating fighting, but conferring upon them the right to self-defense in the event of an attack. This is so because God does not love the *mu'tadīn*, that is, "those who begin fighting, whether in sacred or non-sacred territory" (*al-mubtadi'īn bi-'l-qitāl fī 'l-ḥill wa-'l-ḥarām*). If the pagans were to initiate hostilities, Muslims should fight them wherever they may be found and expel them from Mecca just as they had been expelled, because they associate partners with God, and the worship of idols is a graver matter than fighting in the Sanctuary. *Wa-lā tuqātilūhum* means "do not begin hostilities near the Sacred Mosque until they first commence fighting there" (*bi-'l-ibtidā'*). If they should do so, then they should be fought against—for such is the recompense of the unbelievers. *Fa-in intahaw* in Qur'ān 2:192 means, according to the *Tanwīr*, that if they abandon polytheism and repent, then God will forgive and show mercy to the one who repents and dies in this state of repentance. Otherwise, Muslims may fight the polytheists anywhere, provided that they commence hostilities (*bi'l-ibtidā' minhum*), until there is no more associationism with God in the Sanctuary, and it is replaced by Islam and the worship of the one God in the Sanctuary (*fī-'l-ḥaram*). *Fa-in intahaw* in Qur'ān 2:193 means that if they should desist from fighting in the Sanctuary, then the believers no longer have a reason to continue to fight against them, except against those who do wrong (*al-ẓālimīn*). *Al-ẓālimīn* here is clearly glossed in the *Tanwīr* as a reference to those who initiate killing (*al-mubtadi'īn bi-'l-qatl*). Qur'an 2:194 refers to the sacred month in which the believers entered Mecca intending to perform the *'umra*. Instead, they were prevented from doing so by the pagan Meccans, who initiated hostilities against them in the Sanctuary, thus committing a clear act of aggression. The Muslims are urged in this verse to fear God as they engage in fighting in this context and to keep in mind that God helps the devout in gaining victory.[42]

'Abd al-Razzāq's *tafsīr* offers us a very brief commentary on some of these verses. Thus for *al-fitna ashaddu min al-qatl*, he says that "polytheism (*al-shirk*) is worse than killing." He also reports from Ma'mar, relating from Qatāda, that the initial prohibition against fighting near the Sanctuary was abrogated by the permission given in Qur'ān 2:190 to fight the polytheists wherever one may encounter them. Once again on the authority of Qatāda, he relates from Ma'mar that "fight them until there is no more *fitna*" means "until there is no more polytheism." With regard to Qur'ān 2:194, 'Abd al-Razzāq, like Muqātil, says that it refers to the year of al-Ḥudaybiyya when the Prophet and his Companions were prevented from performing the *'umra* in Mecca, but agreed with the pagan Meccans to return the following year during the same month.[43]

With regard to Qur'ān 2:190, **Hūd b. Muḥakkam** says that this verse was revealed before the command to fight all the polytheists was given [a reference to Qur'ān 9:36 is given here]; prior to that, Muslims would fight only those who fought them. *Lā ta'tadū* means "do not transgress in your battles by fighting those who do not fight you or those with whom one has concluded treaties or to whom one has granted protection." Then, he says, God revealed Qur'ān 9:5 [44] (to be discussed in the next chapter); thereby implying that this verse did away with these restrictions, although this is not explicitly stated by him.[45]

As for Qur'ān 2:191, Ibn Muḥakkam glosses *fitna* as meaning *shirk* in this context (*wa-'l-fitna hāhunā al-shirk*) and refers to Mujāhid, who was of the opinion that being enticed away from faith in God was harder upon the believer than fighting. The rest of the verse that forbids Muslims from initiating fighting near the Sacred Mosque is understood as such, on the authority of unnamed exegetes (*qāla ba'ḍ al-mufassirīn*). But then, continues Ibn Muḥakkam, the revelation of Qur'ān 9:5 made fighting licit in "sacred and profane places" and at the Sacred Mosque itself "until they [the pagans] bear witness that there is no god but God and Muḥammad is the messenger of God."[46]

"But if they desist" in Qur'ān 2:191 means if the polytheists desist "from fighting you and enter into your religion." *Fitna* in the next verse (2:193) means "polytheism" (*shirk*); the second occurrence of "but if they desist" in this verse is also a reference to polytheism. *Al-ẓālimīn* is glossed as those who do not say, "There is no god but God."[47] By consistently understanding the wrongdoing of the polytheists as inhering in their polytheism, rather than in their aggression, Ibn Muḥakkam thus tacitly endorses the idea of Muslims continuing to fight them until they abandon their polytheism and embrace Islam.

The next verse, Qur'ān 2:194, is a clear reference to the events at al-Ḥudaybiyya; Ibn Muḥakkam references Mujāhid here. "Those who aggress against you aggress against them to a similar extent" is understood on the authority of al-Kalbī to contain divine permission for the Muslims to defend themselves if they are attacked first near the Ka'ba, as was feared the year before al-Ḥudaybiyya. Al-Suddī is similarly cited.[48]

In exegesis of Qur'ān 2:193, the early Shī'ī exegete **al-'Ayyāshī** (d. ca. 320/932) records the interpretation that the wrongdoers (*al-ẓālimīn*) were none other than the descendants of those who had killed al-Ḥusayn. In a less particularist vein, al-'Ayyāshī also reports on the authority of 'Alā' b. al-Fuḍayl that the next verse allowed Muslims to fight back in the event that the polytheists attacked first.[49]

Al-Ṭabarī records the opinions of some unnamed authorities who considered this verse to have been the first revelation giving Muslims permission to fight.[50] In comparison with our earlier commentaries, al-Ṭabarī's exegesis records a wide variety of interpretive positions, some at odds with others, and allows us to chart certain developments over time that are extremely important for our purposes. We therefore deal with his exegesis of this critical cluster of verses at some length below.

Qur'ān 2:190, al-Ṭabarī notes, was understood by some unnamed exegetes as commanding the believers to fight the pagan Meccans only after the latter had initiated hostilities and to desist from combat when they (sc. the pagan Meccans) refrained from fighting. But, he comments, al-Rabī' b. Anas and Ibn Zayd had been of the opinion that the ninth chapter (*al-Tawba or al-Barā'a*) of the Qur'ān had abrogated this verse. Other unnamed exegetes had maintained that no part of this verse was abrogated, and that the aggression forbidden in it, a categorical prohibition, applied specifically to women and children.[51] A new construal of the nonaggression clause now emerges in al-Ṭabarī's exegesis—that of the immunity of noncombatants. Ibn 'Abbās is quoted by al-Ṭabarī as having said, "[Y]ou should not kill women, children, the elderly, and the one who offers peaceful greetings and restrains his hand. If you do so, you have resorted to aggression" (*fa-qad i'tadaytum*). Furthermore, 'Umar b. 'Abd al-'Azīz is said to have written to 'Adiy b. Artaḥ, one of his military commanders, and interpreted this verse as "Do not fight those who do not fight you; that is, women, children, and monks." Al-Ṭabarī asserts that this statement of 'Umar is the most fitting interpretation because there is no incontrovertible evidence that the meaning of this verse was abrogated, as some have maintained.[52]

Al-Ṭabarī then proceeds to offer his own exegesis of Qur'ān 2:190 as follows: The verse commands the believers, he says, to fight in the way of God—that is, His path, which He has clearly delineated and His religion, which He has revealed to His worshipers—"in obedience to Me and what I have prescribed for you in My religion." God urges them to invite "with [their] hands and tongues" those who turn away from His religion in arrogance until they come to obey Him or pay the *jizya* willingly if they are one of the scriptuaries. The meaning of "Do not commit aggression" means that one should not kill children or women or those who pay the *jizya* from among the People of the Book and the Zoroastrians. Those who transgress these limits and hold licit what God has clearly forbidden regarding these groups of people are those who are indicated in "Indeed God does not love those who transgress."[53]

This critical debate among early and later exegetes concerning what constitutes aggression is more clearly evident in al-Ṭabarī's discussion of the next three verses, Qur'ān 2:191–193. With regard to Qur'ān 2:191, al-Ṭabarī explains it as meaning that the believers should not initiate fighting with the polytheists near the Sacred Mosque until they initiate hostilities. Once the polytheists have begun to fight, Muslims should fight and slay them, for that is the just recompense for them in this world, while eternal disgrace awaits them in the next. This was the opinion of Qatāda and al-Rabī', says al-Ṭabarī. *Al-fitna* in this verse refers to associating partners with God, which is more severe than fighting. As this is not the usual general signification of the word *fitna*, al-Ṭabarī acknowledges that the root meaning of this word is "trial" or "tribulation." He proceeds to attempt to harmonize these two disparate significations in the following way: "The trials of the believer in regard to his religion so that he falls away from it and associates partners with God after his embrace of Islam is much harder and more harmful for him than being killed while firm in his religion, stalwart and unwavering in it," says al-Ṭabarī. Mujāhid, Qatāda, al-Rabī', and al-Ḍaḥḥāk are among those who subscribed to this view. Ibn Zayd is quoted by al-Ṭabarī as offering a minority opinion—holding that *fitna* referred to unbelief (*kufr*, rather than *shirk*).[54]

As for Qur'ān 2:192, it means that "if the unbelievers who fight you desist from fighting and from their lack of faith in God, and abandon all that and repent, then God pardons the sins of the one who believes in Him and repents of his associationism, and turns to God away from his previous sins in the past." God will be merciful toward such a repentant individual and reward him. This was the opinion of Mujāhid, who understood "if they cease" to mean "if they repent"—that is, repent of their associationism.[55]

The word *fitna* in Qur'ān 2:193 is generally held to be the equivalent of *shirk* ("associationism," "polytheism") as in Qur'ān 2:191, explains al-Ṭabarī, so that the verse may be understood to command Muslims to fight those polytheists who fight them until there is no more polytheism and they worship God alone. Qatāda, Mujāhid, al-Suddī,[56] and Ibn 'Abbās were among those who glossed *fitna* as *shirk*, whereas Ibn Zayd glossed it as *kufr*. As for the interpretation of "and religion belongs to God," al-Ṭabarī refers to al-Rabī', who commented that it means "until only God is worshiped." Al-Rabī' cited the *ḥadīth* in which Muḥammad is quoted as saying, "I have been commanded to fight people until they say 'There is no god but God,' perform the prayers, and pay the obligatory alms. When they do that, they have protected their blood and wealth from me except for what is due on it, and their reckoning is with God." Qatāda is said to have similarly interpreted this verse.[57] The significance of this strand of interpretation cannot be underestimated. The redefinition of *fitna* exclusively as "polytheism" (or "unbelief" according to a minority viewpoint) in Qur'ān 2:193 changes the parameters of the combative *jihād* and allows military activity to be waged against polytheists *because of their polytheism*, and not because of the disturbance or violence they foment. In regard to Qur'ān 2:191, al-Ṭabarī had acknowledged that the primary meaning of *fitna* is trial/tribulation, with its attendant connotations of disturbance and violence. The deployment of the above *ḥadīth* on the authority of al-Rabī', which anchors al-Ṭabarī's preferred understanding of this critical verse, is noteworthy. After him, this particular report became fairly commonly invoked in this context to lend support to the position that Muslims were henceforth required to fight non-Muslims on account of the latter's lack of belief or absence of correct belief, rather than on account of their prior resorting to violence against Muslims.

But one "problem" (from al-Ṭabarī's point of view) still remains: how to categorically establish the assumed imperative in Qur'ān 2:193 to fight polytheists on account of their polytheism and neutralize the explicit proscription in 2:190 against the initiation of hostilities by Muslims? Not unexpectedly, the answer is abrogation. Al-Ṭabarī marshals support for this position by referring to Qatāda and al-Rabī', who is said to have been of the opinion that Qur'ān 2:190 had been abrogated by Qur'ān 2:193. According to another report from Qatāda, the verse was abrogated by Qur'ān 9:5.[58] As is his custom, al-Ṭabarī helpfully records dissenting opinions: Thus he notes that other exegetes, like Mujāhid, had maintained that Qur'ān 2:190 remained normative and unabrogated (*muḥkama*). Given the overall tenor of his commentary on this cluster of verses, al-Ṭabarī chooses to throw his weight behind those who said that Qur'ān 2:190 had been abrogated by Qur'ān 2:193, as well as by Qur'ān 9:5.[59]

The full implications of Qur'ān 2:193 are summarized by al-Ṭabarī as follows: The verse means that when those among the unbelievers who fight the believers cease fighting "and enter into your religion [Islam] and hold to what God has imposed as religious obligations and abandon their previous worship of idols, then refrain from aggression, fighting, and striving (*jihād*) against them." Fighting is to be carried out against those who do wrong (*al-ẓālimīn*). Significantly—and ominously—*al-ẓālimīn* is specifically glossed here not as "the oppressors" or "the wrongdoers," which are among the usual meanings assigned to this term and so understood by a number of earlier exegetes (as recorded in the *Tanwīr*, for example, noted above), but as "those who associate partners with God, and those who abandon adoration of Him and worship [beings] other than God." And, continues al-Ṭabarī, if someone should ask, "Can one attack *al-ẓālimīn*," then the answer is, as given in the verse, "There is no aggression except against *al-ẓālimīn*." Once again, Qatāda is invoked as a corroborating authority who is reported to have defined the *ẓālim* as one who refuses to say, "There is no god but God." Al-Rabī' and 'Ikrima are also said to have hewed to similar interpretations.[60] Given their views, the Successors Qatāda b. Di'āma (d. 117/735), al-Rabī' b. Anas (d. 139/756), and 'Ikrima (d. ca. 105/723–724) may be regarded as constituting an early group of "hawkish" exegetes intent on deriving a Qur'anic mandate for fighting against polytheists *qua polytheists*, rather than for their initial aggression. In order to justify their position, these exegetes proceeded to impose this unprecedented and uncharacteristic meaning of "polytheists" on the lexeme *al-ẓālimīn*.[61]

With his customary comprehensiveness, al-Tabarī goes on to record views that are diametrically opposed to these hawkish ones, allowing us to appreciate the contested nature of such interpretations in the early period. Thus, he records, certain exegetes, like Mujāhid, maintained that the Qur'anic assertion "there is no aggression except against the wrong-doer" clearly means "do not fight except those who fight." Al-Suddī, further maintained that "God does not like aggression/initiation of attacks [even] upon wrong-doers or anyone else (*inna allāh lā yu ḥibbu al-'udwān 'alā al-ẓālimīn wa-lā 'alā ghayrihim*), and that fighting is allowed only against those who initiate hostilities and only "to the extent that they aggress against you."[62] Al-Suddī's statement in particular constitutes a noteworthy rejection of any kind of equivocation regarding the Qur'anic prohibition against the initiation of hostilities by Muslims under any circumstance, particularly on confessional/religious grounds, and points to the necessity of observing the rules of proportionality when retaliating against a prior act of violence.

The proportionality of one's armed response to that of the adversary is also an important concern in 2:194; once again, al-Ṭabarī points to a range of interpretive positions among the exegetes. According to Ibn 'Abbās, this verse was revealed in Mecca when the Muslims were few in number and too weak to subdue the polytheists, who reviled and physically hurt them. Thus God allowed the Muslims to retaliate to the extent to which they were hurt, or to be patient, or to forgive, the latter being the ideal (*amthal*) response, according to Ibn 'Abbās. When the Prophet emigrated to Medina, and God increased him in strength, and rescued Muslims from their victimhood and gave them control of their own affairs, He commanded them not to attack one another like the people of the pre-Islamic period.[63]

But others maintained that the verse was Medinan and allowed believers to fight those among the polytheists who fought them. Those who subscribed to this interpretation included Mujāhid (this agrees with what we previously noted according to Mujāhid's extant *tafsīr*);al-Ṭabarī agrees with this interpretation, because the verses preceding Qur'ān 2:194 have to do with fighting the unbelievers, which was allowed only after the *hijra*. The remainder of the verse is also Medinan, as fighting was not permitted in the Meccan period. The meaning of "Those who attack you retaliate against them to the extent to which they attack you" may be compared to "Fight in the path of God those who fight you." The resulting meaning is that "whoever attacks you in the Sanctuary and fights you, attack and fight him to the extent of his act of aggression," according to the law of *talionis* (*qiṣaṣ*). But, according to al-Ṭabarī, this verse was abrogated by Qur'ān 9:36. Others have maintained that the meaning of this verse is "Whoever aggresses against you—that is, whoever is hostile toward you and inflicts a wrong—you may attack him—that is inflict harm on him to the same extent—in exact retribution (*qiṣaṣ*) for what he did to you, without transgressing the limits (*lā ẓulman*)."[64] These latter exegetes appear not to have considered this verse abrogated by any other. The verse concludes, al-Ṭabarī continues, with an assurance to the believers that those who adhere to these limits are the pious ones, and God is with the pious who revere Him, carry out the religious obligations, and avoid what is forbidden.[65]

Al-Ṭabarī's detailed exegesis of this critical cluster of verses constitutes a valuable repository of an important spectrum of early views on the legitimate reasons for resorting to armed combat that progressively became elided in later exegetical works and that find scant reference in the influential juridical literature, a point we will return to in the Conclusion.

Post-al-Ṭabarī Exegetes

In the following century, **al-Wāḥidī** in his exegesis of Qur'ān 2:190 also refers to al-Rabī' and Ibn Zayd as early authorities who had maintained that this was the first verse to be revealed concerning fighting. At the time of its revelation, says al-Wāḥidī, the Prophet would fight those who fought and desist from those who desisted. *Wa-lā ta'tadū* means that one should neither initiate attacks nor launch a surprise assault before a proclamation of summons (*qabla taqdīm al-da'wa*) is made, for "God does not love aggressors." Aggression also consisted of inhumane conduct during warfare, for as Ibn 'Abbās had declared, "Do not kill women, children, the elderly, and the one who proffers you peaceful greetings and restrains his hand [from attacking]; if you do that, you have committed aggression."[66] Qur'ān 2:191 means that one may slay the unbelievers when one comes upon them and expel them from Mecca from where the believers were expelled, for their polytheism constitutes a greater offense in the sight of God than their being slain. The verse concludes by forbidding Muslims from initiating hostilities, specifically in the Sanctuary, until the polytheists attack. When they do, they are to be resisted with force wherever they may be.[67]

Wa-in intahaw in the next verse means, al-Wāḥidī continues, that if the unbelievers abandon their unbelief and accept Islam, then God will pardon their previous adherence to polytheism. In Qur'ān 2:193, *fitna* refers to *shirk*, so that the meaning of the verse is that the unbelievers should be fought until they accept Islam, for *jizya* cannot be accepted from those who worship idols; obedience and worship is due to Him alone. If they refrain from unbelief, then they can no longer be attacked (*fa-lā 'udwān*), killed, or enslaved. Excepted are those who persist in their wrongdoing (*al-ẓālimīn*), that is, the unbelievers whose continuing unbelief constitutes an act of aggression, and therefore its recompense is also aggression (here, al-Wāḥidī references Qur'ān 42:40, which states that the requital of evil is an evil like it).[68]

According to Ibn 'Abbās as related by 'Aṭā' [b. Abī Rabāḥ], al-Wāḥidī continues, Qur'ān 2:194 allows believers to fight the unbelievers when the latter resort to fighting during the sacred month. Al-Zajjāj had stated that their violation of the sanctity of the month invited a like response. Al-Wāḥidī then inserts a caveat saying that this principle of *talionis* does not allow Muslims to initiate fighting (*'alā sabīl al-i'tidā'*), but only allows them to retaliate to the same extent as the aggressor, as the rest of the verse indicates (*fa-'tadū 'alayhi bimithlimā i'tadā 'alaykum*). The response is also termed "aggression" (*i'tidā'*) because it is in retaliation for an initial act of aggression. The verse ends by adjuring the believer to obey God and avoid what is forbidden and thus earn His help and support.[69]

In this highly significant commentary, al-Wāḥidī thus upholds a somewhat modified principle of nonaggression according to which Muslims may not attack polytheists first, at least not without a formal summons to accept

Islam, and may not target noncombatants once hostilities have ensued. The absolute proscription against initiating fighting, according to al-Wāḥidī, continues to apply particularly in the sacred sanctuary. In retaliating, Muslims may not exceed the level of aggression perpetrated against them by the enemy. Once fighting has commenced, Muslims are required to continue to fight the polytheists until they renounce *both* their hostility and their associationism. It seems that by al-Wāḥidī's time, *fitna* is generally equated with "polytheism"; he has no reference to the early debates concerning what exactly the polytheists are expected to refrain from in *wa-intahaw* in Qur'ān 2:191 and 2:193, as detailed in al-Ṭabarī's extensive commentary. Al-Wāḥidī's views on the rules of warfare thus coincide to a large extent with classical legal formulations of proclaiming and waging war, as explained in *siyar* works from the third/ninth century and onward.

Al-Zamakhsharī in the sixth/twelfth century outlines three competing ways of looking at Qur'ān 2:190 as follows: (1) It refers to the Prophet's abstention from fighting against all those who did not fight, and fighting only those who did; or (2) it refers to his fighting those who resorted to combat, and desisting from traditional noncombatants, such as women, children, the elderly, and monks; or (3) it refers to his fighting all the unbelievers whose resistance to Islam constituted an act of aggression in itself, whether they actually physically fought or not. Al-Zamakhsharī essentially endorses the third interpretation when he states that Qur'ān 2:190 was abrogated by Qur'ān 9:36 (which states, "Fight against all the polytheists" [*kāffatan*]).[70] His preference for the third option signals a widespread acceptance of this position by the exegetes of his day, in contrast to earlier scholars.

The command *wa-lā ta'tadū* in Qur'ān 2:190 prohibits Muslims from initiating fighting or from fighting against those who do not fight, such as women, the elderly, and children, and those with whom the Muslims have concluded a treaty (*'ahd*), and from launching a surprise attack without a formal summons. If the Muslims are attacked, they may fight the unbelievers wherever they may encounter them.[71] Of particular note is al-Zamakhsharī's interpretation of *fitna* specifically in this verse and his recognition of the contested meanings of this critical term. Unlike the majority of the exegetes we have already discussed, with the exception of al-Ṭabarī, al-Zamakhsharī glosses *fitna* as "trials and tribulations which descend upon man and causes him to suffer."[72]

However, in Qur'ān 2:191, al-Zamakhsharī understands *fitna* to refer to polytheism (*shirk*), and the phrase "religion is for God" means that it is sincerely for Him and "Satan has no part in it." The verse also commands that one must not attack those who refrain from fighting, for that would constitute an act of aggression (*'udwān*) and injustice (*ẓulm*). The clause "except for those who do wrong" may refer to either those who have ceased fighting but remain wrongdoers (*al-ẓālimīn* in the original; al-Zamakhsharī does not indicate the nature of this wrongdoing as did al-Ṭabarī painstakingly before him), or those who do wrong by continuing to engage in hostilities; he expresses no preference for one interpretation over the other.[73] Finally, he says, Qur'ān 2:194 refers to the events at al-Ḥudaybiyya and the substitution of the lapsed sacred month in 5/628 for the observed sacred month the following year, thus setting up the principle of exact retaliation for violation of the rules of sanctity (*ḥurma*). The verse also commands that believers may not transgress the imposed limits in implementing the *lex talionis*.[74]

Al- Rāzī's views: Al-Rāzī comments that Qur'ān 2:190 is to be read in light of the preceding verse, which emphasizes *taqwā* (roughly "God-consciousness") as "a means of knowing God the Exalted" and as "a means of obeying God." God has commanded in this verse, he continues, the severest aspect of *taqwā* and the most difficult for the human self to bear—fighting the enemies of God.[75] But the questions remain: Why and how?

In response to why one should fight, al-Rāzī begins by commenting that the specific occasion of revelation was the year of al-Ḥudaybiyya and recapitulates the main events associated with this year that provided the impetus for fighting.[76] With regard to how one should fight, al-Rāzī, like al-Zamakhsharī, advances three strands of interpretation in reference to Qur'ān 2:190 that are, however, somewhat different in detail. First, citing Ibn 'Abbās, al-Rāzī comments that one should fight only those who fight—whether that is construed as those who actually resort to armed combat or display hostile intention by forcibly preventing Muslims from performing the pilgrimage [the reference is to al-Ḥudaybiyya]. Second, one should fight only those who have the ability and skill to engage in fighting. The third position is that one should fight those capable of fighting, except for those who are inclined to peace (*siwā man janaḥa li-'l-salm*; cf. Qur'ān 8:61). Perhaps uncharacteristically for his time and in a significant departure from some of his immediate predecessors, al-Rāzī expresses a preference for the first viewpoint attributed to Ibn 'Abbās because that is the closest, he stresses, to the obvious meaning of the verse, in his view. Al-Rāzī goes on to add categorically that the divine imperative in Qur'ān 2:190 is directed at *actual*, not *potential*, combatants, meaning that the verse allows fighting only against those who have actually commenced fighting, and not against those who are able and prepared to fight but have not yet resorted to violence.[77] This represents a rather trenchant critique of the prevailing juridical position in al-Rāzī's time, which had all but abandoned the categorical Qur'anic principle of nonaggression through legal and hermeneutical legerdemain.[78] Against those who would maintain that "God Almighty had given the command to fight them [sc. the polytheists] unconditionally" (*amara allāhu ta'ālā bi-qitālihim 'alā 'l-iṭlāq*), al-Rāzī records the counterargument of the Mu'tazila, who had commented that God would not have stated, "Indeed God does not love those who commit aggression" (*inna allāh lā yuḥibb al-mu'tadīn*) if "aggression" (*al-i'tidā'*) occurred with God's approval and according to His wish.[79]

As for *al-fitna ashaddu min al-qatl*, according to Ibn 'Abbās, *fitna* referred to a lack of belief (*al-kufr*) in God. Unbelief was termed *fitna*, because it represents corruption (*fasād*) on earth, which leads to injustice and turmoil. The injustice specifically perpetrated by the unbelievers consisted of preventing the Muslims from the Sacred Mosque, which was an offense worse than resorting to fighting there, for they strove to forbid worship and obedience to God, for which purpose alone humans and the Jinn were created. A believer's renunciation of his faith would be a more grievous act than killing for a just cause.[80]

With regard to 2:192, al-Rāzī draws the reader's attention to the fact that, although the preceding verse may suggest that fighting must continue even if the enemy combatant were to stop and repent, this verse clearly establishes that in such a situation, the injunction to fight and kill the enemy lapses. He adduces as further evidence Qur'ān 8:38, which states, "Say to those who disbelieve that if they should stop (*yantahū*), they will be forgiven what has preceded," and proceeds to record the contradictory interpretations of Ibn 'Abbās and al-Ḥasan al-Baṣrī. According to the former, Qur'ān 8:38 refers to refraining from fighting, whereas the latter was of the opinion that it referred to abandoning polytheism. The argument advanced in support of Ibn 'Abbās's position is as follows: Because the intention behind the granting of permission to fight was to prevent the unbelievers from fighting, then in this context, it is more plausible to understand this verse as referring to the cessation of fighting. Those who agreed with al-Ḥasan argued that the unbeliever does not attain God's forgiveness and mercy by renouncing fighting, but rather by renouncing unbelief. This highly significant part of al-Rāzī's commentary clearly conveys to us that the purview of *fa-intahaw* was vigorously debated in the early period; eventually, the point of view attributed to al-Ḥasan would become the prevalent one, particularly in hawkish juridical circles. Al-Rāzī's advocacy of Ibn 'Abbās's position indicates to us that a strict adherence to the nonaggression clause prohibiting the initiation of fighting by Muslims remained a credible position through al-Rāzī's time, and that this group of exegetes, including al-Rāzī himself, defended their position through a cross-referential reading of related Qur'anic verses, as evident in his invocation of Qur'ān 8:38 in this context.[81]

The term *fitna* in Qur'ān 2:191 and 2:193 may be interpreted in two ways, continues al-Rāzī. First, it may be understood to mean polytheism and unbelief (*al-shirk wa-'l-kufr*), which led to the persecution of the Companions in Mecca so that a number of them had to flee to Abyssinia and then had to emigrate to Medina when the persecution continued. The second interpretation, according to Abū Muslim,[82] is that *fitna* refers to violent acts (*al-jurm*), for God had commanded the believers to fight the unbelievers until the latter desisted from fighting. The unbelievers' initiation of hostilities constituted a great trial for the believers that required self-defense.[83]

As for His saying, "And if they should desist," it means that if the polytheists should desist from what had caused them to be fought against, "whether that be their unbelief or their [initiation of] hostilities," then it is no longer permissible to engage them in combat, as also stated in Qur'ān 8:38, continues al-Rāzī. The rest of the verse, which says, "There is to be no enmity/aggression except against those who oppress/are unjust (*al-ẓālimīn*)," can be understood to mean that if the polytheists desist from polytheism, then they are not to be attacked. In other words, only those who do not abandon polytheism may continue to be fought, for by persisting in their unbelief, they are unjust to themselves (*al-ẓālimīn*), as indicated in Qur'ān 31:13, which states, "Indeed polytheism is a great injustice" (*ẓulm 'aẓīm*). If Muslims were to persist in fighting the pagan Meccans after they had abandoned polytheism and aggression, then they would become the aggressors.[84]

With regard to Qur'ān 2:193, al-Rāzī once again indicates the different ways in which exegetes have understood this verse. Some were of the opinion that this verse abrogated Qur'ān 2:191, with which al-Rāzī disagrees. The reason for his disagreement is that Qur'ān 2:191 contains a general injunction, whereas Qur'ān 2:193 contains a specific proscription against the initiation of fighting near the Sacred Mosque, which would violate its sanctity. He agrees with al-Shāfi'ī that a specific injunction takes precedence over a general injunction, regardless of whether the former precedes or follows the latter ("and God knows best").[85]

As for Qur'ān 2:194, it allows believers to attack those who attack them to the same extent, and God will help and support those who are sincere believers.[86] In this part of his commentary, it appears that al-Rāzī continues to maintain the general nonaggression clause so that Muslims may not ever initiate fighting, but once fighting has started against the pagans, then it must be continued until they abandon both their polytheism and aggression, for one presupposed the other in the case of the Meccan Arabs, and both were conducive to injustice.[87]

Al-Qurṭubī's views: In al-Qurṭubī's exegesis, we get an even fuller and detailed exposition of the multiple, often contradictory, views held by the scholars in relation to Qur'ān 2:190–194, confirming to us once again the close attention paid to these verses because of their significance for the articulation of legal and ethical norms governing the waging of the combative *jihād* in various historical periods. Thus al-Qurṭubī reports that early authorities like Ibn 'Abbās, 'Umar b. 'Abd al-'Azīz, and Mujāhid, considered Qur'ān 2:190 with its proscription against initiating hostilities against polytheists to be universally binding and unabrogated (*muḥkama*) by any other verse in the Qur'ān. Abu Ja'far al-Naḥḥās (d. 338/950), the author of *I'rab al-qur'ān*, agreed with this and said that this was the more correct (*aṣaḥḥ*) interpretation, for it was in accordance with the *sunna* and reason. This position finds support in a *ḥadīth* from Ibn 'Umar, according to which the Prophet, upon noticing a slain woman during one of his military campaigns (*maghāzihi*), expressed his revulsion and forbade the killing of women and children, as has been related by prominent authorities (*al-a'imma*). From the viewpoint of reason, the verbal noun of the third verbal form *fi'āl/mufā'ala* requires that there be a recipient of the action implied in the verb; thus fighting (*qitāl/muqātala*) can be waged only against those who fight back. It therefore cannot be waged against women, children, and other noncombatants, like monks, the chronically ill (*al-zamnā*), the elderly, and peasants/serfs, who are not to be killed. This is in accordance with what Abū Bakr had counseled Yazīd b. Abī Sufyān when he was dispatched to Syria, as recorded by Mālik b. Anas and others.[88] Al-Qurṭubī then goes on to give a lengthy, detailed treatment of the various juridical views on the status of these noncombatant groups during a battle[89] that need not be reproduced here.[90]

The command "do not aggress/commit violence" (*wa-lā ta'tadū*) in Qur'ān 2:190 was interpreted by unnamed exegetes as proscribing fighting for worldly reasons, such as zealotry and gaining renown, instead of seeking to please God (*li-ghayr wajh allāh*). There are also those who say that *lā ta'tadū* means "do not fight those who do not fight." This latter meaning, however, al-Qurṭubī says, has been abrogated by the command to fight all the unbelievers (cf. Qur'ān 9:36).[91] *Fitna* in Qur'ān 2:191 refers to the persecution visited upon the Muslims with the intention of making them relapse into unbelief, an act that is worse than killing. Mujāhid understood *fitna* in this sense, although others said that unbelief and associating partners with God was a graver and more heinous offense than resorting to fighting.[92] In regard to Qur'ān 2:193, two main issues are foregrounded, one having to do with its status and the other with its specific meaning. First, there are those who regard this as an abrogating verse and understand it to contain a commandment to slay every polytheist everywhere. Opposed to them are those who do not consider Qur'ān 2:193 to be an abrogating verse and understand it to mean that the unbelievers may only be fought when they initiate fighting (*fa-in qātalūkum*). al-Qurṭubī favors the first interpretation and asserts that the verse is to be understood as containing an absolute commandment to fight, regardless of whether the unbelievers initiate fighting or not (*wa-huwa amr bi-qitāl muṭlaq lā bi-sharṭan yabda' al-kuffār*). This is borne out by the statement "And religion is for God" in the same verse and by the *ḥadīth* in which the Prophet says, "I have been commanded to fight people until they say 'there is no god but God.' " Thus both the verse and this *ḥadīth* indicate that "the reason for fighting is unbelief" (*anna sabab al-qitāl huwa 'l-kufr*). This is why God has said, "Until there is no more *fitna*," where *fitna* refers to "unbelief" (*kufr*). The objective of fighting is the eradication of unbelief (*'adam al-kufr*), asserts al-Qurṭubī. According to Ibn 'Abbās, Qatāda, al-Rabī', al-Suddī, and others, *fitna* here refers to "polytheism" (*al-shirk*) and the harm to the unbelievers that ensued from it. He notes, however, that the basic meaning of *fitna* is "trial and test," harking back to the "testing" [refining] of silver in fire in order to separate the dross from it.[93]

Second, al-Qurṭubī continues, *fa-in intahaw* refers to abandoning unbelief, either by embracing Islam (in the case of pagans) or through the payment of *jizya* in the case of the People of the Book. Otherwise, both groups are to be fought because they are unjust/wrongdoers (*wa-hum ẓalimūn*), and "there is no aggression except against them" (*wa-lā 'udwān illā 'alayhim*). The reason it is called aggression is because it is the counterpart of the kind of aggression the unbelievers resort to against the believers, as indicated in Qur'ān 42:40 ("the requital of evil is evil like it"). The "wrongdoers" (*al-ẓālimūn*) may be interpreted in two ways: (1) those who initiate fighting; and (2) those who adhere to unbelief (*kufr*) and [the attendant] harm (*fitna*).[94] As for Qur'an 2:194, according to al-Ḥasan, when the unbelievers were determined to fight the Prophet, this verse came down, allowing the believers to fight and defend themselves (*fa-abāḥa allāh bi-'l-āya mudāfa'atahum*), even in the Sanctuary under such circumstances.[95]

The array of views recorded by al-Qurṭubī (not reproduced here in their entirety) once again conveys to us the contested meanings of these verses through the formative and late medieval periods, with the absolutely no-aggression school firmly pitted against those who sought to qualify and nullify the no-aggression injunction with a variety of hermeneutic and legal stratagems, not least of all through abrogation. As we observed, early authorities, such as Mujāhid and al-Suddī, unequivocally subscribed to the view that these verses explicitly prohibit Muslims from initiating hostilities, regardless of time and place. Although al-Ṭabarī records these early views, he shows a clear preference for the pro-*naskh* school; after him, this hermeneutical strand appears to have become the predominant one. al-Qurṭubī's own robust partiality for the position that fighting may continue against polytheists until they renounce their beliefs is reflective of the prevailing legal (but not exegetical) near-consensus of his time on this matter.[96]

Additional Reasons for Fighting: Qur'ān 9:12–13

In addition to the reasons contained in Qur'ān 22:39–40 and 2:191–193, which legitimated resorting to fighting by Muslims, verses in Qur'ān 9:12–13 make clear that violation of contracts coupled with hostile behavior on the part of the polytheists and their initiation of fighting had provided grounds for military action on the part of Muslims during the time of the Prophet, as discussed below:

> Qur'ān 9:12–13 state: If they break their pacts (*aymānahum*) after having concluded them and revile your religion, then fight the leaders of unbelief for they do not honor oaths; perhaps they will desist (*yantahūn*). Will you not fight a people (*qawman*) who violated their oaths (*lā aymāna lahum*) and had intended to expel the Messenger and commenced [hostilities] against you the first time (*wa-hum bada'ūkum awwala marra*)?

Almost all the exegetes surveyed by us (with the exception of selected Shīʿī exegetes) stress that the violation of pacts by the polytheists, their denigration of Islam, hostile intent toward Muḥammad, and their initial act of aggression toward Muslims had made fighting against them necessary.

In his very brief comments on Qur'ān 9:13 preserved for us, **Mujāhid b. Jabr** glosses *aymānahum* as "their pact" (*'ahdahum*) violated by the polytheists, who are also censured for expelling the Prophet. It is the Quraysh who initiated fighting when they attacked the allies of Muḥammad, he states.[97]

Muqātil b. Sulaymān remarks that Qur'ān 9:12 refers to the Meccan polytheists who violated their agreement with the Prophet to desist from fighting for two years. Instead of observing the truce, they secretly armed the Banū Kināna and goaded the latter to attack the Banū Khuzāʿa, who had made peace with Muḥammad. As a result, "the Prophet, peace and blessings be upon him, deemed it licit to fight them" (*fa-'staḥalla al-nabiyy ṣallā allāhu 'alayhi wa-sallam qitālahum*). These polytheists had also belittled Islam. The leaders of unbelief are identified by Muqātil as the leaders of Quraysh: namely Abū Sufyān b. Ḥarb, al-Ḥārith b. Hishām, Suhayl b. ʿAmr, ʿIkrima b. Abī Jahl, and others.[98] The next verse refers to the same incident concerning Kināna and Khuzāʿa, he continues, and denounces the Quraysh for descending upon the Dār al-nadwa, conspiring to either kill the Prophet, shackle him, or expel him.

The Quraysh commenced hostilities when they marched to Badr to fight the Muslims.[99]

The ***Tanwīr al-miqbās*** says that Qur'ān 9:12 refers to those Meccans who broke the pacts they had concluded with Muslims and reviled the religion of Islam. As a consequence, Muslims were given the command to fight the leaders of the Quraysh, namely Abū Sufyān and his cohorts, in order to dissuade them from habitually violating their oaths. The following verse (9:13) similarly emphasizes the imperative to fight those who had reneged on their word and had attempted to kill the Messenger when they rushed into the Dār al-nadwa. It was the Meccans who had initiated hostilities by supporting their ally Banū Bakr in their war preparations against the Banū Khuzā'a, who had allied themselves with Muḥammad. The verse contains the admonition that if the Companions of Muḥammad are true believers, asserts the *Tanwīr*, they will fear God rather than the Qurayshīs.[100]

Hūd b. Muḥakkam similarly understands this verse to contain an indictment of the leaders of Quraysh (his list is similar to that of Muqātil), for they had violated the treaty that existed between them and the Prophet and had expelled him from Mecca. *Aymān*, as it occurs in the verse, is clearly a reference to a pact (*'ahd*), he says. *La'allahum yantahūna* is explained as "Perhaps whoever is not killed among them will desist from his unbelief in fear of being killed."[101]

Ibn Muḥakkam refers next to the *Tafsīr* of al-Kalbī, which explained these verses in the context of al-Ḥudaybiyya and the violation of the treaty by the Meccans, providing the occasion of revelation for Qur'ān 9:12. Al-Ḥasan al-Baṣrī in his commentary on the following verse had similarly emphasized the initial contravention of the pledge by the polytheists when they initiated an attack on the allies of the Prophet (*wa-hum bada'ūkum awwala marra*). This required a military response from Muḥammad and his Companions. Qur'ān 9:13 contains a warning to the Companions that, if they are indeed believers, they should fear God more than their enemies under such circumstances.[102]

In contradistinction to the exegetes above, the Shī'ī exegete **al-'Ayyāshī**, on the authority of Ja'far al-Ṣādiq (Abū 'Abd Allāh) identifies Ṭalḥa and al-Zubayr as "two of the imāms from among the imāms of unbelief," moving the historical locus for Qur'an 9:12 improbably from the time of the Prophet to the caliphate of 'Alī.[103]

In his commentary on Qur'ān 9:12, **al-Ṭabarī** says that it is a critique of those among the Quraysh who violated the terms of their pact with Muḥammad that they would not fight the Muslims or provide aid to their enemies; additionally, these Qurayshīs had defamed Islam. The leaders of the unbelievers thus had to be fought against to cause them to desist from providing aid to the enemies of Muslims and from reviling Islam. Al-Ṭabarī notes that most exegetes agree with this interpretation, although they differ on the precise identification of the leaders of the unbelievers[104] and on whether to read *al-aymān* or *al-īmān* in 9:13. On the latter point, al-Ṭabarī notes that exegetes from the Ḥijāz, Iraq, and elsewhere read the word as *aymān* in reference to oaths/pledges (*'uhūd*). But al-Ḥasan al-Baṣrī is said to have read it as *īmān* (lit. "faith"), with the resultant meaning being "they do not have Islam" (*la islāma lahum*). This reading also permits the understanding "do not offer them safe conduct," if the verbal noun *īmān* is construed to mean "offering protection." Al-Ṭabarī endorses the reading *aymān* as correct, the plural of *yamīn*, in specific reference to oaths/pledges.[105]

The next verse adds to the polytheists' list of sins their expulsion of the Prophet and their commencement of hostilities during the battle of Badr. Others, like Mujāhid, say it is because they began to fight the Banū Khuzā'a, who were the allies of Muḥammad. The verse concludes, comments al-Ṭabarī, by warning that Muslims should fear God more than they do the polytheists.[106]

In **al-Wāḥidī**'s commentary on these verses, we occasionally see significant departures from these early exegeses on a number of points. Like his predecessors surveyed here, he glosses *aymān* as oaths (*qasam*) made by the Qurayshī polytheists that they proceeded to violate and then followed these violations with defamation of Islam. The leaders of unbelief were the chiefs of Quraysh; the list of names coincides with the one provided by Hūd b. Muḥakkam. According to Yaḥyā b. Ziyād al-Farrā' (d. 207/822; author of the *Ma'āni 'l-qur'ān*), *aymān* refers to "pacts" (*'uhūd*), but he also accepted the possibility of it referring to *īmān*, so that it would mean "they do not have Islam" (*la islām lahum*). Unlike al-Ṭabarī, al-Wāḥidī concedes that this is a plausible interpretation, for polytheists do not have faith like the scriptuaries (*ahl al-dhimma*). This interpretation is further supported by the occurrence of the phrase *a'immat al-kufr*, which underscores their lack of faith, he says. Proceeding from this interpretation, al-Wāhidī then makes the case that *la'allahum yantahūn* means to desist from unbelief, not from violating oaths. He invokes the authority of Ibn 'Abbas, who is quoted as saying, "in order that they refrain from associating partners with God" (*kay yantahū 'an al-shirk bi-'llāh*). Believers (*al-mu'minīn*) are thus exhorted to fight them.[107] This interpretation, we should note, represents a radical departure from the views of earlier exegetes of this important verse. Its attribution to Ibn 'Abbās is highly suspect; none of our earlier exegetes, especially al-Ṭabarī, known for his conscientious recording of variant perspectives, documents this view.

Qur'ān 9:13 is understood by **al-Wāhidī** as stating that fighting those who break their pledges is more worthy than fighting other kinds of unbelievers, because it prevents others from doing the same. Here, *aymānahum* is clearly a reference to pledges because the historical backdrop to this verse is the truce of al-Ḥudaybiyya, says al-Wāhidī, which the polytheists violated by providing aid to the Banū Bakr against the Khuzā'a, the allies of the Prophet. Al-Wāḥidī concurs that the verse also refers to their plot to kill Muḥammad at the Dār al-nadwa and that it censures the polytheists for initiating fighting at Badr.[108]

In the sixth/twelfth century, **al-Zamakhsharī** more or less conforms to the interpretation advanced by al-Wāḥidī in the following manner: He says the phrase *a'immat al-kufr* in Qur'an 9:12 stresses that the people thereby intended had reneged on their pledges in their state of polytheism out of defiance and aggression, flouting the conventions of honor and fidelity prevalent among Arabs. Reading Qur'ān 9:12 in the context of its preceding verse (which states, "If they should repent, perform the prayers, and give *zakāt*, then they are your brothers in religion and we explain the signs for a people who are knowledgeable"), al-Zamakhsharī says that these leaders had previously become believers, performed the prayer, paid the *zakāt*, and become the brothers of Muslims in faith. But then they violated their oaths to remain faithful (*wa-nakathū ma bāya'ū 'alayhi min al-īmān*) and to honor their pacts (*wa-'l-wafā' bi-'l-'uhūd*), resorting instead to maligning "the religion of God" and declaring "the religion of Muḥammad to be nothing"—these are the leaders of unbelief. Al-Zamakhsharī discusses whether *al-aymān* or *al-īmān* should be the preferred reading in the last part of Qur'ān 9:12; he endorses the variant reading *al-īmān*.[109] If someone should remonstrate that this reading is implausible, because the same verse cannot contradictorily maintain that the pagan Meccans had faith and did not have faith, al-Zamakhsharī responds that the verse should be understood to mean that the polytheists were only feigning belief and thus did not in reality have faith (*lā imāna lahum 'alā 'l-ḥaqīqa*). He records the opinion of Abū Ḥanīfa that the oath of the polytheist was not really an oath, contradicted by al-Shāfi'ī, who said that it *did* constitute a real oath, for, as the use of the term *nakth* indicates, the verse accuses the polytheists of not abiding by their oaths. Al-Shāfi'ī thereby implies that the charge of violation holds only if the polytheists had contravened something that was valid and binding.[110]

Given this interpretive trajectory, it is not surprising that al-Zamakhsharī further interprets *la'allahum yantahūn* as a reference to the polytheists desisting from their state of unbelief, rather than their propensity to contravene their oaths in order not to be fought against, an interpretation with substantial doctrinal and legal implications.[111]

Al-Rāzī also debates the validity of the readings *aymānahum* versus *īmānahum*, but unlike al-Zamakhsharī, states a clear preference for the first reading because it is the more common one (*al-qirā'a al-mashhūra*) and because the entire verse deals with those who violate their pledges (*nāqiḍī 'l-'ahd*). God has singled out the leaders of the polytheists to be fought against, he says, because they goad their followers into committing wrong acts. In regards to the occurrence of *aymān* in Qur'ān 9:13 specifically, he entertains the three interpretive strands that we have already referenced: (1) The word is to be read as *īmān*, according to the Syrian Qur'ān-reciter Ibn 'Āmir (d. 118/736),[112] so that it could refer to either (2) a lack of faith on the part of the polytheists, or (3) an interdiction against their being granted safe conduct (*amān*). Al-Rāzī notes the contrary views of Abū Ḥanīfa and al-Shāfi'ī concerning the validity of the unbeliever's oath. He remarks, quite logically, that the verse would not have employed the verb *nakathū* if the oaths of the polytheists had not been valid oaths, "for if they [the oaths] had not been [properly] concluded (*mun'aqidan*) then it would not have been accurate to describe them as having been violated/contravened." However, al-Rāzī, like al-Wāḥidī and al-Zamakhsharī before him, sides with those who were of the opinion that "perhaps they may desist" is to be explained in the context of "the leaders of unbelief." Thus the verse is to be understood as commanding fighting unbelievers until they cease to disbelieve (*an takūna al-muqātala sababan fī 'ntihā'ihim 'amma hum 'alayhi min al-kufr*), rather than because they break their pledges.[113]

The next verse continues by enumerating three reasons for fighting the polytheists, says al-Rāzī, each of which on its own constitutes grounds for fighting them: (1) their violation of the terms of the treaty of al-Ḥudaybiyya by aiding the Banū Bakr against the Khuzā'a; (2) their seeking to evict the Prophet, either from Mecca at the time of the *hijra* according to one school of thought, or from Medina when they approached him for consultation and connived together to kill him, according to another; and (3) their initiation of hostilities at Badr and their vow not to leave until they had "uprooted Muḥammad and those with him." The verb *bada'ūkum* in Qur'ān 9:13 draws attention to the fact that the aggressor is unequivocally the greater offender (*tanbīhan 'alā anna 'l-bādi' aẓlam*).[114]

Al-Qurṭubī offers a lengthier and more detailed legal discussion of the rights of polytheists, as argued by the classical jurists in relation to these two verses, the full details of which need not unnecessarily engage us here. It is important to note, however, that he glosses *al-nakth* as *al-naqḍ* ("violation/infringement") in relation to oaths and pacts and *wa-ṭa'anū fī dīnikum* as the warfare and rebellion instigated by polytheists against Islam.[115] al-Qurṭubī furthermore understands the phrase *lā aymāna lahum* as a reference to the breaking of their pledges by the polytheists, but he records the minority opinion of Ibn 'Āmir, who understood it as *lā imāna lahum*, meaning "they have no Islam/faith" or possibly "they have no safe conduct." In regard to the phrase *la'allahum yantahūn*, al-Qurṭubī cites the opinion of al-Kalbī, who had maintained that the verse referred to the Treaty of al-Ḥudaybiyya, which was rescinded when the Banū Umayya began to provide arms and supplies to their allies, the Banū Kināna, against the Banū Khuzā'a, who had allied themselves with the Prophet. The phrase therefore expresses the hope that the polytheists will renounce "their unbelief, their wrongdoing, and the harm they inflict on Muslims." In other words, the verse declares that the reason for fighting polytheists was "to repel their aggression so that they may desist from fighting us and enter into our religion"[116]; this nicely achieves a synthesis of the two contradictory interpretations of the verb *yantahū*.

Like his predecessors, al-Qurṭubī understands Qur'ān 9:13 to be a reference to the leaders of the Quraysh. who compelled the Prophet to come out of Medina in order to fight the Meccans, who had violated their pledge, a reference to al-Ḥudaybiyya. Al-Ḥasan al-Baṣrī was of the opinion that *bada'ūkum* referred to the polytheists' initiation of fighting when they began to arm the Banū Bakr against the Khuzā'a in violation of the terms of the treaty. Al-Qurṭubī also notes the different interpretive strands—others had maintained that the historical backdrop to the verses was the battle of Badr, and yet others said that it was a reference to the polytheists' attempts to prevent Muḥammad from carrying out the pilgrimage the year before al-Ḥudaybiyya, which constituted an act of hostility.[117]

Concluding Remarks

Our diachronic survey of Qur'ān 9:12–13 clearly establishes that, roughly in the first four centuries of Islam, a majority of the exegetes understood these verses as criticizing the polytheists for their violation of pledges they had concluded with Muslims, rather than for their religious predilections, and for having subsequently initiated fighting against the Muslims. The introduction of the variant reading of *īmān* to replace *aymān* in Qur'ān 9:13 by al-Wāḥidī on the authority of the Syrian *qāri'* Ibn 'Āmir became quite prevalent, however, among later exegetes, signaling, among other things, a drastic change in the self-understanding of Muslims versus non-Muslims. Such a radically altered interpretation, which appears to have gained ground in the post-al-Ṭabarī period, would add a new theological dimension to the range of legitimate reasons for which Muslims could go to war against non-Muslims. It also allowed for the convenient neutralization of the final condition mentioned in

Qur'ān 9:13—that legitimate armed retaliation should be in response to the initiation of fighting by an implacably hostile and duplicitous enemy.[118] This is a point we will dwell upon further in our concluding chapter in view of its far-reaching ramifications for understanding the purview of the military *jihād* and the historical trajectory of interfaith relations.

III

The Ethics of Fighting, Refraining from Fighting, and Peacemaking

IN ADDITION TO verses discussed in the previous chapter that have to do primarily with legitimate reasons for engaging in fighting, the Qur'ān also contains verses that prescribe specific conduct during warfare, the manner of terminating hostilities, and making peace with enemies. Some of the most frequently cited verses in connection with the ethics of war and peace are discussed below under the following rubrics: (1) obligation to fight under justified circumstances; (2) abstention from and termination of hostilities; and (3) peacemaking.

Obligation to Fight under Justified Circumstances

When war is duly constituted for justified and legitimate reasons (the most significant of which were discussed in the previous chapter), fighting becomes a moral obligation that no adult male believer may shirk without extenuating reason. Qur'ān 2:216, 9:5, and 9:29 are among the most frequently discussed verses understood to emphasize this conditional religious duty, as is discussed below. Qur'ān 4:95 further describes how the combative *jihād* should be undertaken by the believers in Medina—"with their wealth and their selves"—a locution that lends itself to multiple interpretations. As will become evident in our survey of exegetical works, when and exactly upon whom the commandment to fight was binding and how this duty should be discharged remained subjects of lively debate through the centuries.

> Fighting has been prescribed for you even though you find it displeasing. Perhaps you dislike something in which there is good for you and perhaps you find pleasing that which causes you harm. But God knows and you do not. (Qur'ān 2:216)

We have only brief comments preserved on this verse from our earliest exegetes.

Muqātil b. Sulaymān says that the verse made fighting "obligatory for you" (*furiḍa 'alaykum*), just as fasting had been prescribed. Fighting may represent a hardship (*mashaqqa*) for the believers, but God has made conquest, booty, and martyrdom its end results (*fatḥ wa ghanīma wa-shahāda*). The believers may prefer to refrain from *jihād* (*al-qu'ūd 'an al-jihād*), but as a result they forgo victory and the spoils of war.[1]

The ***Tanwīr al-miqbās*** explains this verse as prescribing (*furiḍa*) fighting for Muslims *specifically during the time of the Prophet's military campaigns* (*fī awqāt al-nafīr al-'āmm ma'a 'l-nabī*), despite their dislike for "fighting in the path of God" (*al-jihād fī sabīl allāh*). If they should choose to refrain from *jihād*, then they will not attain martyrdom and booty, which is the understanding of *khayr* in this context. But God knows "that *jihād* is better for you" and that refraining from it "is a source of harm for you."[2] Compared to Muqātil, who appears to have understood fighting to be an injunction laid upon Muslims in general, the *Tanwīr* restricts the applicability of this injunction to the time of Muḥammad during his specific military campaigns. This is a highly significant interpretation of the purview of the military *jihād* that continued to be transmitted and discussed by later exegetes, as we will see shortly.

'Abd al-Razzāq in his extant commentary deals only with the clause *wa-huwa kurh la-kum* in this verse and glosses it as "a hardship for you."[3]

In his *tafsīr*, **Hūd b. Muḥakkam** refers to al-Ḥasan al-Baṣrī, who was of the opinion that *al-jihād fī sabīl allāh* was one of those activities that believers used to dislike, although it is a good deed before God. Ibn Muḥakkam also refers to al-Kalbī, who had mentioned that the combative *jihād* was at first voluntary (*taṭawwu'an*) and then became mandatory in Medina. Another report from an unnamed source is recorded that counseled an unnamed individual to continue to look after his mother instead of joining the military campaign against Kark (undertaken during the time of the second 'Abbasid caliph Manṣūr), "unless the enemy were to attack you [directly], in which case fighting would become obligatory for you."[4] In this report, which became much cited in the later literature, filial duty is deemed to be more urgent than military defense and therefore more morally excellent in the specified circumstances.

In the briefest of remarks preserved for us, **Ibrāhīm al-Qummī** comments that Qur'ān 2:216 was revealed in Medina and abrogates Qur'ān 4:77, which says, "Hold back your hands [establish worship and pay the obligatory alms]. . . ."[5]

In his more detailed commentary on this verse, **al-Ṭabarī** glosses *kutiba 'alaykum al-qitāl* as "prescribed for you is fighting against the polytheists" (*al-mushrikīn*), even though it is displeasing to the believers. He then proceeds to delineate significant differences of opinion among scholars in the formative period regarding the duty of fighting, and offers more fulsome evidence, in comparison with the *Tanwīr*, that the combative *jihād* was understood by a number of early authorities to be restricted only to the time of Muḥammad. Thus, al-Tabarī records, Ibn Jurayj had reported that he had asked 'Aṭā' [b. Abī Rabāḥ] whether Qur'ān 2:216 made fighting (*al-ghazw*) obligatory for people in general. 'Aṭā' replied that it did not and that it was prescribed only for those [*ūlā'ika*, sc. Companions] at that time (*ḥīna'idhin*).[6] Al-Ṭabarī also records a report from Abū Isḥāq al-Fazārī (d. ca. 188/804; other death dates are also given),[7] who had questioned al-Awzā'ī (d. 157/774)[8] about this verse and whether it applied to all people. Al-Awzā'ī replied that he did not know. "But," he continued, "the leaders and the general populace (*al-'āmma*) cannot abandon it. As for the individual man himself, then no."[9] As late as the third quarter of the second/eighth century, therefore, leading scholars remained doubtful that fighting was a prescribed *religious* duty for Muslims after the time of the Companions, whether individually or collectively. Al-Awzā'ī's equivocal response clearly conveys to us that he deemed fighting to be an obligation that the leader and the general population could not abandon—not on religious but pragmatic grounds and for reasons of commonweal.

Al-Ṭabarī goes on to report that unnamed others said that fighting is an individual duty until enough people (*al-kifāya*) are available to undertake it, at which time such a duty is no longer obligatory for the rest of the Muslims. This is comparable to the duty of offering funeral prayers, and washing and burying the body, in the opinion of Muslim scholars in general. Al-Ṭabarī agrees with this point of view as a consensus of opinion can be adduced for it and because of Qur'ān 4:95, which states, "God has preferred those who strive with their wealth and their selves with a degree over those who do not similarly strive (*al-qā'idīna*, lit. "the sedentary ones") and has promised goodness (*al-ḥusnā*) for both" (see also our extended discussion of this verse below). Thus God informs in this verse, he says, that the strivers accrue merit (*al-faḍl*), but that both they and the sedentary people earn goodness. If, al-Ṭabarī argues, the *qā'idīn* had failed to fulfill an essential duty, they would have earned a bad recompense, not a good one.[10] From this cross-referential reading of the Qur'anic text, the conclusion emerges: Fighting is not to be regarded as a religious obligation for an individual Muslim, but rather as an act of supererogation, since the pious person who abstains from fighting is also promised goodness in the hereafter.

Al-Ṭabarī further records the views of Dā'ūd b. Abī 'Āṣim,[11] who had maintained that "it [fighting] was an obligatory duty (*farḍ wājib*) for Muslims until the Last Hour." Dā'ūd is said to have remarked to the Companion Sa'īd b. al-Musayyab, "I have come to learn that fighting (*al-ghazw*) is obligatory (*wājib*) for people!" Sa'īd b. al-Musayyab did not respond, and Dā'ūd b. Abī 'Āṣim went on to assume that if the former had disagreed with this statement, he would have made his opinion clear.[12] From the presentation of these varying views, al-Ṭabarī concludes that *kutiba* in the verse refers to a collective duty (*farḍ kifāya*) and not an individual one (*farḍ 'ayn*) (as also became the prevailing legal consensus).

As for the rest of the verse, al-Ṭabarī says that it counsels the believers not to recoil from fighting, which perhaps may be a good thing for them, and that by electing to abstain from taking part in the military *jihād*, they may be choosing what is bad for them. Al-Suddī had commented that the verse indicates that the Muslims used to detest fighting; the *khayr* mentioned in the verse refers to possible booty, victory, and martyrdom as a result of fighting.[13] Al-Ṭabarī also cites Ibn 'Abbās, who had related that the Prophet had counseled him to be satisfied with whatever God decrees, "even though it be contrary to your desire" and recited this verse as proof-text.[14] According to these early exegetes, then, believers should show a pragmatic *preference* for fighting, because the verse, interpreted through the prism of a cost-benefit analysis, allows one to infer that the benefits of fighting, often material, far outweigh its inconvenience, difficulty, and risk. Such an inference should cause Muslims to volunteer for such an advantageous, even lucrative activity, but these verses themselves (Qur'ān 2:216 and 4:95) do not require it, notes al-Ṭabarī significantly.

In the fifth/eleventh century, **al-Wāḥidī** continues to endorse the early position that fighting as a religiously prescribed duty was temporally circumscribed. He too quotes 'Aṭā' b. Abī Rabāḥ, who had understood Qur'ān 2:216 to refer specifically to the Companions of the Prophet because *only fighting with the Prophet* (emphasis mine) was an obligatory duty. It was not permissible to refrain from fighting when the Prophet himself undertook *jihād* against the enemy. Al-Wāḥidī adds that, in his time, this duty is understood to be a collective one (*annahu min furūḍ al-kifāya*).[15]

In his very brief commentary on this verse, **al-Zamakhsharī** states that the verse means that it is possible that believers dislike all that they have been commanded to do (he does not single out fighting here), because humans are inclined to shirk their duties and disobey God. But God knows wherein lies goodness and welfare for them, while they know not, concludes al-Zamakhsharī.[16]

As one has come to expect, **al-Rāzī** has a much more extensive commentary on this verse and provides for us a valuable account of the changing interpretive trajectory for this critical verse. He begins by underscoring that Muḥammad had been forbidden to fight during the Meccan period. But, after the *hijra*, he was given permission to fight those who fought him from among the polytheists, and then to fight them in general (*'āmmatan*). Al-Rāzī acknowledges, however, like al-Ṭabarī, that widely divergent opinions have historically existed among the scholars. Thus the Syrian scholar Makḥūl[17] is said to have sworn at the Ka'ba that *ghazw* (the term is used here very likely in contrast to defensive *jihād*) was obligatory in general. According to the Medinan scholars Ibn 'Umar and 'Aṭā', however, this verse imposed the duty of fighting on the Companions of Muḥammad "at that time only" (*fī dhālika 'l-waqt faqaṭ*), that is, solely during the lifetime of the Prophet.[18] Once again, it becomes clearly apparent from al-Rāzī's exegesis that Syrian scholars like Makḥūl presumably in the context of continuing Umayyad military engagements with the Byzantines allowed for a general injunction to fight to be read into this verse in contradistinction to Ḥijāzī scholars outside of the Umayyad orbit, such as 'Aṭā' b. Abī Rabāḥ and Ibn 'Umar, who inferred no such broad religious mandate and restricted the imposition of the duty to fight on the Companions of the Prophet alone.

Al-Rāzī refers specifically to the commentary of 'Aṭā' b. Abī Rabāḥ, who had maintained that *kutiba* in the verse may refer to the imposition of a duty for one time only and *'alaykum* was a reference only to those who had been present at the time of the verse's revelation. Al-Rāzī himself, however, supports the derivation of a general injunction to fight from this verse, for he asserts that *kutiba* and *'alaykum* both mean "God imposes duties." *'Alaykum* ("upon you" [plural]), he explains further, means the imposition of duties upon both those who are present and those who will come later, as in Qur'ān 2:178, which states, "Prescribed (*kutiba*) for you is the law of *talionis* (*qiṣaṣ*)" and Qur'ān 2:183, which states, "Prescribed for you is fasting."[19] Compared with his predecessors, this is a new line of reasoning initiated or adopted by al-Rāzī clearly to countervail the views of those who had argued that the commandment to fight *as a religious obligation* had lapsed after the time of the Prophet.[20]

Al-Rāzī then goes on to ponder the vexing question of whether the verse should be understood to prescribe fighting as a duty incumbent upon individuals (*al-a'yān*) or on the collectivity (*al-kifāya*)? Given the tenor of his discussion, it is not surprising that he endorses the position that it is imposed on individuals, for, he comments, the verse says "upon you [plural]," which is to be interpreted as "[obligatory] upon each and every one of you," as were *qiṣaṣ* and fasting. To those who challenge this line of argument by pointing to Qur'ān 4:95 (he clearly has al-Ṭabarī in mind although he is not specifically named), which promises reward to both those who fight and those who do not fight, thereby suggesting that the obligation (*farḍ*) imposed in Qur'ān 2:216 may be regarded as having been abrogated or qualified by Qur'ān 4:95, al-Rāzī simply states that he does not accept this instance of abrogation as there is no proof (*dalīl*) for it. He is similarly dismissive of those who adduce as proof-text Qur'ān 9:122, which states, "Let not all the believers go out to fight," as abrogating Qur'ān 2:216 and establishing the collective nature of fighting. Al-Rāzī indirectly admits that his is a minority opinion, for he goes on to note that according to the consensus of his day, fighting was one of the collective obligations, unless the polytheists were to enter the lands of Muslims, in which case *jihād* at that time would become obligatory for all ("and God knows best").[21] Al-Rāzī's commentary on this significant verse makes abundantly clear that in his own perilous era (the Third and the Fourth Crusades were launched during his lifetime), the more hawkish position understandably had greater appeal for him and prompted him to promote fighting as an individual religious duty against the general juridical consensus of his time.

In the following century, **al-Qurṭubī**'s exegesis is very similar to that of al-Rāzī. He equates *kutiba* in the verse with *furiḍa* and notes that during the Meccan period, Muḥammad was given permission to fight only after the *hijra* and only those among the polytheists who resorted to arms (cf. Qur'ān 22:39); subsequently, he was given permission to fight them in general. Like a number of the exegetes we have already discussed, al-Qurṭubī also records the early variations in scholarly views regarding those who are intended in this verse. Thus he relates that according to some, the verse referred specifically to the Companions of the Prophet, and that fighting with the Prophet was individually imposed only on them. When the revealed law became fully determined, then the obligation is said to have become a collective one. This position had been maintained by 'Aṭā' and al-Awzā'ī; al-Qurṭubī cites the by-now-familiar report from 'Aṭā' as related by Ibn Jurayj as a proof-text. A majority of scholars, including Ibn 'Aṭiyya, have affirmed that the first imposition of fighting was also as a collective duty. Ibn 'Aṭiyya had also maintained, along with Sufyān al-Thawrī, that "*Jihād* is a voluntary act" (*al-jihād taṭawwu'*), notes al-Qurṭubī.[22]

Al-Qurṭubī's account of Sa'īd b. al-Musayyab's views is worthy of attention. According to our exegete, Ibn al-Musayyab is reported to have declared that *jihād* was a duty enjoined upon every individual Muslim for all time, as was related by the well-known Shāfi'ī jurist al-Māwardī (d. 450/1058). This report is at variance with the version recorded by al-Ṭabarī circa early fourth/tenth century, according to which Ibn al-Musayyab remained silent when pointedly asked by Dā'ūd b. Abī 'Āṣim whether fighting was an obligatory duty for everyone. Al-Qurṭubī's version indicates that eventually, Ibn al-Musayyab's silence had become rescripted as an unequivocal endorsement of fighting as a divinely mandated obligation, apparently by the time of al-Māwardī to whom this version is ascribed. One might surmise that for juridical purposes in the context of international relations, this latter version would prove more useful as a proof-text.

It is telling that al-Qurṭubī ends his exegesis of this verse by pointing out that, because *jihād* was abandoned in al-Andalus and the Muslims there had become fearful of fighting and resorted to fleeing before the onslaughts of the enemy, the enemy had gained control of their land and subjected them to imprisonment, killing, captivity, and enslavement. Without doubt, al-Qurṭubī's enthusiasm for the view that fighting was a religiously prescribed, individual duty is at least partially explained by the circumstances of his own historical period, when Muslims were being progressively expelled from al-Andalus in the wake of a muscular Christianity. "We are from God and to Him we return!" he exclaimed in horror at this tragic dénouement.

> Qur'ān 9:5: When the sacred months have lapsed, then slay the polytheists (*al-mushrikīn*) wherever you may encounter them. Seize them and encircle them and lie in wait for them. But if they repent and perform the prayer and give the *zakāt*, then let them go on their way, for God is forgiving and merciful.

This verse (often along with Qur'ān 9:29 discussed below) is frequently cited in a decontextualized and ahistorical manner in certain kinds of literature—particularly in the contemporary period—to support the view that the Qur'ān itself promotes global military conquest that must be carried out to eventually impose Islam on all.[23] As our ensuing discussion shows, Muslim exegetes in different historical periods subscribed to a range of views concerning the applicability of this verse and the people intended as referents in it.

Muqātil b. Sulaymān understands the "sacred months" to be a reference to twenty days during Dhū 'l-Ḥijja and thirty days during the following month of Muḥarram. The *mushrikūn* are those with whom there is no pact (*'ahd*), who may be fought wherever they are to be found, in sacred or profane territory, except during the above fifty days. Muslims are commanded to "apprehend them" (*khudhūhum*), seek them out (*wa-'ḥṣurūhum*), and lie in wait for them on every path as long as they are unbelievers (*wa-hum kuffār*). But if they should repent of their polytheism (*min al-shirk*) and offer prayers and the obligatory alms, then they are to be left alone and not wronged in any way. As a consequence, God will forgive them their sins committed while they were polytheists and grant them mercy in Islam.[24]

Very similar views are expressed in the ***Tanwīr al-miqbās***[25] and by **Hūd b. Muḥakkam.**[26]

Al-ʿAyyāshī glosses "if they repent" as "if they believe," in which case they [sc. the polytheists] are to be considered brothers in religion; otherwise, fighting or entry into Islam are the two choices available for them.[27] **Furāt** comments that, according to ʿAlī b. Abī Ṭālib, when the four months have elapsed and the terms of the treaties with the polytheists have ended, the verse allows the polytheists to be fought in sacred and non-sacred territories.[28]

Al-Ṭabarī understands the verse to command the slaying of polytheists wherever they may be found on earth, in sacred or non-sacred territory, and—in an important departure from Muqātil's views—also during holy or non-holy months. The polytheists are to be imprisoned and prevented from moving about freely in Islamic realms and from entering Mecca unless they accept Islam.[29] If, however, they renounce their polytheism and their rejection of the prophethood of Muḥammad, affirm the oneness of God, and perform the obligatory duties of a Muslim, then they may freely move about in Islamic lands and enter the Sacred Mosque. All their previous sins are consequently forgiven by the merciful God.[30]

Al-Ṭabarī then proceeds to refer to certain other scholars who had resorted to the by-now familiar hermeneutic of abrogation to explain away, not the following verse Qur'ān 9:6 (see our discussion below), but Qur'ān 9:5. Thus, al-Ṭabarī records, al-Ḍaḥḥāk and al-Suddī had maintained that Qur'ān 9:5 was abrogated by Qur'ān 47:4, which states in relation to the polytheists: "whether by a handsome release afterwards or by ransom."[31] A rival camp, which included Qatāda, asserted the exact reverse: that Qur'ān 9:5 had abrogated Qur'ān 47:4.[32] At this point, al-Ṭabarī weighs in and says that the correct interpretation is that Qur'ān 9:5 is not abrogated (*wa-laysa dhālika bi-mansūkh*). He clarifies what he means by "abrogation" (*al-naskh*)—it is the nullification of a previously established commandment (*nāfī ḥukm qad kāna thubita*) by another commandment (al-Ṭabarī does not specifically say a "later" commandment). It is not correct to assume, he continues, that God had commanded the slaying of polytheists in every circumstance and then nullified this commandment by ordering their release (*wa-lā ʿalā wajhi 'l-mann ʿalayhim*). Rather, ransom, release, and putting to death remained possible options in relation to polytheists, as established since the first battle fought at Badr by Muḥammad.[33]

Al-Wāḥidī barely dwells on Qur'ān 9:5 and simply refers to Ibn ʿAbbās's view that the polytheists may be taken captive and are to be prevented from traveling about, unless they embrace Islam.[34] Al-Wāḥidī does not refer to this verse as abrogating any other verse in the Qur'ān.

Al-Zamakhsharī also pays scant attention to this verse. In his brief commentary, he glosses "the sacred months" as those during which the violators of their pledges (*al-nākithīn*) can move about freely. *Fa-'qtulū 'l-mushrikīn* is a reference to "those who betray you and rise up against you" (*alladhīna naqaḍūkum wa-ẓaharū 'alaykum*), who may be killed in holy and non-holy places and taken captive, and restricted in their movements. Worthy of note is al-Zamakhsharī's depiction of the polytheists who should be fought against as specifically being those who break their pledges and display a priori hostility to Muslims—not polytheists in general.[35] Like al-Wāḥidī, al-Zamakhshari does not consider this to be an abrogating verse.

Al-Rāzī discusses several matters in connection with Qur'ān 9:5. First, in comparison with Qur'ān 9:2 (which states, "travel the earth for four months"), he concludes that the sacred months are four, during which fighting and killing have been forbidden. When these months have passed, al-Rāzī continues, the polytheists may be killed wherever they are found and at any time, or they may be taken captive and prevented from reaching the Ka'ba.[36]

With regard to the rest of the verse, al-Rāzī injects into his commentary the opinions of al-Shāfi'ī, who had declared on the basis of this verse that whoever abandons prayer may be put to death, adding an unexpected legal and doctrinal dimension *concerning Muslims* to his discussion. According to al-Shāfi'ī, the life of such a lapsed Muslim may be spared, however, if he should meet the following three combined conditions: (1) repentance of unbelief; (2) performance of prayer; and (3) the payment of *zakāt*. Al-Rāzī takes note of the dissenting opinions of those [unnamed] who remonstrate that this verse requires one to believe in the necessity of these religious obligations, rather than the actual observance of them.[37] This unprecedented commentary clearly shows that, compared with earlier exegetes, al-Rāzī, invoking the authority of al-Shāfi'ī, has extended the purview of this verse from its original context in reference to the Arab polytheists of Muḥammad's time to a more general and ahistorical one in relation to Muslims who do not observe required religious duties. It is worthy of note that, even at this late date, al-Rāzī does not designate this verse as *āyat al-sayf*, nor does he assert that this verse had abrogated other verses in the Qur'ān that preach conciliation and peaceful relations with non-Muslims in general.

Al-Qurṭubī refers to the Mu'tazilī scholar al-Aṣamm, who understood Qur'ān 9:5 to be directed specifically at polytheists with whom Muslims had no treaty and who could not be fought until the four sacred months had elapsed.[38] Al-Qurṭubī himself, however, considers the commandment *fa-'qtulū 'l-mushrikīn* as a general one concerning polytheists, although on the basis of the *sunna*, restrictions are imposed on the killing of women, children, and others. Qur'ān 9:29 (see further our discussion below) allows the People of the Book to pay the *jiyza*, which concession is not allowed to the "worshipers of idols" (*'abadat al-awthān*). Although *fa-'qtulū 'l-mushrikīn* on the surface allows any manner of killing, specific *ḥadīth*s forbid mutilation, he notes.[39]

With regard to the abrogating function of Qur'ān 9:5, al-Qurṭubī, like al-Ṭabarī, points to a lively debate among the exegetes. According to al-Ḥusayn b. Faḍl, this verse had abrogated all other verses in the Qur'ān that advocate peaceful resistance and patience (*al-iʿrāḍ wa-'l-ṣabr*) in the face of harm caused by enemies.[40] However, al-Ḍaḥḥāk, al-Suddī, and 'Aṭā' were of the opinion that Qur'ān 9:5 was abrogated by Qur'ān 47:4; while Mujāhid and Qatāda maintained that Qur'ān 9:5 had abrogated Qur'ān 47:4 and that polytheist prisoners should be killed. Ibn Zayd had firmly maintained, however, that both verses were unabrogated (*muḥkamatan*), with which interpretation al-Qurṭubī concurred. For, he said, all three options—unconditional release, putting to death, and ransom were allowed by the Prophet since the battle of Badr. The verse also permits restricting the movements of polytheists in Muslim lands, unless express permission is given them to enter such lands in safety.[41]

It is noteworthy that al-Qurṭubī spends more time explicating this verse than most of his predecessors, indicating that military ethics and strategies and the need to justify them on the basis of scriptural warrants were more of a pressing issue during his time in al-Andalus. The imminent danger posed to Muslims by advancing Christian armies there leads al-Qurṭubī to read into Qur'ān 9:5 a rather latitudinarian attitude toward the adoption of rather extreme measures. Thus on the basis of the word *marṣad* in this verse (which he explicates by means of the poetry of 'Āmir b. al-Ṭufayl and 'Adiy), he finds in it a warrant for preemptively slaying the enemy before he is invited [to accept Islam] (*jawāz ightiyālihim qabla 'l-daʿwa*),[42] thereby going against the preponderant legal consensus of his day.

The command to kill polytheists lapses, continues al-Qurṭubī, when they repent and perform the prayers and give the *zakāt*; not merely by repenting of their previous sins. He adduces as proof-text the *ḥadīth* in which the Prophet states that he has been ordered to fight until the people say the *shahāda* and perform the prayer and give the *zakāt*, in which case they win protection for their lives and property except for what is due on it (*illā bi-ḥaqqihā*). Al-Qurṭubī proceeds to explain that *ḥaqq* in this *ḥadīth* refers to three things: unbelief after faith, fornication after chastity, and the taking of a life. He affirms that a majority of the Companions and Successors were of the opinion that anyone who deliberately misses a prayer and refuses to make it up, and publicly declares that he does not pray, is to be deemed an unbeliever, and his life and property are no longer protected. Mere repentance unaccompanied by prayer and almsgiving does not grant the individual immunity, according to al-Qurṭubī.[43] Like al-Rāzī, therefore, al-Qurṭubī indicates that Qur'ān 9:5 has been effectively uncoupled from its original historical context with its internal reference to the

Arab polytheists and redeployed by later exegetes as a proof-text in the context of legal discussions concerning the status of nonobservant Muslims.

It is highly significant that al-Qurṭubī does not call this verse *āyat al-sayf*, as was also the case with his predecessors, nor does he refer to anyone using this designation already. We encounter this designation first in our survey of exegetical works in the *tafsīr* of the eighth/fourteenth century exegete Ibn Kathīr (d. 774/1373), where he states, "This noble verse is the verse of the sword."[44] Ibn Kathīr's commentary on this verse indicates to us a partiality that had developed by the Mamluk period for the derivation of an expansive, general mandate from otherwise historically circumscribed Qur'anic verses (as so understood by a number of earlier exegetes) to fight or punish all those deemed enemies of Islam (including lapsed Muslims) in the later period. Qur'ān 9:5 became deployed above all as a proof-text to implement this assumed mandate.

> Qur'ān 9:29: Fight those who do not believe in God nor in the Last Day and do not forbid what God and His messenger have forbidden and do not follow the religion of truth *from among* (*min*) those who were given the Book until they proffer the *jizya* with [their] hands in humility.

Mujāhid's extant brief comment on this verse merely identifies the occasion of revelation as the battle of Tabūk.[45]

In his slightly longer commentary, **Muqātil b. Sulaymān** says that the verse is directed at "those who do not believe in the oneness of God nor in the resurrection when actions will be judged."[46] Moreover, these people do not forbid wine or swine flesh, prohibitions against which have been made explicit in the Qur'ān. They are also culpable for not adhering to Islam, "because any religion other than Islam is false." These people are the Jews and Christians who, when they pay the *jizya* in person (*'an anfusihim*), willingly and humbly (*madhlūl*), are pardoned and exempted from [military] service, but if it has to be taken from them by force, then they are not to be given any concession, he asserts.[47]

The ***Tanwīr al-miqbās*** says that the referents in this verse do not believe in the joys of heaven and do not forbid what God and His messenger have forbidden, and that this is a reference to the Torah. "They do not follow the true religion" means that they do not submit to the one God. The people to whom the Book was given are the Jews and Christians who, while standing, are to offer with their own hands the *jizya* into the hand [of the receiver] in meekness.[48]

Hūd b. Muḥakkam comments that *dīn al-ḥaqq* in this verse is "the religion of Islam" (*dīn al-islām*) and that it commands that the People of the Book be fought until they either embrace Islam or pay the *jizya*. He refers to Mujāhid's comment that the last part of the verse had to do with the Prophet's expedition to Tabūk (as noted above). Ibn Muḥakkam adds that the *jizya* was taken personally from the People of the Book once a year and from all polytheists except for the Arabs (*wa-jāmi' al-mushrikīn mā khalā 'l-'arab*), if they agreed to do so, and refers to historical precedents for this view.[49]

Al-Qummī records that when Ja'far al-Ṣādiq was asked in connection with this verse how much *jizya* should be assessed on the People of the Book, he replied that it should be in accordance with what they can pay from their wealth, the payment of which protects their freedom and lives.[50] *Wa hum ṣaghīrun* implies that they should feel shame in paying the *jizya*, so that they eventually will feel impelled to embrace Islam.[51]

Al-'Ayyāshī records a report narrated by Ḥafṣ b. Ghiyāth from Ja'far b. Muḥammad from his father, who said that this verse was revealed concerning the *ahl al-dhimma*, abrogating a previous verse concerning them, Qur'ān 2:84, which stated, "Speak a good word to the people." *Dhimmīs* who live in Islamic territory must henceforth either be fought or the *jizya* taken from them.[52]

Al-Ṭabarī comments that God addressed the Prophet and his Companions in this verse and urged them to fight those people who do not believe in God, or in heaven or hell, and who do not truly obey God, that is they do not obey Him as do Muslims. These are Jews and Christians. "Those who have been given the Book," that is, the Book of God, are the "people of the Torah and the Gospel." The *jizya* is the head-tax that they pay to Muslims, from hand to hand, in return for their protection. *Wa-hum sāghirūn* means they are humble and subjugated (*maqhurūn*). Al-Ṭabarī says that the historical context for the revelation of this verse was war with Byzantium, and soon thereafter Muḥammad undertook the campaign of Tabūk, as maintained by Mujāhid and others.[53] Already in al-Ṭabarī's commentary we note considerable attention being paid to the legal minutiae of collecting the *jizya*,[54] a matter that considerably exercised the jurists but that need not engage us here. Jews and Christians are treated as undifferentiated collectivities by him; no distinction is made between hostile and peaceable factions within them. Furthermore, their legal subjugation and general inferiority to Muslims on a doctrinal basis are stressed. As we know from the works of other scholars from the third/ninth century onward (such as al-Jāḥiẓ (d. 255/869), the growing influence and prominence of *dhimmīs* in the major urban centers of the 'Abbasid empire at this time contributed to Muslim resentment against them, which appears to have become progressively codified in legal and official decrees governing relations between Muslims and non-Muslims.[55]

In his fairly brief remarks on this verse, **al-Wāḥidī** says that the verse was revealed concerning Jews and Christians from among the People of the Book whose faith is not like the faith of monotheists (*ka-īmān al-muwaḥḥidīn*), because they do not believe in the Qur'ān and in the prophethood of Muḥammad.[56] The People of the Book pay the *jizya*, which is what is due from someone who has concluded a contract. According to Ibn 'Abbās, they should pay the *jizya* with their own hands and not have it sent, arriving on foot and not mounted on an animal.[57]

Al-Zamakhsharī's commentary is very similar to that of his predecessors, in which he identifies "the religion of truth" as Islam, which the People of the Book do not follow. In return for exemption from fighting, they have to pay the *jizya* willingly with their own hands. Al-Zamakhsharī also proceeds to delineate in detail the categories of people who have to pay the *jizya* and the amounts they have to pay. These detailed regulations signal to us once again the considerable attention paid to the legal status of the *dhimmī*s at this time and a heightened sense of confessionalism on the part of Muslims vis-à-vis the People of the Book.[58]

Al-Rāzī identifies this verse dealing with the People of the Book as parallel to other verses that deal with the treatment of polytheists. Al-Rāzī identifies the *ahl al-kitāb* as consisting of Jews, Christians, Samaritans (al-Samīra), Sabians, and Zoroastrians, and displays considerable interest in doctrinal differences between these groups and Muslims.[59] In his opinion, the People of the Book are to be fought until they submit or until they give the *jizya*, mainly because they do not believe in God correctly. He accuses most of the Jews of being anthropomorphists (*mushabbiha*), because they believe that whatever/whoever exists, including God, must have or be incarnate in a corporeal form. Al-Rāzī concedes that similar differences of opinion have also sprung up among Muslims, and he denounces the majority of scholastic theologians who, by having differed on the question of the attributes of God, are also guilty of having denied His [true] existence. If someone should remonstrate that there are other Jews who are truly monotheistic (*muwaḥḥada*), al-Rāzī readily acknowledges that they are not indicated in this verse. But the *jizya* is due on them anyway, he says, because one should not make distinctions among them.[60]

As for the Christians, their belief in the Trinity and incarnation and monism is tantamount to rejection of [true] divinity (*yunāfī al-ilāhiyya*).[61] Both groups deny bodily resurrection and are therefore guilty of not believing in the Last Day. "They do not forbid what God and His messenger forbid" may mean that Jews and Christians do not forbid what the Qur'ān and Muḥammad's *sunna* forbid, or it may also mean, as maintained by Abū Rawq (d. 140/757),[62] that they do not abide by the laws of the Torah and the Gospel respectively, and they change them and promulgate laws of their own making.[63] In our survey so far, al-Rāzī is the first to indicate in detail that there were differences of opinion among Muslim scholars regarding to which laws the People of the Book should proclaim their adherence. Abū Rawq's remarks in particular indicate that there were Muslim authorities, particularly in the early period, who questioned the applicability of Qur'anic injunctions to the People of the Book, and who maintained instead that they are to be judged by their own scriptures—a position, one may add, that is more consistent with the Qur'ān itself[64] and early historical praxis.[65] Like al-Zamakhsharī, al-Rāzī also dwells extensively on the various details of the collection of the *jizya*, as well as its amounts, the manner of collecting it, and treatment of the concerned *dhimmī*.[66]

Al-Qurṭubī's extensive commentary on this verse is noticeably different in tone and content from that of his predecessors; we can only refer to a number of highlights from his discussion. He notes, for example, that the *ahl al-kitāb* are so named in this verse "out of respect for their book" and because "they are knowledgeable about monotheism, the messengers, the revealed laws (*al-sharā'i'*), and religious sects (*al-milal*), and especially about the mention of Muḥammad, peace and blessings be upon him, and his religion and community." But when the *ahl al-kitāb* rejected Muḥammad and Islam, they committed an enormous sin, and after being duly warned of their transgression, a substitution for fighting was created, which was the payment of the *jizya*. The phrase "those who were given the *kitāb*" was meant to underscore the fact that the advent of Muḥammad and Islam was written down in the Torah and the Gospel.[67]

Al-Qurṭubī next discusses at considerable length which groups, according to various scholars, qualify to pay the *jizya*.[68] As for the last part of the verse (*'an yad wa-hum ṣāghirūn*), al-Qurṭubī replicates a number of the explanations offered by his predecessors. On the issue of treatment of the *ahl al-dhimma*, however, he notably includes the following reports as a caveat: According to Muslim b. Ḥajjāj, the Companion Hishām b. Ḥakīm b. Ḥizām[69] was once walking by a group of Nabateans in Syria who had been made to stand in the sun when the order to "pour oil on their heads" was given. When Hishām inquired into their case, he was told that they had withheld the *jizya*. Hishām remonstrated that he had heard the Prophet say, "Indeed God will punish those who punish humans in the world." Hishām then went to see 'Umayr b. Sa'd, the ruler at that time in Palestine, and narrated this *ḥadīth* before him, and 'Umayr gave the order for them to be released. Al-Qurṭubī continues by saying that "our scholars" [sc. jurists in Andalusia] were of the view that if the *jizya* was withheld by the *ahl al-dhimma* despite being able to pay it, then it was a punishable offense, but if they were incapable of making the payment, then it was not permissible to punish them. Inability to pay the *jizya* nullified the requirement to do so, he continues; the rich may not remit it on behalf of the poor. Al-Qurṭubī concludes this section by relating another *ḥadīth*, as transmitted by Abū Dā'ūd from Ṣafwān b. Salīm (alive ca. 132/749),[70] which relates that Muḥammad had said, "Whoever oppresses the one who has entered into a pact [with Muslims; *mu'āhid*^{an}] or disparages him or imposes on him a responsibility beyond his ability or takes something from him with animus (*bi-ghayr ṭayyib al-nafs*), then I will be his (sc. the *dhimmī*'s) advocate on the Day of Judgment."[71] Clearly, the harsh measures introduced by a number of jurists for collecting the *jizya* were not to the liking of everyone. Al-Qurṭubī's comments are clearly intended to provide an important corrective to the more discriminatory and punitive attitudes that had surfaced among Muslim authorities, as reflected in this kind of literature.

Once again, exegeses of Qur'ān 9:29 are revealing of changing Muslim self-perceptions and communal identities vis-à-vis other, particularly monotheistic, religious communities. The partitive preposition *min* in the verse clearly indicates that specific contingents from among the People of the Book who are wrongdoers are being referenced here and not Jews and Christians in their entirety.[72]

Mujāhid's early linkage of this verse to the battle of Tabūk specifically points to hostile Byzantine Christians as the historical referent. Notwithstanding the wording of this verse, a majority of the exegetes starting already with Muqātil, as we saw, went on to infer a blanket criticism of scriptuaries, leading to an elaborate code of conduct governing the payment of the *jizya* in rather humiliating circumstances. Notably, in spite of the perilous times in which he lived, al-Qurṭubī's own multi-faith environment in Muslim Spain seems to have predisposed him to invoke more irenic and humane *ḥadīth*s commanding compassion for the *dhimmī* in the Muslim's protection, in contradistinction to practically all the exegetes surveyed above who were anxious to articulate the superior legal and confessional status of Muslims in their more religiously segregated societies.

Striving with One's Wealth and Self

There are several verses—all regarded as Medinan—that refer to the striving of the believers in the path of God with their wealth and their selves. Once again, because of length constraints, we cannot discuss how each of these verses was understood by exegetes over time. A diachronic survey of some of the most important exegeses of a key verse, Qur'ān 4:95, containing a version of this collocation, will, however, adequately convey to us the general scope of its meanings as understood by influential exegetes. This verse, believed to have been revealed in 4/625, sets up a general and highly significant contrast between the "sitters" and "strivers" (*al-qā'idūn* and *al-mujāhidūn*) that is worthy of our attention. Qur'ān 4:95 states:

> Those among the believers who sit at home who are not blind and those who strive in the path of God with their wealth and their selves are not the same. God has preferred those who strive with their wealth and their selves by a degree (*daraja*) over the sitters but to each He has promised goodness. But God has distinguished the strivers from the sitters [by the promise of] a great reward.

Qur'ān 4:95 is understood by **Muqātil b. Sulaymān** to express divine preference for those who strive with their wealth and their selves over those who are "sitters" without a legitimate reason. However, God has promised a generous reward—paradise—for both the striver and the "excused sitter" (*al-qā'id al-ma'dhūr*). The verse affirms that those who were unable to emigrate due to extenuating circumstances are not the same in rank as those who were able to do so, says Muqātil; nevertheless, they earn a handsome recompense in the next world.[73] It is noteworthy that Muqātil makes no specific reference to fighting in this verse as a component of the striving of the believers with their wealth and their selves against their enemies; the focus is instead on emigration.

In the briefest of remarks preserved on Qur'ān 4:95, **'Abd al-Razzāq** says that "the sitters" are those who abstained from taking part in the battle of Badr.[74] Here we have an early explicit connection made between Qur'ān 4:95 and fighting, specifically at Badr.

Hūd b. Muḥakkam preserves al-Barā' b. 'Āzib's commentary that Qur'ān 4:95 had been revealed in connection with Ibn Umm Maktūm, who had lamented that because of his blindness, he would not be able to reach the same level of moral excellence as the activist strivers. Al-Ḥasan al-Baṣrī compared the verse to Qur'ān 48:17, which similarly grants exemptions to those with physical afflictions. Although the verse grants one higher degree of excellence to the strivers over those who are sedentary, it promises to both "goodness," which is paradise. Ibn Muḥakkam remarks that this verse was revealed after the military *jihād* was declared to be voluntary (*taṭawwu'an*). He further records a *ḥadīth* in which the Prophet states that God is obligated to forgive whomever has prayed and given *zakāt* and died without having associated anything with Him, whether he had "striven" or "was sedentary" (*jāhada aw qa'ada*).[75]

Very briefly, **al-Qummī** comments that Qur'ān 4:95 refers to the greater merit of the strivers over the sitters, except for those who have a chronic disability; he does not refer to the exact nature of striving here.[76]

In his exegesis of Qur'ān 4:95, **al-Ṭabarī** sets up a striking contrast between *al-qā'idūn* and *al-mujāhidūn fī sabīl allāh* that is of interest to us. The former are described by him as "those who believe in God and His messenger" but prefer the easy life, "remaining in their homes away from the hardships and discomforts of traveling and journeying on earth, and [refraining] from confronting the enemies of God in their struggle for the sake of God (*bi-jihādihim fī dhāt allāh*) and fighting them in obedience to God (*wa-qitālihim fī ṭā'at allāh*)." The latter are those who strive to make the word of God ascendant by expending their energy to the utmost in fighting the enemies of God and the enemies of their religion with their wealth, which they spend in order to foil the machinations of the enemies of Islam; and with their selves by directly engaging them in battle.[77] Those who suffered from a physical affliction such as blindness were, however, exempt from the combative *jihād*; the cause of revelation once again centers on Ibn Umm Maktūm and the exemption (*rukhṣa*) that he had wished for.[78] The *mujāhidūn* in this verse enjoy a degree in rank above the *qā'idūn*, who are exempt from the military *jihād*, al-Ṭabarī continues; both, however, will be rewarded with *al-ḥusnā*, glossed as "paradise" (*al-janna*). In comparison to the sitters-at-home without a legitimate excuse, the *mujāhidūn* earn a great reward (*ajr*^{an} *'aẓīm*^{an}).[79]

Al-Wāḥidī notes, like al-Ṭabarī, that when Qur'ān 4:95 was first revealed, Ibn Umm Maktūm had lamented that on account of his blindness, he would be prevented from being an activist striver. A subsequent revelation inserted the exemption *ghayr ulī 'l-ḍarar* into the verse, which excluded those who had an ailment from "emerging [to fight]" (*al-khurūj*). The *mujāhidūn* and the *qā'idūn* without a legitimate exemption were not equal, al-Wāḥidī goes on to say; those "sitters" who had a genuine affliction were, however, considered to be the equivalent of "the strivers." But, according to the rest of the verse, God grants a higher status to those who strive with their wealth and their selves over those who do not, even if the latter are prevented from doing so for legitimate reasons; each still earns *al-husnā*, that is, paradise, as maintained by Muqātil. According to 'Abd Allāh b. Muḥayrīz (d. 99/717),[80] the difference in the recompense earned by the *mujāhidūn* and the *qā'idūn* without a legitimate excuse was much greater—as much as seventy degrees (*sab'ūna daraja*).[81] It is noteworthy that, unlike al-Ṭabarī, al-Wāḥidī does not explicitly link military activity or a specific battle to Qur'ān 4:95.

Al-Zamakhsharī understands the collocation *al-mujāhidūn fī sabīl allāh* in Qur'ān 4:95 to be a specific reference to those who fight in the path of God, and *al-qā'idūn* as those who desist from fighting. No blame accrues, however, to those who suffer from some affliction. Like al-Wāḥidī, al-Zamakhsharī recognizes that the verse promises "goodness" (*al-ḥusnā*), glossed as paradise, to both the *mujāhidūn* and the *qāʿidūn*, but the former enjoy a degree of precedence over the latter. Unlike al-Wāḥidī, al-Zamakhsharī in this context invokes the opinion of Ibn ʿAbbās, who had stated that the verse referred specifically to those who failed to fight at Badr. Al-Zamakhsharī also notes that Muqātil was of the opinion that the verse referred to Tabūk.[82]

Al-Rāzī mostly replicates the essence of the exegeses of his predecessors concerning the strivers and the sitters, the exemption granted to those with physical ailments who cannot take part in the military *jihād*, and the difference in status between them, which need not be repeated here.[83] What is exceptional is that for al-Rāzī, the military *jihād* in the context of this verse is *less* meritorious than striving to verbally invite people to Islam. Thus, in comparison with ʿAlī b. Abī Ṭālib whose *jihād* consisted of fighting, the *jihād* of Abū Bakr was [carried out] by verbally summoning to religion [*bi 'l-daʿwā ilā al-dīn*]. The latter "type of *jihād* was of the practice of the Prophet, upon him be blessings and peace" and therefore considerably superior, he comments.[84] It should be noted that this view was in fact quite prevalent among the Muʿtazila and other scholars with rationalist leanings (like al-Rāzī), who tended to discount the military *jihād* in favor of intellectual endeavors and reasoned argumentation, which in their view entailed greater and more meritorious effort.[85]

Al-Qurṭubī in his brief commentary on Qur'ān 4:95 quotes Ibn ʿAbbās, who described the *qāʿidūn* as those who did not take part in Badr, as opposed to those who did; their status was consequently not equal. For al-Qurṭubī, *jihād* as it occurs in this last verse is thus primarily combative.[86]

This brief survey of the exegeses of Qur'ān 4:95 is revealing of the highly important fact that a number of exegetes, both early and later, specifically understood the nature of striving in this verse in a non-combative sense, so that the phrase *al-mujāhidūn fī sabīl allāh* is primarily understood to refer to those who emigrated to Medina and/or summoned unbelievers to Islam. From ʿAbd al-Razzāq on, though, most exegetes tended to privilege the military sense of striving and yoked the verse to the battle of Badr.

Abstention from and Termination of Hostilities

> Qur'ān 60:7–9: Perhaps God will place affection between you and those who are your enemies for God is powerful and God is forgiving and merciful. God does not forbid you from being kind and equitable to those who have neither made war on you on account of your religion nor driven you from your homes; indeed God loves those who are equitable. God forbids you however from making common cause with those who fight you on account of your religion and evict you from your

homes and who support [others] in driving you out. Those who make common cause with them are wrong-doers.

Mujāhid briefly comments that Qur'ān 60:8 means that Muslims should pray for mercy for the people mentioned in the verse, do good to them, and be equitable toward them. These are the people, he continues, who had believed in Mecca but did not emigrate. As for Qur'ān 60:9, it refers to the unbelievers of Quraysh.[87]

Muqātil b. Sulaymān comments that Qur'ān 60:7 counter-balances earlier revelations that had counseled Muslims to forsake Meccan unbelievers, even if they were relatives, as Abraham had been counseled before them. When God perceived the severity of this command for Muslims, says Muqātil, He revealed this verse. When the people of Mecca embraced Islam (that is, after the fall of Mecca), Muslims mixed with them and intermarried. The Prophet himself married Umm Ḥabība, the daughter of Abu Sufyān. This is the "affection" (*mawadda*) mentioned in the verse, which God is capable of bringing about, continues Muqātil. He forgave the sins of the pagan Meccans when they repented and embraced Islam, and showed mercy toward them after their submission. In the next verse (60:8), God granted a concession about maintaining relations with those who did not wage war against Muslims and did not aid the polytheists, commanding Muslims to bless them and act justly toward them by fulfilling the terms of their agreements with them. Such amity was, however, forbidden in the case of Meccan unbelievers who had evicted Muḥammad and his companions out of hatred for Islam, as well as in the case of those who had aided them; Muslims may not form alliances with them, for that would constitute an act of wrongdoing. But, says Muqātil, the sword verse (9:5) had abrogated these two verses (60:8–9).[88] Here, significantly, we have the abrogation of a critical conciliatory verse in the Qur'ān attributed to a very early exegete from the Umayyad period.

The ***Tanwīr al-miqbās*** says that according to Qur'ān 60:7, God has promised to create bonds of kinship and marriage between Muslims and those among the people of Mecca who had opposed them in their religion; thus Muḥammad had married Umm Ḥabība (bt. Abī Sufyān b. Ḥarb) after the fall of Mecca. God does not forbid Muslims from befriending and helping those who do not fight them because of their religion and do not drive them out from their homes in Mecca or aid others in doing so. Muslims should rather bless and help such people and behave justly with them by observing their treaties with them. Such peaceable people included the Khuzā'a, the people of Hilāl b. 'Uwaymir, Khuzayma, and Banū Mudlij, who concluded a peace treaty with the Prophet before the year of al-Ḥudaybiyya, according to the terms of which they promised not to fight or expel Muslims from their homes. Muslims are forbidden, however, to form alliances with those Meccans who fight them on account of their religion and uproot them from their homes; if they were to do so, they would wrong themselves (*al-ḍārrūna li-anfusihim*).[89] There is no reference to the abrogated or unabrogated status of this verse in the *Tanwīr*.

'Abd al-Razzāq in his very brief commentary on Qur'ān 60:8 says that the verse had been abrogated by Qur'ān 9:5,[90] signaling to us that by the early third/ninth century, this interpretation had taken root.

Hūd b. Muḥakkam comments that Qur'ān 60:7 commands the believers to maintain their bonds of kinship with their polytheist relatives and to be kind and just with them, especially in supporting them with their wealth. According to the usual occasion of revelation cited for this verse as contained in the *Tafsīr* of al-Ḥasan al-Baṣrī, Qur'ān 60:7 was revealed after the command to fight the polytheists had been given. A number of concerned Muslims thereupon came to the Prophet and sought his counsel regarding how they should treat their pagan relatives; this verse was subsequently revealed. Mujāhid, however, was of the opinion, Ibn Muḥakkam continues, that the verse referred to those Muslims who had remained behind in Mecca and had not yet emigrated to Medina (as noted above). The following verse, Qur'ān 60:9 is a clear reference to the unbelievers at Mecca who drove the Muslims out of there.[91] Clearly reflecting a perspective that had gained ground by his time, Ibn Muḥakkam, like 'Abd al-Razzāq, also states that this verse was abrogated by Qur'ān 9:5 and additionally by Qur'ān 9:36.[92]

In his very brief remarks preserved for us, **al-Qummī** says that the verse refers to the time when the people of Mecca embraced Islam and the Companions began to intermarry with them, the example being set by Muḥammad's marriage to Umm Ḥabība.[93]

Al-Ṭabarī says that Qur'an 60:7 refers to those among the pagan Meccans who embraced Islam and consequently became the friends and allies of Muslims. Those who were of this opinion included Ibn Zayd.[94] The verse goes on to declare that God is certainly capable of planting such affection among people, and He is forgiving and merciful toward those polytheists who repent of their sins, as was the view of Qatāda. God further commands Muslims to treat with kindness and justice those among the Meccans who do not fight them or expel them from their homes. There is, however, a difference of opinion regarding exactly who is intended in this verse. Some exegetes, like Mujāhid, were of the opinion that the verse referred to those who had believed in Mecca but did not emigrate, and who were to be treated with kindness and justice by other Muslims. Others were of the view that the verse referred to a different group of Meccans altogether. Thus 'Abd Allāh b. Zubayr was of the view that the verse was a reference to Asmā' bt. Abī Bakr whose mother, Qutayla bt. 'Abd al-'Uzzā, had not converted to Islam. When Qutayla once came bearing gifts for Asmā', the latter spurned them and prevented the former from entering into her presence, "unless the Messenger of God, peace and blessings be upon him, were to give permission." 'A'isha mentioned the event to Muḥammad, and subsequently Qur'ān 60:8 was revealed, enjoining kindness to peaceful non-Muslims.[95]

Yet other exegetes were of the view that the verse referred to Meccan polytheists who did not war against Muslims or expel them from their homes, but that it had been abrogated by the later commandment to fight them. Thus, according to Ibn Wahb, Ibn Zayd had commented that this verse had been abrogated by the commandment to fight and that polytheists were henceforth to be given the choice of either the sword or Islam. Qatāda is said to have similarly commented on this verse.[96] As we observed previously, Ibn Zayd and Qatāda were often on record for their belligerent views, and their partiality for advocating the abrogation of conciliatory verses yet again does not come as a surprise. Ibn Zayd's view that Qur'ān 60:7 refers to pagan Meccans who had accepted Islam further renders the distinction between peaceful and non-peaceful polytheists moot and potentially allows the military *jihād* to be carried out against them *qua* polytheists.

Al-Ṭabarī expresses his preference at this point and says that the most appropriate exegesis of this verse is as follows: God has not forbidden Muslims from acting kindly and fairly toward all those from any and every religion and creed who do not fight them and do not expel them from their homes. Al-Ṭabarī also summarily dismisses the suggestion that this verse is abrogated, for the verse clearly permits the faithful to be kind to "the people of war" (*ahl al-ḥarb*), whether blood relatives or not, who bear no ill-will toward Muslims and as long as such relationships do not compromise the security of Muslims. The truth of his commentary, says al-Ṭabarī, is borne out by the cause of revelation concerning Asmā' bt. Abī Bakr and her mother. For God loves those who are equitable (*al-munṣifīn*), who give people their due rights, are personally just to them, and do good to those who are good to them.[97]

As for Qur'ān 60:9, it forbids believers from helping and befriending those from among the unbelievers in Mecca who fight them over religion and evict them from their homes. Those who do so are wrongdoers and violate the command of God; this was the view of Mujāhid.[98]

In his brief commentary, **al-Wāḥidī**, like a number of his predecessors, understands Qur'ān 60:7 to be a reference to those Meccan polytheists who embraced Islam after the fall of Mecca; they included Abū Sufyān b. Ḥarb, Abū Sufyān b. al-Ḥarth, al-Ḥarth b. Hishām, Suhayl b. 'Amr, and Ḥakīm b.

Ḥizām, who had been the leaders of the unbelievers and previously implacably hostile toward Muslims. But God is able to effect change from hostility to affection after repentance and conversion, states al-Wāḥidī. The verse that follows is a reference to those unbelievers who observe their treaties with Muslims and are thus to be treated kindly, providing categorical evidence that relations between Muslims and polytheists are to be characterized by kindness, although military alliances are forbidden (*wa-hādha yadullu 'alā jawāz al-birr bayna al-muslimīn wa' -l-mushrikīn wa-in kānat al-muwālah munqaṭi'a*). As for the last part of Qur'ān 60:8, al-Zajjāj (d. 311/923) had remarked that Muslims should behave equitably toward unbelievers and fulfill their agreements with them, but must not form alliances with them to the detriment of Muslims.[99]

Like Muqātil b. Sulaymān, **al-Zamakhsharī** comments that Qur'ān 60:7 showed mercy to those Muslims who had severed their relations with pagan relatives by holding out the hope of reconciliation and renewal of affection between them. This happened after the fall of Mecca when its people embraced Islam and Muḥammad married Umm Ḥabība, for God, al-Zamakhsharī comments, is capable of changing hearts and facilitating affection between people who were erstwhile enemies.[100]

The next two verses counsel goodness toward those who do not fight Muslims and, while not prohibiting charity toward those who do fight Muslims, forbids the formation of [military] alliances with them, stresses al-Zamakhsharī (*la yanhākum 'an mabarrat hā'ulā', innama yanhākum 'an tawālī hā'ulā'*). Al-Zamakhsharī concludes by emphasizing that the command *wa-tuqsiṭū* in Qur'ān 60:8 requires Muslims to treat non-Muslims justly (*bi-'l-qisṭ*) and without oppression (*wa-lā tuẓlimuhum*). It is an excellent command, he enthuses, for through such equitable behavior, Muslims protect themselves from the wrongdoing of the polytheists (*wa-yataḥāmū ẓulmahum*), a situation that is comparable to the fraternal relationship among Muslims themselves.[101]

Like Muqātil and al-Zamakhsharī before him, **al-Rāzī** understands Qur'ān 60:7 as a softening of the previous command to Muslims to sever relations with the polytheists; he in fact quotes Muqātil in full here.[102] He goes on to indicate the differences of opinion that had emerged concerning the identification of "those who do not fight you." The majority are of the opinion that it refers specifically to those who concluded treaties with the Prophet, such as the Banū Khuzā'a, and who pledged not to fight or evict him, in return for which Muhammad counseled Muslims to treat them kindly and to adhere to their agreement. This was the view of Ibn 'Abbās, the two Muqātils [sc. Muqātil b. Sulaymān[103] and Muqātil b. Ḥayyān], and al-Kalbī. The other possible referents are Meccan Muslims who did not emigrate (according to Mujāhid); women and children (no specific attribution); and Asmā' bt. Abī Bakr (according to 'Abd Allāh b. al-Zubayr).[104]

Al-Rāzī notes that Qatāda had deemed this verse to have been abrogated by Qur'ān 9:5, but he himself disagrees with this interpretation. Al-Rāzī instead concludes by stressing, like al-Wāḥidī before him, that this verse makes evident that "kindness and charity are permissible between polytheists and Muslims," but disallows [military] alliances. Furthermore, Muslims must behave justly with non-Muslims, whether they are kinsfolk or not, according to Ibn 'Abbās, and honor their agreements, according to Muqātil.[105]

Compared with earlier exegetes, **al-Qurṭubī** adds nothing new to his discussion of Qur'an 60:7. With regard to Qur'ān 60:8, he regards it, like most of his predecessors, as a concession to Muslims who wished to maintain good relations with their polytheist relatives. He notes Ibn Zayd's view that this verse was applicable in the early period of Islam but was then abrogated; Qatāda had also maintained that it was abrogated by Qur'ān 9:5. The majority of exegetes, affirms al-Qurṭubī, are of the view that Qur'ān 60:8 is unabrogated and valid for all time (*muḥkama*), arguing for this status on the basis of the incident concerning Asmā' bt. Abī Bakr and her mother and Muḥammad's kind interactions with the Banū Khuzā'a.[106]

Al-Qurṭubī records a number of valuable reports that delineate for us the complex relationships between Muslims and non-Muslims over time and therefore the contested purview of the military *jihād*. Thus he notes that al-Qāḍī Abū Bakr [al-Jaṣṣāṣ, d. 370/981] in his *Kitāb al-aḥkām* had mentioned that the best of jurists (unnamed) had maintained that a Muslim son must bear the expenses of his unbelieving father, a position that the good *qāḍī* himself disapproved of because he thought it went too far [in showing kindness to a non-Muslim]. Al-Qurṭubī further refers to the example of another *qāḍī*, Ismā'īl b. Isḥāq (d. 282/896),[107] who treated a *dhimmī* with respect (*akramahu*) when the latter entered into his presence. When some of those who were present took exception at that, Ismā'īl recited Qur'ān 60:8.[108] As for the next verse, al-Qurṭubī comments, it is a reference to the most hostile Meccan polytheists who had fought the Muslims on account of their religion and helped others in expelling them from their homes. It is forbidden for Muslims to take them as allies, supporters, and close friends (*yattakhidhuhum awliyā' wa-anṣār^{an} wa-aḥbāb^{an}*).[109] Among the post-Ṭabarī exegetes surveyed, al-Qurṭubī is the most explicit and adamant in maintaining that the exhortation in Qur'ān 60:8 to be kind to those who had caused Muslims no harm was applicable to everyone who belonged in this category, regardless of their religious affiliation, and that the command was unambiguous and valid for all time.

> Qur'ān 9:6: If anyone from among the polytheists asks you for protection, grant it to him so that he may hear the word/speech of God (*kalām Allāh*), then escort him to a place of safety for him. That is so because they are a people without knowledge.

This verse immediately following the so-called sword verse appears almost startlingly dissonant, because it countermands the seemingly absolute, general injunction to "slay the polytheists wherever you may find them" in the preceding verse. In seeming contrast, this verse advocates courteous, even deferential, behavior toward the same Arab polytheists who show a willingness to learn about the Qur'ān and evince no hostility toward Islam and Muslims per se.

Mujāhid said that this verse guarantees the safety of people in general (*insān*) who came to listen to the Prophet recite from the Qur'ān until they had returned to the place of refuge whence they came.[110]

The ***Tanwīr al-miqbās*** says that the verse commands the Prophet to grant safe conduct to anyone from among the polytheists who asks for it, so that he may hear the recitation of the speech of God. If he does not believe (sc. embrace Islam), then he is to be granted safe passage back to his land (*waṭanahu*). This is so because they are a people ignorant of the commandments of God and His oneness.[111]

Hūd b. Muḥakkam similarly comments that the polytheist who requests safe conduct from Muslims in order to listen to the word of God is to be so granted and returned unharmed to his place of origin, whether he embraces Islam or not. This was the view of Mujāhid, for example. Al-Kalbī is quoted as saying that the verse referred instead to a group of polytheists who wished to renew their pact with Muḥammad after the sacred months had passed. When Muḥammad asked them to profess Islam, offer prayers, and pay the *zakāt*, they refused, and the Prophet let them return safely to their homes. Ibn Muḥakkam further notes that al-Ḥasan al-Baṣrī had remarked thus on the status of this verse: "It is valid and unabrogated (*muḥkama*) until the Day of Judgment."[112]

Al-Qummī affirms briefly that this verse asks Muslims to recite the Qur'ān to the polytheist, explain it to him, and not show him any opposition until he returns safely.[113] It is worth noting that **Furāt** regards Qur'ān 9:6 as abrogating Qur'ān 9:5 and thus overriding the seemingly blanket injunction concerning the polytheists contained in the latter verse. In this he agrees with many of his predecessors that the polytheist who wishes for safe conduct in order to listen to the word of God should be so granted and then peacefully escorted back to his home, regardless of whether he had embraced Islam or not.[114]

Al-Ṭabarī says that in this verse God counsels Muḥammad, "If someone from among the polytheists (*al-mushrikīn*)—those whom I have commanded that you fight and slay after the passage of the sacred months—were to ask you, O Muḥammad, for safe conduct in order to listen to the word of God, then grant this protection to him so that he may hear the word of God and you may recite it to him." Such an individual, according to the verse, is to be subsequently escorted back to his place of safety even if he rejects Islam and fails to believe after the Prophet's recitation of the Qur'ān before him. Scholars in the past who have agreed with this general interpretation include Ibn Isḥāq, al-Suddī,[115] and Mujāhid (as above).[116]

The occasion of revelation is given in one report from Sa'īd [b. Jubayr], according to which, Muḥammad once went out to battle and faced the enemy. One man from among the polytheists stepped forward and the Muslims began to reach for their spears. The man said, "Withdraw your weapons from me, and let me listen to the word of God." They asked, "Do you believe that there is no god but God and that Muḥammad is His servant and messenger, and that you forsake other gods and renounce al-Lāt and al-'Uzzā?" He replied, "I bear witness before you that I have done so."[117] This occasion of revelation, in contradistinction to the exegeses given above that had assumed the pagan status of the Qur'ān listener, appears to attempt to effect a semantic and doctrinal reconciliation between the two consecutive verses, Qur'ān 9:5 and 9:6, a point that is not explicitly made, however, by al-Ṭabarī.

Al-Wāḥidī comments very briefly that, should someone from among the same group of polytheists request safe conduct and refuge among Muslims so that he may listen to the word of God and learn of its positive commandments and interdictions, he is to be so granted and escorted back to a place of safety. This is so because they are an ignorant people, and so should be given protection and the opportunity to acquire knowledge and perhaps submit to Islam.[118]

In his similarly brief commentary, **al-Zamakhsharī** explains this verse quite literally—that if one of the polytheists, with whom no pact (*mīthāq*) exists, were to request safe conduct from the Muslims in order to listen to the Qur'ān, then he should be granted it so that he may reflect upon God's words. Afterward, he is to be escorted back to his home where he feels safe. This, al-Zamakhsharī says, is established practice for all time. Al-Ḥasan al-Baṣrī had similarly maintained that this verse is "valid till the Day of Resurrection." Al-Zamakhsharī notes without comment that al-Suddī[119] and al-Ḍaḥḥāk had regarded this verse as being abrogated by its immediately preceding verse (Qur'ān 9:5).[120]

Al-Rāzī gives a cause of revelation different from that recorded by al-Ṭabarī, on the authority of Ibn 'Abbās, who relates that a polytheist man asked 'Alī b.

Abī Ṭālib, "If we wished to approach the Messenger after the end of this period (the four sacred months) in order to listen to the word of God or for some other reason, will we be killed?" 'Ali replied in the negative and recited this verse, affirming the granting of safe conduct to him so that he may listen to the Qur'ān.[121] Unlike previous exegetes, al-Rāzī further comments that this verse indicates that imitation of precedent (*al-taqlīd*) is not sufficient in religion, and that critical inquiry (*al-naẓar*) and the seeking of proofs (*al-istidlāl*) are indispensable requirements within religion. If emulation of precedent were enough, he argues, then this verse would not have granted a respite to this unbeliever, and he would have been merely given a choice between professing his belief [in Islam] or death. As this did not occur, it confirms that Muslims are required to offer safe conduct to such a person and thereby assuage his fears and allow him the opportunity to deliberate upon the proofs of religion. How long such a respite should last is not known; perhaps it should be determined according to prevalent custom (*bi-'l-'urf*), he says.[122]

In comparison with his predecessors, **al-Qurṭubī** offers a detailed and sophisticated legal discussion of the concept of *amān* in the context of this verse; this is not of immediate concern to us.[123] Al-Qurṭubī next discusses the status of the verse and notes that al-Ḍaḥḥāk and al-Suddī were of the opinion that it had been abrogated by the preceding verse, Qur'ān 9:5. But al-Ḥasan al-Baṣrī and Mujāhid had maintained that the verse was unabrogated and a binding precedent until the day of judgment (*hiya muḥkama sunna ilā yawm al-qiyāma*). Al-Qurṭubī dismisses as invalid the views of those who say that this verse's injunction was valid only for the four months mentioned in the preceding verse. On the basis of the occasion of revelation cited by Sa'īd b. Jubayr (as previously discussed) and on the authority of 'Alī b. Abī Ṭālib, al-Qurṭubī concludes that this verse is *muḥkam* and valid for all time.[124]

Peacemaking

The quintessential Qur'anic verse concerning peacemaking is 8:61, which states, "And if they should incline to peace (*wa-in janaḥū li-'l-salm*), then incline to it [yourself] and place your trust in God; for He is all-hearing and all-knowing."

Mujāhid said that this verse is a reference to "peacemaking" (*al-ṣulḥ*) in regard to the Jewish tribe of Banū Qurayẓa.[125]

Muqātil b. Sulaymān says that if they—a reference to the Qurayẓa—should desire peace (*al-ṣulḥ*), then you should desire it as well (*fa-aridhu*). But then, says Muqātil, the verse was abrogated by Qur'ān 47:35, which states, "Do not waver nor call for peace while you have the upper hand." The Prophet, continues

Muqātil, had ended his recitation of Qur'ān 8:61 by exhorting Muslims to trust in God, for He is with them in victory if they [the opposite side] should violate the peace (*naqaḍū al-ṣulḥ*), and He is all-hearing when they desire peace and are cognizant of it.[126]

The ***Tanwīr al-miqbās*** explicates *wa-in janaḥū li-'l-salm* as "if the Banū Qurayza should incline to peace (*al-ṣulḥ*) and desire peace," then Muḥammad should also incline to it or desire it, and place his trust in God regarding their possible violation or allegiance to the peace agreement. God after all can listen in on their speech, and He is knowledgeable of their potential perfidy or trustworthiness.[127]

In his brief comments, **Hūd b. Muḥakkam** says that *al-silm/salm* in this verse refers to peacemaking (*al-ṣulḥ*). Mujāhid had understood the referent in this verse to be the Banū Qurayẓa. Ibn Muḥakkam also notes that some exegetes were of the opinion that this verse had been abrogated by Qur'ān 9:5, but he expresses no preference himself.[128]

Al-'Ayyāshī understands the verse in a highly particularist vein. He records a report from Muḥammad al-Ḥalabī, who on the authority of Abū 'Abd Allāh (sc. Ja'far al-Sādiq) had glossed *al-salm* in the verse as obedience to the Imām.[129] **Furāt** offers the terse commentary that Qur'ān 8:61 had been abrogated by Qur'ān 47:35, as was also maintained by Muqātil (as previously noted).[130]

Al-Ṭabarī says that God in this verse addresses the Prophet and counsels him that if he should fear treachery and perfidy on the part of a group of [unspecified] people (*qawm*), then he should withdraw from them and fight them. But "if they should incline to making peace with you and abandon warfare" (*wa-in mālū ilā musālamatika wa mutārakatika al-ḥarb*), either through entry into Islam, or payment of the *jizya*, or through the establishment of friendly relations (*muwāda'a*), then you should do the same for the sake of peace and peacemaking (*min asbāb al-silm wa-'l-ṣulḥ*).[131] Those who have supported this exegesis include Qatāda, who glossed *al-silm* as *al-ṣulḥ* but who also maintained that this verse had been abrogated by Qur'ān 9:5 and 9:36.[132] 'Ikrima and al-Ḥasan al-Baṣrī stated that Qur'ān 9:29 had abrogated this verse; al-Suddī made no mention of its abrogation.[133] Ibn Isḥāq's commentary as recorded by al-Ṭabarī is somewhat novel; he understood *al-salm* as a reference to Islam and therefore interpreted the verse as counseling that the opposite side should be granted peace terms based on their submission to Islam (*fa-ṣāliḥhum 'alayhi*). Ibn Zayd was of the opinion that the verse commanded making peace with the opposite side (*fa-ṣāliḥhum*), but then the military *jihād* abrogated this commandment.[134]

As is his wont, al-Ṭabarī then proceeds to assess the validity of these various perspectives. He comments that Qatāda's statement, echoed by others, to the effect that this verse had been abrogated cannot be supported on the basis of the Qur'ān, the *sunna*, or reason. An abrogating verse, he continues, is one that nullifies the injunction/prescription contained in an abrogated verse in every aspect. If it does not meet this essential criterion, then it cannot function as an abrogating verse. Qur'ān 9:5 cannot abrogate Qur'ān 8:61 because the latter concerns the Banū Qurayẓa (as maintained by Mujāhid, he notes), who were Jews and therefore one of the *ahl al-kitāb*. God has permitted believers, he says, to make peace with the People of the Book and abandon fighting them when *jizya* is taken from them. Qur'ān 9:5, on the other hand, has to do *only* with Arab polytheist idolaters from whom *jizya* cannot be taken. Neither verse invalidates the injunction contained in the other, and both remain unabrogated (*muḥkam*) concerning their specific content.[135] The rest of the verse, concludes al-Ṭabarī, assures Muḥammad that he need only place his faith in God when making peace with "the enemies of God," for He hears and knows all that transpires during such negotiations.[136]

Al-Wāḥidī comments that the general meaning of the verse is that one should incline to peace (*al-ṣulḥ*) when the other side inclines to it. According to al-Kalbī, the verse referred to the Qurayẓa, but al-Ḥasan [al-Baṣrī] understood it to be a reference to the polytheists. Al-Wāḥidī further remarks that most exegetes believe that this verse had been abrogated by Qur'ān 9:5.[137] This last comment by al-Wāḥidī, juxtaposed with al-Ṭabarī's clearly delineated position on the *muḥkam* status of Qur'ān 8:61, suggests that in the intervening century between the two exegetes, the pro-abrogation position had gained considerable ground.

Al-Zamakhsharī refers to Ibn 'Abbās who believed that Qur'ān 8:61 was abrogated by Qur'ān 9:29 (the *jizya* verse),[138] whereas Mujāhid had maintained that it was abrogated by Qur'ān 9:5 (this is not recorded, however, in Mujāhid's published *tafsīr*). Mujāhid had also said that the verse referred to the Qurayẓa (as previously mentioned). Al-Zamakhsharī affirms that the truth of the matter is that, in each case, the Imam determines whether it is to the benefit of Muslims to engage in peace or in war, for neither fighting nor truces (*al-hudna*) are absolutely prescribed or proscribed. Al-Zamakhsharī thus invokes a calculus of pragmatic benefit and rational considerations—rather than assumed doctrinal ones—to determine the efficacy, moral or otherwise, of war and peacemaking. The verse furthermore assures believers, he concludes, that they need not fear treachery from their enemies, for God is privy to all that they do.[139]

Al-Rāzī has, uncharacteristically, a fairly brief commentary on this verse. He says that after the preceding verse (Qur'ān 8:60) exhorted Muslims to assemble their forces against the enemy, should the same enemy incline to peace, then Muslims are commanded to accept their offer of peace (*fa-'l-ḥukm qubūl al-ṣulḥ*). He notes that Qatāda had considered these verses to be abrogated by Qur'ān 9:5 and 9:29, but that others (not named by him) had stated that this verse was not abrogated; the verse in fact contains a command to make peace when there is benefit in it (*al-āya ghayr mansūkha lākinnahā taḍammanat al-'amr bi-'l-ṣulḥ idhā kāna al-ṣalāḥ fīhi*). The verse ends with the assurance of God's help and support for the believers in case the enemy violates their pact with them. Al-Rāzī notes that Mujāhid had been of the opinion that the verse was revealed in regard to the Banū Qurayẓa and Banū Nadīr. Al-Rāzī comments, however, that the verse's allusion to these two tribes does not preclude it being understood in a broader and more general sense.[140]

Al-Qurṭubī remarks that if the adversary inclines to peaceableness (*al-musālama*), that is to say, peacemaking (*al-ṣulḥ*), then Muslims should also incline to it. The word *al-salm*, as it occurs in this verse (although some like al-A'mash and al-Mufaḍḍal read it as *al-silm*), and the related word *al-salām* are the equivalents of *al-ṣulḥ*.[141] He notes the differences of opinion among scholars regarding the status of the verse—thus al-Suddī and Ibn Zayd (contrary to what other exegetes reported from the latter) maintained that if the enemy invited you to peace, then you should respond in kind; and that the verse was not abrogated, but Qatāda and 'Ikrima had been of the opinion that Qur'ān 9:5 and 9:36 had abrogated 8:61 and that the entire ninth chapter had abrogated the possibility of amicable relations (*muwāda'a*) with the enemy unless they were to utter the *shahāda*.[142]

He then lists a variety of opinions concerning the length of time allowed for such truces, ranging from one to ten years. The early Andalusian jurist Ibn Ḥabīb (d. 238/852) relating from Mālik b. Anas, however, said that the length could be for any specified or unspecified period of time (*wa-ilā ghayr mudda*). According to a *ḥadīth* recorded by al-Bukhārī, Muslims may also make peace with polytheists and conclude truces with them without levying any taxes on them. Furthermore, they may conclude peace agreements according to which they themselves pay tribute to the enemy.[143]

It should be noted here that Ibn Kathīr (d. 774/1373) in the late eighth/fourteenth century also affirms the unabrogated status of this verse and states that its principle of peacemaking was exemplified by the Prophet during the events of al-Ḥudaybiyya.[144]

Concluding Remarks

Fighting was a complex subject then, as was its cessation. As this chapter shows, both religious and pragmatic imperatives were invoked by Muslim scholars in delineating the purview of the military *jihād* and to articulate an ethics of initiating and ending armed combat on the basis of the critical verses discussed here. Once again, it is evident that the specific sociopolitical circumstances of our exegetes were frequently decisive in shaping their views, an awareness of which allows us to appreciate the highly contingent—and contested—nature of these discourses. Tensions between dovish and hawkish camps continue to manifest themselves in this exegetical material, especially in connection with the controversial hermeneutical tool of *naskh*, which was wielded by certain exegetes to privilege more belligerent readings of the Qur'ān. Al-Ṭabarī's caveat that a verse may function as an abrogating one only in relation to another verse which deals with the same matter is highly significant for it imposes a check on the potentially arbitrary deployment of this powerful device, particularly for ideological reasons. His critique of those like 'Ikrima, Qatāda, and Ibn Zayd — our usual hawks — who had asserted that Qur'ān 8:61 had been abrogated by selected verses from the ninth chapter of the Qur'ān that deal with different groups of people and circumstances is particularly apt. The non-abrogation position in connection with Qur'ān 8:61 continued to be maintained by later exegetes like al-Zamakhsharī, al-Rāzī, and Ibn Kathīr, indicating that the pro-*naskh* position was hardly credible to all.

In the next chapter, we take up the matter of martyrdom as an equally complex phenomenon related to *jihād*, both in combative and non-combative contexts. As with *jihād*, our discussion seeks to recuperate a variety of contested meanings ascribed to martyrdom and trace the evolution and significance of the concept's variegated inflections over time.

IV

Dying in the Path of God

CONSTRUCTING MARTYRDOM

MARTYRDOM, ESPECIALLY IN the military sense, is an inchoate concept in the Qur'ān, not encapsulated by any single, specific term. The term *shahīd* used almost exclusively in extra-Qur'anic literature to refer to a martyr, military or otherwise, does not occur in the Qur'ān in this sense. *Shahīd* and its cognate *shāhid* in the Qur'ān refer to a legal witness or an eyewitness, and it is used for both God and humans in appropriate contexts (e.g., Qur'ān 3:98; 6:19; 41:53). The Qur'anic locution most commonly understood to refer to the martyr is *man qutila fī sabīl allāh* ("one who is slain in the path of God"), along with its variants. This locution is therefore not without ambiguity, and it does not explicitly refer to the military martyr, although the Qur'anic contexts for a number of verses employing this phrase suggest it. Another less commonly occurring concept of selling or bartering (*yashrī/yashrūn*) one's self or the life of this world for the hereafter may be connected to the notion of martyrdom.

It is only in the post-Qur'anic literature—exegetical, *ḥadīth*, juridical, and literary hortatory works—that the term *shahīd* explicitly acquires the specific meaning of "one who bears witness for the faith," particularly by laying down his or her life. Extraneous, particularly Christian, influences may be suspected in this semantic evolution.[1] Muslim encounters with Levantine Christians in the late seventh century very likely contributed to this semantic development. Arthur Jeffrey has pointed to the probable influence of the cognate Syriac word for martyr-witness, *sahedo*, on the Arabic *shahīd* and the latter's subsequent acquisition of the secondary and derivative meaning of "martyr."[2] The fact that we encounter the term *shahīd* in the sense of martyr-witness only in extra-Qur'anic literature establishes the later development of this strand of meaning.

There are nine Qur'anic verses that refer to either dying or being killed in the path of God, and two more that refer to bartering one's life in this world for the next. Some of these verses have been interpreted to glorify dying on the battlefield and to specifically promote a cult of military martyrdom, even though, as will become evident, the Qur'ān seeks to prevent the formation of such a cult. Two verses in this group ambiguously employ the term *shuhadā'* (plural of *shahīd*). Due to length constraints, the exegeses of a smaller selection (six in total) of frequently cited verses in the context of martyrdom are discussed in this chapter, allowing us to gain at least a general understanding of the range of interpretations that have been preserved for us in pre-modern Qur'ān commentaries about this topic. These verses are all deemed to be early Medinan revelations from roughly before the fifth year of the *hijra*.

Exegeses of Qur'ān 3:157–158; 4:74; and 22:58

> Qur'ān 3:157–158: If you are slain in the path of God or die (*wa-la in qutiltum fī sabīl allāh aw muttum*), then there is pardon and mercy from God better than what they amass [in this world]. Whether you die or are slain (*wa-la in muttum aw qutiltum*), you will be assembled before God.

Muqātil b. Sulaymān (d. 150/767) comments briefly that when believers are slain in the path of God or die without being slain (*fī ghayr qatl*), then they are assured of forgiveness from God for their sins and His mercy, which are better than their accumulated wealth. They are warned about the Day of Resurrection in the next verse, regardless of their manner of dying.[3]

In contradistinction to Muqātil, the author/redactor of ***Tanwīr al-miqbās*** (from roughly before the fourth/tenth century?) understands this verse to be addressing the lukewarm or hypocritical Muslims (*yā ma'shar al-munāfiqīn*), reminding them that whether they are slain in the path of God or die in their homes while being sincere [in their faith] (*wa-kuntum mukhliṣīn*), God will pardon their sins and spare them punishment, all of which is better than what they have amassed as wealth in this world. And whether they die in their own land or while traveling or are slain in some military campaign (*fī ghazāh*), they will be gathered before God.[4] Both Muqātil and the *Tanwīr al-miqbās* understand the verse as promising equally generous rewards to the righteous believer who dies on or off the battlefield.

In his very brief comments on this verse, **Hūd b. Muḥakkam** (d. ca. 290/903) says that it promises forgiveness of sins for those who are slain in the path of God or die naturally. *Raḥma* in the verse specifically refers to paradise (*janna*), which is better than anything in the world.[5]

Al-'Ayyāshī (d. ca. 320/932) records a report from the Companion Jābir b. 'Abd Allāh, who said that he asked the fifth Imām Abū Ja'far about the meaning of Qur'ān 3:157. The latter proceeded to explain the phrase "the path of God" as a reference to 'Alī and his progeny. Whoever is slain or dies while professing allegiance to them, said Abū Ja'far, is slain or dies in the path of God.[6] **Furāt b. Ibrāhīm** (fl. second half of third/ninth century) comments similarly on this verse.[7] In this specifically Shī'ī understanding of the critical phrase *fī sabīl allāh*, which emphasizes fealty to the imāms, we continue to find affirmation of the general early position that the pious believer is assured of heavenly reward, regardless of the manner of death.

Al-Ṭabarī (d. 310/923) says that God addresses His faithful believers (*'ibādahu al-mu'minīn*) in these two verses, who are counseled to strive in the path of God and fight His enemies, secure in the knowledge that if they should be slain in battle or die while traveling, they are promised pardon and mercy. Dying in the path of God (*anna mawtan fī sabīl allāh*) or being slain for His sake (*aw qatlan fī 'llāh*) was better than all the accoutrements of the good life on earth that they had collected and that held them back from striving in His path and meeting the enemy.[8]

The remaining post-Ṭabarī exegetes—al-Wāḥidī (d. 468/1076);[9] al-Zamakhsharī (d. ca. 538/1144);[10] al-Rāzī (d. 606/1210);[11] and al-Qurṭubī (d. 671/1273)[12]—similarly continue to emphasize that, whether believers are slain while fighting in the path of God or die of other natural causes, they are equally deserving of God's forgiveness and mercy in the hereafter.

> Qur'ān 4:74: Let those who barter (*yashrūn*) the life of the world for the hereafter fight in the path of God. Whoever fights in the path of God and is killed or is victorious, we shall offer him a great reward.

In his very brief comment, **Muqātil** says that this verse affirms that, regardless of whether the believer is slain or is victorious over the enemy, his [or her] reward is equally abundant in paradise.[13]

The ***Tanwīr al-miqbās*** indicates a difference of opinion regarding how the first part of this verse should be read. According to one school of thought, the verse is addressed to the Hypocrites and commands them to fight in His path out of obedience to God and reprimands them for having chosen this world over the next. (The verb *sharā/yashrī* can mean, depending on the context, either to buy or to sell.) But others say that this verse was revealed in reference to sincere believers who sell (*yabī'ūn*) the life of this world for the next, exhorting them to fight in the path of God and prefer the hereafter over the present world. Both the one who is martyred (*yastashhidu*, used as a gloss on *yuqtalu*) and the one who is victorious will be given abundant reward in paradise.[14]

Hūd b. Muḥakkam briefly glosses "a great reward" as "paradise," and then proceeds to relate *ḥadīths* that promise abundant rewards to those who fight and perish in the path of God.[15]

The injunction "Let them fight in the path of God" means, according to **al-Ṭabarī**, "[to fight] for the religion of God and for the summoning [of the unbelievers] to it." The phrase "those who barter the life of the world for the hereafter" means "Those who sell their lives in this world for the reward of the next and for what God has promised the people who obey Him in such matters." Their "selling" consists of what they spend of their wealth in order to secure the pleasure of God by fighting against those who are among His enemies and striving resolutely against them. The last part of the verse promises that those who fight (*man yuqātil*) the enemies of God in order to "establish the religion of God and to make God's word supreme" and are either killed or triumph will be given a mighty recompense and reward. The adjective (*ʿaẓīm*^{an}) to describe the reward (*ajr*^{an}) indicates an extent the measure or value (*mablaghahu*) of which cannot be fathomed by humans.[16] It should be noted that the terms *shahīd and shahāda* are not used by al-Ṭabarī here in reference to those who are killed while fighting.

Unlike Muqātil and al-Ṭabarī, but reminiscent of the *Tanwīr al-miqbās*, **al-Wāḥidī** in his brief exegesis of this verse explicitly introduces the terms *shahāda* (clearly with the meaning of military martyrdom) and *shahīd*. He says that this verse refers to those "who choose paradise over existence in this world and so strive to seek martyrdom in the path of God" (*fa-yujāhidūn ṭalaban li-'l-shahāda fī sabīl allāh*). The next part of the verse affirms that both the one slain "as a martyr" (*shahīdan*) and the victor are assured of divine reward.[17]

Al-Zamakhsharī in his *Kashshāf* says that this verse cautions those who purchase the life of this world at the expense of the hereafter to be sincere in their belief in God and His apostle and fight the true fight in the path of God (*wa-yujāhidū fī sabīl allāh ḥaqqa 'l-jihād*). Those who sell their lives in this world are believers who prefer the next world over the present and exert themselves for its sake; they are firm and sincere in their belief and they fight, for which they have been promised a great reward.[18]

Al-Rāzī says that the verb *yashrūna* generally means to "sell" (*yabīʿūna*) but, according to another school of thought, *yashrūn* is also equivalent to *yashtarūn* ("to buy"). The verse may therefore be understood to address the Hypocrites who had desisted from fighting during the battle of Uḥud and to exhort those who have preferred this world over the next to fight. Al-Rāzī expresses his reservations about this interpretation, as it would imply that the verse is suggesting that the Hypocrites, who purchase the life of this world at the expense of the next, should resort to fighting so that they may attain happiness and honor in this world by vanquishing the enemy and collecting booty.[19] The second part of the verse, continues al-Rāzī, means that those who die fighting the unbelievers and those who triumph will be given a great reward that will be pure, everlasting, and glorious. Such a promise serves to embolden the fighter (*mujāhid*) and prevents him from fleeing the battle.[20]

Al-Qurṭubī says that the first part of the verse is addressed to the believers, commanding them to fight the unbelievers in the path of God. The verb *yashrūna* is equivalent to *yabī'ūna* (to sell/barter), meaning that these believers have expended themselves and their wealth for God in order to attain their reward in the hereafter. The second part of the verse means that one who fights in the path of God and is slain will be given a great reward. Al-Qurṭubī explicitly glosses *fa-yuqtal* ("is slain") as *fa-yastashhid*, that is, "to be martyred." The fighter who is not slain triumphs over the enemy and is entitled to the spoils of war, he comments.[21]

The verse thus suggests that both the slain (*shahīd*) and the victorious fighter are equal in merit. Here, al-Qurṭubī cites a *ḥadīth* from Abū Hurayra, recorded by Muslim in his *Ṣaḥīḥ*, in which the Prophet says, "God has vouchsafed for the one who goes out in His path, that is to say for the one who has ventured forth only 'on account of *jihād* in My path, faith in Me, and acceptance of My messengers,' either a guaranteed entrance into Paradise or return to his place of residence whence he emerged, attaining his rightful reward or booty."[22]

A comparison of all these exegeses on Qur'ān 4:74 reveals that it was still not common until al-Ṭabarī's time to refer to the one slain in the path of God as *shahīd*. Al-Wāḥidī is the first in our survey to explicitly use *shahīd* in reference to a battlefield martyr, and this usage resurfaces in al-Qurṭubī's commentary. All the exegetes in our survey affirm that fighting in the path of God when urged to do so by the Prophet was without doubt a highly meritorious activity, and the victor and the slain were assured of the same posthumous rewards, with no privileging of the battlefield martyr.

> Qur'ān 22:58: Those who emigrated in the path of God and then were slain or died (*thumma qutilū aw mātū*), God will provide handsome provisions (*rizqan ḥasanan*) for them; indeed God is the best of providers.

Muqātil briefly comments that the verse assures those who emigrated to Medina and afterward were either killed or died of a generous provision (*rizqan karīman*) from God in the hereafter. The verse was revealed in reference to a group of Muslims who said to Muḥammad, "We fight the polytheists and we slay some of them (*fa-naqtul minhum*) and are not martyred (*lā nastashhid*);

thus martyrdom is denied us (*fa-mā lana shahāda*)." Then God assigned all of them together to Paradise.[23] Here in this early *tafsīr*, we appear to have already a clear articulation of the concept of military martyrdom in relation to Qur'ān 22:58, as indicated by the use of the lexemes *nastashhid* and *shahāda*. There is, however, no indication yet that the military martyr is superior to other believers who die of natural causes.

In his similarly brief remarks, **Hūd b. Muḥakkam** says that the verse affirms that those who were killed or died in their beds after the *hijra* were assured of paradise.[24]

Al-Ṭabarī similarly understands this verse to refer to those who departed from their native lands and families in order to serve God and undertake *jihād* against His enemies. Whether they were subsequently killed or died, God will confer on them abundant reward "in His gardens" on the Day of Judgment, for He is the best and most generous of providers. This verse was specifically revealed in regard to certain Companions who differed regarding the status of those who perished in the path of God. Some were of the opinion that the one who was slain and the one who died were of the same status, whereas others maintained that the one who was slain had achieved greater merit (*afḍal*). Consequently, this verse was revealed in order to inform Muhammad that **both** the one who is slain and the one who dies naturally in the path of God attain the same reward in the hereafter.[25]

Al-Wāḥidī very briefly remarks that the verse refers to those who emigrated from Mecca to Medina and afterward were killed while fighting or died. According to al-Suddī, the *rizq* that they are promised refers to the provisions of Paradise.[26]

Just as briefly, **al-Zamakhsharī** comments that the verse regards all the emigrants from Mecca to Medina to be equally meritorious, regardless of whether they subsequently were killed during the early battles or survived and died later. God is fully cognizant of their status and confers His reward on them equally.[27]

In his lengthier commentary on this verse, **al-Rāzī** makes the following pertinent remarks: The verse promises a generous reward specifically for the Meccan emigrants (*al-muhājirīn*) and serves to aggrandize their status (*tafkhīman li-sha'nihim*).[28] As for "the generous provision," it clearly refers to the bounties of paradise; but he also notes the views of al-Aṣamm (d. ca. 200/815), the early Mu'tazilī theologian, who thought it referred to "knowledge and understanding" (*al-'ilm wa-'l-fahm*), while the early Kufan scholar al-Kalbī (d. 204/819) thought it referred to booty. Al-Rāzī finds both views implausible because the verse refers to the posthumous reward of the believers for their emigration in the path of God—whether they are slain or die naturally in its course—and therefore it must be, he concludes, a reference to the joys of paradise.[29] It is worthy of note that al-Rāzī unambiguously points to emigration itself as the activity undertaken in the path of God referred to in this verse that confers merit on the believer, regardless of his subsequent manner of dying. Fighting is not coupled with emigration here.

As for His saying, "Then they were slain or they died," it means that His promise (*wa'd*) encompasses both of these groups equally, al-Rāzī continues. At the basic linguistic level, the verse does not indicate either preference or equal status for these two groups and does not on its surface support those who say that the one slain in the military *jihād* and the one who dies in his bed (*wa-'l-mayyit 'alā firāshihi*) are equal in moral status. This understanding of an equal status finds support in a *ḥadīth*, however, from Anas b. Mālik in which Muḥammad had remarked, "The one who is slain in the path of God the Exalted (*al-maqtūl fī sabīl allāh ta'ālā*) and the one who dies of natural causes in the path of God (*al-mutawaffā fī sabīl allāh bi-ghayr qatl*) are the equal of one other in regard to the blessings and reward [which they are entitled to]." It has also been related, al-Rāzī comments, that a group of Companions asked the Prophet whether they, after having fought with him and survived, would be with him in the next world like those who had been slain and given their promised reward. This verse (and the following) was then revealed to indicate the equal status of these two groups.[30]

Al-Qurṭubī says that the verse singles out those Meccan emigrants who were either slain or died in order to show preference and honor for them (specifically 'Uthmān b. Maz'ūn and Abū Salama b. 'Abd al-Asad) over all others. Some were of the opinion that one who is slain in the path of God is better (*afḍal*) than the one who dies of natural causes (*māta ḥatfa anfihi*), but the revelation of this verse explicitly affirmed, comments Qurṭubī, that both were equal in status (*al-āya musawwiya baynahum* [sic]) and that God would accord both a handsome provision in the hereafter. In spite of that, al-Qurṭubī notes, the law came to indicate the superior status of the slain (*anna 'l-maqtūl afḍal*).

Al-Qurṭubī then proceeds to provide valuable documentation of a range of views held by scholars concerning the status of the military martyr. According to some [unnamed] scholars, both the one who is slain in the path of God and the one who dies in the path of God are equally regarded as martyrs (*shahīd*), but the slain individual enjoys a distinctive status because of what he suffered for the sake of God (*wa-lākinna li-'l-maqtūl maziyya mā aṣābahu fī dhāt allāh*). But other [unnamed] scholars stated that they were equal (*humā sawā'*), adducing as a proof-text Qur'ān 4:100, which states, "Whoever emerges from his home in order to emigrate to God and His apostle, and is then overtaken by death, his reward is already assured of with God." He also lists the *ḥadīth* concerning Umm Ḥarām, who was thrown from her riding mount and died as a consequence rather than being slain (*mātat wa-lam tuqtal*), and the Prophet said addressing her, "You are among the first [rank of believers] (*anti min al-awwalīn*)." Both Qur'ān 4:100 and the *ḥadīth* above are clearly valuable proof-texts for affirming the high status of the non-combative martyr.[31]

Al-Qurṭubī adduces another significant report in the same vein in which Ibn al-Mubārak (reporting from Fuḍāla b. 'Ubayd) relates that two men died at the same place, one after having been wounded by a mangonel during a military campaign and the other of natural causes. Fuḍāla sat down by the corpse of the latter man, and it was said to him: "You abandoned the martyr (*al-shahīd*) and did not sit by him?" He replied, "I do not care in which of the two graves I am raised up in." Then he recited Qur'ān 22:58.[32] But there are others, al-Qurṭubī points out, who argued that the slain individual enjoyed a higher status according to the *ḥadīth* in which Muḥammad was asked, "Which *jihād* is more meritorious (*afḍal*)?" He replied, "[The *jihād* of] one whose blood flows and whose steed is hamstrung." If such an individual is deemed to be "the best of martyrs" (*afḍal al-shuhadā'*), then, al-Qurṭubī claims, one who does not meet his end in this manner is deemed to be less meritorious (*mafḍul*).[33]

Al-Qurṭubī's valuable documentation of these debates concerning the status of the military martyr versus that of the naturally dying pious individual once again points to a hearty politics of piety in the early period that pitted pro-militancy groups against non-militant ones. His commentary indicates the greater reliance on particularly *faḍā'il al-jihād* reports by the first group to undermine the explicit meanings of verses, such as Qur'ān 22:58, that make no *prima facie* distinction in status between the naturally deceased and the fallen in battle. The cult of military martyrdom by al-Qurṭubī's time appears to be well-entrenched, and its establishment necessitated such a hermeneutic stratagem to circumvent an otherwise transparent stricture in Qur'ān 22:58 against the very construction of such a cult.

Exegeses of Qur'ān 2:154 and 3:169

> Do not say regarding those who are slain in the path of God that they are dead (*wa lā taqūlu li-man yuqtal fī sabīl allāh amwāt[un]*); rather they are alive (*bal aḥyā'*) but you are not aware (Qur'ān 2:154) and Do not consider as dead those who are slain in the path of God (*lā taḥsabanna 'lladhīna qutilū fī sabīl allāh amwāt[an]*); rather they are alive (*bal aḥyā'*) and given sustenance in the presence of their Lord (*'inda rabbihim yurzaqūn;* Qur'ān 3:169).

With regard to 2:154, **Muqātil** says it was revealed in reference to those fourteen Muslims who were slain at Badr, eight from among the Anṣār and six from among the Muhājirūn, whose names he then lists. The revelation of this verse served to inform the believers that those who were slain in the path of God were not dead but alive, reaping their rewards in paradise in the presence of God. The souls of the martyrs (*al-shuhadā'*), Muqātil says, reside near the lotus tree closest to the throne of God (*sidrat al-muntahā*).[34] As for Qur'ān 3:169, it was also revealed concerning those killed in the battle of Badr, says Muqātil, who are not to be regarded as dead, but rather as alive, enjoying the fruits (*al-thimār*) of heaven. According to an unattributed *ḥadīth*, God renders the souls of the martyrs as green birds that flit about in heaven under the candelabra suspended over the divine throne.[35] When they alight on these candelabra, continues Muqātil, God appears before them and asks them three times if He can provide for anything more. The third time, they wish aloud that their souls could be returned to their bodies, so that "we may fight in your path again." On having experienced God's generosity toward them, they wish to go back and inform their brethren of the joys that await them and to counsel them that if they should encounter fighting, "they should hasten themselves toward martyrdom" (*sāri'ū bi-anfusihim ilā 'l-shahāda*). The revelation of Qur'ān 3:169 was intended to convey information about their situation in heaven to their brethren on earth, concludes Muqātil.[36]

The author of ***Tanwir al-miqbās*** briefly comments that Qur'ān 2:154 refers to those faithful who were slain during the battle of Badr. They are not like the other dead, but alive in heaven and enjoying its bounties. The exceptional honor that is bestowed on them is not known to us.[37] Qur'ān 3:169 is a reference to those slain at Badr and at Uḥud, who are not dead, but alive and blissfully happy in the presence of God.[38]

In his *Tafsīr*, **'Abd al-Razzāq** says in reference to Qur'ān 2:154 that the souls of the martyrs are in the form of either white birds or green birds who eat from the fruits of paradise and take refuge in the candelabra under the divine throne.[39] He cites similar reports in regard to Qur'ān 3:169[40] and does not dwell further on the significance of this avian symbolism for the construction of military martyrdom.

In general, the image of the green bird housing the soul of the martyr seems to have become prevalent in the later exegetical literature,[41] as we also note in **Hūd b. Muḥakkam**'s commentary on Qur'ān 2:154.[42] Ibn Muḥakkam further describes three possible outcomes for "the one who strives in the path of God" (*al-mujāhid fī sabīl allāh*): (1) The one killed in the path of God remains alive and provided for (*ḥayy^{an} marzūq^{an}*); (2) the one who returns victorious earns from God a great reward; and (3) the one who dies naturally (*wa-man* *māta*) is granted by God a handsome provision (*rizq*^{an} *ḥasan*^{an}).[43] It is noteworthy that our author's expansive definition of "the one who strives in the path of God" encompasses all pious Muslims who struggle to carry out God's commands and die in the course of this struggle—regardless of whether they carry it out in their homes or on battlefields.

In regard to Qur'ān 3:169, Ibn Muḥakkam comments that some unnamed exegetes were of the opinion that the verse was revealed concerning the Medinan Hypocrite 'Abd Allāh b. Ubayy b. Salūl. According to another occasion of revelation, one of the Companions is said to have wished out loud that he would be given knowledge of what had happened to "our brothers who were slain in the path of God on the day of Uḥud;" subsequently, this verse was revealed.[44]

There are no comments preserved in **al-'Ayyāshī**'s *Tafsīr* on Qur'ān 2:154, but he records the following cause of revelation for Qur'ān 3:169 on the authority of Abū Ja'far, as related by Jābir: A man came to the Prophet and said that he wished to be active in *jihād*. Muḥammad advised him to fight in the path of God (*fa-jāhid fī sabīl allāh*) and outlined for him the following consequences: If he were killed, he would remain alive in the presence of God and handsomely provided for; if he died a natural death later, he would still attain his reward in the hereafter; and if he were to return as a victor from the battlefield, he would later meet his Lord purged of his sins.[45] These three outcomes for the *mujāhid*, who is clearly a military warrior here in **al-'Ayyāshī**'s understanding, are similar to the ones identified by Ibn Muḥakkam above.

In **al-Ṭabarī**'s discussion of these two verses, we find a much more detailed topography of the next world and a more extensive taxonomy of the heavenly rewards awaiting specific categories of believers, indicating the extent to which this issue had begun to exercise the minds of exegetes and the extent of literary embellishment that had emerged by the late third/ninth century in narratives concerning martyrdom. He begins by commenting that in Qur'ān 2:154, God addresses the believers and exhorts them to seek His help while patiently obeying Him in their *jihād* against their enemies, forsaking all that constitutes disobedience to Him and in carrying out the rest of their religious obligations. They are also commanded not to say that those who are slain in the path of God are dead (*mayyit*), for the dead are lifeless and deprived of their senses, unable to enjoy pleasures and experience bliss. Rather, "those among you and from the rest of My creation who are killed in the path of God are alive in My presence, [immersed] in life and happiness, [enjoying] a blissful existence and glorious provisions, exulting in what I have bestowed on them of My bounty and conferred on them of My generosity." Like his predecessors, al-Ṭabarī also lists the ubiquitous reports variously describing the souls of martyrs taking the form of green or white birds, alive in the presence of their Lord, and enjoying the fruits of heaven and the smell of its fragrance, even though they are not actually within paradise.[46] For the one who strives/fights in the path of God (*li-'l-mujāhid fī sabīl allāh*), he furthermore identifies three possible outcomes and rewards that are identical to those described by Ibn Muḥakkam.[47]

But what if someone remonstrates that the generous compensation promised to the "one slain in the path of God" (*al-maqtūl fī sabīl allāh*) is also generally applicable to any pious believer? According to a number of reports, the Prophet had described similar rewards reserved for all righteous believers and the punishment that the unbelievers would face. So what if anything, asks this interlocutor, distinguishes the state of the one killed (*al-qatīl*) in the path of God from the rest of humanity, believers and unbelievers, who, according to these reports, are all alive in Barzakh (the intermediary world after death between this one and the next), albeit in vastly different conditions?[48]

The answer to this question is as follows, continues al-Ṭabarī: The martyrs are distinguished from other believers by the fact that they alone are privy to the delicious food of heaven in Barzakh before their resurrection and which they continue to savor after their resurrection; this is how God has privileged them over everyone else. He records a report from Ibn 'Abbās, which relates that the martyrs are near Barīq, a river at the gate of paradise, in a green dome (according to another version, in a green garden), where they are given their provisions from heaven morning and night. Yet another report relates that the souls of the martyrs are in the white domes of paradise. In each dome, two wives (*zawjatān*) await. Every day their sustenance comes in the forms of a bull and a whale. The bull contains every kind of fruit in heaven, and the whale contains every kind of drink available in paradise.[49]

Al-Ṭabarī then proceeds to reply to those who protest that these rather hyperbolic reports cited by him cataloging the pleasures awaiting the martyrs are not mentioned in Qur'ān 2:154, which merely gives information about their state—whether they are dead or alive. Al-Ṭabarī agrees that Qur'ān 2:154 simply forbids humankind to say that the martyrs are dead and does not give further information about their state. The exegetical reports he cites are to be understood rather as providing details about the pleasures enjoyed by the martyrs that are alluded to by God in the related verse, Qur'ān 3:169, which refers to their provision (*yurzaqūn*).[50] Qur'ān 3:169, al-Ṭabarī continues, is specifically related to those Companions killed at Uḥud. The verse served to inform Muḥammad that he should not regard them as dead, that is, devoid of feeling and the ability to feel pleasure. Rather, "they are alive in My presence, delighting in My sustenance, exulting and rejoicing in what I grant them from My generosity and mercy, bestowing on them the abundance of My reward and provisions."[51]

In regard to Qur'ān 2:154, **al-Wāḥidī** briefly explains that people used to say that those who had been killed in the path of God were dead and no longer able to enjoy the good things of the world. This verse was revealed to counter such assertions. In connection with His saying, "they are alive," the exegetes cited the *ḥadīth* in which Muḥammad said, "The souls of the martyrs are lodged inside green birds who flit about among the fruit-trees of paradise and drink from its rivers, taking refuge at night among the lighted candelabra hanging by the Divine Throne."[52] As for Qur'ān 3:169, al-Wāḥidī cites the *ḥadīth* recorded by Muqātil, according to which the martyrs express a wish to return to earth, with variants attributed to Ibn ʿAbbās, ʿAbd Allāh [b. Masʿūd], and Jābir b. ʿAbd Allāh.[53]

In his very brief commentary, **al-Zamakhsharī** cites the following statement from al-Ḥasan al-Baṣrī in reference to Qur'ān 2:154:

> Indeed, the martyrs are alive in the presence of God, their provisions laid out before their souls. Thus, they are engulfed by happiness and bliss just as fire is laid out before the souls of the Pharaoh's people morning and night. And they are engulfed by pain.[54]

As for Qur'ān 3:169, al-Zamakhsharī comments that the verse essentially refers to those who are slain in the path of God and are alive and eat and drink like normal living human beings; this serves to underscore the exceptionally blissful existence they are granted by God.[55]

Al-Rāzī has a typically lengthy exposition on Qur'ān 2:154, and grapples with the theological significance of this particular subject by his time. He discusses extensively what the possible implications are of this verse for understanding the state of the martyrs after physical death, the full details of which are not possible for us to reproduce here. Instead, a summary of some of his most important points is given below.

Al-Rāzī says that the majority of commentators are in agreement that those who are obedient to God (*al-muṭīʿīn*) attain their reward in their graves, even though their bodies are lifeless. He refers to al-Aṣamm, who had said that this verse contains a riposte to "the polytheists who do not know that the one who is killed for the faith of Muḥammad, upon him be peace and blessings, is alive in the faith and guided by His Lord." Other verses that can be adduced to support such statements include Qur'ān 82:13–14; 4:145; 22:56; 40:11, 46; 71:25.[56]

He next rehearses some of the debates already familiar to us concerning whether a special status reserved only for the martyrs is indicated here and whether they enjoy their reward physically in heaven or spiritually in their graves. Al-Rāzī believes that the verse does indicate a special status for the martyrs, although their status is lower than that of the prophets and the truthful ones (*al-nabiyyīn wa-'l-ṣiddiqīn*; cf. Qur'ān 4:69).[57] He also inclines toward the view that the martyrs enjoy their rewards spiritually, for no one will be physically resurrected until the Day of Judgment, and the disembodied soul is capable of experiencing pain and pleasure. On the Day of Resurrection, the souls will be united with their bodies, leading to a "fusion of the physical states with the spiritual."[58]

With regard to Qur'ān 3:169, al-Rāzī says that the verse was revealed to counter the assumption that *jihād* leads to being killed (*al-qatl*), as was said about those who left for the battle of Uḥud, and of course being killed is something undesirable (*makrūh*) and to be avoided. Being killed, however, continues al-Rāzī, is determined by God, as is natural death; there is no avoiding either when ordained by God. But the verse provides another cogent response to allay such anxieties: that being slain in the path of God is not something undesirable. How can it be undesirable when the slain individual is alive with God after his death and destined for an honorable status and closeness to God? What intelligent person will then assert that this manner of dying is undesirable?[59]

This verse, continues al-Rāzī, was specifically revealed concerning those slain at Badr and Uḥud, and to reprimand the Hypocrites who had desisted from taking part in the fighting because of their fear of being killed. God elucidated the merits of fighting in these battles in this verse so that it would serve as an impetus for Muslims to emulate those who had fought (*jāhada*) in these campaigns and were slain. Those who forsake *jihād* may or may not attain the good things of this world, which are paltry and contemptible, but those who embark upon it have without doubt attained the bounties of the next world, which are great and everlasting, proving that undertaking *jihād* is better than forsaking it.[60]

The obvious signification of the verse is that those who are slain are alive, whether physically or metaphorically. Al-Rāzī proceeds to recapitulate here some of the debates concerning how this state of being alive should be understood, some of which have been briefly dealt with above and need not further occupy us here.[61]

Al-Qurṭubī defers the full treatment of "martyrs and the laws pertaining to them" until his exegesis of the related verse, Qur'ān 3:169. In brief, he comments in regard to Qur'ān 2:154 that when one says that the martyrs are alive, it does not mean that "they will be brought to life" (*sa-yaḥyūn*), for that is true of everyone. Rather, it refers to some different state, as indicated by His saying, "But you are not aware," and means that the martyrs are dead and alive at the same time, a state that cannot be compared to any other.[62]

With regard to Qur'ān 3:169, al-Qurṭubī says that the verse concerns "the martyrs of Uḥud" (*shuhadā' Uḥud*), although others like Ibn Isḥāq said that it referred to Bi'r Ma'ūna, while yet others thought it was a reference to Badr. God intended Uḥud to serve as a test to distinguish the hypocrite from the sincere believer (*al-munāfiq min al-ṣādiq*), and that whoever was slain while fighting was assured of a noble status and life in His presence. He cites a *ḥadīth* from Jābir in which the Prophet assures him that his father who had suffered martyrdom (*ustushhida*) had been granted a special audience with God and that when he wished that people on earth would know of his fate, the verse was revealed.[63] In general, the verse sought to give comfort to those still alive who were lamenting the fate of the slain lying in their graves, while they continued to savor the good things of this world.[64]

Like al-Rāzī, al-Qurṭubī next launches into a discussion of what "being alive" after having been killed means, citing many of the same authorities as the former. Interestingly, he includes the martyrs with prophets, scholars, callers to prayer, market inspectors (*muḥtasibīn*), and Qur'ān reciters (*ḥamalat al-qur'ān*), whose bodies "are not consumed by earth" (sc. do not decay). Additionally, he lists the various funerary practices (bathing the body, manner of praying over the deceased, etc.) that developed because of the special status accorded to the martyr, and the differences of opinion regarding these practices among legal scholars.[65] The extended legal discussion about different categories of martyrdom and the special treatment to be accorded to these various types of martyrs by those responsible for their burials indicate the importance accorded to this subject in juridical discourses by al-Qurṭubī's time.

Al-Qurṭubī goes on to list several *ḥadīth*s and reports in this section, some of which were not listed by the other exegetes we previously surveyed, that further elucidate the fate of the martyr in the next world. He lists a *ḥadīth* that declares that a martyr's debt, unlike his other sins and shortcomings, will not be erased, and another *ḥadīth*, not directly pertaining to a martyr, that warns that righteous deeds alone will not save the believer from the Fire if he or she has also slandered or cursed a person, spilled blood, or engaged in backbiting. Both these *ḥadīth*s have the effect of imposing a ceiling on the otherwise unusually exalted status ascribed to the martyr in the next world.[66]

As for the *rizq* that the martyrs will enjoy in the hereafter, it includes closeness to God, a noble status before Him, and the opportunity to engage in seemly praise of Him. Their souls will exult in the good things of paradise, a state that will be enhanced when they are eventually reunited with their bodies.[67]

Concluding Remarks

Our comparison of early and later exegeses of Qur'ān 2:154 and 3:169 clearly reveals how a cult of military martyrdom progressively developed in response to post-prophetic historical circumstances, the impetus for which was anachronistically read back into these verses (as was also the case with Qur'ān 22:58), despite the lack of overt reference in them to the military martyr, and to any assumption of their higher status vis-à-vis other believers who die, for example, while emigrating in the path of God.[68] The process of establishing this cult started quite early, as we observed. Although not mentioned in the Qur'ān, bounteous posthumous pleasures earmarked primarily for military martyrs are fancifully elaborated upon by the exegetes to indicate their special status in the next world, starting already in the Umayyad period as evident from the *tafsīr* of Muqātil. No doubt, the lure of such pleasures was expected to serve as additional enticement for what appears to be at least a segment of the population that was reluctant to enlist in the imperial armies of the Umayyads (and later the 'Abbasids), as our study seems to indicate. Other than pietist concerns, this reluctance may also have been instigated by traditional tribal rivalries and disagreements over specific policies.[69] Many of the exegetes in our survey helpfully document that the progressive high esteem accorded to the "one slain in the path of God" – frequently conflated with the military martyr – at the expense of the non-military martyr, such as the emigrant, was questioned by some. The physical, especially gastronomic, pleasures outlined in some detail awaiting the military martyr in specific reports were also regarded by some as fanciful embellishments, as al-Ṭabarī records, since they had no basis in the Qur'ān, which merely informs that the martyr is to be regarded as alive rather than dead in the next world. The Mu'tazila distinctively understood the bountiful provisions promised in Qur'ān 22:58 as a reference to knowledge and understanding rather than material pleasures, an interpretation that was clearly intended as a rebuke to the *ahl al-ḥadīth* and their over-reliance on reports that must have appeared to the Mu'tazila to be of dubious provenance and content. The variety of perspectives that remain available to us through these exegetical works sheds critical light on the competing constructions of martyrdom through Islamic history and their broader theological and socio-ethical implications.

Identifying the Shuhadā': Exegesis of Qur'ān 4:69

As we noted, the singular *shahīd* is never used in the Qur'ān for a martyr, military or otherwise. The Qur'anic plural *shuhadā'* is frequently translated into English as "martyrs," which is clearly an anachronistic understanding, since it is logical to assume that the plural should be semantically linked to the singular. The following section discusses the exegeses of an important Qur'anic verse that employs *al-shuhadā'* as a specific category of righteous believers.[70] Once again, comparison of early and late exegeses allows us to trace how this critical term underwent significant transformations in meaning through time.

> **Qur'ān 4:69**: Whoever obeys God and the Messenger are with those upon whom God has conferred His bounty: prophets (*al-nabiyyīn*), veracious people (*al-ṣiddiqīn*), witnesses (*al-shuhadā'*), and righteous people (*al-ṣaliḥīn*). They are the best of companions.

Muqātil b. Sulaymān said that this verse concerns a man from among the Anṣār named 'Abd Allāh b. Zayd b. 'Abd Rabbihi al-Anṣārī, who once remarked to the Prophet, "When we leave your presence to return to our families, we long for you, and nothing seems to benefit us until we return to you. I think of your [lofty] status in paradise—how then can we see you if we enter heaven?" The verse was then revealed. The four categories of people mentioned in the verse are identified by Muqātil as follows: *al-nabiyyīn*, those who were granted prophethood (*bi-'l-nubuwwa*); *al-ṣiddiqīn*, those who were endowed with veracity (*bi-'l-taṣdīq*) and who were first to believe in and help the prophets; *al-shuhadā'*, those slain in the path of God as martyrs (*al-qutlā fī sabīl allāh bi-'l-shahāda*); and *al-ṣāliḥīn*, the believers who are the denizens of heaven (*ya'nī al-mu'minīn ahla 'l-janna*).[71]

Like Muqātil, **Hūd b. Muḥakkam** says that the verse was revealed in response to the concern expressed by a number of Muḥammad's unnamed contemporaries that after death, they would be separated from him. Unlike Muqātil, however, Ibn Muḥakkam does not provide us with a definition of the categories of people named in the verse.[72]

The ***Tanwīr al-miqbās*** similarly says that this verse was revealed to reassure the Companions that they would not be separated from Muḥammad in the next world, and that whoever obeyed God in carrying out the religious obligations and obeyed the Prophet in regard to the *sunna* would be in heaven with all those whom God has blessed. The heavenly dwellers include Muḥammad and others among the prophets (*al-nabiyyīn*), the best of the Companions of Muḥammad (*al-siddiqīn*), those who were martyred in the way of God (*alladhīna ustushhidū fī sabīl allāh;* a gloss on *al-shuhadā'*), and the righteous from Muḥammad's community (*al-sāliḥīn*). This is God's favor upon them (*al-faḍl min allāh*), as the next verse affirms.[73]

Al-Qummī understands *al-nabiyyīn* in the verse to refer to Muḥammad; *al-ṣiddiqīn* to ʿAlī; *al-shuhadāʾ* to al-Ḥasan and al-Ḥusayn; and *al-ṣāliḥīn* to the imāms.[74] Al-ʿAyyāshī records a report in which Abū ʿAbd Allāh (sc. Jaʿfar al-Ṣādiq), not unexpectedly, identified the imāms as the *ṣiddiqūn* and the *shuhadāʾ*, while the followers of the imāms are the *ṣāliḥūn*.[75] According to one lengthy report recorded by **Furāt** on the authority of the well-known first/seventh century Shīʿī transmitter Asbagh b. Nubāta (d. second half of first/seventh century) in exegesis of this verse, the best of creation are the messengers (*al-rusul*), among whom Muḥammad is the best; followed by the legatee to the Prophet, ʿAlī, who is the best of all legatees; followed by the *shuhadāʾ*, the best among whom is Ḥamza, the leader of the martyrs; followed by Jaʿfar b. Abī Ṭālib, nicknamed "he of the two wings"; the two grandsons al-Ḥasan and al-Ḥusayn, the masters of the youth of Paradise; Fāṭima; and the Mahdī.[76]

According to **al-Ṭabarī**, the verse says that those who submit to the commands of God and the Prophet and sincerely seek to fulfill them while desisting from all that is forbidden by God will be with the prophets, whom God has blessed with His guidance and success for their obedience, in this world and in the next when they enter paradise. As for *al-ṣiddīqūn*, the plural of *al-ṣiddīq*, al-Ṭabarī indicates that there is a difference of opinion concerning its meaning. Some say that *al-ṣiddīqūn* refers to the followers (*tubbāʿ*) of the prophets in general, for they believed in their message and followed their ways (*manāhijahum*) after them until their deaths.[77] Others cited a *ḥadīth* from the Companion Miqdād, who related that Muḥammad had stated that the *ṣiddīqūn* are those who affirm the truth (*hum al-muṣaddiqūn*).[78] Al-Ṭabarī acknowledges that the chain of transmission of this report is sound, but as the report does not emanate from anyone else, he is inclined to discount it. It is preferable, he says, to understand *al-ṣiddīq* as "one who affirms his speech through his actions" (*al-muṣaddiq qawlahu bi-fiʿlihi*).[79]

As for *al-shuhadāʾ*, it is the plural of *shahīd*, which refers to "the one killed (*al-maqtūl*) in the path of God" and receives this name because "he undertakes to bear witness to the truth on the side of God until he is killed." The *sāliḥīn*, plural of *ṣāliḥ*, are all those whose private and public attributes and acts are righteous (*kullu man ṣalaḥat sarīratuhu wa-ʿilāniyyatuh*).[80] As for the last part of the verse concerning companionship, al-Ṭabarī cites a number of reports in which the Prophet assures his Companions that they would be able to see him and interact with him in heaven despite the difference in their statuses.[81]

The term *ṣiddīqūn*, according to **al-Wāḥidī**, refers to all those who believe in what God has commanded without a shred of doubt and believe in the prophets, according to Qurʾān 57:19, which states, "Those who believe in God and His prophets are the *ṣiddīqūn*." He cites the opinion of al-Kalbī who understood *al-ṣiddīqūn* as a reference to "the most excellent of the Companions of the Prophet" (*afāḍil aṣḥāb al-nabiyy*), whereas Muqātil was of the opinion that the *ṣiddīqūn* were the first to believe in and help the prophets (as noted earlier).[82] The *shuhadā'* refer to those who are killed in the path of God, and the *ṣāliḥīn* are the rest of the Muslims. All of them will be the companions of the prophets in paradise, as indicated by the Qur'anic term *rafīq*^{an} that occurs in the verse, comments al-Wāḥidī.[83]

Al-Zamakhsharī also says that the *ṣiddīqūn* are the most excellent of the Companions, especially those who were among the earliest to affirm the truth, such as Abū Bakr, in their speech and action, which served to encourage other believers to be obedient. Because of their exceptional status, the *ṣiddīqūn* have been promised the companionship of those elect who are the closest to God and have the highest status in His presence. Al-Zamakhsharī further cites the report concerning Thawbān (although with slight variants) as the occasion of revelation for this verse.[84]

Al-Rāzī typically offers us a rich and dauntingly detailed exposition of this verse, the main points of which we now try to distill as succinctly as possible. In general, he says, the verse affirms that all those who obey God and the Prophet will attain a high status and a noble recompense from God. Al-Rāzī proceeds to explain what this obedience entails and the kind of closeness to God one may aspire to as a consequence, the details of which need not detain us here.[85]

With regard to the four groups of people mentioned in the verse, he says that most are agreed that the prophets constitute a category different from the other three. Some are of the opinion that the remaining three categories are interchangeable and that the traits signified by them can be found in a single individual or group of people. Al-Rāzī inclines to the view that each category is distinctive from the other and describes a specific type of person or people (*ṣinf min al-nās*). Thus the term *al-ṣiddīq* is applied to the one who is habitually and most notably truthful, a noble and distinctive trait in a believer. Some say that the *ṣiddīqūn* are the most excellent Companions of the Prophet; *al-Ṣiddīq* is after all the name given to the one who was the first to believe in Muḥammad—that is, Abū Bakr—thus setting an example for the rest of the people.[86] After his early acceptance of Islam, Abū Bakr went on to "struggle in regard to God" (*jāhada fī 'llāh*), which caused several later, prominent Companions, such as 'Uthmān b. 'Affān, Ṭalḥa, al-Zubayr, 'Alī, and others to embrace Islam. Compared to the physical *jihād* of 'Alī during the Medinan period, Abū Bakr's nonviolent *jihād* in Mecca was much more meritorious, for it is well-known, continues al-Rāzī, that *jihād* during a period of weakness is more excellent than *jihād* during a period of strength.[87] The Qur'ān also points to the high status in general of those endowed with the quality of veracity, as in Qur'ān 19:54, 56; and 39:33.[88]

With regard to *al-shuhadā'* and *al-shahāda* (which concerns us most), al-Rāzī begins by protesting (one assumes against the prevailing opinion of his time) that it is not permissible to understand *shahāda* here as a reference to the state of "a person killed by an unbeliever." There are at least three reasons for stating this, he says. First, this verse indicates that the merit accruing to *shahāda* is enormous. So how can it refer to being killed by an unbeliever when such an act of slaying is the result of wrongdoing by one who has no standing with God? Second, the believers are wont to beseech God, asking Him to "grant us *al-shahāda.*" If *al-shahāda* here is a reference to being killed by an unbeliever, then such a believing individual has asked God that he be slain in this manner, and that is not permissible, for "to ask that the act of [his] slaying proceed from the unbeliever is itself unbelief. So how can he ask of God something that is [tantamount to] unbelief?" Third, according to a *ḥadīth*, the Prophet said that one who dies from a stomach ailment (*al-mabṭūn*) is a *shahīd*, as is the one who dies from drowning (*al-gharīq*). Thus we learn, al-Rāzī says, "that *al-shahāda* does not refer to being killed." Rather, *al-shahīd* must be understood to be the equivalent of the active participle *al-shāhid*, referring to one "who witnesses to the truth of the religion of God the Exalted, sometimes through logical argumentation and proof (*bi-'l-ḥujja wa-'l-bayān*) and at other times with the sword and the spear." The *shuhadā'* are those who establish justice (*al-qā'imūna bi-'l-qisṭ*), continues al-Rāzī, as is borne out in Qur'ān 3:18, which states, "God Himself is a witness that there is no god but He, as are the angels and the people of learning, establishing justice." The one killed in the path of God is a witness (*shahīd*) to the extent that he has exerted himself in aiding the religion of God and borne witness that it is the truth and distinct from falsehood.[89]

Finally, the *ṣāliḥūn*, in brief, are those who are righteous (*ṣāliḥan*) in their belief and actions. Although every *shahīd* is a righteous person, al-Rāzī says, every righteous person is not necessarily a *shahīd*, that is, one who publicly witnesses to the truth of God's religion, whether through logical proofs or fighting. Every *shahīd* is not a *ṣiddīq*, but every *ṣiddīq* is a *shahīd*, because *ṣiddīq* refers to someone who has preceded others in faith and serves as an example for them through public witness to his or her faith. There is thus a distinct hierarchy of moral excellence adumbrated in this verse, with the prophets at the top and the *ṣāliḥūn* at the bottom, each learning about religion from the category of people immediately above them.[90] It should be stressed here that al-Rāzī's discussion of the proper and comprehensive semantic content of the terms *shahīd* and *shuhadā'* in particular is enormously important and challenges what became the more common ascription of the meaning of military martyr/s to these terms.

Al-Qurṭubī cites the reports concerning various Companions who expressed their sorrow at being separated from the Prophet as providing the occasions of revelation for this verse. With regard to the specific categories of people mentioned in the verse, al-Qurṭubī understands *ṣiddīq* as someone who is extremely devoted to the truth or in affirming the truth in general, and one who implements what he says with his tongue. Some, he notes, have understood this term as referring to the most notable among those who followed the prophets and among the earliest to affirm their prophethood, as in the case of Abū Bakr al-Ṣiddīq. *Al-shuhadā'* here has been understood to refer to 'Umar, 'Uthmān, and 'Alī, and the *ṣāliḥīn* to the rest of the Companions. Others have understood *al-shuhadā'* to refer to those killed in the path of God and the *ṣāliḥīn* as referring to the righteous people in the community of Muḥammad. Al-Qurṭubī is of the opinion that these terms refer broadly to "every righteous person and *shahīd*" (it is not clear if he specifically means witness or martyr here).[91] Al-Qurṭubī thus affirms most of the points discussed by al-Rāzī without contributing anything substantially new to the exegesis of Qur'ān 4:69.

Concluding Remarks

This diversity of views in the exegetical literature concerning the identity of the Qur'ānic *shuhadā'* is highly important and allows us to reconstruct a broader repertoire of meanings for this term in variegated historical circumstances. It also allows us to trace the rise of a cult of martyrdom that privileged the military martyr over all other believers. It is clear that the understanding of the Qur'anic *shuhadā'* as exclusively "military martyrs" started quite early but remained contested through al-Qurṭubī's period (seventh/thirteenth century). Al-Rāzī in particular preserves for us a critical range of non-combative meanings assigned to this term and vigorously queries the meaning of "military martyrs" assigned to *shuhadā'* in Qur'ān 4:69 and asserts its basic meaning of "witnesses." He emphasizes that contrary to popular assumption, the *shuhadā'*—whether understood broadly as witnesses or more narrowly as military martyrs—are not the most morally excellent of people in the Qur'anic milieu; in this verse, they are trumped not only by the *nabiyyūn* (understandably), but also by the *ṣiddīqūn*. The latter group of people earn their privileged position because of their fearless devotion to the truth, which they are not afraid to affirm and bear witness to with their tongues. Al-Rāzī thus understands the *ṣiddīqūn* to subsume the *shuhadā'*, who similarly bear witness to the truth but who cannot attain the moral excellence of the former. This is because the *ṣiddīqūn* are endowed with the quality of singular devotion to the truth which they struggle to proclaim in the face of severe obstacles and dire consequences, as exemplified by Abū Bakr, who carried out this form of non-violent *jihād* in Mecca, deemed by our exegete to be more meritorious than the martial exploits of ʿAlī b. Abī Ṭālib in the Medinan period. Al-Rāzī's valorization of non-martial jihād in the case of Abū Bakr is of course at least partially colored by sectarian concerns against the backdrop of the Sunnī resurgence during the Saljuq period. It is also a corrective to what he clearly perceives to be an excessive reverence for the combative jihād and military martyrdom in certain circles of his time.

A diachronic study as ours thus decisively challenges the understanding of martyrdom in the Islamic context as a static and monolithic concept, unconnected to specific socio-historical circumstances which shaped its variegated inflections through time. As we will see in the next chapter, the shifting semantic landscape pertaining to *jihād* and martyrdom that we have uncovered so far in our study of exegeses is mirrored to a considerable extent in the *ḥadīth* literature as well, and it is similarly exhumed through a comparison of early and late *ḥadīth* works.

V

Jihād *and Martyrdom Compared in Early and Later* Ḥadīth *Literature*

OUR REVIEW OF the exegetical literature in the previous chapters brings into relief the diversity of views that existed in the early period concerning a number of important issues in regard to the military *jihād*. These include, above all, the conditions under which fighting (*qitāl*) as a specific aspect of *jihād* becomes obligatory and upon whom; the moral and ethical restrictions placed on the carrying out of the combative *jihād*; and the permissibility of engaging in fighting at all after the death of the Prophet and under rulers perceived to be morally reprobate. Discussion of these issues became more streamlined in later exegeses and, as we saw, more circumscribed views of *jihād* and of the related concept of martyrdom became manifest in these later works, emphasizing above all their military aspects.

These trends find similar reflection in the *ḥadīth* literature. Comparison of early (from before the late third/ninth century) and late *ḥadīth* works clearly reveals that there were competing definitions of how best to strive in the path of God, engendered by the polyvalence of *jihād* in the Qur'ān. Similarly, early *ḥadīth* works, in contrast to later ones, ascribe a broader range of meanings to the specific Qur'anic locutions *man qutila fī sabīl allāh/alladhīna qutilū fī sabīl allāh* and to the terms *shahīd* and *shuhadā'* that are often not replicated in later works. Thus the extant *ḥadīth* literature from before the period of compilation of the six great authoritative Sunni *ḥadīth* collections (*al-kutub al-sitta*) remains for us an invaluable source for retrieving some of the earliest construals of *jihād* and *shahāda*.

The preservation of the broader semantic content of these terms in diverse early works in comparison with later sources allows us to speculate on the probable historical and sociopolitical reasons for the subsequent circumscription of their meanings. The questions that may be fruitfully posed here are the following: In what post-Qur'anic contexts did the combative aspect of *jihād* become foregrounded, very nearly to the exclusion of other aspects in official circles? How does the *ḥadīth* literature help us illuminate this process of transformation and recreate the probable circumstances in which these changes took place? The following discussion does not claim to be an exhaustive study of the *ḥadīth* literature with a view to answering these questions definitively. Our purpose is rather to broadly canvass and selectively compare the contents of early and later *ḥadīth* works and thereby provide a sense of some of the diachronic transformations occurring in the conceptualizations of these terms. A more detailed analysis of our diachronic study of the *ḥadīth* literature is presented in the Conclusion.

Competing Views on Jihād *and Martyrdom in Early* Ḥadīth *Literature*

The *Muṣannaf* of ʻAbd al-Razzāq al-Ṣanʻānī (d. 211/827)[1]

The *Kitāb al-jihād* section in this early *ḥadīth* compilation by ʻAbd al-Razzāq al-Ṣanʻānī preserves a number of reports attributed to prominent figures of the first two centuries of Islam that convey multiple, contested meanings of the moral imperative "to strive in the path of God." Among such prominent figures are the Ḥijāzī scholars Ibn Jurayj (d. ca. 150/767), ʻAbd Allāh b. ʻUmar (d. 73/693), ʻAmr b. Dīnār (d. 126/743), and Sufyān al-Thawrī (d. 161/778), who was one of ʻAbd al-Razzāq's teachers. These scholars were known for their personal exemplary piety and, sometimes, opposition to the Syrian Umayyad rulers.[2] A number of reports emanating from them and others, selectively discussed below, record important early perspectives on the parameters of *jihād* that became occluded in later works. Full *isnād*s of these reports are occasionally provided when pertinent to our discussion.[3]

One such report is transmitted by ʻAbd al-Razzāq from Ibn Jurayj, who related that he had once inquired of ʻAṭā' b. Abī Rabāḥ whether fighting (*al-ghazw*) was obligatory for all. To this question, ʻAṭā' and ʻAmr b. Dīnār, who was also present, are said to have replied, "We do not know."[4] This report notably encodes the equivocation of early pious authorities about fighting in Umayyad armies with unscrupulous commanders, an equivocation we saw documented in exegetical works as well. A similar hesitancy in endorsing the military *jihād* as an obligatory duty is evident on the part of another well-known early Ḥijāzī scholar, Saʻīd b. al-Musayyab (d. 94/713), who was queried by the Meccan Dā'ūd b. Abī ʻĀṣim as to "whether fighting is obligatory on everyone" (*al-ghazw a-wājib ʻalā al-nās ajmaʻīn*). The former is said to have remained silent (*fa-sakata*).[5] This last report is certainly quite archaic, conveying a clear skepticism on the part of a number of early, particularly Ḥijāzī, authorities as to whether the military *jihād* constituted a religious obligation.

Other reports—prophetic and non-prophetic—preserve a lively, early debate about what constitutes *jihād*. The term is generally used in these cases without the definite article, indicating a broader spectrum of meanings nestled within it. One such *ḥadīth* is narrated by 'Abd al-Razzāq from Ma'mar from 'Abd al-Karīm [b. Mālik] al-Jazarī (d. ca. 127/744),[6] who related that a man once came to the Prophet and told him, "I am a timid man; I cannot bear [the idea] of encountering the enemy." Muḥammad replied, "Shall I not indicate to you a *jihād* in which there is no fighting (*a-lā adulluka 'alā jihād lā qitāl fīhi*)?" When the interlocutor expressed eagerness, the Prophet continued with "The *ḥajj* and the *'umra* are incumbent upon you." A variant *isnād* replaces Ma'mar with Ibn Jurayj,[7] while a variant report, whose *isnād* replaces Ma'mar with Sufyān al-Thawrī, quotes Muḥammad as describing the piligrimage as "a *jihād* which requires no physical strength" (*jihād lā shawka fīhi*).[8] The key transmitters of the variants of this significant *ḥadīth* are all pietists from the Umayyad period who quote Muḥammad as affirming that, first of all, unlike the military *jihad*, the *ḥajj* and the *'umra* are religiously mandated duties; second, *jihād* may be carried out in different ways; and, finally, that it was not shameful or sinful for a man to shun military activity if he had no inclination or aptitude for it. It is worth noting here that this report occurs as a variant in later standard *ḥadīth* compilations counseling *only women* to substitute the pilgrimage for the military *jihād*,[9] signifying the extent to which valor on the battlefield became construed over time as a near-essential ingredient of the adult Muslim male's moral excellence in certain circles.

The multiple significations of the phrase *fī sabīl allāh*, frequently conjoined to *al-jihād*, are heralded in a noteworthy report recorded in 'Abd al-Razzāq's *Muṣannaf*, which relates that a number of the Companions were sitting with the Prophet when a man of muscular build, apparently a pagan from the tribe of Quraysh, came into view. Some of those gathered exclaimed, "How strong this man looks! If only he would expend his strength in the way of God!" The Prophet asked, "Do you think only someone who is killed [sc. in battle] is engaged in the way of God?" He continued, "Whoever goes out in the world seeking licit work to support his family is on the path of God; whoever goes out in the world seeking licit work to support himself is on the path of God. Whoever goes out seeking worldly increase (*al-takāthur*) has gone down the path of the devil" (*fa-huwa fī sabīl al-shayṭān*)."[10] This report is noteworthy for at least two reasons. First, it contains a clear rebuttal to those who would understand "striving in the way of God" in primarily military terms. It praises instead the daily struggle of the individual to live his or her life "in the way of God," which infuses even the most mundane of licit activities with moral and spiritual significance, and thus worthy of divine approbation. Second, the report emphasizes the importance of personal intention in determining the moral worth of an individual's act. Correct *niyya* or intention determines the moral valence of an act, stressed in the famous *ḥadīth*, "Actions are judged by their intentions."[11] Because the meritorious nature of an individual's striving for the sake of God is contingent upon purity of intent, one may understand this report as counseling caution against accepting at face value ostentatious pietism or assuming that what appears to be a pious activity to humans—such as the claim to be waging a true *jihād*—will be deemed as such by God, who alone can know the true intention of an individual.

A particularly hawkish figure in the Umayyad period is the previously encountered Syrian jurist Makḥūl al-Dimashqī (d. between 112/730 and 119/737), who is said to have himself participated in military campaigns.[12] Several reports attributed to him in the *Muṣannaf* advocate relentless military activity as obligatory *jihād*. One such report is recorded by ʿAbd al-Razzāq from the Syrian scholar Saʿīd b. ʿAbd al- ʿAzīz (d. 167/783),[13] who heard Makḥūl relate the following *ḥadīth*: "The Messenger of God, peace and blessings be upon him, said, 'If from among the members of a household no one emerges as a warrior (*ghāz*[in]), nor do they outfit [someone] as a warrior, or designate someone as such, then God will surely afflict them with a calamity before death.'"[14] Another *ḥadīth* of similar tenor is related by Makḥūl from Abū Umāma, who quoted the Prophet as saying, "Fighting in the path of God (*al-jihād fī sabīl allāh*) is obligatory for you, for it is a door among the doors of Paradise and God thereby dispels grief and distress."[15] Finally, according to a report that ʿAbd al-Razzāq heard from an unidentified man, Makḥūl is said to have faced the *qibla* and sworn ten times that "Fighting (*al-ghazw*) is obligatory for you."[16] The stridency of Makḥūl's position as conveyed particularly in this report paradoxically establishes its contested nature in its time.

Counter-reports are recorded by ʿAbd al-Razzāq that assert the obligatory nature of the usual religious requirements and thereby challenge what clearly appeared to many as an unwarranted glorification of the military *jihād*. One report narrated by ʿAbd al-Razzāq from Sufyān al-Thawrī relates that Abū Ḥayyān and others had asserted, "The greater and the lesser pilgrimage are incumbent upon you."[17] Both Sufyān al-Thawrī and Abū Ḥayyān al-Taymī (d. 145/762)[18] are early pietist Kufan authorities; the former is on record as having regarded only the defensive *jihād* to be permissible,[19] a stance that could not have been popular in official Umayyad and certain juridical circles. Interestingly, a harmonizing report is attributed to ʿUmar b. al-Khaṭṭāb, who states that three types of travel are incumbent upon the believer—the greater and lesser pilgrimages, and *jihād* in the path of God.[20]

A report notable for categorically asserting that the usual religious duties are the most important and cannot be displaced by the military *jihād* is related by 'Abd al-Razzāq on the authority of al-Ḥawārī b. Ziyād. According to this report, Ibn Ziyād said that once, when he was sitting with 'Abd Allāh b. 'Umar, a young man came up to him and asked, "Why are you not taking part in *jihād* (*a-lā tujāhid*)?" Ibn 'Umar did not answer and turned away from him, and then responded: "Indeed Islam is founded upon four supports—performance of prayer, giving of the required alms—and no distinction is made between the two; fasting during the month of Ramadan; and pilgrimage to the Sanctuary for the one capable of undertaking it. *Jihād* and voluntary charity are among the good (recommended) actions (*wa-inna 'l-jihād wa-'l-ṣadaqa min al-'amal al-ḥasan*)."[21] A variant report includes Sufyān al-Thawrī in the *isnād* and is attributed to the Companion Hudhayfa b. al-Yamān, who affirms that Islam is founded on eight parts—the two parts of the *shahāda*, prayer, *zakāt*, fasting, pilgrimage, the commanding of the good, and prohibition of wrong—and "whoever has no part in this has failed."[22] The first report related by Ibn Ziyād from 'Abd Allāh b. 'Umar clearly challenges what is perceived as an excessive valorization of military activity in the Umayyad environment and reiterates the traditional religious duties as the most important. The second report, related by Sufyān al-Thawrī from Hudhayfa, makes no mention of the military *jihād* and instead emphasizes the broad moral imperative of commanding the good and preventing evil—what might be regarded as a more capacious view of *jihād*.

Filial and familial devotion, according to other reports, is the best of *jihāds* and distinctly superior to the military variety. In a *ḥadīth*, as related once again by 'Abd Allāh b. 'Umar, the Prophet counseled a man who wished to fight to tend instead to his living parents, for "striving is in regard to them" (*fa-fīhima jihād*).[23] In a variant *ḥadīth* related by the Basran Successor Muslim b. Yasār, Muḥammad advises a young man to return to his family and look after his young children "for one carries out a good *jihād* in regard to them" (*fa-inna fīhim mujāhid ḥasan*).[24] Two other variants, one attributed to al-Ḥasan al-Baṣrī and the other to Muḥammad b. Ṭalḥa, emphasize service to one's mother over the combative *jihād*.[25]

These reports asserting the primacy of non-combative religious acts strongly indicate that, in general, pious and abstemious Ḥijāzī scholars like 'Abd Allāh b. 'Umar, 'Aṭā' b. Abī Rabāḥ, and Ibn Jurayj, less consistently, Kufan scholars like Sufyān al-Thawrī, and occasionally, Basran scholars like al-Ḥasan al-Baṣrī, tended to be against the military adventurism of the Syrian

Umayyads and refused to participate in the effort underway in pro-Umayyad circles to glorify military activity, particularly at the expense of the cultivation of the usual religious virtues and practices as must have appeared to them.[26] Battles fought for worldly reasons were dubbed *jihād* by the Umayyad (and post-Umayyad) rulers to legitimize them in the eyes of the public, a trend that appears to have been clearly challenged by these and other scholars. In contrast to this pietist contingent, mostly Syrian scholars, like Makḥūl, are on record as having adopted more hawkish views (noted above) and eager to impute considerable religious merit to military activities carried out on behalf of the Umayyads.

The not-easily-resolved moral dilemma of serving under reprobate leaders emerges in a few reports in ʿAbd al-Razzāq's *Muṣannaf*, which specifically express ethical qualms concerning fighting in the Umayyad armies. Granted, Islamic realms have to be defended against outside aggressors, but are such acts vitiated by fighting under military commanders whose moral standing is less than stellar? Such qualms are gingerly allayed in one such report attributed to Abū Ḥamza al-Ḍabʿī(?), who is said to have lamented to Ibn ʿAbbās, "We go on campaigns (*naghzū*) with these commanders/rulers (*al-umarāʾ*) but they [only] fight seeking [the gains of] the world." Ibn ʿAbbās counseled him to fight for "your portion in the hereafter."[27] Another relevant report is attributed to Kahmas (d. 149/766),[28] who said that he asked al-Ḥasan [al-Baṣrī] for his advice on fighting with the Umayyads. Kahmas complained to the latter, "We fight with the commanders although we know nothing about their [true] affairs, except that we refrain from fighting when they do, and we fight when they do." Al-Ḥasan replied, "Fight with the Muslims against their enemies."[29] These Companion and Successor reports of Umayyad provenance cautiously express support for the military campaigns of the Umayyad rulers and brand their enemies as the enemies of Muslims in general. At the same time, they also testify to strong reservations on the part of the pious that taking part in the military campaigns spearheaded by rulers—widely perceived as impious—qualified as "fighting in the path of God."[30]

Other reports, attributed once again to prominent religious figures of the late first–second/seventh–eighth centuries, however, forcefully make the point that pious Muslims should have no compunctions about fighting in the Umayyad armies, based on the precedents set by some of the most illustrious Companions and Successors. Thus the Basran scholar Ibn Sīrīn (d. 110/728) is said to have related that the famous Companion-warrior Abū Ayyūb al-Anṣārī would campaign with Yazīd b. Muʿāwiya—the Umayyad ruler of Karbalāʾ infamy no less! According to this report, when Abū Ayyūb fell ill, Yazīd was in his company and, full of solicitude, asked the former if he was in need of anything. Abū Ayyūb replied that he wished to be buried in Byzantine territory. After his death, Yazīd is said to have complied with his wishes and taken part in Abū Ayyūb's burial arrangements.[31] Yazīd's commendable association with a Companion renowned for his virtue and valor confers on the former a patina of religious piety and potentially grants him, on the one hand, absolution for his dastardly role in the Karbalā' massacre, and on the other, establishes his moral credentials to be the leader of a legitimate *jihād*.

Serving in the standing Umayyad army and thus evincing loyalty to the Umayyads appears to have been promoted in official circles as an act of moral excellence in this period. This is suggested in a report attributed to the prominent Successor al-Sha'bī (d. 103/721), who was asked by Jābir whether professional soldiers were more morally excellent (*afḍal*) than volunteers or vice versa. Al-Sha'bī responded that the professional soldiers were more morally excellent, for volunteers can leave whenever they want.[32] Al-Sha'bī's pro-Umayyad sentiments should not come as a surprise; originally from Kufa, he was first in the employ of the Umayyad Caliph 'Abd al-Malik b. Marwān and later served as *qāḍī* under 'Umar b. 'Abd al-'Azīz.[33]

Pro-Umayyad bias becomes most transparent in those *faḍā'il al-jihād* reports that vigorously promote the merits of *ribāṭ* or armed vigilance on the frontiers of the Islamic realms against enemy incursions, a practice that began in the post-prophetic period and became common during the Umayyad period. One particularly hyperbolic report is attributed to Salmān al-Fārisī, who encouraged Shuraḥbīl b. al-Samaṭ in his vigils by quoting the following *ḥadīth*: "*Ribāṭ* for one day in the path of God is better than fasting and standing in prayer for a month. Whoever dies as a *murābiṭ* in the path of God is protected from the torments of the grave and his good deeds multiply until the Day of Judgment."[34] Another report purports to convey the following exhortation from 'Umar b. al-Khaṭṭāb: "*Al-ribāṭ* is prescribed for you for it is the best of military activity."[35]

We know from various historical sources that naval campaigns against the Byzantines were strenuously promoted from the very early Umayyad period; Mu'awiya's shipbuilding activities are documented by several historians.[36] According to several reports in the *Muṣannaf*, these naval campaigns of the Umayyads appear to have been distinctly unpopular in pietist circles and invited the same kind of criticism that their ground campaigns did.[37] Thus 'Abd al-Razzāq relates a significant report according to which Ibn Jurayj queried 'Aṭā' b. Abī Rabāḥ about campaigning at sea, at which the former expressed his dislike and replied, "I am fearful [of them]" (*akhshā*).[38] Other pious objectors included Sa'īd b. al-Musayyab and 'Umar b. al-Khaṭṭāb, both of whom are quoted as expressing repugnance for naval campaigns.[39]

A counter-offensive appears to have been launched by the pro-naval campaign camp as encoded in several reports that hyperbolically advance campaigning at sea as the most meritorious of military activities, trumping in particular the land-based *ribāṭ*. A *ḥadīth* narrated by ʿAlqama b. Shihāb al-Qushayrī[40] quotes Muḥammad as saying, "Whoever was not able to campaign with me let him campaign at sea; for indeed the reward for one day at sea is the equivalent of the reward for a month on land. . . ."[41]

According to another significant *ḥadīth*, as related by ʿAbd al-Razzāq[42] on the authority of the preacher (*al-qāṣṣ*) ʿAṭāʾ b. Yasār (d. between 94–104/712–722),[43] the wife of the Companion Ḥudhayfa reported that once Muḥammad fell asleep in her presence and woke up laughing. When she asked in concern if "you are laughing on my account, O Messenger of God," Muḥammad replied, "No, rather on account of a contingent of people from my community who will set out for campaigns at sea—their likeness will be that of kings upon thrones." Muḥammad then fell asleep a second time, continued ʿAṭāʾ, and once again woke up laughing. Ḥudhayfa's wife inquired about the reason a second time, and he answered that his delight was due to "a group of people who will emerge from my community to fight at sea; they will return with little booty but with their sins forgiven." She asked that the Prophet impore God to make her a member of this group and he did. Later, she did take part in the campaign led by al-Mundhir b. al-Zubayr to Byzantium and died there. This *ḥadīth* is recorded by al-Bukhārī in his *Ṣaḥīḥ* (see below); its inclusion signals his approval of its chain of transmission, but apparently with little regard for the tendentiousness of its content. Reports advocating naval campaigns multiply in the later *Muṣannaf* work of Ibn Abī Shayba, as we will soon see.

A number of the *ḥadīths* and *akhbār* that occur regularly in later collections in exaggerated praise of the combative *jihād* are already found in ʿAbd al-Razzāq's *Muṣannaf*. One such example is the *ḥadīth* narrated by Jābir that quotes Muḥammad as saying, "Whoever is wounded in the path of God will arrive bleeding on the Day of Judgment—his aroma will be that of musk and color that of blood."[44] Another frequently occurring *ḥadīth* in the later literature attributed to al-Ḥasan al-Baṣrī is included by ʿAbd al-Razzāq in which the Prophet states, "Coming and going in the path of God is better than the world and what is in it."[45] These two *ḥadīth*s are recorded in al-Bukhārī's *Ṣaḥīḥ* and other standard collections as well.

Several reports promise abundant rewards to both the victorious warrior and the military martyr. According to Maʿmar and al-Kalbī, the Prophet described the souls of martyrs as assuming the shape of green birds who flit about in paradise and alight upon candelabra hanging below the divine throne.[46] In another *ḥadīth* related by the Companion al-Miqdām b. Maʿdī

Karib al-Kindī, Muḥammad promises nine distinctive rewards reserved for the military martyr: (1) forgiveness from God at the first drop of blood; (2) display of his seat in paradise; (3) bedecking with the adornment of faith; (4) protection from the torments of the grave; (5) marriage with a dark-eyed damsel; (6) safety from the "great terror" [of Judgment Day]; (7) the placing of a crown of honor on his head, each sapphire in it better than the whole world and its contents; (8) marriage with seventy-two dark-eyed damsels; and (9) intercession on behalf of seventy of his relatives.[47]

As this purported *ḥadīth* (in various versions) has gained notoriety in recent times, it is worth dwelling on its chain of transmitters here to determine its status among *ḥadīth* scholars. The *isnād* consisting of primarily Syrian transmitters from Ḥimṣ is as follows: ʿAbd al-Razzāq from Ismaʿīl b. ʿAyyāsh from Buḥayr b. Saʿd from Khālid b. Maʿdan from al-Miqdām b. Maʿdī Karb al-Kindī. The Syrian transmitter Ismāʿīl b. ʿAyyāsh (d. 182/798), also known as Ibn Sulaym al-Ḥimsī, was known for his prolific transmission of reports—"tens of thousands," according to one account,[48] many of which of non-Syrian provenance were deemed to be weak and vitiated by frequent interpolation of both the chains of transmission and the contents, according to al-Bukhārī and others. He is described by some as "upright and most knowledgeable of people about Syrian *ḥadīth*,"[49] but most of the reports that have been attributed to him were deemed "strange" (gharīb) by the reliable authorities (*thiqāt*) of Medina and Mecca and shunned by the Iraqis. Ibn Khuzayma and others had declared that his *ḥadīth*s could not be used as proof-texts.[50] Buḥayr b. Saʿd al-Suḥūlī al-Ḥimṣī is another Syrian transmitter who narrated reports primarily from Khālid b. Maʿdan and Makḥūl, and only those reports of his that were specifically of Syrian provenance were generally deemed to be reliable.[51]

The next transmitter, Khālid b. Maʿdan b. Abī Kurayb al-Kilāʿī al-Shāmī al-Ḥimṣī (d. ca. 103/721), was a Syrian Successor, generally regarded as a *thiqa* and held in high esteem by the Syrian jurist al-Awzāʿī. Khālid b. Maʿdan was, however, prone to relating *mursal* reports (lacking the name of the Companion who would have heard it directly from the Prophet) and did not personally meet a number of the Companions from whom he claimed to be transmitting, as was the opinion of the well-known *muḥaddith* Aḥmad b. Ibrāhīm al-Ismāʿīlī (d. 371/981).[52] Finally, the Companion al-Miqdām b. Maʿdī Karb al-Kindī (d. ca. 86/705), also known as Abū Yaḥyā al-Kindī, settled in Ḥimṣ and narrated reports from staunch warriors like Khālid b. al-Walīd, Abū Ayyūb al-Anṣārī, and others.[53]

The strong Syrian cast to this report, transmitted in this case by authorities specifically based in Ḥimṣ, an important *jund* (province) during the Umayyad period,[54] is not unexpected in a *faḍāʾil al-jihād* report from this period that, as its exaggerated tone leads us to believe, is clearly promoting an unpopular activity. Ratcheting up other-worldly benefits to enhance the lure of joining Umayyad armies, to put it somewhat cynically perhaps, was an understandable tactic under the circumstances. *Isnād* scrutiny reveals the dubious reputations of many of its transmitters—Ismā'īl b. 'Ayyāsh and Khālid b. Ma'dan in particular—that undermine the reliability and probative value of this *ḥadīth.* Its inclusion in 'Abd al-Razzāq's *Muṣannaf* indicates its early provenance, but not its unimpeachability (at least of its *isnād*); unlike other *faḍā'il al-jihād* reports contained in the *Muṣannaf,* this one did not make its way into the famous collections of al-Bukhārī and Muslim. Al-Tirmidhī, who does include a version of this purported *ḥadīth* in one recension of his *Sunan,* classifies it as *ḥasan ṣaḥīḥ gharīb,* indicating its restricted circulation in the early period, despite what he deemed to be an acceptable chain of transmission.[55]

The archaic nature of many of the *faḍā'il* reports in the *Muṣannaf* of 'Abd al-Razzāq in praise of the military *jihād* is established by the fact that it is the warrior (*al-ghāzī*) who is usually compared to the pious non-combatant worshipper to establish the former's religious merit. Reports in praise of the combatant occurring in later *ḥadīth* compilations often reverse this equation and hold up the *ghāzī* as the moral yardstick to whom other devout but non-combatant Muslims are compared and frequently found wanting. Thus a *ḥadīth* narrated by Abū Hurayra likens the [true] *mujāhid* ("for only God knows who truly strives in His path") to the prayerful, fasting individual (*ka-'l-qā'im al-ṣā'im*). Such a true *mujāhid* is vouchsafed paradise should he perish; otherwise, he returns safely to receive his wages or booty.[56] In these reports, the pious worshipper is held up as the ideal to whom the warrior is compared and weighed against.

Definitions of Shahīd

A number of non-prophetic reports in the *Muṣannaf* of 'Abd al-Razzāq relate competing definitions of *shahīd.* It is noteworthy that several of these archaic reports preserve the most expansive, non-combative significations of the term *shahīd.* One report attributed to the Companion Abū Hurayra states that the *shahīd* is one who, were he to die in his bed, would enter heaven. The explanatory note that follows states that it refers to someone who dies in his bed and is without sin (*lā dhanb lahu*).[57] In another memorable report, Mujāhid reports, "Every believer is a witness" (*kull mu'min shahīd*), and then cites as proof-text the following Qur'anic verse: "Those who believe in God and His messengers are the veracious ones and witnesses"[58] (*hum al-ṣiddīqūn wa 'l-shuhadā'*; Qur'ān 57:19). Here we have attestation from an early exegete for understanding the Qur'anic *shuhadā'* as a broad reference to righteous believers who bear witness to the truth, presumably in the way they lead their lives, rather than to military martyrs, as would become the common understanding in a later period.

Several *ḥadīths* and non-prophetic reports specifically challenge those who would emphasize dying on the battlefield as the primary understanding of martyrdom. In one such *ḥadīth* narrated by ʿAbd Allāh b. Nawfal, Muḥammad is quoted as saying, "The one who dies [of natural causes] in the path of God is a martyr" (*al-mayyit fī sabīl allāh shahīd*).[59] One Companion report from Ibn Masʿūd enumerates three kinds of *shahāda* or martyrdom: death as a result of (1) falling off a mountaintop; (2) being devoured by wild animals; and (3) drowning at sea.[60] Another non-prophetic report attributed to the wife of Masrūq b. al-Ajdaʿ declares that there are four types of martyrdom: (1) the plague: (2) parturition or delivery of a child; (3) drowning: and (4) a stomach ailment.[61] Significantly, there is no mention of martyrdom being earned by dying on the battlefield in this early report. An expanded version of this report, however, originating with Abū Hurayra, quotes the Prophet as adding to this list "being killed in the path of God (*al-qatl fī sabīl allāh*)."[62] It is noteworthy that this expanded version containing five definitions of a *shahīd* is recorded later in the *Ṣaḥīḥ* of al-Bukhārī, as we will see shortly.[63]

Relatively few reports in the *Muṣannaf*, compared to later works, record the exaggerated merits of military martyrdom; one example is attributed to Abū Hurayra, who quotes the Prophet as saying, "Whoever dies as a *murābiṭ* dies as a martyr (*shahīd*), and is protected from the torments of the grave, is given his provisions from paradise, and reaps the benefits of his [good] deeds."[64] The paucity of such reports in this early work indicates to us that the cult of martyrdom took somewhat longer to develop, the evidence of which is to be found in the later *ḥadīth* collections from the third/ninth century onward.

The *Muṣannaf* of Ibn Abī Shayba (d. 235/849)

Abū Bakr ʿAbd Allāh b. Muḥammad b. Ibrāhīm b. ʿUthmān al-ʿAbsī al-Kūfī, known as Ibn Abī Shayba, was a traditionist and historian from Iraq, descended from a long line of religious scholars. He studied in al-Ruṣāfa and other places in his quest for knowledge, settled in Baghdad, and died in Kufa. Among his students were Ibn Māja, and his numerous works, besides the *Muṣannaf*, included *Kitāb al-taʾrīkh*, *Kitāb al-fitan*, and *Kitāb al-tafsīr*. The *Muṣannaf*, also known as the *Kitāb al-Musnad*, was declared to be of "canonical" status in the Maghrib along with the authoritative *ḥadīth* compilations of al-Bukhārī, Muslim, Mālik, Abū Dāʾūd, and others.[65]

The extensive section on *jihād* (*Kitāb al-jihād*) in Ibn Abī Shayba's *Muṣannaf*, like ʿAbd al-Razzāq's work, attests to competing early views regarding which activities undertaken "in the path of God" are to be considered the most religiously meritorious and a range of perspectives about the purview of martyrdom. Once again, many of these reports are Syrian in origin and, as in the case of 'Abd al-Razzāq's *Muṣannaf*, often encode pro-Umayyad sympathies in their apparent eagerness to promote the legitimacy of Umayyad military campaigns.

The section begins by recounting several variants of the *ḥadīth* (also found in 'Abd al-Razzāq's *Muṣannaf*) in which the Prophet asserts, "Coming and going in the path of God is better than the world and what is in it." The first variant is related on the authority of Ibn 'Abbās, and the context given is the battle of Mu'ta (8/629). The second variant is attributed to Sahl b. Sa'd, the third to Abū Ayyūb, the fourth to Abū Hurayra, and the last to Anas b. Mālik. Only the third variant has the following, different wording: "Coming and going in the path of God is better than what the sun rises and sets upon."[66] Its ascription to Abū Ayyūb, the Companion who fearlessly fought against the Byzantines and died in Byzantine realms, is likely to raise our suspicion that the original version of the *ḥadīth* set against the battle of Mu'ta is now being co-opted to legitimize Umayyad military activity as fighting in the path of God.

The very high valuation of *jihād* as "better than the world and what is in it" in the reports cited above is contested, however, by a *ḥadīth* recorded by Ibn Abī Shayba, in which the Prophet when asked by 'Abd Allāh b. Mas'ūd about the best or the most morally excellent act, replied, "Prayer at its appointed time," followed by "filial devotion to one's parents," and finally, "*jihād* in the path of God."[67] In this hierarchy of pious and devotional activities, the combative *jihād* is soundly trumped by prayer and filial piety. The full *isnād* of this *ḥadīth* is as follows: Ibn Abī Shayba (referred to as Abū Bakr) reporting from 'Alī b. Mushir from [Abū Isḥāq] al-Shaybānī from al-Walīd b. al-'Ayzār from Sa'd b. Iyās Abī 'Amr al-Shaybānī from 'Abd Allāh [b. Mas'ūd]. Highly noteworthy is the Kufan background of each of these narrators; Kufa, as we recall, was, in addition to the Ḥijāz, a principal pietist site of resistance to the Umayyads and their military activity. This is of course not always a predictable geographical feature but, in general, this "topography" of anti-Umayyad sentiment can be sustained.

In the majority of reports in this collection, it is the "warrior in the path of God" who is compared to the prayerful, abstemious person, unambiguously indicating that through the early Umayyad period, "fighting in the path of God" was more commonly considered to be either inferior or at most morally equivalent, rather than superior, to supererogatory prayer and fasting; the latter activities constituted the moral yardstick. In the later period, the equation was sometimes made in the reverse (see below), indicating a progressively higher moral valuation of the combative *jihād* in influential circles vis-à-vis more common, quotidian acts of piety.

This process of inversion is already evident in a few reports recorded by Ibn Abī Shayba that compare the relative merits of supererogatory fasting and prayer and the undertaking of the military *jihād*. One such report is narrated by Abū Mu'āwiya[68] from Suhayl b. Abī Ṣāliḥ (d. ca. 84/703) from his father from Abū Hurayra, who said that a number of unspecified people asked Muḥammad about "an activity that would be the equivalent of *jihād* in the path of God." The Prophet replied, "You will not be able to bear it." When they protested to the contrary, he said that the equivalent of the fighter in the path of God was the fasting, prayerful individual, who is obedient to the commandments of God and who does not slacken in his zeal for fasting or in spending for charity, until the warrior returns to his family.[69] Inclusion of such infrequent reports in Ibn Abī Shayba's *Muṣannaf* provides valuable evidence of a progressive transformation in a fundamental paradigm of piety, already underway by the late second/eighth century. It should be noted that Suhayl b. Abī Ṣāliḥ's reputation as a *ḥadīth* transmitter is extremely mixed; the famous *ḥadīth* critic Yaḥyā b. Ma'īn, among others, did not consider his reports to be valid as proof-texts.[70]

A number (not all) of the *ḥadīth*s recorded by Ibn Abī Shayba in praise of the military *jihād* give specific contexts for the utterance of these statements. Upon returning with Muḥammad from Tabūk, Mu'ādh b. Jabal is said to have asked the Prophet to inform him about "the pinnacle (*dharwa*) of Islam." He replied, "Its pinnacle is *jihād* in the path of God" (*al-jihād fī sabīl allāh*).[71] Explicit references to specific battles fought by the Prophet that form the backdrop to a number of these *ḥadīth*s in praise of *jihād* convey to the reader that the applicability of these statements is limited to these particular events. In other words, Muḥammad is praising the valor and dedication of his followers during these specific battles fought "in the way of God"—a phrase that is clearly meant to signal that these Muslims fought with the right intention and for a just cause under the leadership of a righteous prophet, who by virtue of his office was privy to infallible directives from God. As we recall, the importance of right intention and establishing just cause for fighting was strongly emphasized by many of the early exegetes previously surveyed, and this is reflected to a considerable extent in the early *ḥadīth* literature as well.

These prerequisites for a legitimate *jihād*—just cause, right intent, and righteous leadership—could be easily fulfilled during the Prophet's time. Could such a situation, however, be replicated in the post-prophetic period in the absence of a truly righteous leader, the purity of whose motives could not be impugned in any way? The doubts we saw expressed by the pious in 'Abd al-Razzāq's *Muṣannaf* concerning fighting "in the way of God" under dissolute Umayyad rulers indicate that at least some were indeed concerned that battles in their time were being waged for base motives and were not religiously meritorious acts at all. Such "slackers" and "doubters" would have to be convinced that the Umayyad rulers were in fact fighting "in the way of God." One obvious way to do this was to circulate *ḥadīths* and non-prophetic reports exhorting the faithful to rally to the Umayyad side by discounting the importance of the personal probity of the military and political leaders, as we caught a glimpse of in 'Abd al-Razzāq's *Muṣannaf*. Another was to take *ḥadīths* already in existence that refer to specific battles fought under the Prophet and generalize these statements to any military campaign fought under any (at least ostensibly) Muslim leader. The level of exhortation was occasionally raised to new emotive levels in these reworked *ḥadīths*, leading us to conclude that the targeted audience was quite reluctant to fall in with Umayyad ambitions. These hortatory attempts could be quite transparently blatant, as *isnād* scrutiny reveals. A number of these reports have chains of transmission that, beyond the first-generation Companion, contain the names of distinctive Umayyad and Syrian personalities, some of whom, like the Syrian jurist al-Awzā'ī, Khālid b. al-Walīd and Mu'āwiya, were known for their enthusiasm for campaigning against the Byzantines. The names of other prominent Umayyad personalities, like 'Umar b. 'Abd al- 'Azīz, Makḥūl (d. 13/731), Ibn Sīrīn, and lesser members of the Umayyad dynasty, also feature occasionally in the *isnāds* of these reports.

An example of such a hortatory *ḥadīth* with a rather dubious pedigree is as follows: 'Abd Allāh b. Mubārak (reporting from al-Awzā'ī from Yaḥyā b. Abī Kathīr from Abū Sa'īd al-Khudrī) related that the Prophet had remarked, "Those who press themselves into the first row [on the battlefield] and do not turn their faces until they are killed are those who are frolicking in the highest pavilions (*al-ghuraf al-'ulyā*) of paradise. Your Lord laughs [in pleasure] at them. Indeed when your Lord laughs at a people [in pleasure], there is no reckoning for them."[72] We are not too surprised to find that the Basran transmitter Yaḥyā b. Abī Kathīr (d. between 129/746 and 132/749), who links al-Awzā'ī to Abū Sa'īd al-Khudrī, was accused of lying about his authorities (*tadlīs*) and relating *mursal* reports. According to Abū Ḥātim, the only Companion Yaḥyā had come into contact with was Anas, and that was only through a dream![73]

Furthermore, two features of this report are worth dwelling on. First, the *isnād* contains the names of 'Abd Allāh b. al-Mubārak and al-Awzā'ī; the former was a pious, "ascetic" warrior who wrote a well-known work cataloging the merits of the combative *jihād* (discussed in the next chapter) and who took part in military activities against the Byzantines. The latter scholar was a pro-Umayyad jurist, who served in the government in al-Yamāma in Syria.[74]

There are in fact a number of reports in Ibn Abī Shayba's *Muṣannaf* with this specific *isnād*. Second, this report consciously borrows Qur'anic vocabulary to set up a competing hierarchy of moral excellence that privileges the combative aspects of *jihād* over its non-combative ones. In the Qur'ān, "the paradisiacal pavilion" (*al-ghurfa*; for example, Qur'ān 25:75)[75] and "recompense without measure or reckoning" (*ajrahum bi-ghayr ḥiṣāb*; Qur'ān 39:10; cf. 40:40) are promised specifically and exclusively to those who are patiently forbearing (*al-sābirūn*; cf. our discussion of this verse in chapter 7). Reassignment of these Qur'anic posthumous rewards away from the non-combative pious Muslim to the unflinching Muslim warrior defending Umayyad realms against outside aggressors leads to a corresponding devaluation of the moral excellence of the former.

A high estimation of *ṣabr* is, however, evident in a prophetic report that states that the one who patiently endures the abusive behavior of a neighbor is equally beloved of God as the one who fights the enemy and is either slain or is victorious, as well as the one who attends to prayer even while traveling.[76] This *ḥadīth* emanates from Abū Dharr, the Companion famed for his self-effacing piety. Another *ḥadīth* firmly yokes *ṣabr* to being killed in the path [of God],[77] making it an even more meritorious activity. In this *ḥadīth* narrated by 'Abd Allāh b. Abī Qatāda from his father, the Prophet in response to a query from Qatāda's father assures him that were he to be slain in the path of God while patiently accepting his lot (*ṣābiran muḥtasiban*) and without ever retreating, God would forgive all his sins except for his debts.[78]

A number of reports specifically weigh and compare the relative merits of undertaking the combative *jihād* and performance of the *ḥajj*, encoding for us valuable shifting and competing views in this period on what constitutes the more meritorious religious activity. Thus one report related by the Kufan traditionist Wakī' b. al-Jarrāḥ (d. 197/812)[79] states that "Departing in the path of God is better than ten pilgrimages for the one who has already performed the *ḥajj*."[80] This report, attributed to the Companion Anas b. Mālik, regards the combative *jihād* as superior to non-obligatory pilgrimages (i.e., those performed after the one pilgrimage incumbent upon the Muslim capable of undertaking it). Another report, also narrated by Wakī' states that taking part in a military campaign (*safra/ghazwa*) is better than "fifty pilgrimages."[81] Two distinctive features of this latter report are worthy of note: First, it is attributed to the Companion 'Abd Allāh b. 'Umar, who was sometimes harnessed as a purveyor of pro- 'Uthmāniyya/Umayyad perspectives.[82] Second, compared to the first report from Wakī' it appears to be unequivocal in its endorsement of the combative *jihād* as the more meritorious religious activity in comparison with the required *ḥajj*, since it does not make clear that this report specifically concerns the individual who has already performed one required pilgrimage. As other early sources, like the *siyar* work composed by the Kufan jurist Abū Isḥāq al-Fazārī (d. after 185/802), preserve reports that assert that the *ḥajj* was more excellent than *jihād* as a religious activity,[83] we may reasonably conclude that the 'Abd Allāh b. Umar report is a late one. The report attributed to Anas may be regarded as a transitional one.

Several laudatory *ḥadīths* and non-prophetic reports occur in the *Muṣannaf* of Ibn Abī Shayba that specifically praise *ribāṭ* as being more meritorious than other acts of devotion. Thus, according to 'Īsā b. Yūnus who related a *ḥadīth* attributed to Salmān al-Fārisī (whose *isnād* contains the name of the hawkish Syrian jurist Makḥūl), the Prophet said, "*Ribāṭ* for a day in the path of God is better than fasting for a month and standing up [for prayer during its nights]. Whoever dies as a *murābiṭ* will be spared the punishment of the grave and his virtuous acts will encompass him until the Day of Judgment."[84] This highly laudatory report bears comparison with the reports we discussed earlier that consider *jihād* in the way of God to be equivalent to prayer and fasting, rather than more meritorious. A Companion report from Abū Hurayra that has al-Awzā'ī's name in the *isnād* proclaims, "If you carry out *ribāṭ* for three [days], then one may worship as one pleases."[85] Other *ḥadīths* in which Muḥammad asserts that the period of fulfilment of *ribāṭ* is forty days are equipped with preponderantly Syrian-Umayyad *isnāds*. One such *isnād* lists 'Īsā b. Yūnus reporting from Mu'āwiya b. Yaḥyā al-Ṣadafī from Yaḥyā b. al-Ḥārith al-Dhimārī from Makḥūl.[86] 'Īsā b. Yūnus b. Abī Isḥāq (d. ca. 187/802), who is a frequent source for Ibn Abī Shayba of pro-*ribāṭ* reports, was originally from Kufa but settled in Syria. He is said to have undertaken the pilgrimage and *ribāṭ* in alternate years and taken up residence at the frontiers (*al-thughūr*), where he also died.[87]

How important *ribāṭ* had become in the Umayyad period is indicated in a distinctive report that equates *ribāṭ* carried out on horseback with the giving of charity in exegesis of Qur'an 2:274, which cites, "Those who spend their wealth at night and during the day, secretly and openly." It is related by the later Kufan scholar Zayd b. al-Ḥabbāb (d. 203/818)[88] and attributed to Sahl b. 'Ajlān al-Bāhilī, who remarked, "Whoever carries out *ribāṭ* on horseback in the path of God, and does not do so in order to gain renown and prestige, is among those who spend their wealth day and night."[89] Other significant reports encode recognition of the fact that *ribāṭ* could be particularly arduous and dangerous along the coast; coastal *ribāṭ* is thus portrayed as morally superior to land-based *ribāṭ* in these hortatory reports. Once again, 'Īsā b. Yūnus is quoted, this time relating on the authority of Abū Hurayra a variant of the report cited above in which the Companion promises rewards in the grave for *ribāṭ* until the Day of Judgment, except that 'Īsā b. Yūnus this time refers specifically to vigilance on the coast (*sāḥil al-baḥr*).[90] In another report, ʿAbd Allah b. ʿAmr b. al-ʿĀṣ remarked that taking part in sea campaigns was more beloved to him than spending a single coin in the path of God.[91]

An even more explicit report leaves no doubt in the reader's mind that during the Umayyad period, naval campaigns began to take precedence over land forays. As a consequence, this preferred military activity of the time is presented as the more religiously meritorious activity in specific reports that continued to be disseminated in the later period. According to the later Kufan scholar Isḥāq b. Manṣūr al-Salūlī (204/819), the earlier Kufan scholar Yaḥyā b. ʿIbād b. Shaybān (d. ca. 120/737) is reported to have remarked, "The superiority (*faḍl*) of the one who fights on sea (*al-ghāzī fī 'l-baḥr*) over the one who fights on land is comparable to the superiority of the one who fights on land over the one who sits at home."[92] Clearly, there were Umayyad supporters among Kufan scholars as well. Reports advocating the merits of naval campaigns were also usefully disseminated in the ʿAbbasid period by al-Salūlī and others.

Finally, Ibn Abī Shayba includes a number of reports that exist in the earlier Muṣannaf of ʿAbd al-Razzāq. Thus we have a reference to the report that stated Makḥūl would face the *qibla* and swear for ten days that "fighting [*al-ghazw*] is incumbent upon you." But whereas in ʿAbd al-Razzāq's *Muṣannaf*, the report was attributed to an unidentified man, in Ibn Abī Shayba's *Muṣannaf*, it is attributed to the Basran scholar Muḥammad b. Bakr (d. ca. 203/818) narrating from Ibn Jurayj from Maʿmar.[93] Muḥammad b. Bakr b. ʿUthmān al-Bursānī, also known as Abū ʿUthmān al-Baṣrī, is generally regarded as a *thiqa*, who frequently transmitted from Ibn Jurayj and others, and from whom Aḥmad b. Ḥanbal and Yaḥyā b. Maʿīn, among others, related reports.[94]

It is also Muḥammad b. Bakr who informs us that Saʿīd b. al-Musayyab appeared to have disagreed with Makḥūl's position on the obligatory nature of the military *jihād*, a report we encountered earlier in ʿAbd al-Razzāq's *Muṣannaf*. In Ibn Abī Shayba's version, Muhammad b. Bakr related from Ibn Jurayj who said that Dāʾūd [b. Abī ʿĀṣim] had informed him that when he asked Ibn al-Musayyab whether fighting (*al-ghazw*) was obligatory on all the people (*ʿalā 'l-nās ajmaʿīn*), he remained silent (*fa-sakata*). Dāʾūd appears to have interpreted this silence as tacit affirmation on Ibn al-Musayyab's part and announced his intention to carry out *ribāṭ*.[95]

A similar hesitancy to unequivocally endorse fighting as obligatory is apparent in the case of the Ḥijāzī scholars ʿAṭāʾ b. Abī Rabāḥ and ʿAmr b. Dīnār, as was also recorded by ʿAbd al-Razzāq in his *Muṣannaf*. In Ibn Abī Shayba's version, their interlocutor is Ibn al-Mubārak (instead of Ibn Jurayj), and he asks them whether *al-ghazw* was a required duty; both of them replied, "We do not know."[96] In this cluster of reports, we note once again a significant divergence in views attributed to Ḥijāzī scholars (equivocal or tacitly against) and Syrian scholars (generally in favor) on the obligation to fight.

In another report, Ibn Fuḍayl relates that 'Umar had stated that faith had four props: prayer, alms-giving, *jihād*, and integrity (*al-amāna*).[97] Worthy of note is that the term *jihād* (without the definite article) is used here instead of the more frequent *ghazw*, and therefore it is more likely a broader reference here to a general striving in the path of God. A report from 'Ā'isha suggests that some people did not take part in military campaigns (*fa-lā yaghzūnā*) more out of cowardice than out of a willful shirking of religious duty, conveying the view that *jihād* was elective and contingent upon personal preference.[98] We also encounter the highly significant report in which a certain Yazīd b. Bishr al-Saksakī[99] relates that he traveled to Medina and visited 'Abd Allāh b. 'Umar there. An Iraqi man came to Ibn 'Umar and reproached him in the following manner: "What is the matter with you that you perform the *ḥajj* and *'umra* but have abandoned fighting in the path of God (*al-ghazw fī sabīl allāh*)?" To which Ibn 'Umar responded, "Fie on you! Faith is founded on five: that you worship God, perform the prayer, give *zakāt*, perform the pilgrimage and fast during Ramadan. This is according to what the Messenger of God, peace and blessings be upon him, [has] told us. After that *jihād* is fine (*thumma al-jihād ḥasan*)."[100] This report, like the variant recorded earlier by 'Abd al-Razzāq, is a resounding reprimand to those who harbor an excessive regard for the military *jihād* as a religious obligation. It contains a firm reminder that the essential duties for a Muslim remain the five pillars (in Ibn Abī Shayba's version, the first pillar of faith is added); the military *jihād*, if one should choose to engage in it, is, according to this report, a voluntary act, which by its very nature could not displace any one of the five pillars as a fundamental obligation for the faithful.

Interestingly and significantly, Ibn Abī Shayba records another report in which none other than Ibn 'Umar extols the merits of *jihād*. It is narrated by Mu'ādh (from Ibn 'Awn from Nāfi'), who stated that Ibn 'Umar would go on military campaigns himself and would remark that *jihād* in the path of God was the best action after prayer.[101] Once again, the existence of these two reports encoding contradictory positions allows us to speculate that Ibn 'Umar is being invoked as an early authority in certain quarters to lend credence to contested views on the excellence of *jihād* versus the excellence of more common and basic acts of piety. It is worthy of note that in comparison with the first report from Ibn 'Umar, which asserts that all five pillars of Islam are ahead of *jihād* in moral excellence, only prayer precedes *jihād* in merit in the latter report.

Martyrdom

Like 'Abd al-Razzaq's *Muṣannaf*, Ibn Abī Shayba's *Muṣannaf* also evidences a diversity of early and competing views on what constitutes martyrdom and who qualifies for it. This work, like its predecessor, attests to both combative and non-combative perspectives on martyrdom, but goes even further in ascribing exaggerated posthumous rewards to the military martyr in particular. Most of these reports are non-prophetic and often attributed to a Companion or Successor; only a few are ascribed to the Prophet.

One such *ḥadīth* (a *mursal* report) is narrated by the Basran scholar Ḥātim b. Wardān (d. 184/800)[102] from another Basran transmitter Yūnus [b. 'Ubayd Allāh][103] from the Successor al-Ḥasan [al-Baṣrī]. In this *ḥadīth*, Muḥammad is quoted as saying that the average [pious] person after death is pleased with his [or her] reward in the hereafter and has no desire to return to this world. But when he becomes aware of the abundance of good things (*al-na'īm*) that await the martyr (*al-shahīd*), then he yearns to go back in order to be slain.[104] Here the *shahīd* is specifically identified as a military martyr, whose moral status in this report is higher than that of an average believer. Another non-prophetic report assigns specific, detailed rewards to the military martyr denied to any other. It is narrated by, once again, Ḥātim b. Wardān from the Syrian-Basran transmitter Burd b. Sinān (d. 135/752)[105] from Makḥūl, who states, "The martyr has six distinctive features in the presence of God: God forgives his sins as soon as the first drop of his blood strikes the earth; he will enjoy the vestments of faith; he will marry a dark-eyed celestial damsel (*al-ḥūr al-'ayn*); a door to paradise will open for him; he will be spared the torments of the grave; and, finally, he will be kept safe from the greatest fear—that of the Day of Resurrection."[106] Once again, we notice a general trend of Syrian and Basran scholars to promote the merits of combative *jihād* and military martyrdom. We may recall that a variant version of this report attributed to al-Miqdām b. Ma'dī Karib al-Kindī that confers nine distinctions on the martyr was recorded earlier by 'Abd al-Razzāq.[107]

But, as in 'Abd al-Razzāq's *Muṣannaf*, other *ḥadīths* and non-prophetic reports challenge such a circumscribed understanding of martyrdom and its purview. Thus the Kufan transmitter 'Abd Allāh b. Numayr (d. 199/814)[108] relates the following *ḥadīth* attributed to Abū Hurayra:

> I heard the Messenger of God, peace and blessings be upon him, ask, "Who do you regard as *shahīd*?" Those present replied, "One who is slain in the path of God (*al-maqtūl fī sabīl allāh*)." The Prophet exclaimed, "Then the martyrs of my community would be few indeed! The one who is slain (*al-qatīl*) in the path of God is a martyr; the one

who is felled to the ground from his mount in the path of God is a martyr; the one who drowns in the path of God is a martyr; and the one who is stricken by pleurisy in the path of God."[109]

In a variant *ḥadīth* narrated by Wakīʿ on the authority of the Companion ʿUbāda b. al-Ṣāmit, the Prophet asks a similar question of his Companions regarding who are to be counted among the martyrs. When they identified the one who fights in the path of God and is then slain as a martyr, Muḥammad exclaimed that the martyrs of his community would be too few in number. He proceeded to include among martyrs, beside the one slain in the path of God, the one who dies from a stomach ailment and the woman who dies during childbirth.[110]

Two other variant non-prophetic reports are worthy of note. One related by once again Wakīʿ on the authority of the Companion ʿAbd Allāh b. Masʿūd includes the one who drowns in the sea, or falls from the mountain, or is eaten by wild animals among "the martyrs in the presence of God on the Day of Resurrection."[111] The final variant is reported by the Basran transmitter ʿAbd al-Wahhāb b. ʿAbd al-Majīd al-Thaqafī (d. 194/809)[112] on the authority of the Kufan Successor Masrūq b. Ajdaʿ (d. 63/682), who related, "The plague, the stomach [ailment], parturition, drowning, and whatever afflicts a Muslim constitutes martyrdom (*shahāda*) for him."[113] In all these reports with a preponderance of Iraqi transmitters, martyrdom in the path of God is expansively construed as death resulting from any kind of suffering and pain endured by the faithful during their earthly existence. The last five variant reports do not specifically use the phrase *fī sabīl allāh* for the non-combat-related afflictions and injuries, as does the immediately preceding one (excerpted above), but the implication is nevertheless clear: Earthly suffering for the righteous leading to death places practically all of life's hardships conducive to death within the purview of martyrdom, a view explicitly stated in the last report from Masrūq (who, it is important to note, as also reported by ʿAbd al-Razzāq, did not specifically include dying on the battlefield as constituting a type of martyrdom).

A significant report recorded by Ibn Abī Shayba contains an early challenge to a potential cult of martyrdom. Its *isnād* is Kufan; the report is narrrated by the Kufan *mawlā* Khālid b. Mukhallad (d. 213/828)[114] from ʿAlī b. Ṣāliḥ (d. ca. 151/768)[115] from his father, who reported that the Successor al-Shaʿbī (d. 103/721) had stated, "The victor in the path of God is better than the one who is slain" (*al-ghālib fī sabīl allāh afḍal min al-maqtūl*).[116] Al-Shaʿbī's statement begs comparison with a *ḥadīth* also recorded by Ibn Abī Shayba with a mixed Iraqi chain (narrated by Yazīd b. Hārūn from the highly regarded Basran transmitter Hishām al-Dastawāʾī [d. ca. 152/769][117] from Yaḥyā b. Abī Kathīr from ʿĀmir al- ʿUqaylī[118] from his father) from Abū Hurayra, who related that the Prophet had remarked, "The first three of my community who will enter heaven were presented before me: the martyr, the pious slave who is not distracted by the pleasures of life from obeying his Lord, and the virtuous poor person with dependents."[119] The martyr here need not be an exclusive reference to the military type; in any case, these three individuals are deemed to be completely morally equivalent. In contrast to the statement by al-Sha'bī recorded above, this *ḥadīth* glorifies sincere self-sacrifice in the service of God, however it may be accomplished. In some later, especially *faḍā'il al-jihād*, works (as we will see in chapter 6), the status of the military martyr would be considerably aggrandized vis-à-vis pious, non-combative Muslims in highly tendentious reports.

Competing Views on Jihād *and Martyrdom in the* Ṣaḥīḥayn

The *Ṣaḥīḥ* of al-Bukhārī (d. 256/870)

Compared with these early *Muṣannaf* works, the tenor of the reports in the chapter entitled *Kitāb al jihād wa-'l-siyar* in al-Bukhārī's *ḥadīth* compilation is rather different. First of all, it contains only prophetic reports regarding a much narrower range of topics related to the combative *jihād*, preparations for it, and conduct during it. According to the compiler's criteria, the Companion reports that were amply recorded by 'Abd al-Razzāq and Ibn Abī Shayba have been effectively weeded out. From our perspective, this streamlining process has rendered al-Bukhārī's's collection less useful for tracing the progressive transformation in the meanings of *jihād* and *shahāda* and for exhuming competing views among the earliest Muslims regarding their semantic and legal purview. The work, however, still preserves a modest range of early competing views on the necessity of *jihād* and its relation to other religious activities, which we now discuss briefly.

A *ḥadīth* narrated by 'Abd Allāh b. Mas'ūd, previously recorded by Ibn Abī Shayba regarding the merits of various pious acts relative to one another (see above), is also included by al-Bukhārī. According to this report, when 'Abd Allāh b. Mas'ūd queried the Prophet regarding the best action, he replied, "Prayer at its appointed time." When Ibn Mas'ūd asked, "And then?" Muḥammad replied, "Devotion (*birr*) to parents." Ibn Mas'ūd repeated, "And then?" to which the Prophet responded, "*Jihād* in the path of God." He did not add anything else to that, records al-Bukhārī.[120] Obligatory acts of worship, like the daily prayers, and devoted service to one's parents continue to outweigh fighting in the path of God, according to this report.

The greater moral excellence of filial devotion compared to *jihād* is unambiguously underscored in another *ḥadīth* narrated by Ādam [b. Abī Īyās;

d. 221/835] on the authority of ʿAbd Allāh b. ʿUmar, who related that a man came to Muḥammad and asked the latter's permission to take part in fighting (*fī 'l-jihād*). The Prophet asked, "Are your parents alive?" The man replied, "Yes." The Prophet advised, "Then strive [or do *jihād*] with regard to them" (*fa-fīhima fa-jāhid*).[121]

Al-Bukhārī's chapter on *jihād* encodes the by-now-familiar competing views on what constitutes the best of supererogatory acts. According to a *ḥadīth* narrated by Abū 'l-Yamān (from Shuʿayb from al-Zuhrī f rom ʿAṭā' b. Yazīd al-Laythī from Abū Saʿīd al-Khudrī), Muḥammad was once asked who was the best among people (*ayyu 'l-nās afḍal*). He replied, "A believer who strives in the path of God with his self and his wealth." "Then who?" he is asked. The Prophet replies, "Then a believer who [lives] in a ravine (*shiʿb*) reverencing God and averting wrongdoing on his part from reaching the people." In another *ḥadīth* with an identical *isnād* up to al-Zuhrī, who then transmits from Saʿīd b. al-Musayyab relating from Abū Hurayra, the Prophet remarked, "The fighter in the path of God—and God knows best who fights in His path—is like the fasting, prayerful one (*ka-mathal al-ṣā'im al-qā'im*). And God has vouchsafed for the fighter in His path a generous reward by causing him to enter Paradise or causing him to return safely with a recompense (*ajr*) or booty (*ghanīma*)."[122] In both these *ḥadīths* we detect a tension between activist and quietist definitions of striving in the path of God and the concern for setting up a hierarchy of moral excellence that evaluates the relative merits of both.

Interestingly, Qur'an 3:200 is firmly yoked to the post-prophetic activity of *ribāṭ* in the heading of section #715. The *ḥadīth* in question is now the familiar one that extols the *ribāṭ* of one day in the path of God as being better than the world and what it contains.[123] The *Ṣaḥīḥ* also records the *ḥadīth* previously encountered in ʿAbd al-Razzāq's *Muṣannaf* in praise of naval warfare, in which the Prophet expresses joy over the future prospect of "a contingent of people from my community who will ride the seas like kings astride their thrones...."[124]

Suicide is categorically forbidden according to a noteworthy report recorded by al-Bukhārī. In this *ḥadīth* related by Abū Hurayra, the Prophet is quoted as consigning to hellfire a man who had fought valiantly in a battle, was wounded, and then took his own life because he could not stand the pain.[125] Another noteworthy *ḥadīth* from Ibn ʿAbbās asserts that there was no more migration (*hijra*) after the fall of Mecca, but that *jihād* with the proper intention would continue.[126] The content of this *ḥadīth* clearly challenges the amorphous group of people we encountered earlier who maintained that there was no more military *jihād* after the time of the Prophet, since it was an obligation solely placed upon him and the Companions .

Compared to the two earlier *Muṣannafs*, al-Bukhārī's *Ṣaḥīḥ* records primarily *ḥadīths* that specifically praise the military *jihād* and describe the posthumous rewards promised to the military martyr in particular. References to non-combative martyrdom and its virtues occur, but are noticeably fewer in this section on *jihād* and *siyar*, indicating to us the streamlining of these topics during this period of *ḥadīth* compilation and the winnowing away of reports containing non-combative significations of *jihād*. Typically, these latter reports would then be placed in chapters titled *riqāq*/*raqā'iq*, *zuhd*, etc.[127] Among such reports included in the *Kitāb al-jihād* section of the *Ṣaḥīḥ* is a noteworthy one narrated by Abū Hurayra in which Muḥammad declares martyrs to be of five kinds: those who die from the plague, from stomach ailments, from drowning, from being crushed to death [perhaps by a falling wall], and by suffering martyrdom in the path of God (*wa-'l-shahīd fī sabīl allāh*).[128] In another report transmitted by Anas b. Mālik, the Prophet states that "The plague is [a source of] martyrdom (*shahāda*) for every Muslim."[129]

In comparison with the earlier *Muṣannafs*, more reports recorded in the *Ṣaḥīḥ* assign a privileged status to military martyrs with special rewards in the hereafter earmarked for them alone; some of these reports were not previously encountered by us. In a *ḥadīth* narrated by Abū Hurayra, the Prophet says the following: "Whoever believes in God and His Messenger, performs the prayers, and fasts during Ramadan, God is obligated to cause him to enter paradise, whether he strove/fought (*jāhada*) in the path of God or remained sedentary in the land he was born in." When the people gathered commented, "O Messenger of God, may we not give these good tidings to the people?" the Prophet continued, "There is in heaven hundred levels (*mi'ata daraja*) which God has prepared for those who fight in the way of God (*al-mujāhidīn fī sabīl allāh*); the distance between each level is like the distance between the sky and the earth."[130] A *ḥadīth* on the authority of Samura [b. Jundub] states that there is an "abode of martyrs" (*dār al-shuhadā'*),[131] which is the best and most excellent of abodes in the hereafter.[132] Another *ḥadīth* narrated by Anas b. Malik asserts that only the martyrs among the pious will wish to return to earth and be killed repeatedly in order to continue to multiply the abundant posthumous rewards awaiting them, a variant *mursal* version of which, emanating from al-Ḥasan al-Baṣrī, we encountered earlier in Ibn Abī Shayba's *Muṣannaf*.[133] Anas is also said to have reported from the Prophet that "Coming and going in the path of God is better than the world and what is in it."[134]

One *ḥadīth* on the authority of Abū Hurayra declares that whoever is wounded in the path of God (and God knows best who is truly wounded in His path) will be resurrected on the Day of Judgment with the color of blood and breath of musk.[135] Those who are on the "path of God" are identified in one *ḥadīth* related by Abū Mūsā [al-Ash'arī] as "those who fight so that the word of God may be supreme."[136] The circulation of such *ḥadīths* signals a heightened attempt in a number of influential circles to underscore the unique, even greater, moral status of the soldier and the military martyr, noticeably departing thereby in tenor and content from sections on *jihād* contained in the two aforementioned *Muṣannafs*.

Some *ḥadīths* warn, however, that the exalted status of the soldier should not lead to the deliberate courting of martyrdom on the part of the faithful by seeking to confront the enemy. One such *ḥadīth* on the authority of 'Abd Allāh b. Abī Awfā relates that the Prophet during a military campaign would customarily wait till the sun had tilted toward the West and then address his troops with these words: "Do not wish to meet the enemy, O People, and ask forgiveness of God. When you meet them, be forbearing (*fa-'ṣbirū*) and know that paradise lies below the shade of the swords."[137] In truncated form, "paradise lies below the shade of the swords" appears to be an unqualified endorsement of warring. Within the context of the full *ḥadīth*, however, the overall meaning is that one should attempt to avoid armed combat; when such combat becomes unavoidably necessary under certain legitimate conditions, then one should fight patiently and earnestly, for which there is heavenly reward.

The *Ṣaḥīḥ* of Muslim b. al-Ḥajjāj (d. 261/875)

A great number of *ḥadīths* in Muslim's chapter on al-*jihād wa-'l-siyar* have to do with the division of spoils, the minutiae of which need not engage us here. An additional section on the "merits of *jihād* and departing in the path of God" (*bāb faḍl al-jihād wa-'l-khurūj fī sabīl allāh*) is included within the chapter that follows in the *Ṣaḥīḥ* on statecraft (*bāb al-imāra*), signifying the intimate connection that was assumed between the state and warfare.

At the beginning of the section *al-jihād wa-'l-siyar*, Muslim records two *ḥadīths* that expressly forbid seeking to engage the enemy in battle. The first is attributed to Abū Hurayra and quotes the Prophet as saying, "Do not wish to meet the enemy; when you meet them, be patient." The second is attributed to 'Abd Allāh b. Abī Awfā; the text (but not the *isnād*) is identical to the version recorded by al-Bukhārī referred to above.[138]

Two noteworthy *ḥadīths*, one from 'Abd Allāh [b. Mas'ūd] and the other from Ibn 'Umar, forbid the killing of women and children during battles.[139] Two other reports from Ibn 'Abbās emphasize the Prophet's specific proscription against the killing of children.[140] But a contradictory report (not recorded by al-Bukhārī), three variants of which are all attributed to Ibn 'Abbās relating from the Companion al-Ṣa'b b. Jaththāma, states that when

Muḥammad was asked (interlocutor not named) about the status of "the children of polytheists" in the context of warfare, he replied, "they are one of them."[141] One of the variants lists 'Abd al-Razzāq transmitting from Ma'mar from al-Zuhrī in its *isnād*, but we did not encounter this *ḥadīth* in his extant *Muṣannaf*.

Reports detailing the merits of *jihād* and dealing with prescribed and proscribed conduct during battle occur not in this *jihād wa-siyar* chapter, but in a subsequent, separate section entitled *bāb fadl al-jihād wa-'l-khurūj fī sabīl allāh*, as previously mentioned. The contents of most of these reports are by now familiar to us: expressing the desire to repeatedly fight and be slain in the path of God (from Abū Hurayra);[142] the characterization of returning from *jihād* as being better than the world and everything within it (five variants attributed variously to Anas b. Mālik, Sahl b. Sa'd al-Sā'idī, Abū Hurayra, and Abū Ayyūb);[143] and describing the martyr as one who is still bloodstained upon resurrection but emitting the fragrance of musk (from Abū Hurayra)[144] and who wishes to return to earth upon discovering the posthumous merits accruing to military martyrdom (from Anas b. Mālik).[145]

Other hierarchies of moral excellence are suggested in various reports contained in the *Ṣaḥīḥ*; according to Abū Qatāda, faith in God and striving (*al-jihād*) in the path of God are equally the most meritorious of actions (*afḍal al-a'māl*). Here *jihād* is clearly military in nature, for the *ḥadīth* continues with an unnamed man asking if all his sins would be forgiven if he were slain in the path of God. The answer was in the affirmative, with the exception of debts. Several variants of this well-known *ḥadīth* are given.[146] One *ḥadīth* related by Abū Hurayra states that fighting in the path of God on horseback was the best way to earn one's livelihood (*min khayr ma'āsh al-nās lahum*).[147] A cluster of variant reports from Anas b. Mālik quotes Muḥammad as expressing his approval for those among his community who fight at sea.[148]

As we also observed in regard to al-Bukhārī's *Ṣaḥīḥ*, collation of these various reports listed above extolling the merits of *jihād* in Muslim's collection does not yet suggest the **greater** moral excellence of the military *jihād* vis-à-vis the more predictable and supererogatory acts of worship, as would become more common in later *faḍā'il al-jihād* works; they suggest either its secondary importance to faith, prayer, and fasting or their equivalence. This order of moral excellence is strongly indicative of the relatively archaic nature of these *ḥadīth*s recorded in the *Ṣaḥīḥayn*. However, a handful of reports in Muslim's *Ṣaḥīḥ* attempt to reverse this hierarchy. One is attributed to Abū Sa'īd al-Khudrī, who related that the Prophet had affirmed that "a man who strives in the path of God with his wealth and his self" was more morally excellent than the Muslim who had taken refuge in an isolated ravine (*shi'b min* *al-shiʿāb*) to worship God exclusively and to avoid causing harm to people,[149] a *ḥadīth* we had already countered in al-Bukhārī's *Ṣaḥīḥ*. Such vaunting *ḥadīth*s are a minority in Muslim's *Ṣaḥīḥ* (as they are in al-Bukhārī's); their relative paucity suggests the rarity of their occurrence and limited circulation in the early period. The fact that *ribāṭ* emerged as a military stratagem well after the death of the Prophet allows one to credibly posit a late provenance for reports in exaggerated praise of such activity.

The extraordinary rewards reserved for the military martyr are familiarly depicted in one Companion report from ʿAbd Allāh b. Masʿūd, who in exegesis of Qur'ān 3:169 describes the souls of martyrs as ensconced within green birds, who are given candelabras suspended over the divine throne, and who flit about as they please, their every desire satisfied.[150] Several *ḥadīth*s in Muslim's *Ṣaḥīḥ* affirm the certainty of generous posthumous rewards for those who perish on the battlefield.[151] Those who may be deemed as truly fighting in the path of God are those who fight so that "the word of God may be supreme," as related in a *ḥadīth* from Abū Mūsā al-Ashʿarī.[152] According to a significant cluster of reports related by a variety of Companions, there will always be a contingent of Muslims fighting for the truth (*yuqātilūn ʿalā 'l-ḥaqq*) until the Day of Judgment.[153] Those who fight for personal glory and fame are destined, however, for hellfire, as related in a *ḥadīth* from Abū Hurayra.[154] Finally, one report exhorts that one should take part in military campaigns when one can and when there is no legitimate justification for not doing so. In this *ḥadīth*, the Companion Abū Hurayra states that whoever dies without having taken part in a military campaign, and who had never resolved to do so, dies as a kind of hypocrite.[155] Those who suffer from a physical disability—illness[156] or blindness,[157] for example—have a natural exemption from fighting, however. It is noteworthy that ʿAbd Allāh b. al-Mubārak, whose name occurs in the *isnād*, appends the caveat that the *ḥadīth's* injunction applied only at the time of the Prophet. Unmoored from its original context, however, one can see how this *ḥadīth* could be deployed to establish a higher moral evaluation of the military *jihād* as a religiously prescribed activity in absolute terms.

With regard to martyrdom and its purview, Muslim preserves reports that are as expansive as some recorded in the two *Muṣannaf* works of ʿAbd al-Razzāq and Ibn Abī Shayba. For example, a *ḥadīth* narrated by Sahl b. Ḥunayf (from his father and grandfather) states that whoever asks God sincerely (*bi-sidq*) for martyrdom (*al-shahāda*), will be granted the status of a martyr, even if such an individual were to die in his or her bed.[158] A variant *ḥadīth* narrated by Anas b. Mālik quotes the Prophet as saying that whoever implores God sincerely for martyrdom will be granted it, even if he does not actually attain it.[159] In both these *ḥadīths*, the terms martyrdom and martyr are clearly being used in a very broad sense, that is, in relation to any manner of death of a pious person in general. These more expanisve meanings are confirmed in the *ḥadīth* narrated by Abū Hurayra (previously encountered in al-Bukhārī's *Ṣaḥīḥ*) in which Muḥammad enumerates five kinds of martyrs: those who die from the plague, from a stomach ailment, from drowning, from being crushed [by a falling structure], and dying in the path of God.[160] Another *ḥadīth*, also narrated by Abū Hurayra, quotes the Prophet as defining the one slain on the battlefield, the one dying [of natural causes] in the path of God, and the one fatally stricken by plague or by a stomach ailment as making up "those who are killed in the path of God." A variant from Ibn Miqsam adds the victim of drowning to this list.[161]

The Sunans of Ibn Māja, Abū Dā'ūd, al-Tirmidhī, and al-Nasā'ī

Due to length constraints, we offer here a bird's-eye view of these major *ḥadīth* works compiled after Muslim b. Ḥajjāj. By the third–fourth/ninth–tenth centuries, there was already a well-established corpus of *ḥadīths* concerning *jihād*, which were reproduced to a considerable extent in practically every major compilation, with some occasional divergences and inclusions of *ḥadīths* not previously encountered by us. These additional features are highlighted in our discussion of the following works.

The *Sunan* of Ibn Māja al-Qazwinī (d. 273/886)

Ibn Māja has a fairly lengthy section entitled *Kitāb al-jihād* in his *Sunan*.[162] It is a chapter combining *faḍā'il al-jihād* and *siyar* reports. He records *ḥadīths* in praise of *jihād*, with an emphasis on the virtues of *ribāṭ* and fighting at sea and in praise of martyrdom and the merits accruing to the *shahīd*, as well as *ḥadīths* that refer to typical *siyar* matters: the division of spoils; the immunity of noncombatants, particularly of women and children; the permissibility of asking non-Muslims for assistance; and the treatment of prisoners of war, etc.

Some of the *faḍā'il al-jihād* reports are already familiar to us from earlier *ḥadīth* compilations and are not repeated here. With regard to martyrs, as in Muslim's *Ṣaḥīḥ*, four types of martyrs are identified in a *ḥadīth* attributed to Abū Hurayra: one who is killed in the path of God; one who dies [naturally] in the path of God; one who dies from a stomach ailment; and one stricken by plague. A variant from Abū Ṣāliḥ adds the victim of drowning to the list.[163] We also find the *ḥadīth* narrated by Sahl b. Ḥunayf from his father in which

Muḥammad remarks that one who sincerely petitions God for martyrdom will attain it even if he dies in his bed.[164]

With regard to *ribāṭ* and fighting at sea, we encounter some of the familiar *ḥadīths* or variants thereof (e.g., the one from Umm Ḥaram in which Muḥammad approvingly describes Muslims in the future riding the high seas like "kings of the waves.")[165] But unlike most *ḥadīths* in the *Ṣaḥīḥayn*, which posited at best a moral equivalence between supererogatory acts of worship and the combative *jihād*, Ibn Māja includes reports that grant military activity a higher religious rank vis-à-vis supererogatory acts of piety. Thus, according to Anas b. Mālik, the Prophet is said to have remarked that a night's vigilance in the path of God is **more** meritorious than the fasting of a man and support of his family for a thousand years, a year equaling 360 days and a day equaling a thousand years![166] This exaggerated numerical trope alone indicates to us that *ribāṭ* has exponentially grown in religious importance by Ibn Māja's time in certain circles.

Other *ḥadīths* in praise of the combative *jihād* in general and of both land-based *ribāṭ* and fighting at sea have similarly become quite hyperbolic in tone in comparison with the *faḍā'il* reports in the *Ṣaḥīḥayn*.[167] Two *ḥadīths* assign considerably exaggerated merits to fighting at sea over *ribāṭ* on land, suggesting to us a possible escalation in these debates by Ibn Māja's time. Once again, Abū Umāma reports that the Prophet had commented that the one who dies at sea is the equivalent of two martyrs on land, and while the land-based martyr has all his sins forgiven except for his debts, the martyr at sea has his debts forgiven as well.[168] As the editor of this volume, Muḥammad Nāṣir al-Dīn al-Albānī points out, this is a "very weak" report; one of its transmitters, 'Ufayr b. Ma'dan al-Shāmī, was impugned by al-Bukhārī, al-Nasā'ī, and Ibn Ḥanbal, among others. Another *ḥadīth* from Abū 'l-Dardā', also deemed *ḍa'īf*, declares campaigning at sea to be the equivalent of ten land-based campaigns.[169] It is clear that Ibn Māja's later compilation includes hortatory reports that are more frequently encountered in *faḍā'il* al-*jihād* treatises that were either not available or had not become widely circulated during the time of al-Bukhārī and Muslim, or which they had rejected on account of their blatant tendentiousness.

Other tendentious *ḥadīths* recorded by Ibn Māja suggest a lively professional rivalry waged by different factions of the military—the cavalry versus the archers, for example. A cluster of reports[170] clearly deems the cavalry to be superior. In one such report, according to Tamīm al-Dārī, the Prophet had commented that whoever tethers his horse in the path of God and then prepares its fodder with his own hand earns a merit for each grain that he touches.[171] Another cluster of reports[172] eulogizes the archers as the most meritorious among those who fight; one explicitly quotes Muḥammad as saying that archery was preferable to him than fighting on horseback (*wa-an tarmū aḥabbū ilayya min an tarkabū*).[173] A notable *ḥadīth* emanating from Ibn 'Abbas reminds Muslims that Ishmael "your forefather, was an archer."[174]

The *Sunan* of Abū Dā'ūd al-Sijistānī (d. 275/888)

Abū Dā'ūd also has a fairly lengthy section entitled *Kitāb* al-*jihād* in his *Sunan*.[175] As in Ibn Māja's collection, the bulk of the reports enumerate the merits of *jihād*, placing emphasis on fighting at sea and carrying out *ribāṭ*. There are also *faḍā'il* reports about military martyrdom, the tone of which is similarly hyperbolic in comparison with earlier *ḥadīth* works. Like Ibn Māja, Abū Dā'ūd also includes familiar *siyar* reports that discuss *inter alia* the division of spoils, the permissibility of women's presence on the battlefield, and the treatment of noncombatants, etc.

An unprecedented *ḥadīth* included by Abū Dā'ūd serves as a significant benchmark for a progressively escalating estimation of the status of the military martyr. Attributed to the Companion 'Ubayd b. Khālid al-Sulamī, it states that the Prophet made two men brothers of one another; one of them was slain (it is assumed on the battlefield) and the other died (sc. of natural causes) a week or so after the former. Several of the Companions prayed at the latter's grave. When Muḥammad asked them what they had uttered, they replied that they had prayed for his forgiveness and that he would be united with his companion. At that, the Prophet exclaimed that the prayers, the fasting, and the deeds of the two men in general were not comparable, for "Indeed, [the difference] between them is like that between the sky and the earth." This report gives us pause in connection with our previous discussion of Qur'ān 3:157–158 and Qur'ān 22:58, in which the equal moral status of the pious Muslim, in this world and the hereafter, was asserted regardless of his or her manner of dying. This *ḥadīth* clearly undermines the Qur'anic equivalence established between these two types of martyrs and ascribes instead a vastly superior position to the military martyr. The content of this purported *ḥadīth* signals to us a dramatic transformation in the construction of piety in Muslim discourses by the late third/ninth century, as evident in this exaggerated exaltation of the military martyr at the expense of the non-military one.

The *Sunan* of al-Tirmidhī (d. 279/892)

The *Sunan* of al-Tirmidhī has an even more extensive section on *jihād* and related issues. There is one separate chapter on *siyar* (*Kitāb al-siyar*);[176] followed by a chapter on the merits of *jihād* (*Kitāb faḍā'il al-jihād*);[177] which in turn is followed by yet another chapter on simply *jihād* (*Kitāb al-jihād*).[178] Many of al-Tirmidhī's *ḥadīths* are similar to those recorded by Abū Dā'ūd in his *Kitāb al-jihād*; al-Tirmidhī sorts them further according to the specific content of the reports.

Two *ḥadīths* concerning the rewards reaped by the military martyr are worthy of our attention, especially because they are not recorded by the other five authoritative *ḥadīth* compilers. One of them is narrated by Abū Hurayra, who relates that three groups of people are guaranteed entrance into paradise: (1) a martyr (*shahīd*); (2) a chaste and pure person; and (3) a slave who excels in worship of God and offers wise counsel to his masters.[179] In this report, there is an equivalence of merit between the military martyr and the non-martial pious person. The second *ḥadīth* emanates from 'Umar b. al-Khaṭṭāb in which he states that he heard Muḥammad enumerate four types of martyrs (*al-shuhadā'*): (1) a believing man of strong faith who meets the enemy with resolute and honest intent and is slain—he is the best kind; (2) a believing man of strong faith who on encountering the enemy falters due to a twinge of cowardice and is slain—he is of the second rank; (3) a believing man who mixes good deeds with bad but meets the enemy with honest intent and is slain—he is of the third rank; and (4) a believing man who sins against himself but meets the enemy with resolute intent and is slain—he is of the fourth rank.[180] What is noteworthy about this *ḥadīth* from 'Umar is that it has replaced the five to seven categories of non-military martyrs (as enumerated in the previously mentioned reports recorded by al-Bukhārī and Muslim) with only military ones.

Al-Tirmidhī's three fairly extensive chapters devoted to myriad issues concerning *jihād* and ancillary issues signal to us the great significance attached to this topic by his time. The detailed regulations collectively contained in the reports that were available to him by the late third/ninth century attest to the close attention paid during this period to the minutiae of fighting and military martyrdom in particularly legal and administrative contexts. Al-Tirmidhī's tripartite division of the *jihād* material in his collection reflects an attempt on his part to establish some manner of thematic coherence in a burgeoning literature.

The *Sunan* of al-Nasā'ī (d. 303/915)

The *Kitāb al-jihād* in this authoritative *sunan* work[181] is primarily a collection of *faḍā'il* reports concerning *jihād* and martyrdom. It lacks the *siyar* reports regarding treatment of prisoners and of noncombatants, and division of booty, etc., found in most other *ḥadīth* sections of this sort. But like the *faḍā'il/kitāb al-jihād* sections of the previously mentioned collections, al-Nasāʾī's compilation reproduces the usual reports having to do with the merits of striving with one's self and wealth in the path of God, the necessity of proper intention when so striving, the posthumous rewards reserved for the martyr, and the merits of *ribāṭ* and fighting at sea, etc. One *ḥadīth* not previously encountered merits special attention because it attests to a higher evaluation of the fighter in the path of God in a hierarchy of pious people. It is narrated by the Companion Fuḍāla b. ʿUbayd, who said that he had heard Muḥammad guarantee for those who had believed in him, embraced Islam, and emigrated, a house on the periphery and another in the middle of paradise. But for those who had believed in him, embraced Islam, and fought in the path of God (*jāhada fī sabīl allāh*), he vouchsafed not only a house on the periphery and in the middle of paradise, but also a house in its highest pavilions (*fī aʿlā ghuraf al-janna*). In this *ḥadīth*, *jihād* clearly trumps the *hijra*, the act of migration from Mecca to Medina during the time of Muḥammad, which is otherwise the seminal event in the inauguration of the Islamic era. Noteworthy, moreover, is the co-optation of the pavilions (*ghuraf*) of paradise as rewards for military activity, an honor reserved in the Qur'ān exclusively for the godfearing (Qur'an 39:20), the patiently forbearing (Qur'ān 25:75; here the singular *ghurfa* is used), and in general, for those who believe and do good deeds (Qur'ān 29:58), as had been previously noted by us in regard to ʿAbd al-Razzāq's *Muṣannaf*. The transferral of this highest celestial reward to the pious combatant from the pious non-combatant represents a stark subversion of the Qur'anic hierarchy of moral excellence adumbrated in the above verses. One suspects that such a scripturally mandated hierarchy of moral excellence was deemed to be out of step with the hardheaded political realism of the later period, which advocated a strong military as a deterrent against actual and potential aggressors, hence the attempt to pragmatically reconfigure this moral hierarchy.

In his brief section on the topic of martyrdom (*bāb mas'alat al-shahāda*), al-Nasāʾī includes a *ḥadīth* from ʿUqba b. ʿĀmir in which the Prophet enumerates the five types of martyrs, as also recorded earlier by ʿAbd al-Razzāq, Ibn Abī Shayba, al-Bukhārī, Muslim, and Ibn Māja, from different narrators.[182] Al-Nasāʾī further includes the *ḥadīth* narrated by Suhayl b. Ḥanīf, also included by Muslim, in which the Prophet affirms that whoever sincerely asks God for the status of a martyr will be granted it, even if he or she dies in bed.[183]

A *ḥadīth* not encountered by us previously is recorded by al-Nasāʾī; it appears to encode early debates concerning which groups of people were entitled to be called martyrs. In this report narrated by al-ʿIrbāḍ b. Sāriya, one of the *ahl al-ṣuffa*,[184] the Prophet says that military martyrs (*al-shuhadāʾ*) and those who died naturally in their beds (*al-mutawaffawna ʿalā furūshihim*) would wrangle in the following manner before God regarding those who had perished from the plague (*yutawaffawna min al-ṭāʿūn*):

> The martyrs will say, "Our brothers were slain (*qutilū*) as we were slain," and those who had died in their beds will say, "Our brothers died (*mātū*) in their beds as we died." Our Lord will say, "Look at their wounds: if their wounds are similar to the wounds of those who were slain, then they are one of them and with them." And lo! their wounds were similar to their wounds.[185]

This report is highly significant because it establishes that (1) the issue of whether individuals dying nonviolently in their beds may qualify for martyrdom on a par with warriors was being debated in the earliest period, as the internal reference to the *ahl al-ṣuffa* might suggest, and/or that it remained a contested issue well into al-Nasāʾī's time; and (2) those who perish from non-battlefield afflictions may earn the right to be called martyrs only if it was proven that their afflictions were as severe as those suffered by military martyrs. It is not surprising that, as one of the non-combatant *ahl al-ṣuffa*, ʿIrbāḍ propagates this report (or this report is ascribed to him to ensure credibility) that implicitly questions whether the suffering of the military martyr should become the standard against which the sufferings of all others are to be measured before being granted the imprimatur of martyrdom.

Notably new in al-Nasāʾī's collection are accounts of the Prophet's premonition of future military campaigns in Iraq and Persia. Because of Muḥammad's prior approval of such campaigns and by their inclusion in this section, these campaigns are to be regarded as instances of legitimate *jihād* (the caption, however, reads *Bāb ghazwāt al-turk wa-'l-ḥabasha*). In the case of the Turks and the Ethiopians, the Prophet had counseled in one *ḥadīth* that they be left alone as long as they left Muslims alone.[186] With regard to India, according to the Companion Thawbān [b. Bujdud], Muḥammad reportedly said there were two contingents from among Muslims who would be saved from hellfire, one that campaigned in India (*ʿiṣāba taghzū 'l-hind*) and the other that will be with Jesus [at the end of time].[187] The Prophet's prescient knowledge and approval of these military campaigns after his death allows for their depiction as legitimate and meritorious religious activities, clearly intended to serve as mimetic precedents for later generations of Muslims. The *isnād* of this report from Thawbān includes the Syrian (Ḥimṣī) transmitter Baqiyya b. al-Walīd (d. ca. 197/812), who has a rather unsavory reputation among *ḥadīth* critics for deliberately concealing reports from reliable sources and relating instead reports from weak authorities, a propensity that, in the opinion of Ibn Qaṭṭān, greatly "vitiated his probity."[188]

Concluding Remarks

Our survey reveals that a number of highly significant reports containing contested perspectives on *jihād* preserved in the two early *Muṣannaf* works of Ibn 'Abd al-Razzāq and Ibn Abī Shayba are either completely missing from later works or exist in reworked forms. These two collections are therefore particularly important as transitional works that allow us to monitor the crystallization of the *faḍā'il al-jihād* genre during the critical Umayyad period. Through comparison with the later *ḥadīth* works, we are able to more firmly document the evolving paraenetic and hortatory functions of a number of the reports recorded in these collections. Furthermore, our close reading of the Six Books reveals that a stable repertoire of *ḥadīth*s concerning *jihād* and martyrdom had emerged by the third/ninth century; these tended to be replicated in standard and other [Sunnī] compilations of *ḥadīth*. But the later *sunan* works of al-Tirmidhī, Abū Dā'ūd, Ibn Māja, and al-Nasā'ī, in comparison with the two *Ṣaḥīḥ*s of al-Bukhārī and Muslim, further show that *faḍā'il* reports promising exaggerated posthumous rewards to the military martyr continued to be added to and put in circulation after the third/ninth century. These developments testify to a continuing robust politics of piety among various groups in the medieval period as they sought to define their earthly relations to one another on the basis of moral excellence and precedence in Islam, even as they contemplated their fates in the next world.

VI

Jihād *and Martyrdom in Early and Late Treatises on the Merits of* Jihād

MANY OF THE reports and perspectives concerning *jihād* and martyrdom found in the early *ḥadīth* compilations of ʿAbd al-Razzāq and Ibn Abī Shayba are replicated to a considerable extent in early works on the merits of *jihād* composed during the Umayyad period. The composition of these treatises on *jihād* in itself is testimony to the growing importance of this topic by the second/eighth century. As with the *ḥadīth* literature, comparison of these early and late compositions on the merits of *jihād* are revealing of progressive, critical transformations in the inflections of this term and of martyrdom.

One of the earliest extant examples of such literature is the *Kitāb al-Jihād* of ʿAbd Allāh b. al-Mubārak. In comparison with the *Muṣannafs* of ʿAbd al-Rāzzaq and Ibn Abī Shayba, it is a slightly earlier work and a similarly valuable repository of early multiple and shifting views of the combative *jihād*.

Early Works from the Second/Eighth and Third/Ninth Centuries

The *Kitāb al-Jihād* of ʿAbd Allāh Ibn al-Mubārak (d. 181/797)

ʿAbd Allāh b. ʿAbd al-Raḥmān Ibn al-Mubārak al-Ḥanzalī was a Khurasanian merchant who also devoted himself to religious scholarship. He was a friend of Abū Isḥāq al-Fazārī (d. ca. 186/802), the author of an early *siyar* work. Among his teachers were Abū Ḥanīfa, Sufyān al-Thawrī, and Mālik b. Anas, whose *al-Muwaṭṭaʾ* he transmitted. He reportedly narrated *ḥadīths* from about a thousand teachers, some of which are recorded by Muslim in his *Saḥīḥ*. Known for his pious, abstemious lifestyle, Ibn al-Mubārak is said to have undertaken pilgrimage and the military *jihād* on the land frontiers (*thughūr*) in alternate years. The *Kitāb al-Jihād* is the earliest extant treatise on the military *jihād* and its merits; in al-Andalus, this work was also known as *Kitāb faḍl al-jihād*.[1]

A number of the reports recorded by Ibn al-Mubārak often emphasize the right intention (*niyya*) for engaging in *jihād* in the path of God. In one such Companion report, ʿUmar b. al-Khaṭṭāb's authority is invoked to drive home the critical point that one should fight only for the sake of God. This report narrated by Muḥammad b. Sufyān (a frequent transmitter via Saʿīd b. Raḥma from Ibn al-Mubārak) states that ʿUmar b. al-Khaṭṭāb once appeared at a gathering in the Prophet's mosque in Medina in which the people were talking about an expedition that had "perished in the path of God" (*halakat fī sabīl allāh*). One of those present commented that the people in the expedition were God's agents (*ʿummāl allāh*) who had perished in His path and, therefore, their reward was assured with Him. But another interjected that only God knew their true state, and that they would be compensated according to what they had justly earned. When ʿUmar became aware of what they were discussing, he remarked, "Indeed there are some people who fight out of a desire for this world, while others fight for glory and renown, and yet others who fight only reactively. But there are those who fight 'desiring/seeking the face of God,' and they are the martyrs (*al-shuhadāʾ*)."[2]

This report contains an explicit caveat that *jihād* as a moral and religious duty was not to be undertaken for profane and frivolous purposes, and as a term it must not be deployed to legitimize military adventurism in pursuit of worldly objectives, such as earthly fame and glory. The term "desiring/seeking the face of God" (*ibtighāʾ wajh allāh*) in conjunction with fighting, as occurs in the report from ʿUmar, sets up a moral line of demarcation (not legally or otherwise enforceable) between justified and unjustified armed combat. It is highly relevant to point out here as well that the phrase *ibtighāʾ wajh rabbihim* is used in the Qurʾān in conjunction with *ṣabr* (Qurʾān 13:22) and not with the combative *jihād*. Ibn al-Mubārak's appropriation of a slight variant of this phrase in connection with fighting confers upon this activity a higher degree of moral excellence and indicates a conscious reformulation on his part of a predominant Qurʾanic paradigm of piety.

We also encounter a number of *ḥadīth*s and other kinds of reports in Ibn al-Mubārak's work that establish a moral equivalency between fighting in the path of God and the usual or supererogatory religious acts, reminiscent of similar reports contained in the *Muṣannaf*s of ʿAbd al-Razzāq and Ibn Abī Shayba. In one such *ḥadīth* from Abū Hurayra, the Prophet affirms that the fighter in the path of God is like the devout person who fasts and prays continuously until he [sc. the fighter] returns.[3] In another report, the Companion ʿUthmān b. Abī Sawda offers a harmonizing exegesis of Qurʾān 56:10, which states, "Those who precede are the ones who precede (*wa-'l-sābiqūn al-sābiqūn*)." 'Uthmān said that the verse refers to "the first of those who frequent the mosque" and "the first of those who depart in the path of God, the Exalted, the Mighty."[4]

It is noteworthy that in a number of these reports, it is the pious warrior who is being compared to the non-combative pious believer in order to assess the former's religious merit, as we similarly observed in early *ḥadīth* compilations. What this clearly indicates is that through Ibn al-Mubārak's time, the piety of the non-combative believer continued to constitute the standard against which the moral excellence of the pious combatant was judged. Other reports posit the moral equivalence of fighting in the path of God to essential religious obligations performed for the sake of God, such as prayer and fasting. But already we begin to detect an overall shift in emphasis in this treatise, with more reports now extolling the greater moral excellence of the military *jihād* over more routine devotional acts, such as prayer and fasting, which are not recorded by either 'Abd al-Razzāq or Ibn Abī Shayba and are not to be found in the later authoritative *ḥadīth* compilations of al-Bukhārī and Muslim. This is significant because, first of all, it implies the more limited circulation of these reports, and second, it conveys to us that they were not deemed sound or reliable enough to be included in the two *Ṣaḥīḥ*s. Some of these reports allow us to track a major shift by the time of Ibn al-Mubārak in the moral valuation of *jihād* as military combat and the martyrdom earned as a consequence.

In one such report, Abū Hurayra asks, "Can any one of you stand [in prayer] unwaveringly and fast without breaking it while alive?" Someone exclaimed, "O Abū Hurayra, who can possibly tolerate this?" He replied, "By the one in whose hand is my soul, one day of the fighter in the path of God (*al-mujāhid fī sabīl allāh*) is better than it."[5] In another Companion report, 'Uthmān b. 'Affān promotes specific military campaigns and addresses his people as follows: "It has become clear, by God, that you have become diverted from [carrying out] *jihād*, so that [now] it has become an imperative for me and you. Whoever wishes to go to Syria, let him do so; whoever wishes to go to Iraq, let him do so; whoever wishes to go to Egypt, let him do so. Indeed a day [in the life] of the fighter in the path of God is like a thousand days for the one who fasts without eating and the one who unflaggingly remains standing [in prayer]."[6] In this report, the bar has been raised to astronomical levels for the non-*mujāhid*. Whereas a number of earlier reports established a moral equivalence between fighting in the path of God and constant prayer and fasting, this report and the two immediately above categorically establish the far greater superiority of fighting in the path of God over more common, non-combative acts of religious devotion. It is worthy of note that the text of this report provides us with a specific historical context—the early Arab conquests—as the specific background for the generation and circulation of these hortatory reports. Another noteworthy feature of this report is that 'Uthmān is made to specifically label the early Islamic military forays into Syria, Iraq, and Egypt as *jihād*. Its *isnād* contains the name of Abū 'l-'Ubayd, who had served as the *ḥājib* [chamberlain] of the Umayyad Caliph Sulaymān b. 'Abd al-Mālik (d. 99/717); the report thus strongly indicates that attempts were made in Umayyad ruling circles to circulate reports that bestowed religious luster and legitimacy upon their wars of conquest.[7]

As we recall, a number of reports in Ibn Abī Shayba's *Muṣannaf* record the considerable equivocation of several early authorities concerning *jihād* as a religious obligation (*wājib*). Such reports do not occur in Ibn al-Mubārak's work. One Successor report attributed to al-Ḍaḥḥāk b. Muzāḥim not only does not display any such equivocation, it proceeds to make a categorical pronouncement on the obligatory nature of fighting. The report is narrated by Muḥammad b. Sufyān on the authority of al-Ḍaḥḥāk, who reported that when Qur'ān 2:216, which states, "Fighting has been prescribed for you even though it is displeasing to you," was revealed, "The people of certitude (*ahl al-yaqīn*) did not prefer anything else to *jihād*; they loved it and desired it...." He ends by saying, "And *jihād* is one of the divinely ordained obligations" (*wa-'l-jihād farīḍa min farā'iḍ allāh*).[8] The absence of more equivocal or contradictory reports in Ibn al-Mubārak's work suggests that such reports had been sifted away so as not to dilute al-Ḍaḥḥāk's preferred point of view, which clearly accorded with our author's position.

The greater moral excellence of the fighter in the path of God vis-à-vis Muslims engaged in other pursuits is made evident in *ḥadīths* and reports in which, in response to the question "Who is the best of people (*khayr al-nās*)?" or the equivalent thereof, either the Prophet or a Companion indicates that it is the *mujāhid*. One such *ḥadīth* has the following *isnād*: Ibrāhīm from Muḥammad b. Sufyān from Sa'īd from Ibn al-Mubārak from Ḥammād b. Salāma from Hishām b. 'Amr and al-Fazārī from an unknown person (*fulān*) from 'Umar b. al-Khaṭṭāb. 'Umar related that he was in the presence of the Prophet along with a large assembly of people, when a man asked, "O Messenger of God, who has the most favored status (*khayr manzila*) with God, the Exalted and Mighty, after His prophets and His friends (*aṣfiyā'ihi*)?" Muḥammad replied, "The fighter in the path of God, the Exalted, the Mighty, with his self and his wealth until he is summoned by God, while astride his horse and holding its rein." The *mujāhid* is followed by the one who excels in his worship of God and restrains people from wrongdoing.[9] The *isnād* is particularly weak because it refers to an unknown person (*fulān*) as the direct transmitter from 'Umar, vitiating the report's status as a proof-text, according to the rules of *ḥadīth* criticism. Al-Fazārī (d. after 186/802), who transmits from *fulān*, was a student of the Syrian jurist al-Awzāʿī (d. 157/774) and the author of a *siyar* work.[10]

A highly important variant of this *ḥadīth* contextualizes the creation of such hierarchies of moral excellence and intimates to us that these were not meant to be absolute hierarchies. This variant report has an *isnād* that is identical to that of the immediately preceding *ḥadīth* up to Ibn al-Mubārak, who related from Sufyān b. ʿUyayna from Ibn Abī Najīḥ from Mujāhid, who said that a woman called Umm Mubashshir asked the Prophet about the best of people before God. He replied, "The man on horseback who frightens the enemy and they [the enemy] frighten him." But then Muḥammad gestured toward the Ḥijāz and said, "The man who stands up in prayer and gives of his wealth what is due to God, the Exalted, the Mighty."[11]

What are we to make of this second remark? It appears to set up a competing hierarchy of moral excellence based on where one is located and on the exigencies of these particular circumstances. It is not made explicitly clear where the man on horseback is, but if we allow for an obvious anachronism, we may conclude that he is guarding the frontiers of Syria against the Byzantines. Given the urgent nature of this activity, it acquires the status of the most religiously meritorious activity in the Syrian-Umayyad context. In contrast to Syrians, people in the Arabian Peninsula do not have to bestir themselves to defend their territory against enemy incursions. According to situational ethical reasoning, therefore, the report indicates that the usual devotional acts continue to be the most meritorious for Ḥijāzīs.

As we saw in the *Muṣannafs* of ʿAbd al-Razzāq and Ibn Abī Shayba, *ribāṭ* as a specific dimension of fighting in the path of God becomes foregrounded as a highly meritorious religious activity. Like Ibn Abī Shayba, Ibn al-Mubārak records a report in exegesis of Qurʾān 3:200, which states, "O those who believe, be patient and exhort one another to patience and be resolute" (see a previous discussion of this verse in chapter 1). This Successor report is related by al-Ḥasan al-Baṣrī who commented on this verse, "He has commanded them to be patiently forbearing in their religion and not to abandon it on account of hardship or ease, in happiness and sorrow. And He commanded them to bear patiently with the unbelievers and to be resolute with the polytheists."[12] A variant Successor report is attributed to Qatāda, who said, "Bear patiently with the polytheists and engage in *ribāṭ* in the path of God."[13] The first report in its understanding of *rābiṭū* remains close to the Qurʾanic signification of "being firm and resolute," whereas the second report anachronistically reads into this passage the specific Umayyad activity of manning the frontiers against enemy incursion.

In the above reports extolling the merits of fighting in the path of God, one is likely to assume that when *jihād* is compared with prayer and fasting, the latter two refer to supererogatory acts and not to the prescribed daily prayers and the obligatory fast of Ramadan. But one report recorded by Ibn al-Mubārak makes clear that *ribāṭ* as a specific way of fighting in the path of God is being compared to the required fast during Ramadan and deemed to be morally equivalent. It is related by the Syrian Shuraḥbīl b. al-Samaṭ al-Kindī,[14] who had been engaged in *ribāṭ* for a long time. One day, Salmān al-Fārisī happened to arrive at the fortress where Ibn al-Samaṭ was maintaining his vigil. Realizing that the latter was homesick and longing for his wife, Salmān attempted to shore up his spirits by saying that he had heard the Prophet remark, "*Ribāṭ* for a day and night or a day or a night is like fasting during the month of Ramaḍān and standing up for prayer during it. Whoever dies while engaged in *ribāṭ* will earn an equivalent reward and sustenance...."[15] It should be noted that Shuraḥbīl served as Mu'āwiya's *'āmil* (agent/governor) in Ḥimṣ for almost twenty years; when we add to that his partiality for *ribāṭ*, the impetus for exaggerated praise of such activity becomes evident in this context.

An even more laudatory *ḥadīth* is related by Fuḍāla b. 'Ubayd b. Nāqidh from his father 'Ubayd, who said he heard the Prophet say, "For everyone who dies, his deeds are sealed at the point in time when he died, except for the *murābiṭ* in the path of God, the Exalted, the Mighty. Rather his deeds continue to grow until the Day of Judgment and he is protected from the trials of the grave."[16] Fuḍāla b. 'Ubayd (d. ca. 53/672), one of the Anṣār, may be considered to have had a vested interest in adducing purported *ḥadīth*s that, by ascribing aggrandized posthumous rewards to the *murābiṭ*, could serve as possible inducements for young men to enlist in the Umayyad army. Fuḍāla himself participated enthusiastically in Mu'āwiya's army and was appointed the commander of military expeditions by the caliph and to the judgeship of Damascus.[17] It is worthy of note that the content of this *ḥadīth* from Fuḍāla b. 'Ubayd directly challenges the better-known *ḥadīth* recorded by Muslim b. Ḥajjāj (d. 261/875), according to which the Prophet said, "If a human being dies, then his good deeds stop except for three: continuous charity (*ṣadaqa jāriya*), beneficial knowledge, or a righteous child who prays for him."[18] All the activities referred to in this well-known *ḥadīth* are non-combative in nature; the version attributed to Fuḍāla sets up a competing paradigm of piety that foregrounds military activity and martyrdom.

Other variants of this *ḥadīth* from Fuḍāla are given. One such *ḥadīth* related by the Companion 'Aqaba b. 'Āmir (with a truncated *isnād*) says that it is the "one who dies in the path of God" (*alladhī yamūt fī sabīl allāh*) whose deeds will continue till the Day of Judgment.[19] This variant, broader locution "one who dies in the path of God" allows for a larger cross-section of pious people to be included in its purview, because it is not the warrior who is being specified; the usual Qur'anic locution frequently understood to be in reference to the warrior-martyr, as we recall, is *man qutila/yuqtal fī sabīl allāh* (i.e., "one who is slain in the path of God," rather than "one who dies in the path of God"). Comparison of this *ḥadīth* from 'Aqaba with the one from Fuḍāla strongly suggests that such reports were being circulated in the early Umayyad period to establish the greater moral excellence of specific groups vis-à-vis others. 'Aqaba, like Fuḍāla, also lived during the time of Mu'āwiya, but he had stronger pietist credentials than the latter, with a better claim to Islamic priority (*sābiqa*), having converted to Islam early and emigrated to Medina. He was a Qur'ān reciter and compiled a *muṣḥaf* in Egypt that apparently survived in its original form until Ibn Ḥajar's time. He was dispatched to Egypt to take part in a military expedition by Mu'āwiya under Maslama b. Mukhallad, but seems to have had a falling-out with him.[20] Given his background and scholarly credentials, 'Aqaba might be expected to have a more "holistic" perspective on moral excellence, rather than a much narrower one focusing on martial exploits, reflected in the purported *ḥadīth* emanating from him. It is possible to suggest that those in the Umayyad period lacking in the traditional requisite *sābiqa* attempted to make up for it by promoting the greater merits of military exploits, in which they enjoyed an advantage. By elevating military activities above others, they hoped to establish an alternative construction of moral precedence.[21]

Naval warfare assumes great importance as a highly meritorious activity in Ibn al-Mubārak's *Kitāb al-jihād*, as it does in the two *Muṣannafs* of 'Abd al-Razzāq and Ibn Abī Shayba. A *ḥadīth* is related by 'Alqama b. Shihāb al-Qushayrī, who said that he heard the Prophet recommend, "Whoever could not attain campaigning with me, let him campaign in the sea. Indeed fighting for a day in the sea is better than fighting for two days on land. The reward of a martyr in the sea is equivalent to the reward of two martyrs on land. Indeed the best of martyrs before God the Exalted, the Mighty, are those people whose boats have capsized."[22] Once again, reports like this clearly indicate a distinctive "politics of piety" fully launched by Ibn al-Mubārak's time in putative *ḥadīths* like these, particularly of the *faḍā'il* type, in which a particular religious activity or moral attribute is championed by one group over another kind of religious activity or moral attribute championed by another group, both using a very similar idiom and style, especially in the invocation of heavenly rewards for the activity or attribute in question. In this dubious *ḥadīth*, the Prophet himself is inserted into the text to mediate the relative merits of fighting on land versus on sea and allows naval warriors to trump land warriors. As we noted in chapter 5, al-Balādhurī in his *Futūḥ al-buldān* had commented that the Arab population in general was loath to relocate to the coast in the early Umayyad period even when urged by Mu'āwiya and other Umayyad rulers to do so. This situation thereby impelled Mu'āwiya to move Persians to the coastal towns. These reports championing naval warfare could have been circulated to great effect in order to induce the reluctant populace to take part in these campaigns.[23]

In another report included by Ibn al-Mubārak, the famous Companion Abū Ayyūb al-Anṣārī is invoked to enhance the merit of Umayyad naval campaigns. According to a report related by Ibn Lahī'a (d. 174/790), the Umayyad *maghāzī* scholar Abū 'l-Aswad (d. ca. 131/748)[24] informed him that he took part in naval campaigns during the time of Mu'āwiya, and Abū Ayyūb would accompany them. Ibn Lahī'a also reported that Mu'āwiya would lead expeditions to the island of Rhodes during the time of 'Uthmān, and another famous Companion, Ka'b al-Aḥbār, would accompany him.[25] That this kind of ardent advocacy of naval warfare clearly grated on some nerves is evident from a Companion report that explicitly takes issue with it. In this report, Ibn 'Umar is quoted as remarking that campaigning astride his quiet, docile camel was much more preferable to him than taking to the sea.[26]

Martyrdom

Ḥadīths and other kinds of reports that preserve the early expansive meanings of *shahīd* and *shahāda*, as recorded in the two *Muṣannafs* of 'Abd al-Rāzzaq and Ibn Abī Shayba, are also found in Ibn al-Mubārak's treatise. Thus, in a *ḥadīth* narrated by the Companion 'Atīk b. al-Ḥārith, the Prophet asked some of his Companions on the occasion of 'Abd Allāh b. al-Ḥārith's death what they regarded as martyrdom (*al-shahāda*). They said that it was being killed in the way of God. The Prophet then responded, "The martyrs are seven. Other than being killed in the path of God, one who dies of a stomach ailment is a martyr, one who drowns is a martyr, the one who is stricken by plague is a martyr, one who is struck dead by having something fall on him (*ṣāḥib al-hadm*) is a martyr, one who is burned fatally is a martyr, and the woman who dies during pregnancy is a martyr."[27] According to a report about 'Abd Allāh b. Mas'ūd, the Companion is said to have remonstrated in the following manner when he heard a martyr being described in his presence solely as one who had died while fighting: "Your martyrs would then be very few indeed." He went on to say that whoever dies from falling off a mountaintop, or from drowning in the sea, or from being attacked by wild animals will be considered a martyr on the Day of Judgment.[28] This last report is a slight variant of the *ḥadīth*, recorded by both 'Abd al-Razzāq and Ibn Abī Shayba, in which the Prophet makes a very similar assertion about martyrs.

A variant of this report in which the principal interlocutor, either Muḥammad or one of his Companions, asks the question as to who may be considered a martyr, is also attributed to 'Umar b. al-Khaṭṭāb. This report is related by Masrūq, who said that someone commented in 'Umar's presence, "Felicitations to the one upon whom God has conferred martyrdom." At that, 'Umar asked, what in the opinion of the people present constituted martyrdom? They said, "Campaigning in the path of God" (*al-ghazw fī sabīl allāh*). 'Umar replied, "That is too much" (*inna dhālika la-kathīr*). When prompted to define a *shahīd*, he said it was the one "who consecrates his self [to God]" (*alladhī yaḥtasib nafsahu*).[29] This is probably about the most expansive definition of a martyr one may find in this kind of literature, in addition to the one we encountered in 'Abd al-Razzāq's *Muṣannaf*, according to which a *shahīd* is one who dies in his or her bed without sin. Finally, a variant of the report enumerating the different types of martyrs is attributed to a certain Hujayra al-Akbar, who is said to have identified the five following categories of *shahīd*: one who is slain in the path of God, one who drowns in the path of God, one who is stricken by the plague in the path of God, one who is felled by a stomach ailment, and the woman who dies during labor.[30] Such expansive definitions of a martyr contained in these archaic reports are not always reproduced in later *faḍā'il al-jihād* works and preserve for us the more malleable constructions of martyrdom in the early priod.

Kitāb al-jihād by Ibn Abī 'Āṣim (d. 287/900)

Abū Bakr Aḥmad b. 'Amr b. Abī 'Āṣim al-Ḍaḥḥāk al-Shaybānī al-Nabīl al-Ẓāhirī was born in 206/822 and spent many years studying in Baṣra. He later moved to Iṣfahān, where he served as *qāḍī* between 269/882 and 282/895. In addition to his mastery of *fiqh*, he was also acknowledged as a scholar of *ḥadīth*. Ibn Abī 'Asim was known for his abstemiousness and is said to have written over three hundred works, including a *Kitāb al-awā'il* treatise, works on *zuhd* and *dhikr*, and *ḥadīth*.[31]

In this *faḍā'il al-jihād* work separated by almost a hundred years from Ibn al-Mubārak's treatise, we continue to find reports extolling *jihād* in the broadest sense of exerting oneself to serve God. Thus Ibn Abī 'Āṣīm records the following *ḥadīth* narrated by Ibn Abī Shayba from Fuḍāla b. 'Ubayd, who quoted the Prophet as saying, "The *mujāhid* is one who exerts himself for the sake of God" (*man jāhada nafsahu li-'llāh*).[32] Such a *mujāhid* is praised in another *ḥadīth* recorded by Ibn Abī 'Āṣim as being the best among people. It is related by the Medinan (later Syrian) transmitter 'Aṭā' b. Yazīd al-Laythī (d. 105/723)[33] from Abū Sa'īd al-Khudrī, who reported that a man once asked Muḥammad,

"O Messenger of God, who is the best of people (*ayy al-nās afḍal*)?" The Prophet replied, "A believer who strives with his self and his wealth in the path of God" (*mu'min yujāhid bi-nafsihi wa-mālihi fī sabīl allāh*).[34]

However, we also simultaneously observe a more heightened concern with establishing the greater excellence of the combative *jihād* over other acts of piety in a number of the reports assembled in this work. As before, the *isnād*s of a number of these reports point to their Syrian-Umayyad provenance and suggest to us an ideological motivation for their circulation. An example of such a report is transmitted on the authority of 'Ubāda b. al-Ṣāmit (related by al-Ḥawṭī [d. 281/894][35] from Ismā'īl b. 'Ayyāsh[36] from Abū Bakr b. Abī Maryam [d. 156/772] from the Prophet's servant Abū Sallām from the Companion al-Miqdām b. Ma'dī Karib from 'Ubāda) and quotes Muḥammad as saying, "Fight (*jāhidū*) in the path of God, for *jihād* in the path of God is one of the doors of heaven, by means of which God grants deliverance from sorrow and tribulations." The *isnād* is mostly Syrian and regarded as highly problematic by a number of scholars, as helpfully noted by the editor.[37] For example, Abū Bakr b. Abī Maryam, a Ghassānid from Ḥimṣ, has a particularly poor reputation among *ḥadīth* critics, generally dismissed by them as "weak" and "amounting to nothing" (*lā shay'*), possessed of a faulty memory, and whose reports were to be avoided (*matrūk*).[38]

Another laudatory report is one we have encountered before; attributed to Abū Dharr, the Prophet states in it, "The summit of the peak of Islam is *jihād* in the path of God; only the most excellent attain to it." It should be noted that according to the *ḥadīth* critics Yaḥyā b. Ma'īn and Abū Ḥātim, the mostly Syrian, strongly pro-Umayyad *isnād* of this *ḥadīth* is deemed to be particularly weak among the final three links: 'Alī b. Yazīd (d. ca. 120/737) relating from al-Qāsim b. 'Abd al-Raḥmān (d. 112/730) relating from the Companion Abū Umāma.[39] Both Damascenes 'Alī b. Yazīd and al-Qāsim b. 'Abd al-Raḥmān are highly problematic transmitters. The former is severely criticized by the *rijāl* experts for the general unreliability of his reports; al-Bukhārī, for example, described his *ḥadīth*s as unacceptable and weak (*munkar, ḍa'īf*).[40] The latter, al-Qāsim, was a *mawlā* of the Umayyad family of Abū Sufyān b. Ḥarb, and is criticized by *ḥadīth* critics for transmitting unacceptable reports (*manākīr*).[41]

Ibn Abī 'Āṣim continues to include *ḥadīth*s that compare the *mujāhid* to the prayerful, abstemious individual, indicating the latter's moral precedence over the former. One such *ḥadīth* with an exemplary *isnād* is narrated by Sa'īd b. al-Musayyab from Abū Hurayra, who heard Muḥammad say, "Indeed the likeness of the fighter in the path of God is the one who stands [in prayer] while fasting, humbly bowing, and prostrating."[42] Two variant reports, one attributed to Abū Hurayra and the other to Nu'mān b. Bashīr, affirm the same.[43]

But there are also reports that reverse the equation, making the *mujāhid* and his actions the yardstick for evaluating piety. In a rather lengthy report with a distinctively Syrian *isnād*, 'Abd al-Raḥmān b. 'Awf is quoted as asking the Prophet how he could attain the status of those who fight in military campaigns, and Muḥammad replied that he would never be able to do that. When 'Abd al-Raḥmān asked if it would be possible to do so through fasting, prayer, or alms-giving, the Prophet asked, "Are you able to stand [in prayer] without ever sleeping or fast without ever eating until they [sc. the fighters] depart?" When 'Abd al-Raḥmān replied in the negative, Muḥammad remarked, "Even if you were to do that, you would not achieve their status!"[44] The report's *isnād* is as follows: narrated by al-Ḥawṭī from Abū 'l-Mughīra from Ṣafwān b. 'Amr from Khālid b. al-Walīd al-Saksakī, who heard some men from Damascus, who had spoken to Ibn Abī Kabsha in Baṣra, who claimed to have met the Prophet. The *isnād*'s weakness—especially with its reference to unidentified men from Damascus—is evident, and the text's paraenetic intent is clear: to rouse the population to fight for the unpopular Umayyad rulers. The Ḥimṣī Ṣafwān b. 'Amr b. Haram al-Saksakī (d. ca. 155/771) was an important source of *faḍā'il al-jihād* traditions for Ibn al-Mubārak, Abū Isḥāq al-Fazārī, Ismā'īl b. 'Ayyāsh, and others.[45]

The Umayyad milieu for the propagation of many of the *faḍā'il* reports concerning *jihād* is most transparently apparent in the reports that express extravagant praise for *ribāṭ* and naval expeditions, as previously observed in Ibn Abī Shayba's *Muṣannaf* (chapter 5) and Ibn al-Mubārak's *Kitāb al- jihād*. In a *ḥadīth* with a heavily Syrian *isnād* attributed to the Companion 'Irbāḍ b. Sāriya (d. ca. 75/694), who resided in Ḥimṣ,[46] the Prophet states, "Every action of an individual stops when he dies, except in the case of the one who does *ribāṭ* (*al-murābiṭ*) in the path of God; indeed, for him, his actions are made to multiply and its recompense is granted him until the Day of Judgment."[47] The Syrian context, specifically Beirut, is made plainly evident in another report extolling the merits of *ribāṭ* attributed to the Companion Salmān al-Fārisī. In this report emanating from al-Qāsim Abū 'Abd al-Raḥmān, Salmān addresses the people of Beirut and, in order "that God may remove any disinclination on your part towards *ribāṭ*," proceeds to recite to them the following *ḥadīth*, "*Ribāṭ* for a day is [equivalent to] fasting for two months. Whoever dies as a *murābiṭ* will be spared the tribulations of the grave and given the recompense of the best of his deeds until the Day of Resurrection."[48] The historian Abū Zur'a al-Dimashqī (d. 280/893) records this report, which he is said to have heard from Ibn al-Mubārak in the year 213/828, in his chronicles. When he related this report with its *isnād* to Ibn Ḥanbal, the latter discounted the possibility of al-Qāsim Abū 'Abd al-Raḥmān, a client of Khālid b. Yazīd b. Mu'āwiya, having ever met Salmān.[49] Al-Qāsim Abū 'Abd al-Raḥmān is the same as al-Qāsim b. 'Abd al-Raḥmān (d. 112/730), whom we encountered before, and whose dubious reputation we indicated. The purpose of these spurious *faḍā'il* reports is clearly to exhort Muslim men to undertake *ribāṭ* on behalf of the Umayyads. Once again, the importance of such an activity for the Umayyad elite and the reluctance of the populace to undertake it on behalf of their unpopular rulers are suggested by the prolific nature of these reports and their promise of exaggerated rewards for those who fulfil this duty.[50]

As we noted in regard to the two *Muṣannafs* of 'Abd al-Razzāq and Ibn Abī Shayba, there are also purported *ḥadīths* that specifically praise *ribāṭ* on the coasts and deem it to be more morally excellent than land-based *ribāṭ*. One such *ḥadīth* with a predominantly Syrian *isnād* is transmitted by the previously mentioned al-Ḥawṭī and 'Amr b. 'Uthmān on the authority of Anas b. Mālik, who related that the Prophet had said, "Whoever performs *ribāṭ* for a night on the coasts of the sea [has performed an action] more excellent than what a man can do for his family for a thousand years. The year has 360 days and each day is the equivalent of a thousand years."[51] As the editor Abū 'Abd al-Raḥmān points out, Ibn al-Jawzī had dismissed this *ḥadīth* as unreliable, and Ibn Māja had included this report in his compilation in spite of his expressed concern that it was fabricated. Both Sa'īd b. Khālid and Ibn Shabūr, whose names occur in the *isnād*, were described as unreliable transmitters by a majority of *ḥadīth* critics.[52] Like al-Ḥawṭī, 'Amr b. 'Uthmān b. Sa'īd b. Kathīr b. Dīnār al-Ḥimṣī (d. 250/864) was a Syrian transmitter who was furthermore identified as a *mawlā* of the Banū Umayya.[53]

Another *ḥadīth* categorically pronounces coastal *ribāṭ* to be superior to land-based *ribāṭ*. It is attributed to Umm al-Dardā', who quoted the Prophet as saying, "Whoever carries out *ribāṭ* for three days anywhere along the coasts belonging to Muslims will be given the recompense of a full year's [land-based] *ribāṭ*."[54] The *isnād* contains the name of the prolific Syrian transmitter Ismā'īl b. 'Ayyāsh (d.182/798), also known as Ibn Sulaym al-Ḥimsī who had acquired a reputation for transmitting weak reports, as previously noted in chapter 5.[55]

Martyrdom and Martyrs

In a *ḥadīth* emanating from 'Umar b. al-Khaṭṭāb, the Prophet is quoted as saying:

> The martyrs are four: [first] a believer of good faith (*jayyid al-imān*) who meets the enemy while believing in God and fights until he is killed—he is the one that people will strain their necks to gaze at on the Day of Judgment. [Second] a believing man who mixes the good

with the bad in his actions, meets the enemy while believing [in God], and he is as if felled by a mighty thorn from the acacia tree when the arrow of a stranger strikes and kills him. Next is a believing man who meets the enemy and fights, has faith in God and is killed—he will be in the third level [of Paradise]. [Finally] a believing man who commits excesses against himself, meets the enemy and has faith in God, fights and is killed—he will be in the fourth level.[56]

Interestingly, as in Ibn al-Mubārak's work, the four types of martyrs in this *ḥadīth* are all combatants. This report appears to have displaced in importance, at least in *faḍā'il al-jihād* works, the *ḥadīth* recorded in earlier compilations (the *Muṣannaf* s of 'Abd al-Razzāq and Ibn Abī Shayba, for example), which refer to five types of martyrs, four of whom were non-military martyrs. The *isnād* of this *ḥadīth*—Abū Bakr b. Abī Shayba from Zayd b. al-Ḥabbāb[57] from 'Abd Allāh from 'Aṭā' b. Dīnār from Abū Yazīd al-Khawlānī from Fuḍāla b. 'Ubayd al-Anṣārī from 'Umar b. al-Khaṭṭāb—is regarded as weak by *ḥadīth* experts, particularly on account of Abū Yazīd al-Khawlānī, whose particulars, such as his given name, are unknown. Al-Tirmidhī recorded this report, categorizing it as a good (*ḥasan*) but rare *ḥadīth* (*gharīb*), known only through the transmission of 'Aṭā' b. Dīnār (126/744).[58] It is worth noting that 'Aṭā' b. Dīnār, a Qur'ān commentator and *muḥaddith*, relied heavily on the reports of Sa'īd b. Jubayr (d. 95/714), an exegete who had composed one of the earliest *tafsīrs* specifically for the Umayyad Caliph 'Abd al-Mālik.[59] A putative *ḥadīth*, with unambiguous praise for various types of military martyrs, that promises absolution for all kinds of sins upon death would have been very useful, however, in exhorting people to enlist in the armies of the Umayyad period.[60] Sa'īd's reports, as transmitted through 'Aṭā', could be—and certainly were—effectively deployed toward this end.

Traces of the suffering non-military martyr remain in the following report related by Abū Burda b. Qays from his brother Abū Mūsā, who had heard the Prophet say, "O God, let my community perish by dying in the path of God through piercing [by a lance/sword] or the plague."[61] The clever play on the Arabic words (*bi-'l-ṭa'n wa-'l-ṭā'ūn*) in this *ḥadīth* (not found in any of the six authoritative Sunnī collections or previously encountered by us in the works surveyed so far) pithily harmonizes reports that variously allow for martyrdom to be attained as a result of being the victim of both military and non-military sources of affliction.[62]

A number of reports that we encountered in earlier works that include non-military definitions of martyrdom are not to be found in Ibn Abī 'Āṣim's treatise. Instead, Ibn Abī 'Āṣim records a report that appears to be a reworked version of these earlier *ḥadīths*; its content challenges the possibility of assigning martyrdom to a non-combatant. This report—not surprisingly—has a predominantly Syrian *isnād*; it is related by the now-familiar al-Hawtī from Baqiyya from 'Abd al-Raḥmān b. Thābit b. Thawbān from his father, who attributed it to Makḥūl al-Shāmī reporting from 'Abd al-Raḥmān b. Ghanān from Abū Mālik al-Ash'arī from the Prophet, who said, "Whoever departs in the path of God and either dies or is slain is a martyr. Should his horse or mule [throw him and] cause him to break his neck, then he is a martyr. Or if he is bitten by a snake or he dies in his bed in whatever manner God decrees for him, then he is a martyr."[63] What is noteworthy about this report is that it appropriates the various non-combative ways of dying or of being killed in relation to *any* individual, male or female, as enumerated in the archaic version recorded, for example, in the two early *Muṣannafs*, and applies them solely to the one who fights in the path of God. In other words, the warrior who dies of causes other than wounds inflicted on the battlefield may still be considered a martyr, according to this report; by implication, it thereby excludes the non-combatant who dies of natural and non-martial causes from being so considered. As might be expected, the *isnād* of this purported *ḥadīth* is very weak. The Ḥimṣī transmitter Baqiyya b. al-Walīd, for example, was notorious for fabricating reports from his teachers (as previously discussed in chapter 5), and Ibn Thawbān is considered in general to be a weak transmitter.[64] Makḥūl's hawkish views have been noted before, and he is clearly the key link in this *isnād*.

The exalted status of military martyrs is affirmed in the promise of abundant reward for them in the hereafter in a number of prophetic reports. One such *faḍā'il* report is related by al-Hawtī from Ismā'īl b. 'Ayyāsh from Buḥayr b. Sa'd from Khālid b. Ma'dan, but ends with Kuthayr b. Murra transmitting from Nu'aym b. Ḥammār, who reported that a man once came to Muḥammad and asked him, "Who is the best of martyrs?" He replied, "Those who meet people [standing] in rows and who do not turn their faces until they are killed. These are the ones who are cavorting in the highest pavilions (*fī 'l-ghuraf al-'ulyā*) of paradise. Your Lord laughs at them; whenever your Lord laughs at a servant in a battlefield then there is no reckoning for him."[65] This *faḍā'il* report is not to be found in any of the six authoritative compilations; al-Bukhārī referred to this *ḥadīth* not in his *Ṣaḥīḥ*, but in his *al-Ta'rīkh al-kabīr*, and pronounced it to be defective.[66] Of great importance to us is the description of these unflinching martyrs as residing in the grandest pavilions (*ghuraf*) in paradise—once again, representing the appropriation of an honor and idiom reserved in the Qur'ān for those who are patiently forbearing (cf. Qur'ān 25:75; also 29:58; 34:37; 39:20 for righteous believers in general), as noted earlier.

Despite the glorious station reserved in the hereafter for the genuine martyr, according to most reports recorded by Ibn Abī ʿĀṣim, one *ḥadīth* categorically prohibits the willful seeking of martyrdom. This is attributed to ʿAbd Allāh b. Abī Awfā, who wrote that "the Prophet, peace and blessings be upon him, counseled, 'Do not wish to meet the enemy. When you do meet them, be patiently forbearing; indeed paradise is under the shade of the swords.'"[67] This *ḥadīth*, as noted before, is included by al-Bukhārī and Muslim, among others, and generally deemed to be reliable.[68]

Interestingly, Qur'ān 2:195 ("Do not cast yourselves into destruction with your own hands"), understood prima facie to contain a proscription against taking one's own life, is reinterpreted in a non-prophetic report to refer to a different kind of [self]-destruction (*tahluka*). This *ḥadīth* is related by al-Ḍaḥḥāk b. Abī Jābira, who said that the Anṣār used to give alms generously; then one year, they were afflicted by a misfortune, and they desisted from giving charity. At that, God caused Qur'ān 2:195 to come down.[69] This re-reading of the verse allows the relevant term *tahluka* to be understood as the posthumous punishment reserved for those who are miserly, and not for those guilty of self-inflicted death. Such an interpretation potentially allows for the conscious seeking of martyrdom, in circumvention of both Qur'anic and sunnaic prohibitions of the same. It should come as no surprise to us then that the *isnād* of this report has been impugned by *ḥadīth* critics. Among the transmitters of this report are the Basrans Ḥammād b. Salama (d. 167/783), whose *ḥadīths* were repudiated by al-Bukhārī,[70] and Dā'ūd b. Abī Hind (d. ca. 140/757), who was criticized for falsely attributing reports to Anas b. Mālik and described by Aḥmad b. Ḥanbal as being prone to relating confused and contradictory reports.[71]

Later Treatises from the Fourth/Tenth Century and Beyond

Kitāb qudwat al-ghazī by Ibn Abī Zamanīn (d. 399/1009)

The *Qudwat al-ghāzī* is a hybrid work, straddling the *faḍā'il* and *aḥkām* genres, a combination that is not unusual in this later period. For our discussion here, we focus primarily on the *faḍā'il al-jihād* sections of this work, which constitute its bulk. The work was the composition of Abū ʿAbd Allāh Muḥammad b. ʿĪsā al-Murrī, also known as Ibn Abī Zamanīn, a Mālikī jurist and *muḥaddith* from Elvira, Spain. He wrote a number of works on *fiqh* and *zuhd* and was the author of a commentary on Mālik's *al-Muwaṭṭa'* and a digest of Saḥnūn's *al-Mudawwana*.[72]

The *faḍā'il al-jihād* genre is a well-established one by this period—the late fourth/tenth century. Most of the works belonging to this genre contain by-now-familiar *ḥadīths* and reports extolling the variegated merits of combative *jihād* and martyrdom. Thus Ibn Abī Zamanīn records the previously encountered *ḥadīth*, "Fighting (*al-jihād*) in the path of God is one of the gates of heaven...,"[73] and the one stating that standing in battle ranks is better than worship for seventy years.[74] Moving beyond these frequently quoted *ḥadīths*, we focus on reports not encountered in our survey so far, allowing us to further speculate on the continuing development of this genre. It should be noted that, for the most part, Ibn Abī Zamanīn does not give detailed *isnāds* for these reports, making it more difficult for us to assess their probable provenances and paraenetic intents.

Many of these reports testify to a more heightened insistence on the superior merit of the combative *jihād* vis-à-vis other, more common, devotional practices. One such report narrated by ʿAṭā' al-Khurasānī relates that a man once came to the Prophet and asked him whether particular acts of his could measure up to the acts of the *mujāhid fī sabīl allāh*. When Muḥammad inquired about the nature of these acts, the man replied, "I stand [in prayer] at night and I fast all day." The Prophet remarked, "That is but like the sleep of one asleep in the path of God."[75] The Syrian ʿAṭā' b. Abī Muslim al-Khurasānī (d. 133/750) was known for his *mursal* reports, especially from Ibn ʿAbbās, and frequently quoted by Syrian authorities, such as Ibn Jurayj and al-Awzāʿī. This *ḥadīth* is not recorded in the six authoritative Sunnī compilations and occurs mainly in *jihād* treatises, such as the one by Ibn al-Naḥḥās (d. 814/1411; see further below). Al-Bukhārī included ʿAṭā' among the weak transmitters (*al-duʿafā'*); Yaḥyā b. Maʿīn faulted him for his mistakes in transmission and considered his reports inadmissible as proof-texts; and al-Dāraquṭnī and other *ḥadīth* critics refused to mention him in their *rijāl* works.[76]

Another *ḥadīth* without an *isnād* is recorded by Ibn Abī Zamanīn, who quotes the Prophet as saying, "The weapons of the Muslim are weighed every Thursday and Monday. If he has prepared it for God, then his merits increase. If, however, he has prepared it for Satan, his demerits increase."[77] As might be expected, this report with its unusual reverence for military hardware is not to be found in the early *muṣannaf* works or in the six authoritative Sunnī *ḥadīth* collections.[78]

We also find in Ibn Abī Zamanīn's treatise what has now become fairly commonplace reports in *faḍā'il al-jihād* works that praise the merits of both land-based and coastal *ribāṭs*. Most of the *faḍā'il* reports in the *Qudwat al-ghāzī* suggest that the combative *jihād* in general, and *ribāṭ* in particular, is more meritorious than common supererogatory acts of devotion. One such report attributed to Abū Hurayra states that *ribāṭ* for one night along the sea coast is more beloved to him than spending "the night of power" (*laylat al-qadr* during Ramaḍān) in one of the two mosques—the Grand Mosque in Mecca or the mosque of the Prophet in Medina.[79] Such exceptionally hyperbolic reports are not found in earlier *ḥadīth* compilations. Their occurrence in later treatieses on *jihād* clearly indicates that the manufacturing and circulation of such vaunting reports continued unabated through the ninth and tenth centuries, particularly in response to new military threats from the Byzantines during this time. Particularly in the second half of the tenth century, there was a renewed Byzantine offensive against the maritime and land frontiers controlled by the 'Abbasids.[80] These hostile encounters must have provided the impetus for the continuing manufacture and circulation of more *faḍā'il al-jihād* reports in specific praise of coastal *ribāṭ* calculated to rouse the population to fight against the ever-encroaching Byzantine enemy.[81] The vaunting nature of many of these reports further testifies to a continuing vibrant dialectics among various groups on the construction of moral excellence and its ramifications for the organization of society through the height of the 'Abbasid period.

A fairly extensive section in Ibn Abī Zamanīn's treatise deals with the important ethical dilemma of having to fight under dissolute rulers. How may one discharge the necessary religious duty to defend Islamic realms against external aggression and square one's conscience with the fact that one has to serve under morally reprobate commanders? The reports in this section, here mostly equipped with complete *isnāds*, are highly significant in that they allow us to reconstruct to a considerable degree the circumstances of the early debates among pious Muslims concerning the validity of such acts. In one such report, the Mālikī jurist Saḥnūn (d. 240/854) relates from Ibn al-Qāsim, who stated:

> It has reached me that Mālik [b. Anas] used to dislike fighting the Byzantines (*jihād al-rūm*) with these rulers. But when it was the time of Mar'ash and the Byzantines did what they did, he [sc. Mālik] retreated from his position [literally, his speech] and said, "There is no harm in conducting *jihād* with them; for if *jihād* with them were to be abandoned, that would be injurious for the people of Islam."

Ibn Abī Zamanīn adds the postscript: "This is what Mālik arrived at and it is what all the leaders of Muslims are agreed upon."[82]

Mar'ash, called Germanikeia by the Byzantines, was destroyed by Constantine V in 129/746, as reported by al-Balādhurī and Theophanes.[83] The Syrian-Umayyad provenance of this juridical position, which justifies an otherwise morally dubious course of action for pragmatic reasons of military defense, is firmly established in this report attributed to Mālik b. Anas.

Other reports go further in creating a weightier pedigree for this juridical opinion by attributing it to the Companions as a collectivity, and now not only obliterating in them any suggestion of moral quibble over the legitimacy of fighting under the Umayyads, but mandating such fighting as a required religious duty. A report with a Syrian *isnād* is related by Asad b. Mūsā from Thawr b. Yazīd from Makḥūl, who said:

> It was asked of the Companions of the Messenger of God, peace and blessings be upon him, when they were afflicted with oppression, "Do you campaign with these [rulers] while they do what they do?" And each of them replied, "Campaign according to your share in Islam. If they resort to deception, do not deceive; if they commit treachery, do not commit treachery; if they cause destruction (*wa-in afsadū*), do not cause destruction; if they are rebellious, do not rebel. Fight for your portion in the hereafter and leave them to fight for their share of the world. And beware of causing harm to the faithful!"[84]

All three Syrian transmitters of this report have mixed reputations. Asad b. Mūsā b. Ibrāhīm b. al-Walīd b. ʿAbd al-Malik b. Marwān al-Umawī (d. 212/827) was regarded as having related unacceptable reports and was described as weak in his transmission by Ibn Ḥazm and others.[85] Thawr b. Yazīd b. Ziyād al-Kilāʿī (d. ca. 153/770) was from Ḥimṣ, whose transmission was rejected by Mālik b. Anas, although others considered him reliable.[86] Finally, Makḥūl al-Shāmī, the near-ubiquitous Damascene jurist in these contexts, is said to have narrated many *ḥadīths* that were *mursal*. Although Ibn Ḥajar considered Makḥūl to be a *thiqa* despite the latter's propensity to relate *mursal* reports, Ibn Saʿd regarded him as weak in his narration, while al-Dhahabī accused him of forging *ḥadīths*. However, influential scholars like al-Awzāʿī, ʿIkrima, and al-Ḥajjāj b. Arṭa'a (d. ca. 145/762) narrated from Makḥūl, as a result of which his reports gained considerable currency and became recorded in influential *ḥadīth* compilations.[87]

In one *ḥadīth* with a full *isnād*, a blatant attempt is made to draw a parallel between the battles fought during the Prophet's lifetime and military campaigns undertaken by the Umayyads. It is narrated by Asad b. Mūsā once again from Baqiyya b. al-Walīd from al-Zuhrī from ʿUbayd Allāh b. ʿAbd Allāh b. ʿUtba b. Masʿūd, who related that the Prophet said, "There will spring up after me a group who will harbor doubts about *jihād*. The one who undertakes *jihād* at that time will have [the reward] of the one who undertakes *jihād* with me today."[88] As indicated before, both Asad b. Mūsā and Baqiyya have less-than-stellar reputations as *ḥadīth* transmitters; the Ḥimṣī transmitter Baqiyya (d. ca. 197/812) was known for his prolific fabrication of *isnād*s and indiscriminate transmission of *ḥadīth*s from unreliable sources.[89] Al-Zuhrī was the famous Medinan scholar generally trusted by the *ḥadīth* specialists; however, he was very close to the Umayyad rulers and known to have held *ḥadīth* dictation sessions attended by senior Umayyad officials, who frequently recorded his reports.[90] A pro-Umayyad bias on the part of al-Zuhrī would therefore not be unexpected in such a situation. Finally, ʿUbayd Allāh b. ʿAbd Allāh is described as having been prone to relating *mursal* reports, as in this case.[91]

Another report gives us a hint as to what kinds of people may have been opposed to the military adventurism of the Umayyads. It is narrated by al-Ṭalḥī from ʿAbd al-Raḥmān b. Zayd b. Aslam from his father, who reported that the Prophet had remarked:

> *Al-jihād* will remain sweet and verdant as long as rain drops fall from the sky. There will come a time for people when the reciters of the Qur'an (*qurrā'*) among them will say, "This is not the time for *jihād* (*laysa hādha bi-zamān jihād*)." Whoever reaches that time [will have reached] the best of times for *jihād*. [The people gathered] asked, "Someone will [actually] say that?" He replied, "Yes, the one upon whom is the curse of God, His angels, and all the people."[92]

The main link in this *isnād*, ʿAbd al-Raḥmān b. Zayd (d. 182/798), is universally described as relating weak and unreliable reports, as maintained by Aḥmad b. Ḥanbal, al-Nasā'ī, Ibn al-Jawzī, and others.[93] As we have noted before, Ibn Zayd, like his father Zayd b. Aslam, was known for his particularly belligerent views, and a number of our reports advocating the superior merit of military activity are attributed to him. Despite the assessment of the *isnād*, the report is of considerable value to us in identifying one of the groups opposed to fighting under the Umayyads—the *qurrā'*, usually identified as the Qur'ān reciters.[94] This term, it should be noted, also appears to have been used broadly to refer to pious, abstemious groups of people, often variously referred to as *nussāk*, *zuhhād*, etc. in the literature.[95] It is very likely that the term is being used here in this broader sense. The perspectives of these early pious groups appear to have been quite anti-statist and anti-militarist, particularly in the Umayyad context, and they continued to be disseminated well after them.

In addition to Ibn Zayd, Asad b. Mūsā, whose dubious credentials we referred to above, appears quite frequently in the *isnād*s of these reports, which sternly warn against ever abandoning fighting. One report similarly condemning those who say "there is no *jihād*" (*la jihāda*) in later times is narrated by Asad b. Mūsā from Juwaybir from al-Ḍaḥḥāk from Ibn 'Abbās.[96] As the editor points out, Juwaybir b. Sa'd al-Azdī (known as Abū 'l-Qāsim al-Balkhī; d. between 140/757 and 150/767) was described by al-Nasā'ī and al-Dāraquṭnī as someone to be avoided (*matrūk*), while Ibn Ma'īn dismissed him as "amounting to nothing" (*laysa bi-shay'in*).[97] It is also known that the Successor al-Ḍaḥḥāk b. Muzāḥim al-Hilālī (known as Abū 'l-Qāsim al-Khurasānī; d. between 102/720 and 105/723), although described as a *thiqa* by Aḥmad b. Ḥanbal, related *mursal* reports and was said not to have heard anything directly from any Companion, including Ibn 'Abbās.[98]

Asad b. Mūsā's name occurs in the *isnād* of another report that specifically advocates fighting alongside the notorious Umayyad governor of Baṣra, al-Ḥajjāj b. Yūsuf. In this report, Muḥammad b. 'Abd al-Raḥmān b. Yazīd asks his father whether he had fought during the time of al-Ḥajjāj. The reply is memorable: "O my son, I have met men whose revulsion for al-Ḥajjāj was greater than yours towards him; yet they would not ever renounce fighting with him under any circumstance."[99] Asad's name is similarly to be found in the *isnād* of another report that relates that the celebrated Companion Abū Ayyūb al-Anṣārī, who had fought at Badr, initially had misgivings about joining the campaigns of Yazīd b. Mu'āwiya, but soon thought better of it and began to participate in them, dying later in Byzantium.[100] The central link in this *isnād* is the Basran Naṣr b. Ṭarīf, who is said to have been repudiated as "one of the people of falsehood" by *rijāl* experts and whose *ḥadīths* were declared to be invalid for use as proof-texts.[101]

Finally, Asad b. Mūsā (along with al-Uwaysī) related from Ismā'īl b. 'Ayyāsh from 'Abd al-Quddūs from al-Ḥasan [al-Baṣrī] that the Prophet had stated, "Islam is founded upon the *jihād* being continuous since [the time] God sent His messenger until the last group of Muslims who will fight the anti-Christ. It [the duty of *jihād*] is not diminished by the injustice of the one who is unjust nor by the justice of the one who is just."[102] A more forthright counter-response to those who expressed concern about fighting with dissolute rulers cannot be found. Not surprisingly, the *isnād* of this *mursal* report is rather weak; it is weakened by the inclusion of the names—not unexpectedly—of Asad b. Mūsā and Ismā'īl b. 'Ayyāsh, in addition to that of the Ḥimṣī transmitter 'Abd al-Quddūs b. al-Ḥajjāj al-Khawlānī, also known as Abū 'l-Mughīra (d. 212/827).[103]

All these tendentious reports then were circulated to challenge those who had strong moral scruples about fighting with the worldly Umayyads—and, after them, with the worldly 'Abbasids as well[104]—and who harbored grave reservations about the moral legitimacy of such military activity. The intensity of the polemics directed against those sections of the population who considered a legitimate *jihād* to be impossible under such reprobate rulers indicates to us—once again paradoxically—the strength and continuity of this oppositional, pious contingent and the cogency of its position.

Aḥkām al-jihād wa-faḍā'ilihi by 'Izz al-Dīn 'Abd al-'Azīz b. 'Abd al-Salām al-Sulamī (d. 660/1262)

The Syrian Shāfi'ī jurist and Ash'arī theologian'Izz al-Dīn 'Abd al-'Azīz b. 'Abd al-Salām b. Abī 'l-Qāsim b. al-Ḥasan al-Sulamī al-Dimashqī was recognized as the *mujtahid* of his time and was called *Sulṭān al-'ulamā'* after his death. Al-Sulamī was also very interested in Sufism and for the last twenty years of his life spent in Egypt, he would frequently visit the Sufi master Abū 'l-Ḥasan al-Shādhilī (d. 656/1258) and attend *samā'* sessions. At first appointed as preacher and *qāḍī* at the great mosque of 'Amr b. al-'Āṣ in Fusṭāṭ, he later resigned and embarked on a career as a teacher of Shāfi'ī law at the Ṣāliḥiyya madrasa established in Cairo by the Mamluk ruler Najm al-Dīn Ayyūb (d. 647/1249).[105]

Despite having *aḥkām al-jihād* in the title, al-Sulamī's treatise is not a conventional legal exposition of *jihād*—it notably does not deal with the division of booty or the levying of taxes on conquered populations, for example. This treatise is almost completely based on citations of relevant Qur'anic verses and *ḥadīths*, from which the author extrapolates (or the reader is led to extrapolate) broad injunctions concerning the proper performance of the military *jihād* and its abundant merits, as is typical of most literary *faḍā'il al-jihād* works.

Al-Sulamī was writing in a period of great turmoil, with Islamic realms besieged externally by the Crusaders and Mongols and wracked internally by the corruption of some of the Mamlūk rulers, all of which "struck at the core of the Muslim polity and sapped its strength."[106] In this charged atmosphere of fear and insecurity, it is not surprising that al-Sulamī's treatise begins with urgent exhortations to the faithful to take up arms against the rapacious invaders. The author commences by proclaiming that "the best of works after faith in God is *jihād* in the path of God because it is a means towards destruction of the enemies of God and the earth's cleansing of them. . . ."[107] He marshals as his proof-texts Qur'ān 9:41,which states, "Strive (*jāhidū*) with your wealth and selves in the path of God," as well as Qur'ān 2:216, which prescribed fighting for the Companions against the Meccan polytheists.[108] He also cites the *ḥadīth*, "Strive (*jāhidū*) against the polytheists [*al-mushrikīn*] with your wealth and tongues," which means, al-Sulamī comments, "Be stern with them in [your] speech." These proof-texts establish for him the moral imperative for resisting the aggression of the new "polytheists" of al-Sulamī's time—the Crusaders and the Mongols. The believers, like the first generation Muslims, must be roused to assume this critical duty, he says. Qur'ān 4:84 and 8:65, which commanded the Prophet to "exhort the believers" (*ḥarriḍ al-mu'minīn*) to fight against the pagan Meccans, are deployed in this new historical context to prod Muslims out of their lethargy to fight for their very existence in the eighth/fourteenth century against the powerful, destructive armies of the Crusaders and the Mongols.[109]

In this vein, al-Sulamī next proceeds to detail the merits of the combative *jihād* and emphasizes the exalted station reserved in the next world for those who fight in the way of God (Qur'ān 4:74; cf. 4:95–96). He refers to a *ḥadīth* related by Abū Sa'īd al-Khudrī that affirms that only the believer who undertakes the military *jihād* in the way of God may aspire to an exceptional status in paradise; the distance between the status of the *mujāhid* and non-*mujāhid* is comparable to the distance between the heavens and the earth.[110] Some of the *ḥadīths* cited by al-Sulamī in praise of *jihād* occur in authoritative *ḥadīth* collections, such as the *Ṣaḥīḥ* of al-Bukhārī, a number of which we discussed earlier (see chapter 5) and need not engage us here further. The *faḍā'il* reports that he assembles in this work focus on, among other issues, the necessity of making proper preparations for military campaigns, the importance of having sincere intentions when undertaking *jihād*, keeping vigil at night in the path of God, and being resolute against the enemy. Some of these reports also catalog the merits of fasting while fighting, achieving either victory or martyrdom in the path of God, and enduring the travails (*mashāqq*) of undertaking the military *jihād*.[111]

A proper *jihād* should be undertaken, according to al-Sulamī, with the sincere intention to serve God alone and to fight "so that the word of God is ascendant"—only such a warrior is deemed to be "in the path of God."[112] Muslims also fight in the path of God for the sake of the weak and the oppressed (*al-mustaḍ'afīn*; Qur'ān 4:75) and to liberate their prisoners of war.[113] Al-Sulamī lists a *ḥadīth* in which Muḥammad counsels against committing treachery and mutilating bodies. If an allied party commits treachery, stern measures are to be taken against them, including their expulsion. When battle commences, Muslims must remain united, firm, and unrelenting with the enemy.[114] They must not wrangle among themselves, for that would inevitably lead to failure; rather they must patiently persevere for "God is with the patient" (Qur'ān 8:46).[115]

Al-Sulamī further stresses the cultivation of patience during fighting, referencing Qur'ān 2:270, 3:200, and 2:177, and the necessity of imploring God for His assistance (cf. Qur'ān 3:159).[116] As for seeking an end to hostilities, Muslims should not sue for peace while they have the upper hand (cf. Qur'ān 48:35); but if the other side inclines toward peace, "then incline towards it and trust in God" (cf. Qur'ān 8:61).[117] He deems the cutting down of trees and the destruction of homes in enemy territory permissible, if this leads to the adversary's demoralization and dishonor, referencing Qur'ān 59:5.[118] Al-Sulamī further emphasizes the necessity of taking proper counsel from learned people, specifically during military campaigns (based on Qur'ān 3:159, which states, "Pardon them, ask forgiveness for them, and consult them in [various] matters"), and more generally in every realm of behavior (*fī kull taṣarruf*), in emulation of the Prophet.[119]

The emphasis on scriptural warrants in this treatise for exhorting the populace to fight against the onslaughts of the Crusaders and the Mongols conveys to us the sense of urgency on al-Sulamī's part and the sanctity of such an undertaking. Despite such urgency, however, our author maintains great concern for establishing righteous intent, purpose, and conduct during defensive *jihād* against foreign aggressors.

Kitāb al-ijtihād fī ṭalab al-jihād by Ibn Kathīr (d. 774/1373)

This short treatise, separated by over a century from al-Sulamī's work, was written specifically for the *amīr* Manjaq b. 'Abd Allāh, Sayf al-Dīn al-Yūsufī (d. 776/1374), the Syrian deputy of the Mamlūk sultan al-Nāṣir Muḥammad b. Qalawūn in Damascus, by the well-known Syrian Mamluk historian and *muḥaddith* 'Imād al-Dīn Ismā'īl b. 'Umar b. Kathīr, who was a student of Ibn Taymiyya (see below).[120] Ibn Kathīr was responding to a request by the *amīr* that "I write down what was feasible [on my part] from the Book (the Qur'ān), the *sunna*, and reliable reports regarding the carrying out of *ribāṭ* along the fortified Islamic frontiers, so as to rouse their inhabitants by means of the rewards that God has prepared for them [for carrying out this duty]. . . ."[121] The enemy was the Crusaders, specifically the Franks of Cyprus, who were laying siege to the Lebanese-Syrian coast at the time.

Like al-Sulamī before him, Ibn Kathīr adduces several Qur'anic verses and various *ḥadīths* as proof-texts to point to the essential duty of fighting to defend the frontiers of Islam. The Qur'anic verses are, in order of appearance, 9:123; 9:29; 9:14–15; 47:1–9; 61:10–13; 9:111–112; and 9:19–22, all of which refer to striving or fighting in the path of God. Whereas al-Sulamī had propounded the merits of the combative *jihād* in general, Ibn Kathīr stresses in particular the merits of undertaking *ribāṭ* in his selection of *ḥadīths*. Most of the *ḥadīths* he lists in exhortation of *ribāṭ* have been previously noted by us in our discussion of earlier works. For example, he includes the *ḥadīth* recorded by al-Bukhārī on the authority of Sahl b. Sa'd al-Sa'idī: "*Ribāṭ* for one day in the path of God is better than the world and what is upon it." He also records the *ḥadīth* contained in *Ṣaḥīḥ Muslim*, which declares the *ribāṭ* of one day in the path of God to be better than fasting and praying for a month. According to another *ḥadīth* recorded by Aḥmad b. Ḥanbal, the reward for carrying out *ribāṭ* continues to multiply even after death, protects one from the tribulations of the grave, and so forth.[122] Ibn Kathīr also includes the one report from Umm al-Dardā' that declares that *ribāṭ* for three days along the coast was the equivalent of a whole year's land-based *ribāṭ*.[123]

The invocation of the *ḥadīth* above advocating *ribāṭ* along the coast takes on great urgency in view of the fact that Ibn Kathīr specifically denounces in this treatise the Crusader invasion of the coastal city of Alexandria, Egypt, in the month of Muḥarram in the year 767/1365. He bemoans the fact that, due to the lack of vigilance on the part of the inhabitants and the absence of the Mamluk deputy from the city, the Franks (*al-faranj*) had charged into Alexandria, plundered its wealth, slain its men, imprisoned the women and children, and caused general destruction and mayhem. They were finally beaten back by "the advent of the banners of Islam and the recitation of verses of might and succor against them. . . . "[124]

A similar fate befell the Crusaders when they attacked Tripoli (Tarābulus) and laid siege to its coast at the beginning of 769/1367. The Crusaders subsequently attacked 'Īyas, a coastal town in southern Asia Minor, but their advance was once again successfully repelled by the Muslims. The importance of defending the coastline—whereby the Franks had gained access to Muslim realms—and being vigilant in general across the frontiers becomes patently clear in Ibn Kathīr's account of these various Crusader onslaughts during his time. At one point in his narrative, he describes the Muslim army heroically fending off the Frankish assault "while being patiently steadfast and ever-vigilant at the frontiers" (*muṣābiran murābiṭan muthāgiran*), in conscious invocation of Qur'ān 3:200 and explicitly yoking military activity to *ṣabr* and *ribāṭ*.[125] Ibn Kathīr's use of key, highly emotive words from the *faḍā'il al-jihād* literature to describe the exemplary courage of the Muslim soldiers proves to us his familiarity with the idiom of this literature. It also demonstrates to us the well-established nature of this idiom, which our author skillfully manipulated in order to more effectively goad the population into rising up against the invaders.

As part of this literary construction, Ibn Kathīr casts these latter-day Muslim-Christian hostile encounters as essentially a continuation of events that occurred during the lifetime of the Prophet and the era of the Rightly Guided Caliphs. Thus he refers to Muḥammad's abortive expedition to Tabūk, Syria, in the last year of his life as a harbinger of later Muslim excursions into Syria and beyond.[126] Military forays into Iraq and Syria during Abū Bakr's time, the conquest of Jerusalem (Bayt al-maqdis) under ʻUmar, and Muʻāwiya's conquest of Cyprus, for example, are all cited as historical precursors of contemporary military engagements.[127] Such an uninterrupted pedigree reaching back to the time of the *salaf* (the Pious Forebears), of course, grants greater moral luster to these Mamluk campaigns and casts them as part of a larger cosmic design to stave off disorder and iniquity in the world, and they are thus inevitably blessed by Providence. Lest the atrocities of the Crusaders on capturing Jerusalem in 493/1099 be repeated, when they massacred almost 70,000 of "worshipful, abstemious, and humble Muslims," the Muslim polity must exercise great vigilance, cautions Ibn Kathīr, particularly along its vulnerable shores where the Franks first made their incursions.[128] As was true during the Umayyad period, so it was true in Ibn Kathīr's time—*ribāṭ*, particularly along the coast, was the key to a successful defensive strategy against ferocious invaders, a strategy we already saw vigorously endorsed in the reports praising the merits of coastal *ribāṭ* circulating from the late first/seventh century onward.

Ibn Kathīr ends this short treatise by focusing on the importance of the city of Damascus in this heroic battle against evil in his own time—highly appropriate (and necessary) in a hortatory work written at the behest of the city's ruler. Our author refers to the *ḥadīth* of the Companion al-Nawās b. Samʻān (who later settled in Syria) and others, as recorded in the *Ṣaḥīḥ Muslim*, according to which Jesus will descend from the heavens at the end of time and alight upon the eastern minaret in Damascus at the time of the dawn prayer, while it is besieged by the armies of the anti-Christ. This is an indication, he says, that Damascus will remain the abode of faith, security, and stability until the coming of Jesus.[129] Such a divine guarantee was meant to assure the Muslims of Ibn Kathīr's time that they would survive the Crusader onslaughts, as long as they fulfilled their required role as defenders of Islamic realms.

Mashāriʻ al-ashwāq ilā maṣāriʻ al-ʻushshāq by Ibn al-Naḥḥās (d. 814/1411)

Aḥmad b. Ibrāhīm b. Muḥammad al-Dimashqī al-Dumyatī, better known as Ibn al-Naḥḥās, was originally from Syria and then settled in Dumyat (Damietta) in Egypt during the time of the later Crusades. Details about his life are fairly sketchy. Timur Lane's attack on Damascus in 1400 may have played a role in our author's departure from Syria. In 1411, he died in a Crusader raid on Egypt.

This Mamlūk work also shows a preoccupation—typical for its time—with the necessity of waging the combative *jihād* to rid the Muslim world of its external enemies—the Crusaders who at this time had occupied Cyprus and continued to raid the Syrian and Egyptian coastal areas, as well as the Mongol hordes. The first chapter is thus concerned with establishing the necessity of fighting against the unbelievers (*al-kuffār*) and warning against abandoning this duty in one's lifetime. Ibn al-Naḥḥās cites Qur'ān 2:216, 244, 251; 9:5, 29; and 22:40 in support of this imperative. He also cites two *ḥadīths*; in one, Muḥammad promises to fight people until they bear witness to the oneness of God, and in the other, declares the combative *jihād* to be a duty for Muslims under any and every ruler, regardless of whether he is just or unjust, the equation being drawn with the permissibility of praying behind any Muslim regardless of his moral probity.[130] Other *ḥadīths* cited by Ibn al-Naḥḥās similarly underscore the obligation to fight against the enemies of Islam.[131] Such an obligation is understood to be a collective duty (*farḍ kifāya*) that must be carried out once a year.[132] The collective duty becomes an individual one in case of an attack on Muslim lands.[133]

As to be expected, there is an extensive section on the merits of the military *jihād* and those who undertake it (*faḍl al-jihād wa-'l-mujāhidīn fī sabīl allāh*). Reports variously place the military *jihād* below faith, the required prayers, and filial devotion; or below faith alone; or create a moral equivalence between resolute faith, taking part in a military campaign not marred by illegal appropriation of the spoils (*ghulūl*), and a properly executed pilgrimage.[134] In other reports, *jihād* is declared to be more meritorious than (1) giving the call to prayer; (2) offering water to pilgrims during the *ḥajj*; and (3) undertaking the lesser pilgrimage.[135] Yet other reports maintain that the combative *jihād* was the best of all actions without exception (*'alā 'l-iṭlāq*); that *jihād* was the most beloved of all actions to God; that the fighter (*mujāhid*) was the best of all people; and that no one was able to carry out a deed that was the equivalent of *al-jihād fī sabīl allāh*.[136]

Certain *faḍā'il* reports in the *Mashāri' al-ashwāq* assert the absolute superiority of the combative *jihād* over the *ḥajj*,[137] a position that is interpreted by Ibn al-Naḥḥās to mean that *jihād* is better than the optional or voluntary pilgrimage. If, however, *jihād* should be transformed into an individual duty, then, he says, it takes absolute precedence over the required pilgrimage because of its urgent nature.[138] Other reports included by Ibn al-Naḥḥās assert the superiority of campaigning at sea over land;[139] and praise the virtues of "spending in the path of God" (*al-nafaqa fī sabīl allāh*),[140] of making adequate preparations for military forays,[141] and of undertaking *ribāṭ*, among other military activities.[142] In fact, it is noteworthy that each and every activity connected with fighting is deemed highly meritorious and assured of a heavenly reward in an appropriate report, usually prophetic. Thus the archer reaps the reward equivalent to that earned by someone who manumits a slave and is vouchsafed paradise.[143]

Horse racing in preparation for battle is commendable,[144] as is excelling in horsemanship and the use of weapons.[145] Fighting in organized rows is laudable,[146] and it is meritorious to be wounded in the path of God.[147]

Ibn al-Naḥḥās deals with the important question of whether the individual who rushes out to battle to confront a superior army could be considered guilty of committing suicide or resorting to self-destruction (*al-tahluka*), categorically proscribed in Qur'ān 2:195 ("Do not cast yourselves into destruction with your own hands"). The answer is no for the following reasons: According to one report from al-Barā' b. al-'Āzib, "the man who meets the enemy and fights until he is killed" is not guilty of *tahluka*, for God says in another verse, "Fight in the path of God; you are responsible only for yourselves" (Qur'ān 4:84). According to al-Barā', Qur'ān 2:195 has to do with financial expenditure (*al-nafaqa*).[148] Another report makes more explicit this particular meaning of *tahluka*. It emanates from the Successor al-Qāsim b. Mukhaymara (d. ca. 100/718), who defined *tahluka* as "the abandonment of expenditure in the path of God" and stated that such a term could not be applicable to the man who "attacks tens of thousands [of enemy troops]—in that there is no qualm."[149] Ibn Mukhaymara was a transplanted Kufan who moved to Syria to carry out *ribāṭ* and was close to Umayyad ruling circles, allowing us to credibly impute to him the motivation of self-interest for preferring this particular interpretation of Qur'ān 2:195.[150] We recall that Ibn Abī 'Āṣim in his book on *jihād* had also included a report that had advanced a similar understanding of *tahluka*, and whose *isnād* similarly contained the name of transmitters with dubious motivations. Other reports recorded by Ibn al-Naḥḥās praising those who charge into battle even under unfavorable circumstances emanate from either a Companion or a Successor; the Prophet's own speech or conduct is not cited to set the precedent for such actions.

Like some earlier scholars, Ibn al-Naḥḥās weighs the respective merits of those who die [naturally] in the way of God and those who are killed [on the battlefield] (*al-mayyit fī sabīl allāh wa-'l-maqtūl*). He refers to the well-known *ḥadīth* concerning Umm Haram, who was felled from her riding mount and proclaimed to be a martyr by the Prophet. Despite this and other similar *ḥadīths*, Ibn al-Naḥḥās expresses a clear preference for the school of thought that considers those killed on the battlefield to be more meritorious. In defense of this latter position, he cites the report according to which Muḥammad was queried as to which *jihād* was more excellent, and he replied, "When your steed is hamstrung and your blood spills out." Furthermore, Ibn al-Naḥḥās continues, reason suggests to people in general that the one slain on the battlefield is more excellent than the one who dies elsewhere, and that the one who intends to carry out a deed is better than the one who intends to do so but subsequently dies without realizing his intention, even if his reward is the same as that of the slain individual. Even if one who dies [naturally] in the path of God were to receive the same reward as military martyrs (*al-shuhadā'*), such a person is still referred to as "dead" or "deceased" (*mayyit*), which the slain person never is. God Himself forbade that in Qur'ān 2:154 when He stated, "Do not say regarding those slain in the path of God that they are dead—they are rather alive." Moreover, only the one slain in the path of God is rewarded for the wounds he suffered by being resurrected on the Day of Judgment with his blood still flowing, "its color the color of blood and its aroma the aroma of musk," something that is denied to those who simply die.[151]

Other critical differences between the *mayyit* and the *maqtūl*, according to Ibn al-Naḥḥās, are that the latter wishes to return to earth upon becoming aware of the exalted status of the military martyr in the next world, and he is assured of forgiveness of all sins unlike the former. Furthermore, his body is not washed and prayed over, for his sins have already been forgiven. To those who would remark that the word *shahīd* is applied to both types equally, he remonstrates that in common usage the term is reserved exclusively for "the one slain in the path of God." Other distinctions are that the soul of the *maqtūl*, unlike that of the *mayyit*, is lodged inside a green bird in paradise; the *maqtūl* is not subject to any tribulations in the grave and is able to intercede for others. The slain military martyr (*al-shahīd al-maqtūl*) sees the dark-eyed celestial damsel before his blood dries, unlike the *mayyit*, even though both attain *shahāda*. Thus, although Ibn al-Naḥḥās concedes that those who die from a stomach ailment, the plague, drowning, or in a fire are all called *shuhadā'*, none of them may attain the elevated and unique status of the military martyr because of the travails he undergoes in waging war.[152] Ibn al-Naḥḥās's extensive discussion of the relative merits of the military and non-military martyr clearly indicates to us the vigor with which this topic was still being debated in his time. Against the backdrop of relentless attacks by the deadly foes of his time—the Crusaders and Mongols—there was no doubt in our author's mind that military defense of Islamic realms and dying while engaged in it were the most morally excellent and religiously meritorious deeds in his contemporary environment.

In the rest of his treatise, Ibn al-Naḥḥās emphasizes the importance of hewing to the classical rules of proper conduct before, during, and after a military campaign. The *mujāhid* must therefore be knowledgeable about the legal and normative rules concerning warfare.[153] If he should be guilty of *ghulūl* (which he defines as stealthily siphoning off a part of the spoils before its formal division) and subsequently die in battle, he is not to be considered a *shahīd*.[154] Ibn al-Naḥḥās affirms the general proscription against killing women and children who do not fight, indicates the legal differences of opinion concerning other groups of people, and discusses the use of deadly weapons such as mangonels, the cutting of trees and crops, the remuneration of soldiers, the treatment of prisoners of war, and other issues related to conduct during and after warfare.[155]

Ibn al-Naḥḥās concludes his treatise by referring to the well-known *ḥadīth* recorded by al-Bukhārī, Muslim, ʿAbd al-Razzāq, and others in which the Prophet forbids expressing a desire to meet the enemy.[156] He also includes *ḥadīths* in which Muḥammad proscribes the mutilation of bodies, burning by fire, resorting to treachery, and breaking of pledges, for these, Ibn al-Naḥḥās records, are all great moral infractions before God.[157] Our author ends with a heartfelt plea to Muslims to adhere to these lofty principles of conduct and seek God's forgiveness for their shortcomings.[158]

Concluding Remarks

As with the *ḥadīth* literature, a careful reading of the micro-discourses contained within the early and late treatises on the merits of *jihād* discussed in this chapter demonstrates that a broad range of views existed in the early period regarding the repertoire of meanings to be ascribed to *jihād* and the moral valence of the activities signified by the term. Changing historical circumstances and growing Muslim vulnerability to external attacks colluded to sharply delimit this spectrum of meanings assigned to *jihād* and elide its broader, particularly non-combative, dimensions over time—an understandable development given the fraught historical contexts in which this literature emerged. The plentiful existence of the kind of hortatory reports discussed in this chapter underscores the centrally important role that military activity under the rubric of *jihād* came to play within the imperial policies of the Umayyads, the ʿAbbasids and their successors. *Faḍāʾil al-jihād* reports exhorting Muslims to undertake the military *jihād*, and especially land and coastal *ribāṭ*, as the most morally excellent activity, become particularly strident during the Mamluk period characterized by continuing Crusader and Mongol attacks. When these larger historical contexts become uncoupled from some of these *faḍāʾil al-jihād* works, their content can, as it has, conduce to the essentialist view that Islam is inherently militant. Such decontextualized material can also be deployed, as it has been in our own time, to create a powerfully compellingly narrative about the normativity of violence to be directed against non-Muslims, as will become apparent in chapter 8.

Although the scholars discussed in this chapter mostly emphasized the military dimensions of *jihād* in the dangerous world in which they lived, other scholars wrote edifying literary works in which they gave prominence to the cultivation of patient forbearance as an essential ingredient of human striving in the world and as the perennial feature of *al-jihād fī sabīl allāh*. We turn our attention to a representative sampling of them in the following chapter.

VII

The Excellences of Patient Forbearance

COUNTER-NARRATIVES ON STRIVING IN THE PATH OF GOD

THE ATTRIBUTE OF *ṣabr* (translated here as "patience" or "patient forbearance") was valued by pre-Islamic Arabs and continued to be valorized in the Islamic period. The verb *ṣabara* had the original meaning of "to bind"; thus *ṣabara nafsahu* yielded the meaning of "to bind oneself" or hence to "control oneself" and thus be patient in the face of life's vicissitudes.[1] In Qur'anic discourse, *ṣabr* in this sense of stoic patient forbearance is an important component and dimension of the overall enterprise known as *al-jihād fī sabīl allāh*. Quietist and activist resistance to wrongdoing as encoded in the dyads *jāhadū/ṣabarū* and their derivatives are equally valorized in specific verses (cf. Qur'ān 3:142; 16:110; 47:31, etc.). Generous posthumous rewards are promised in the Qur'ān to believers for the conscious inculcation of patience and forbearance. In the Qur'anic context, patient forbearance is an attribute not only of the peaceful, non-militant striver in the path of God, but also of the combatant who takes up arms in response to the aggression of the enemy. *Ṣabr* is the constant, defining attribute of the believer in any and every circumstance which aids him or her in carrying out the simplest to the most arduous of quotidian and exceptional tasks in obedience to God. *Ṣabr* in the Qur'ān is thus inevitably tied to *jihād*, broadly construed as the ongoing human struggle on earth.

To reconstruct more holistically early competing perspectives on what constitutes *al-jihād fī sabīl allāh* and who most efficaciously strives in the path of God, we therefore have to take into account how *ṣabr* as a component of *jihād* found reflection in the non-legal writings of Muslims concerned with such issues. If *ṣabr* is understood mainly as the non-combative and internal dimension of *jihād* (what is later called *jihād al-nafs*), then it is not surprising that we find inadequate or no reflection of it in standard juridical works and political treatises in which the focus on *jihād* was primarily in the context of external relations with non-Muslim polities, and thus inevitably military in nature. Discourses on the merits of inculcating and practicing *ṣabr* as an internal moral and psychological attribute of the pious believer belonged more appropriately to the realm of religious ethics and social conduct (broadly *akhlāq* and *adab* in Arabic), not to the hardheaded realms of international law and Realpolitik. *Ṣabr* after all could be neither legislatively mandated nor enforced by the state. But moral and ethical treatises composed by scholars of various stripes could and did propound this essential trait in the believer, and its moral priority could be wielded as a tool to challenge a perceived excessive emphasis on externalized, physical, and ritualized manifestations of piety and religiosity. By extension, it is possible to suggest that, starting already from the Umayyad period, emphasis upon *ṣabr* in certain circles as the pervasive and most important dimension of striving in the path of God was intended to be a moral and ethical corrective to the predominantly militarist and aggressive definitions of *jihād* and martyrdom promoted in administrative and juridical circles. These perspectives extolling patient forbearance are being retrieved here primarily from the exegeses of specific Qur'anic verses that refer to *ṣabr* and the "excellences of patience" literature.

In this first part of the current chapter, as a complement to Qur'ān 3:200, which contains references to various dimensions of *ṣabr* (discussed in detail in chapter 1), one more key Qur'anic verse (39:10) from the middle to late Meccan period will be discussed. This verse is often invoked in the ethical literature generally and in the *faḍā'il al-ṣabr* literature specifically to underscore the scriptural basis for the inculcation of the attribute of patient for bearance. More important, this verse explicitly promises generous and exceptional rewards in the hereafter *exclusively* to the *ṣābirūn*, a fact little noted outside of the "excellences of patience" genre, overshadowed as this verse is in the general literature on *jihād* by other verses exhorting believers to struggle physically with their lives and wealth and fight against wrong-doing and consequently reap bounteous heavenly rewards. The implication of Qur'ān 39:10 for an alternate hierarchy of moral excellence deserves further exploration. We focus here at the micro-level on how some of the principal exegetes have interpreted Qur'ān 39:10, followed by a discussion of Qur'ān 16:110 and 3:142, which conjoin *ṣabr* to *jihād*. Once again, the emphasis is on diachronic comparison of these interpretations to tease out the subtle and not-so-subtle transformations in these micro-discourses.

In the second part of this chapter, we focus on the ways in which *ṣabr* as a normative attribute of the pious is described and endorsed in specific literary works that belong to the larger "excellences of patience" genre.

The Recompense of Patient Forbearance: Exegeses of Qur'ān 39:10

Qur'ān 39:10: O my servants who believe—fear your Lord! For those who do good in this world is goodness and God's earth is wide. Indeed the patient/steadfast ones will be given their reward without measure (*innamā yuwaffā al-ṣābirūn ajrahum bi-ghayr ḥisāb*).

Muqātil b. Sulaymān (d. 150/767) briefly comments that the first part of this verse means that believers who perform good deeds (*al-'amal*) will be given paradise (*al-janna*). God's wide earth refers to the city of Medina. He assumes that the meaning of the patient/steadfast ones (*al-ṣābirūn*) is clearly apparent and does not offer a further explanation of who are intended by this term. He understands the last part of the verse to indicate that the reward of the *ṣābirūn* is "paradise and their [unlimited] provisions within it."[2]

Hūd b. Muḥakkam (d. ca. 290/903) understands "those who do good" (*alladhīna aḥsanū*) in this verse as a reference to those who believe (*āmanū*). The *ḥasana* in this world is a reference to "what God gives them of goodness (*khayr*) in the world," that is, their "seemly obedience" (*ṭā'a ḥasana*) to Him in this world, as well as to the goodness they reap in the next world. God's wide earth has to do with the territory to which Muslims were commanded to emigrate (cf. Qur'ān 29:56). The *ṣābirūn* are those who are steadfast in their obedience to God and in their avoidance of disobedience to Him; their reward is paradise. The phrase *bi-ghayr ḥisāb* means that there is no reckoning for them in paradise (*lā ḥisāba 'alayhim fī 'l-janna*); here Ibn Muḥakkam references Qur'ān 40:40, which also contains this phrase.[3] It should be noted that the referents in Qur'ān 40:40 are pious men and women in general who have faith and are therefore guaranteed entrance into heaven.[4] Like the patiently forbearing in Qur'ān 39:10, they too will be given provisions without measure.

In his exegesis of this verse, **al-'Ayyāshī** (d. ca. 320/932) records a *ḥadīth* related by Ja'far al-Ṣādiq in which the Prophet states, "When the scrolls [of deeds] are unfurled and the scales are raised [on Judgment Day], there will be no raising of scales for the people of tribulations nor will the scrolls be unfurled for them." Then Muḥammad recited this verse.[5]

Al-Ṭabarī (d. 310/923) says that the verse commands the Prophet to say to the believers that, if they obey God and avoid disobeying Him, then they will reap *al-ḥasana*, which is variously understood to refer to paradise by a majority of scholars or goodness in this world, such as health (*al-ṣiḥḥa*) and vigor (*al-'āfiya*), as maintained by the early exegete al-Suddī (d. 128/745). The reference to God's wide earth is understood by al-Ṭabarī to contain a command for believers to "emigrate from the land of polytheism to the land of Islam," as was the understanding of another early exegete Mujāhid b. Jabr (d. 104/722).[6]

Like Muqātil, al-Ṭabarī says that the last part of this verse promises that "the people of patient forbearance" (*ahl al-ṣabr*) will be given their reward without measure in the hereafter for what they endured in this world. He refers to Qatāda b. Di'āma (d. 118/736), who had understood the verse to make clear that there would be no "weighing and apportioning" of the reward due to the people of patient forbearance.[7] Both Muqātil and al-Ṭabarī understand "patience" or "patient forbearance" to be a general attribute of righteous believers in the face of life's trials.

Al-Wāḥidī (d. 468/1076) glosses "Those who do good" as those who place their belief in the oneness of God and perform good deeds, for which they reap paradise. He refers to Ibn 'Abbās, who interpreted the statement "And God's earth is wide" to mean that God intended for Muslims to leave Mecca and emigrate to a safe place (cf. Qur'ān 4:97). He also promises to amply reward those who are steadfast in their religion and who do not abandon it in spite of the persecution they face as a consequence. The verse was specifically revealed in reference to Ja'far b. Abī Ṭālib and his companions who would not abandon their religion when they were severely persecuted for adhering to it; instead, they persevered patiently and emigrated, in this case to Abyssinia. Al-Wāḥidī thus establishes a specific connection between emigration in the face of persecution and the exercise of patience/steadfastness, as exemplified by Ja'far b. Abī Ṭālib.

As for "their reward will be without measure," the early exegete 'Aṭā' b. Abī Rabāḥ (d. 114/732) is said to have understood this statement to mean that their reward will be such "as could not be imagined by the mind nor could be described." Al-Wāḥidī further quotes Muqātil, who had commented that this phrase meant that the reward of the believers will be paradise and "their provisions within it will be limitless."[8]

Al-Zamakhsharī (d. ca. 538/1144) prefers the understanding that *al-ḥasana* refers to the reward reaped by the believers in the hereafter; thus it is unambiguously a reference to paradise, which by definition is a reward that defies description. He rejects al-Suddī's interpretation of *al-ḥasana* as a reference to worldly rewards like health and vigor on syntactic grounds.[9] As for the part that says, "And God's earth is wide," it urges believers, when they are prevented from carrying out good deeds (*al-iḥsān*) in their own lands, to emigrate to other realms, thus "emulating the prophets and the righteous peoples in their emigration to a foreign land, so that they may increase in righteousness and obedience." Al-Zamakhsharī understands the *ṣābirūn* to be specifically those who patiently bore the pain of separation from their homeland and kinsfolk and other trials and afflictions because of their obedience to God and their great virtue. "Without measure" means that no weight or proportion can be assigned to the reward that such virtuous people earn. The Companion Ibn ʿAbbās had appropriately remarked, "The calculations of the calculator cannot attain to it [sc. to such reward] nor can it be known." The Prophet himself had remarked,

> The scales will be raised and the people of alms will be brought forward and their compensations will be given with due measure. Likewise with [the people of] prayer and pilgrimage. Then the people of [who underwent] trials will be brought in and the scales will not be raised for them nor will their record [of deeds] be unfurled. Rather their reward will be heaped upon them without measure.

Upon seeing the extent of the reward for the people of trials, those who had been spared such tribulations would wish that they had suffered a similar fate on earth.[10]

Al-Rāzī (d. 606/1210) has a lengthy explanation of this verse; what follows is a summary of his main points that are directly relevant to our concerns.

Like many of his predecessors, al-Rāzī ponders whether this verse refers to reward in this world or the next.He concludes by favoring the meaning of *al-ḥasana* as "paradise," because the majesty, permanence, and elevated status indicated by this word have nothing to do with the debased and ephemeral conditions of this world, but are instead related to the noble, secure, and eternal conditions of the next. Borrowing practically verbatim from al-Zamakhsharī's commentary, al-Rāzī comments that the statement "And God's earth is wide" contains within it an exhortation to believers to emigrate from their land like the prophets and righteous people before them, when they can no longer fulfill their religious duties in it, to a different land where they are able to do so.[11]

Al-Rāzī thus understands *al-ṣābirūn* to refer specifically to those who were patient during their exile from their homeland and relatives, and who steadfastly endured the anguish and tribulations visited upon them as they strove to obey God. As a result, they have earned "reward without measure," which locution can be understood in three primary ways, he comments. First, according to al-Jubbāʾī (d. 303/916), the well-known Muʿtazilī scholar, this phrase means that the patient will be given the reward they deserve and more besides, which will be without measure. Reward that is strictly deserved is after all measured reward. The later Muʿtazilī theologian al-Qāḍī ʿAbd al-Jabbār (d. 415/1025) disagreed with this position and commented that even if these believers were given only their deserved compensation, it would still be "reward without measure" for there is no excess in compensation. Second, al-Rāzī continues, religious merit (*al-thawāb*) has three qualities. The first of them is that it earns for the righteous eternal reward. "Reward without measure" means "reward without limit," for everything that can be measured is finite. Whatever is infinite or limitless (*lā nihāya lahu*) is beyond measure. The second is that such earned merit in itself confers the entirety of benefits (*manāfi' kāmila*) upon the faithful, the essence of which the human intellect cannot comprehend. Thus the Prophet had said, "There is in paradise what no eye has seen, no ear has heard, and what no heart has perceived." Such reward exceeds what a human can imagine and expect; this is the probable meaning of "reward without measure," says al-Rāzī. A third aspect is that the reward of the people of tribulation (*ahl al-balā'*) has been interpreted to be beyond assessment by means of weights and scales. Here al-Rāzī refers to al-Zamakhsharī who had commented that in contrast to the people given to much prayer and alms-giving and who are rewarded in exact measure, the people who had undergone much tribulation will receive their reward without measure, so much so that people who had enjoyed more favorable conditions on earth would be envious of their greater reward.[12]

Al-Qurṭubī (d. 671/1273) says that the first part of this verse counsels the Prophet to warn the believers that they should avoid disobeying God. According to Ibn 'Abbās, the specific referent is Ja'far b. Abī Ṭālib and all those who emigrated with him to Abyssinia. The *ḥasana* refers to both their obedience and reward in paradise. Those exegetes who were of the opinion that the believers attained good in this world maintained that this was in addition to the reward they would reap in the next world. Such worldly rewards included health, vigor, victory, and the spoils of war. Al-Qushayrī (d. 465/1072) thought *al-ḥasana* only referred to reward in the hereafter, because the unbeliever also enjoyed the good things of this life. Al-Qurṭubī weighs in at this point and says the believer partakes of the good things of this life along with the unbeliever, but also earns paradise when he or she gives thanks for these bounties. In this world, *al-ḥasana* is seemly praise [of God for His bounties], whereas in the next, it refers to the just recompense (*al-jazā'*) for the believer. Like most other exegetes, al-Qurṭubī concludes that the verse contains an imperative to emigrate, specifically from Mecca, to a safe place.[13]

As for the critical last part of the verse, he understands *bi-ghayr ḥisāb* to mean "without measure/estimation" (*bi-ghayr taqdīr*). Some exegetes explained this phrase as referring to "additional reward" (*yuzād 'alā 'l-thawāb*), occurring without pursuit or demand, as one demands the good things of this world, notes al-Qurṭubī. Others said that the phrase *al-ṣābirūn* refers to those who fast (*al-ṣā'imūn*), as may be inferred from the following *ḥadīth qudsī*, in which God says, "Fasting is for Me alone, and I will reward it," implying boundless reward. According to Mālik b. Anas, however, this verse refers in a more general sense to patient forbearance in the face of the vicissitudes of this world and its sorrows. Without doubt, all those who patiently submit to their trials and avoid what has been prohibited will be given their reward without measure. Al-Qatāda had also emphasized the limitless nature of this kind of reward.[14] Al-Qurṭubī then narrates from Anas b. Mālik the *ḥadīth* recorded by al-Zamakhsharī in which the people of trials are described as earning their reward without measure when compared with the people of prayer and charity.[15]

As our survey shows, all the commentators discussed above generally understand the *sābirūn* to be those who struggle to obey God in adverse circumstances and bear life's tribulations with fortitude. The overwhelming majority of commentators also specifically connect this verse to emigration primarily to Medina, because of the unusual hardship and the pain of separation from loved ones that it entailed; al-Wāḥidī, however, connects it to Ja'far b. Abī Ṭālib and his emigration to Abyssinia. Al-Qurṭubī does not see an obvious connection in this verse between emigration and patience. Rather, he understands *ṣabr* in the general sense of being steadfast in the performance of essential religious obligations, including fasting based on a *ḥadīth qudsī*, with additional merit accruing from being patient during life's chronic vicissitudes.

It is noteworthy in this Meccan verse that fighting is not yet understood to be one of life's tribulations, and therefore *sabr* is not specifically yoked to it as it is later in the Medinan revelations. "Reward without measure" clearly trumps all other kinds of rewards in the Qur'ān and is earmarked solely for the *ṣābirūn*, who in the context of this verse stand head and shoulders above other righteous Muslims for having borne with equanimity the fierce persecution and exceptional afflictions heaped upon them in Mecca for their faith alone. Al-Zamakhsharī's comment, that when others see the extent of the reward reserved for the *ahl al-balā'*, they would wish that they had suffered a similar fate on earth, is highly significant. This topos of "reward envy" is highly reminiscent of the case of the military martyr who, on viewing his bounteous recompense in the hereafter, wishes to return to earth to keep adding to his martial feats and counsel others to do the same by inciting in them a desire to reap the same rewards. Once again, we discern the construction of competing paradigms of moral excellence that pit the non-combative, pious individual against the combative one.

Derivatives of jhd *and* ṣbr *together*

In this section, we deal with two Qur'anic verses (16:110 and 3:142) that couple derivatives from these two roots. Their exegeses by various commentators from different historical periods and different doctrinal persuasions provide us with a valuable window into how these verses came to be understood in variegated contexts, as we now proceed to discuss.

> As for those who emigrated after having been persecuted, then strove (fought) and were steadfast (*thumma jāhadū wa-ṣabarū*), then indeed your Lord is merciful and forgiving after that. (Qur'ān 16:110)

This early Medinan verse (as its context reveals)[16] was generally understood in the early period to refer to a specific group of Companions who were subjected to severe persecution in Mecca by the pagans and who later migrated to Medina and strove with the Prophet, as indicated by **Muqātil** and **Hūd b. Muḥakkam.**[17] Muqātil comments that the verse was specifically revealed in regard to several Companions: 'Ayyāsh b. Abī Rabī'a al-Makhzūmī, Abū Jundal b. Suhayl b. 'Amr al-Qurashī from the Banū 'Āmir b. Lu'ay, Salāma b. Hishām b. al-Mughīra, al-Walīd b. al-Mughīra al-Makhzūmī, and 'Abd Allāh b. Usayd al-Thaqafī, who emigrated to Medina after their persecution in Mecca. There they strove with Muḥammad and were steadfast after their persecution, for which God forgave all their past sins and showed mercy toward them.[18]

Al-Qummī simply says that the verse was revealed in reference to 'Ammār b. Yāsir.[19]

Al-Ṭabarī understands this verse to refer to

> those who emigrated from their homes and dwellings and their kinsfolk from among the polytheists and moved away from them to the homes and dwellings of Muslims (*ahl al-islām*) and to the people commanding their allegiance (*ahl wilāyatihim*), after having endured the persecution of the polytheists among whom they had been some of the most prominent members. Then they strove (*jāhadū*) against the polytheists after that with the sword in their hands and by their tongues by declaring themselves to be free of them and of what they worshiped besides the one God, and were patiently forbearing during their striving (*ṣabarū 'alā jihādihim*).[20]

It is noteworthy that al-Ṭabarī offers us a specific definition of *jihād* in this particular context, one that entailed both physical combat against the polytheists and public, verbal declarations of their dissociation from them. He continues that because of what they had endured, God promised them forgiveness and mercy in spite of their having uttered words of disbelief during their persecution in Mecca. This was so because their hearts had remained firm in their faith, and they had subsequently repented of their involuntary public apostasy.[21] According to Ibn Isḥāq, al-Ṭabarī records, the verse was revealed in reference to the Companions ʿAmmār b. Yāsir, ʿAyyāsh b. Abī Rabīʿa, and al-Walīd b. al-Walīd, while others, such as al-Ḥasan al-Baṣrī, were of the opinion that it referred specifically to Ibn Abī Sarḥ, who had apostatized and taken refuge with the pagan Meccans.[22]

In his brief commentary on this verse, **al-Wāḥidī** says that it was revealed concerning the weak (*al-mustadʿafīn*) among the faithful in Mecca who were tortured and forced to recant. Then this oppressed group made the *hijra* to the Prophet after their persecution and, according to Ibn ʿAbbās, they then strove/fought with Muḥammad and remained steadfast in their religion and *jihād*. Despite their public abjuration of Islam, they were forgiven by God. Ibn ʿĀmir read *futinū* as *fatinū*, which would mean that they oppressed their souls by their forced public professions of disbelief. At this time, it would have been considered an act of oppression because the concessionary or exculpatory verse (*al-rukhṣa*) concerning such involuntary acts had not yet been revealed, comments al-Wāḥidī.[23]

In his even briefer comments, **al-Zamakhsharī** states that the verse refers to ʿAmmār and his companions and what they endured of persecution and coercion into unbelief.[24]

Al-Rāzī[25] and **al-Qurṭubī**[26] reproduce in essence the same discussions concerning this verse recorded by al-Ṭabarī and al-Wāḥidī.

To sum up, Qur'ān 16:110 is understood by all the exegetes as maintaining a distinction between patient forbearance in the face of persecution and tribulations in Mecca and active striving during and after the *hijra*. As in Qur'ān 39:10, patience and striving in Qur'ān 16:110 are strongly linked to the act of emigration and the travails encountered while undertaking it, to which the new dimension of *qitāl* is added in the Medinan period. The early exegetes Muqātil and Hūd b. Muḥakkam understood striving (*jāhadū*) in the broadest sense and did not explicitly include fighting as a manifestation of it, although arguably that is to be inferred because the verse is Medinan. From al-Ṭabarī onward, however, it became customary to understand the verse as explicitly referring to fighting, as well as verbally proclaiming one's faith and dissociating oneself from the polytheists. Patient forbearance continues to be a desideratum in the post-*hijra* period, as a constant attribute of the believer in generally adhering steadfastly to Islam and specifically when undertaking the military *jihād*.

Did you think that you would enter heaven while God has yet to know those who strive (*jāhadū*) among you and those who are patient (*al-ṣābirīn*)? (Qur'ān 3:142)

Muqātil b. Sulaymān comments that this Medinan verse[27] means that God addressed the community of Muslims and informed them that they cannot assume they will enter heaven while He has yet to determine who among them truly strives in the path of God among people, and who among them are patient in the midst of tribulations. Muqātil here clearly distinguishes the *ṣābirīn* (quietists) from the *mujāhidīn* (activists). In his understanding, the former refers in general to all those who remain steadfast when faced with life's afflictions, whereas the latter is a specific reference to those who actively struggle for the sake of God. Here Muqātil does not state explicitly if "those who strive" refers more narrowly to those who fight for His sake.[28]

Hūd b. Muḥakkam very briefly remarks that this verse is comparable to Qur'ān 2:214, which states, "Did you think that you would enter heaven while there has not come upon you the like of that which afflicted those before you? Trials and tribulations fell upon them." This comparison reveals that Ibn Muhakkam understands Qur'ān 3:142 to be primarily referring to the vicissitudes of life that believers are generally subjected to as a trial from God.[29]

Al-Ṭabarī's commentary is very similar to Muqātil's: God addresses the Companions of Muḥammad and warns them that they cannot attain a noble and elevated status in His presence until it has become clear who is "the striver among you in the path of God according to what He has commanded you." The *ṣābirīn* in the verse are described as those who patiently endure trials and tribulations of all sorts.[30] Like Muqātil, al-Ṭabarī also maintains a distinction between the category of activist strivers (*mujāhidūn*) in the path of God, without mentioning what specific actions are connoted by this broad term, and the category of quietly forbearing believers (*ṣābirūn*) in the midst of afflictions, both of whom, he says, will be rewarded in the next world. In both Muqātil's and al-Ṭabarī's exegeses, these two groups of people are furthermore equal in merit to one another, and the *mujāhidūn* are not valued higher than the *ṣābirūn* (or vice versa).

Al-Ṭabarī further records that, according to Ibn Isḥāq (d. 150/767), when God says in this verse, "Did you reckon that you would enter heaven," He is asking, "and thereby attain a noble status in regard to my [promised] compensation while I have yet to test you with trials and afflict you with hardships so that I may know the sincerely believing among you and the patiently forbearing in all that happens to them for my sake (*fiyya*)?"[31] Ibn Isḥāq's commentary thus seemingly collapses any distinction between the *mujāhidūn* and the *ṣābirūn* and considers both groups of people so described as engaged in a general struggle to earn divine approbation by manifesting their sincere faith while patiently enduring life's tribulations. This is in contrast to Muqātil's and al-Ṭabarī's understanding, which maintains a distinction between these two categories.

We encounter a major interpretive leap when we reach **al-Wāḥidī** writing in the fifth/eleventh century. In contrast to Muqātil and al-Ṭabarī, al-Wāḥidī understands this verse to refer specifically to the battle of Uḥud in which God addresses those who were vanquished: "Did you think that you would enter heaven like those who were killed and exerted their utmost, and remained steadfast while enduring grievous pain and injury—[sc.] without following in their footsteps and enduring what they endured?"[32] Even though God knows the unknown, al-Wāḥidī comments, He has to ascertain the sincerity of believers in fact. In this brief commentary, al-Wāḥidī affirms that the lexeme *jāhadū* is to be understood more narrowly as fighting, and *ṣabr* is the quality evinced by sincere believers defending their faith on the battlefield, specifically during the battle of Uḥud in this case.

Al-Zamakhsharī[33] and **Fakhr al-Din al-Rāzī** similarly understand the combative *jihād* to be indicated in this verse and patience as the necessary quality for enduring its travails. Al-Rāzī says further, "It would not be possible for humans to attain happiness and paradise by neglecting this [act of] obedience."[34] As for the phrase, "So that He may know the patiently forbearing," the conjunction *waw* at the beginning of this phrase indicates that entry into paradise cannot occur if one abandons steadfastness during the combative *jihād*. The exegete Abū 'Amr[35] understood the *waw* to be the *waw* of *ḥāl* (indicating simultaneity of action), says al-Rāzī, so that the phrase means "you fight while you are steadfast."[36]

Al-Qurṭubī understands this verse to be a reference to the battle of Uḥud, and his commentary is almost a verbatim repetition of al-Wāḥidī's.[37]

In summation, our survey reveals that Muqātil and al-Ṭabarī maintained a clear distinction between the *ṣābirūn* and the *mujāhidūn* as those who patiently bear life's afflictions and strive actively for the sake of God, respectively. Along with Hūd b. Muḥakkam, these two exegetes furthermore did not identify fighting as a specific component of the striving of the *mujāhidūn*. The four post-Ṭabarī exegetes—al-Wāḥidī, al-Zamakhshari, al-Rāzī, and al-Qurṭubī—are, however, in agreement that *jāhadū* in this verse is an unambiguous reference to the military *jihād*, and that *ṣabr* is the necessary attribute that accompanies it and for which one receives posthumous reward. The specific historical context given is the battle of Uḥud. For these later commentators, the close proximity of the two terms in Qur'ān 3:142 facilitates the link between military combat and patience, the latter being a necessary element during the former.

The Faḍā'il al-Ṣabr *("Excellences of Patience") Literature*

The juridical-statist construal of *jihād* primarily as armed combat (*qitāl*) against non-Muslims, a view that had become ascendant by the second/eighth century, did not efface the earlier multiplicity of views regarding the term's meanings. Competing views challenging the predominantly legal understanding of *jihād* as military activity in support of the state appear to have emanated particularly from pietist circles as a corrective to what appeared to them as the state's unseemly glorification of the military *jihād* and apparent disregard for its moral underpinnings, as a number of our sources suggest. Such early "dissenters" in the late first/seventh through the third/ninth centuries were not necessarily pacifists or ascetic-mystics (this period is well before the rise of institutional Sufism). They appear to have been rather pious ethicists, moralists, and scholars in general—those often referred to in the literature as *ahl al-'ibāda* or *'ubbād*—who appear inter alia to have taken exception to the reduction of *jihād* to essentially *qitāl* by certain jurists and by the state's perceived willful disregard for establishing just cause for the military *jihād*. This trend would become even stronger in later Sufi circles after the fourth/tenth century.

The counter-narratives generated by these pietist, often anti-establishment, groups constitute in part a genre called *faḍā'il al-ṣabr*, which refers to "the excellences or virtues of patience/forbearance." It is a genre that is meant to be contraposed to the far better-known genre of *faḍā'il al-jihād*. As the name suggests, works of the former type extol the virtues of patience, forbearance, and fortitude, seeking to foreground the practice and exercise of these qualities as important aspects of piety in general and of struggling in the path of God, often invokng Qur'anic precedent, as we already discussed in chapter 1 in connection with Qur'ān 3:200. The *faḍā'il al-ṣabr* genre appears not to have been very prolific, if the extant literature is any indication. Standard *ḥadīth* collections do not typically have a section devoted to listing reports in praise of patience. In contrast, reports enumerating the merits of combative *jihād* are usually grouped into an essential chapter in such works.[38] There are, however, a few treatises on this topic, as well as chapters in larger works of ethics on the merits of *ṣabr*, usually coupled with the attribute of gratitude (*shukr*) to God. Such works illuminate for us the significance of this trait for religio-social activism of a non-martial type and therefore establish its direct and indirect association with *jihād*, as broadly conceived. Our discussion below of such compositions is necessarily selective due to length constraints.

Ibn Abī 'l-Dunyā and the Merits of Patient Forbearance

An early monograph available to us on the merits of patience and forbearance is the third/ninth century work of Abū Bakr 'Abd Allāh b. Muḥammad Ibn Abī 'l-Dunyā (d. 281/894), called *al-Ṣabr wa-'l-thawāb 'alayhi* ("Patience and the Rewards for It"). Renowned for his piety and abstemiousness, Ibn Abī 'l-Dunyā was a popular teacher and became the tutor of several 'Abbasid princes, including of the caliphs al-Mu'tadid and al-Muqtafī in their youth. He was the author of over one hundred works, of which only roughly twenty have survived. He lived and died in Baghdad.[39]

Most of Ibn Abī 'l-Dunyā's works, like the current one under discussion, deal with ethics and the cultivation of exemplary virtues, such as patience, humility, trust in God, charity, etc. *Al-Ṣabr wa-'l-thawāb 'alayhi* is remarkable for having preserved from a relatively early period *ḥadīths*, Companion reports, and other kinds of anecdotes that eulogize the attribute of *ṣabr* as superior to other qualities and give assurance of bounteous rewards in the hereafter for those who possess and manifest this attribute. In this work, patience above all is defined as an essential aspect of faith (*al-īmān*). Thus, according to 'Alī b. Abī Talib, patience in relation to faith is in the position of the head to the body, with the implication that faith itself would be gravely impaired if patience were to be severed from it. Subsequently, 'Alī went even further and proclaimed that whoever lacks patience, also lacks faith.[40] *Ṣabr* is also non-aggressive and non-retaliatory, according to some. Thus, according to Ḥawshab,[41] al-Ḥasan al-Baṣrī declared, "O mankind, do not cause harm; if you are harmed, be patiently forbearing!"[42] Al-Ḥasan also considered those who suppressed their anger as commendably self-restrained and greatly forbearing (*al-kāẓim al-sabūr*).[43] According to the Kufan pietist (*al-'ābid*) Muḥammad b. Sūqa,[44] patiently awaiting deliverance (*al-farāj*) from a trial is an act of worship.[45]

From a social-consequentialist perspective, the practice of *ṣabr* may be understood as promoting political and social quietism in specific historical circumstances. Advocating the inculcation of *ṣabr* could be and was indeed interpreted by some as evincing pro-Umayyad sympathies in the early period, as the practice of this attribute would discourage rising up in political revolt against tyrannical rulers.[46] But it is also possible to argue that these trends—the valorization of *ṣabr*, its promotion as the single most important human attribute the manifestation of which is necessary in practically every imaginable situation, and the abjuration of, at least unnecessary and unethical, physical aggression—in themselves may be regarded as constituting civil, non-aggressive forms of protest against the injustices of the day. In certain circumstances, it was a more morally efficacious way of resisting wrongdoing and, therefore, of carrying out *jihād*. When may one resort to physical means to challenge wrongdoing, and when not? The answer is suggested in a *ḥadīth* recorded by Ibn Abī 'l-Dunyā and narrated by Suday b. 'Ijlān al-Bāhilī in which the Prophet states, "If you should see a matter that you are not able to change, be patiently forbearing (*fa-'ṣbirū*) until God Himself changes it."[47] *Ṣabr* is not in itself conducive to quietism or worse, passivity. It has both activist and quietist dimensions depending on the choices and circumstances that confront a given individual possessed of certain aptitudes and level of empowerment that would allow him or her to effect change in the status quo. *Ṣabr* is the one indispensable attribute of the human being in the journey through life and negotiation of its uneven course, as emphasized by Ibn Abī 'l-Dunyā. Since trials and tribulations are a constant staple of life, "the believer is in need of patience as much as he is in need of food and drink."[48]

This perspective is affirmed in *ḥadīths* and other kinds of reports and anecdotes that point to the greater moral excellence of those who possess *ṣabr*. In one such *ḥadīth* recorded by Ibn Abī 'l-Dunyā with an impeccable *isnād* reaching down to Abū Sa'īd al-Khudrī, Muḥammad is reported as having stated, "Whoever is patient (*yaṣbir*), God will grant him solace (*yuṣabbiruhu*), and no one has been granted anything better or more abundant than patience."[49] Another *ḥadīth* related by 'Amr b. al-'Ās quotes the Prophet as follows:

> When God will gather together creation [on the Day of Judgment] a caller will cry out, "Where are the people of patient forbearance" (*ahl al-ṣabr*)? A group of people, few in number, will rise and hasten towards paradise. The angels will meet them and inquire, "We see you rushing towards paradise—who are you?" They will reply, "We are the people of patient forbearance." They [sc. angels] will ask, "What did your patience consist of?" They will respond, "We used to patiently persevere in obeying God and were steadfast in not disobeying Him." Then it will be said to them, "Enter paradise—the best of recompense for those who have acted [well]."[50]

Other reports explicitly proclaim that those practicing the virtues of veracity and patience are equivalent in moral status to the military martyr. Ibn Abī 'l-Dunyā records a statement attributed to 'Abd al-'Azīz b. Abī Rawwād (d. 159/775), a pious *mawlā* of Khurasanian descent, who related, "A statement affirming the truth (*al-qawl bi -'l-ḥaqq*) and patience in abiding by it is equivalent to the deeds of the martyrs."[51] Another report goes further and establishes the moral superiority of the patient, forbearing individual over all others, including the military martyr. He quotes this report on the authority of a certain ʿIṣma Abī Ḥukayma, who related:

> The Messenger of God, peace and blessings be upon him, wept and we asked him, "What has caused you to weep, O Messenger of God?" He replied, "I reflected on the last of my community and the tribulations they will face. But the patient from among them who arrives will be given the reward of two martyrs (*shahīdayn*)."[52]

This report categorically challenges other, better-known reports that assign the greatest merit to military martyrs, and posits instead a different, non-martial and nonviolent understanding of virtuous self-sacrifice. The affirmation of a greater reward for the patiently forbearing individual in the next world is also a validation of his or her higher moral status in *this* world.[53] As we mentioned earlier, such "dissenting" traditions are usually not found in the standard juridical and *ḥadīth* works, but in edifying literature that deals with ethics, character, and the spiritual formation of the believer. We should also note that it is the *ahl al-ṣabr* who are usually on the defensive in such works; the status of the patient non-combative person is more frequently compared to that of the military warrior, and the greater merit of the former is asserted in relation to the latter. In earlier works such as Ibn al-Mubārak's *Kitāb al-jihād*, the comparison was more frequently made in the reverse, indicating that it was the pro-military camp that was in the minority and on the defensive in the earlier period.

Many of the *faḍāʾil al-ṣabr* reports contained in Ibn Abī ʾl-Dunyā's work testify in fact to the existence of competitive discourses on the constitutive aspects of piety by his time. These reports typically emphasize the superiority of patience and forbearance over all other traits and activities, which by implication would include the military *jihād*. One such report is attributed to Abū ʿImrān al-Jūnī,[54] who stated, "After faith, the believer (*ʿabd*) has not been given anything more meritorious (*afḍal*) than patience with the exception of gratitude, but it (sc. patience) is more meritorious of the two and the fastest of the two to reap recompense (*thawāb*) [for the believer]."[55] A similar report attributed to Sufyān b. ʿUyayna (d. ca. 196/811) says, "The believers (*al-ʿibād*) have not been given anything better or more meritorious than patience, by means of which they enter heaven."[56] These reports are at odds with other, more frequently quoted reports that claim that falling on the battlefield brings swift and immeasurable heavenly rewards to the martyr. As noted earlier, one of the best-known reports on the issue of compensation for the *shahīd* is recorded by Muslim and Ibn Māja (d. 273/887) in their two authoritative *ḥadīth* collections, which states that all the sins of the martyr will be forgiven except for his debt.[57]

It is noteworthy that Ibn Abī 'l-Dunyā records a report found in praise of patience that invokes language very similar to that found in a report attributed to the Successor Abū Mijlaz[58] in praise of the military *jihād*, as recorded by 'Abd al-Razzāq in his *Muṣannaf.* According to this latter report, when Abū Mijlaz overheard a reader reciting Qur'ān 4:95, he commented that the higher rank promised in the verse to those who strive with their selves and their wealth over the sedentary was in fact "seventy ranks, and between each two levels, [a distance of] seventy years is reserved for the emaciated charge horse."[59] The report recorded by Ibn Abī 'l-Dunyā containing similar hyperbolic language in praise of patience is attributed to 'Alī b. Abī Ṭālib, who relates:

> The Messenger of God, peace and blessings be upon him, said, "Patience is of three kinds: patience during tribulations; patience in obedience to God, and patience in avoiding sin. Whoever has patience during a tribulation until he averts it by the seemliness of his forbearance, God will ordain for him three hundred levels [of recompense]; the distance between each level would equal that between the sky and the earth. And whoever has patience in obedience to God, God writes down for him six hundred levels; the distance between each level would equal that between the boundaries of the earth till the edge of the divine throne. And whoever has patience in avoiding sin, God prescribes for him nine hundred levels; the distance between each level is twice the distance between the boundaries of the earth up to the edge of the divine throne."[60]

'Alī's report considered together with the report attributed to Abū Mijlaz by 'Abd al-Razzāq suggests that there were efforts made to counter the kind of excessive glorification of the merits of military activity in certain quarters. The similar idiom contained in these two reports in terms of how many levels or ranks the armed combatant and the patient, forbearing individual striving in the path of God would earn or rise to in the hereafter suggests the vaunting nature of these reports and their conscious positing of opposed hierarchies of moral excellence.

Al-Ghazālī's Views on *Ṣabr*

Abū Ḥāmid Muḥammad al-Ghazālī (d. 505/1111), the famous *mujaddid* of the fifth/eleventh century, needs little introduction. Trained as an Ash'arī theologian, he suffered the equivalent of a nervous breakdown at the height of his professional career when he was assailed by doubts concerning the value of academic scholarship. This triggered a lengthy spiritual odyssey, at the end of which al-Ghazālī embraced Sufism and the experiential knowledge it engendered as the true path to God.[61]

To retrieve his valuable perspectives on *ṣabr*, we focus on his *Kitāb al-ṣabr wa-'l-shukr*, the thirty-second chapter of his magnum opus *Iḥyā' 'ulūm al-dīn*. Al-Ghazālī begins this chapter by asserting that faith (*al-imān*) is composed of two halves: patience and gratitude. These attributes are also part of the beautiful divine names: *al-Ṣabūr* and *al-Shakūr*. One who is ignorant of the truth of patience and gratitude is thus ignorant of the two essential components of faith and is consequently deprived of the possibility of drawing close to God, for one draws close to Him only through faith, asserts al-Ghazālī.[62]

Al-Ghazālī stresses that over seventy verses in the Qur'ān refer to *ṣabr*, its merits, and the reward earned by the believer for cultivating this attribute. He adduces several of these Qur'anic verses as proof-texts to establish the excellence of patience (*faḍīlat al-ṣabr*), as selectively referred to below. Verses that affirm that patient forbearance leads to positive consequences in this world and the next include Qur'ān 32:24, which states, "We appointed from among them leaders who guide according to our command when they were patiently enduring"; Qur'ān 7:137, which states, "Your Lord's fair word was fulfilled for the Children of Israel for what they had borne in patience and we destroyed all that the Pharaoh and his people had done"; Qur'ān 28:54, which states, "These will be given their reward twice over because they endure patiently and ward off evil with good and spend from what we provide"; and the well-known Qur'ān 39:10, which states, "Those who are patient will be given their reward without measure." This last verse, al-Ghazālī explains, stresses that unlike other deeds and attributes that are rewarded according to a certain measure, patience and forbearance are not subject to such limitations. One significant reason for this is that fasting is part of *ṣabr*, indeed it is half of *ṣabr*. And from among all the acts of worship, God designated fasting as the one act that is deserving of special, divine recognition, for He has informed us, "Fasting is for Me [alone] and I will reward it."[63]

The superiority of patience is established in various *ḥadīth*s and other reports, continues al-Ghazālī. Thus the Prophet asserted, "Patience is half of faith."[64] According to another *ḥadīth* narrated by Ibn 'Abbās, when Muḥammad came into the presence of the Anṣār, he asked them, "Are you believers (*mu'minūn*)?" When they remained silent, 'Umar spoke up: "Yes, O Messenger of God." He asked, "And what is an indication of your faith?" They said, "We give thanks during times of ease and are patient during times of hardship and we are content with what befalls us." The Prophet exclaimed, "By the Lord of the Ka'ba, [these are] believers!" According to a report, 'Umar b. al-Khaṭṭāb is said to have written to Abū Mūsā al-Ash'arī the following: "Be patient. Know that patience is of two kinds, one of them better than the other. Patience during calamities is good, but better than that is steadfastly avoiding what God the Exalted has forbidden. Know that patience is the foundation of faith. That is so because reverence for God (*al-taqwā*) is the most excellent of pious acts and reverence for God [is only established] through patient forbearance."[65]

Using well-established Sufi terminology, al-Ghazālī describes patience as one of the way stations (*maqām*) of religion, and a stop among the many stops for the traveler (on the path to God). He says all the way stations (*maqāmāt*) of religion are fashioned from three things: knowledge (*ma'ārif*), states (*aḥwāl*), and deeds (*a'māl*). Knowledge is the basis that generates states, which in turn generate deeds. He adds lyrically, "Knowledge is like the trees, states like the branches, and deeds like the fruit. This is a constant [dynamic] in all the stops along the way for the traveler to God."[66] Faith sometimes has to do specifically with knowledge and at other times with all three. Thus patience, as an essential component of faith, is contingent upon one's prior knowledge and current state.[67]

Patience is specifically a human attribute (*khāṣṣiyāt al-ins*), al-Ghazālī continues, denied to animals because of their deficient natures and to angels because of their perfection. Humans in their youth are like animals in that there is a preponderance of instincts in them at this stage, and they lack patience. Through God's infinite mercy, two angels are sent to the human at the onset of puberty, "one of which guides him and the other strengthens him," thereby elevating the human from the level of animals. Then there ensues a fierce struggle in the human soul between the "army" (*jund*) championing carnal instincts on one side and the army fighting on behalf of religious piety on the other. Patience, our author asserts, is required in the successful waging of "war" by the "troops" of religiosity over those of base carnal desires.[68]

The explicitly martial imagery invoked by al-Ghazālī in his description of this primal spiritual battle in the human soul is quite vivid and dramatic and underscores his conscious appropriation of militant vocabulary in order to invert its conventional meanings. Thus he says:

> Let us call this trait—which distinguishes humans from animals with regard to suppressing the carnal instincts and overcoming them—a religious incentive (*bā'ithan dīniyan*), and let us call the desire to succumb to base appetites the carnal incentive (*bā'ith al-hawā*). Let it be understood that the battle waged between the religious and the carnal

> incentives is subject to vicissitudes, and the locus of this battle is the individual's heart. The religious incentive emanating from the angels aids the party of God the Exalted and the carnal incentive emanating from the devils aids the enemies of God the Exalted. Patience is an expression of the perseverance of the religious incentive in its confrontation with the carnal incentive. If it perseveres until it overcomes and prevails over opposed carnal instincts, then the party of God has triumphed and becomes affiliated with the patient ones (*al-ṣābirīn*). If it should flag and weaken so that the carnal instincts vanquish it and it does not resolutely repel it, then it becomes affiliated with the followers of devils.[69]

The external cosmic battle between the forces of good and evil that will persist until the last times has been completely internalized by al-Ghazālī and transferred to the "battle-ground" of the human heart. To rephrase this, the external military *jihād* of the jurists that theoretically has to be waged against the enemies of God (sc. of the state) until the end of time has become transmuted into a relentless spiritual struggle in al-Ghazālī's exposition of the basic human duty to strive in the path of God.

Al-Ghazālī maintains that no one can persist in patience through difficult and easy times except through strenuous struggle (*illā bi-juhd jahīd*) and indefatigable effort; this persistence is called *taṣabbur. Taṣabbur,* wedded to reverence for God (*al-taqwā*) and a firm conviction in the positive consequences resulting from it, ultimately leads to the effortless inculcation of patience in the human soul. This has been promised by God in Qur'ān 92:5–8, which states, "As for those who give [alms], are God-fearing, and believe in the good, we will facilitate ease for them." The strong man, after all, easily vanquishes the weaker one with little effort. This is how the battle (*al-muṣāra'a*) between the religious and the carnal incentives is conducted, representing the battle between the troops of the angels and the devils, comments al-Ghazālī. Constant cultivation of patience leads to satisfaction or contentment (*al-riḍā*), which is a higher stage or way station (*maqām*) than patience. This is what the Prophet indicated when he said, "Know that much good inheres in patient forbearance of what you dislike."[70]

Ṣabr is particularly needed in carrying out obligatory and supererogatory religious duties (*al-ṭā'āt*). Three of such duties are mentioned in Qur'ān 16:90, which says, "Indeed God has enjoined justice and kindness (*iḥsān*) and the giving [of alms] to kinsfolk." Justice is mandatory (*farḍ*), says al-Ghazālī, *iḥsān* is supererogatory, while the giving of alms to relatives is a manifestation of one's noble character (*al-murū'a*) and familial loyalty. The performance of all these duties requires patience and forbearance.[71]

But greater patience is required in abstaining from all those matters expressly forbidden by God (*al-ma'āṣī*), to which we are urged by carnal impulses. As mentioned once again in Qur'ān 16:90, "He forbids lewdness (*al-faḥshā'*), reprehensible behavior (*al-munkar*), and injustice/rebellion (*al-baghy*)." The merits of such patient abstinence is evident in the *ḥadīth* in which Muḥammad says, "The emigrant (*al-muhājir*) is one who emigrates from what God has forbidden and the striver (*al-mujāhid*) is one who strives against his self."[72] Al-Ghazālī next proceeds to develop a threefold typology of patience adumbrated in the Qur'ān as follows: first, patience in carrying out the positive injunctions of God; second, in refraining from matters forbidden by Him; and third, in exercising self-restraint during the misfortunes that befall one, particularly during the earliest moments of a tragic event. The first type has three hundred levels or degrees (*daraja*), the second six hundred, and the last nine hundred. The last type of patience is displayed mainly by the prophets, for it is the hardest on the soul.[73]

Al-Ghazālī also singles out patient endurance of the harm inflicted by other people as "one of the highest levels of patience." He quotes from the Gospel (al-Injīl) as follows: "Jesus, the son of Mary, upon him be peace, said, 'It was said to you before—a tooth for a tooth, a nose for a nose, but I say to you, do not return evil with evil but rather to the one who strikes your right cheek turn to him the left cheek, and whoever takes your cloak, give him your shawl. . . . "[74] This statement, al-Ghazālī comments, enjoins patient forbearance in the face of injury by others. Such forbearance is deemed great because it is exercised in the presence of the religious and carnal impulses, as well as anger, that are provoked on such occasions.[75]

Like the authors of the *faḍā'il al-jihād* treatises discussed in the previous chapter, al-Ghazālī takes notes of Qur'ān 3:200, which states, "O those who believe, be patient and forbearing and firm; and reverence God so that you may succeed." He says that this verse has been explained to mean "Be patiently forbearing in God (*fī 'llāh*), be patiently forbearing with others through God (*bi-'llah*), and be firm with them with God (*ma'a 'llāh*)." It has also been said, he continues, that patience for the sake of God (*al-ṣabr li-'llāh*) is freedom [from reliance on others and on material things] (*ghanā'*); patience through God (*al-ṣabr bi-'llāh*) is survival (*baqā'*); patience with God (*al-ṣabr ma'a 'llāh*) is fidelity (*wafā'*); and patience away from God (*al- ṣabr 'an allāh*) is estrangement (*jafā'*). Here al-Ghazālī sees no reflection of the military *ribāṭ* in this critical verse (unlike some of his contemporaries), but stays close to the earlier meanings of these three verbs within the context of the Qur'ān as counseling the exercise of patience, fortitude, and forbearance.

In al-Ghazālī's exposition of *ṣabr* in the *Iḥyā'*, we thus see a dramatic transformation in the semantic and behavioral purview of the concept of *al-jihād fī sabīl allāh*, especially in comparison with the predominant juridical construals of this locution in our author's time. *Jihād* is unequivocally conflated with *ṣabr*, challenging the primarily legal conflation of *jihād* with *qitāl* and reviving one of the principal Qur'anic significations of the term. Moreover, the principal site for staging *jihād* shifts from the earthly battleground to within the human heart and/or soul. Such a transformation would strike a highly emotional chord within Islamic realms, and practically universal receptivity to it would become codified in the much-quoted *ḥadīth* dividing *jihād* into greater (physical/combative) and lesser (spiritual/non-combative) ones. This transformation is not al-Ghazālī's achievement alone of course, nor does he particularly break new ground in doing it. But by eloquently and methodically invoking and reworking Qur'anic themes of patience and forbearance and foregrounding them as the essential ingredients of the true unending *jihād*, al-Ghazālī offers us one of the most persuasive explanations of why this must be so. *Ṣabr*, as an irreducible component and product of faith, is the main bulwark against the forces of evil. Without *ṣabr*, no other attribute or deed is meaningful and may in fact become contaminated by hubris and other base inclinations. The militant language employed by al-Ghazālī in this discussion of *ṣabr* is arguably best understood as a conscious rejoinder to the proponents of the military *jihād*, establishing that the "militantly" patient and forbearing individual is engaged in a more arduous, and therefore more meritorious, battle against even more trenchant enemies. It is significant that the *Iḥyā'* has no section on the merits of the combative *jihād*, implying that it has no role to play in al-Ghazālī's project of the revivification of the religious sciences, at least at the individual level.[76] "The fighter in the path of God" who merely engages external enemies is then no match for "the travelers [on the path] to God" (*al-sālikīn ilā 'llāh*). The latter are "armed" along the various way stations with the more powerful weapons of patience and resolute forbearance against more debilitating internal foes in a holistic quest for God. In al-Ghazālī's exposition, there is no higher struggle and calling for the believer.

'Uddat al-ṣābirīn wa-dhakhīrat al-shākirīn, by Shams al-Dīn Muḥammad b. Qayyim al-Jawziyya (d. 751/1350)

A famous student of Ibn Taymiyya, the well-known Damascene Hanbalī jurist Ibn Qayyim al-Jawziyya was also considerably influenced by mysticism, as this work attests. A prolific author, he was a teacher of the next generation of influential scholars, such as Ibn Kathīr and Ibn Ḥajar al-ʿAsqalānī. His legal thought remains particularly popular in Wahhābī and Salafī circles today.[77]

In the introduction to this work, Ibn Qayyim al-Jawziyya begins by engaging in an eloquent paean to the attribute of *ṣabr* and its centrality in the Qur'anic discourse of piety and in the human being's relationship to God and to his or her fellow beings. The first paragraph of this introduction after the customary salutations is translated in full below, because it captures in essence the tenor of our author's main arguments developed in the rest of the book:

> Indeed God the exalted has made *ṣabr* [like] a race-horse which never stumbles and [like] a sharp sword which never misses [its target], and [like] an army which never suffers defeat, and [like] an impregnable fortress fortified against destruction and fissure. Victory (*al-naṣr*) and it are full-blooded siblings, for victory goes along with patience as does relief with distress, and hardship with ease. It is by far the most helpful [attribute] for the one among men who possesses it. Its position in relation to success (*al-ẓafar*) is that of the head to the body, for the All-Truthful, All-Trustworthy One in the unambiguous verses of the Book has guaranteed for those endowed with patience the awarding of their recompense without measure. He has informed them that He is with them through His guidance, His mighty help, and His clear victory. The Almighty said, "Be patiently forbearing, for God is with those who are patient" (*al-ṣābirīn*). By virtue of "this withness" (*bi-hādhihi 'l-maʿiyya*), the patiently forbearing are successful in attaining the goodness of this world and the hereafter, and thus His external and internal bounties. He Who is glorified has made leadership in religion dependent upon patience and conviction (*bi-'l- ṣabr wa-'l-yaqīn*). The Almighty said, and through His speech the rightly-guided are guided, "We have set up leaders from among them who follow Our command when they are patient and who have firm belief in Our signs."[78] (Qur'ān 32:24)

The blatantly martial undertone to the first part of this passage, otherwise an encomium to the essentially nonviolent trait of patient forbearance, is reminiscent of al-Ghazālī's invocation of the armies of God versus those of the devil who fight for supremacy within the conflicted human soul. Once again, such martial imagery should not come as a surprise to us when viewed within the larger dialectical matrix of such works. In this work, Ibn Qayyim, like al-Ghazālī, also (re)configures *jihād* as essentially the practice of and adherence to *ṣabr* and borrows the idiom of military *jihād* to express the intensity of the spiritual struggle within the human soul. He too talks about the religious instinct versus the carnal instinct. When the former is strong and predominant, it can easily vanquish "the army of passion." This situation only comes about with the constant cultivation of patience and forbearance, Ibn Qayyim says, that leads to victory in this world and the next. These are the kind of people referred to in Qur'ān 41:29–30, where the angels address the righteous believers after their death: "Do not fear and do not grieve, but rejoice in heaven which you have been promised. We are your friends in the life of this world and in the next." These are the people, affirms Ibn Qayyim, who have attained to "withness" with God along with the patiently forbearing ones (*al-ṣābirīn*), and "who have striven with regard to God in true striving (*jāhadū fī 'llāh ḥaqqa jihādihi*; cf. Qur'ān 22:78) and are the rightly-guided."[79]

Ibn Qayyim al-Jawziyya does not devalue the external combative *jihād* when and where there is a need for it and deems it a highly meritorious act in such specific contexts, but, like al-Ghazālī, he regards *ṣabr* as trumping all other traits and considers its active inculcation the best of all deeds under *all* circumstances, taking his cue from the high Qur'anic valuation of this attribute and its cultivation. In his estimation, the relentless internal human struggle to be patiently enduring of life's vicissitudes is a bloodless, yet more exacting, battle.

From scrutiny of other Qur'anic verses that reference *ṣabr* and its derivatives, Ibn Qayyim establishes the inevitability and paramount importance of practicing *ṣabr* in every sphere of life for the believer who wishes to be successful in this world and the next. For example, on the basis of Qur'ān 16:126, which states, "If you are patiently forbearing, then that would be good for the patient," *ṣabr* is to be understood as clearly conducing to goodness (*khayr*). On the basis of Qur'ān 3:120, which states, "If you are patiently forbearing and God-fearing (*tattaqū*), then their machinations will not hurt you at all; indeed God encompasses what they do," the inculcation of *ṣabr* and *taqwā* is an effective shield against the evil stratagems of the most formidable enemy. Qur'ān 3:146, which states, "And God loves the patiently forbearing (*al-ṣābirīn*)," establishes the greatest inducement (*a'ẓam targhīb*)—earning the love of God—for practicing *ṣabr*. According to Qur'ān 2:45, which states, "Ask the help [of God] with patience and through prayer; that is a great [imposition] except for those who are humble," believers are urged to seek help patiently and through prayer when confronted with life's difficult challenges and the hardships of religion. Another verse, Qur'ān 41:34, which states, "Good and evil are not equal; repel [evil] with that which is better/best (*aḥsan*) so that the one between whom and you there is enmity may become as if he were a close friend," informs us, says Ibn Qayyim, that wrongdoing is thwarted most effectively by morally superior deeds, and only those who are patiently forbearing resort to this practice. Qur'ān 42:43, which states, "And indeed those who are patient and forgive, that is surely among the most resolute of affairs," exhorts that patience be wedded to forgiveness to create a moral and behavioral synergy that is always productive and beneficial (*lā tabūr*).[80]

Because of this centrality of *ṣabr* in human lives established in the Qur'ān, Ibn Qayyim calls it the essential "harness of the believer" (*ākhiyat al-mu'min*), which drives his or her faith. One who lacks patience, he says, lacks faith. Faith consists of two halves: One half consists of patience (*ṣabr*) and the other of gratitude (*shukr*), as also maintained by al-Ghazālī.[81] One who desires the salvation of his or her soul and wishes to attain happiness cannot ignore these essential and basic attributes. Like al-Ghazālī, he describes patience as being of three kinds: (1) patience in carrying out the commands of God; (2) patience in refraining from forbidden and undesirable acts; and (3) patience in the seemly acceptance of what befalls us over which one has no control. This was the counsel given by the prophet Luqman to his son (cf. Qur'ān 31:17), and it is what the spiritual master 'Abd al-Qādir al-Jīlānī advised in his *Futūḥ al-ghayb*, remarks Ibn Qayyim.[82]

Like al-Ghazālī, Ibn Qayyim also takes special note of Qur'ān 3:200. Ibn Qayyim comments that the verse commands believers to be patient in themselves (*aṣbirū*), to be forbearing (*ṣābirū*) with their adversaries, and firm and resolute (*rābiṭū*) in their adherence to patience and forbearance. All these qualities are governed by God-fearing piety (*taqwā*), upon which one's salvation and success (*al-falāḥ*) depend. Ibn Qayyim further takes note of the fact that *al-murābaṭa* has come to mean guarding the frontiers where incursions by external enemies may take place. But in this specific Qur'anic verse, he asserts, it means guarding the frontiers of the heart so that base desires and the devil cannot enter it and thus rob it of its supremacy.[83] Here we have a specific analogy drawn between the resoluteness engendered by patient forbearance and the resoluteness displayed by the warrior patrolling the borders. Both play an essential role in warding off internal and external enemies that cause havoc to the proper ordering of life. But once again, like al-Ghazālī, Ibn Qayyim does not read into this verse a physical, combative meaning, despite its apparent prevalence in scholarly circles by his time (as per our survey of exegeses of this verse in chapter 1).

Other significant verses in this context are Qur'ān 13:19–22, which state:

> As for the one who knows that what has been revealed to you from your Lord is the truth like the one who is blind? Those possessed of insight take heed; [they are] those who fulfill their pacts with God and do not violate their agreement and those who join what God has commanded to be joined, and those who are in awe of their Lord and fear an evil reckoning. They are those who are patient *for the sake of God*, perform the prayers, and spend of what we have bestowed on them secretly and

openly and they ward off evil with good—they are those for whom is assured the reward of paradise.

Of note is that the phrase "for the sake of God" (emphasis added) used in connection with *sabr* is expressed in the Arabic as *ibtighā' wajh rabbihim*. This is a phrase (in a variant form) that we encountered in Ibn al-Mubārak's work *Kitāb al-jihād*, previously discussed in chapter 6, but in conjunction with the combative *jihād*. As we noted then, this represents a conscious borrowing on Ibn al-Mubārak's part of the original Qur'anic locution and its subsequent annexation to military activity to add greater moral luster to the concept of "fighting in the path of God." For Ibn Qayyim, the verse "And those who are patient for the sake of God" means that it is not enough for one to possess the quality of *ṣabr*; one should also evince it "sincerely for His sake" alone.[84] As with fighting for the sake of God, patience and forbearance for the sake of God were also contingent on correct and sincere intentions.

The above verses, Ibn Qayyim comments further, deal with all the issues pertaining to submission to God and faith (*al-islām wa-'l-īmān*). They furthermore refer to all the deeds that have been commanded and proscribed, and they underscore the importance of patience during life's tribulations. All verses that conjoin *taqwā* to *ṣabr* (for example, Qur'ān 2:45; 2:153; and 3:200), he says, affirm three essential matters: the truth or reality of God-fearing piety, the commission of good deeds, and avoidance of forbidden matters. It is remarkable that in this commentary on Qur'ān 13:19–22, which, according to Ibn Qayyim, encompass *all* matters pertaining to submission to God and faith, he makes no attempt to include fighting in the path of God as one of these essential matters. In accordance with the wording of these verses, the emphasis is rather on prayer and charity, the doing of good to compensate for evil, preserving familial and other bonds, and honoring one's commitments.[85]

Moreover, Ibn Qayyim points out that Qur'ān 90:18, which states, "Then those who are among the believers and exhort one another to patience and mercy, are the people of the right hand," means that "He, the Glorified, has designated the people of the right hand as the people of patience and mercy who practice these qualities and enjoin them on others." Furthermore, patience has been compared to prayer, one of the basic pillars of Islam and supports of faith, in Qur'ān 2:45, which states "Seek help [of God] with patience and prayer." Patience is also deemed the equivalent of "pious deeds" (*bi-'l-a'māl al-ṣāliḥa*) in general in Qur'ān 11:11.[86]

The *ḥadīth* literature similarly eulogizes *ṣabr*, and Ibn Qayyim provides several examples of such prophetic statements, many of which we have encountered before.[87] He also documents sayings in praise of patient forbearance attributed to prominent Companions and Successors, especially those renowned for their abstemious and scrupulous lifestyles, such as 'Umar b. al-Khaṭṭāb, 'Alī b. Abī Ṭālib, 'Umar b. 'Abd al-'Azīz, al-Ḥasan al-Baṣrī, Aḥmad b. Ḥanbal, the pious Syrian jurist Maymūn b. Mihrān, also known as Abū Ayyūb (d. ca. 116/734)[88] from al-Raqqa, Mujāhid b. Jabr, Ibn al-Mubārak, the Basran pietist Muṭrif b. 'Abd Allāh al-Shikhkhīr, and others.[89] These names give us an idea of the kind of pietist circles from which a number of these *faḍā'il al-ṣabr* reports apparently emanated in the late first/seventh to early second/eighth centuries. Ibn Ḥibbān's characterization of al-Shikhkhīr (who died at the beginning of al-Ḥajjāj's reign) in his *Kitāb al-thiqāt* as one of the *'ubbād* and *zuhhād* of his time would be a typical one for most of these transmitters.[90]

Concluding Remarks

Any project that wishes to reconstruct more holistically early competing perspectives on what constitutes *al-jihād fī sabīl allāh* and who among Muslims (or more broadly, among humans) most efficaciously strives in the path of God must also include discussions of *ṣabr* and its centrality in the construction of the "technologies of the self"[91] in the Islamic milieu. Inclusion of such counter-narratives in our discussion allows us to retrieve competing views of *jihād* and martyrdom that found inadequate reflection in standard juridical, exegetical, and *ḥadīth* literature, but were unquestionably relevant for the construction of an ethical and moral worldview for the pious Muslim. As discussed above, some of the reports and anecdotes contained in the *faḍā'il al-ṣabr* literature consciously invoke the idiom and ethos of the *faḍā'il al-jihād* literature, suggesting that the former was often generated in dialectical engagement with the latter. Taking its cue from the Qur'ān, the two *faḍā'il* genres, variously extolling the merits of patient forbearance and armed combat to resist and contain wrongdoing, came to represent countervailing definitions of how best to struggle for the sake of God, and they established competing, but also complementary, paradigms of religious piety and ethical behavior.

VIII

Modern and Contemporary Debates on Jihād *and Martyrdom I*

POLITICAL AND MILITANT PERSPECTIVES

MODERN AND CONTEMPORARY perspectives on *jihād* and its purview are sometimes both similar to and idiosyncratically different from the variegated early, classical, and late medieval understandings of *jihād* and martyrdom. As with earlier views, these later perspectives are conditioned by the socio-historical milieus in which they were shaped and are being shaped. We selectively deal with these views below, focusing primarily on those that have been deemed influential and far-reaching in their impact in recent times.

This chapter deals with modern and contemporary thinkers who have emphasized the military aspect of *jihād* over all others and have foregrounded the combative *jihād* as a religious duty to be waged against those deemed in general to be a threat to the physical and spiritual well-being of Muslims. Chronologically, we begin in the early twentieth century during the height of European colonial occupation of a broad swath of the Islamic world, go through the post-colonial period starting roughly in the mid-twentieth century, and end in the post-September 11 period in the early twenty-first century. Cataclysmic changes during these periods, over which they often had little control, evoked strong and varied responses from a number of Muslim scholars, thinkers, and activists concerned with their debilitating aftermaths.

Although in the nineteenth century the military *jihād* made a comeback as legitimate self-defense against Western colonizers,[1] a notable development in the early twentieth century was the reconfiguration of *jihād* as a means of effecting sociopolitical reform in Muslim-majority societies by the removal (with violence or other means) of indigenous authoritarian, secular governments. This is a new dimension to *jihād* not encountered in the pre-modern period. Legitimate political rebellion (i.e., with due cause) was usually termed *baghy* by the classical and medieval jurists[2]; despite recognition of its potential legitimacy, rebellion against lawful authority, however, was greatly discouraged. Illegitimate political rebellion (i.e., without due cause) was categorically proscribed and equated with highway robbery, brigandage, and what in today's parlance we would call "terrorism" (*ḥirāba*).[3] Unlike contemporary times, armed uprising against a well-entrenched government, however tyrannical it might be perceived to be, was usually not justified under the rubric of *jihād* in the pre-modern period. This development alone marks a radical departure from pre-modern juridical and political thought.

The Rise of Political Islam and Post-Colonial Jihād *in the Twentieth Century*

The following section focuses on the views of three principal ideologues of what has been termed "political Islam" or "Islamism" in the twentieth century—Ḥasan al-Bannā, Abū 'l-'Alā' Mawdūdi, and Sayyid Quṭb. Their views on *jihād* are particularly influential in Islamist circles. We then describe the views of post-Quṭb militant activists in the late twentieth century, in whose radical rhetoric *jihād* has become the equivalent of a no-holds-barred cosmic struggle against all those who stand in their way (and thus, to their thinking, in God's way). One particular militant tract entitled *al-Farīḍa al-ghā'iba* captured our attention because of its influence in certain extremist circles. The main highlights of this work are discussed in this chapter; a detailed refutation of it by a prominent mainstream religious scholar is presented in the next chapter. The chapter concludes with an account of post-September 11 militant narratives of *jihād* as unending sacred violence directed against all those regarded as unjust and godless.

The Views of Ḥasan al-Bannā (d. 1368/1949)

Ḥasan al-Bannā, a teacher, preacher, and political activist, was a graduate of the Dār al-'ulūm in Cairo and founder of the organization called al-Ikhwān al-Muslimūn (the Muslim Brotherhood) in Egypt in 1928. In the wake of British imperialism and the abolition of the caliphate in 1924 by the Republican Turks, the Ikhwān was established to mount a campaign of reform against the perceived materialism and secularism of its day and politically empower ordinary Egyptian people against what was deemed to be the corrupt indigenous elite subservient to the West. As a man of learning, al-Bannā emphasized transformation of the individual and society through education, as well as political activism to bring about change in Egyptian society. As relations with the Egyptian government deteriorated, al-Bannā was shot to death by the then-prime minister on February 12, 1949, ensuring his status as "the martyr of the nation" and the continued influence of his thought in certain Islamist circles.[4]

Al-Bannā wrote a short essay on *jihād* titled *Risālat al-jihād*, which is the focus of our attention. In this essay, he emphasizes the obligatory nature of *jihād* for every Muslim, "from which there is no escape, and no flight," and for which Muslims are expected to attain success and ample reward in this world and the next. Those who abandon this duty reap humiliation and disgrace on earth and punishment in the hereafter, asserts al-Bannā.[5] *Jihād* for him is primarily the military defense of the truth (*al-ḥaqq*) that the Muslim community undertakes as one united bloc (*ṣaffan wāḥidan*), as one finds "in the religion of Islam, its teachings, the verses of the Glorious Qur'ān, the sayings of the great Messenger, peace and blessings be upon him...."[6] In support of this position, he cites several Qur'anic verses, including Qur'ān 2:216; 3:156–158; 3:169–175; and 4:71–78. Through these verses, he says, the Qur'ān urges Muslims to fight in order to defend the weak (*li-ḥimāyati 'l-du'afā'*) and liberate the oppressed (*takhlīṣ al-maẓlūmīn*), and reprimands those who linger behind out of cowardice and refrain from fighting. Al-Bannā regards the above verses as setting up a parallel between fighting and prayer, fasting, and the other pillars of Islam. He goes on to quote several verses from the eighth and ninth Qur'anic chapters (al-Anfāl and al-Barā'a/al-Tawba) that exhort Muslims to fight against their enemies from among the pagan Meccans and the People of the Book (Qur'ān 9:29). Al-Bannā states that the basis of "the military spirit" (*al-rūḥ al-'askariyya*) rests upon two matters that he believes are indicated in the Qur'ān: obedience and organization (no specific verses are cited to support this view). These Qur'anic imperatives taken together establish for him the excellences of *jihād* and the generous recompense promised to those who undertake this duty.[7]

Al-Bannā turns his attention next to the *ḥadīth* literature. He records a number of reports occurring in the *faḍā'il al-jihād* sections of the six Sunnī authoritative *ḥadīth* compilations that enumerate the merits of *jihād* and martyrdom, many of which we have previously noted.[8] Thus he refers to the *ḥadīth* in which the martyr is described as being resurrected in the hereafter with the color of blood and the fragrance of musk; the one in which paradise is described as being under the shade of the swords; and the one in which the fighter in the path of God is likened to the constantly praying, fasting individual, etc. Al-Bannā duly notes the merits of fighting on horseback and at sea, and guarding the frontiers, and includes the report that states that martyrdom is granted to the one who sincerely desires it, even if that person dies in his bed. Those who spend their money in the path of God receive seven hundred times the usual reward. He focuses fairly extensively on the status and merit of the military martyr, recording, for example, the *ḥadīth* reported by Abū Dā'ūd (but not by al-Bukhārī and Muslim) that the martyr may intercede on behalf of seventy members of his family.[9] Al-Bannā in fact displays quite a bit of familiarity with *faḍā'il al-jihād* reports that occur in standard *ḥadīth* collections and in popular treatises, like the *Manāzi' al-ashwāq ilā maṣāri' al-'ushshāq* (as he titles it).[10]

Al-Bannā is also quite familiar with the legal rulings of the classical jurists and the positions of different legal schools concerning the necessity of the military *jihād* and the proclamation and conduct of war.[11] He describes the difference between *jihād* as a collective versus individual obligation and cites authoritative juridical pronouncements on this matter. Essentially, he says, the military *jihād* is a collective duty for the Islamic community for propagating the faith; it becomes an individual obligation when it is necessary to repel the direct attack of unbelievers on it. This is the situation in which Muslims now find themselves in, for they are, al-Bannā says, "humiliated by others and ruled by unbelievers; their lands are overrun, and their dignity violated. Their adversaries decide their matters, and the laws of their religion in their own lands have been suspended, in addition to their inability to propagate their faith."[12] Al-Bannā reminds his co-religionists that "before this oppressive age," the elite of previous eras—the scholars, ascetics, and professionals, like Ibn al-Mubārak, the Ṣūfī 'Abd al-Wāḥid b. Zayd (d. 177/793),[13] and the *salaf* in general—did not abandon the military *jihād*.[14]

Why should Muslims fight? It is important for al-Bannā to establish the just and moral nature of the cause for which Muslims have been exhorted to fight, and this cause is none other, he says perhaps somewhat unexpectedly, than the establishment of peace (*al-salām*). Being in a state of preparedness (*al-isti'dād*), he claims, is the best way to guarantee peace.[15] A just and peaceful world is attained only "when the word of God is ascendant" (*kalimat allāh hiya al-'ulyā*). Once again, this is the only reason people should engage in *jihād* in the way of God, as affirmed in a *ḥadīth* recorded by five of the six most reliable *ḥadīth* compilers, asserts al-Bannā. If one fights for fame and/or worldly gain, one cannot be assumed to have fought in the way of God.[16]

Just conduct during battle is also emphasized by al-Bannā, in emulation of the precedents set by early Muslims. He points to the Qur'anic imperative for hewing to fair and humane conduct during the waging of war as established by Qur'ān 5:8, which states, "And do not let the hatred of a people towards you cause you to swerve from justice: be just, that is closest to godly piety." When righteous Muslims fight, they therefore do not commit aggression or acts of injustice, al-Bannā asserts. They do not mutilate, or steal, or plunder wealth; they do not violate the sanctity (of people or places) or cause harm in general.

He continues, "They [sc. Muslims] are in their wars the best of warriors, just as in their peace they are the most virtuous of peacemakers." Al-Bannā quotes a number of *ḥadīths* forbidding acts of violence and destruction.[17]

Al-Bannā acknowledges the greater *jihād*, which in contrast to the lesser *jihād*, that is, fighting the enemy, is defined as the *jihād* of the heart or the soul. He warns, however, that the famous *ḥadīth* that proclaims the superiority of the greater *jihād* in no way diminishes the importance of fighting and making necessary preparations for it. The *ḥadīth* in any case is acknowledged to have a weak chain of transmission going back to the Companion Jābir. Even if the *ḥadīth* was deemed to be sound, continues al-Bannā, it is still not to be understood as advocating the renunciation of the combative *jihād* and of being in a state of preparedness to defend the lands of the Muslims and repel the hostilities of unbelievers. Rather, the report is correctly understood to point to the necessity of striving against one's carnal self in order to consecrate all of one's acts to God.[18]

Jihād also encompasses the broad ethical imperative of enjoining the good and forbidding the wrong, as expressed in the *ḥadīth*: "Among the greatest *jihād* is a word of truth before an unjust ruler." Al-Bannā, however, adds that the greatest of martyrdom and rewards for the *mujāhidūn* are reserved for the one who "kills or is killed in the way of God."[19]

Finally, al-Bannā ends his treatise with an entreaty to fellow Muslims to not be afraid to die an honorable death in defense of their lands and religion; in return, they will gain eternal life in the next world and perfect bliss.[20] The pathos of his plea is particularly resonant in the context of the colonial situation and its immediate aftermath in which Muslims, having suffered subjugation at the hands of hostile European Christians, are implored to prevent the recurrence of such a debacle through armed deterrence and self-defense.

The Views of Abul A'la Mawdudi (d. 1400/1979)

The South Asian activist Abul A'la Mawdudi has been very influential in twentieth-century Islamist circles. Although he was at best sporadically educated in the traditional religious sciences, his influence derives not from any exceptional reputation as a religious scholar, but rather from his forceful, charismatic personality and his uncanny ability to articulate in an emotive Islamic idiom the sociopolitical concerns of his co-religionists in a colonial context. The destiny of Muslims, he came to believe, was to create a specifically Islamic state in which Muslims would be free to live and govern themselves according to Islamic principles. Along with about seventy-five persons, Mawdudi formed the Jamaat-i Islami party in 1941 and was elected its leader, or *amīr*. The new party's mission was to create a virtuous cadre of Muslims (*Salih Jamaat* in Urdu) who would assume leadership of their community and rebuild Muslim civilization and culture in post-colonial South Asia.[21]

A tract on *jihād* written by Mawdudi has been partially translated into English from the original Urdu as "*Jihād* in Islam."[22] Although not a translation of the original work in its entirety, it provides us with at least the rudimentary, broad contours of Mawdudi's thinking on this topic.

In this tract, Mawdudi defines *jihād* in its broadest sense as follows: "To exert one's utmost endeavour in promoting a cause."[23] This exertion or struggle is not like other struggles, however, because it is carried out "for the cause of God," meaning that it "is undertaken for the collective well-being of mankind."[24] It is not equivalent to war (*ḥarb*);[25] rather it is a broad, multilayered term that allows for the welfare of humankind to be achieved through both peaceful and military means.[26] In his Qur'ān commentary, Mawdudi asserts that *jihād* "for the cause of God" does not allow forcible conversion of non-Muslims to Islam;[27] in fact, it specifically allows non-Muslims "perfect freedom of religious belief and permits them to act according to their creed."[28] It does not, however, grant them the right to administer state affairs in accordance with laws and practices that are antithetical to Islamic ones, for such a situation would "fatally affect the public interest from the viewpoint of Islam."[29] *Jihād* further calls for the political and territorial expansion of Islam because only under a single, worldwide "Islamic State" can humanity "benefit from the ideology and welfare programme" of Islam.[30]

Against the backdrop of British colonization of India and rising Hindu and Muslim nationalism of his time, *jihād* in the way of God, in Mawdudi's conceptualization, thus becomes yoked to a revolutionary doctrine that contains for Muslims "an invitation to join a movement of social revolution."[31] This revolution is to be waged against the forces of injustice and evil, which have been set in motion not only by hostile non-Muslims, but also by imperfect Muslims. Muslims (of the right-thinking kind) constitute a Revolutionary Party whose objective

> is to expend all the powers of body and soul, your life and goods in the fight against the evil forces of the world, not that having annihilated them you should step into their shoes, but in order that evil and contumacy should be wiped out and God's law should be enforced in the world.[32]

According to this worldview, the prophets were all revolutionary leaders, and Muḥammad was the greatest revolutionary leader of all. The distinction between these prophets as revolutionary leaders and general run-of-the-mill revolutionaries is that the former act "under direct Guidance of their Lord" and are above the usual human proclivity to favor one group or class over another.[33] Their true followers (Mawdudi and his cohort, for example), who constitute "the Muslim Party" (apparently interchangeable with the *umma*),[34] are charged with setting up an Islamic government, not only in one territory, "but to extend the sway of Islamic system all around as far as its resources can carry it."[35] According to Mawdudi, this mandate was already established and implemented during the lifetime of the Prophet and the Rightly Guided Caliphs. In conformity with their practices, Muslims in the modern world, besieged by hostile non-Muslims, must strive earnestly to spread the word of God and Muslim rule. The vehicle for doing this is the "Islamic State" and the means for achieving this goal is *jihād*. Thus, according to Mawdudi, "Islam is a revolutionary ideology and programme which seeks to alter the social order of the whole world and rebuild it in conformity with its own tenets and ideals." *Jihād* primarily "refers to that revolutionary struggle and utmost exertion which the Islamic Party brings into play to achieve this objective."[36]

In this revolutionary sense, it is irrelevant, Mawdudi maintains, to ask whether *jihād* is offensive or defensive, for these terms are meaningful only in the context of wars between nation-states and countries with specific territorial boundaries. Since the Islamic *umma* is transnational and not circumscribed by territorial parameters, concepts of "attack" and "defense" do not apply to it. *Jihād*, he claims, is simultaneously offensive and defensive. It may be regarded as offensive "because the Muslim Party assaults the rule of an opposing ideology," but it is also defensive "because the Muslim Party is constrained to capture state power" so that it may defend its principles.[37] For Mawdudi, *jihād* then is ultimately an ideological struggle to be waged by all means, military and non-military, to ensure the realization of what he deems to be essential Islamic principles through the establishment of what he calls the Islamic State, whether the rest of the world (including the rest of his coreligionists) acquiesce in this venture or not.[38]

The Views of Sayyid Quṭb (d. 1386/1966)

The Egyptian political activist and ideologue Sayyid Quṭb was greatly influenced by the writings of Mawdudi, available in Arabic translation.[39] Trained initially as a literary critic at the Dār al-ʿulūm in Cairo, with no scholarly religious education, he is said to have been radicalized during his trip to the United States in the 1940s due to the materialism and loose morals he encountered there, as well as the racism that he experienced firsthand. Upon his return to Egypt, Quṭb joined the Muslim Brotherhood and became a vocal and prominent critic of the Nasser government and its secular policies. Accused of plotting to assassinate Nasser, Quṭb was thrown into prison and tortured, which caused him to become more militant in his thinking. While in prison, he wrote two of his most important works: the fiery revolutionary tract *Ma'ālim fī 'l-ṭarīq* and his Qur'ān exegesis *Fī ẓilal al-qur'ān* in which he delineates his vision of the perfect Islamic society. He was executed in 1966, but his works continue to be studied and disseminated in radical Islamist circles to this day.[40]

In the chapter titled "al-Jihād fī sabīl allāh" in *Ma'ālim fī 'l-ṭarīq*, Quṭb takes strong exception to those who would maintain that "Islam [sic] does not undertake *jihād* except in defense (*li-'l-difā'*)." This is the slogan, he says derisively, of "those who have been defeated spiritually and intellectually" (*mahzūmūn rūḥiyyan wa-'aqliyyan*) by the adverse circumstances confronting Muslims of his time and who mistakenly believe that they are enhancing the image of Islam by denuding it of "its program" (*manhajihi*)—which is to remove all tyrants/tyrannical/unjust systems (*ṭawāghīt*) from the face of the earth. Such a program is meant to ensure that all of humankind would worship the one God and no other, not by forcing them to do so, but by putting an end to all other "reigning political systems" or by subjugating them, so that these other systems agree to either pay the *jizya* or declare their submission. Their populaces are free, however, to accept or reject "this creed" (*hādhihi al-'aqīda*). The objective of Islam is unchanging—to win over all humanity to the worship of the one God—and "this movement" must therefore be perennially engaged in its pursuit. This was the mission of the Prophet Muḥammad "since the first day," declares Quṭb, and there can be no negotiation or flexibility concerning this fundamental tenet (*hādhihi al-qā'ida*). Whoever resists this hegemonic mission of Islam, as conceived by Quṭb, must be ruthlessly fought until death or capitulation.[41]

This is fundamentally the purpose of *jihād*—which is mainly combative and offensive—geared toward, as Quṭb frames it, "the liberation (*taḥrīr*) of humanity on earth from the worship of [other] humans."[42] Islam, he declares yet again, is not just a belief or creed (*'aqīda*); it is a public proclamation of the liberation of human beings from the worship of humans; it seeks to achieve this by putting an end to "human sovereignty or governance" (*ḥākimiyyat al-bashar*) and replacing it with true worship of the one God. This is manifested on earth by the establishment of the law of God and His authority (*sharī'at allāh wa-sulṭānihi*), thus setting people "free" (*aḥrār*) from the "worship" of (or bondage to) other humans.[43]

It is worthy of note that this language of "liberation" pervades the chapter on *jihād* and the entire *Ma'ālim*, imparting a certain chiliastic or messianic tenor to the whole work. This tenor is furthermore heightened by the invocation of "the kingdom of God" (*mamlakat allāh*) to be established on earth that will replace "the kingdom of man" (*mamlakat al-bashr*).[44] These terms are not indigenous to Islamic thought. In conjunction with the term "liberation" (*taḥrīr*), these locutions betray a strong debt to twentieth-century Christian liberation theologies, suffused with messianic fervor, as well as to Marxist-socialist notions of totalitarian political systems.

The waging of *jihād*, according to Quṭb's understanding, is unending and relentless; it is both "*jihād* of the sword" (*al-jihād bi-'l-sayf*) and "*jihād* of proof/elucidation" (*al-jihād bi-'l-bayān*). Quṭb is quick to assert that the latter type does not suggest a "defensive war," however; such a notion is trumpeted only by those "Muslim defeatists" who cringe before the "cunning onslaught" of Orientalists. *Jihād* may be considered to be defensive only insofar as it seeks to defend human beings themselves against all the factors that curtail their freedom and prevent their emancipation, including political systems based on economic exploitation, racism, and elitism that existed before the advent of Islam, and forms of which still persist in "the contemporary period of Jāhiliyya."[45]

All these obstacles to human freedom and progress are to be removed by force; it is foolhardy to imagine that such impediments to human freedom may be removed by *jihād* of the tongue alone, states Quṭb. *Jihād* through argumentation can only occur among individuals living under a righteous government upholding the laws of God. It is in this context that the Qur'anic injunction of "Let there be no compulsion in religion (*al-dīn*)" (2:256) is upheld. No individual may be forced to accept any creed (*'aqīda*), but societies and nations of the world must yield to a *pax Islamica*, in which religion (*al-dīn*) must be for God alone (*yakūn al-dīn fīhā kulluhu li-'llāh*).[46] This signifies that Islam is not merely a belief or creed; it is rather a complete "program" (*manhaj*) of social and political activism that must efface all other modes of living and governance, because they stand in the way of the complete liberation of humankind.[47] Apparently, it escaped Quṭb's attention—even though he laboriously sets up this distinction between *'aqīda* and *dīn*—that Qur'ān 2:256 specifically prohibits compulsion in *dīn*, which, according to his understanding, is the very thing that must be imposed by force on people everywhere!

Quṭb acknowledges that "the greater *jihād*" (*al-jihād al-akbar*), referring to the struggle against one's carnal self (*al-nafs*), also exists. This entails fighting against one's base desires and passions, as instigated by Satan, and against the narrow, self-serving interests of one's own family or community, in order to establish God's authority on earth and to efface all other forms of authority that usurp it.[48] In his conceptualization, the *jihād al-nafs* has become purely instrumental, which prepares the properly-formed Muslim primarily to undertake the *jihād al-sayf*. Quṭb does not state this explicitly, but it is clear from the

Ma'ālim that he has subverted the traditional hierarchy and made the lesser *jihād* in fact the greater one.

Late Twentieth-Century Militant Construals of Jihād

Quṭb's fiery call to armed insurrection against Nasser's government (and by extension all autocratic governments) in the name of human freedom and social justice resonated with others who similarly saw themselves as politically and socially disenfranchised victims in the twentieth century. Not everyone so marginalized was moved to resort to militancy, of course; but as with Communism before it, the sociopolitical utopia promised by political Islam was appealing to many who lived in humanly-degraded conditions under repressive governments in many Muslim-majority societies. The memory of the humiliations that had been visited on Muslim peoples by European Christian colonizers remained strong through the middle of the twentieth century and was revived in the late twentieth century by fresh, Western, primarily American, incursions into the Middle East during the late twentieth century—particularly during the first and second Gulf Wars. The creation of the Jewish state of Israel in 1948 by Western powers on what had been Arab land for centuries, resulting in the displacement of hundreds of thousands of Palestinians, was another painful reminder of the political disenfranchisement of Muslims on a global scale. The 1967 and 1973 Arab-Israeli Wars that resulted in even more loss of Arab land to the Jewish state, further exacerbating the Palestinian refugee problem, created added grievances in their wake. Recent American support for repressive governments in the Middle East and elsewhere in the Islamic world, and the post-September 11 invasion and occupation of Iraq under now-discredited *casus belli* have fueled dismay and disillusionment with the West as a whole among considerable segments of Muslim populations. Under such disquieting, even cataclysmic, circumstances, violence deemed to be in the service of human freedom and the reclamation of human dignity can be regarded as a highly redemptive act of religiosity, even its apotheosis. Past history provides copious examples of such redemptive acts of violence, often self-sacrificial, throughout time.[49]

The Views of Muḥammad 'Abd al-Salām Faraj

Quṭb's death at the hands of his persecutors, as viewed by his supporters, was a redemptive act of self-sacrifice in the cause of a higher good, worthy of emulation by those who admired him. One such admirer was Muḥammad 'Abd al-Salām Faraj, the Egyptian author of a radical militant tract titled *al-Farīḍa al-ghā'iba* ("the Lapsed Duty"); the duty in question is the combative *jihād*. Faraj was one of the militants belonging to the group *al-Jihād wa 'l-takfīr*, which assassinated Nasser's successor, Anwar Sadat, in 1982, after he signed a peace treaty with Israel. The tract essentially exhorts Muslims to revive the military *jihād* because they are besieged by external and internal enemies—non-Muslims and Muslim "apostates," respectively. Faraj heaps scorn on the scholars of his time because, in his opinion, they have encouraged Muslims to abandon this critical duty. He says, "*Jihād* [struggle] for God's cause, in spite of its extreme importance and its great significance for the future of this religion, has been neglected by the *'ulamā'* [leading Muslim scholars] of this age. They have feigned ignorance of this duty, but they know that it is the only way to the return and establishment of the glory of Islam anew."[50]

To establish the imperative of the combative *jihād*, Faraj relies on the well-established practice of selectively quoting Qur'anic verses and *ḥadīth*s that may be interpreted as exhorting the faithful to fight continually against those deemed to be their intractable enemies. Predictably, the sword verse, Qur'ān 9:5 (and in one instance, Qur'ān 2:216) is cited by Faraj and is understood by him to have abrogated 114 verses in 48 (or 54) chapters of the Qur'ān that advocate conciliation and forbearance with one's adversaries, apparently on the authority of late medieval scholars such as Ibn Ḥazm and Ibn Kathīr. Faraj notes the dissenting opinion of al-Suyūṭī, who regarded Qur'ān 2:109, which states, "So forgive and pardon them [in reference to a specific wayward contingent from among the People of the Book who mischievously seek to entice Muslims away from their faith] until God makes His judgment apparent" as unabrogated; this verse would therefore impose considerable restrictions on the deployment of Qur'ān 9:5 as mandating perpetual warfare against non-Muslims. Faraj, however, proceeds to say that even if the unabrogated status of Qur'ān 2:109 is conceded, it does not mitigate in any way the duty to carry out the military *jihād*. Since Faraj wishes to privilege the understanding of *jihād* as unrelenting warfare against non-Muslims and "dissident" Muslims, he does not (or cannot) attempt to reconcile the meaning of these two verses. Instead, he invokes a *ḥadīth* in which the Prophet remarks, "*Jihād* will continue until the Day of Resurrection."[51] This, it should be noted, is not an unexpected tactic in these kinds of militant discourses, in which *ḥadīth*s are often deployed to undermine the meaning of a Qur'anic verse, such as 2:109, that is inconvenient for them. Furthermore, *jihād* as it occurs in this *ḥadīth* is understood to be a reference to its combative aspect only.

Faraj's militancy is constructed, however, primarily on the basis of Ibn Taymiyya's pronouncements against the Mongols—now generalized to all "lapsed" Muslims—and to a lesser extent, on the other Mamluk scholar Ibn Kathīr's similar indictment of the Mongols in his Qur'ān commentary. Faraj speaks approvingly of Ibn Taymiyya's *fatāwa* in which he condemns the Mongols as apostates from Islam who still adhere to their tribal law (*yasak*) and draws a comparison between them and the unrighteous rulers of his time in Muslim-majority societies.[52] The chilling purpose of this comparison is clear: Faraj and his cohort derive a mandate thereby to justify in their minds the assassination of Egyptian President Sadat (and potentially other Muslim rulers) deemed to have lapsed from Islam.

Carrying out *jihād* on the extensive scale that these extremists have in mind would require state apparatus and a regular army. Accordingly, Faraj stresses the importance of establishing an Islamic state and the revival of the historical caliphate of the Rightly-Guided Rulers. As the Qur'ān makes no reference to any form of government, including the caliphate, Faraj cites the one *ḥadīth*, narrated by Ibn Ḥanbal, in which Muḥammad predicts that the rightly-guided caliphate will follow the age of prophethood, after which governance will degenerate into kingship. According to this solitary *ḥadīth*, a righteous, millenarian caliphate will subsequently be revived, during which plenitude and joy will fill the earth.[53] On the basis of this slim textual evidence, Faraj proceeds to establish the normative necessity of reviving this idealized caliphate for contemporary Muslims.

A tension now becomes evident in Faraj's thought—if the Islamic state steered by the rightful caliph is necessary to wage this all-out war against the forces of evil, where do Faraj and his cohorts derive the legitimacy to stage **their** *jihād* against the unjust majority in the absence of the Islamic state? The answer lies in their invocation of situation *in extremis*—the current situation of Muslims has become so dire and desperate, being assailed as they are by ungodly forces (internal and external) who covet their land and assault their dignity, that the combative *jihād*, they argue, is now essentially an act of self-defense. It has therefore become a *farḍ 'ayn*, an urgent individual obligation. Under normal conditions, all those who needed the permission of their guardians to take part in the collective, non-defensive *jihād*—the dutiful son of his parents, the wife of her husband, the slave of his or her master—no longer need do so.[54] Fighting the "near enemy" (specifically Arab governments) takes priority over fighting the "far enemy" (Western governments); thus "we have to establish the Rule of God's Religion in our own country first. . . ."[55] The contingent of God's true warriors, a beleaguered minority in the Islamic world, will eventually establish the Islamic State, states Faraj, and give the lie to those who say that the ideal Muslim community will come about through peaceful propagation of the faith.[56]

Because Faraj is aware that this construction of *jihād* as relentless, no-holds-barred warfare against the enemy within and without is bound to meet with censure from mainstream Muslim scholars, he attempts to preempt their arguments by railing against those who would argue that the pursuit of knowledge is also part of *jihād* and that in the contemporary period of religious ignorance, it is the best kind of struggle and a religious obligation. Faraj counteracts this line of argument by simply asserting that Qur'ān 2:216 states, "Prescribed for you is fighting." Predictably, he uncouples this verse from its original historical purview (see our discussion of this verse in chapter 2) and regards it as an absolute injunction for Muslims, valid for all times and places. Faraj also records a number of *faḍā'il* reports that praise the combative *jihād*. He takes specific aim at the scholars of al-Azhar, who were among his most vociferous critics, dismissing them as not equal to those who fight physically. After all, he remarks derisively, their learning and academic credentials availed them nothing "when Napoleon and his soldiers entered al-Azhar on horseback."[57]

Faraj is loath to allow that the internal, spiritual *jihād* may be considered to be more important than the physical, combative *jihād* and that the former is of greater priority than the latter. He says that those who are proponents of this view misunderstand Ibn al-Qayyim's intent in identifying three kinds of *jihād*—against one's soul, against the devil, and against unbelievers and hypocrites. These are not to be considered successive phases of *jihād*, but rather its three aspects, says Faraj. He also asserts that Ibn al-Qayyim dismissed the *ḥadīth* that refers to the greater versus the lesser *jihād* as fabricated.[58]

Faraj concludes his screed by reviewing the classical rules of launching a *jihād* and humane conduct during warfare. Not unpredictably, he privileges the exceptions devised by a number of jurists to these rules and lists only those reports that lend support to these exceptions, so that, according to Faraj's manual, one should now preferably launch an attack without prior warning, kill women and children who live with combatants, and cut down and burn trees.[59] According to Faraj, such measures are justified if one engages in *jihād* with pure intention and complete sincerity, with no thought of material gain.[60] The seeking of political power (usually eschewed by classical scholars), however, is exempted from this stricture against worldly gain through military activity. In the extremist creed of Faraj and his cohort, this vaunted purity of intent appears to offer absolution from violation of the general rules of humane conduct governing warfare that had been carefully crafted by Muslim jurists in the classical period, for in their conceptualization of the correct world order, there is no higher and purer goal for Muslims than to establish the Islamic political utopia of their imagination on this earth—at whatever cost.

The Views of Āyatullāh Rūḥullāh Khomeini (d. 1410/1989)

Āyatullāh Khomeini is best known as the architect of the Islamic Revolution in Iran in 1979. Born in Khomein in southwestern Iran in 1902, he studied with the well-known scholar ʿAbd al-Karīm Hāʾirī in Qom and launched his own teaching career there, becoming recognized as a prominent jurist (*faqīh*) and *mujtahid*. Unlike many other jurists of his time, however, Khomeini became active in political affairs and took part in strenuous opposition to several secularizing and westernizing policies of the Iranian government. The Shah of Iran imprisoned Khomeini in 1963 and then had him exiled from Iran. Khomeini made his way to Turkey and then to Najaf in Iraq before his triumphant return to Iran in February 1979. The monarchy was abolished, and Iran was declared to be an Islamic Republic under a guardian jurist (*valī-ye faqīh*).[61]

Khomeini wrote a short treatise titled *jihād al-nafs aw al-jihād al-akbar*, which is the focus of our study here.[62] In this work, he describes the centrality of *jihād* as continual human striving on the authority of al-Ḥusayn b. ʿAlī, the second Shīʿī *imām*, as follows:

> Life is belief and struggle in the path of freedom and liberation and in order to restore usurped rights; a struggle to help the weak and the oppressed; a struggle to repel the oppressors and tyrants; a struggle in the path of elevation, vigor, strength, virtue, and honor.[63]

Jihād in Khomeini's conceptualization is thus essentially a social and political struggle against injustice and oppression that ultimately leads to a movement of political liberation—mirroring the views of Sunni activists like Mawdudi and Quṭb.[64] As far as their objectives are concerned and frequently in their terminology and rhetoric, modern Shīʿī and Sunnī political activists share much common ground.

Khomeini addresses his treatise primarily to the scholars who are to be the vanguard of the coming revolution against unjust rulers. He says to them, "On your necks lie a heavy duty," and "you are not like other people."[65] Their responsibility differs from the rest of humanity, for the scholar who is righteous in his behavior with people is the primary cause of the well-being of the people. When the scholars are able to carry out all their actions for the sake of God and have cleansed their hearts of love for the world, then they will be able to mount an effective resistance (*al-muqāwama*) against their unscrupulous rulers.[66] It is the very spiritual and moral transformation of the scholars—their internal *jihād*—that represents the greatest threat to the colonizers (here the term refers to the Shah and his cohort), hence their aversion toward the religious universities that produce such scholars, states Khomeini. Such scholars will proceed to galvanize Muslims around the world, particularly their youth, in order to defend Islam and themselves against this encroaching colonialism by hostile and irreligious indigenous rulers.[67] The *jihād* of the self is an absolutely vital prelude to engaging in the *jihād* against political tyranny, and Shīʿī scholars, like Quṭb's learned, righteous Sunnī elite, must lead the way.

Khomeini emphasizes this critical point in his other writings as well. In his "Lectures on Sūrat al-Fātiḥa," he states that "All forms of *jihād* that may be waged in the world depend on this greater *jihād*; if we succeed in the greater *jihād*, then all our other strivings will count as *jihād*, and if not, they will be satanic."[68] The external *jihād*, after due attention is paid to the internal *jihād*, must be undertaken against those he regards as "tyrannical rulers and governments." The waging of *jihād* against such external enemies is not, ipso facto, a militant enterprise. In one of his essays, "Program for the Establishment of an Islamic Government," he defines this *jihād* as essentially a program of nonviolent resistance and withholding of cooperation from unjust rulers. Following in the footsteps of the Shīʿī Imāms who had adopted such methods of resistance, Khomeini advocates that "all relations with such rulers be severed and that no one collaborate with them in any way."[69] Illegitimate war is waged by imperialist governments, such as the Shah's monarchy and the American government, that foster injustice and arrogance in the world, as opposed to a properly constituted *jihād* that is waged on behalf of the weak and oppressed in order to restore a just sociopolitical order.[70] Imperialist and unjust governments are labeled by Khomeini as *ṭāghūt*, a term also common in radical Sunni treatises.[71] Once again, we note the shared political idiom and sensibilities between Shīʿī and Sunnī political activists of the twentieth century.

Post-September 11 Milieu: The Rhetoric of Terror

Extremist construals of *jihād* and martyrdom in more recent history do not differ very much in detail from those offered by Muḥammad Faraj. Scrutiny of the public statements of Usāma bin Lādin (d. 1432/2011), the acknowledged mastermind behind the September 11, 2001 attacks, yields a virulently strident manifesto of revenge and punishment, amounting to a scorched-earth policy against all those deemed to be unrighteous by him and his cohorts. Once again, the enemy is both "lapsed" Muslims and unregenerate non-Muslims, who have collectively laid siege to the small minority of "true" Muslims who have taken it upon themselves to redeem the world. According to what has become a common extremist litany of accusations, the situation of Muslims is dire because "Western Crusader" invaders and their Zionist allies occupy Muslim territory, and Muslim blood is shed copiously in Bosnia-Herzegovina, Chechnya, Palestine, Kashmir, and elsewhere.[72]

Wronged Muslims must thus fight back in self-defense with a no-holds-barred attitude; this defensive *jihād*, as he constructs it, is therefore an individual obligation from which no one is exempt. In a declaration of war published by Bin Lādin in *Al-Quds al-ʿArabī*, a London-based newspaper, in August 1996, titled "Declaration of Jihad against the Americans Occupying the Land of the Two Holy Mosques: Expel the Heretics from the Arabian Peninsula," he proclaimed:

> You are not unaware of the injustice, repression, and aggression that have befallen Muslims through the alliance of Jews, Christians, and their agents, so much so that Muslims' blood has become the cheapest blood and their money and wealth are plundered by the enemies. Your blood has been spilled in Palestine and Iraq.... That alerted Muslims to the fact that they are the main target of the Jewish-crusade alliance aggression, and all the false claims about human rights fell under the blows and massacres committed against Muslims everywhere.[73]

Bin Lādin glorifies fallen militants, such as ʿAbd Allāh ʿAẓẓām, as martyrs for the cause, and like Faraj before him, he often appeals to the authority of Ibn Taymiyya to legitimize his violent manifesto,[74] as well as to the Qur'ān commentary of Ibn Kathīr.[75] Viewed through this vengeful lens, the dire circumstances in which *jihād* is to be carried out by the beleaguered minority of "true Muslims" make permissible all kinds of violent actions. The accusation of terrorism is thus meaningless to Bin Lādin, and the wrongheaded label is rather to be worn with pride. After September 11, 2001, Bin Lādin praised the attack on the United States and described it as having ensued from his own incitement to terror. He proclaimed chillingly:

> And they [the attackers] have done this because of our words—and we have previously incited and roused them to action—in self-defense, defense of our brothers and sons in Palestine, and in order to free our holy sanctuaries. And if inciting for these reasons is terrorism, and if killing those that kill our sons is terrorism, then let history witness that we are terrorists.[76]

In November 2002, in a document titled "Letter to America," Bin Lādin further argued that both civilian and military targets in the United States could be legitimately attacked because the citizens of a democratic state are assumed to have given their consent to the policies of the government elected by them. He wrote, "Thus, if we are attacked, we have the right to return the attack... whoever has killed our civilians, we have the right to kill theirs."[77]

Not unlike Samuel Huntington and his "clash of civilizations" theory,[78] Bin Lādin subscribed to the idea of irreconcilable ideologies dividing the Muslim world and the West; his war against the West is therefore ideological, metaphysical, and total. As Faisal Devji remarks, "Al-Qaeda's very deliberate description of the jihad as a metaphysical struggle between Christianity, Judaism and Islam should be seen for what it is—an effort to define the terms of global social relations outside the language of state and citizenship."[79] It is this conception of a global, metaphysical war against the West (and those perceived to be its minions in the Islamic world, such as the Saudis) that sets al-Qā'ida apart from nationalist militant movements that strive overall for political liberation, rather than to score ideological points with the West as an undifferentiated collectivity.[80]

A highly illuminating explanation of the rationale for the waging of this global war against those perceived to be the ruthless enemies of Muslims is offered in a treatise composed by a prominent al-Qā'ida ideologue, Abū Yaḥyā al-Lībī. We now examine the contents of this treatise.

Nathr al-jawāhir fī munāqashāt al-mu'tariḍ 'alā tafjīrat al-jazā'ir—radd 'alā maqāl al-shaykh nāṣir al-'umar by Abū Yaḥyā al-Lībī (d. 2012)

Abū Yaḥyā al-Lībī, a Libyan national, was until his recent death a high-ranking official and top strategist within al-Qā'ida. Also a preacher, he was reputed to have studied Islamic jurisprudence and theology for two years in Mauritania. After his dramatic escape in 2005 from the Bagram Airbase in Afghanistan, where he had been held captive by American troops, al-Lībī's standing within al-Qā'ida rose higher than ever. Al-Lībī used several aliases; he signed off on this particular manifesto issued in 2007 as Ḥasan Qā'id, listed after his real name.[81]

This tract is a rebuttal to an essay written by al-Shaykh Nāṣir al-'Umar, a Saudi religious scholar and jurisconsult (*mufti*), published under the title of *al-Mawqif min al-tafjīr fī bilād al-muslimīn*. The incident referred to in this latter essay is a series of bomb attacks (including suicide bombings) that were carried out in Algeria during 2007. Al-Lībī's refutation of al-'Umar's essay is in the format of statement and counterstatement: After listing a usually brief critical remark or question from the latter, the former offers a lengthier rebuttal to it, creating in the process an unambiguously hard-line defense of violent attacks upon civilians.

When his interlocutor expresses his ignorance of the reasons and justifications for carrying out these deadly attacks, al-Lībī proceeds to answer him in the following manner after deriding him for his ignorance: He cites Qur'ān 2:193 ("Fight them until there is no more *fitna* and religion is for God; and if they should desist, then there should be no more aggression except against the wrongdoers"), which, according to him, provides one of the principal justifications for resorting to large-scale violence. He asks, "Do you see—and the answer is obvious—whether God's religion in Algeria is entirely for God—in regard to law, legislation, politics, relations [perhaps of the international sort?], economy, society, personal affairs, freedoms, punishments, culture and communications, peace, war—etc."[82] As any intelligent person will concede that such is not the case, who would dare to prevent this from happening? Rather, al-Lībī asserts, the people of Algeria are clamoring for an "Islamic State" (*dawla islāmiyya*); they flock to the streets to demonstrate in favor of it and "the horizons reverberate with their statements." But, he declares, the cowardly minions of France persist in their reprehensible ways, continue to disassociate religion from government, and become even more tenaciously committed to secularism—publicly rejecting everything that has to do with divine revelation and truth (*bi-'l-shar' wa-'l-ḥaqq*).[83]

Al-'Umar next counters by saying that it is one thing to attack American military sites and munitions depots in combat zones such as Iraq and Afghanistan and justify it as legitimate retaliation against "an infidel occupier" (*kāfir muḥtall*), but what excuse do they have for violently attacking innocent civilians living in either Muslim or non-Muslim societies, an act clearly proscribed in the religious texts of Islam and in the legal edicts of well-known scholars? In Qur'ān 28:15, Moses is depicted as being filled with remorse when he slew "the oppressive unbelieving Egyptian in an infidel land whose ruler was the Pharaoh," and considered himself a wrongdoer, even though his killing had been unintentional. What excuse then do "these self-exculpators who wade into the blood of Muslims and of protected people" have? Ibn 'Arabī is known to have asked that, when the killing of an animal without just cause has been proscribed in Islam, how can one even begin to justify the killing of any human being, or specifically a Muslim, or any righteous, God-fearing person? *Jihād*, continues al-'Umar, is indeed a continuous obligation until the Day of Judgment, but it is a conditional duty restricted to specific regions today, such as Palestine and Iraq, where Muslims are under attack. It in no way makes licit the blood of Muslims in general or allows for terrorizing the civilian population as a collectivity.[84]

In response, al-Lībī not unexpectedly marshals the *ḥadīth*, "I have been commanded to fight people until they say 'There is no god but God…,'" and mentions that it was deployed by Abū Bakr to legitimize fighting against those who had withheld their *zakāt* payment. Fighting is therefore even more appropriate, concludes al-Lībī, against those who prohibit "all or most of the laws of Islam" and adopt "the religion of secularism" (*dīn al-ʿilmāniyya*) by separating religion from politics.[85] Al-Lībī also references Ibn Taymiyya, who is reported to have said that anyone who abandons a single required religious obligation that has been established by incontrovertible proof can be fought against legitimately. The scriptural warrant for this argument is again, not unexpectedly, assumed to be Qur'ān 2:193, which states, "Fight them until there is no more tumult (*fitna*), and religion, all of it, is for God."[86] Al-Lībī concludes by exhorting "my fighting brothers in Algeria and others beside them to persist in the path of *jihād* unflaggingly" in order to inflict a crushing defeat upon "Pharaoh and his forces."[87]

Al-Lībī cites another Qur'anic verse (4:75) which states, "Why do you not fight in the path of God while the weak among the men, women, and children cry out, 'Our Lord, deliver us from this town whose people are oppressive, and send to us from your presence an ally, and send to us from your presence a supporter!'" He remarks that this verse should be understood to refer to all people who live in grinding poverty and who have been disenfranchised by tyrannical and unjust ruling elites, whose deliverance from such oppressive circumstances is "one of the greatest reasons for *jihād*." The law of the jungle these abject people live under must be replaced by the law of the Generous Provider so that they may no longer be deprived of God's mercy and justice and "may seek shelter in His shade."[88]

Al-ʿUmar protests that the violent actions perpetrated by the attackers are in violation of the fundamental stipulations of the Sharīʿa, despite the attempts of the militants to make such actions palatable by ostensibly appealing to the religious law. Their criminal actions are rather motivated only by sheer reactive impulse (*maḥḍ hawā*) and a rank desire to seek unbridled vengeance for the inequities they believe they are subjected to, he remonstrates. In spite of their religious trappings, they are under the sway of their base carnal selves (*al-nafs al-ammāra*), and they invoke religion "without insight or knowledge." None of the militants is known to have formally studied with recognized scholars or to have studied the objectives of the law (*maqāsid al-sharīʿa*), yet, laments our scholar, they wish to establish an Islamic state without having sought the counsel of a knowledgeable religious leader![89]

Al-Lībī replies by declaring that the sphere of *jihād* leaves no room for introspection, inactivity, and peaceableness; he and his cohorts are rather impelled to action by "the blood of the sons of this community, their sweat, and their struggles," included among whom are scholars and students who have been imprisoned by the "tyrants" (*al-ṭughāt*), at the head of whom is the Saudi royal family. These [true] scholars have attempted to defend the Muslim community with their bodies just as they have done with their pens. While the latter activity is called for in times of stability and prosperity, the former is what is needed in the present situation of crisis and danger. Al-Lībī accuses his interlocutor and his scholar colleagues of failing in their duty to set up an Islamic state and to assume leadership of the community "by means of their knowledge and actions."[90]

Jihād for al-Lībī is thus irreducibly a military duty to be undertaken by right-thinking male Muslims like himself, who follow—as they prefer to imagine themselves—in the steps of the great biblical prophets and the Prophet Muḥammad in their attempts to vanquish what they often describe as the pharaonic forces of evil that threaten to extinguish the light of truth. Because the end clearly justifies the means, *jihād* in the conceptualization of these vengeful militants has ineluctably become a cosmic, holy war to be waged relentlessly against all perceived enemies as the enemies of God, unfettered by the normative juridical standards of humane conduct during warfare and by the rules of proportionality devised by the classical Muslim jurists and invoked in desperation by his interlocutor.

Fiqh al-jihād by Yūsuf al-Qaraḍāwī

The views of the controversial Egyptian Qatar-based scholar and cleric Yūsuf al-Qaraḍāwī are deemed to be quite influential in the Arabic-speaking world, particularly on today's fraught issues of religiously inspired violence, martyrdom, and terrorism. Al-Qaraḍāwī appears as a regular guest on the Qatari television station al-Jazīra's popular program "Sharī'a and Life." An Azhari-trained religious scholar, al-Qaraḍāwī has been a member of the Muslim Brotherhood since its founding by Hasan al-Bannā. He emigrated to Qatar in 1961 and has been very active in shaping the religious educational system there and in continuing his *da'wā* work. A prolific writer, he is the author of over 120 books dealing with *fiqh*, theology, and a wide spectrum of contemporary issues, such as Islamic finance, Muslim minority rights, women's rights, and politics.[91]

Discussion of the recent hefty tome authored by al-Qaraḍāwī titled *Fiqh al-jihād* is included under this chapter's rubric with some misgivings. *Fiqh al-jihād* is more appropriately a work that occupies a middle space between the kind of writings described in this chapter and those described in the following one. In comparison with most of the works referred to in this chapter, al-Qaraḍāwī's book is far more interpretively nuanced and shows a greater historical awareness of pre-modern juridical trends. Such a historical and diachronic approach leads him to challenge in this work the relentlessly bellicose interpretations of the militants. Having already drawn attention by both publicly condemning the September 11 attacks and publicly condoning suicide attacks by Ḥamas militants against armed and unarmed Israelis, al-Qaraḍāwī defies pigeonholing exclusively as either an unabashed proponent of radicalism or a consistently principled opponent of militant extremism.

Like most of the modern classically trained scholars we describe in the next chapter, al-Qaraḍāwī begins his massive tome by stressing the polyvalence of the term *jihād* and its inflections during the Meccan period, and bemoaning the reduction of its meanings to simply "fighting." *Jihād*, he continues, refers rather to a Muslim's utmost exertion of effort and strength in order to resist evil and banish falsehood, starting with striving against the evil in his soul as a result of satanic enticements, to proceeding to resisting the wrongdoing found in the society around him, and ending with combating evil wherever it may be found to the best of his ability. *Jihād* is carried out by the heart through proper intention and resolve, by the tongue through summoning to God and explaining [the truth], and by the intellect through reflection and expression of opinions. Al-Qaraḍāwī thus identifies three primary types of *jihād*: (1) striving against the external enemy; (2) striving against the devil; and (3) striving against the carnal self.[92] These three types of *jihād*, he says, are indicated in Qur'ān 22:78; 9:41; and 8:72, and in various *ḥadīths*.[93]

Al-Qaraḍāwī acknowledges that "fighting" has now become the predominant meaning of *jihād*, and this kind of *jihād* may be divided into two types: defensive (*jihād al-daf'*) and preemptive or offensive (*jihād al-ṭalab*). He defines the first as resisting the enemy when he enters and occupies Islamic realms or when he aggresses against the lives, property, and dignity of Muslims without necessarily entering their territory but through de facto occupation, which is now occurring, he remarks, through foreign aerial bombardment of Muslim territory and the use of long-range missiles from afar. It also involves resisting the enemy when he oppresses Muslims on account of their beliefs, denies them freedom of religion, and attempts to force them to abandon their faith through persecution, so that the weak among them cry out to their Lord for deliverance "from the people of this town who are oppressors" and who plead, "Grant to us from Your presence a protector and an ally" (Qur'ān 4:75). Armed resistance to such an arrogant and unjust enemy—returning force for force—is what is termed "defensive *jihād*," states al-Qaraḍāwī, as was conducted by the Prophet and his Companions during the battles of Uḥud and Khandaq, and as was manifest during the Algerian resistance to French occupation and is now currently underway in the Palestinian resistance to Zionist attacks.[94]

As for the preemptive or offensive *jihād*, al-Qaraḍāwī continues, it is carried out while the enemy is still in his territory and "we are the ones who seek him out and pursue him, either to expand the territory of Islam or to secure it, so that we, rather than he, initiates [fighting]." Such a preemptive strike may also be made to convey the message of God to the people in enemy territory and remove the obstacles that prevent the communication of such a message to them, or to liberate people from tyrannical governments. This was the kind of *jihād*, he says, that was carried out by the Companions and after them during the period of Muslim conquests.[95]

Al-Qaraḍāwī next offers a noteworthy discussion of whether *jihād* is considered to be an obligatory or an optional duty according to revealed law. Here he privileges the views of famed jurist Abū Bakr al-Rāzī al-Jaṣṣāṣ (d. 371/981), who has preserved a diversity of early views on this critical topic in his *Aḥkām al-qur'ān*. Al-Jaṣṣāṣ had referenced the positions of Ibn Shubruma (d. ca. 144/761),[96] Sufyān al-Thawrī, and others who had maintained that *jihād* was a voluntary, not an obligatory, duty. Al-Qaraḍāwī understands their positions to be in specific reference to fighting (*al-qitāl*) and the preemptive or offensive *jihād* (*jihād al-ṭalab*). Qur'ān 2:216, which states, "Fighting has been decreed for you," refers to fighting as a recommended, rather than a mandatory, act according to a report attributed to Ibn 'Umar. The report originates with Maymūn b. Mihrān, who related that when he was in the presence of Ibn 'Umar, a man came to 'Abd Allāh b. 'Amr b. al-'Āṣ and asked him about the obligatory duties (*al-farā'iḍ*). Within earshot of Ibn 'Umar, 'Abd Allāh answered by enumerating the five pillars, followed up by *al-jihād fī sabīl allāh*. Ibn 'Umar became enraged and responded by naming only the five pillars and deliberately leaving out *jihād*. According to another report, Ibn Jurayj asked 'Aṭā' [b. Abī Rabāḥ] if military activity (*al-ghazw*) was obligatory (*wājib*) for people. Both 'Aṭā' and 'Amr b. Dinār replied, "We do not know."[97] (See our discussion of these early reports in chapter 5.)

Other scholars like Abū Hanifa, Abū Yusuf, Muḥammad [al-Shaybānī], and Mālik [b. Anas] held that *jihād* was a collective duty. Sufyān al-Thawrī's statement to the effect that *jihād* was not an obligatory duty (*laysa bi-farḍ*), although there was no consensus regarding its abandonment is construed by al-Qaraḍāwī as an endorsement of the position that the preemptive *jihād* is a collective obligation. The defensive *jihād* remains an obligatory duty, as is clearly indicated in Qur'ān 2:216, stresses al-Qaraḍāwī. He takes issue with the position of Ibn Shubruma, as reported by al-Jaṣṣāṣ, that Qur'ān 2:216 only recommends it (*annahu 'alā 'l-nadab*) because, in his view, that would contravene the obvious meaning of the words contained in the verse.[98] This distinction between "the *jihād* of defense" (*jihād al-daf'*) and "the *jihād* of preemption" (*jihād al-ṭalab*) remains a critical one for al-Qaraḍāwī. According to a practically universal consensus among scholars, the first type of *jihād* in response to legitimate concerns about security and fear for the lives and property of Muslims is obligatory for the whole community (*'alā kāffat al-umma*). Legal differences of opinion arose in regard to these vital questions: Can Muslims continue to engage in military campaigns against an enemy who poses no immediate threat and makes no hostile overture? Can Muslims undertake military forays against such an enemy until he submits to Islam or pays the *jizya*? Clearly, a number of early scholars such as Ibn 'Umar, 'Aṭā', 'Amr b. Dinār, and Ibn Shubruma were of the view that Muslims and their Imām may not undertake military expeditions against such an enemy and in fact should desist from fighting them (*'an yaq'udū 'anhum*).[99]

Others said, however, that the Imām and Muslims in general should continue to undertake military expeditions against non-Muslims until they embrace Islam or pay the *jizya*. Among them is Makḥūl, who had sworn that military campaigns (*al-ghazw*) were mandatory, whereas Ibn Shihāb al-Zuhrī had maintained that *al-jihād* had been commanded by God for the people and could be carried out either "through fighting or by desisting from fighting" (*ghazwan aw qa'dan*) (i.e., it would be required for some Muslims to engage in armed combat, while others whose services were not so required would refrain from fighting)—in other words, comments al-Qaraḍāwī, military activity was deemed by al-Zuhrī to be a *farḍ kifāya*.[100]

Al-Qaraḍāwī also refers to the report recorded by Ibn Abī Shayba in his *Muṣannaf* (previously mentioned in chapter 5) on the authority of Yazīd b. Bishr al-Saksakī, according to which, Ibn 'Umar affirms the five basic pillars of Islam, after which, he says, *jihād* is fine (*thumma 'l-jihād ḥasan*). A similar *mursal* report was recorded by 'Abd al-Razzāq. Al-Qaraḍāwī interprets Ibn 'Umar's assessment of *jihād* in the following manner: Because the Qur'ān does not mention *jihād* in connection with the essential characteristics of pious believers in relevant passages in chapters 2, 8, 13, 23, 25, 51, 114,[101] it is then reasonable to assume that *jihād* is hardly a required duty in every circumstance. It becomes obligatory for specific purposes: (1) to fend off aggressive enemies; (2) to prevent turmoil and rebellion in religious matters; (3) to come to the aid of the weak and oppressed; and (4) as defense against the danger presented by a relentlessly aggressive enemy. Under such conditions, the combative *jihād* is a collective duty upon the community.[102]

Al-Qaraḍāwī next assesses the validity of the early position that fighting was restricted only to the time of the Prophet, as reported by Abū

Ja'far al-Naḥḥās about 'Aṭā' and as attributed to Ibn al-Mubārak, for example. Al-Qaraḍāwī somewhat enigmatically interprets this as meaning that, although fighting may not be required of the generations of Muslims after the Companions, it does not mean that *jihād* as a general concept should be absent from the consciousness of Muslims. He references al-Jaṣṣāṣ, who was of the opinion that Qur'ān 2:216 prescribed fighting only for its immediate addressees (i.e., the Companions) especially when understood in the context of other verses, such as Qur'ān 2:183, 190–191; and 9:36, which specifically refer to fighting the pagan Arabs when they began to fight Muslims. Al-Qaraḍāwī endorses al-Jaṣṣāṣ's essential reasoning that the particularities of these verses do not allow for a broader, ahistorical commandment—an injunction to fight everyone—to be extrapolated from them.[103]

Through this profuse documentation of contested views in the early period, only partially listed here, al-Qaraḍāwī clearly wishes to challenge "the reader who imagines that the matter [sc. *jihād*] has been firmly agreed upon (*muttafaq 'alayhi*) and that there was no controversy regarding it." After this detailed discussion, al-Qaraḍāwī arrives at the conclusion that some form of *jihād* against unbelievers (*jihād al-kuffār*) remains individually binding on the Muslim, whether it is carried out "by his hand, his tongue, his wealth, and his heart" ("and God knows best"), as was the stated view of the influential Ḥanbalī jurist Ibn Qayyim in his *Zād al-ma'ād*. The non-defensive military *jihād*, according to the overwhelming majority of jurists, as exemplified by Ibn Qudāma, remains a *farḍ kifāya*. Such a collective obligation is to be discharged by the Imām by conducting military expeditions once a year into enemy territory, a position with which al-Qaraḍāwī concurs. It is clear, therefore, that although al-Qaraḍāwī acknowledges and describes in great detail the diversity of early conceptualizations of the military *jihād* as a religious obligation, he ultimately endorses the later legal consensus that developed regarding its purview, particularly in the Ḥanbalī school of law.[104]

The state is responsible for making sure that this *farḍ al-kifāya* is discharged on behalf of the Muslim community through its yearly military expedition, continues al-Qaraḍāwī; today the state is primarily responsible for keeping its military forces—army, navy, and air force—in a state of preparedness. Should the state be incapable of carrying out this function—whether due to its nonexistence, or because it has renounced Islam, or because it has been occupied by enemy forces, as occurred in Afghanistan under the Communist government—then, al-Qaraḍāwī declares, it behooves individuals or civic organizations to select a group of people who will undertake this duty while fully adhering to the conditions of a legitimate *jihād* outlined by the jurists.[105] Of great interest to us is that he also refers to "the *jihād* of patience and forbearance" (*jihād al-ṣabr wa-'l-muṣābara*), a formulation that is not to be encountered in the usual legal treatises, whether pre-modern or modern. This kind of *jihād*, asserts al-Qaraḍāwī, was practiced by Muḥammad and his Companions when they preached and summoned to Islam and patiently bore persecution at the hands of the pagan Meccans until they were eventually forced to emigrate.[106]

In the third major chapter of the book, al-Qaraḍāwī ponders the all-important question of whether relations between Muslims and non-Muslims are to be characterized by "peace or war" (*al-silm am al-ḥarb*). Are Muslims restricted to fighting only those non-Muslims who are hostile and violate the sanctity of their lives and property? In other words, the critical question is: Why should Muslims fight unbelievers—because of their unbelief or because of their aggression against Muslims? As this has become perhaps an all-consuming question of our time, we offer here some discussion of al-Qaraḍāwī's views on it.

He begins by bemoaning the fact that, although pre-modern and modern scholars have disagreed on the answer to this question, only one perspective seems to have gained ascendancy in the view of many—that Islam commands fighting against all those who oppose it, whether they are pagan idol-worshipers or one of the People of the Book (Jews or Christians), or simply irreligious, until they submit to Islam or meekly pay the *jizya*. Such a momentous question, he remarks, deserves deep reflection and critical rereading of foundational texts, and not mere transmission of the views of one scholar or another. Such a reappraisal involves *inter alia* holistic reading of the Qur'ān, careful matching of secondary principles to primary ones, interpreting specific texts in the context of larger objectives, and a process of discussion, weighing of the evidence, analysis, and authentication that should result in a preference for a perspective or opinion that is most in conformity with revealed texts and their purpose and with the greater good of the Muslim community.[107]

The difference of opinion that primarily exists concerns the preemptive *jihād* (*jihād al-ṭalab*), notes al-Qaraḍāwī, because there is unanimity among all schools of law concerning the obligatory nature of the defensive military *jihād* (*jihād al-daf'*), which is waged to liberate the territories of Islam from the aggression of occupiers.[108] The differences on this point are sharpest between those he calls "moderates" (*al-mu'tadilīn*) and "extremists" (*al-mutashaddidīn*). He accuses the extremists of misrepresenting the views of the moderates by depicting them as a camp completely opposed to the preemptive *jihād*. This is contrary to the truth, he asserts, because the genuine moderates, as opposed to those who are "pacifists" (*mustakinīn*), "capitulators" (*al-mustaslimīn*), and "defeatists" (*al-inhizāmiyyīn*), support preemptive *jihād* for the following reasons: (1) to ensure the unimpeded propagation of the message of Islam among people who are prevented by their tyrannical rulers from listening to the truth and in whose lands Muslim missionaries are murdered, as happened, for example, under the Byzantine emperors; (2) to ensure the safety of the Islamic State (*al-dawla al-islāmiyya*) and secure its borders; (3) to come to the aid of the weak and the defenseless (*al-mustaḍʻafīn*), whether they are relatives or minority groups, **Muslim or non-Muslim** [emphasis added], living under despotic and oppressive rule, especially when they request such assistance (cf. Qur'ān 4:75), a meritorious humanitarian act recognized as such in all religions; and finally (4) the banishment of aggressive, arrogant polytheism (*al-shirk al-muḥārib al-mutajabbir*) from the Arabian peninsula and its preservation "as a free nation purely for Islam and its people," a position for which he claims to find scriptural warrant in Qur'ān 9:5.[109]

The main (and only) point of contention that remains between the moderates and the extremists is the treatment of peaceable non-Muslims of goodwill, who do not fight Muslims on account of their faith, or evict Muslims from their homes, or evince malevolence toward Muslims in their speech and actions. Should such people be fought against or not? The moderates or those who are inclined to peace or the so-called defensive camp (*al-difāʻiyyīn*) assert that they are not to be fought against, since they have not carried out any actions that would merit a military response. They base their opinion on several verses in the Qur'ān: 2:190; 2:256; 3:64; 4:90–91; 5:13; 8:60–61; 9:6–7; 15:94; 16:125; 16:127; and 46:35. All these verses and others beside them are used by the moderates as proof-texts to make the point that Islam is peaceful toward those who are peaceful toward it, and opposes only those who display opposition to it, and does not fight except those who fight it and prevent the peaceful propagation of its message and persecute believers for their faith.[110]

The radicals, continues al-Qaraḍāwī, hew to the exact opposite opinion, dismissing these numerous verses with a simple and dangerous stratagem: by declaring them to be abrogated by part of a single verse known as "the sword verse." On this basis, this "aggressive camp" (*al-hujūmiyyūn*) considers it permissible to attack non-Muslims—or more pejoratively, unbelievers—simply because of their lack of true belief and not because of aggressive and malevolent acts on their part. Their "unbelief" in itself is construed as a threat to Muslims and therefore sufficient cause for fighting them.[111] Al-Qaraḍāwī then proceeds to detail the worldwide destruction these extremists have wrought on the basis of this nihilist philosophy and their willful disregard of relevant United Nations resolutions, the detailed discussion of which need not engage us here.[112] Al-Qaraḍāwī also goes on to discuss the historical evidence for the existence of these two camps—advocates of peace and advocates of war—and their views through time, based particularly on their interpretations of some of the key Qur'anic verses mentioned above, the full details of which, again, need not be given here in the interests of brevity.[113]

Views on So-Called Martyrdom Operations

The origins of modern so-called martyrdom operations (*al-'amaliyyāt al-istishhādiyya*), according to some accounts, may be traced back to the actions of a thirteen-year-old Iranian boy, Mohammed Hossein Fahmideh, during the Iran-Iraq War of 1980–1988. In November 1980, Fahmideh is said to have attached rocket-propelled grenades to his chest and blown himself up underneath an Iraqi tank, an act for which he was declared a martyr and national hero by Ayatollah Khomeini.[114] Others trace its genesis to Lebanon in the early 1980s.[115] The term *'amaliyyāt istishhādiyya* is said to have been coined in the spring of 1994, however, when Hamas carried out suicide attacks in Israel; it is a term that is now routinely used for such activities.[116]

Hard-line Islamists and radical ideologues have a range of opinions on the legitimacy of suicide bombings and on the topic of whether they conform by any stretch of the imagination to the classical legal definitions of military martyrdom and the parameters of military *jihād*. Although a number of them acknowledge that such acts are legally acts of suicide and therefore unequivocally proscribed by Islamic law, others devise ingenious explanations to get around this proscription in an attempt to classify them as legitimate, even obligatory, acts of self-defense in specific circumstances.[117]

An example of such an ideologue is 'Abd al-Mun'im Muṣṭafā Ḥalīma, better known as Abū Baṣīr al-Tarṭūsī, a Syrian cleric whose views are often cited in discussions of suicide attacks. He declares in his online article *Maḥādhīr al-'amaliyyāt al-istishhādiyya aw al-intiḥāriyya*[118] that martyrdom operations, in his opinion, are closer to suicide than to martyrdom and are therefore illicit and forbidden (*ḥarām*). He cites particularly Qur'ān 4:29 ("Do not kill yourselves, indeed God is merciful towards you") and Qur'ān 2:195 ("Spend in the way of God and do not cast yourselves into destruction with your own hands") to establish the prohibition against taking one's life. He also quotes several *ḥadīths* that sternly forbid suicide, including "Whoever takes his own life with something in this world will be tormented by it on the Day of Resurrection" (recorded by Muslim).[119] Abū Baṣīr acknowledges the utter impermissibility of taking innocent human life, Muslim or non-Muslim, according to several Qur'anic verses (e.g., 4:93; 17:33; and 48:25) and *ḥadīths*. When one *ḥadīth* states, "Whoever hurts a believer there is no *jihād* for him," how, Abū Baṣīr asks, can one even begin to justify intentional killing when one is not even allowed to cause any harm? He also notes the *ḥadīth*, "Whoever kills a man from among the *ahl al-dhimma* will not encounter the fragrance of heaven," which protects non-Muslims from wrongful assault. The categorical prohibition against murder of innocents established by such clear, incontestable proof-texts (*adilla muḥkama qaṭʿiyya*) cannot be dismissed or refuted by more ambiguous proof-texts or by a weaker argument, he asserts.[120]

Abū Baṣīr next discusses the position of those who make a case for the legitimacy of suicide attacks by appealing to the legal arguments about *al-tatarrus*—the use of Muslim civilians as human shields by the non-Muslim enemy in order to dissuade Muslims from launching a military attack against them. He stresses, however, that the legal arguments that were articulated on *al-tatarrus* allow a Muslim military assault under strict conditions in circumscribed situations; if any one of these conditions is violated, then recourse to *al-tatarrus* is no longer valid. This is especially true when the aggression of the enemy can be repelled by other means, and when resorting to *al-tatarrus* would result in greater harm and danger than not doing so. This is in accordance with the legal principle that a greater evil may be avoided by allowing a lesser evil in times when these are the only options.[121]

Abū Baṣīr then proceeds to postulate circumstances in which resorting to killing Muslim civilians in enemy territory becomes the only categorical and inevitable option (*qaṭʿiyya wa-yaqīniyya*)—that is, a last-resort option to ensure the greater good (*al-maṣlaḥa al-rājiḥa*). In such a case, the circumstances are so dire that such an option can no longer be postponed and deliberated. If circumstances have not deteriorated to such a crisis point, and there is time and opportunity for civilians to be safely evacuated, then one may not, states Abū Baṣīr, mount an attack on the enemy in such a situation and expose noncombatants to harm. According to this line of argument, when the previously mentioned conditions have been met, only then may the *mujāhid* attempt to repel the enemy, even if civilians are thereby endangered. His intention must remain solely to target the enemy combatant, not the Muslim civilian population (*wa-niyyatuhu wa-qaṣduhu al-ʿaduw wa-laysa al-tars*). If noncombatants suffer harm as a consequence, then it is to be deemed collateral damage, and the *mujāhid* is not to be blamed. This was the opinion of al-Qurṭubī, says Abū Baṣīr, who had considered such an alternative permissible exclusively in the face of an intractable, vicious enemy who could only be vanquished under such circumstances, and when failure to adopt such an extreme measure would lead to two undesirable outcomes: (1) the murder of the Muslim civilian population at the hands of the enemy; and (2) enemy encroachment into Muslim territory and occupation of it, progressively leading to the annihilation of Muslims and the extinction of Islam.[122]

Abū Baṣīr then goes on to pose the essential question: Are current martyrdom operations hewing to these conditions and restrictions so that they may be considered a legitimate last-resort option against an intractable enemy? The answer is a categorical no—which he proceeds to soften slightly by acknowledging the nobility of the intent and desire of "the brother *mujāhid*" to sacrifice himself, his wealth, and everything he owns in the path of God—such a wish is to be accorded utmost respect, he says. However, "this unique and exceptional young man" who resorts to self-immolation of this sort must be prevented, continues Abū Baṣīr, from resorting to measures that will lead to the judgment of suicide against him, causing him and those who goaded him into such actions to forfeit the next world. Such a young man must instead be given plenty of opportunity to engage in *jihād* "in an authentic manner" (*bi-ṣūra ṣaḥīḥa*)—by which Abū Baṣīr means the conventional ways of fighting and inflicting damage on the enemy—and protected from being enticed by those who would coerce him into taking part in martyrdom operations for the following two reasons. First, from a theological point of view, when these youths unwittingly agree to blow themselves up, they are in fact committing suicide and disobeying God, as religious texts trenchantly warn. Second, from a military strategic view, such young men are being killed during a single operation, depleting the number of youthful warriors in the ranks of Muslims. These considerations, scriptural and strategic, lead Abū Baṣīr to proscribe suicide bombings and declare them impermissible.[123]

It is worth noting that Abū Baṣīr concludes by positioning himself between two diametrically opposed groups: religious scholars who categorically forbid suicide bombings and declare their perpetrators to have committed suicide and thus deserving of punishment in the next world, and groups that declare them to be martyrs and worthy of reward in the next world. He considers both positions to be too absolute and thus weak. Even though he considers martyrdom operations to be closer to suicide and therefore reprehensible, Abū Baṣīr recognizes an exception to this general proscription. Should the perpetrator of a suicide attack interpret his actions to be in conformity with the conditions and restrictions (as outlined before by Abū Baṣīr concerning *al-tatarrus*), then he hopes and prays that the suicide bomber will be deemed a martyr (*arjū an yakūn shahīdan*), his sins forgiven, and given his due reward. If, however, the attacker knows of the usual proscription against suicide and is not convinced that the proscription has lapsed because of exceptional emergency circumstances and is in fact riddled with doubts about the licitness of his actions—but proceeds to carry them out anyway—then such a person has in fact committed suicide and is assured of hellfire, according to scriptural warrants. If the suicide bomber's actions destroy the lives of innocent people in addition to his, then he has also committed murder and violated the rights of other human beings, for which suitable penalties should be imposed (presumably on his heirs).[124]

More Views on Martyrdom Operations

Although Abū Baṣīr's views on suicide bombings as outlined above are complex, and his arguments betray a deep moral conflict, other writers have displayed far less ambivalence and adopted a more favorable stance toward such actions. One such influential author is Nawwāf al-Takrūrī, who published his *al-'Amaliyyāt al-istishhādiyya fī 'l-mīzān al-fiqhī* in 1997, a work that has been reprinted several times. Like Abū Baṣīr, al-Takrūrī is fully aware of the scriptural prohibitions against suicide and the consequent legal and ethical obstacles for justifying martyrdom operations. He enumerates instead practical and tactical reasons for endorsing attacks of this sort along the following lines: They inflict the highest number of casualties on the enemy without exacting a similar loss of life among Muslims; they level the playing field against a militarily superior enemy, such as Israel; and they instill fear and despair in the heart of an otherwise intractable enemy.[125] With their backs against the wall, such a hopelessly outgunned people *in extremis* are granted, according to al-Takrūrī, a moral exception to the standard juridical proscriptions against self-immolation and the killing of noncombatants.

This line of reasoning has been repeated most controversially by the previously discussed author Yūsuf al-Qaraḍāwī, who has generated a flurry of largely negative publicity in the global media. In 2002, al-Qaraḍāwī declared martyrdom operations to be the new defensive weapon of the weak against aggressive tyrannical forces and therefore a manifestation of the highest form of *jihād*. Willful taking of one's own life is justified under such circumstances, he claimed, because the vastly superior enemy forces are thereby intimidated and harmed. According to such criteria, suicide attacks are legitimate against Israelis, and the general rules of noncombatant immunity do not apply to them, because Israel is essentially a military society in which every man and woman can be called on at any moment to serve in the army. By the same criteria, the terror attacks of September 11, 2001, were not justified because they were not carried out in self-defense, and they resulted in the deaths of many genuine civilians, including many Muslims.[126]

Among contemporary militant ideologues, Abū Muḥammad 'Āṣim al-Maqdisī is one of the most influential, and he has legitimized suicide bombings as a proper manifestation of military *jihād* in specific circumstances. He has expressed his conviction that the pronouncement of suicide is reserved only for those who kill themselves in disobedience to God for personal reasons and who hasten death "because he was impatient during tribulations or injury, etc.," not for those youths in Palestine who blow themselves up to inflict harm on Israelis and on "apostates who have fortified the aggression of the Jews, Americans and other unbelievers on Muslim lands." In fact, such an action subsumed under the duty of *jihād*, according to al-Maqdisī, "becomes confirmed and obligatory if it occurs in an occupied and extorted [sic] Muslim land as is the case in Palestine."[127] The following three caveats apply, however: (1) the latest technological methods in explosive devices should be used to minimize the number of victims on the Muslim side; (2) the operations should focus on military targets and avoid the intentional targeting of children; and (3) the motive for resorting to such actions should be for the purpose of establishing a true and general public benefit and avert a categorical harm, not a probable one. If one can kill the enemy without resorting to suicide bombings, then "sacrificing the self is not permitted, because it is not a necessity and because it can be accomplished by other means."[128] In view of the incursions of unbelievers into Muslim territory, aided by apostates such as the Saudis, the military *jihād* is now to be regarded as "a valid act of worship that is permissible at any time."[129]

In such accounts generated by a number of militant activists and "cyber-shaykhs," cultic reverence for self-immolation confers upon the non-state Muslim militant actor, at least cognitively, a trump card over the non-Muslim enemy that deploys a conventional army and considerably outguns and outnumbers him. Judged by a calculus of strategic and psychological benefits, the willful taking of one's life that brings in its wake harm to the enemy and deters him from inflicting future attacks upon Muslim targets is no longer a selfish act of suicide. In these meta-narratives granting exoneration to self-immolators, their acts are reconfigured as acts of altruism that apparently level—however gruesomely and temporarily—the playing field for a wounded and humiliated group of people.[130] These militants have but one life to give for their cause; the cult of self-inflicted martyrdom is intended to infuse that life with religio-political meaning, most determinedly in defiance of those who challenge and denigrate their intentions and actions.

IX

Modern and Contemporary Debates on Jihād *and Martyrdom II*

PRIVILEGING HISTORY, CONTEXT, AND POLYSEMY

IN SHARP CONTRAST to most of the modern thinkers and activists on whom we focused in the previous chapter, the scholars and activists discussed in this chapter are distinguished by their inclination to engage the concept of *jihād* in a more diachronic and holistic manner and to emphasize its historically conditioned, multilayered significations through time. In other words, while acknowledging that armed combat may be, has been, and will continue to be a necessary feature of *jihād* under specific, highly circumscribed circumstances, this group is inclined to stress that it is by no means the only signification or the most important aspect of this multivalent term, particularly in the contemporary world. When compared with many of the political ideologues and militants described in chapter 8, these scholars and thinkers typically display a more *longue-durée* historical approach to the topic of *jihād* and tend to emphasize the variegated discourses and praxis that have grown up around it through changing times and sociopolitical circumstances.

We begin by focusing on well-known writers who articulated their views before September 11, 2001, followed by a discussion of those who composed their works in the aftermath of these attacks. The pre-September 11 group includes Muḥammad ʿAbduh, Jamāl al-Bannā, Jawdat Saʿīd, and Saʿīd Ramaḍān al-Būṭī; the post-September 11 group includes ʿAlī Jumʿa, Wahiduddin Khan, and Ṭāhir-ul-Qadrī. The writings of Muhammed Fethullah Gülen discussed here straddle this temporal divide. Once again, we must of necessity be highly selective, even as we try to be generally representative in presenting these views.

Early Modern Perspectives on Jihād *and Martyrdom*

Muḥammad ʿAbduh (d. 1323/1905), the great modernist Egyptian scholar and reformer of the nineteenth century, needs little introduction. Educated at al-Azhar and greatly influenced by the thinking of Jamāl al-Dīn al-Afghānī (d. 1315/1897), he was appointed the Grand Mufti of Egypt in 1317/1899, a position he held until his death. He is counted as one of the original Salafi reformers of the nineteenth century, an attribution that, in its early modern incarnation, implied a critical and dynamic engagement with the Islamic past and its religio-intellectual tradition in the process of negotiating modernity and its concerns.[1]

Although ʿAbduh did not write specifically on *jihād* itself, his views (as partially refracted through Rashīd Riḍā) may be reconstructed from his Qurʾān commentary *Tafsīr al-manār*. ʿAbduh's recorded commentary on the critical Qurʾān verses 2:190–193, 9:5, and 9:29 allows us to gain a sufficiently comprehensive window into his perspectives on the purview of the combative *jihād*.

In his interpretation of Qurʾān 2:190–93, ʿAbduh refers to the Treaty of al-Ḥudaybiyya as providing the historical backdrop for the revelation of these verses, citing al-Wāḥidī as his specific authority. ʿAbduh emphasizes that Qurʾān 2:190 allowed fighting as "defense in the path of God so as to allow unimpeded worship of Him in His house" and as a warning against those who break their oaths and seek to entice Muslims away from their faith. *Wa-lā taʿtadū* is interpreted by him to contain a proscription both against initiation of hostilities by Muslims and attacking traditional noncombatants such as women, children, the elderly, the infirm, and "those who proffer you peace"; it additionally prohibits causing destruction to crops and property.[2]

The next verse (2:191) is understood to be a specific reference to the pagan Meccans who had driven Muḥammad and his Companions out of their homes in Mecca and prevented their subsequent attempt to peacefully perform the pilgrimage in the year of al-Ḥudaybiyya. The right granted to Muslims to defend themselves in the face of Meccan hostility and faithlessnes was therefore a divine act of mercy toward them in their hour of helplessness, comments ʿAbduh. He says that the right to fight in self-defense, as is clearly the case here, undermines the assertions of those who maintain, out of willful ignorance, that Islam was spread by the sword.[3] *Fitna* in Qurʾān 2:191 is specifically glossed as the torments visited upon the Muslims as a consequence of their beliefs—expulsion from their homes and confiscation of their property, for example. ʿAbduh cross-references Qurʾān 29:2 here to underscore the meaning of *fitna* as "tribulations" and Qurʾān 22:39 to establish the reasons (oppression, eviction from home, etc.) that render fighting in self-defense permissible.[4]

'Abduh notes that a number of classical jurists had understood *fitna* to be the equivalent of *shirk* or associationism, an interpretation that he does not find tenable, primarily because it does not fit within the context of the verse. Likewise, he does not accept the interpretation that Qur'ān 2:191 abrogates the preceding verse. Those who advanced such an interpretation, he remarks, clearly did not find it to their liking that fighting was conditional on the prior aggression of the polytheists (*al-mushrikīn*) and that it was meant to ensure the security of believers in the practice of their faith (*wa-li ajl amn al-mu'minīn fī 'l-dīn*), and not for the sake of religion itself. Its abrogating status is also rejected by 'Abduh because, he argues, these verses were revealed as a cohesive unit in reference to one event. "If they should desist" in the next verse refers to the polytheists either desisting from violence or renouncing their polytheism and embracing Islam.[5]

Qur'ān 2:193 reaffirms the meaning of *fitna* as the persecution visited upon believers in order to force them to renounce their religious beliefs and worship. "So that religion may be for God" (*wa-yakūn al-dīn li-'llāh*) is compared to *wa-yakūn al-dīn kulluhu li-'llāh* in Qur'ān 8:39 and interpreted to mean that the religion/religiosity of each individual should be sincerely for the sake of God and not motivated by the fear of any human being. The believers furthermore have the right not to be enticed away from their religion or persecuted because of it or cajoled and flattered into renouncing it. Once again, the historical context must be kept in mind, stresses 'Abduh; Mecca at the time of the revelation of the Qur'ān was the stronghold of polytheism, and the Ka'ba the repository of idols. While the polytheist was free and unencumbered in his belief, the monotheist believer was in a state of subjugation and oppression. If the polytheist were to desist from fighting and violence, then hostility against him also ceases, because aggression against him is carried out only to make him renounce his violent, oppressive ways (*li-anna 'l-'udwāna innamā yakūn 'alā al-ẓālimīn ta'dīban lahum li-yarji'u 'an ẓulmihim*) and for no other reason, he stresses.[6]

'Abduh rejects the interpretation that the so-called sword verse (Qur'ān 9:5; alternatively, Qur'ān 8:38) had abrogated the more numerous verses in the Qur'ān that call for forgiveness and peaceful relations with non-Muslims. Citing the views of al-Suyūṭī, 'Abduh argues that in the specific historical situation with which the verse is concerned—with its references to the passage of the four sacred months and the pagan Meccans—other verses in the Qur'ān advocating forgiveness and nonviolence were not abrogated by it, but rather placed in temporary abeyance or suspension (*laysa naskhan bal huwa min qism al-mansa'*) in that specific historical circumstance. *Naskh* implies the abrogation of a command, which is not the case here. Rather, the command contained in Qur'ān 9:5 was in response to a specific situation at a specific time in order to achieve a specific objective and has no effect on the injunction contained in, for example, Qur'ān 2:109, which states, "Pardon and forgive until God brings about His command," in regard to a different set of circumstances and objectives.[7]

'Abduh is critical of those who would see the injunction contained in Qur'ān 9:5 with its clear reference to Arab polytheists as being applicable in any way to non-Arab polytheists or to the People of the Book. The latter are referred to very differently in the Qur'ān, as in Qur'ān 5:82,[8] and in *ḥadīths*, such as the one that counsels leaving Ethiopians (as well as Turks) alone as long as they leave the Muslims alone. He bemoans the fact that if jurists had not read these verses and *ḥadīths* "from behind the veil of their juridical schools," they would not have so egregiously missed the fundamental point made throughout the Qur'ān and in sound *ḥadīths* that "the security to be obtained through fighting the Arab polytheists according to these verses is contingent upon their initiating attacks against Muslims and violating their treaties. . . ."[9] 'Abduh goes on to point out that the very next verse, Qur'ān 9:6, offers protection and safe conduct to those among the polytheists who wish to listen to the Qur'ān.[10] The implication is clear—polytheists and non-Muslims in general who do not wish Muslims harm and display no aggression toward them are to be left alone and allowed to continue in their ways of life.

With regard to Qur'ān 9:29 (called by some the second sword verse, or *jizya* verse), 'Abduh notes that most commentators are agreed that it was revealed on the occasion of the military campaign in Tabuk, and this verse specifically deals with the People of the Book, as opposed to Qur'ān 9:5, which deals only with Arab polytheists. The verse occasions a fairly lengthy disquisition on specific beliefs and practices of various factions within Christianity and Judaism criticized by the Qur'ān, followed by an extended discussion of the nature of *jizya* and its objectives,[11] the minutiae of which need not be discussed here. What is more directly relevant to us is 'Abduh's subsequent definition of *jihād* and elaboration of its purview in the context of this verse.

'Abduh identifies three different types of *jihād*: (1) struggle against the external enemy (*mujāhadat al-'aduw al-ẓāhir*); (2) struggle against the devil (*mujāhadat al-shayṭān*); and (3) struggle against the soul (*mujāhadat al-nafs*). All three types are included in the following Qur'anic injunctions: "Strive in regard to God as is His due" (Qur'ān 22:78); "Strive with your wealth and selves in the path of God" (Qur'ān 9:41); and "Those who believed, emigrated, and strove with their wealth and their selves in the path of God" (Qur'ān 9:72).

Two *ḥadīths* attest furthermore to the manner of carrying out *jihād* by the hand and the tongue, one in which Muḥammad says, "Struggle against your passions (*ahwā'akum*) as you struggle against your enemies," and the other in which he says, "Strive against the unbelievers with your hands and your tongues." The latter *ḥadīth*, continues 'Abduh, stresses the primacy of *jihād* of the tongue—that is, of attesting to the truth by means of amassing evidence and compelling arguments.[12]

The above proof-texts and others belie the arguments made by Orientalist scholars and those who follow them that *jihād* is reducible to fighting against non-Muslims in order to forcibly effect their conversion.[13] 'Abduh points to Qur'ān 2:256 ("There is no compulsion in religion") and other verses that allow fighting only against those who initiate fighting and that command Muslims to incline to peace when the adversary inclines to peace as proof-texts; all of them establish the falsity of imputing such a reductive meaning to *jihād*.[14] Wars fought for material gain and for the shedding of blood, as was common among ancient kings, or for revenge and out of religious animus, as in the case of the Crusades, or for the purposes of confiscating the possessions of the weak and demeaning human beings, as evident in the European colonial wars of his time, are all forbidden by Islamic law. 'Abduh acknowledges that the military *jihād* may be carried out to bring non-Muslims under the rule of Islam; but this does not grant Muslims the right to resort to "oppression, the shedding of blood, and siphoning off the wealth of those who accept it [sc. Muslim rule] from other communities in contrast to the well-attested practices of the European colonizers. . . ." Muslims are instead exhorted to treat non-Muslims under their jurisdiction with justice and fairness, and even to provide for the destitute among such people.[15]

The only kind of legitimate war on which there is unanimity among Muslim scholars is the defensive war when proclaimed by the Imām in the event of an attack upon Muslim territory, asserts 'Abduh. The Muslim populace must obey him in such a case and make the necessary preparations for effective military resistance. War is an unfortunate fact of human life. However, Islam alone effected one of the most important humane reforms in history by forbidding the waging of war for the purposes of enforcing religious conversions, pillaging other people's wealth, and establishing personal or national dominion over others, stresses 'Abduh. Islamic law mandates humane conduct during battle and prohibits attacks on noncombatants, mutilation of bodies, and destruction of the environment. Chafing under European colonial rule, 'Abduh forcefully contrasts these humane injunctions to the self-serving, exploitative policies he sees perpetrated by Western colonialists, who concoct various "schemes in order to ruin morals and religions" and to establish their tyranny over subject peoples. The defensive war against prior aggression is an individual duty, the legitimacy of which is acknowledged by all nations of the world, concludes 'Abduh.[16]

Refutations of al-Farīḍa al-Ghā'iba

Al-Farīḍa al-Ghā'iba, discussed in the previous chapter, elicited a number of refutations by some of the leading scholars and clerics of the time, particularly those associated with al-Azhar University. A useful summary of the forceful refutation composed by the then-Grand Mufti of al-Azhar, Shaykh Jādd al-Ḥaqq, is provided by Johannes Jansen in his translation of Faraj's work.[17] In this section, we discuss the views of another influential scholar, Jamāl al-Bannā, who composed a detailed refutation of the *Farīḍa* in 1984.

Jamāl al-Bannā: Challenging Militancy

The Egyptian thinker and prolific author Jamāl al-Bannā is the youngest brother of Ḥasan al-Bannā and, unlike his brother, known particularly for his socially liberal views. His refutation of the *Farīḍa* is pointedly titled *al-Farīḍa al-ghā'iba: jihād al-sayf am jihād al-'aql?*[18]

Al-Bannā begins his treatise by praying for forgiveness for the author of *al-Farīḍa al-ghā'iba* and his cohorts, who in their ignorance and hubris, assume—like the assassins of the third Caliph 'Uthmān b. 'Affān—that they have committed a good deed.[19] He identifies two main cruxes in the *Farīḍa* on which hinge Faraj's arguments: (1) the allegations of *takfīr* and *al-ridda*; and (2) the depiction of fighting (*al-qitāl*) as the ideal means to establish the Islamic State. He proceeds to refute both.

In regard to the accusation of apostasy, al-Bannā emphasizes that Qur'ān 4:116 states that only the sin of associating partners with God is unforgivable. Additionally, several well-attested *ḥadīths* affirm that an individual who utters the Muslim creedal statement is henceforth to be regarded as a Muslim, regardless of other blameworthy acts committed by him or her. A significant *ḥadīth* transmitted by the Companion Ḥudhayfa b. al-Yamān (d. ca. 36/656) asserts that anyone who testifies to the oneness of God will be saved from the Fire. In total disregard of such unassailable proof-texts, the author of the *Farīḍa* hurls accusations of apostasy arbitrarily and randomly, without any kind of corroboration or witness, as required, for example, by Qur'ān 24:4, which asks believers to produce four witnesses before an allegation may be deemed to be credible, al-Bannā reminds. The famed scholar Abū Ḥāmid al-Ghazālī in his book *al-Tafriqa bayn al-īmān wa 'l-zandaqa*[20] had warned against the arbitrary leveling of accusation of unbelief and counseled that it was far better to spare the lives of thousands of unbelievers than to wrongly shed the blood of a single Muslim.[21]

Rather than following the historical precedents of the Prophet and the early Muslims, al-Bannā continues, the author of the *Farīḍa* has instead embarked upon the path of the Khawārij, who were the first to resort to *takfīr* against ʿAlī b. Abī Ṭālib and his followers, as well as against his adversaries and those who had committed a major sin. ʿAlī however did not in return accuse them (or the supporters of Muʿāwiya) of unbelief, but rather uttered the following memorable words: "One who seeks the truth and misses it is not like the one who seeks falsehood and attains it."[22] The significant point therefore made by al-Bannā is that the Companions themselves refrained from resorting to *takfīr*, and it is their practice that sets the normative standard. By violating this standard, today's extremists are no better than the Khawārij, who are universally condemned by Muslims for their intolerance and violence.

Al-Bannā distinguishes between religious or doctrinal apostasy and political apostasy. The kind of apostasy generally deemed to be punishable by the jurists was of the political kind, usually termed *ḥirāba*, although there were considerable legal differences of opinion on this matter.[23] He notes that the Qur'ān itself does not mandate any this-worldly punishment for religious apostasy but defers punishment until the next (çf. Qur'ān 2:217). There is, however, the *ḥadīth* attributed to Ibn ʿAbbās in which Muḥammad is quoted as saying, "Whoever changes his religion, have him put to death." This *ḥadīth*, however, is regarded as one of the solitary ones (*āḥād*); al-Bannā notes that most jurists are of the opinion that *ḥudūd* punishments may not be administered on the basis of solitary reports, and that unbelief (*al-kufr*) in and of itself was not considered to be grounds for shedding blood. This is in accordance with Qur'ān 2:256, which forbids compulsion in religion. Only when unbelief manifests itself in overt acts of violence and hostility against Muslims (*muḥārabat al-muslimīn*) can it be deemed punishable, for it is then the equivalent of political treason. It is on such a political basis that Abū Bakr justified the *ridda* wars and why ʿAlī eventually fought the Khawārij.[24] As for the *ḥadīth* narrated by Ibn ʿUmar in which the Prophet states, "I have been commanded to fight people until they bear witness that there is no god but God and that Muḥammad is the Messenger of God, perform the prayers, and offer the obligatory alms; if they were to do that, they would protect their blood and property from me, except for what is due on it to Islam, and their reckoning is with God," al-Bannā remarks that this is not a generally applicable report. There is wide agreement among Muslim scholars that the referent in this *ḥadīth* is specifically the Arab polytheists, and that its content is therefore not applicable to the People of the Book or to non-Arab polytheists. Furthermore, one can adduce as counter-evidence *ḥadīths* that do not prescribe any kind of punishment for not performing the required prayers, such as the one that relates that the Banū Thaqīf asked Muḥammad to grant them a reprieve from praying; the Prophet refused to do so but also did not prescribe any punishment for those who so desisted.[25]

Al-Bannā next criticizes the militant interpretation of *jihād* as primarily *qitāl* and its glorification of fighting as "the only way to resurrect and rejuvenate the lofty edifice of Islam" and remove "the tyrants of this earth."[26] The primary proof-text offered by the author of the *Farīḍa* to support this position is the *ḥadīth* that states, "Whoever fights so that the word of God is supreme is in the path of God." Al-Bannā points out that the *ḥadīth* in its entirety does not support the *Farīḍa*'s contention that God's word must thereby be established through both offensive and defensive battles. The full *ḥadīth* provides a larger context for this statement: The Prophet was asked who among the following men was truly in the path of God—the man who fights out of valor and zeal; the man who fights for booty; or the man who fights for renown or prestige. To which question, the Prophet gave the reply as quoted above. Al-Bannā comments that the full, contextualized *ḥadīth* stresses that, only when one fights for the sake of the highest Islamic principles, may one be considered to be in the way of God, and not when fighting out of national chauvinism or in pursuit of worldly gain and standing.[27]

Al-Bannā disparages the extremist claim that fighting is now an individual duty for every Muslim, because the enemy in the guise of political leaders now resides within Islamic realms. Al-Bannā notes that this position represents a dramatic departure from classical juridical thought that had defined *jihād* as an individual duty only in the event of a direct attack by an external non-Muslim enemy upon Muslim territory or occupation of it. Opposition to the ruler was subsumed under the heading of "Rebellion against the Ruler" (*al-khurūj ʿalā ʾl-ḥākim*) and was not deemed *jihād*. The extremists compound this error by assigning the highest priority to fighting against Muslim rulers, who are regarded as having failed to obey God's rulings by not resisting colonization. According to them, the colonization of Muslim lands has been facilitated by such pusillanimous rulers. Al-Bannā finds the logic of this argument to be perverse; he notes that colonization preceded the rise of such rulers, who are themselves the product of colonization, not its facilitators. Once again, extremist rhetoric of this kind is reminiscent of the views of the Khawārij in early Islam, who regarded ʿUthmān and ʿAlī as "disobedient" rulers and therefore unbelievers who could licitly be killed. Examples of extremist "reasoning" of this kind, says al-Bannā, "reveals to us how narrow-mindedness, blind chauvinism, and ignorance, which go together, lead to falling into strategic and fundamental error. . . . " Al-Bannā does not accept the *Farīḍa*'s premise that the so-called sword verse had abrogated numerous Qur'anic verses "which decree inviting to Islam with wisdom and good counsel and attribute to God the final adjudication of differences on the Day of Judgment." In any case, he remarks, the sword verse was directed only at polytheists and not at the People of the Book.[28]

Against the assertions of the *Farīḍa*, al-Bannā points to historical examples from early Islam of humane conduct during the combative *jihād*, particularly in relation to noncombatants, such as women, children, and the elderly, who must not be molested; in the treatment of prisoners; in its prohibition against the mutilation of bodies; and in the establishment of rules for the equitable distribution of spoils. Extremists, however, have focused only on a few exceptional circumstances when the Prophet was forced to deal harshly with some of his most intractable enemies and had ordered the cutting down and burning of trees, for example. Al-Bannā remonstrates that such exceptions when recounted should be noted as specific exceptions to the general rules of conduct during warfare and not misleadingly labeled as "Islamic Strategies" by the author of the *Farīḍa*.[29] *Jihād* is not reducible to merely "*jihād* of the sword," as in the *Farīḍa*. On the basis of Qur'anic evidence, it is clear that *jihād* is also connected to alms-giving (*jihād bi-'l-māl*); the exhortation to carry out *jihād* by means of one's wealth precedes mention of *jihād* "with one's selves," as in Qur'ān 8:72, which states, "Those who believed and emigrated and strove with their wealth and their selves . . . " (cf. also Qur'ān 9:20; 9:88; 4:95; and 49:15).[30]

In contrast to these hawkish extremists, al-Bannā refers to unnamed liberal scholars who maintain that in Islam, the default situation is peace, not war, and Muslims are not allowed to fight others merely on the basis of religious differences. The Qur'ān permits fighting only under one of the following conditions: defense against wrongdoing and oppression (*al-ẓulm*); containing chaos and social disorder (*al-fitna*); and protecting freedom of religious propagation (*ḥimāyat al-da'wā*). The battles fought during the lifetime of the Prophet were fought only for these reasons, as referenced in the Qur'ān itself. During such legitimate battles, the strict rules concerning the protection of the lives of noncombatants and against initiating aggression were scrupulously observed. If the combative *jihād* was for the purpose of forcibly converting non-Muslims to Islam, then these behavioral and ethical restrictions on how *jihād* is to be conducted would not have existed, argues al-Bannā. Furthermore, the successful propagation of a religion occurs not at the point of a sword but through genuine conviction and inner faith, as categorically indicated in Qur'ān 2:256 and elsewhere.[31]

The *dār al-ḥarb* is comprised of nations that are hostile to Islam, aggress against Muslims, and violently prevent the propagation of Islam; under such circumstances, Muslims have the right to retaliate and defend themselves. Non-Muslim nations that do not initiate hostilities against Muslims or prevent the peaceful dissemination of Islam may not be fought against, and Muslims are required to establish amicable relations with them.[32] Qur'ān 5:51, which counsels Muslims not to take the People of the Book as "allies" (*awliyā'*), a verse the extremists like to cite as a general prohibition against befriending non-Muslims, must be understood in this historical vein. The verse warned against only those Jews and Christians who had conspired against Muslims and intended them harm during specific historical events. A blanket indictment of them would not make sense in view of the fact that the Qur'ān allows, for example, Muslim men to marry Jewish and Christian women and live with them in harmony. Al-Bannā repeats and further elaborates upon many of these arguments in the rest of his treatise; these arguments underscore the fundamental points of difference between what he depicts as the supremacist, violent manifesto of the extremists and the historically contextualized, irenic arguments of liberal, rational scholars like himself.[33] He ends this section by passionately proclaiming as follows:

> The successful groups are those which are licit and out in the open and follow rational ideas, not individuals, and which refute baseless ideas and replace them with sound views. In their struggle, they adhere to legitimate means and distance themselves thoroughly from anything that smacks of secrecy and conspiracy and that inclines to violence and terrorism.[34]

General Works on Jihād*: Pre-September 11 Period*

We now turn our attention to a monograph on *jihād* written by Muḥammad Sa'īd Ramaḍān al-Būṭī in 1993. Al-Būṭī (b. 1348/1929) is an influential Syrian jurist, public intellectual, and television preacher, who obtained his doctorate from al-Azhar University in 1385/1965. He served as dean of the Sharī'a faculty at Damascus University for some time and continues to teach there to this day.[35]

Al-Būṭī begins his important work titled *al-Jihād fī 'l-islām* by directly challenging the prevalent assumption that *jihād*, which he describes as "a fundamental part of Islamic legal rulings and prescriptions," was prescribed only in the Medinan period after the *hijra* and that it did not exist as a concept and requirement in the Meccan period. Not so, he says. The Meccan phase of the Prophet's career "was filled with *jihād*" as was the Medinan phase, as the Qur'ān itself testifies in al-Furqān, a Meccan chapter, "Do not obey the unbelievers and strive against them mightily with it" (25:52). Another verse states, "Indeed God will be merciful and compassionate towards those who emigrated after they were persecuted, and then strove and were steadfast" (Qur'ān 16:110). A majority of scholars, including al-Ḥasan al-Baṣrī, 'Ikrima, 'Aṭā'[b. Abī Rabāḥ], and Jābir, maintained that the entire sixteenth chapter was revealed in Mecca; the *hijra* must therefore be understood in this verse as a reference to the emigration to Abyssinia. Because most people tend to define *jihād* in a combative sense, and since the combative *jihād* was permitted only in the Medinan period, this has led to the erroneous assumption that *jihād* in general was commanded only after the emigration to Medina. This misconception has occurred, al-Būṭī continues, because the multivalence of the term *jihād*, evident during the Meccan period, has been lost, and *jihād* came to acquire specific circumscribed meanings after this period due to the contingencies of particular historical circumstances.[36]

However, one of the most important types of *jihād* was practiced in early Islam—the summoning of the polytheists by the Prophet (and after him by his Companions) to the Truth (*bi-da'wātihim ilā 'l-ḥaqq*) and their verbal refutation of the practices of the pagan Arabs and their forefathers. Their resoluteness in speaking words of truth to counter wrongdoing, despite the persecution and the hardships that they encountered as a consequence, is also among the most important types of *jihād*. Another important component of the *jihād* of the early Muslims, al-Būṭī continues, was their constant engagement with the Book of God and reflection upon it (*al-tabṣīr bi-kitāb allāh*) and their fearless proclamation of the message contained within it, without any regard for the dangers that consequently engulfed them. These most important forms of *jihād* were set in motion by Qur'ān 25:52, which specifically refers to this kind of striving with the Qur'ān and its proofs and characterizes it as "a mighty striving" (*jihādan kabīran*), indicating its central, distinctive nature among the various forms of *jihād*. These various forms of striving that have nothing to do with fighting constitute the foundation and essence of *jihād*, as further indicated in the aforementioned Qur'ān 16:110, a Meccan verse with the exhortation to "strive and be steadfast," which must be understood in this non-combative sense.[37]

Ḥadīths, such as the one in which Muḥammad says, "The best *jihād* is a word of truth before a tyrannical ruler" and "the best *jihād* is your striving against your self and desires for the sake of God Almighty," provide further corroboration of these non-combative significations, continues our author. Al-Būṭī invites the reader to reflect on these proof-texts and to come to the realization that this aspect of *jihād*, firmly established in Mecca at the dawn of Islam, is the origin and source of the various dimensions it acquired in subsequent periods.[38]

The essential meaning of *jihād* as established during the Meccan period remained in force throughout the Medinan period, continues al-Būṭī. New developments in their changed circumstances required Muslims to take up new tasks in Medina. These new developments were of two types: the rise of the first cohesive Muslim community under the aegis of a state system led by the Prophet Muḥammad; and the unique composition of this society that included the Meccan emigrants, the Medinan helpers, and Jews, all of whom pledged to coexist in peace, according to the provisions of the charter (*al-wathīqa*) drawn up by the Prophet and dictated to his Companions. The Medinan polity represented the first "abode of Islam" (*dār al-islām*), with a well-defined territory the inhabitants of which were entrusted with its defense—this was the new dimension of *jihād* in Medina.[39]

Al-Būṭī does not accept the theory which states that the concept of *jihād* evolved through different stages, with the final pronouncement on its nature abrogating previous Qur'anic injunctions concerning it, as was the case with the issue of wine consumption. Rather, two types of *jihād* remain valid for all times depending on the situation: (1) in one set of circumstances, *jihād* is essentially preaching Islam with the tongue (*da'wā bi-'l-lisān*), with unflagging patience in the face of potential harm; and (2) in a different set of circumstances, *jihād* means fighting those who prevent the carrying out of this *da'wā*. Neither of these two types, he comments, is the equivalent of *jihād* understood as fighting against those who refuse to bear witness in the oneness of God and who resist the summons to it.[40] Understood in this manner, there is a huge chasm separating legitimate *jihād*, the *jihād* of *da'wā*, which is eternal, and the violent rebellions of the contemporary period that beguile young people. Similarly, continues al-Būṭī, a huge gulf separates "true or real peace" (*al-silm al-ḥaqīqī*), the achievement of which is one of the driving forces behind a legitimate *jihād*, and an illusory peace born of capitulation that undermines the legitimacy of *jihād*.[41]

The source of *jihād*'s "sacredness" (*qudsiyyatuhu*) lies in the fact that it represents a path toward attaining the truth and bringing others to it, and therefore a way of distancing oneself and others from falsehood. When a variety of factions claim to have exclusive accessibility to the truth, the remedy is to be found at the table of negotiation and dialogue, states al-Būṭī, conducted with seriousness, objectivity, and sincerity. This should not lead to relativism; such a process of negotiation and dialogue does not entail abandonment of "the established truth" (*al-ḥaqīqa al-thābita*). Rather, *jihād* leads to uncovering this truth and summoning to it—this obligation is "the summit of the sacred struggle" (*ṣinw al-jihād al-muqaddas*).[42]

To those who may ask, Where is the proof that this duty of inviting to God through proper education regarding the principles of Islam and commanding good and forbidding wrong are the bases for the rules and regulations of *jihād*?, al-Būṭī answers thus: These foundational imperatives of *jihād* are asserted, he says, in numerous works of *fiqh*, such as the *Minhāj* of al-Nawawī (d. 676/1278) and the *Aqrab al-masālik* of Aḥmad al-Dardir (d. 1201/1786). Ibn Rushd (d. 595/1198) in his prolegomena to the Book of *Jihād* identifies four types of *jihād*: *jihād* of the heart, the tongue, the hand, and the sword. He explicated the *jihād* of the tongue as commanding right and forbidding wrong, as referenced by Qur'ān 9:73 ("O Prophet, strive against the unbelievers and the hypocrites…"). Ibn Rushd was of the opinion that striving against the unbelievers was accomplished by means of the sword and against the hypocrites by means of the tongue. Al-Būṭī qualifies this latter opinion by suggesting that the *jihād* of the sword against unbelievers must follow an initial verbal invitation to Islam and the presentation of cogent proofs on its behalf. Unbelievers may be fought against only when they attempt to prevent the propagation of Islam in a hostile manner and threaten those who undertake such activity.[43] According to this fundamental definition, *jihād* is therefore a matter of peaceful propagation of Islam (*al-tablīgh*) and as such is not a concern solely of the leader of the Muslim polity, but rather an activity incumbent upon each individual Muslim.[44]

It is in this larger context that al-Būṭī then proceeds to deconstruct the *ḥadīth*, "I have been commanded to fight people until they bear witness 'There is no god but God…,' " a report that was included by al-Bukhārī and Muslim on the authority of 'Abd Allāh b. 'Umar. The principal problem with this *ḥadīth* is that its chain of transmission is characterized as *gharīb* (literally "rare," "strange," "obscure"); despite this deficiency, the *ḥadīth* was accepted by the two aforementioned compilers. However, Aḥmad b. Ḥanbal did not include this *ḥadīth* in his collection, despite his intimate familiarity with the two *Ṣaḥīḥs*, while Ibn Ḥajar recorded the names of those scholars who discredited the reliability of this *ḥadīth*, particularly on the basis that, had Ibn 'Umar really known of this *ḥadīth*, then his father, the second Caliph 'Umar, could not have conceivably argued with Abū Bakr about fighting those who had withheld the payment of *żakāt*.[45] Al-Būṭī admits that these criticisms in themselves will not constitute irrefutable proof that the *ḥadīth* is weak, especially since al-Bukhārī and Muslim accepted these two *ḥadīths*. How then to attempt to explain the text of the *ḥadīth* in the context of his overall premise that inviting to Islam must only take place in a non-coercive and dialogic manner?

Al-Būṭī lists two predominant explanations of this *ḥadīth*, accompanied by his own analysis of them. According to the first school of thought, which al-Būṭī describes as the weakest of these positions, non-coercive *da'wā* was practiced in the early years of Islam before the command for combative *jihād* was revealed. Therefore, the sword verse and this *ḥadīth* abrogated the previous understanding of *da'wā* and mandated the legitimacy of fighting polytheists (*qitāl al-mushrikīn*) and forcibly bringing them into Islam. The second school of thought, to which the majority of jurists and exegetes adhere, maintains that those Qur'anic verses that indicate invitation to Islam must be effected without coercion remain unabrogated and that Ibn 'Umar's *ḥadīth* does not contradict the content of these verses. These scholars justify this position in one of two ways: One group says that the people addressed in the above *ḥadīth* are specifically pagan idol-worshipers and those regarded as rebellious heretics (*al-wathaniyyūn wa-man fī ḥukūmihim ka-'l-malāḥida*). All others are exempt according to Qur'anic verses that otherwise forbid coercion in religious matters, such as the well-known "There is no compulsion in religion" and Qur'ān 60:8, which states, "God does not forbid you from being kind to those who do not oppose you in religion. . . ." Al-Būṭī adds in a footnote that this was the principal view of the Shāfi'ī and Ḥanafī schools and the majority of Ḥanbalī jurists. A second group of scholars were of the view that inviting to Islam permitted absolutely no coercion in regard to any group of people—whether they were scriptuaries or not. The command to kill the polytheists in Qur'ān 9:5 was predicated on their violent hostility (*al-ḥirāba*), not on their unbelief (*al-kufr*). This was the view of Mālik and his companions, al-Awzā'ī, and a considerable number of other jurists.[46]

Al-Būṭī agrees with this second group of scholars from the non-abrogation school. He points out that the so-called sword verse is followed by this: "If anyone from among the polytheists should ask for refuge from you, grant him such a refuge so that he may hear the word of God, then conduct him to safety; that is because they are a people who do not understand." Al-Būṭī comments that if Qur'ān 9:5 is understood to command the fighting of polytheists until their death or their acceptance of Islam, then such a command is countermanded by the very next verse that exhorts Muslims to offer refuge and safe conduct to polytheists while they are in their state of polytheism. He dismisses as irresponsibly arbitrary the view of those who suggest that Qur'ān 9:5 abrogates Qur'ān 9:6; this goes against the usual rule of abrogation that a later verse may supersede an earlier verse, and he stresses that their understanding of Qur'ān 9:5 contradicts other, more numerous verses of the Qur'ān that were later revelations and the praxis of the Companions. An example of such a verse is Qur'ān 9:13, which states, "Will you not fight a people who violate their pledges and are intent on expelling the Messenger, while they initiated aggression against you? Do you fear them while God is more worthy of being feared, if you were truly believers?" (See our discussion of this verse in chapter 3.) Al-Būṭī points out that the verse clearly establishes the following reasons for engaging polytheists in battle: their reneging on oaths, their breaking of treaties, and their initiation of treachery and hostility. Such verses categorically establish that the proclamation of war against the polytheists in Qur'ān 9:5 is predicated on their hostility, not on their lack of belief. Al-Būṭī further adduces several *ḥadīths* and Companion reports as proof-texts that describe the Prophet, as well as a number of his Companions, as counseling kindness toward polytheist relatives and non-relatives who displayed no aggressive behavior. Once again, all of these proof-texts provide further affirmation that the only legitimate reason for fighting any group of people is *al-ḥirāba*—that is, on account of their unrelenting hostility and initiation of aggression, and not on account of their religious beliefs or lack thereof.[47]

The seemingly problematic *ḥadīth* related by Ibn 'Umar, "I have been commanded to fight people until they bear witness that there is no god but God..." has led to a grave misunderstanding of its meaning because most people do not take note of the fundamental distinction between the two verbs *uqātil* and *aqtul* and tend to confuse and/or conflate the two, continues al-Būṭī. The first would mean "[that] I fight" and the second would mean "[that] I kill." If the second verb had occurred in the *ḥadīth*, then that would indeed have been contrary to the texts of numerous Qur'anic verses and *ḥadīths* that prohibit coercion in matters of religion. The actual verb *uqātil* as it occurs in the *ḥadīth* is not contrary to these texts because it broadly means, according to the third verbal form, "to fight someone who opposes you," and more narrowly means "to fight someone who attacks you first with intent to kill." For it is the aggressor (*al-bādi'*) who is called *qātil*, and "the one who resists the aggressor" is called *muqātil*." On the basis of this linguistic analysis, it is compellingly established that the purpose of fighting in this *ḥadīth* is defending oneself in response to a prior act of aggression. The proper meaning of the *ḥadīth* may then be rendered as follows:

> I have been commanded to prevent any act of aggression [directed] at my summoning of the people to faith in the oneness of God, even if this prevention of aggression against this summoning is accomplished through fighting the aggressors, for that is a duty I have been commanded to [undertake] by God, and which must be carried out.

Al-Būṭī draws on a number of other *ḥadīths* and the opinions of other authorities to further establish that this fundamental distinction between *qatala* and *qātala* (and their various derivatives) is a critical one, and the blurring of this distinction can (and has) engendered grave misunderstandings of the purpose and purview of the military *jihād*.[48]

It is important to point out that al-Būṭī does not find convincing the argument of those scholars who maintained that Qur'ān 9:5 and the *ḥadīth* from Ibn 'Umar (*umirtu an uqātila*...) concerned pagan Arabs exclusively and not the People of the Book. He considers this line of argument to be faulty primarily because what is at issue here is not the question of religious belief, but rather aggression on the part of the people involved, regardless of who they may be. According to al-Būṭī—and this, he observes, was also the position of Mālikī jurists, al-Awzā'ī, and other scholars—there can be no dilution of the basic Qur'anic position that religion is a matter of free choice, and absolutely no one without exception can be compelled in such a matter. Our author is very forceful on this point.[49] It is for all these reasons that al-Būṭī faults the modern crop of Islamists who have distorted the real meaning and purpose of *jihād* beyond recognition because of their worldly political aspirations and scant knowledge of religious matters.[50]

By no means, al-Būṭī asserts, does the right to engage in legitimate combative *jihād* translate into a right to stage a revolution or wage a military campaign to bring about an Islamic State, as contemporary Islamists believe. The Prophet, continues al-Būṭī, did not fight to establish an Islamic State; he fought to defend one after God had already granted it to him. One can only defend what exists, after all, not what *may* potentially exist.[51]

Al-Būṭī concludes by summarizing what he calls "the most important principles of peace and war" in regard to *jihād*: First and foremost, world peace (*al-silm al-'ālamī*) is the pivot around which the laws of Islam and its regulations revolve. The clearest assertion of this fundamental principle is contained in Qur'ān 2:208, which states, "O those who believe, enter into peace (*al-silm*) altogether, and do not follow the steps of Satan, for he is an avowed enemy to you." Peace, however, he stresses, "cannot exist nor grow except under the aegis of justice (*al-'adāla*)." Logic and history both confirm this relationship, and most people are aware of this intrinsic connection. Such a profound concern for the establishment of justice is of necessity linked to removal of the causes of injustice—this, al-Būṭī asserts, is the fundamental rationale for *jihād*, which is primarily undertaken for both the removal of these causes of injustice and the construction of just societies. Seeking peace (*ṣulḥ*) without seeking justice can result in blameworthy acquiescence and capitulation (*al-istislām*) to wrongdoing and oppression; "just peace" (*al-salām al-'ādil*) is never achieved under conditions of continuous usurpation of the rights of others.[52] This means that Israelis today who occupy Palestinian territory and areas in southern Lebanon (note: the latter was true at the time of the writing of al-Būṭī's book) should legitimately be resisted and fought against.[53] Al-Būṭī had stressed earlier that this resistance is not directed at them because they are Jews, but because they are oppressors. The Prophet Muḥammad punished members of the Jewish tribe Banū Qaynuqā' only after evidence of their treachery and hostility became apparent and they clearly posed a danger to all.[54]

Al-Būṭī affirms that sincere advocacy of peace must of necessity include a sincere advocacy of justice and earnest efforts to bring about the realization of just peace.[55] Justice, al-Būṭī reminds, is due to all according to the Qur'anic vision, not just to Muslims. He rather grandly and memorably sums up the role that Muslims must assume in the future for all humanity in the service of their faith and their calling to establish just peace:

> The time has come for us to realize that this Islam—when we do wrong to it we wrong ourselves—does not transgress against the right of any community (*umma*), does not suppress the genuine freedom of any people, and is not founded on any kind of chauvinism or racism. It is rather a shield to protect the rights of all those who are endowed with rights. It is the citadel which defends the freedom of every religious group and people; it is the singular means for realizing the highest civilizational ideal for humans.[56]

Post-September 11 Works on Jihād *and Martyrdom*

We begin this section by focusing on 'Alī Jum'a, the current mufti (chief jurisconsult) of Egypt and professor of Islamic jurisprudence at al-Azhar University in Cairo, Egypt. Widely regarded as an influential voice of reason and moderation, he wrote *al-Jihād fī 'l-islam*[57] in 2005, as a rebuttal to typical militant conceptualizations of the combative *jihād*.

In this book, Jum'a begins by highlighting the Qur'anic verse 21:107, which addresses the Prophet Muḥammad thus, "We have sent you only as a mercy to the worlds," thereby setting the tone for this slim book. Jum'a emphasizes that the temporal and spatial scope of this verse is vast, embracing every era and every place and applicable to every generation of people, believer and nonbeliever, Arab and non-Arab. The quality of mercy possessed by the Prophet is thus "general and comprehensive" (*'āmma shāmila*), he says; this colored his temperament and actions toward every living being around him.

Jum'a then proceeds to define *al-jihād fī 'l-islām* as "a licit war" (*ḥarb mashrū'a*) as deemed by "intelligent people" (*al-'uqalā' min banī 'l-bashar*). It is, furthermore, "the purest form of wars" (*min anqā anwā' al-ḥurūb*) when the following criteria are taken into consideration: (1) its objective; (2) its manner of execution; (3) its conditions and precise rules; (4) its [manner of] termination; and finally (5) its consequences and achievements.[58] Both the theory and praxis of *jihād*, he says, are clearly articulated in Islam. But despite this clarity, because of chauvinism and ignorance of the truth of Islam, the true nature of *jihād* has been obfuscated and distorted among Muslims, so much so that Muslims themselves are prone to assert that Islam was spread by the sword and that it exhorts to war and violence. Jumʿa says it is sufficient to counter such false allegations by pointing to the divine injunctions contained in the Qur'ān that command justice and fairness. He takes issue with Western authors like Thomas Carlyle, who propagated the idea that Islam had spread by the sword. To the views of Carlyle he counterposes those of the French historian Gustave LeBon, who in his book *Arab Civilization* pointed out that Islam had spread primarily through peaceful proselytization (*bi-'l- daʿwā*) after the Arab conquests, and particularly in places not conquered by military force, such as China.[59] Jumʿa emphasizes that during the thirteen-year nonviolent phase of Muḥammad's prophetic career in Mecca, conversions to Islam took place through peaceful propagation of the faith alone.[60]

Jumʿa lists several Qur'anic verses[61] (some of which we have discussed in previous chapters), 2:190–191; 192–193; 2:216–217; 3:146; 3:169; 3:195; 4:74–75; 4:90; 8:7–8; 8:17; 8:39; 8:47; 8:61; 8:70; 9:5–7; 9:111; 22:39–40, and *ḥadīths*[62] that define the parameters of a legitimate *jihād*. One memorable *ḥadīth* narrated by Saʿīd b. Jubayr describes the military campaigns of Muslims after the time of the Prophet as "your fighting for worldly power," in contrast to Muḥammad's military activity launched to contain the moral disorder (*al-fitna*) created by the polytheists.[63] Another *ḥadīth* recorded by al-Tirmidhī from al-Nuʿmān b. Muqrin relates that Muḥammad would counsel his military commanders to fear and revere God and to look out for the well-being of those Muslims with them. The rest of the *ḥadīth* provides a detailed protocol for engaging in combat with (Meccan) polytheists by summoning them first to Islam and desisting from fighting them if they should accept the invitation, or resorting to fighting if they should refuse, and refraining from mutilation or excessive violence or killing children.

These carefully chosen Qur'anic verses and *ḥadīths* allow Jumʿa to make the following observations regarding "the objective(s) of warfare in Islam":

1. To repel aggression and to defend oneself
2. To ensure propagation of the word of God and to provide opportunity for the weak to embrace it
3. To demand the restoration of usurped rights
4. To aid truth and justice

The following conditions and restrictions on war are thereby established:

1. Observance of clear, honorable rules of conduct with regard to means and objectives
2. Prohibition against fighting noncombatants and avoidance of aggression against civilians
3. Cessation of hostilities when the opposite camp inclines to peace and desists from fighting, except in the case of those who persist in wrongdoing/oppression (*illā ʿalā ʾl-ẓālimīn*)
4. Protection and humane treatment of prisoners-of-war
5. Protection of the environment—under this proviso, animals must not be killed except for an expressly beneficial purpose; trees may not be cut down, nor may crops and fruit-bearing trees be laid waste; wells and water in general may not be polluted; and houses may not be destroyed
6. Guarantee of freedom of religion for monks and hermits in their monasteries and cells; no hostility may be displayed toward them[64]

A licit *jihād* undertaken for noble motives and executed according to these rules of honorable conduct leads to the following commendable outcomes:

1. Individual inculcation of decency, bravery, and chivalry
2. The removal of tyrants who oppress people, and whose wrongdoing leads to "corruption on earth after its reform" (cf. Qurʾān 7:56; 7:85)
3. The affirmation of justice and freedom for all people, regardless of their beliefs
4. The advancement of the common good over individual benefit
5. The realization of appropriate defensive measures for the protection of people in their nations

The exemplary application of these rules governing *jihād* was illustrated during the battles fought by the Prophet himself, continues Jumʿa. After a fairly lengthy discussion of violent battles described in the various books of the Old Testament that need not be discussed here, he details in contrast the gradual evolution from conciliatory and nonviolent responses of Muslims in Mecca toward the pagan Meccans (cf. Qurʾān 43:89) to resorting to armed combat in self-defense and defense of their faith against hostile adversaries shortly after the emigration to Medina, as evident in Qurʾān 22:39–40. Neither desire for revenge nor rancor motivated the Prophet and his followers, remarks Jumʿa, but rather the principled desire to set aright what was wrong, like "the surgeon who places his scalpel at the site of the affliction to uproot it, without affecting the sound organs. . . . "[65]

Jum'a anticipates a possible question that may be posed to Muslims today: What is their argument to those who point out that most nations agree that conflicts are better adjudicated today through arbitration, rendering wars null and void, whereas "this Qur'ān of yours exhorts you to *jihād* and to undertake it eagerly"? The answer would be: "We [Muslims] marshal [as our proof-text] in this age the Almighty's words, 'If they should incline to peace, then incline to it also and place your trust in God, for He is the all-hearing and all-knowing'" (Qur'ān 8:61). This verse, he says, indicates the eternal wisdom and abiding miracle of the Qur'ān in that it foresaw a future world where global nonviolence was a possibility. Jum'a therefore suggests that the combative *jihād* was necessary for self-defense in a pre-modern, war-ridden world; against such a historical backdrop, the Qur'ān (and the *sunna*) permitted fighting out of necessity while imposing humane and ethical restrictions on waging war. In the modern world governed (at least theoretically) by international treaties and contracts, Qur'ān 8:61 is the more appropriate proof-text to be invoked in mandating peaceful relationships among nations.[66]

Jum'a next analyzes in great detail the major and minor military campaigns carried out by Muḥammad and concludes that they were mainly directed against fourteen Muḍar tribes, who were among the Prophet's kinsmen. The conclusion he reaches at the end of his analysis is that these military engagements for the most part represented limited familial or intertribal conflict instigated by the hostility demonstrated by these Muḍar tribes toward the early Muslims. This analysis affirms that these campaigns did not represent all-out war against Arabs as a whole, nor were they intended to effect their conversion en masse to Islam.[67] A closer look at each of these military campaigns firmly establishes, says Jum'a, that "conversion to Islam by the sword" did not occur during these battles; Muḥammad was instead known to have told his enemies, "Go—for you are free," without imposing any strictures on them to accept Islam.[68]

This extended analysis leads Jum'a to further conclude that there were several salubrious consequences of the Prophet's military *jihād*: First, it put an end to the pre-Islamic practice of plunder and pillage and led to general stability and security in a region that was "more than twice the size of France." Second, it replaced hostility and rancor with bonds of fraternity and spirituality. Third, it established the practice of consultation (*al-shūrā*) in place of authoritarianism (*al-istibdād*). Jum'a also stresses that, based on Muḥammad's example, Muslims must strictly observe their agreements with non-Muslims, unless they fear treachery on the latter's part (cf. Qur'ān 8:58).[69]

Jum'a concludes his treatise by providing documentary evidence that conversion to Islam among non-Arab peoples advanced very slowly in Iran, Iraq, Syria, Egypt, and Muslim Spain, and that Muslims did not become majorities in these areas until well into the fourth/tenth century. Such evidence proves that the early Arab conquests were not wars of forcible conversion. In Jum'a's view, Muslims historically have been more sinned against than sinning. He ends by asserting, "The history of Muslims is unsullied; they [Muslims] in fact petition for their rights with fairness and apology, even though they have not done anything up to the contemporary period that requires an apology."[70]

Jihād *as Primarily Nonviolent Struggle*

There are several contemporary scholars who have focused in their written works on the peaceful activism they understand to be the predominant meaning of *jihād*. A number of such scholars and thinkers typically emphasize the virtue of patient forbearance as the most important aspect of *jihād*, and therefore of nonviolent resistance to wrongdoing, particularly when committed by the state/government, whether comprised of indigenous rulers or foreign occupiers. This modern emphasis on nonviolent public activism as the best manifestation of *jihād* has been espoused by some well-known and less well-known figures. One of the more prominent names from the twentieth century is that of the Pashtun leader Syed 'Abd al-Ghaffar Khan (d. 1988). He organized a peaceful resistance movement called the Khudai Khidmatgar ("the Servants of God") against the British colonizers of India, arguing that Muslims should adopt nonviolence against oppression on the basis of their own scriptural directives and the historical praxis of the early Muslims that emphasized *ṣabr*.[71] For a closer study of this school of nonviolence based on published materials, we select three scholars and activists who are arguably the best known and most prolific among contemporary writers on this topic: Jawdat Sa'īd, Maulana Wahiduddin Khan, and Fethullah Gülen.

Jawdat Sa'īd (b. 1931): He is a well-known Syrian writer and thinker known for his pacifist views derived from his reading of the Qur'ān, particularly of the story of Adam's two sons, as elaborated below. He obtained a degree in Arabic language from al-Azhar University and eventually settled in Bir Ajam in the Golan Heights, where he lives in the ancestral family house.

In the English translation of his work titled *Non-Violence: The Basis of Settling Disputes in Islam*,[72] Sa'īd grounds his nonviolent understanding of *jihād*, glossed as the struggle to resist wrongdoing, in his reading of the Qur'anic verses 5:27–31, which give an account of the violent altercation between Adam's two sons:

> And recite to them the story of Adam's two sons, in truth, when they both offered a sacrifice [to God], and it was accepted from one of

> them but was not accepted from the other. Said [the latter], "I will surely kill you." Said [the former], "Indeed, God only accepts from those who are righteous [who fear Him]. If you should raise your hand against me to kill me—I shall not raise my hand against you to kill you. Indeed, I fear God, Lord of the worlds. Indeed, I want you to obtain [thereby] my sin and your sin, so you will be among the companions of the Fire. And that is the recompense of wrongdoers." And his soul permitted him to murder his brother, so he killed him and became among the losers. Then God sent a crow searching [i.e., scratching] in the ground to show him how to hide the private parts of his brother's body. He said, "O woe to me! Have I failed to be like this crow and hide the private parts of my brother's body?" And he became of the regretful.[73]

Among the relevant ethical and moral imperatives that Sa'īd derives from these verses are (1) that a Muslim should not call for murder, assassination, and/or any provocative acts that may lead to the commission of such crimes; (2) that a Muslim should not present his opinion to others by force or yield to others out of fear of any such force; and (3) that a Muslim in his or her pursuit to spread the word of God "must not diverge from the true path which was set forth by the prophets from beginning to end."[74] The third inference indicates Sa'īd's understanding of *jihād* as an essentially nonviolent enterprise undertaken by Muslims for the purpose of bearing witness to the truth and justice of their faith and to propagate it—in other words—to carry out *da'wā*, which he defines as "an act of calling... to Islam."[75]

Muslims, continues Sa'īd, are primarily entrusted with speaking "the words of truth under any condition."[76] In this context, he refers to the *ḥadīth* in which Muḥammad affirms that the best *jihād* is speaking a word of truth to a tyrannical ruler. Our author further suggests that while being a witness to truth in this manner, a Muslim may not resort to violence, even apparently in self-defense. He refers to the *ḥadīth* in which Sa'd b. Abī Waqqāṣ asked the Prophet what he should do if someone were to come into his house and "stretches his hand to kill me?" The answer was, "Be like Adam's [first] son"; and then Muḥammad recited Qur'ān 5:27–31.[77]

But what about the combative *jihād* that the Qur'ān clearly permits under certain conditions? Sa'īd does not deny that these verses exist, but states that their commands are not applicable in the absence of a properly formed Islamic community, which is currently the situation in which Muslims live. A properly formed Islamic community is one in which truth and justice reign, inhabited by Muslims "who call for the construction of the Islamic society, its reformation or protecting it against the elements of corruption." They are furthermore those

> who have enough courage to declare their creed and everything they believe in, and who are openly denouncing what they believe to be wrong in a clear way (thus reaching [sic] the distinct propagation of Islam).... They are the kind of people who, for their cause, persevere patiently with the oppression of others when they are subjected to torture and persecution.[78]

Such patient, nonviolent activism in the face of oppression and injustice and in the absence of the properly constituted Islamic community is the only form of *jihād* that can be carried out by Muslims today, asserts Sa'īd. Such nonviolent activism is in emulation of all the prophets mentioned in the Qur'ān who patiently endured the harm visited upon them by their own people because of their preaching the truth.[79] Muslims are primarily charged today with preaching the message of God and reforming humans, which can never be accomplished by force as stated in the verse: "Let there be no compulsion in religion" (Qur'ān 2:256).[80] Sa'īd calls those who advocate unconditional violence in the name of Islam "preachers of terrorism" whose vicious ideology "must be quelled with any possible means."[81] Evil cannot be erased by violence, however; evil can only be eradicated by the establishment of justice, and justice is served by the best form of *jihād*—the proclamation of truth.[82] Sa'īd stresses that such truth should be presented on the basis of reason and should conform to Qur'anic evidentiary standards, as stated in Qur'ān 2:111: "Say, 'Produce your proof, if you should be truthful.'"[83] The Qur'anic exhortation to acquire knowledge through reflection and travel ("Travel through the land and observe how He began creation," Qur'ān 29:20) requires fundamental cognitive and spiritual changes among Muslims today that constitute the prelude to broader social transformations (cf. Qur'ān 8:53).[84] Violence is a disease that afflicts us all and threatens to engulf us unless a comprehensive revolution changes human attitudes, "especially since we are still bound within the phase of the belief in the accusations which the Angels launched against Adam, as being a creature who promotes destruction and corruption."[85] This is the message and mission that Sa'īd wishes to convey to the youth in particular, so that they may be able to bring about necessary peaceful transformations.

Wahiduddin Khan (b. 1925): He is a contemporary Indian scholar of Islam who is the president of the Islamic Centre in New Delhi, India. For fifteen years, he was a member of the Jamā'at-i Islāmī founded by Mawdudi in 1941, but he broke with the latter because of fundamental disagreements concerning the relation between Islam and politics. Khan emphasized, unlike Mawdudi, that *tawḥīd* and peaceful submission to God were at the heart of all things Islamic, and not political and economic reform.[86]

In his book *The True Jihad: The Concept of Peace, Tolerance and Non-Violence*[87] written in the aftermath of September 11, Khan stresses, much like Jawdat Sa'īd, that the main purpose of Islam is the peaceful propagation of the faith (*da'wā*), and that political and social reform are at best secondary concerns that would inevitably result from the spiritual reformation of Muslims. He begins this short treatise by pointing to Qur'ān 22:78, which exhorts the believer to "strive for the cause of Allah as it behooves you to strive for it." *Jihād*, derived from the Arabic root *jhd*, points to this earnest struggle for the sake of God, a term that eventually came to be applied to the early battles in Islam as well, as they were part of this overall struggle. Strictly speaking, the term for fighting is *qitāl*, and not *jihād* per se. On the basis of the *Musnad* of Aḥmad b. Ḥanbal, he identifies the *mujāhid* as "one who struggles with himself for the sake of God," as "one who exerts himself for the cause of God," and as "one who struggles with his self in submission to the will of God." *Jihād* is therefore essentially a peaceful struggle against one's ego and against wrongdoing in general.[88]

Khan proceeds to establish the peaceful essence of *jihād* by invoking the following proof-texts: Qur'ān 25:52 ("Do not yield to the unbelievers, but fight them strenuously with it [the Qur'ān]"), which establishes that *jihād* is essentially a peaceful, nonviolent struggle to establish the truth because "no military activity is referred to in this verse. . . ." A *ḥadīth* narrated by 'Ā'isha, recorded by al-Bukhārī, quotes Muḥammad as expressing a preference for the easier of any two options. Because war is a hardship, this *ḥadīth* encodes the superiority of the peaceful struggle for truth. The Prophet's biography reveals that he never initiated hostilities and that he went to great lengths to avoid them. Examples from his life that support this interpretation are as follows: (1) In the Meccan period, Muḥammad was primarily concerned with challenging polytheism through peaceful verbal means; (2) even when, during the thirteen-year Meccan period, the Quraysh became his arch-enemy and prominent members of the tribe conspired to kill him, he avoided any physical confrontation and resorted instead to migration to Medina; (3) the battle of the Trench is a stellar example of avoiding unnecessary violence; as is (4) the Treaty of al-Ḥudaybiyya, which the Prophet signed with the pagan Meccans in order to avoid the shedding of blood; and (5) the peaceful conquest of Mecca at a time when the Muslims were militarily strong testifies to the preference for nonviolent methods over violent ones to promote truth and justice. These examples provide testimony, states Khan, that "the position of peace in Islam is sacrosanct, while war in Islam is allowed only in exceptional cases when it cannot be avoided."[89]

Muslim advocacy of the principle of nonviolence today recognizes "that the commands of the shariah change according to altered situations."[90] In the pre-modern period, war was a way of life; now we are able to imagine and implement peaceful strategies for conflict resolution. Khan scoffs at the "*jihād* movements" of the contemporary period for their glorification of violence; in these changed circumstances, "launching out on a violent course of action is not only unnecessary, but also unIslamic."[91] A movement, he says derisively, cannot be deemed a *jihād* "just because its leaders describe it as such."[92] A properly constituted *jihād* must fulfill the essential conditions decreed by Islamic law. The combative *jihād*, which is essentially *qitāl* (glossed as "armed struggle"), is an activity relating wholly to the state, and it cannot be placed in the same category as acts of worship, such as prayer and fasting. There is no room, he emphasizes, for non-state warfare, because war, and it must be defensive war, may be declared only by the ruling government. Noncombatants may not be targeted. On this basis, Khan sternly condemns the perpetrators of the September 11 attacks. He also proscribes the carrying out of suicide bombings, which he declares to be a complete departure from Islamic norms and religiously sanctioned practices.[93] "According to Islam we can become martyrs, but we cannot court a martyr's death deliberately,"[94] Khan comments.

The Qur'ān makes a fundamental distinction between "the enemy" and "the aggressor," continues Khan. Believers have not been granted the right to wage unprovoked wars against their enemies; the Qur'ān actually commands them to wage peace against them instead. How? Qur'ān 41:33–34 instructs them: "And good and evil deeds are not alike. Repel evil with good. And he who is your enemy will become your dearest friend."[95] Khan discerns in these verses a clear Qur'ānic mandate for "turning one's enemy into a friend through peaceful means, instead of declaring him an enemy and then waging war against him." Muslims may resort to fighting only if the enemy attacks them first and only when all efforts at reconciliation and peaceful resolution of the conflict have failed. Muslims are clearly forbidden to initiate wars except in response to a prior act of violent aggression, as in Qur'ān 22:38 ("Permission to take up arms is hereby given to those who are attacked because they have been wronged") and in Qur'ān 9:13 ("They were the first to attack you").[96]

How should Qur'anic verses that command fighting be understood? Khan emphasizes the original historical context of the revelation of some of these verses. Qur'ān 2:191, which states, "Slay them wherever you find them," does not mandate unprincipled total violence, but is rather applicable only "to those who have unilaterally attacked the Muslims" and "does not convey the general command of Islam."[97] The peaceful teachings of the Qur'ān are far more numerous and have to do broadly with the worship of God, morality, and justice. The Hindu and Christian scriptures also contain passages exhorting to violence, he continues, but that did not prevent Mahatma Gandhi from preaching a general message of nonviolence founded on the *Baghavad Gita* or prevent Jesus from promulgating peaceful values of love and humility. Similarly, commands to fight in the Qur'ān are to be understood as "specific to certain circumstances" and "not meant to be valid for all time to come." How else could the Prophet have been described as "a mercy for all mankind" (Qur'ān 21:107)?[98]

Qur'ān 16:5 promises that "Those who seek to please God will be guided by Him to 'the paths of peace.'" The Qur'ān also eulogizes patience (*ṣabr*) as a human virtue, promising reward for it that is beyond measure (Qur'ān 39:10). *Ṣabr* is the equivalent of nonviolence as understood in the modern period. The absolute higher valuation of nonviolence over violence is further indicated in a *ḥadīth* in which the Prophet remarks, as recorded by Abū Dā'ūd, "God grants to *rifq* (gentleness) what he does not grant to *'unf* (violence)."[99]

It is in this overall context that the concept of *jihād*, as occurs in the Qur'ān and *ḥadīth* literature, must be understood, continues Khan. Nonviolent activism awakens the human conscience, referred to in the Qur'ān as *nafs lawwāma* (Qur'ān 75:26; lit. the "reprimanding self/soul"), which results in "an awakening in people of introspection and self-appraisal." Recourse to violence awakens the ego, called *nafs ammāra* in Qur'ān 12:53, "which necessarily results in a breakdown of social equilibrium" and leads to "the breaking of social traditions in the launching of militant movements."[100] Nonviolent activism allows for gradual, incremental changes with enduring benefits, as was evident in the life of the Prophet, as well as during the succeeding generations of Muslims. The spread of Islamic learning and the peaceful propagation of Islam throughout the world testify to the success of nonviolent activism.[101]

Jihād today is therefore best carried out through *da'wa*, which, says Khan, "is another name for a peaceful struggle for the propagation of Islam." In fact, today "Islamic activism" is none other than "*da'wah* activism."[102] Muslims are not able "to join the mainstream in modern times" because of their violent attitudes today. Even if only a small proportion of Muslims resorts to violence, the majority of Muslims by failing to disown their violent co-religionists are indirectly culpable, says Khan.[103]

> As soon as Muslims take to the path of nonviolent Islam, they will be able to become equal partners with other communities.... People, instead of dreading them, will welcome them in every field, he remarks.[104]

Khan ends his treatise by making a plea for tolerance that allows for a diversity of opinions to flourish and that expresses "the noble side of a man's character."[105] A spirit of tolerance conduces to peace, which is "the only religion for both man and the universe."[106] Ideally, peace should be accompanied by justice. But so strong is the imperative toward nonviolence in Islam, Khan asserts, that one may settle for peace first, even if it falls short of justice, as was exemplified by Muḥammad's agreement to the terms of al-Ḥudaybiyya, which were unfavorable toward Muslims. This acceptance of a lopsided peace treaty did, however, lead to the establishment of justice and made the waging of war to attain it unnecessary. He reminds us that "God calls to the Home of Peace" (Qur'ān 10:25) and there is no other way to realize God's will.[107]

Muhammed Fethullah Gülen (b. 1941): He is a well-known and rather controversial contemporary Turkish Muslim thinker, author, and activist. He is the founder of the *hizmet* ("altruistic service") movement (generally known as the Gülen movement), which emphasizes peaceful social reform primarily through education, interfaith dialogue, and peaceful coexistence of peoples of different faiths and cultures. This philosophy and worldview undergirds a growing network of Gülen schools, spread throughout the world. Gülen currently lives in exile in Pennsylvania in the United States.[108]

Gülen grounds his views on *jihād* and peaceful coexistence of different faith and cultural communities in Qur'anic and sunnaic proof-texts. As a practitioner of *taṣawwuf*, he emphasizes the importance of the greater internal *jihād*, without disavowing the necessity of the lesser external *jihād* in specific situations. Thus in his explication of the distinction between these two forms of struggling in the path of God, Gülen says:

> The internal struggle (the greater *jihād*) is the effort to attain one's essence; the external struggle (the lesser *jihād*) is the process of enabling someone else to attain his or her essence. The first is based on overcoming obstacles between oneself and one's essence, and the soul's reaching knowledge, and eventually divine knowledge, divine love, and spiritual bliss. The second is based on removing obstacles between people and faith so that people can choose freely between belief and unbelief.[109]

The effort to attain one's essence, as Gülen puts it, is therefore a perennial one, and the greater *jihād* is waged daily by the individual to fight against one's carnal self (*nafs*), which if unchecked prompts wrongdoing. The acquisition of knowledge that leads to love for God and one's fellow beings is an important part of this process of self-realization, he stresses.[110] Gülen's definition of the lesser or external *jihād* as "the process of enabling someone else to attain his or her essence" is rather unique and worthy of note. The lesser *jihād* in his understanding, therefore, has important social and, one might add, global dimensions, and it challenges those who would primarily construe it as a military endeavor in defense of Islam. Every human act undertaken with noble intention that redounds to the benefit of society and promotes the common good, leading to a genuine transformation of society, is part of the external *jihād*, according to this conceptualization. The external *jihād* must therefore be waged alongside the internal *jihād* to achieve a desired balance, for Gülen says, "If one is missing, the balance is destroyed."[111]

The high estimation in the Qur'ān and *ḥadīths* of *ṣabr* or patient forbearance as an important component of *jihād* finds strong reflection in Gülen's writings. Gülen identifies five categories of patience:

> [E]nduring difficulties associated with being a true servant of God or steadfastness in performing regular acts of worship; resisting temptations of the carnal self and Satan to commit sins; enduring heavenly or earthly calamities, which includes resignation to Divine decrees; being steadfast in following the right path and not allowing worldly attractions to cause deviation; and showing no haste in realizing hopes or plans that require a certain length of time to achieve.[112]

According to this comprehensive definition of patience, it is clearly the single most important component of the internal or greater *jihād*; undertaking it transforms ordinary human beings into God's true friends and worshipers. As a Ṣūfī, he invokes the concept of the final station (*maqām*), or point in one's life, that only "those believers who are the most advanced in belief, spirituality, nearness to God, and who guide others to the truth" attain.[113] "Patience," Gülen affirms, "is an essential characteristic" of these believers during their journey toward God.[114]

Through the patient endurance of all the setbacks and misfortunes in one's life, the individual achieves knowledge of his or her true essence, which as noted above, is understood by Gülen as the primary purpose of the greater *jihād*. Each individual must be repeatedly "sieved" or "distilled," he says, in order to develop one's fullest human potential.[115] He borrows evocative imagery from the well-known Ṣūfī poet Jalāluddīn Rūmī (d. 672/1273) to describe this process of evolution and maturation. In reference to the growth of a grain of wheat from a seed into a loaf of bread that humans may consume for their sustenance, Rūmī remarked that "it must be kneaded, baked in an oven, and, finally, chewed by teeth, sent into the stomach, and digested." The process of moral maturity is a long and arduous one, and only those who are patiently forbearing successfully endure it through the constant waging of the spiritual *jihād* against "one's carnal desires and the impulses of one's temperament."[116]

Finally, Gülen warns against the phenomenon of arbitrary violence and aggression against civilians, that is to say terrorism, which has no place in Islam and militates against its very foundational tenets of reverence for human life and all of God's creation. In an article that he wrote for the *Turkish Daily News* a few days after the attacks of September 11, 2001, titled "Real Muslims Cannot Be Terrorists," Gülen lamented what he regarded as the deplorable hijacking of Islam by terrorists who claimed to be Muslims acting out of religious conviction. He counseled that "One should seek Islam through its own sources and in its own representatives throughout history, not through the actions of a tiny minority that misrepresent it."[117]

The antidote to hatemongering and exclusion, Gülen stresses, is the cultivation of the qualities of forgiveness and tolerance enjoined in the Qur'ān and the revival of moral, holistic education in Muslim-majority societies today.[118] He focuses attention on Qur'ān 3:134, which describes righteous people as "Those who spend benevolently during ease and straitened circumstances, and those who restrain their anger and pardon people; and God loves those who do good to others." Gülen comments that this verse clearly counsels believers to behave with restraint and civility and forgive their adversaries, even in the face of great provocation, and not to resort to hostile behavior.[119] Muḥammad exemplified such behavior in his daily interactions with people. The external *jihād* that the Prophet carried out in his life, Gülen comments, was "an armed struggle... tied to special conditions" and "was the kind of struggle that is sometimes necessary to carry out in order to protect such values as life, property, religion, children, homeland, and honor."[120] In his opinion, fighting in the path of God under such highly restricted conditions can never degenerate into the unprincipled and relentlessly hostile acts of terrorism perpetrated by today's extremists.

Excursus on Martyrdom Operations

In the previous chapter, we briefly discussed the rise of the grisly phenomenon of so-called martyrdom operations in the twentieth century and the justification of these acts of violent self-immolation by a number of militant writers. In contrast to these militants, several prominent Muslim religious scholars and clerics in recent times have categorically condemned suicide bombing and declared them to be unjustified and impermissible under Islamic law. Thus the late well-known scholar of *ḥadīth* Nāṣir al-Dīn al-Albānī (d. 1999) of Syria has been quoted as saying,

> Now we come to suicide missions, we have come to know of this from the Japanese and their likes when a man amongst them would attack an American warship with his fighter jet. He would blow himself up along with his jet...and inflict damage upon the soldiers in that American war ship. We say: Suicide missions in the present time, all of them, are not legislated (by Islam) and all of them are unlawful. They could be of the types (of suicide) which cause a person to remain in the Hellfire eternally. As for suicide missions being (a means of) nearness, by which one seeks closeness to Allah, [that is impossible for] today (we find) that a man fights for the sake of his land or his homeland. These suicide missions are most categorically not Islamic....[121]

The Saudi scholar Muḥammad b. Ṣāliḥ al-ʻUthayman, when asked in 2006 about the legality of suicide attacks, issued a *fatwa* denouncing them. He declared the perpetrators of such attacks to be no different from one who intentionally takes his own life and is therefore deserving of hell, according to a well-known *ḥadīth* recorded by al-Bukhārī.[122] Similar views have been expressed by the late Shaykh ʻAbd al-ʻAzīz Ibn Bāz, who was head of the Saudi commission of senior religious scholars and regarded as the foremost authority on Islam in Saudi Arabia. In an interview with the London-based, Saudi-owned newspaper *al-Sharq al-Awsaṭ*, Ibn Bāz described suicide bombings as illegitimate and said that they "have nothing to do with *jihād* in the cause of God. I am afraid it is another form of killing oneself."[123]

Muḥammad Ṭāhir-ul-Qadrī's Edict against Suicide Bombings

A blistering condemnation of suicide attacks was issued by the Pakistani academic and cleric Muḥammad Ṭāhir-ul-Qadrī on March 10, 2010, that garnered considerable international attention. Ṭāhir-ul-Qadrī is the founding leader of the Pakistan-based organization called Minhāj al-Qur'ān International, with branches in more than ninety countries, and a former professor at the University of Punjab, Pakistan. A prolific author and researcher, he received a classical Islamic education with scholars in Saudia Arabia, Lebanon, the Maghreb, and South Asia.

Ṭāhir-ul-Qadrī's full edict runs into six hundred pages in the original Urdu. A ninety-page synopsis/introduction is available in English translation on the Internet, titled *Fatwa on Suicide Bombing & Terrorism*. The following brief account is based solely on this introduction, which consists of a series of answers given by Qadrī to blunt, probing questions posed by an unnamed interlocutor.[124] When queried about the legitimacy in Islam of using force to spread beliefs and destroy lives and property on account of ideological differences, Qadrī stresses that "Islam is a religion of peace and safety" and that the sacredness of human life and its protection are fundamental concerns of Islamic law. Terrorists acting in the name of Islam violate these fundamental beliefs by seeking to forcibly impose their worldview on others through violence and fear-mongering. Qadrī states, "Terrorism, in its very essence, is an act that symbolizes infidelity and rejection of what Islam stands for. When the forbidden element of suicide is added to it, its severity and gravity becomes [sic] even greater." This has been the unanimous position, he asserts, of scholars throughout the past 1,400 years of Islamic history, and numerous Qur'anic verses and *ḥadīths* support this unequivocal position. Militants, such as al-Qā'ida operatives, are to be regarded as rebels and destined for hellfire.[125]

Qadrī then proceeds to elaborate upon the classical laws concerning the humane conduct of warfare, the immunity of noncombatants during battle, and avoidance of destruction of places of worship, buildings, crops, and trees. Any one who violates these conventions of humane warfare cannot claim to be carrying out *jihād* and "has no relation to Islam and the Holy Prophet."[126] The present-day terrorists are like the Khawārij, he declares, who regarded the killing of Muslims as lawful and thus were beyond the fold of Islam, even though they were punctilious in their observance of religious duties and appeared perhaps more pious than the Companions themselves. Qadrī has harsh words for these early extremists and by extension for today's militants: "The Khawārij were in fact the first terrorist and rebellious group that challenged the writ of the state and raised the banner of armed struggle against a Muslim state."[127] Qadrī's policy recommendations for addressing the problem of militancy include formulating effective measures to remedy the "policies, events, and circumstances the terrorist elements use as fuel for their evil agenda." He also counsels the world powers, and the Pakistani government in particular, to pay attention to the hardships of people and their complaints; otherwise, "real peace will remain merely a dream."[128]

Qadrī directly deals with the contention of militant ideologues that correct intention absolves one of the necessity of adopting correct means in order to realize a just objective. He asserts firmly, "An evil act remains evil in all its forms and content; whatever we may interpret as injustice, this principle remains the same. Therefore, no forbidden action can ever become a virtuous and lawful deed due to goodness of intention."[129] With these words, Qadrī challenges contemporary militant arguments that as long as suicide bombers are carrying out their actions "with good intention and pious motive," then their actions are justified. He refers to Qur'ān 2:39–43, which rejected idol-worship even though it may have been carried out with the intention of drawing close to God, as the pagan Meccans asserted. Although the intention here is noble, the practice of idol-worship, which is inherently abhorrent to monotheist Abrahamic faiths, cannot be justified on the basis of good intention alone. Similarly, terrorist protestations that they strive for justice and reform through their random acts of bloodshed and violence are simply unacceptable.[130]

In Islamic law, lawful objectives can be attained only through lawful means. For example, Qadrī continues, constructing a mosque is always a pious act, but one cannot do so by robbing a bank. The good is never served by evil means. "This is the majesty and purity of the Deen (religion of Islam) that it has purified and reformed both the destination and its path. It has made both objective and method pure and upright," says Qadrī.[131] The famous *ḥadīth*, "Actions are judged according to their intentions," is not intended to "set a wrong thing right," but rather is in reference to "those actions that are proven pious, permissible, and lawful."[132] Actions that are unethical, unjust, and unlawful to begin with cannot be rendered their opposite through good intention alone. Some scholars have also been of the opinion that the resulting actions point to the *a priori* intention of the actor. Qadrī makes the following grim pronouncement:

> So a terrorist's actions speak of his intentions. His killings and destructive activities refer to his foul intention and condemnable ideas and beliefs. His heinous actions cannot stem from pious intentions and beliefs. The bloodshed he causes refers only to a cruel man inside him and not any kind and merciful soul. It is, therefore, evident that whatever false implications and foul justifications these rebels, criminals, evil-mongers, tyrannous brutes may put forth to prove their atrocities as acts of *jihād*, they have nothing to do with the teachings of Islam."[133]

Qadrī's extensive *fatwa* has been reported widely and remains to date one of the most cogent and powerful rebuttals to the violent extremist ideologies crafted by Muslim militants in the recent past. Comparison of the diametrically opposed views offered in chapters 8 and 9 brings into relief the historicizing perspectives of the scholars discussed in this chapter and the widely divergent conclusions they arrive at—with highly important consequences for our present time.

Transition

Our diachronic survey of *jihād* and martyrdom as shifting categories and polysemous concepts that took shape in specific historical and sociopolitical contexts has now come to an end. In the next, concluding chapter, we offer a concise overview of some of the major findings that have emerged from this exploration. Some of the conclusions that have already emerged in previous chapters considerably revise our conventional understanding of *jihād* to date, and they nuance and challenge some of the most widespread assumptions about the ethical and socio-historical purview of this term and its related concepts.

Conclusion

ANALYSIS OF TEXTS: A SUMMATION

IN OUR DISCUSSION of *jihād* and martyrdom, scrutiny of various sources belonging to different genres was prompted by the following broad objectives: (1) to exhume some of the earliest, less well-attested inflections of *jihād* (and its derivatives) from the Qur'ān through a diachronic survey of the exegeses of a wide selection of critical Qur'anic verses, and to thereby trace the changing repertoire of meanings assigned to this term and its derivatives through a comparison of early (first/seventh–third/ninth centuries) and late (fourth/tenth century onward) *tafsīr* literature; (2) to recuperate some of the earliest significations of *shahīd* and its derivatives and explore their shifting semantic trajectory through the comparison of early and late *tafsīr* works; (3) to compare early and late *ḥadīth* and *faḍā'il* works and establish a similarly shifting semantic trajectory for the terms *jihād* and *shahīd/shahāda* in these works, taking into consideration the historical backdrop to these changes to the extent that this is possible; (4) to explore how consideration of the attribute of *ṣabr* (patient forbearance) allows us to understand a crucial, and often overlooked, dimension of the overall Qur'anic enterprise of *jihād*; and (5) to dwell upon modern and contemporary discussions and debates about the parameters of *jihād* and martyrdom and analyze to what extent these modern discourses remain connected to past ones and to what extent they depart from and/or add to them. Our broad conclusions in regard to each of these points are presented below.

Retrieval of the Earliest Meanings of Jihād *and* Shahīd/Shahāda *from Exegetical Works*

Our discussion of the exegeses of the critical verses Qur'ān 22:78, 25:52, 29:69, as well as 3:200, reveals vital, non-combative dimensions attributed to the term *jihād* in the middle Meccan to early Medinan period that have not received due attention in most discussions of this concept. Broad, non-combative meanings for *jihād* in this period are frequently documented, particularly by the earliest commentators: by the two Umayyad exegetes Mujāhid b. Jabr (d. 104/722) and Muqātil b. Sulaymān (d. 150/767); by the author/redactor of the extant *Tanwīr al-miqbās*; by 'Abd al-Razzāq b. Ḥammām (d. 211/827) from the early third/ninth century; and by the early Ibāḍī commentator Hūd b. Muḥakkam (d. ca. 290/903). Early Shī'ī commentators consulted in this study—al-Qummī (d. after 307/919), al-'Ayyāshī (d. ca. 320/932), and Furāt b. Ibrāhīm (fl. second half of third/ninth century)—generally follow a different exegetical trajectory and read into these and other verses favorable references to the *ahl al-bayt* in a particularist vein; but occasionally, they too preserve for us important complementary early perspectives on *jihād*, which sometimes corroborate those of non-Shī'ī scholars.

Thus in regard to Qur'ān 22:78 and 29:69, early exegetes like Muqātil, Ibn 'Abbās, and al-Qummī understand the term *jihād* in these verses as referring to the general struggle of believers to obey God in their actions and to please Him. Al-Ṭabarī's commentary, however, marks a signal transformation in the meanings assigned to the derivates of *jihād* in these verses. In clear contradistinction to earlier authorities whose views he conscientiously preserves, he tellingly expresses a personal preference for assigning combative meanings to the Meccan locutions *jāhidū fī 'llāh/jāhadū fīna* because, he says, they had become the predominant understanding by his time. Al-Ṭabarī's commentary is therefore exceptionally valuable to us in indicating that the progressive privileging of the combative aspects of *jihād* had become almost inexorable by the late third/ninth century in certain scholarly circles. Post-Ṭabarī exegetes, however, continue to record both combative and non-combative meanings of *jihād* in relation to these verses, as we note in the commentaries of al-Zamakhsharī, al-Rāzī, and al-Qurṭubī.

There is more of a consensus among early and later exegetes on the non-combative meaning of Qur'ān 25:52: An overwhelming majority of the exegetes, including al-Ṭabarī, understood the enclitic pronoun in the locution *jāhidhum bihi* to be a reference to the Qur'ān, primarily on the authority of Ibn 'Abbās. The anomalous view that it referred to "the sword" is recorded only in the *Tanwīr al-miqbās*, which additionally records the prevalent understanding that the verse refers to the Qur'ān. This suggests that an alternate, belligerent understanding of *jihād* was suggested by an early pro-combat contingent, but was not deemed to be plausible by most commentators in relation to this verse. The later exegetes al-Rāzī and al-Qurṭubī refer to the anomalous view but dismiss it as untenable, because the verse is universally deemed to be Meccan, whose revelation thus predates the permission given to fight in Medina.

Another highly critical verse—Qur'ān 3:200—allowed commentators from roughly the third/ninth century on to begin to link the attributes of patience and forbearance, as encapsulated in the term *ṣabr* and its derivatives, to combative *jihād* in general and to the military activity of *ribāṭ* specifically. This is in sharp contrast to our earliest commentators—Mujāhid, Muqātil, 'Abd al-Razzāq, Hūd b. Muḥakkam, Furāt, and al-Qummī—who stressed that *ṣabr* and its derivatives in the verse were a reference to patient forbearance in the carrying out of general religious duties, especially in adverse circumstances and in the face of ill treatment by others. Various derivatives of *rbṭ*, and particularly its third verbal form, were understood by early exegetes to refer primarily to sedulous observance of the daily prayers and patient anticipation of them. These non-combative significations are preserved as well by al-Ṭabarī on the authority of early scholars from the second/eighth century, such as al-Ḥasan al-Baṣrī, Qatāda, and Ibn Jurayj. However, once again, we note in al-Ṭabarī's commentary a sharp departure from earlier positions: Both *ṣabr* and *ribāṭ* have now become conjoined in his exegesis to the combative *jihād* and, in the case of *ribāṭ*, specifically to military vigilance on the frontiers. Al-Ṭabarī finds support for this conflation of terms in the commentary of Zayd b. Aslam (d. 136/753), who had referred in this context to 'Umar b. al-Khaṭṭāb and his advice regarding the Byzantine army. Zayd b. Aslam, as we recall, was a legal advisor to the Umayyad Caliph al-Walīd b. Yazīd; his hawkish views no doubt proved useful in the context of hostile Umayyad-Byzantine encounters. In contrast, the earlier Ḥijāzī scholar Abū Salama b. 'Abd al-Raḥmān (d. ca. 104/722), not known to have consorted with the Umayyads, stressed the non-combative significations of *rabṭ* and its derivatives in Qur'ān 3:200. After al-Ṭabarī, the view that Qur'ān 3:200 contained a reference to the post-prophetic military activity of *ribāṭ* became the dominant one, as revealed in our survey.

In the Medinan period, Qur'ān 22:39 is the first revelation, according to most exegetes, to allow the believers to finally bear arms in order to defend themselves against their Meccan persecutors. All the exegetes surveyed in chapter 2 affirm that *qitāl*, now a new dimension of *jihād* introduced in this verse, is defensive in nature and in response to prior aggression by the enemy. The use of the passive verb *yuqātalūna*—"those who are fought against/those against whom fighting is initiated"—in the verse clearly underscores this highly important aspect of legitimate armed combat in the Qur'anic context. The right to profess belief in the one God and to defend this right when violently encroached upon is stressed in all the commentaries consulted there; a number of early authorities believed that Muslims should exercise this right on behalf of other persecuted monotheistic communities as well. The close attention paid to the specific names of the houses of worship for these monotheistic communities is revealing of a deep and abiding concern on the part of our exegetes for defining the relationship between Muslims and Qur'anically-recognized scriptuaries. In a significant cluster of reports from early authorities preserved by al-Ṭabarī, we observe more inclusive and irenic interpretations of this verse vying with more exclusive and confessional ones, as particularly evident when comparing, for example, al-Ḍaḥḥāk's expansive understanding of *masājid* as referring to all houses of worship in contrast to Qatāda's more restrictive one. It should be noted that the doctrines of *taḥrīf* and *naskh* invoked by al-Rāzī and al-Qurṭubī to create a more polemical narrative against the People of the Book were not invoked by earlier exegetes in connection with these verses. Against the backdrop of the onslaught of the Crusaders in the Levant and the military forces of the Reconquista, respectively, al-Rāzī's and al-Qurṭubī's views are decidedly more confessional and anxiously exclusionary. Despite the explicit wording of Qur'ān 22:40 and in striking contrast to the understanding of several early authorities, they confidently discern in it a divine privileging of Islam and mosques vis-à-vis other monotheistic religions and their houses of worship and nullify the verse's ecumenical potential.

One of the most significant clusters of verses concerning the combative *jihād* in the Medinan period is Qur'ān 2:190–194. Early authorities, such as Mujāhid and al-Suddī, unequivocally subscribed to the view that these verses explicitly forbid Muslims from ever initiating aggression against anyone, including obvious wrongdoers/oppressors (*al-ẓālimīn*), in any place, sacred or profane. The *Tanwīr* notably understands these verses to grant Muslims permission to fight the polytheists, provided that the latter initiate hostilities (*bi'l-ibtidā' minhum*). According to a majority of scholars prior to the late third/ninth century, the Qur'anic proscription against initiating fighting in these verses was understood to be absolute. To get around this categorical proscription, several exegetes from after the second/eighth century, as we observed, had to resort to abrogation as a hermeneutic tool to nullify this explicit command. We first see this process underway in Hūd b. Muḥakkam's *tafsīr* in roughly the late third/ninth century and fully elaborated—as we might expect by now—in al-Ṭabarī's commentary. Even though al-Ṭabarī records the views of Mujāhid and al-Suddī and acknowledges that this cluster of verses centered on the events at al-Ḥudaybiyya sets specific, strict limitations on armed combat for the faithful, al-Ṭabarī proceeds to nullify a number of these restrictions by considering them to be abrogated by verses occurring in different chapters referring to escalated hostilities in different contexts and time periods (Badr, Uḥud, etc.) Earlier authorities cited by al-Ṭabarī himself, such as the Successors al-Rabī' (d. 139/756) and 'Ikrima (d. 104/722), had made an exception to the nonaggression clause in the case of the Meccan polytheists, understood by them to be identical to the Qur'anic *al-ẓālimūn/īn*. The progressive understanding of *fitna* and *ẓulm* as specifically referring to "associationism" and/or "unbelief," rather than broadly to "trials" and "wrongdoing," respectively, was critical in facilitating the legal-historical understanding of the military *jihād* in certain circles as religiously motivated (a point emphasized later by Muḥammad 'Abduh). It is noteworthy that al-Rabī' and 'Ikrima are not cited however as having declared any of the verses in this cluster to have been abrogated, particularly by verses from the ninth chapter, as would become fairly common in exegetical works from the time of al-Wāḥidī onward.

This process, however, was not ineluctable. Al-Zamakhsharī continues to maintain in the fourth/tenth century that Muslims may not ever initiate fighting on the basis of Qur'ān 2:190. However, he also maintains—by referencing Qur'ān 9:36 at this point—that once the polytheists have initiated aggression, Muslims may as a consequence fight against all of them, that is, against all polytheist groups, regardless of whether they are individually or as contingents hostile or peaceable. Al-Rāzī in the early sixth/twelfth century upholds the general nonaggression clause so that Muslims may not ever initiate fighting, but once fighting has commenced against the pagans, then it must be continued until they abandon both their polytheism and aggression, for one presupposed the other. Al-Qurṭubī expresses similar views, signaling to us the continuing general acceptance of the nonaggression clause as binding among influential scholars in the later period.

The hermeneutical spectrum available for Qur'ān 9:12–13 reveals a similar general divergence between early and late exegetes in understanding the purview of the military *jihād*. The early exegetes Mujāhid, Muqātil, the author/redactor of *Tanwīr al-miqbās*, and Ibn Muḥakkam understand these verses as allowing Muslims to fight those polytheists who had violated their pacts (*aymānahum*) with them, had denigrated Islam, and initiated hostilities against them. None of them lists a possible alternate reading for the second occurrence of *aymān* in Qur'ān 9:13. The first time we encounter the suggestion of the variant reading *īmān* for *aymān* is in al-Ṭabarī's commentary, which attributes this reading to al-Ḥasan al-Baṣrī but then dismisses it. The first exegete in our survey to consider this reading plausible with its drastically altered implications is al-Wāḥidī, on the basis of the interpretation of al-Farrā' (d. 207/822), author of the*Ma'āni 'l-qur'ān*; this interpretation was also supported by al-Zamakhsharī after him. Al-Rāzī notes this alternate reading on the sole authority of, not surprisingly, the Syrian-Umayyad *qāri'* Ibn 'Āmir (d. 118/736), but he supports the reading of *aymān* as the more logical and appropriate one. He partially accepts, however, the novel interpretations of al-Wāḥidī and al-Zamakhsharī, when he understands *fa-'ntahū* to mean desisting from unbelief, rather than desisting from breaking pledges. Such an interpretation, which appears to have become pervasive in the post-al-Ṭabarī period, had far-reaching implications for the Muslim understanding of warfare—it gradually (and ominously) added a theological dimension to the range of legitimate reasons for which Muslims could go to war against non-Muslims. The Syrian-Umayyad provenance of this variant reading should perhaps not surprise us, since it could be adduced as scriptural support for Umayyad military excursions against the Byzantines in particular and for the justification of preemptive military attacks on non-Muslims *qua* non-Muslims, an interpretation that also could—and did—fortuitously legitimize similar campaigns during the ʿAbbasid and subsequent periods. This development, in comparison with earlier works, represents a major exegetical departure in conceptualizing the military *jihād*, which in the Qur'anic milieu as we have established, is strictly defensive and to be undertaken in response to a prior attack by an implacably hostile enemy. Without recourse to the hermeneutical ruse of *naskh*, the Qur'anic text considered as a whole clearly conduces to the position that it is not the religious affiliation of an adversary but rather its commission of hostile actions that legitimates a proportional counter-attack on the part of Muslims.

Along with Qur'ān 2:190, Qur'ān 9:13 offers the most explicit iteration of this scriptural condition for resorting to armed combat—the initiation of hostilities by the opposite camp (*wa-hum bada'ūkum awwala marratin*). It is thus entirely reasonable for us to conclude that classical juridical views on the combative *jihād* as part of the law of nations (*siyar*) exerted considerable influence on the formulation by a number of exegetes of the radical justification for fighting non-Muslims on the basis of religious affiliation—in blatant contravention of Qur'anic injunctions. Al-Rāzī's recording of the contrary views of Abū Ḥanīfa and al-Shāfiʿī on the legality of oaths made by unbelievers in fact indicates to us the great interest taken by exegetes in influential juridical debates and their occasionally subversive impact upon exegeses of the Qur'ān.

We find these broad trends toward a progressive privileging of the combative *jihād* as an essential religious duty to be replicated repeatedly in our discussion of additional Qur'anic verses that deal with the ethics of fighting, refraining from fighting, and peacemaking, as discussed in chapter 3. A diachronic survey of the exegeses of Qur'ān 2:216 unearths a critical early position on fighting that became nearly completely forgotten or ignored in the later period. This verse, which describes fighting as a prescribed duty (*kutiba ʿalaykum al-qitāl*), instigated a discussion among exegetes as to who exactly was being addressed in the pronominal suffix *kum*. Whereas Muqātil understood the addressed to be all believers in general, the *Tanwīr al-miqbās* restricts it to only the Companions during the time of the Prophet's military campaigns. Al-Ṭabarī provides further valuable documentation that this position as outlined in the *Tanwīr* was subscribed to by the early Medinan authorities Ibn Jurayj and 'Aṭā' b. Abī Rabāḥ. Al-Rāzī adds to this list the name of another Medinan scholar, 'Abd Allāh b. 'Umar, who had similarly maintained that the duty of fighting was imposed on the Companions alone. Contrasted to these Medinan scholars is the early Syrian authority Makḥūl, who is said to have sworn at the Ka'ba that fighting (he uses the word *ghazw*, no doubt to set up a contrast to defensive fighting) was obligatory. His student, the well-known Syrian jurist al-Awzā'ī (d. 157/774), was more equivocal—and pragmatic—in his views, as reported by al-Ṭabarī. In the fifth/eleventh century, al-Wāḥidī is on record as endorsing the early position that fighting as a religiously prescribed duty applied only to the Companions, citing 'Aṭā' b. Abī Rabāḥ as his authority. Other early authorities, like Ibn 'Aṭiyya and Sufyān al-Thawrī cited by our exegetes, construed the military *jihād* in general as a voluntary (*taṭawwu'*) and collective act. On the basis of this substantial documentation, one may conclude that this interpretation of Qur'ān 2:216 as being applicable to only the Companions was hardly a minority and negligible one in Islamic history. As late as the fifth/eleventh century, our sources indicate that this remained a credible and dominant view subscribed to by influential scholars, and that there was considerable resistance on the part of some scholars to the attempts of other scholars to aggrandize the status of fighting as a religious duty incumbent on *all* believers for all time. Al-Rāzī, however, in the early sixth/twelfth century asserts that "in spite of what 'Aṭā' said," the verse in its use of *'alaykum* is to be understood as imposing the duty of fighting on both those who were present at the time of its revelation and those who will come later. Vulnerability to powerful external enemies during the Seljuq period was certainly an important factor in this exegetical transformation; al-Rāzī must have been prompted to adopt this line of reasoning against the backdrop of the Third and Fourth Crusades launched during his lifetime. Al-Qurṭubī hews to very similar views; in his case, his concern to establish fighting as an individual duty on the basis of this verse is prompted by the precarious situation in which Muslims in al-Andalus find themselves in the face of the Reconquista.

Our discussion of Qur'ān 9:5—which in our own time has acquired in certain circles the status of the quintessential belligerent verse threatening non-Muslims generally with annihilation—reveals that until the Seljuq period, the verse was not the subject of much attention in general and that its injunction was understood to be applicable to the Prophet's time only. Thus the exegetes in our survey clearly understood the *mushrikūn* mentioned in this verse to refer to those Meccan polytheists with whom the first generation of Muslims did not have pacts. The phrase "If they repent" (*fa-in tābū*) is however generally understood to refer to their renunciation of polytheism, which is regarded as the source of their aggression. Al-Ṭabarī understands this verse to allow fighting specifically the Meccan Arab polytheists everywhere and at any time and asserts its unabrogated status, in contrast to early exegetes like al-Ḍaḥḥāk and al-Suddī, who were of the opinion that Qur'ān 47:4, which states in relation to the polytheists, "whether by a handsome release afterwards or by ransom," had abrogated Qur'ān 9:5. Al-Ṭabarī maintains that both verses were to be invoked together in creating a protocol for dealing with enemy prisoners of war, who may thereby be either released (with or without a ransom) or put to death. This debate is noteworthy, especially because it records little-known views of early exegetes that challenge the preeminent position accorded to Qur'ān 9:5 by the Mamluk period as practically the abrogating verse *par excellence* in the context of the military *jihād*.

After al-Ṭabarī, it is highly significant that al-Wāḥidī and al-Zamakhsharī both pay scant attention to Qur'ān 9:5, as the verse was unambiguously understood by them to refer to the treatment of the polytheists during Muḥammad's time and thus to have no further applicability in their own time and place. As noted, this situation changes with al-Rāzī, who proceeds to introduce a legal dimension into his commentary on this verse concerning the status of *Muslims,* who are not otherwise mentioned in it. These Muslims are described by him as delinquent in carrying out their religious obligations and, on the authority of al-Shāfi'ī, may be deemed to be unbelievers and, if unrepentant, may be put to death, al-Rāzī states. It is worth noting that contemporary extraneous concerns about the legal status of nonobservant Muslims are being read back into this verse in the sixth/twelfth century, and accommodation of these concerns appears to have been achieved by reinterpreting the *mushrikūn* in this verse as lapsed Muslims—a significant (and dangerous) departure from the views of earlier exegetes. Since there are no more Arab polytheists who are clearly the historical referent in Qur'ān 9:5, the verse is redeployed in this ahistorical manner by certain later scholars to negotiate the boundaries of Muslim religio-communal identity and to adjudicate legal and doctrinal issues pertaining to Muslims themselves. Very similar views to those of al-Rāzī are expressed by al-Qurṭubī in his own precarious circumstances during the late seventh/thirteenth century in al-Andalus.

It is also extremely significant that up until al-Qurṭubī, no exegete in our survey refers to Qur'ān 9:5 as the *āyat al-sayf,* nor is anyone mentioned as using this designation. We first encounter this designation in the commentary of the eighth/fourteenth-century Mamluk exegete Ibn Kathīr (d. 774/1373), as briefly noted in chapter 3. Ibn Kathīr's characterization of this verse as such indicates to us that, by the Mamluk period when Islamic realms were under continuous assault by the Crusaders and the Mongols, many scholars felt impelled to derive a general, expansive mandate from Qur'ān 9:5 and other such historically circumscribed Qur'anic verses (as frequently indicated by earlier exegetes) to fight and punish all those who posed a threat to the well-being of Muslims, including over time those regarded as lapsed Muslims.

Qur'ān 9:29 is regarded by all the exegetes in our survey (except Mujāhid) as referring broadly to Jews and Christians who are required to humbly pay the *jizya*. Mujāhid briefly links this verse to the battle of Tabūk, thereby implying that the scriptuaries referenced in this verse are specifically hostile ones, like the Byzantine Christians. The partitive *min* ("from among") in this verse conduces, after all, to the meaning that only *some* of the People of the Book who are wrongdoers are the objects of divine criticism here. It is in Ibn Muḥakkam's commentary that we first see the phrase *dīn al-ḥaqq* in this verse explicitly glossed as "the religion of Islam" (*dīn al-islām*), worthy of comparison with the more expansive view recorded in the *Tanwīr al-miqbās* that "they do not follow the true religion" means that they do not submit to the one God. The *Tanwīr*'s gloss *prima facie* conveys the understanding that the verse does not reprimand believing Jewish and Christian monotheists in general, but only those who violate their own religious commandments and disobey God (the manner of which is not made explicit). Ibn Muḥakkam's particularist views are amplified by al-Ṭabarī, who regards fighting against Jews and Christians as permissible on account of their theological deficiencies. As we had occasion to remark previously, the increasing presence and influence of *dhimmī*s in major Islamic cities from the mid-third/ninth century onward progressively led a number of jurists and scholars in general (like al-Jāḥiẓ [d. 255/869]) to articulate more discriminatory positions against them as a way of asserting the privileged status of a growing Muslim population; al-Ṭabarī's *tafsīr*, composed in this milieu, sometimes reflects such attitudes.

Al-Rāzī, on the other hand, helpfully preserves a spectrum of opinions among Muslim scholars on how to parse key phrases in Qur'ān 9:29 that indicate divine dissatisfaction with certain contingents from among the People of the Book. Although the majority of exegetes in our survey read this verse as containing a blanket condemnation of Jews and Christians because they do not believe as Muslims do, al-Rāzī documents the important views of an early Kufan exegete Abū Rawq ('Aṭiyya b. al-Ḥārith al-Hamadānī al-Kūfī, d. 140/757), who stated that this verse chides those Jews and Christians who do not heed the prescriptions contained in the Torah and the Gospel, respectively.

Abū Rawq's views are more credibly in line with several other Qur'anic verses (Qur'ān 5:44–47; 5:66) that call upon Jews and Christians to follow the Torah and the Gospel, respectively, and other verses that refer to different revealed laws and ways of life existing concurrently with Islam without having been abrogated (e.g., Qur'ān 5:48; 2:89, 101; etc.) However, against the backdrop of a growing sense of communal solidarity among Muslims vis-à-vis non-Muslim populations in their midst, exacerbated by continuing skirmishes with the Byzantine Christians starting in the Umayyad period and continuing through the 'Abbasid period and eventual bloody encounters with the Crusaders from the fifth/eleventh century onward, most exegetes preferred to construe the disobedience of the People of the Book referred to in Qur'ān 9:29 as their disobedience to the laws of Islam, rather than to their own laws—*against* the overall thrust of the Qur'ān itself. Notably, against a growing legal trend to emphasize the inferior status of Jews and Christians vis-à-vis Muslims, al-Qurṭubī warns against mistreating the *ahl al-kitāb*—a term, he stresses, that implies respect for them and their knowledge of God and His messengers—on the basis of *ḥadīth* and early Muslim praxis. As we had occasion to comment earlier, it appears that al-Qurṭubī's multi-faith environment in Muslim Spain fostered this greater respect and compassion on his part for religious minorities who were willing to coexist with Muslims. He articulated these views even in the face of advancing Christian armies in his own time. Evidently, from his first-hand acquaintance with Jews and Christians, he had learned to distinguish between peaceable and hostile members of these communities and consequently did not read into Qur'ān 9:29 a wholesale denunciation of the People of the Book as an undifferentiated collectivity.

Qur'ān 4:95: Our earliest exegete in this survey, Muqātil b. Sulaymān, does not discern a specific reference to fighting in Qur'ān 4:95; the sitters are those who are unable to make the emigration, rather than those who are unable or unwilling to fight, as became commonly assumed in the later period. However, both the strivers, who are the emigrants to Medina, and the excused sitters earn merit for their piety in general. 'Abd al-Razzāq is the first in our survey to link Qur'ān 4:95 to the battle of Badr, thus adding the dimension of fighting to the striving mentioned in this verse, as do Ibn Muḥakkam, al-Ṭabarī, al-Zamakhsharī, and al-Qurṭubī after him. Al-Wāḥidī does not explicitly link military activity or a specific battle to Qur'ān 4:95. It is noteworthy that al-Rāzī understands Qur'ān 4:95 to valorize intellectual and non-combative striving on behalf of Islam over military exploits. This constellation of exegetical perspectives offers us a valuable window into the polysemy of the Qur'anic term *jihād*, progressively compromised but not completely effaced by the crystallization of the predominant military meaning attached to the term.

Qur'ān 60:7–9: A majority of the exegetes surveyed affirm that Qur'ān 60:7–9 remain unabrogated, and their injunctions to treat peaceful non-Muslims justly and kindly remain valid for all times. Muqātil b. Sulaymān, 'Abd al-Razzāq, and Ibn Muḥakkam are among the early exegetes who stated that Qur'ān 60:7–9 had been abrogated by Qur'ān 9:5; Qatāda and Ibn Zayd—the expected "hawks"—are referenced as early authorities advocating this view. Exegetes surveyed from al-Ṭabarī onward, however, are forceful in affirming the unabrogated status of Qur'ān 60:7–9. These later exegetes, from al-Wāḥidī to al-Qurṭubī, appeal to an impressive cluster of other early authorities—Ibn 'Abbās, Mujāhid, Muqātil b. Ḥayyān, and al-Kalbī—in support of their position. This diversity of views, once again, testifies to vigorous contestations in the early period regarding the parameters of the military *jihād* and our survey establishes that the non-aggression position remained a robust one through the centuries.

Qur'ān 9:6: Another early and highly important exegetical divide becomes apparent in our discussion concerning Qur'ān 9:6: Al-Ḍaḥḥāk and al-Suddī are said to have maintained its abrogation by Qur'ān 9:5, while Mujāhid and al-Ḥasan al-Baṣrī affirmed its continuing validity. The early Shī'ī exegete Furāt unusually maintains that Qur'ān 9:6 had abrogated Qur'ān 9:5. All the exegetical works surveyed by us—from Mujāhid's to al-Qurṭubī's—uphold the commandment in Qur'ān 9:6 to offer safe conduct to peaceful non-Muslims *as an enduring and binding one*. Interestingly, however, with the exception of Furāt, none of the commentators following him suggest that a later consecutive verse could have abrogated an earlier one—as was suggested by some in connection with the Qur'anic cluster 2:190–194—so that Qur'ān 9:6 as the later verse in the sequence would have abrogated Qur'ān 9:5. Instead, remarkably, al-Ḍaḥḥāk and al-Suddī are quoted as postulating that an earlier verse (9:5) had abrogated a later one (9:6)—a position that is inconsistent with the general principle of *naskh* but consistent with the ideology of expansionist *jihād*. This inconsistency however is highlighted much later by Muḥammad 'Abduh in his commentary.

Qur'ān 8:61: With regard to this verse, al-Qurṭubī's documentation of a variety of legal opinions on the permissibility of making peace with non-Muslims and the terms and duration of such agreements clearly reveal that such rules were not considered absolute and that Muslim rulers in fact had considerable leeway in determining when, where, how, and why they should conclude treaties and pacts with non-Muslims. Al-Zamakhsharī had also previously underscored these flexible, even ad-hoc, aspects of peacemaking between Muslims and non-Muslims. Among early authorities, the Successor Qatāda b. Diʿāma (ca. 117/735) adopted a typical hawkish position, as reported in particular by al-Ṭabarī, and maintained that Qur'ān 8:61 was abrogated by Qur'ān 9:5 and 9:36. Al-Ṭabarī's unequivocal defense of the unabrogated status of Qur'ān 8:61 and the reasons he advances for rejecting Qur'ān 9:5 as an abrogating verse in this case are particularly noteworthy. The hawkish, pro-abrogation position in relation to this verse remained a minority contested one, as we observed. Even Ibn Kathīr during the fraught Mamluk period endorsed the verse's *muḥkam* status and upheld its injunction to make peace with those who are so inclined.

Taken as a totality, the variety of opinions recorded by the principal exegetes surveyed on this important verse demonstrates that the reasons advanced by various Muslim authorities over time for entering into peaceful agreements with non-Muslims heeded both religious and pragmatic imperatives. Both prophetic precedent and the calculus of worldly benefit for the Muslim polity could be invoked in implementing the commandment contained in Qur'ān 8:61 to incline to peace with one's adversaries. Muḥammad's own flexible *sunna* in concluding treaties with various non-Muslim groups and levying *jizya* on them—or not—offered a range of options to later Muslim authorities, a range that was sometimes, but not always, replicated in juridical works.

Finally, all these verses taken together in this section on the Qur'anic text clearly establish that the military *jihād* in the Qur'ān itself is most categorically **not** holy war[1] that is fought to **impose or even propagate** Islam,[2] as it may be undertaken only in just **defense** of a religious community (not necessarily restricted to Muslims, especially according to Qur'ān 22:39–40) that has been subjected to violent persecution and prior aggression by implacably hostile forces. Qur'ān 8:61, 9:6, and 60:7–9 in particular make clear that fighting may continue only as long as the adversary engages in fighting, and that Muslims must resort to peaceful arbitration when the other side, regardless of its religious affiliation, sues for one. The invocation of *naskh* by some scholars testifies to the ingenuity of a belligerent faction that was determined to find scriptural sanction for war in the service of empire that may be fought preemptively on ostensible theological grounds, thereby overriding clear Qur'anic injunctions that forbid the initiation of fighting by Muslims and unambiguously declare unprovoked fighting as illegitimate aggression (especially *wa-lā taʿtadū* in Qur'ān 2:190). Such hermeneutic legerdemain on the part of this faction no doubt conveniently provided a mandate—*a posteriori*—for the wars of conquest that ensued after the Prophet's death, whose worldly impetus and imperial provenance were only too apparent to certain pietist groups, as we observed.

Recuperation of Some of the Earliest Significations of *Shahīd* and Its Derivatives

With regard to martyrdom, our diachronic analysis of exegeses of key Qur'anic verses (Qur'ān 3:157–158; 4:74; and 22:58) in chapter 4 reveals a progressively higher moral valuation of military martyrdom in tandem with the aggrandized status of the military *jihād* over time. With regard to Qur'ān 3:157–158, all the commentators in our survey affirm that these verses make no distinction in the assignment of merit and posthumous reward between the believer who dies of natural causes and the believer who is slain in the path of God (the latter understood predominantly by them to be the military martyr). These verses and their early exegeses thus serve as a highly important corrective to the cult of military martyrdom that emerged in certain quarters, roughly after the second/eighth centuries, emphasizing as it does sincerity of faith and purpose as the common link between the pious combatant and the pious noncombatant and downplaying the importance of military activity in itself.

Qur'an 22:58 similarly asserts, and specifically in the case of the Muhājirūn, that whoever among them is slain or dies of natural causes will be given handsome provisions (*rizq*) by God in the next world. The verse is understood by our exegetes to point to the greater status of the Muhājirūn as a whole over other early Muslims, or of specific Companions from among them. As in Qur'ān 3:157–158, the emigrant martyred on the battlefield is not assigned a higher status than the emigrant who dies naturally. Here the common link between them is their act of emigration in the path of God, an arduous act of faith that when undertaken out of the sincerest intention is worthy of generous recompense in the next world. Al-Qurṭubī in particular draws our attention to the contested definitions of a martyr in the path of God. He acknowledges that despite this verse, some legal scholars in particular went on to assert that the believer who is slain on the battlefield is better than the believer who dies naturally, so that the *sharī'a* as interpreted by these jurists came to reflect this point of view. Their view, however, al-Qurṭubī points out, clearly contradicts not only this verse, but also Qur'ān 4:100, which speaks of the reward due to the emigrant who dies on the way "to God and His apostle," as well as a number of *ḥadīths* that, on the basis of Qur'an 22:58, assert the absolute moral equivalence between the believer who dies a natural death and the believer slain on the battlefield. Those who would argue for the higher status of the slain martyr referred to one *ḥadīth* in particular in which Muḥammad affirms that the *jihād* of the one who perishes on the battlefield is superior. This entire discussion is highly significant because it underscores the contested definitions of martyrdom through time and the progressively higher moral valuation of the military martyr that occurred in contrast to the earliest period. This trend is clearly encoded in certain *ḥadīth*s that, **in spite of** countervailing Qur'anic pronouncements, made firm distinctions in status between the military and non-military martyr. The growing influence of these legal and exegetical *ḥadīths* is signaled in the preferential legal treatment that came to be accorded to the military martyr over the non-military one.

In our survey, Qur'ān 4:74 is one verse that emphasizes the meritorious nature of fighting when it is deemed to be morally justified (in the path of God). All the exegetes surveyed are in agreement that the verse promises great reward to such a pious warrior, regardless of whether he triumphs over the enemy or is slain by him. The act of "bartering" this world for the next is not equated with the conscious seeking of martyrdom, but is rather a reference here to sacrifices made on the battlefield in a righteous cause that could entail death. Al-Ṭabarī, however, significantly explains the injunction "Fight in the path of God" in this verse to mean fighting "for the religion of God and the summoning [of the unbelievers] to it," an equation that is certainly not made explicit in the verse but appears to have become the accepted legal rationale for the combative *jihād* by his time and the preferred understanding of what constituted fighting in the path of God. It is also worthy of note that al-Wāḥidī, unlike Muqātil and al-Ṭabarī before him, specifically conflates the term *shahīd* with "one who is slain" as it occurs in the verse, establishing that by his time (late fifth/eleventh century), *shahīd* is the term used preponderantly to refer to the military martyr and conflated with the Qur'anic locution *man qutila fī sabīl allāh* and its variants.

A comparison of early and later exegeses of Qur'ān 2:154 and 3:169 is further revealing of how a cultic reverence for military martyrdom progressively came to be articulated and read back into these verses, despite the lack of overt reference in them to first, the military martyr, and second, any assumption of their higher status vis-à-vis other believers who die, for example, while emigrating in the path of God. We note that by the time we get to al-Ṭabarī, a full-fledged doctrine appears to have emerged regarding the exceptional rewards and status conferred upon the fighter in the path of God (*al-mujāhid fī sabīl allāh*) in general, whether he is slain or victorious and dies later of natural causes. Most valuably, al-Ṭabarī records the objections raised by some in assigning such an exalted status specifically to military martyrs when the Qur'anic verses themselves make no such explicit reference. Al-Ṭabarī responds to these objections by invoking the authority of Companion reports that detail the posthumous pleasures reserved exclusively for military martyrs as an indication of their privileged status and the sensate nature of their being alive. The paraenetic intent of some of these reports that catalog the various pleasures reserved only for the slain fighter (i.e., to exhort the faithful in the post-prophetic period to continue to undertake the combative *jihād* for the cause of Islam) is explicitly mentioned in the report emanating from Ibn Isḥāq recorded by al-Ṭabarī. This is also emphasized by al-Rāzī, who further indicates to us that this particular exegesis remained contested in his time. The increasing attention paid to military martyrs and their legal status is reflected in al-Qurṭubī's reference to an elaborate taxonomy of martyrs that had emerged by his time and the observance of special funerary practices for different categories of martyrs.

The construction of a hierarchy of moral excellence became a deep and abiding concern of Muslims of various stripes in the early period, based on the Qur'anic concept of *sābiqa* or Islamic precedence. *Sābiqa*, as we have discussed elsewhere,[3] was predicated on a typical constellation of pious acts and virtues—including early conversion to Islam, veracity, charity, and courage, for example. Preoccupation with this concern frequently caused Muslims to seek answers to the following broad questions: Who are the most morally excellent people (Muslims), and how do we recognize and rank their excellences? Exegeses of Qur'ān 4:69 reveal sustained scholarly reflection on the status of martyrs/witnesses (*al-shuhadā'*) in relation to the prophets, the *ṣiddīqūn*, and righteous people (*al-ṣaliḥūn*) in general. As early as Muqātil b. Sulaymān, *al-shuhadā'* in this verse is understood to be a reference to "[military] martyrs" (*al-qutlā fī sabīl allāh bi-'l-shahāda*). Muqātil feels no obligation to explain why this plural noun should suddenly refer to martyrs in this verse when its singular *shahīd* consistently and exclusively refers to "a [legal/eye-] witness" throughout the Qur'ān. Muqātil's interpretation of *shahīd/shuhadā'* establishes for us that these Qur'anic terms had already been appropriated by the middle–late Umayyad period to refer primarily to the military martyr, who, as al-Ṭabarī explains later, "undertakes to bear witness to the truth on the side of God until he is killed." Although most of the exegetes surveyed affirm that the verse promises that these three groups of morally excellent people will be together in heaven, suggesting an equivalence in status for the *shuhadā'*, the *ṣiddīqūn*, and the *ṣāliḥūn* as companions of the prophets, al-Zamakhsharī insists that the *ṣiddīqūn* are the most excellent of the Companions, as exemplified by Abū Bakr, who very early affirmed the truth of Muḥammad's message (and it is implied under very adverse circumstances) and thus paved the way for others to accept Islam, a view that is shared to some extent by al-Rāzī. This is a view that runs counter to the later predominant perspective, well-entrenched by the turbulent Mamluk period, that came to generally valorize fighting and dying on the battlefield as the highest form of service to Islam.

Furthermore, al-Rāzī's affirmation that, according to its basic meaning, *shahīd* is the equivalent of the active participle *shāhid*, which refers to one "who witnesses to the truth of the religion of God the Exalted, sometimes through logical argumentation and proof and at other times with the sword and the spear," is highly significant. It challenges the more common and facile equation that progressively came to be drawn between *shahāda* and expiring on the battlefield.

Comparison of Early (Before Third/Ninth Century) and Late (Fourth/Tenth Century Onward) *Ḥadīth* and *Faḍā'il al-jihād* Works

Ḥadīth Works

The broad trends identified in the *tafsīr* literature on *jihād* and martyrdom are replicated to a large extent in the *ḥadīth* literature. A comparison of early and later literature in chapter 5 reveals that in the early period, a broader range of meanings was ascribed to the specific locutions *al-jihād fī sabīl allāh, man qutila fī sabīl allāh/alladhīna qutilū fī sabīl allāh* and to the terms *shahīd* and *shuhadā'*, and that these significations were contested by various groups. The two early *Muṣannaf* works by 'Abd al-Razzāq al-Ṣan'ānī (d. 211/827) and Ibn Abī Shayba (d. 235/849) preserve a number of highly significant reports containing multiple perspectives on *jihād* and martyrdom that are either completely missing from later works or exist in reworked forms. Both compilations are important therefore as transitional works that allow us to monitor the crystallization of the *faḍā'il al-jihād* genre in the Umayyad period when it was first taking shape.

Isnād scrutiny in particular reveals that the division in perspective along regional lines that we first observed in the *tafsīr* literature is corroborated in the early *ḥadīth* literature as well. In general, pietist scholars like 'Abd Allāh b. 'Umar, 'Aṭā' b. Abī Rabāḥ, Ibn Jurayj, 'Amr b. Dīnār, and 'Abd Allāb b. 'Umar from the Ḥijāz, Sufyān al-Thawrī, and Abū Ḥayyān al-Taymī (d. 145/762) from Kufa and occasionally Basran scholars like al-Ḥasan al-Baṣrī tended to be against what must have appeared to them as unseemly glorification of military activity in pro-Umayyad circles, at the expense of the cultivation of the usual religious virtues and duties. We discern this trenchant critique in several memorable Companion reports, such as the one related by al-Ḥawārī b. Ziyād from Ibn 'Umar in which the latter categorically denounces the promotion of the combative *jihād* as a religious duty over and above the five pillars and asserts that fighting is at best a voluntary and optional activity. The reticence of Sa'īd b. al-Musayyab, 'Aṭā' b. Abī Rabāḥ, and 'Amr b. Dīnār in endorsing fighting as a religious obligation, as reported in Abd al-Razzaq's and Ibn Abī Shayba's *Muṣannafs*, is telling. These early reports convey to us that the cult of the military *jihād* and martyrdom that was being promoted during the Umayyad period did not go unchallenged, nor was it inexorable or fully formed during the first two centuries of Islam.

In contrast to this pietist "dovish" contingent, the Syrian scholar Makḥūl championed military activity as a religiously meritorious, even mandated, duty. As we recall, in a noteworthy report included by Ibn Abī Shayba, Makḥūl is said to have sworn for ten days facing the *qibla* that "fighting [*al-ghazw*] is incumbent upon you" (a report also recorded by al-Ṭabarī, as noted). Makḥūl's energetic insistence on this point is paradoxically strongly suggestive of the strength and prevalence of the "dovish" camp.

Contemporary Umayyad concerns further find blatant reflection in reports circulated during this time period, such as the ones that vigorously promote *ribāṭ* and/or naval expeditions as the most meritorious form of military activity. These reports also encode a robust rivalry between the *murābiṭūn* and the navy in the first/seventh century. Even though *ribāṭ* and naval expeditions are post-prophetic developments, we traced the efforts in pro-Umayyad circles to elevate these forms of Umayyad military engagements to the level of "fighting in the path of God" (i.e., equal in merit to the unimpeachable battles fought during the Prophet's time). Promotion of military activity by the Umayyads as a highly commendable act of religiosity could be—and was—useful for compensating for their lack of *sābiqa* in the conventional sense. These reports may thus be understood to codify a concerted effort on their part to invent an alternative, essentially martial, paradigm of moral excellence that, as we have observed in our survey, ultimately proved to be highly enduring.

With regard to martyrdom, several *ḥadīth*s and non-prophetic reports specifically challenge those who would emphasize dying on the battlefield as the primary meaning of being slain in the path of God. The early *ḥadīth* collections in particular offer variegated definitions of those who are slain or die in the path of God—they include those who die from painful afflictions and illnesses in addition to the military martyr, as well as the pious believer who dies peacefully in his or her bed. In tandem with the *tafsīr* literature, the *ḥadīth* literature begins to offer more fulsome descriptions of the bounteous rewards awaiting the righteous military martyr. Already ʿAbd al-Razzaq's *Muṣannaf* contains the report that promises exaggerated celestial rewards, including seventy-two damsels, to the fallen warrior. The strong Syrian cast to this report, transmitted in this case by authorities specifically based in Ḥimṣ, an important Umayyad military province, is not unexpected in a *faḍāʾil al-jihād* report from the Umayyad period that, as its exaggerated tone leads us to believe, is clearly promoting an unpopular activity among a population reluctant to fall in with its military ambitions. Ratcheting up other-worldly benefits to enhance the lure of joining Umayyad armies was, to put it perhaps somewhat cynically, an understandable ruse under the circumstances. *Isnād* scrutiny reveals the dubious reputations of Isma'īl b. 'Ayyāsh and Khālid b. Ma'dan, in particular, that undermine the reliability and probative value of this purported *ḥadīth*. Its inclusion in 'Abd al-Razzāq's *Muṣannaf* indicates its early provenance but not its unimpeachability; unlike some of the other *faḍā'il al-jihād* reports contained in the *Muṣannaf*, this one did not make its way into the coveted collections of al-Bukhārī and Muslim. Al-Tirmidhī, who is alone among the six compilers to include this *ḥadīth* in his *Sunan*, according to one recension, classifies it as *ḥasan ṣaḥīḥ gharīb*, indicating its restricted circulation in the early period, despite what he deemed to be an acceptable chain of transmission.

As became apparent in the *tafsīr* literature, the *ḥadīth* and *faḍā'il* literature bear testimony to a progressive attempt to co-opt Qur'anic praise of *ṣabr* and its virtues and redirect it toward the combative *jihād*. In the Qur'ān, "the paradisiacal pavilion" in one instance (*al-ghurfa* in Qur'ān 25:75) and "recompense without measure" (*ajrahum bi-ghayr ḥiṣāb*; Qur'ān 39:10) are promised specifically and exclusively to those who are patiently forbearing (*al-sābirūn*). This process of cooptation becomes evident, for example, in a notable report recorded by Ibn Abī Shayba (whose *isnād* contains the names of 'Abd Allāh b. al-Mubārak and al-Awzā'ī), in which the highest pavilions (*al-ghuraf al-'ulyā*) of paradise are promised to the unflinching warrior, in what appears to be a clear case of one-upmanship vis-à-vis the *sābirūn*.

Several reports recorded in the two *Muṣannafs* and other *ḥadīth* works cautiously examine the moral propriety of fighting and taking human life under the command of reprobate military leaders, especially when balanced against the urgent need to defend Islamic realms against the encroachments of outside aggressors. As we saw in chapter 6, the moral dilemma presented by these competing considerations is decisively resolved in the first/seventh century by Mālik b. Anas, who is said to have changed his mind on the permissibility of fighting with Umayyad rulers after the Byzantine attack on the town of Mar'ash, as reported by the Māliki jurist Saḥnūn. Mālik realized at that time that if Muslims refrained from defending their lands under the impious Umayyads because of their ethical qualms about fighting with them, they would become vulnerable to increasing Byantine attacks, such as the bloody one at Mar'ash. A course of action that would normally be deemed morally dubious becomes justifiable on purely pragmatic grounds of commonweal; this view would become the predominant legal position, as noted by the Granadan jurist Ibn Zamanīn (d. 399/1008).

Compared to the two earlier *Muṣannafs*, later *ḥadīth* compilations, starting with al-Bukhārī's *Ṣaḥīḥ*, record more *ḥadīths* that contain effusive praise of the military *jihād* and the posthumous rewards promised to the military martyr in particular. References to non-combative martyrdom and its virtues occur, but are noticeably fewer in the *kitāb al-jihād* sections. Because *jihād* in this period is customarily discussed in the context of *siyar* (international law), we also see more legal *ḥadīths* dealing with issues of prisoners of war, division of spoils, etc., included in standard *ḥadīth* compilations. Our scrutiny of these individual collections led to the isolation of a number of reports that signal specific concerns that have come to the fore in the period of their circulation. One such noteworthy *ḥadīth* from Ibn 'Abbās recorded by al-Bukhārī asserts that there was no more migration (*hijra*) after the fall of Mecca, but that *jihād* with the proper intention would continue. The content of this *ḥadīth* clearly challenges the group of people we encountered earlier who had maintained that the military *jihad* was a prescribed duty *only* for the Companions during the time of the Prophet, and had lapsed after his death. This is a position that we now know to have been ascendant at least until the Seljuk period, based on our survey of the exegeses of Qur'ān 2:216 in particular in chapter 3. Without doubt, the text of this *ḥadīth* seeks to undermine the early, entrenched view that fighting was a conditional obligation imposed upon Muḥammad and his followers only.

The later *sunan* works of al-Tirmidhī, Abū Dā'ūd, Ibn Māja, and al-Nasā'ī reveal that a basic corpus of *ḥadīths* concerning *jihād* and *shahāda* had emerged by the fourth/tenth century; these were reproduced to a considerable extent in practically every standard compilation of *ḥadīths*. The construction of competing paradigms of moral excellence continues to be evident in the later collections of Ibn Māja, Abū Dā'ūd, and al-Nasā'ī in which the military martyr's posthumous status becomes considerably aggrandized when compared with earlier works. *Isnād* scrutiny of a number of these tendentious *faḍā'il al-jihād* reports often reveals the presence of transmitters with less than sterling reputations among *ḥadīth* critics, like the Ḥimṣī transmitters Thawr b. Yazīd (d. ca. 153/770) and Baqiyya b, al-Walīd (d. ca. 197/812), 'Abd al-Raḥmān b. Zayd (d. 182/798), Asad b. Mūsā (d. 212/827), and others.

Faḍā'il al-jihād Works

The *Kitāb al-Jihād* of Ibn al-Mubārak, the oldest extant treatise of its type, contains several reports, like the early *Muṣannafs* of 'Abd al-Razzāq and Ibn Abī Shayba, that compare the pious warrior to the non-combative pious believer. Through Ibn al-Mubārak's time therefore, the piety of the non-combative believer continued to constitute the standard against which the moral excellence of the pious combatant was judged. Other reports consider fighting in the path of God to be morally equivalent to the performance of essential religious duties for the sake of God, such as prayer and fasting. But already we begin to detect an overall shift in emphasis in this treatise, with more reports now extolling the **greater** moral excellence of the military *jihād* over more routine devotional acts, such as prayer and fasting. *Isnād* scrutiny frequently confirms that a number of these purported *ḥadīths* emanate from pro-Umayyad narrators, whose paraenetic intent is to represent Umayyad military activity as legitimate *jihād*. One such report is attributed to 'Uthmān b. 'Affān in which he exhorts Muslims to take part in the Arab conquests in Syria, Egypt, and Iraq and specifically labels them *jihād*. The report has predominantly a Syrian *isnād* and contains the name of Abū 'l-'Ubayd, who had served as the *ḥājib* of the Umayyad Caliph Sulaymān b. 'Abd al-Mālik (d. 99/717).

It is further highly significant that reports contained in the two *Muṣannafs* that document the equivocation of early scholars on the topic of fighting as a mandatory religious obligation or their outright rejection of such a proposition are lacking in Ibn al-Mubārak's treatise. Reflecting its Umayyad environment, *ribāṭ* as a specific dimension of fighting in the path of God, as well as naval campaigns, became foregrounded as highly meritorious religious activities, as also evident in the *Muṣannafs* of 'Abd al-Razzāq and Ibn Abī Shayba. *Ḥadīths* and other kinds of reports that preserve the early expansive meanings of *shahīd* and *shahāda*, as recorded in these two *Muṣannafs*, occur to some extent in Ibn al-Mubārak's treatise.

The process of establishing the greater moral excellence of the combative *jihād* over other acts continues unabated in the following centuries, as we see in the *Kitāb al-jihād* by Ibn Abī 'Āṣim (d. 287/900) and the *Kitāb qudwat al-ghāzī* by Ibn Abī Zamanīn (d. 399/1009). Both works contain *faḍā'il al-jihād* reports that did not occur in earlier treatises, equipped with weak *isnāds* that overwhelmingly betray a Syrian-Umayyad provenance. Despite their unreliable status, the contents of these reports often helpfully encode for us early competing constructions of piety and concerns about their sociopolitical implications for Muslims in the formative period. An example of such a report is the laudatory *ḥadīth* related by Fuḍāla b. 'Ubayd b. Nāqidh from his father 'Ubayd, who said that he had heard the Prophet say that the deeds of all human beings are sealed at the time of their death, except in the case of the *murābiṭ*, whose deeds continue to grow until the Day of Judgment and who is protected from the trials of the grave. As we remarked earlier, Fuḍāla b. 'Ubayd (d. ca. 53/672) had served as military commander under Mu'āwiya, was appointed a judge in Damascus by the caliph, and may justifiably be regarded as having had a vested interest in adducing prophetic reports that proclaimed the virtues of making a career out of military service under the Umayyads. Worthy of note is that this *ḥadīth* is at odds with the better-known *ḥadīth* recorded by Muslim b. Ḥajjāj in which the Prophet testifies that a human being's good deeds continue posthumously only in three cases: continuous charity (*ṣadaqa jāriya*), beneficial knowledge, or a righteous child who prays for him. Equally noteworthy is that all the activities referred to in this well-known *ḥadīth* in Muslim's *Ṣaḥīḥ* are non-combative in nature; the version attributed to Fuḍāla boldly attempts to set up a competing paradigm of piety that emphasizes solely military activity and martyrdom.

That these were malleable hierarchies of moral excellence and contextually calibrated is underscored by the *ḥadīth* in which Umm Mubashshir asked the Prophet about the best of people before God. Muḥammad's response claiming that the indices of moral excellence would vary based on whether one was in the Ḥijāz or in Syria is highly significant, suggesting to us that situational ethical reasoning, rather than assumed absolute religious prescriptions, frequently determined how "bestness" was construed, and that external variables were a considerable factor in these constructions.

Situational ethical reasoning continues to leave its broad imprint on the *faḍā'il al-jihād* treatises of the later Mamluk period. Thus in the *Aḥkām al-jihād wa-faḍā'ilihi*, the fervent exhortations of 'Abd al-'Azīz al-Sulamī (d. 660/1262) to the faithful to engage in armed combat is contextually explained by the fact that the Muslim world at that time was besieged externally by the vicious armies of both the Crusaders and the Mongols. It is therefore hardly surprising that al-Sulamī commences his treatise by declaring unqualifiedly that "the best of works after faith in God is *jihād* in the path of God. . . ." It is for the first time in al-Sulamī's treatise, based on our survey, that we notice the redeployment of specific Qur'anic verses—Qur'ān 2:216 and 8:65, for example, that were understood by a majority of early exegetes to have been applicable only to the pagan Meccans—as pertaining to his contemporary circumstances. The urgency of the times he lived in prompted al-Sulamī to cast the Crusaders and the Mongols as the new polytheists of his time and to rouse the contemporary faithful, like the first-generation Muslims, to resist their aggression while conforming to the classical rules of humane conduct during a legitimate *jihād*.

This hermeneutic project of connecting past history to present circumstances continues unabated through the Mamluk period up to our own times. Ibn Kathīr (d. 774/1373) in his *Kitāb al-ijtihād fī ṭalab al-jihād* casts Syrian encounters with the Crusaders in his time as part of a predictable continuum of events predicated on Christian-Muslim hostility beginning from the time of the first generation of Muslims. Ibn Kathīr points to the massacre of almost 70,000 Muslims by the Crusaders on capturing Jerusalem in 493/1099 as a cautionary tale against relaxing vigilance, especially along the vulnerable shores of Syria and Egypt from where the Franks repeatedly carried out their incursions. Given the specific historical exigencies of his time, Ibn Kathīr stresses the extraordinary merits of coastal *ribāṭ* over land-based *ribāṭ* and other forms of military activity, because it was the most effective defensive strategy against the Christian invaders of this period.

The higher estimation of military *jihād* and martyrdom becomes more hyperbolic and pervasive in later popular *faḍā'il al-jihād* works, especially those composed during the Mamluk period in the context of Crusader and Mongol attacks. This trend is evident in the *Mashāri' 'l-ashwāq ilā maṣāri' al-'ushshāq fī 'l-jihād wa-faḍā'ilihi*, composed by the anti-Crusader warrior Aḥmad b. Ibrāhīm Ibn al-Naḥḥās (d. 814/1411); it contains reports that promise exaggerated rewards, including sensual and carnal ones, to the military martyr, some of which have been deployed to great effect by militants in our own period.

Exploration of the Attribute of *Ṣabr* (Patient Forbearance) as a Critical Dimension of *Jihād*

The Qur'anic valorization of *ṣabr* as, arguably, the quintessential and most desirable trait for humans to possess and nurture in the context of their worldly lives is not usually discussed under the rubric of *jihād*. But, as we have stressed in chapter 7, the Qur'ān frequently couples quietist and activist resistance to wrongdoing in the dyads *jāhadū/ṣabarū* and their derivatives. Accordingly, our survey of key verses that deal with *ṣabr* yields the following conclusions.

With regard to Qur'ān 39:10, the underlying common thread in the commentaries on this verse is as follows: The patient and steadfast believers deserving of boundless divine reward are those who continue to strive to obey God despite adverse circumstances. Such obedience was manifested by the early believers in steadfastly adhering to their faith in the face of severe persecution as well as when they emigrated to safe territory where they could practice their religion unmolested, as the majority of commentators maintain, and/or was manifest in performing the essential but demanding religious duty of fasting, as suggested by a *ḥadīth qudsī* recorded by al-Qurṭubī. In these exegeses, there is no explicit reference to fighting as one of the religious duties undertaken by the *ṣābirūn* or as one of the tribulations endured by them for which they are promised boundless posthumous rewards—perhaps not surprisingly, as the verse is known to be Meccan in origin. But equally surprisingly, there is also no exegetical attempt to annex these rewards to military activity or to consider these verses to have been superseded by verses mandating fighting as a religiously meritorious activity in the later period. Furthermore, the *ṣābirūn/ahl al-balā'* ("people of trials"), who exceptionally reap "reward without measure" in the hereafter for the afflictions they have endured may be usefully juxtaposed to the military martyr, who earns the unique distinction of "being alive" in the next world for his extraordinary feats, allowing for competing paradigms of moral excellence to emerge that have fundamentally shaped the Muslim moral and political imaginary through time.

We also observe a diversity of views among early and late exegetes in regard to Qur'ān 16:110 and 3:142, affirming the multiple valences of the term *jihād*—striving to emigrate; practicing forbearance in the face of life's vicissitudes; and steadfastly fighting intractable enemies – that variously overlap with and complement the significations of *ṣabr*.

The relatively modest *faḍā'il al-ṣabr* literature preserves for us valuable reports in praise of patient forbearance as a counterweight to the *faḍā'il al-jihād* reports that glorify military activity and martyrdom. The treatise *al-Ṣabr wa-'l-thawāb 'alayhi* of Ibn Abī 'l-Dunyā (d. 281/894) is a particularly important repository of reports, prophetic or otherwise, the content of which specifically challenges the exaggerated rewards promised to the military martyr, for example. Reports that describe the *ṣābirūn* as being more meritorious than any other group of people and the earliest group to enter heaven directly challenge those *faḍā'il al-jihād* reports that extol the qualities of the fighter as incomparable and promise him immediate access to paradise on death. We should note that in a number of these *faḍā'il al-ṣabr* reports, it is the patient individual who is compared to the military warrior, whereas in the earlier literature, it is customary to find the equation in the reverse. This is strongly suggestive of the later provenance of a number of these *faḍā'il al-ṣabr* reports and their circulation in response to an earlier corpus of *faḍā'il al-jihād* reports. Comparison of both types of *faḍā'il* reports allows us to retrieve competing views of *jihād* and martyrdom that found inadequate reflection in standard juridical, exegetical, and *ḥadīth* literature, and grants us access to an important dialectical process in the medieval period that is otherwise nearly completely erased in official documents.

The high scriptural valorization of patient forbearance clearly resonated strongly with pietist groups, who would apotheosize this attribute to the exception of others, especially in encountering wrongdoing in the world. This becomes evident in al-Ghazālī's lyrical paean to *ṣabr*, which is infused with a general Ṣūfī veneration for self-abnegation and nonviolence in the sixth/twelfth century. Most noteworthy is how al-Ghazālī (d. 505/1111) completely internalizes and spiritualizes the physical *jihād* of the jurists and theologians and transfers it to the battleground of the carnal self, where the religious/

spiritual impulse struggles mightily with the carnal impulse. Not surprisingly, he finds the highest estimation of the various inflections of *ṣābr* and the indispensability of this trait through all of life's struggles adumbrated in Qur'ān 3:200. Needless to say, he does not endorse the contrived understanding of *ribāṭ* in this verse as referring to military activity of any sort.

Very similar views on the merits of *ṣābr* are expressed by the Damascene Hanbalī jurist Ibn Qayyim al-Jawziyya (d. 751/1350) in the eighth/fourteenth century. Like al-Ghazālī, he too takes special note of Qur'ān 3:200 and memorably remarks that even though derivatives of *rbṭ* have come to connote guarding the military frontiers by his time, in the original Qur'anic context, it means guarding the frontiers of the heart so that base desires and evil insinuations cannot enter it. It is worth adding here that Ibn Qayyim's views on *ṣābr* and—by extension—of *jihād* as well are an important corrective to the image he has acquired in modern radical circles as an assumed proponent of relentless, violent *jihād*. Ibn Qayyim's views further underscore that the non-combative and spiritual meanings of *jihād* were prevalent not only in Sufi circles, as is sometimes dismissively asserted, but clearly remained part of mainstream medieval religious scholarship.

Modern and Contemporary Discussions and Debates about the Parameters of Jihād *and Martyrdom*

In the nineteenth and twentieth centuries, *jihād* reconfigured as essentially armed uprising against oppressive political regimes emerged as an active—and malleable—concept in much of the Islamic world chafing under European colonization. As is true for pre-modern perspectives, these later perspectives on *jihād* and its purview are similarly conditioned by the socio-historical milieu in which they have taken and are taking shape. Our survey conducted in chapters 8 and 9 reveals that modern and contemporary views on *jihād* and martyrdom are sometimes both similar to and idiosyncratically different from the variegated early, classical, and late medieval construals of the same.

In the twentieth century, Ḥasan al-Bannā, Abū 'l-'Alā' Mawdūdi, and Sayyid Quṭb, considered to be the three principal ideologues of what is termed "political Islam" or "Islamism" of the twentieth century, wrote on *jihād* as an important component of modern Islamic revivalism. Very much the products of their time, their writings encode contemporary concerns about political liberation and recuperation of national honor in Qur'anic and sunnaic idioms, and create in the process a powerfully compelling narrative that speaks to the modern colonial and post-colonial subject. *Jihād* in this liberatory sense is to be carried out by the Islamic State and is simultaneously offensive and defensive. It is hard not to detect the influence of early modern European socialist-utopian ideals conducing to global hegemony in their thinking. Although most classical jurists at least theoretically advocated the idea that the Imam must campaign once a year and seek to extend the territorial boundaries of *dār al-islām* through military *jihād*, for the most part, they showed little interest in anything as grandiose as the Sisyphean task of stamping out all other ways of living and governing that exist in the world.

The sense of desperation and militant urgency expressed by Quṭb in particular is multiplied manifold in the tract *al-Farīḍa al-ghā'iba* by 'Abd al-Salām Faraj, a member of the extremist Egyptian group *al-Jihād wa 'l-takfīr*, with no pretensions to any kind of scholarly training. Going further than Quṭb, Faraj has rendered *jihād* into a scorched-earth policy of vengeance, fired by a Maccabean zeal for restoring a mythic, divinely sanctioned world order that will empower him and his cohorts—a beleaguered, righteous minority—against the forces of evil. His methodology for creating this imperative has become a familiar one—selective and decontextualized quoting of Qur'anic verses and *ḥadīths*, supporting the abrogating function of Qur'ān 9:5 (the sword verse) vis-à-vis all other conciliatory verses, and finally, and most important, invoking the situation-*in-extremis* argument, which renders armed combat an individual and immediate obligation, and grants him and his fellow militants considerable license in the means they adopt for carrying out their violent mission.

Ruhollah Khomeini's views are very close to those of Sunnī activists like al-Bannā and Mawdudi and add very little that is new to their discussion of *jihād*. Within Shī'īsm, however, his views mark a radical departure from the classical legal and political tradition, which essentially considered the military *jihād* to be in abeyance in the absence of the rightful Imam of the age. Khomeini moves very close to modern Sunnī thought therefore by resurrecting *jihād* in the twentieth-century Iranian milieu as essentially a protest movement that can be spearheaded by learned scholars (like himself) against politically oppressive regimes. The themes of holistic self-actualization and political liberation suffuse his discussion of *jihād* and marry traditional perspectives on this critical concept to the historical exigencies of twentieth-century Iran.

As for the militant treatises and discourses that have appeared in real and virtual media after the attacks of September 11, 2001, their primary goal is to justify violent acts directed at military and civilian targets indiscriminately, invoking a cosmic calculus of right and wrong and an assumed, exclusive mandate from God. The enemy is both "lapsed" Muslims and non-Muslims in general, who collectively oppose the small, beleaguered minority of "true" Muslims who are entrusted with redeeming the world. Because of the emergency situation in which they imagine themselves, the military *jihād* has become an obligatory act of self-defense and makes permissible all manner of violent reprisals for these extremist factions. The "terrorist" label thus became a badge of honor for Usāma bin Lāden and wanton destruction his calling card. Many of his arguments find reflection in the violent manifesto *Nathr al-jawāhir* of Abū Yaḥyā al-Lībī, who similarly regards the military *jihād* as a global holy war to be waged relentlessly against all perceived enemies as the enemies of God.

We next encounter Yūsuf al-Qaraḍāwī's reflections on *jihād* in his hefty tome *Fiqh al-jihād*. A classically trained scholar at al-Azhar, al-Qaraḍāwī's book displays a greater awareness of the diversity of pre-modern juridical trends and the multiplicity of views that existed in the early period concerning the combative *jihād*. His diachronic, historic approach to the sources results in an interpretively nuanced treatment of *jihād* and leads him to challenge in this work the relentlessly bellicose interpretations of radical militants. It is worth noting that he refers to "the *jihād* of patience and forbearance" (*jihād al-ṣabr wa-'l-muṣābara*), a formulation that is not to be encountered in conventional legal treatises, whether pre-modern or modern, but derived directly from the Qur'ān. His contrast between the position of the "moderates" (*al-mu'tadilīn*) and that of the "extremists" (*al-mutashaddidīn*) is an important contribution to contemporary discussions of such critical matters.

Situational ethics grounded in political realism is carried to its extreme by those who make a case for suicide bombings, or martyrdom operations, an unprecedented phenomenon in the modern Muslim world for which there are no classical legal precedents. We presented the views of the Syrian cleric Abū Baṣīr al-Tarṭūsī, who is clearly conflicted about the legitimacy of such operations, being fully aware of the proscription in Islamic law against the deliberate taking of one's own life. In the end, he weakly opts for holding out the hope of genuinely attaining martyrdom to the one who sincerely believes that his actions are in conformity with the rules of *tatarrus*, while denying it to the one who doubts the legitimacy of his actions. Nawwāf al-Takrūrī, however, justifies suicide bombings as a practical, tactical strategy available to the Palestinians, otherwise hopelessly outgunned by superior Israeli military forces, to inflict casualties on an intractable enemy in dire circumstances. Al-Maqdisī and other "cyber sheikhs" adopt very similar positions on the permissibility of suicide bombings when such acts generally give Muslims under occupation and in dire straits a fighting chance against a formidable enemy. "Proper" intent and considerations of military strategy dissolve moral and ethical reservations about premeditated self-destruction and allow for the rescripting of these acts as altruistic acts of self-sacrifice.

A markedly different tenor pervades the works of the next group of Muslim scholars and activists we discuss. In a nutshell, these writers tend to emphasize the historically conditioned multilayered significations of *jihād* through time and typically display a more longue-durée historical approach to this topic. They are particularly keen on retrieving very early views on the parameters of *jihād* and exhume broader definitions of martyrdom, frequently questioning the classical legal and exegetical perspectives that had emerged over time, perspectives that many of them understand to have skewed the original Qur'anic significations. Thus Muḥammad 'Abduh questions the interpretation of *fitna* in Qur'ān 2:190 by classical jurists as the equivalent of *shirk* or associationism, because such a meaning is not warranted by the context of the verse. He also upholds the absolute nature of the no-aggression clause in Qur'ān 2:190 (*wa lā ta'tadū*) and rejects what he depicts as the arbitrary wielding of the hermeneutic tool of abrogation by exegetes to privilege a more belligerent interpretation. 'Abduh thus mirrors the views of a number of early scholars, such as 'Aṭā' b. Abī Rabāḥ, Sufyān al-Thawrī, and Ibn Shubruma, as well as a number of medieval jurists, in his discussion of the reasons for engaging in legitimate combative *jihād* and rejection of the position that the non-Muslim status of the adversary in itself can constitute a valid *casus belli*. Our own historical survey has established that these perspectives are authentically archaic and firmly grounded in the earliest period of Islam. 'Abduh's frustration with those who would dismiss these positions as new-fangled and apologetic when espoused by modern Muslims is understandable.

The well-known scholar Jamāl al-Bannā draws particularly on his knowledge of the early history of Islam, law, exegesis, and *ḥadīth* to compose his detailed refutation of *al-Farīḍa al-Ghā'iba*. His refutation is a masterpiece of skillful dissection and debunking of the major arguments presented by the *Farīḍa*'s author, whom he takes to task for his ahistorical understanding of *jihād* as a monovalent concept, his decontextualized reading of relevant Qur'anic verses, and his ignorance of basic historical facts and legal concepts, such as apostasy.

Sa'īd Ramaḍān al-Būṭī and 'Alī Jum'a in their respective treatises make very similar arguments against the privileging of the military aspect of *jihād* over all other aspects, especially by jurists and contemporary militants, and marshal some of the same texts to highlight the multivalence of the concept and review the legitimate reasons for fighting and the restrictions placed on it. Both these scholars prove that, equipped with firm knowledge of the sources, one can persuasively dismantle the arguments of not very well-informed ideologues and militants in the contemporary period who have a marked proclivity for making torrid and historically untenable pronouncements on the military reach of *jihād*.

Finally, we need to take note of a more recent trend that began in the twentieth century to emphasize the nonviolent, peaceful aspects of *jihād*, particularly as inhering in the concept of *ṣabr* or patient forbearance, as the primary dimension of *jihād*. Among the principal proponents of this view in recent times are Jawdat Sa'īd, Wahiduddin Khan, and Fethullah Gülen, who all eschew violence as an aberration and/or an idea whose time is past. Violence may be regarded as a last-resort measure against intractable evil and thus would rarely occur, according to this perspective. Sa'īd emphatically maintains that evil cannot be stamped out by violence, but instead by the establishment of justice. Justice in turn is served by the best form of *jihād*—the proclamation of truth. All three authors stress that in the modern world, patient, nonviolent resistance to oppression and injustice is more effective and appropriate for Muslims today. Khan describes adopting the path of nonviolence as reviving the spirit and *sunna* of the Treaty of al-Ḥudaybiyya, referred to in Qur'ān 48:26 as "a clear victory." This description, he says, represents Qur'anic endorsement of dialogue between Muslims and non-Muslims in order to establish peace. Writing in the aftermath of September 11, 2001, Gülen is particularly excoriating of violent extremists who have displayed in their conduct complete, nihilistic disregard for the rules of proportional warfare developed by medieval jurists. This pacifist or near-pacifist strain is genuinely a modern development within Islamic thought and tradition, and is grounded in a recuperation of the Qur'anic emphasis on *ṣabr* as the most important and enduring dimension of holistic *jihād*—a view that was also prevalent in pietist circles in the pre-modern period, as we observed. The writings of these authors represent an interpretively creative rapprochement between Islam's fundamental sources and the violence-ridden modern world that they wish to transform.

On the issue of so-called martyrdom operations, mainstream scholars like Nāṣir al-Dīn al-Albānī and Muḥammad b. Ṣāliḥ al-'Uthayman have condemned them as simply a form of suicide and therefore forbidden under Islamic law. The most detailed and blistering condemnation of such acts to date was composed by the Pakistani cleric Muḥammad Ṭāhir-ul-Qadrī. He particularly takes aim at the argument of some contemporary militants that suicide bombings are justified as long as they are carried out "with good intention and pious motive." He marshals an impressive array of arguments based on the Qur'ān and *ḥadīths* to undermine this and other militant positions. His *fatwa* remains one of the most detailed and cogent refutations to date of justifications for suicide bombing.

Ultimately, as far as their interpretive undertakings are concerned, one of the main differences between the modern thinkers and activists presented in chapters 8 and 9 is their adherence or lack of adherence to the principle of *naskh*, usually translated as "abrogation," in relation to key Qur'anic verses. The irenic and peacemaking thrust of the Qur'an—as upheld by 'Aṭā' b. Abī Rabāḥ in the first/seventh century extending to Muḥammad 'Abduh in the nineteenth century and Jamāl al-Bannā in our own time—is primarily established by taking *all* its verses into consideration, especially in connection with the terms *jihād* and *ṣabr* and their derivatives. Read as an unabrogated whole, the Qur'anic text—simply and purely—advocates only limited, defensive fighting when peaceful overtures and stoic, non-violent resistance have failed and the adversary attacks first. The religious affiliation of the adversary in itself is irrelevant. To establish the opposite premise—that the Qur'ān actually advocates offensive attacks against non-Muslims *qua* non-Muslims regardless of whether they are peaceful or hostile—requires that a majority of verses that counsel peaceful, even amicable relations with non-belligerent non-Muslims be considered null and void. Ultimately, the yet unresolved dispute between militant and irenic factions today—as was also true in the past—hinges on their divergent attitudes towards the Qur'anic text and its interpretation. Should the Qur'an holistically engaged remain the final arbiter and source of Muslim ethical and legal deliberations or must its text be mediated—even truncated—by exegeses that defer to specific historical circumstances for the political and material gain of particular Muslims? The debate continues.

Postscript

The contested multiple conceptualizations of *jihād* and the phenomenon of martyrdom derived through several lenses—scriptural, hermeneutical, ethical, and historical—leads us to the following concluding remarks. *Jihād* (and the accompanying concept of martyrdom) provided, in many ways, a discursive template for pre-modern Muslims (and continues to serve as such for contemporary Muslims) upon which a number of sociopolitical concerns could be creatively ventilated and configured in varying circumstances. The following concerns find reflection in the diverse literatures we have looked at to date, addressing such questions as: Which group of people may be assumed to be the most earnest and best strivers in the path of God—ordinary worshippers, scholars, mystics, and/or soldiers, for example? May one undertake a legitimate military *jihād* under a morally reprobate and therefore potentially illegitimate ruler? Is a legitimate military *jihād* always defensive, or can it be offensive as well under certain conditions, especially if a theology of offensive war can be concocted? How does *ṣabr* serve as an essential ingredient of *jihād* broadly conceived? Is the military *jihād* a religiously required duty or is it primarily voluntary and optional, contingent on the physical constitution and natural proclivities of the individual? Perhaps an even more important set of questions exists, with particular resonance in the contemporary period: Is the military *jihād* to be waged by male Muslims to the end of time until Islam—perceived primarily as a political order in these contexts—becomes a global hegemonic reality? If so, how can such a worldview be reconciled with the no-aggression clause in the Qur'ān, for example? Is it legitimate to wield the hermeneutic device of *naskh* to derive such a worldview in the absence of such reconciliation?

Scholars of many stripes have grappled and continue to grapple with questions of this sort in connection with *jihād* and martyrdom. Their answers, as we noted, often varied and continue to vary by region, historical period, and their political/ideological affiliations. The literatures that emerged in response to such questions plainly reveal to us that anxieties about social and moral status in *this* world on the part of the authors (suggesting to us a progressive secularization of the concept of *jihād* in certain circles as it became unmoored from its Qur'anic base) permeate discussions of *jihād*, as much as anxieties about one's status in the hereafter. Intra-communal and sectarian debates about the parameters of legitimate political and moral authority exercised by the state also occasionally leave broad imprints on texts dealing with *jihād*. The literatures extolling the excellences (*faḍā'il*) of military combat and of patience in particular often encode a number of these concerns in a consciously vaunting manner, creating competing paradigms of piety while invoking, co-opting, and reworking the common idioms—Qur'anic and otherwise—of *jihād* and martyrdom broadly construed. Unraveling the various threads from the discursive fabric of *jihād* and its correlate of martyrdom facilitates a more holistic reconstruction of Islam's past socio-politico-religious history and better establishes its continuities and discontinuities with its fractious present.

Notes

INTRODUCTION

1. See, for example, the art. "Djihād" in the *Encyclopaedia of Islam*, new edition, ed. H. A. R. Gibb (Leiden, 1960–2003; henceforth to be abbreviated as *EI²*), 2:538–540; Majid Khadduri, *War and Peace in the Law of Islam* (Baltimore, MD, 1955); id., *The Islamic Law of Nations: Shaybānī's* Siyar (Baltimore, MD, 1966), Rudolph Peters, *Jihad in Classical and Modern Islam: A Reader* (Princeton, NJ, 1996), among others.
2. Among the relatively few exceptions are Alfred Morabia, *Le Ğihâd dans l'Islam médiéval: Le "combat sacré" des origines au XIIe siècle* (Paris, 1993); Richard Bonney, *Jihād: From Qur'ān to bin Laden* (New York, 2004); and more recently Ahmed al-Dawoody, *The Islamic Law of War: Justifications and Regulations* (New York, 2011). Because of length constraints and the specific methodology adopted in this study emphasizing primary texts, we have not provided an extensive review of the secondary literature on *jihād* and martyrdom, although we do occasionally indicate in the notes our agreement or disagreement with modern authors on specific points.
3. Radical revisionist arguments and speculations in recent decades have provided no compelling reasons for jettisoning the otherwise well-entrenched and widely accepted first/seventh-century provenance for the Qur'anic text. For a sober review of some of the principal debates in Western academia concerning this topic, see H. Motzki, "The collection of the Qur'an: a reconsideration of Western views in light of recent methodological developments," *Der Islam* (2001)78:1–34. For a comprehensive account of the collection of the Qur'ān based on traditional primary sources, see Muḥammad Muṣṭafā al-A'ẓamī, *The History of the Qur'anic Text From Revelation To Compilation: A Comparative Study With The Old And New Testaments* (Leicester, UK, 2003), esp. 67–107.
4. These are the only instances when the word *ḥarb* is employed in the Qur'ān. It is, therefore, hardly a common Qur'anic usage as Reuven Firestone maintains in his *Jihād: The Origin of Holy War in Islam* (Oxford, 1999), 140, n. 23.

5. Contra article "War" in the *Encyclopedia of the Qur'ān* (henceforth abbreviated as *EQ*; Leiden, 2006), 5:456, where it is stated that in the Qur'ān, "all war is assumed to involve religious issues." M. M. Bravmann also unhelpfully glosses *jihād* as "war (for God)" in his *The Spiritual Background of Early Islam: Studies in Ancient Arab Concepts* (Leiden, 2009), 115.
6. This is duly noted by Fred Donner when he states, "The juridical definition, of course, has been a major force shaping the reactions of Muslims toward war over the centuries, but it would be rash to assume that it has been the only one"; see his chapter "The Sources of Islamic Conceptions of War," in *Just War and Jihad: Historical and Theoretical Perspectives on War and Peace in Western and Islamic Traditions*, ed. John Kelsay and James Turner Johnson (New York, 1991), 32. He accordingly warns against the reductionist view "that sees all points of the juridical tradition as direct and organic outgrowths of the Qur'an and the example of the Prophet Muhammad alone"; ibid., 33. Abdulaziz A. Sachedina similarly stresses "the necessity of approaching the topic of war in Islam from a variety of directions: religious texts, history, jurisprudence, and so on"; see his "The Development of *Jihad* in Islamic Revelation and History," in *Cross, Crescent, and Sword: The Justification and Limitation of War in Western and Islamic Tradition*, ed. James Turner Johnson and John Kelsay (Westport, CT, 1990), 35–50.
7. The twentieth-century Egyptian scholar and exegete Maḥmūd Shaltūt in his *Tafsīr al-qur'ān al-karīm: al-ajza' al-'ashara al-ūlā* (Beirut, 1983), 246, equates *al-qitāl fī sabīl allāh* with *al-jihād fī sabīl allāh*.
8. *Ḥadīth* collections are discussed in chapter 5.
9. For an insightful discussion of piety in its diverse inflections and its role in shaping a distinctive Muslim religious ethos and identity during the "High Caliphal" period (ca. 750–945 CE), see Marshall G. S. Hodgson, *The Venture of Islam: Conscience and History in a World Civilization* (Chicago, 1977), 1:359–409.
10. Roy Mottahedeh, "The Shu'ūbīyah Controversy and the Social History of Early Islamic Iran," *International Journal of Middle East Studies*, 7/2 (1976): 161–182. See also Walid Saleh, *The Formation of the Classical Tafsīr Tradition: The Qur'ān Commentary of al-Tha'labī (d. 427/1035)*, 227, where he stresses that "Tafsīr is an integral part of the intellectual landscape of Islam and a study of this literature is fundamental to our understanding of Islamic intellectual history."
11. Cf. the second revised edition of the German scholar Th. Nöldeke's original work by F. Schwally, G. Bergsträsser, and O. Pretzl, *Geschichte des Qorans* (Leipzig, Germany,1919–1938); R. Blachère, *Introduction au Coran* (Paris, 1947), 240–263. For a useful discussion of these systems of classification, see Hanna Kassis, *A Concordance of the Qur'an* (Berkeley, CA, 1983), xxxv–xxxix.
12. Cf. Ira M. Lapidus, *A History of Islamic Societies*, second edition (Cambridge, UK, 2002), 45–196; Hodgson, *Venture of Islam*, 2:12–151.

CHAPTER 1

1. Majid Khadduri, *Islamic Law of Nations*, 5.
2. See the wide-ranging discussion of this Arabic root in Edward Lane, *Arabic-English Lexicon* (Cambridge, UK, 1997), 1:473–474.
3. This full locution does not occur in the Qur'ān itself, as pointed out in the introduction.
4. My list of Arabic roots that have a bearing on *jihād* differs considerably from the one developed by Alfred Morabia in *Le Ğihâd dans l'Islam*,120, where he emphasizes only roots having to do with fighting and hostility. He does, however, cursorily recognize *ṣabr* as a constituent element of *jihād*; see ibid., 175, 293 ff.
5. *Tafsīr Mujāhid*, ed. 'Abd al-Raḥmān al-Ṭāhir b. Muḥammad al-Suratī (Islamabad, Pakistan, n.d.).
6. See Ibn Kathīr, *Tafsīr al-qur'ān al-'aẓīm* (Beirut, 1990), 1:5.
7. Fuat Sezgin, *Geschichte des arabischen Schrifttums* (henceforth abbreviated as *GAS*; Leiden, 1967-), 1:29; and the art. "Mudjāhid b. Djabr al-Makkī, *EI²*, 7:293.
8. For example, al-Dhahabī, *Mīzān al-i'tidāl fī naqd al-rijāl*, eds. 'Alī Muḥammad Mu'awwaḍ and 'Ādil Aḥmad 'Abd al-Mawjūd (Beirut, 1995), 6:25.
9. See further the analyses of this work by F. Leemhuis in his chapter "Mṣ. 1075 Tafsīr of the Cairene Dār al-Kutub and Muğāhid's *Tafsīr*," in R. Peters, *Proceedings of the Ninth Congress of the Union Européenne des Arabisants et Islamisants* (Leiden, 1981), 169–80; and id., "Origins and Early Development of the *tafsīr* Tradition," in *Approaches to the History of the Interpretation of the Qur'ān*, ed. Andrew Rippin (Oxford, UK, 1988), 13–30.
10. My conclusions are therefore markedly different from those of Leemhuis, who did a similar comparison of comments attributed to Mujāhid in al-Ṭabarī's *Tafsīr* with the Dār al-kutub manuscript and found that there were too many divergences. As he points out, however, there were at least eight different recensions of Mujāhid's commentary in circulation in the fourth/tenth century; see Leemhuis, Ms. 1075, 168. Al-Asyūṭī's sources seem to be far closer to the material available to al-Ṭabarī on the basis of my selective examination.
11. For whom, see *GAS*, 1:36–37; art. "Muqātil b. Sulaymān," *EI²*, 7:508–509; Josef van Ess, *Theologie und Gesellschaft im 2. Und 3. Jahrhundert Hidschra: eine Geschichte des religiösen Denkens im frühen Islam* (Berlin and New York, 1992), 2:516–528.
12. *Tafsīr Muqātil b. Sulaymān*, ed. 'Abd Allāh Maḥmūd Shiḥāta (Beirut, 2002).
13. This is derived from the recension of Abū Ṣāliḥ Hudhayl b. Ḥabīb (d. after 190/805), as transmitted by the *qāḍī* 'Abd Allāh b. Thābit (d. ca. 308/920) from his father Thābit b. Ya'qūb; cf. van Ess, *Theologie*, 2:521.
14. C. H. M. Versteegh in *Arabic Grammar and Qur'anic Exegesis in Early Islam* (Leiden, 1993), 48–53, similarly argues for the general veridicality of these early *tafsīrs* based on internal textual evidence in contrast to Andrew Rippin, who

expresses opposing views in "Studying early *tafsīr* texts," *Der Islam* 72 (1995): 310–323. See further Miklos Muranyi's critique of Rippin in his "Visionen des Skeptikers," *Der Islam* 81 (2004):206–217.

15. Cf. art. "'Abd al-Razzāq al-Ṣan'ānī," *Encyclopaedia of Islam*,third edition, ed. Gudrun Krämer et al. (Leiden, 2007- ; henceforth to be referred to as *EI*[3]), 1:7–9 (also available online).
16. *Tanwīr al-miqbās min tafsīr Ibn 'Abbās* (Beirut, 1992). For this discussion, see Andrew Rippin, "*Tafsīr Ibn 'Abbās* and criteria for dating early *tafsīr* texts," *Jerusalem Studies in Arabic and Islam* 18 (1994): 38–83; Harald Motzki, "Dating the so-called *Tafsīr Ibn 'Abbās*: some additional remarks," *Jerusalem Studies in Arabic and Islam* 31 (2006):147–163. See also the discussion in *Tanwīr al-miqbās min tafsīr Ibn 'Abbās,* trans. Mokrane Guezzou and ed. Yousef Meri (Amman, 2007), ii–ix.
17. In this I am in agreement with van Ess, *Theologie*, 1:300–302; and Marco Schöller, "*Sīra* and *Tafsīr*: Muḥammad al-Kalbī on the News of Medina," in Harald Motzki, ed., *The Biography of Muhammad: The Issue of the Sources* (Leiden, 2000), 42–44.
18. Valerie J. Hoffman, *The Essentials of Ibāḍī Islam* (Syracuse, N.Y., 2012), 20; for the Ibāḍīs in general, see ibid., and also the art. "al-Ibāḍīyya," *EI*[2], 3:648–660. Very little biographical information is otherwise available for Ibn Muḥakkam.
19. For whom, see, for example, Ibn Ṣhahrāṣhūb, *Ma'ālim al-'ulamā'*, ed. 'Abbās Iqbāl (Tehran, 1934), 88–89; al-Najāṣhī, *Rijāl* (Bombay, 1899), 247–250.
20. *GAS*, 1:539. For a detailed study of these three early *tafsīrs*, see Meir M. Bar-Asher, *Scripture and Exegesis in Early Islam* (Leiden, 1999).
21. *Jāmi' al-bayān fī tafsīr al-qur'ān* (Beirut, 1997).
22. For more details, see *EI*[2], art. "al-Ṭabarī", 10:11–15; Ulrike Mårtensson, *Tabari: Makers of Islamic Civilization* (London, 2011).
23. *Al-Wasīṭ fī tafsīr al-qur'ān al-majīd*, ed. 'Ādil Aḥmad 'Abd al-Mawjūd et al. (Beirut, 1994).
24. *EI*[2], art. "al-Wāḥidī," 11:48. For a detailed study of al-Wāḥidī and his *tafsīr* works, including his *al-Wasīṭ*, see Walid Saleh, "The last of the Nishapuri School of *Tafsīr*: al-Wāḥidī (d. 486/1076) and His Significance in the History of Qur'anic Exegesis," *Journal of the American Oriental Society* 126 (2006):223–244, and references therein.
25. Saleh, "Last of the Nishapuri School," 232.
26. Al-Zamakhsharī, *Al-Kashshāf 'an ḥaqā'iq ghawāmiḍ al-tanzīl wa-'uyūn al-aqāwīl fī wujūh al-ta'wīl*, eds. 'Alī Muḥammad Mu'awwaḍ and 'Ādil Aḥmad 'Abd al-Mawjūd (Riyadh, 1998).
27. See art. "al-Zamakhsharī," *EI*[2], 11:432–434. For a detailed study of the *Kashshāf* and its author, see Andrew J. Lane, *A Traditional Mu'tazilite Qur'ān Commentary: The* Kashshāf *of Jār Allāh al-Zamakhsharī (d. 538/1144)* (Leiden, 2006).
28. Cf. art. "Fakhr al-Dīn al-Rāzī," *EI*[2], 2:751–755.
29. See art. "Al-Ḳurtubi," *EI*[2], 5:512–513.

30. Muqātil, *Tafsīr*, 237.
31. Hūd b. Muḥakkam al-Huwwārī, *Tafsīr kitāb allāh al-'azīz*, ed. Balḥāj b. Sa'īd Sharifī (Beirut, 1990), 3:214.
32. *Tanwīr al-miqbās*, 384.
33. Al-Ṭabarī, *Tafsīr*, 9:398.
34. Al-Wāḥidī, *Wasīt*, 3:343.
35. Al-Zamakhsharī, *Kashshāf*, 4:362–363.
36. Al-Rāzī, *Al-Tafsīr al-kabīr* (Beirut, 1999), 8:474.
37. Al-Qurṭubī, *Al-Jāmi' li-aḥkām al-qur'ān*, ed. 'Abd al-Razzāq al-Mahdī (Beirut, 2001), 13:59.
38. Muqātil, *Tafsīr*, 3:39–91.
39. *Tanwīr al-miqbās*, 424.
40. Hūd b. Muḥakkam, *Tafsīr*, 3:312.
41. Furāt b. Ibrāhīm, *Tafsīr Furāt al-Kūfī*, ed. Muhammad al-Kāẓim (Beirut, 1992), 1:320.
42. Al-Qummī, *Tafsīr Qummī* (Beirut, 1991), 2:129. For al-Qummī, cf. *GAS*, 1:45 and references cited therein.
43. This is the Successor 'Abd al-Raḥmān Ibn Zayd b. Aslam al-'Adawī al-Madanī, son of the well-known Companion Zayd b. Aslam. Ibn Zayd was known to have composed a Qur'ān commentary that was used by al-Ṭabarī, as well as a work titled *Kitāb al-nāsikh wa-'l-mansūkh*; cf. *GAS*, 1:38.
44. Al-Ṭabarī, *Tafsīr*, 10:161.
45. Al-Wāḥidī, *Wasīṭ*, 3:426. Ibn Zayd is quoted as saying that the first part of the verse meant "Those who strove (*jāhadū*) against those polytheists and fought them (*wa-qātalūhum*) in order to support our religion (*fī nuṣrat dīninā*)."
46. Al-Wāḥidī, *Wasīṭ*, 3:426.
47. Al-Zamakhsharī, *Kashshāf*, 4:462.
48. Al-Rāzī, *Tafsīr*, 9:77.
49. Ibid., 9:77–78.
50. For whom, see *GAS*, 1:32–33; *EI*², 9:762. Ismā'īl 'Abd al-Raḥmān al-Suddī transmitted *ḥadīths* from several Companions and the older Successors. His influential Qur'ān commentary was used by al-Ṭabarī, al-Tha'labī, and others.
51. This is the early Syrian exegete Abū Muḥammad 'Abd Allāh b. 'Aṭiyya b. 'Alī b. Ḥabīb al-Dimashqī (d. 383/993), who derives his name from having been born in the mosque of 'Aṭiyya in Damascus; cf. *GAS*, 1:45. There is also the later Andalusian exegete Ibn 'Aṭiyya (d. 541/1146). It is more likely that al-Qurṭubī has this early exegete in mind, rather than the later Andalusian exegete, as he is citing mainly very early sources here; we are proceeding on this assumption.
52. He is very likely al-Ḥasan b. al-Ḥasan b. al-Ḥasan (d. 145/763), who is said to have been a Zaydī; cf. Abū 'l-Faraj al-Iṣbahānī, *Maqātil al-ṭaalibiyyīn*, ed. A. Ṣaqr (Cairo, 1949), 185.
53. Al-Qurṭubī, *Jāmi'*, 13:324–325.

54. These various non-combative meanings ascribed to derivatives from the root *jhd* in early sources belie the surprising statement made by David Cook in *Understanding Jihad* (Berkeley, CA, 2005), 19, that early Islamic texts do not indicate "that the jihad being described is anything other than military," clearly a hasty and unfounded statement.
55. Unless otherwise stated, translations of Qur'anic verses are my own, although I have freely consulted a number of existing English translations.
56. Muqātil, *Tafsīr*, 3:139.
57. *Tanwīr al-miqbās*, 358.
58. Hūd b. Muḥakkam, *Tafsīr*, 3:128.
59. Furāt, *Tafsīr*, 1:275.
60. Al-Qummī, *Tafsīr*, 2:63.
61. Al-Ṭabarī, *Tafsīr*, 9:191.
62. This is Yūnus b. ʻAbd al-Aʻlā (d. 264/877), an Egyptian scholar who transmitted from Sufyān b. ʻUyayna, ʻAbd Allāh b. Wahb, and al-Shāfiʻī, among others, and from whom Muslim, al-Nasāʼī, Ibn Māja, and others transmitted reports; see Ibn Ḥajar, *Tahdhīb al-tahdhīb*, ed. Khalīl Ma'mūn Shīḥā et al. (Beirut, 1996), 6:271.
63. This is very likely al-Qāsim b. Mabrūr al-Aylī (d. ca. 158/774), a jurist who narrated from his uncle, Talḥa b. ʻAbd al-Malik, from Ibn Jurayj, his contemporary Yūnus b. Yazīd, and others; see Ibn Ḥajar, *Tahdhīb*, 4:506–507; other possibilities cannot be ruled out.
64. Al-Ṭabarī, *Tafsīr*, 9:91.
65. Ibid. The identity of al-Ḍaḥḥāk here is not immediately apparent.
66. Ibid.
67. For whom, see *GAS*, 1:36.
68. Al-Wāḥidī, *Wasīṭ*, 3:281.
69. Ibn al-Mubārak is the author of the well-known *Kitāb al-jihād*, which is discussed in chapter 6. For Ibn al-Mubārak, see the brief entries on him in *GAS*, 1:95, and *EI*[2], 3:879.
70. Al-Wāḥidī, *Wasīṭ*, 3:281.
71. Al-Zamakhsharī, *Kashshāf* 4:214.
72. Al-Rāzī in his *tafsīr* relied heavily on al-Zamakhsharī's commentary, notwithstanding the latter's obvious Muʻtazilī leanings.
73. Al-Rāzī, *Tafsīr*, 8:254–255.
74. Ibid., 8:255.
75. Ibid.
76. Al-Qurṭubī, *Jāmiʻ*, 12:91–92.
77. Most commentators are agreed that chapter 3 (Sūrat Āl ʻImrān) as a whole is early Medinan, revealed during the third and fourth years of the *hijra*; although, as we will see, a number of early authorities cited by our exegetes regarded Qur'ān 3:200 specifically as a Meccan verse.

78. Mujāhid, *Tafsīr*, ed. Abū Muḥammad Asyūṭī (Beirut, 2005), 44.
79. Muqātil, *Tafsīr*, 1:324. Muqātil then goes on to append details of the letter that Muḥammad wrote to the Christians of Najrān and 'Umar's affirmation of it, details of which need not detain us here.
80. He was a student of Ma'mar b. Rashīd and transmitted from Ibn Jurayj, al-Awzā'ī, Mālik b. Anas, Sufyān al-Thawrī, and Sufyān b. 'Uyayna. 'Abd al-Razzāq is said to have harbored pro-'Alid sympathies; cf. *GAS*, 1:99.
81. 'Abd al-Razzāq, *Tafsīr 'Abd al-Razzāq*, ed. Maḥmūd Muḥammad 'Abduh (Beirut, 1999), 1:430.
82. Hūd b. Muḥakkam, *Tafsīr*, 1:343.
83. Furāt, *Tafsīr*, 1:99.
84. For an extensive biography of al-'Ayyashī and the sources for information about his life, see the editorial board's introduction to his *Tafsīr*, 1:1–57 (full bibliography given below).
85. Al-Qummī, *Tafsīr*, 1:136–137; al-'Ayyashī, *Tafsīr*, ed. Qism al-dirāsāt al-islāmiyya; Mu'assasat al-ba'tha (Qum, 1320), 1:309.
86. Al-Qummī, *Tafsīr*, 1:136–137.
87. Al-'Ayyashī, *Tafsīr*, 1:309.
88. For whom, see *GAS*, 1:31–32.
89. This is 'Abd al-Malik b. 'Abd al-'Azīz Ibn Jurayj, the author of a *Kitāb al-Tafsīr* in which he quoted from early authorities like Ibn 'Abbās 'Ikrima and Mujāhid, among others. This *tafsīr* was used by al-Ṭabarī and by al-Tha'labī (d. 427/1035) in his *al-Kashf wa-'l-bayān fī tafsīr al-qur'ān*, for example. Ibn Jurayj was also a well-regarded *muḥaddith* and jurist and the first Meccan to systematically arrange *ḥadīth*; cf. *GAS*, 1:91.
90. Al-Ṭabarī, *Tafsīr*, 3:561–562
91. Muhammad b. Ka'b b. Sulaym al-Quraẓī, said to be the oldest among the Tābi'ūn, had composed a Qur'ān commentary used by al-Tha'labī; cf. *GAS*, 1:32.
92. Al-Ṭabarī, *Tafsīr*, 3:562.
93. Zayd b. Aslam, one of the Successors, was a Qur'ān commentator and one of the most important jurists in Medina of his time. He transmitted reports from 'Ā'isha, Abū Hurayra, Jābir b. 'Abd Allāh, and others, while those who transmitted from him included his son 'Abd al-Raḥmān, Mālik b. Anas, and Ibn Jurayj. Significantly, he was close to the Umayyad Caliph al-Walīd b. Yazīd, who frequently consulted with him on legal matters; cf. *GAS*, 1:405–406.
94. Al-Ṭabarī, *Tafsīr*, 3:562.
95. Abū Salama b. 'Abd al-Raḥmān b. 'Awf b. 'Abd 'Awf al-Zuhrī al-Madanī was known by his *kunya*; his given name may have been either 'Abd Allāh or Ismā'īl. Ibn Sa'd describes him as a "trustworthy, learned man, who transmitted many *ḥadīths*" (*thiqa faqīh kathīr al-ḥadīth*); Abū Zur'a concurred; see Ibn Ḥajar, *Tahdhīb*, 6:351–353.
96. Shuraḥbīl was one of the earliest writers of *maghāzī* and, according to Sufyān b. 'Uyayna, the most knowledgeable of it. Ibn Isḥāq and al-Wāqidī did not transmit

from him, but Ibn Sa'd related from him concerning the *hijra* of the Prophet; cf. GAS, 1:279.

97. Al-Ṭabarī, *Tafsīr*, 3:562. For variant reports, see ibid., 3:562–563. This meaning of *rābiṭū* as "adhering to prayers" (*luzūm al-ṣalawāt*) also occurs in the early Qur'ān commentary of 'Abd Allāh b. Wahb (d. 197/812), *'Abd Allāh b. Wahb (125/743–197/812):* al-Ǧāmi': *tafsīr al-Qur'ān*, ed. Miklos Muranyi (Weisbaden, 1993), 174 (fol. 25a).
98. Al-Ṭabarī, *Tafsīr*, 3:562.
99. Ibid.
100. Ibid. For an extensive discussion of the term *ribāṭ* and its manifold significations, see art. "Ribāṭ," *EI*², 8:493–506. The author of the article, J. Chabbi, rightly emphasizes that "The word needs to be constantly related to a context and a chronology since the sense has been very evolutive"; ibid., 8:493.
101. Al-Wāḥidī, *Wasīṭ*, 1:537–538.
102. For whom, see *GAS*, 1:221–222.
103. Al-Wāḥidī, *Wasīṭ*, 1:538.
104. Ismā'īl b. Ja'far b. Abī Kathīr al-Anṣārī was a Qur'ān reader and a traditionist from Medina. He died in Baghdad where he had been appointed the tutor of 'Alī, the son of the 'Abbasid Caliph al-Mahdī; cf. *GAS*, 1:94.
105. Al-Wāḥidī, *Wasīt*, 1:539.
106. Al-Zamakhsharī, *Kashshāf*, 1:683.
107. Al-Rāzī, *Tafsīr*, 3:473.
108. In his otherwise extensive and illuminating study *Commanding Right and Forbidding Wrong in Islamic Thought* (Cambridge, UK, 2000), Michael Cook makes no reference to *muṣābara* as part of this enterprise. Cook in fact points to the "frequent abrasiveness of forbidding wrong in Islam" and "...the ways in which Muslim scholars link the duty to holy war [sic]..."; ibid., 582. As we can see, however, in al-Rāzī's commentary, quietist and peaceful resistance to wrongdoing as encoded in *ṣabr* and its derivatives is clearly regarded as part of the overall struggle to enjoin what is right and prevent evil. Al-Rāzi does go on to say (as noted in the main text) that the practice of *muṣābara* in the face of wrongdoing may lead to endangering one's life, in which case one is allowed to fight in self-defense—hardly the definition of "holy war" here.
109. Al-Rāzī, *Tafsīr*, 3:473.
110. Ibid., 3:473–474
111. Ibid.
112. Ibid. Similar views are expressed by the twentieth-century exegete Maḥmūd Shaltūt in his *Tafsīr al-qur'ān*, 157–158, where he comments that references to both steadfastness (*al-iltizām*) and the military frontiers (*al-thughūr*) are contained within the term *ribāṭ* and its derivatives.
113. It is not clear which Abū 'Umar this is.
114. Al-Qurṭubī, *Jāmi'*, 4:313–314.

115. Ibid., 4:314.
116. Ibid., 4:315.
117. Ibid.
118. See note 92 above.
119. Scott C. Lucas, *Constructive Critics,* Ḥadīth *Literature, and the Articulation of Sunnī Islam* (Leiden, 2004).
120. For similar observations, see Roy Mottahedeh and Ridwan al-Sayyid, "The Idea of the *Jihad* in Islam before the Crusades," in *The Crusades from the Perspective of Byzantium and the Muslim World,* eds. Angeliki E. Laiou and Roy Parviz Mottahedeh (Washington, D.C., 2001), 23–29. According to their findings, Ḥijāzī jurists in general tended to place greater emphasis on religious practices, such as prayer and mosque attendance, and did not consider *jihād* obligatory for all. But Syrian jurists, like al-Awzāʿī (d. 157/773), held the view that even aggressive war may be considered obligatory, a perspective that was no doubt formed against the backdrop of constant military skirmishes between the Umayyads and the Byzantines along the frontiers. This Syrian preoccupation with the military *jihād* continued into the ʿAbbasid period; cf. van Ess, *Theologie,* 1:68–69. For early Arab perceptions of the Byzantines, see Nadia Maria El Cheikh, *Byzantium Viewed by the Arabs* (Cambridge, MA, 2007), ch. 1; Ahmad Shboul, "Byzantium and the Arabs: The Image of the Byzantines as Mirrored in Arabic Literature," *Byzantine Papers: Proceedings of the First Australian Byzantine Studies Conference,* ed. Elizabeth Jeffreys et al. (Canberra, AU, 1978), 43–68.
121. See also the brief reference by Alfred Morabia to the competing belligerent and non-belligerent interpretations of Qur'ān 3:200 in his *Ğihâd dans l'Islam,* 403–404, note 8.

CHAPTER 2

1. Emphasis mine. It should be noted that even though the Arabic uses the passive verb (*yuqātalūna*) instead of the active (*yuqātilūna*), many English translations inaccurately render the verb as active: for example, those produced by George Sale, A. J. Arberry, and Mohammed Marmaduke Pickthall. The translations of N. J. Dawood, Yusuf ʿAli, M. A. S. ʿAbdel Haleem, and Muhammad Asad, for example, translate the verb correctly as a passive one. Both ʿAli and Asad consequently emphasize the defensive nature of fighting in the verse on account of the passive verb; see Abdullah Yusuf Ali, *The Qur'an: Text, Translation and Commentary* (Elmhurst, NY, 2008), 861 and n. 2816; *The Message of the Qur'ān,* trans. and explained by Muhammad Asad (Bristol, UK, 2003), 570, and n. 57. This critical point is not noted by David Cook, who in his *Martyrdom in Islam* (Cambridge, UK, 2007), 15, mistranslates *yuqātalūna* as "those who fight" and fails to see the significance of this misconstrual (similarly in id., *Understanding Jihad* 7 ff., where he then boldly goes on to construct what he regards as a doctrine of military conquest directly from the Qur'ān itself).

2. Cf. *Abū 'Ubayd al-Qāsim b. Sallām's K. al-nāsikh wa-l-mansūkh*, ed. John Burton (Cambridge, UK, 1987), 67.
3. Mujāhid, *Tafsir*, 169. This report emanates from the Kufan scholar Abū Bishr Warqā' b. 'Umar (d. 160/776), who transmitted the *tafsīr* of the well-known early exegete 'Abd Allāh b. Abī Najīḥ (d. 131/748), which was used by Mujāhid; cf. *GAS*, 1:37.
4. Mujāhid, *Tafsīr*, 170.
5. Muqātil, *Tafsīr*, 3:130.
6. *Tanwīr al-miqbās*, 353.
7. For a discussion of this frequently occurring *isnād* in 'Abd al-Razzāq's *ḥadīth* collection, called *al-Muṣannaf*, see Harald Motzki, "The *Muṣannaf* of 'Abd al-Razzāq al-Ṣan'ānī as a source of authentic *aḥādīth* of the first century A.H.," *Journal of Near Eastern Studies* 50 (1991):1–21.
8. In the published *tafsīr* attributed to the second/eighth century exegete Sufyān al-Thawrī (d. 161/777), Sufyān reporting from the Kufan scholar al-A'mash (d. 148/765) comments briefly on this verse that "it was the first verse to be revealed regarding fighting"; see Sufyān al-Thawrī, *Tafsīr sufyān al-thawrī* (Beirut, 1983), 214.
9. 'Abd al-Razzāq, *Tafsīr*, 2:408.
10. Hūd b. Muḥakkam, *Tafsīr*, 3:119.
11. Ibid.
12. Al-Qummī, *Tafsīr*, 2:59.
13. Furāt, *Tafsīr*, 1:273. His comments on Qur'ān 22:39 have not been preserved for us.
14. Al-Ṭabarī, *Tafsīr*, 9:160. See also the brief discussion of these variant readings in Ibn Mujāhid *Kitāb al-sab'a fī 'l-qirā'āt*, ed. Shawqī Ḍayf (Cairo, 1972), 437.
15. Al-Ṭabarī, *Tafsīr*, 9:161.
16. Ibid., 9:161–162.
17. Ibid., 9:162
18. Ibid., 9:163.
19. Ibid.
20. Ibid., 9:163–164.
21. Some Muslim scholars took a strong interest in monasteries in Muslim lands; see this discussion in Hilary Kikpatrick, "Monasteries through Muslim Eyes: The *Diyārāt* Books," in *Christians at the Heart of Islamic Rule: Church Life and Scholarship in 'Abbasid Iraq*, ed. David Thomas (Leiden and Boston, 2003), 19–37.
22. Al-Wāḥidī, *Wasīṭ*, 3:273.
23. Ibid., 3:272–273.
24. Al-Zamakhsharī, *Kashshāf*, 4:199.
25. Ibid.
26. Al-Rāzī, *Tafsīr*, 8:229.

27. Ibid.
28. Ibid., 8:229–230.
29. Ibid.
30. Ibid.
31. Ibid.
32. Al-Qurṭubī, *Jāmi'*, 12:66.
33. For a quick overview of this hermeneutic concept, see the article "Naskh" in *EI*^{2}, 7:1010–1015.
34. Al-Qurṭubī, *Jāmi'*, 12:67.
35. Ibid., 12:67–68.
36. Ibid., 12:69.
37. Ibid. The verse states, "There are among them those who are unjust to themselves, and those who are just, and those who precede with their good works."
38. See also Ibn Kathīr, *Tafsīr al-qur'ān al-'aẓīm* (Beirut, 1990), 3:219, where he endorses such exclusivist perspectives in the Mamluk period.
39. Mujāhid, *Tafsīr*, 23.
40. This verse states, "If you do not go forth, He will punish you gravely and substitute for you another group of people. You cannot harm Him at all; God has power over everything."
41. Muqātil, *Tafsīr*, 1:167–168. For a detailed account of the events surrounding al-Ḥudaybiyya, see Ibn Hishām, *al-Sīra al-nabawiyya*, ed. Suhayl Zakkar (Beirut, 1992), 2:776 ff.
42. *Tanwīr al-miqbās*, 33.
43. 'Abd al-Razzāq, *Tafsīr*, 1:314–315.44

The first part of this verse states, "When the sacred months have passed, slay the polytheists wherever you may find them..."

45. Hūd b. Muḥakkam, *Tafsīr*, 1:180–181.
46. Ibid., 1:181.
47. Ibid.
48. Ibid., 1:182.
49. Al-'Ayyāshī, *Tafsīr*, 1:193–194.
50. Al-Ṭabarī, *Tafsīr*, 2:196.
51. Ibid.
52. Ibid.
53. Ibid., 2:196–197.
54. Ibid., 2:197–198.
55. Ibid., 2:199–200.
56. Cf. al-Suddī, *Tafsīr al-Suddī al-kabīr*, ed. Muḥammad 'Atā' Yūsuf (al-Manṣūriya, Egypt, 1993), 143.
57. Al-Ṭabarī, *Tafsīr*, 2:200–201.
58. Ibid., 2:198.
59. Ibid., 2:198–199.

60. Ibid., 2:201.
61. As Toshihiko Izutsu points out, the primary meaning of the root *ẓlm* is that of "putting in a wrong place"; in the field of ethics, it acquires the meaning of "to transgress the proper limit and encroach upon the right of some other person"; see his *Ethico-Religious Concepts in the Qur'ān* (Montreal and Kingston, 2002), 164–172. For an insightful discussion of the close semantic link between *ẓulm* and *i'tadā*, see further ibid., 172–174.
62. Al-Ṭabarī, *Tafsīr*, 2:202; cf. al-Suddī, *Tafsīr*, 143.
63. Al-Ṭabarī, *Tafsīr*, 2:205.
64. Ibid., 205–206.
65. Ibid., 2:206.
66. Al-Wāḥidī, *Wasīṭ*, 1:292.
67. Ibid.
68. Ibid.
69. Ibid., 1:293.
70. Al-Zamakhsharī, *Kashshāf*, 1:395–396.
71. Ibid.
72. Ibid.
73. Ibid., 1:397.
74. Ibid.
75. Al-Rāzī, *Tafsīr*, 2:287.
76. Ibid., 2:287–288.
77. Ibid., 2:288.
78. A prominent exception among later jurists was Ibn Taymiyya, who adamantly maintained on the basis of Qur'ān 2:190, which he regards as unabrogated, that the reason (*'illa*) for fighting against the polytheists was their prior act of aggression, not their lack of belief; see a synopsis of his views in *Qā'ida mukhtaṣara fī qitāl al-kuffār wa-muhādanatihim wa-taḥrīm qatlihim li-mujarrad kufrihim*, ed. 'Abd al-'Azīz b. 'Abd Allāh b. Ibrāhīm (Riyadh, 2004), 92 ff. Ibn Taymiyya is quoted as defining aggression (*'udwān*) as "fighting those who did not initiate fighting against us."
79. Al-Rāzī, *Tafsīr*, 2:287–288.
80. Ibid., 2:289–290.
81. Ibid., 2:290–291.
82. It is not clear which Abū Muslim is indicated here; one possibility is Abū Muslim Ibrāhīm b. 'Abd Allāh b. Muslim al-Kajjī al-Baṣrī (d. 292/904), who transmitted from al-Aṣmā'ī; cf. *GAS*, 1:162.
83. Al-Rāzī, *Tafsīr*, 2:291.
84. Ibid.
85. Ibid., 2:291.
86. Ibid., 2:292–293.

87. Cf. with Ibn Taymiyya, *Qā'ida mukhtaṣara*, 102 ff., where he similarly maintains that once fighting has been initiated by the enemy, they can be fought against wherever Muslims encounter them, so that there is no contradiction between Qur'ān 2:190 and 2:191.
88. Al-Qurṭubī, *Jāmi'*, 2:345–346.
89. Ibid., 2:346–347.
90. These details, however, are important for a comprehensive discussion of the ethics of war and peace in Islam, currently beyond the purview of this study.
91. Al-Qurṭubī, *Jāmi'*, 2:347–348.
92. Ibid., 2:348.
93. Ibid., 2:351.
94. Ibid.
95. Ibid., 2:351–352.
96. See also al-Dawoody's discussion of these critical verses and their contested interpretations in *The Islamic Law of War*, 59–62.
97. Mujāhid, *Tafsīr*, 98.
98. 'Abd al-Razzāq in his *Tafsīr*, 2:137, includes the following names as the leaders of unbelief: Abū Sufyān b. Ḥarb, Umayya b. Khalaf, 'Utba b. Rabī', Abū Jahl b. Hishām, and Suhayl b. 'Amr.
99. Muqātil, *Tafsīr*, 2:159–160.
100. *Tanwīr al-miqbās*, 200.
101. Hūd b. Muḥakkam, *Tafsīr*, 2:117.
102. Ibid., 2:118.
103. For these reports and other variants, see al-'Ayyāshī, *Tafsīr*, 2:219.
104. For a discussion of the various possibilities, see al-Ṭābarī, *Jāmi'*, 6:329.
105. Ibid., 6:330.
106. Ibid., 6:331.
107. Al-Wāḥidī, *Wasīṭ*, 2:480–481.
108. Ibid., 2:481.
109. Al-Zamakhsharī, *Kashshāf*, 2:17–18.
110. Ibid., 2:18.
111. Ibid.
112. This is the Damascene *qāri'* 'Abd al-Rāḥmān b.'Āmir al-Yaḥṣibī al-Shāmī; for whom, see Ibn Ḥajar, *Tahdhīb*, 3:359. According to Ibn Mujāhid, Ibn 'Amir was alone in reading *aymān* as *īmān* in this verse; the rest of the *qurrā'* preferred *aymān*; see Ibn Mujāhid *Kitāb al-sab'a*, 312.
113. Al-Rāzī, *Tafsīr*, 5:534–535.
114. Ibid., 5:535.
115. Al-Qurṭubī, *Jāmi'*, 8:77–78.
116. Ibid., 8:79–80.
117. Ibid., 8:80.

118. Failure to holistically take into consideration these verses under discussion here in addition to Qur'ān 9:5 and 9:29 (discussed in the next chapter) and other verses in the ninth *sūra* causes Reuven Firestone to miss out on the importance attached by the Qur'ān to the prior commission of hostilities by the enemy and not their religious affiliation per se as constituting a *casus belli*; see his *Jihad*, 90, where he describes "a ruthless ideological war of religion" being commanded against unbelievers in the ninth chapter reminiscent of Deuteronomy 20:15–18. Not quite.

CHAPTER 3

1. Muqātil, *Tafsīr*, 1:184.
2. *Tanwīr al-miqbās*, 38.
3. 'Abd al-Razzāq, *Tafsīr*, 1:335.
4. Hūd b. Muḥakkam, *Tafsīr*, 1:202–203.
5. Al-Qummī, *Tafsīr*, 1:79–80.
6. Al-Ṭabarī, *Jāmi'*, 2:357.
7. This is Ibrāhīm b. Muḥammad al-Ḥārith al-Fazārī, originally from Kūfa, a highly regarded historian and *muḥaddith*, known for his *Kitāb al-siyar fī 'l-akhbār*; cf. *GAS*, 1:292.
8. Abū 'Amr 'Abd al-Raḥmān b. 'Amr b. Yuḥmid al-Awzā'ī was a well-known Syrian jurist who studied with 'Aṭā' b. Abī Rabāḥ, Qatāda, and al-Zuhrī, among others. His *siyar* work is no longer extant, but we are able to reconstruct some of its content through an existing refutation of it, known as the *Radd 'alā siyar al-Awzā'ī*, written by Abū Yūsuf; cf. *GAS*, 1:516–517; Ibn 'Asākir, *Ta'rīkh madīnat dimashq* (Beirut, 1995), 35:148 ff.
9. Al-Ṭabarī, *Jāmi'*, 2:357.
10. Ibid.
11. Dā'ūd b. Abī 'Āṣim b. 'Urwa b. Mas'ūd al-Thaqafī al-Ṭā'ifī, from whom Ibn Jurayj and Qatāda frequently reported, is generally regarded as a *thiqa*; see Ibn Ḥajar, *Tahdhīb*, 2:116–117.
12. Al-Ṭabarī, *Jāmi'*, 2:357.
13. Cf. al-Suddī, *Tafsīr*, 148.
14. Al-Ṭabarī, *Jāmi'*, 2:358–359.
15. Al-Wāḥidī, *Wasīṭ*, 1:319.
16. Al-Zamakhsahrī, *Kashshāf*, 1:423.
17. Makḥūl b. Abī Muslim Shuhrāb al-Dimashqī, a *tābi'ī*, was a renowned jurist of his time; among his students were al-Awzā'ī and al-Zuhrī. He was closely associated with the Umayyads, having served as a teacher of the Caliph Yazīd b. 'Abd al-Malik; cf. *GAS*, 1:404; Ibn 'Asākir, *Ta'rīkh*, 60:196–235.
18. Al-Rāzī, *Tafsīr*, 2:384.
19. Ibid.
20. It is in this context that the true import of the prophetic report declaring that there was no more *hijra* after the fall of Mecca but that *jihād* would continue

becomes evident; see our reference to this *ḥadīth* as recorded by al-Bukhārī in chapter 5. The report may be understood to have been put into circulation specifically to challenge those who maintained that the duty of fighting had lapsed after the time of the Prophet and to legitimate and promote Umayyad wars of conquest as authentic military *jihād; pace* Patricia Crone, "The First Century Concept of 'Hiǧra'," *Arabica* 41 (1994):352–387.

21. Al-Rāzī, *Tafsīr*, 2:384.
22. Al-Qurṭubī, *Aḥkām*, 3:38–39.
23. A small industry of polemical literature promoting this view has emerged in recent times; see, for example, Cook, *Understanding Jihad*, 10 ff.; and Andrew G. Bostom, *The Legacy of Jihad: Islamic Holy War and the Fate of Non-Muslims* (Amherst, NY, 2008), 125 ff., among others.
24. Muqātil, *Tafsīr*, 2:157.
25. *Tanwīr al-miqbās*, 198–199.
26. Hūd b. Muḥakkam, *Tafsīr*, 2:113–114.
27. Al-'Ayyāshī, *Tafsīr*, 2:218–219.
28. Furāt, *Tafsīr*, 1:163.
29. Al-Ṭabarī, *Jāmi'*, 6:320.
30. Ibid.
31. Al-Suddī, *Tafsīr*, 288.
32. Al-Ṭabarī, *Jāmi'*, 6:320.
33. Ibid.
34. Al-Wāḥidī, *Wasīṭ*, 2:479.
35. Al-Zamakhsharī, *al-Kashshāf*, 3:13–14.
36. Al-Rāzī, *Tafsīr*, 5:528.
37. Ibid., 5:528–529.
38. Al-Qurṭubī, *Jāmi'*, 8:69.
39. Ibid.
40. Cf. Abū 'Ubayd, *Nāsikh*, 67–68, where Qur'ān 9:5 (and Qur'ān 9:29) are already listed as abrogating verses.
41. Al-Qurṭubī, *Jāmi'*, 8:70.
42. Ibid.
43. Ibid., 8:71–72.
44. Ibn Kathīr, *Tafsīr* (Beirut, 1990), 2:322, where he goes on to quote 'Alī b. Abī Ṭālib, who is said to have remarked that the Prophet had been sent with four swords—the first directed at the Arab polytheists, the second at the People of the Book, the third at the Hypocrites, and the fourth at Muslim rebels (*al-bāghīn*), a report that was apparently known to the early Ḥanafī jurist al-Shaybānī (d. 189/804)—cf. Khadduri, *War and Peace*, 74—but does not occur in our earlier exegetical works.
45. Mujāhid, *Tafsīr*, 99. See Fred McGraw Donner, *The Early Islamic Conquests* (Princeton, NJ, 1981), 96–102, where he rehearses some of the traditional reasons for supporting the position that military campaigns to the north, particularly

Syria, had already acquired a special importance toward the end of the Prophet's life and set the stage for the conquests (*al-futūḥ*) that ensued after his death. Our extended discussion of the conception of fighting in the Qur'an and the reasons for which fighting becomes obligatory make this a very doubtful proposition, even though later Islamic sources routinely make this claim.

46. Muqātil, *Tafsīr*, 2:166.
47. Ibid., 2:167.
48. *Tanwīr al-miqbās*, 202.
49. Hūd b. Muḥakkam, *Tafsīr*, 2:125–126. The classic study of the *jizya*, usually (but erroneously) translated into English as "poll tax," remains Daniel C. Dennett, *Conversion and the Poll Tax in Early Islam* (Cambridge, MA, 1950).
50. It should be noted that al-Qummī, unlike his predecessors, understands the phrase *'an yad* as it occurs in this verse to refer to the financial capability of the *dhimmī*, rather than his personal proffering of the *jizya*. For brief discussions of the possible meanings of this ambiguous phrase in modern secondary literature, see, for example, M. Bravmann, "A propos de Qur'an IX-29: *ḥattā yu'ṭū l-ǧizyata wa-hum ṣāghirūna*," *Arabica* 10 (1963), 94–95 (also reprinted in *Der Koran*, 293–294); M.J. Kister, "*'An yadin* (Qur'an IX/29): An Attempt at Interpretation," *Arabica* 11 (1964):272–278; and others. Kister understands *'an yad* to be a reference to the "ability and sufficient means" of the *dhimmī*, which closely accords with al-Qummī's exegesis, not however cited by Kister.
51. Al-Qummī, *Tafsīr*, 1:287–288.
52. Al-'Ayyāshī, *Tafsīr*, 2:228; it is worth noting that al-'Ayyāshī is the first to use the term *dhimmī* in our exegetical survey. For modern scholarly discussions of the concept of *dhimma*, see, for example, C. E. Bosworth, "The Concept of *dhimma* in Early Islam," in *Christians and Jews in the Ottoman Empire: The Functioning of a Plural Society*, ed. Benjamin Braude and Bernard Lewis (New York, 1982), 1:37–51; Mahmoud Ayoub, "Dhimmah in Qur'an and Hadith," *Arab Studies Quarterly* 5 (1983): 172–182; and the art. "Dhimma," *EI*², 2:227.
53. Al-Ṭabarī, *Jāmi'*, 6:349.
54. Ibid., 6:350.
55. Al-Ṭabarī's polemical attitude toward Jews and Christians is discussed by Seth Ward in his article, "A Fragment from an Unknown Work by al-Ṭabarī on the Tradition 'Expel the Jews and Christians from the Arabian Peninsula (and the Lands of Islam),' " *Bulletin of the School of Oriental and African Studies* 53 (1990):407–420. As Ward suggests, the growing presence and influence of the *dhimmīs* in Islamic cities during al-Ṭabarī's time contributed to the desire on the part of some jurists to firmly demarcate the theological and sociological boundaries between Muslims and non-Muslims. The third/ninth century belle-lettrist al-Jāḥiẓ (d. 255/869) in his "al-Radd 'alā 'l-naṣāra" in *Rasā'il al- Jāḥiẓ*, ed. 'Abd al-Salām Hārūn (Cairo, 1979), 3:303–351, clearly indicates that the wealth and what appeared to him as the uppity manners of some of the *dhimmīs* during his

time generated resentment at least among some Muslims. For a recent, particular interpretation of these early socio-historical trends that impacted the formation of Muslim identities in the context of inter-faith relations, especially in the earlier Umayyad period, cf. Fred Donner, *Muhammad and the Believers: At the Origins of Islam* (Cambridge, MA, 2010).

56. Al-Wāḥidī, *Wasīṭ*, 2:489.
57. Ibid.
58. Al-Zamakhsharī, *Kashshāf*, 3:32–33.
59. Al-Rāzī, *Tafsīr*, 6:26.
60. Ibid., 6:23–24.
61. Ibid.
62. This is ʿAṭiyya b. al-Ḥārith al-Hamadānī al-Kūfī, author of a Qurʾān commentary, who was generally considered to be a reliable transmitter; cf., for example, Ibn Ḥajar, *Tahdhīb*, 4:138.
63. Al-Rāzī, *Tafsīr*, 6:25.
64. For example, an important cluster of verses (Qurʾān 5:44–47) calls upon Jews and Christians to judge among themselves by the Torah and the Gospel, respectively. Qurʾān 5:48 specifically refers to different revealed laws and ways of life that exist concurrently with Islam without having been abrogated. Other verses (for instance, 2:89, 101; 5:48; 10:37) affirm that previous revelations are confirmed, rather than superseded, by the Qurʾān.
65. The *ḥadīth* and *sīra* literatures contain examples of Muḥammad adjudicating among the Jews on the basis of their own laws—for example, permitting Jewish rabbis to stone an adulterous Jewish couple according to the punishment prescribed in the Torah; see al-Bukhārī, *al-Ṣaḥīḥ*, ed. Qāsim al-Shammāʿī al-Rifāʿī (Beirut, 1987), 7:580 ff.
66. Al-Rāzī, *Tafsīr*, 6:25–27.
67. Al-Qurṭubī, *Jāmiʿ*, 8:101.
68. Ibid., 8:102–107.
69. For whom, see, for example, Ibn Ḥajar, *Tahdhīb*, 6:26–27.
70. Ibid., 2:547–548.
71. Al-Qurṭubī, *Jāmiʿ*, 8:106.
72. In Arabic, this is known as *tabʿiḍiyya* ("partitive"). As M.A.S. Abdel Haleem points out, whenever *min* occurs in reference to the People of the Book in the Qurʾān, it is partitive, as in Qurʾān 2:178; 3:75, 113; 5:80 and 9:34; see his article "The *jizya* Verse (Q. 9:29): Tax Enforcement on Non-Muslims in the First Muslim State," *Journal of Qur'anic Studies* 14.2 (2012): 75.
73. Muqātil, *Tafsīr*, 1:401.
74. ʿAbd al-Razzāq, *Tafsīr*, 1:473.
75. Hūd b. Muḥakkam, *Tafsīr*, 1:413–414.
76. Al-Qummī, *Tafsīr*, 1:156.
77. Al-Ṭabarī, *Jāmiʿ*, 4:229.

78. Ibid., 4:231–232. In variant accounts, the blind man is not identified as such.
79. Ibid., 4:232–233.
80. For whom, see, for example, Ibn Ḥajar, *Tahdhīb*, 3:251.
81. Al-Wāḥidī, *Wasīṭ*, 2:103–104.
82. Al-Zamakhsharī, *Kashshāf*, 2:132–136.
83. Al-Rāzī, *Tafsīr*, 4:193–194.
84. Ibid., 4:194–195.
85. See further al-Jāḥiẓ, *Risālat al-ʿUthmāniyya*, ed. ʿAbd al-Salām Hārūn (Cairo, 1955), 54–55; and Afsaruddin, *Excellence*, 58–61. Cf. also the manuscript by the influential Māturidī jurist Abū ʾl-Muʿīn al-Nasafī (d. 508/1115) titled *Ǧihād*, Arabe 4589, Ms. Bibliothèque Nationale, fol. 8a, where he notably refers to competing interpretations of this verse between those who understood *al-mujāhidūn* as a reference to "those who strive against unbelievers and therefore are preferred a degree above the sitters" and similarly unnamed "others" (*al-ākharūn*) who maintained that *al-mujāhidūn* referred instead to "those who strive against their selves and that this striving (*hādhihi al-mujāhada*) was the greatest and most noble type of *jihād* [on account of which] they are preferred over the sitters by degrees." Al-Nasafī then cites the famous *ḥadīth* in which the Prophet refers to the greater versus the lesser *jihād*.
86. Al-Qurṭubī, *Jāmiʿ*, 5:324–327.
87. Mujāhid, *Tafsīr*, 293.
88. Muqātil, *Tafsīr*, 4:301–302.
89. *Tanwīr al-miqbās*, 591. For a detailed account of the fall of Mecca in 9/630, see Ibn Hishām, Sīra, 2:843 ff; for reference to Muḥammad's marriage to Umm Ḥabība, see ibid., 2:1060.
90. ʿAbd al-Razzāq, *Tafsīr*, 3:303.
91. Hūd b. Muḥakkam, *Tafsīr*, 4:338.
92. Ibid.
93. Al-Qummī, *Tafsīr*, 2:343.
94. As reported by Yūnus from Ibn Wahb from Ibn Zayd.
95. See, for example, Ibn Saʿd, *al-Ṭabaqāt al-kubrā* (Beirut, 1998), 8:252.
96. Al-Ṭabarī, *Jāmiʿ*, 12:62–63.
97. Ibid., 12:63.
98. Ibid.
99. Al-Wāḥidī, *Wasīṭ*, 4:285.
100. Al-Zamakhsharī, *Kashshāf*, 6:92–93.
101. Ibid., 6:94–95.
102. Al-Rāzī, *Tafsīr*, 10:520.
103. It is possible that al-Rāzī is conflating these two Muqātils and assuming uniformity in their views. In his extant *tafsīr*, Muqātil b. Sulaymān expresses the view that Qurʾān 60:7–9 had been abrogated by Qurʾān 9:5.
104. Al-Rāzī, *Tafsīr*, 10:521.

105. Ibid.
106. Al-Qurṭubī, *Jāmiʿ*, 18:54.
107. A Mālikī judge in Baghdad, he was the author of an *aḥkām al-qur'ān* work; cf. *GAS*, 1:475–476.
108. Al-Qurṭubī, *Jāmiʿ*, 18:54.
109. Ibid., 18:54–55.
110. Mujāhid, *Tafsīr*, 98.
111. *Tanwīr al-miqbās*, 199.
112. Hūd b. Muḥakkam, *Tafsīr*, 2:115.
113. Al-Qummī, *Tafsīr*, 1:282.
114. Furāt, *Tafsīr*, 1:163.
115. Cf. al-Suddī, *Tafsīr*, 288.
116. Al-Ṭabarī, *Jāmiʿ*, 6:321.
117. Ibid., 6:322.
118. Al-Wāḥidī, *Wasīṭ*, 2:479.
119. Al-Suddī, *Tafsīr*, 288.
120. Al-Zamakhsharī, *al-Kashshāf*, 3:14–15.
121. Al-Rāzī, *Tafsīr*, 5:529.
122. Ibid., 5:530–531.
123. Al-Qurṭubī, *Jāmiʿ*, 8:72–73.
124. Ibid., 8:73.
125. Mujāhid, *Tafsīr*, 95.
126. Muqātil, *Tafsīr*, 2:123.
127. *Tanwīr al-miqbās*, 195.
128. Hūd b. Muḥakkam, *Tafsīr*, 2:102.
129. Al- ʿAyyāshī, *Tafsīr*, 2:204.
130. Furāt, *Tafsīr*, 1:278.
131. Al-Ṭabarī, *Jāmiʿ*, 6:278.
132. Ibid.
133. See, however, al-Suddī, *Tafsīr*, 285, where the editor notes that al-Suddī had maintained that Qur'ān 47:35 had abrogated Qur'ān 9:6, as related in *al-Durr al-manthūr* and *Fatḥ al-qadīr*
134. Al-Ṭabarī, *Jāmiʿ*, 6:278.
135. Ibid., 6:278–279.
136. Ibid., 6:279.
137. Al-Wāḥidī, *Wasīṭ*, 2:469.
138. Abū ʿUbayd, *Nāsikh*, 70, lists Qur'ān 9:29 as the abrogating verse, also on the authority of Ibn ʿAbbās.
139. Al-Zamakhsharī, *al-Kashshāf*, 2:595.
140. Al-Rāzī, *Tafsīr*, 5:500–501. Ibn Kathīr, *Tafsīr*, 2:309, is of the opinion that the verse refers rather to Badr.
141. Al-Qurṭubī, *Jāmiʿ*, 8:40–41.

142. Ibid., 8:42.
143. Ibid.
144. Ibn Kathīr, *Tafsīr*, 2:309.

CHAPTER 4

1. *Contra* Michael Bonner, who in his *Aristocratic Violence and Holy War: Studies in the Jihad and the Arab-Byzantine Frontier* (New Haven, CT, 1996), 10, suggests that the direction of influence went the other way. He, however, does not take into consideration the lack of Qur'anic attestation for the concepts of "martyr" and "martyrdom" exclusively in the military sense. See, however, his later work *Jihad in Islamic History* (Princeton, NJ, 2006), 74, where he notes that *shahīd* in the Qur'ān does not refer to a military martyr, although he still translates the plural *shuhadā'*, as occurs in Qur'ān 4:69, as "martyrs"; similarly in Cook, *Martyrdom*, 17, in relation to Qur'ān 3:138–142. Neither offers an explanation as to why the plural noun, in contradistinction to the singular, should suddenly acquire a different, independent meaning.
2. Arthur Jeffrey, *The Foreign Vocabulary of the Qur'an* (Baroda, India, 1938), 187; Ignaz Goldziher, *Muslim Studies*, ed. S. M. Stern and trans. C. R. Barber and S. M. Stern (London, 1971), 350–351; Keith Lewinstein, "The Reevaluation of Martyrdom in Early Islam," in *Sacrificing the Self: Perspectives on Martyrdom and Religion* (Oxford, UK, 2002), 78–79. This relationship obviously needs to be better studied and documented, which is presently beyond the purview of this work. See further on this topic the useful article by A. J. Wensinck, "The oriental doctrine of the martyrs," in his *Semietische Studiën uit de nalatenschap* (Leiden, 1941), 91–113, which establishes striking parallels between Christian and post-Qur'anic Muslim concepts of martyrdom, as well as the article "Shahīd," *EI*[2], 9:104. For a general and comparative study of how "militant and aggressive modes of religiosity became such crucial resources for communal self-fashioning among early Christian and early Muslim communities," see Thomas Sizgorich, *Violence and Belief in Late Antiquity: Militant Devotion in Christianity and Islam* (Philadelphia, 2009), quotation at 4. Sizgorich uncovers interesting congruences, particularly between Muslim and Christian portrayals of ascetic praxis linked to militancy; see especially ibid., 168–195.
3. Muqātil, *Tafsīr*, 1:309.
4. *Tanwīr al-miqbās*, 77.
5. Hūd b. Muḥakkam, *Tafsīr*, 1:325.
6. Al-'Ayyāshī, *Tafsīr*, 1:344.
7. Furāt, *Tafsīr*, 1:98.
8. Al-Ṭabarī, *Tafsīr*, 3:193.
9. Al-Wāḥidī, *Tafsīr*, 1:511–512.
10. Al-Zamakhsharī, *Kashshāf*, 1:646.
11. Al-Rāzī, *Tafsīr*, 3:403–404.

12. Al-Qurṭubī, *Tafsīr*, 4:240.
13. Muqātil, *Tafsīr*, 1:379.
14. *Tanwīr al-miqbās*, 97–98.
15. Hūd b. Muḥakkam, *Tafsīr*, 1:398–399.
16. Al-Ṭabarī, *Tafsīr*, 4:170.
17. Al-Wāḥidī, *Wasīṭ*, 2:80.
18. Al-Zamakhsharī, *Kashshāf*, 2:107.
19. Al-Rāzī, *Tafsīr*, 4:140.
20. Ibid.
21. Al-Qurṭubī, *Jāmi'*, 5:266.
22. Ibid.
23. Muqātil, *Tafsīr*, 3:134.
24. Hūd b. Muḥakkam, *Tafsīr*, 3:124.
25. Al-Ṭabarī, *Tafsīr*, 9:182.
26. Al-Wāḥidī, *Wasit*, 3:278.
27. Al-Zamakhsharī, *Kashshāf*, 4:207.
28. Al-Rāzī, *Tafsīr*, 8:243.
29. Ibid.
30. Ibid., 8:244.
31. Al-Qurṭubī, *Jāmi'* 12:82–83. It is relevant to point out here that some sources suggest that one could also be a "martyr of patience"; cf. al-Mas'ūdī's account of Ḥujr b. 'Ādī's death at the hands of Mu'āwiya in 53/672 in his *Murūj al-dhahab wa-ma'ādin al-jawhar* (Beirut, 1965), 3:3, where Ḥujr is described as "the first of those who have been killed in patient forbearance in (for the sake of) Islam" (*wa-huwa awwal man qutila ṣabran fī 'l-islām*). In al-Ṭabarī's account of Ḥujr's death, the latter is said to have requested that his blood not be washed off from his body, a practice that later became standard for battlefield martyrs; see *Ta'rīkh al-Ṭabarī* (Beirut, 1997), 3:220. I am grateful to Maria Dakake for these valuable references.
32. Al-Qurṭubī, *Jāmi'*, 12:83. Other significant reports are recorded by al-Qurṭubī that similarly affirm the equal status of the believer who dies of natural causes and one who dies on the battlefield.
33. Ibid.
34. Muqātil, *Tafsīr*, 1:151.
35. Cf. Ibn Wahb, *Ğāmi'*, 252 (fol. 5b).
36. Muqātil, *Tafsīr*, 1:314.
37. *Tanwīr al-miqbās*, 27.
38. Ibid., 78–79.
39. 'Abd al-Razzāq, *Tafsīr*, 1:298.
40. Ibid., 1:421.
41. Cf. van Ess, *Theologie*, 4:524–525.
42. Hūd b. Muḥakkam, *Tafsīr*, 1:158–159.

43. Ibid., 1:159.
44. Ibid., 1:331–332.
45. Al-'Ayyāshī, *Tafsīr*, 1:350.
46. Al-Ṭabarī, *Tafsīr*, 2:42.
47. Ibid. See, however, al-Nasafī, *Ǧihād*, 10b, where he expresses the view that *aḥyā'* does not refer to an actual physical state of being alive but is rather a metaphorical allusion to a pleasant final state (*huwa majāz 'an ḥusn 'āqiba*).
48. Al-Ṭabarī, *Tafsīr*, 2:42–43.
49. Ibid., 2:43.
50. Ibid.
51. Ibid., 3:513.
52. Al-Wāḥidī, *Wasīt*, 1:236.
53. Ibid., 1:519–520. In the same century, the Sufi exegete Abū 'Abd al-Raḥmān al-Sulamī (d. 412/1021) records a dramatically different interpretation of Qur'ān 3:169 in his *Ziyādāt ḥaqā'iq al-tafsīr*, ed. Gerhard Böwering (Beirut, 1995), 30, where "those who have been slain in the path of God" are understood to be "those who fight against their desires" and sacrifice themselves in this effort.
54. Al-Zamkhsharī, *al-Kashshāf*, 1:347.
55. Ibid., 1:657–658.
56. Al-Rāzī, *Tafsīr*, 2:125.
57. Al-Sulamī, *Ziyādāt*, 33, quotes Abū 'l-Ḥusayn al-Fārisī (d. 370/981), who similarly places the *nabiyyūn* and the *ṣiddiqūn* above the *shuhadā'*.
58. Al-Rāzī, *Tafsīr*, 2:126–128.
59. Ibid., 3:425.
60. Ibid.
61. Ibid., 3:425–426.
62. Al-Qurṭubī, *Jāmi'*, 2:168–169.
63. Ibid., 4:261.
64. Ibid.
65. Ibid., 4:262–267.
66. Ibid., 4:265–267.
67. Ibid., 4:2.
68. *Contra* the article "Martyr," in *EQ*, 3:282.
69. For this discussion, see M. A. Shaban, *Islamic History: A New Interpretation I A.D. 600–750 (A.H. 132)* (Cambridge, UK, 1971), 120–130.
70. Other verses in which this plural occurs cannot be discussed, once again because of length constraints.
71. Muqātil, *Tafsīr*, 1:388.
72. Hūd b. Muḥakkam, *Tafsīr*, 1:397.
73. *Tanwīr al-miqbās*, 97.
74. Al-Qummī, *Tafsīr*, 1:151.

75. Al-ʻAyyāshī, *Tafsīr*, 1:417.
76. Furāt, *Tafsīr*, 1:112; a variant report is given in ibid., 1:113.
77. Al-Ṭabarī, *Tafsīr*, 4:165.
78. Ibid.
79. Ibid., 4:165–166.
80. Ibid., 4:166.
81. Ibid., 4:166–167.
82. Al-Wāḥidī, *Wasīt*, 2:78.
83. Ibid.
84. Al-Zamakhsharī, *Kashshāf*, 2:104.
85. Al-Rāzī, *Tafsīr*, 4:132–133.
86. See also my discussion of this *laqab* in *Excellence and Precedence: Medieval Islamic Discourse on Legitimate Leadership* (Leiden, 2002), 87–92, 100–102.
87. Similar views are expressed by al-Jāḥiẓ in his *Risālat al-ʻuthmāniyya*, 122–123; and Ibn Ḥazm in *Kitāb al-fiṣal fī 'l-milal wa 'l-ahwā' wa-'l-niḥal*, ed. ʻAbd al-Raḥmān Khalīfa (Cairo, 1347/1928), 4:107.
88. Al-Rāzī, *Tafsīr*, 4:133–135.
89. Ibid., 4:135.
90. Ibid., 4:134–135.
91. Al-Qurṭubī, *Jāmiʻ*, 5:260–261.

CHAPTER 5

1. His brief biography is given in the introduction.
2. Although the Kufan exegete and jurist Sufyān al-Thawrī apparently had relations with the Umayyads (see the art. "Sufyān al-Thawrī," EI^2, 9:770–772), his sojourns in the Ḥijāz and Yemen decisively shaped a number of his views, such as on the combative *jihād*, that cannot be regarded as pro-Umayyad. His anti-ʻAbbasid sentiments are well-documented; see this discussion in Abou El-Fadl, *Rebellion*, 96–98.
3. Full *isnād* scrutiny will be done selectively when necessary (in deference to length constraints) to discuss the probity of individual narrators.
4. Cf. Abū ʻUbayd, *Nāsikh*, 72.
5. ʻAbd al-Razzāq al-Ṣanʻānī, *Al-Muṣannaf*, ed. Ayman Naṣr al-Dīn al-Azharī (Beirut, 2000), 5:118. For variants of these reports given by Ibn Abī Shayba, see below.
6. For whom, see Ibn Ḥajar, *Tahdhīb*, 3:459–460. Al-Jazarī was originally from al-Yamāma and a client (*mawlā*) of the Banū Umayya. Ibn Jurayj, Mālik b. Anas, and Maʻmar were among those who transmitted from him. He was generally regarded as a reliable *ḥadīth* transmitter (*thiqa thābit*).
7. ʻAbd al-Razzāq, *Muṣannaf*, 5:118, #9334.
8. Ibid., 5:120.
9. Cf. al-Bukhārī, *Ṣaḥīḥ*, Kitāb al-ḥajj, 2:639, #1420.

10. 'Abd al-Razzāq, *Muṣannaf*, 5:183, #9641.
11. This *ḥadīth* is recorded by al-Bukhārī, Muslim, Abū Dā'ūd, and others; see A. J. Wensinck, *Concordance et indices de la traditions musulmane* (Leiden, 1988), 7:55.
12. Cf. *GAS*, 1:404; van Ess, *Theologie*, 1:111–113.
13. Sa'īd b. 'Abd al-'Azīz was a well-known Syrian scholar of his time, on a par with al-Awzā'ī, according to a number of sources, and although generally regarded as a *thiqa*, he was said to have mixed up his reports toward the end of his life; see Ibn Ḥajar, *Tahdhīb*, 2:325–326.
14. 'Abd al-Razzāq, *Muṣannaf*, 5:118–119, #9338.
15. Ibid., 5:119, #9341.
16. Ibid., 5:119–20, #9344. Cf. Abū 'Ubayd, *Nāsikh*, 72.
17. 'Abd al-Razzāq, *Muṣannaf*, 5:119, #9340.
18. Yaḥyā b. Sa'īd b. Ḥayyān Abū Ḥayyān al-Taymī was a pious Kufan scholar generally regarded as a *thiqa*. Muslim b. Ḥajjāj had a very high opinion of him (*kūfī min khiyār al-nās*) as did Sufyān al-Thawrī. Yaḥyā is described as inclined to night vigils and constant prayer; Ibn Ḥajar, *Tahdhīb*, 6:134.
19. Mottahedeh and al-Sayyid, "Idea of the Jihad," 26.
20. 'Abd al-Razzāq, *Muṣannaf*, 5:119, #9339.
21. Ibid., 5:119, #9342. Cf. Abū 'Ubayd, *Nāsikh*, 69–70.
22. 'Abd al-Razzāq, *Muṣannaf*, #9343.
23. Ibid., 5:120, #2499.
24. Ibid., 5:121, #2502. For Muslim b. Yasār, see Ibn Ḥajar, *Tahdhīb*, 5:416–417.
25. 'Abd al-Razzāq, *Muṣannaf*, 5:121, #2501 and #2503, respectively.
26. Cf. Cook, *Commanding Right*, 45, where he notes a similar "implicitly political" divide between Kufan and Syrian traditionists, based on the fact that Kufa was the primary site of provincial opposition to the Umayyads based in Syria. See also Afsaruddin, "The Excellences of the Qur'ān: Textual Sacrality and the Organization of Early Islamic Society," *Journal of the American Oriental Society* 122 (2002): 15–16.
27. 'Abd al-Razzāq, *Muṣannaf*, 5:189, #9673.
28. This is Kahmas b. al-Ḥasan al-Tamīmī Abū al-Ḥasan al-Baṣrī, regarded in general as a *thiqa* by Abū Da'ūd, Ibn Ḥibbān, Ibn Sa'd, and others, but deemed weak by Ibn Ma'īn; see Ibn Ḥajar, *Tahdhīb*, 4:576.
29. 'Abd al-Razzāq, *Muṣannaf*, 5:189, #9676.
30. The "impiety" of Umayyad rulers was not simply constructed out of whole cloth by later 'Abbasid historians, as has been suggested by some modern scholars. It is already a strong leitmotif in early reports of Umayyad provenance, such as those contained in 'Abd al-Razzāq's *Muṣannaf* and other works, and clearly reflects a contemporary perspective.
31. 'Abd al-Razzāq, *Muṣannaf*, 5:119, #9671.
32. Ibid., 5:189, #9675.
33. See *GAS*, 1:277; for a more extensive entry, see the art. "al-Sha'bī," EI^2, 9:162.

34. 'Abd al-Razzāq, *Muṣannaf*, 5:190, #9680. Variants are given in ibid., 5:190–191, #9681, #9682.
35. Ibid., 5:191, #9684.
36. According to the early historian al-Balādhurī (d. ca. 279/892), Mu'āwiya embarked upon a project to strengthen Syrian coastal defenses against Byzantine attacks and carried out both land and coastal campaigns against the Byzantines; see his *Futūḥ al-buldān*, ed. M. J. de Goeje (Leiden, 1866, repr. Leiden, 1968), 117. This represented a continuation of Mu'āwiya's policies from his time as governor of Syria; see also Julius Wellhausen, "Arab Wars with the Byzantines in the Umayyad Period," trans. M. Bonner, in *Arab-Byzantine Relations in Early Islamic Times*, ed. Michael Bonner (Aldershot, UK, 2004); Kennedy, *The Great Arab Conquests: How the Spread of Islam Changed the World We Live In* (Philadelphia, PA, 2007), 324–343. For a contemporary account of Mu'āwiya's shipbuilding activities, see Sebeos, *The Armenian History*, trans. R. W. Thompson (Liverpool, UK, 1994), 144.
37. Arabs in general did not want to move to the coastal areas, and therefore Mu'āwiya settled Persians (Furs) there instead, moving them from Baalbak, Ḥims, and Antioch; al-Balādhurī, *Futūḥ*, 117; Kennedy, *The Armies of the Caliphs* (London and New York, 2001) 12.
38. 'Abd al-Razzāq, *Muṣannaf*, 5:192, #9687.
39. See the reports in ibid., 5:192, #9686, #9688, # 9689, and #9690.
40. The *isnād* is 'Abd al-Razzāq reporting from 'Abd al-Quddūs from 'Alqama.
41. 'Abd al-Razzāq, *Muṣannaf*, 5:193–194, #9694.
42. The *isnād* is 'Abd al-Razzāq from Ma'mar from Zayd b. Aslam from 'Aṭā' b. Yasār.
43. For whom, see Ibn Ḥajar, *Tahdhīb*, 4:134. He was a freedman of Maymūna, the wife of the Prophet, and generally regarded as a *thiqa*.
44. 'Abd al-Razzāq, *Muṣannaf*, 5:172, #9594.
45. Ibid., 5:176, #9612.
46. Ibid., 5:177–178, #9619; other variants are given. One such variant, also attributed to al-Kalbī, describes the souls of martyrs assuming the shape of white birds; ibid., 5:177, #9616.
47. Ibid., 5:178, #9622.
48. See Ibn Ḥajar, *Tahdhīb*, 1:263.
49. Ibid., 1:263.
50. The full entry is given in ibid., 1:262–265.
51. Ibid., 1:324.
52. Ibid., 2:75–76.
53. Ibid., 5:508.
54. Cf. the art. "Ḥimṣ," EI^2, 3:397; Hugh Kennedy, *Armies of the Caliphs*, 31.
55. See the editor Ayman Naṣr al-Dīn al-Azharī's comment in 'Abd al-Razzāq, *Muṣannaf*, 5:178, note 7, where he notes that this report was also included by Ibn

Māja in his *Sunan* (see our discussion of this work in this chapter) and by Ibn Ḥanbal in his *Musnad*.

56. ʿAbd al-Razzāq, *Muṣannaf*, 5:171–172, #9593.
57. Ibid., 5:181, #9631.
58. Ibid., #9633.
59. Ibid., 5:180–181, #9629.
60. Ibid., 5:181–182, #9635.
61. Ibid., 5:183, #9638.
62. Ibid., 5:182–183, #9637.
63. Recorded in al-Bukhārī, *Ṣaḥīḥ*, 2:420–421. A variant of this *ḥadīth* attributed to Ibn Ḥafṣ is recorded by ʿAbd al-Razzāq, *Muṣannaf*, 5:183, #9639.
64. ʿAbd al-Razzāq, *Muṣannaf*, 5:192, #9685.
65. Cf. the art. "Ibn Abī Shayba," *EI*², 3:692.
66. Ibn Abī Shayba, *al-Kitāb al-muṣannaf fī 'l-aḥādīth wa-'l-āthār*, ed. Muḥammad ʿAbd al-Salām Shāhīn (Beirut, 1995), 4:207, #19296, #19297, #19298, and #19299.
67. Ibid., 4:207, #19301.
68. It is not clear which Abū Muʿāwiya this is.
69. Ibn Abī Shayba, *Muṣannaf*, 4:208, #19307; see also the variant report in ibid., 4:227, #19472.
70. See Ibn al-Jawzī, *Kitāb al-ḍuʿafāʾ wa-'l-matrūkīn*, ed. Abū 'l-Fidāʾ ʿAbd Allāh al-Qāḍī (Beirut, 1986), 2:30; Ibn Ḥajar, *Tahdhīb*, 2:446–448.
71. Ibn Abī Shayba, *Muṣannaf*, 4:208.
72. Ibid., 4:213.
73. Ibn Ḥajar, *Tahdhīb*, 6:166–167.
74. Cf. the art. "al-Awzāʿī," *EI*, 1:772.
75. In other Qur'anic occurrences of *ghurfa/ghuraf*, they are mentioned as rewards reserved in general for the pious believer, as in Qur'ān 29:58; 34:37; and 39:20.
76. Ibn Abī Shayba, *Muṣannaf*, 4:213–214.
77. Interestingly, this report uses the truncated form *sabīl* rather than *sabīl allāh*, as also occurs below in report #19352.
78. Ibn Abī Shayba, *Muṣannaf*, 4:217, #19383. The *isnād* is Yazīd b. Hārūn from Yaḥyā b. Sa'īd from Sa'īd from ʿAbd Allāh b. Abī Qatāda from his father.
79. See the extensive entry on him in Ibn Ḥajar, *Tahdhīb*, 6:78–82.
80. Ibn Abī Shayba, *Muṣannaf*, 4:214, #19351.
81. Ibid., 4:214, #19352.
82. Even though, as we saw in ʿAbd al-Razzāq's *Muṣannaf*, he is quoted in a number of reports as devaluing the combative *jihād* and emphasizing the usual pillars of Islam.
83. Abū Isḥāq al-Fazārī, *Kitāb al-siyar*, ed. Farūq Ḥamāda (Beirut, 1987), 137, #92, for example.
84. Ibn Abī Shayba, *Muṣannaf*, 4:224–225, #19446.
85. Ibid., 4:224, #19445.
86. Ibid., 4:225, #19450.
87. Ibn Ḥajar, *Tahdhīb*, 4:447–449.

88. Generally regarded as a *thiqa*, he is also said to have been particularly unreliable when relating reports that had chains of transmission containing the names of Sufyān al-Thawrī and other well-known scholars. He is further said to have transmitted unsubstantiated reports (*manākīr*) from unknown sources (*al-majāhīl*); cf. Ibn Ḥajar, *Tahdhīb*, 2:240–241.
89. Ibn Abī Shayba, *Muṣannaf*, 4:214, #19356.
90. Ibid., 4:225, #19447.
91. Ibid., 4:219, #19397.
92. Ibid., 4:231, #19501.
93. Ibid., 4:237, #19550.
94. Cf. Ibn Ḥajar, *Tahdhīb*, 5:47–48.
95. Ibn Abī Shayba, *Muṣannaf*, 4:237, #19551.
96. Ibid., 4:237, #19552.
97. Ibn Abī Shayba, *Muṣannaf*, 4:237, # 19553.
98. Ibid., 4:237, #19555.
99. I could not locate Yazīd b. Bishr in the usual sources.
100. Ibn Abī Shayba, *Muṣannaf*, 4:237, #19556.
101. Ibid., 4:237, #19557.
102. See Ibn Ḥajar, *Tahdhīb*, 1:462. Ḥātim b. Wardān b. Marwān al-Saʿdī, known as Abū Ṣāliḥ al-Baṣrī, served as *imām* of the mosque of Ayyūb and appears to have been generally regarded as a *thiqa*.
103. Ibid., 6:271–272. Ibn Ḥibbān regarded him as someone who made mistakes in his transmissions.
104. Ibn Abī Shayba, *Muṣannaf*, 4:226, #19459.
105. Burd b. Sinān al-Shāmī was a *mawlā* of the Quraysh; originally from Damascus, he settled in Basra. He was a frequent transmitter of reports from Makḥūl, along with Zayd b. Wāqid; al-Awzāʿī was one of his principal transmitters. Although a majority considered Burd to be generally acceptable (*sadūq*; *lā ba's bihi*) despite being a Qādirī, al-Dārimī citing ʿAlī b. Madā'inī considered him to be weak, and Abū Ḥātim described him as "not strong" (*laysa bi 'l-matīn*); Ibn Ḥajar, *Tahdhīb*, 1:328–329.
106. Ibn Abī Shayba, *Muṣannaf*, 4:226, #19460.
107. See above at note 46.
108. See Ibn Ḥajar, *Tahdhīb*, 3:271–272, where he is given a highly favorable assessment by leading *ḥādīth* scholars.
109. Ibn Abī Shayba, *Muṣannaf*, 4:227, #19466.
110. Ibid., 4:227, #19467. For variants, see ibid., #19468, #19469.
111. Ibid., 4:227, #19470.
112. For whom, see Ibn Ḥajar, *Tahdhīb*, 3:504.
113. Ibn Abī Shayba, *Muṣannaf*, 4:227, #19471.
114. Cf. Ibn Ḥajar, *Tahdhīb*, 2:74–75. His reputation is very mixed; although al-Bukhārī and Muslim narrated from him, others like Abū Ḥātim and al-Azdī considered his *ḥadīths* unacceptable (*manākīr*).

115. This is ʿAlī b. Ṣāliḥ b. Ṣāliḥ b. Ḥayy al-Hamdānī, a Kufan transmitter, generally regarded as a *thiqa*, although Ibn Maʿīn is said to have regarded him as weak; cf. ibid., 4:200–201.
116. Ibn Abī Shayba, *Muṣannaf*, 4:237, #19559.
117. Cf. Ibn Ḥajar, *Tahdhīb*, 6:30–31. His full name is Hishām b. Abī ʿAbd Allāh al-Dastawayh, also known as Abū Bakr al-Baṣrī, who is described in glowing terms by Abū Dāʾūd al-Ṭayālisī as "the *amīr al-muʾminīn* of *ḥadīth*." Both al-Dastawayh and al-Awzāʿī were frequent transmitters from Yaḥyā b. Abī Kathīr.
118. He is ʿĀmir b. ʿUqba, also known as Ibn ʿAbd Allāh al-ʿUqaylī, who transmitted primarily from his father and from Abū Hurayra and was considered to be a *thiqa* by Ibn Ḥibbān; cf. Ibn Ḥajar, *Tahdhīb*, 3:53.
119. Ibn Abī Shayba, *Muṣannaf*, 4:236–237, #19549.
120. Al-Bukhārī, *Ṣaḥīḥ*, 4:406.
121. Ibid., 4:474.
122. Ibid., 4:407–408.
123. Ibid., 4:440.
124. Ibid., 4:441; a variant is listed in ibid., 4:408.
125. Ibid., 4:494.
126. Ibid., 4:499.
127. Thus, in the *Kitāb al-riqāq* of his collection, al-Bukhārī records a *ḥadīth* in which *ṣabr* is described as the "best" and "most abundant" of rewards conferred by God; see his *Ṣaḥīḥ*, 7:471, #1335.
128. This *ḥadīth* is very similar to the one recorded by Mālik b. Anas in his *al-Muwaṭṭaʾ*, ed. Bashshār ʿAwad Maʿrūf and Maḥmūd Muḥammad Khalīl (Beirut, 1993), 1:366–367.
129. Al-Bukhārī, *Ṣaḥīḥ*, 4:420–421.
130. Ibid., 4:409.
131. *Shuhadāʾ* here could of course mean "witnesses," but in this context, "military martyrs" seems to be intended.
132. Al-Bukhārī, *Ṣaḥīḥ*, 4:409.
133. See note 116 above.
134. Al-Bukhārī, *Ṣaḥīḥ*, 4:410.
135. Ibid., 4:412.
136. Ibid., 4:414.
137. Ibid., 4:481–482. Two more variants are given; one is also on the authority of ʿAbd Allāh b. Abī Awfā while the other is attributed to Abū Hurayra.
138. Muslim, *Ṣaḥīḥ* (Beirut, 1995), 3:1095–1096, #19, #20.
139. Ibid., 3:1097, #24, #25.
140. Ibid., 3:1139, #137; 3:1150, #140, where the reference is specifically to "the children of polytheists."
141. Ibid., 3:1097–1098, #26, #27, #28.

142. Ibid., 3:1188, #103, #106.
143. Ibid., 3:1191–1192, #112–115.
144. Ibid., 3:1189, #105, #106.
145. Ibid., 3:1190, #108, #109.
146. Ibid., 3:1192–1193, #117, #119, #120.
147. Ibid., 3:1195, #125.
148. Ibid., 3:1205–1207, #160–162.
149. Ibid., 3:1194, #123; for variants, see #122, #124.
150. Ibid., 3:1193–1194, #121.
151. Ibid., 3:1199–1201, #143–48.
152. Ibid., 3:1202, #149, #150, #151.
153. Ibid., 3:1210, #170–177.
154. Ibid., 3:1202–1203, #152. For the importance of correct intention in general, see ibid., 3:1204, #155.
155. Ibid., 3:1205, #158.
156. Ibid., #159.
157. Ibid., 3:1199, #141, #142.
158. Ibid., 3:1204–1205, #157.
159. Ibid., 3:1204, #156.
160. Ibid., 3:1207, #164.
161. Ibid., 3:1207–1208, #165. Cf. also ibid., #166.
162. Ibn Māja, *al-Sunan*, ed. Muḥammad Nāsir al-Dīn al-Albānī (Riyad, 1998), 3:115–177.
163. Ibid., 3:141–142.
164. Ibid., 3:137–138.
165. Ibid., 3:126–127.
166. Ibid., 3:124. The *isnād* ʿĪsā b. Yūnus al-Ramlī from Muḥamamd b. Shuʿayb b. Shābūr from Saʿīd b. Khālid b. Abī al-Ṭawīl who said that he heard Anas b. Malik say that he heard the statement from the Prophet—this formulation, as highlighted, characterizes this *ḥadīth* as *mudallas*—is highly problematic for more punctilious critics. The editor points out that this *ḥadīth* is considered *ḍaʿīf*. For variants, see ibid., 3:121–122; 122–123; 124.
167. Ibid., 3:119.
168. Ibid., 3:128.
169. Ibid., 3:127–128. According to the editor, al-Būṣīrī considered the *isnād* weak, particularly due to the presence of Muʿāwiya b. Yaḥyā and his teacher Layth b. Abī Sulaym.
170. Ibid., 3:132–135.
171. Ibid., 3:135; for other variants from different narrators, see ibid., 3:132–133.
172. Ibid., 3:144–146.
173. Ibid., 3:145.
174. Ibid., 3:146.

175. Abū Dā'ūd, *Ṣaḥīḥ Sunan Abī Dā'ūd*, ed. Muḥammad Nāṣir al-Dīn al-Albānī (Riyadh, 1989), 2:470–536.
176. Al-Tirmidhī, *al-Jāmi' al- Ṣaḥīḥ*, ed. Kamāl Yūsuf al-Ḥūt (Beirut, n.d.), 4:101–140.
177. Ibid., 4:141–163.
178. Ibid., 4:164–188.
179. Ibid., 4:151, #1632.
180. Ibid., 4:152, #1633.
181. Al-Nasā'ī, *Ṣaḥīḥ Sunan al-Nasā'ī*, ed. Nāṣir al-Dīn al-Albānī (Beirut, 1988), 2:646–672.
182. Ibid., 2:665, #2965.
183. Ibid., #2964.
184. For a biography, see, for example, Ibn Ḥajar, *Tahdhīb*, 4:109.
185. Ibid., #2966.
186. Ibid., 2:668–669, #2976.
187. Ibid., 2:668, #2975. Other reports advocating the merits of fighting in India are grouped under the caption *Ghazwat al-hind*.
188. See the lengthy assessment of him in Ibn Ḥajar, *Tahdhīb*, 1:357–359.

CHAPTER 6

1. For a brief biography, see EI^2, 3:879. For an analysis of Ibn al-Mubārak's *Kitāb al-jihād*, see Michael Bonner, "Some Observations concerning the Early Development of Jihad on the Arab-Byzantine Frontier," *Studia Islamica* 75 (1992), 19–31, as well as his *Aristocratic Violence*, 119–125.
2. Ibn al-Mubārak, *Kitāb al-jihād* (Beirut, 1988), 19, #10.
3. Ibid., 29, #37.
4. Ibid., 65, #127.
5. Ibid., 40, #70.
6. Ibid., #71.
7. The religious propaganda waged by the Umayyads on their behalf is established by Wadad al-Qadi, "The Religious Foundation of Late Umayyad Ideology and Practice," in *Saber religioso y poder político en el Islam*, ed. Manuela Marin (Madrid, 1994), 231–273. Sulaymān's father, 'Abd al-Malik b. Marwān (d. 86/705), the fifth Umayyad caliph, was particularly proactive in establishing Islamicizing credentials for his dynasty; see Robert Hoyland, "New Documentary Texts and the Early Islamic State," *Bulletin of the School of Oriental and African Studies* 69 (2006):395–416; and Donner, *Muhammad and the Believers*, esp. chapter 5.
8. Ibn al-Mubārak, *Kitāb al-jihād*, 40, #73.
9. Ibid., 85, #165.
10. For whom, see further M. Muranyi, "Das *Kitāb al-Siyar* von Abū Isḥāq al-Fazārī," *Jerusalem Studies in Arabic and Islam* 6 (1985):67–70; Bonner, "Some Observations," 9–19.
11. Ibn al-Mubārak, *Kitāb al-jihād*, #166.

12. Ibid., 87, #170.
13. Ibid., #171. See also ibid., 89, # 177, where the Prophet counsels former pagans to perform *ribāṭ* and win redemption.
14. Shuraḥbīl b. al-Samaṭ narrated from the Prophet, but his status as a Companion has been doubted; see Ibn Ḥajar, *Tahdhīb*, 2:484–485.
15. Ibn al-Mubārak, *Kitāb al-jihād*, 87, #172.
16. Ibid., 88, #174.
17. When Fuḍāla died, Mu'āwiya was among those who carried his bier; see Ibn Ḥajar, *Tahdhīb*, 4:467.
18. Cf. Muslim, *Saḥīḥ*, 3:1016, #14.
19. Ibn al-Mubārak, *Kitāb al-jihād*, 90, #179–182; cf. also ibid., #181, #182.
20. Cf. Ibn Ḥajar, *Tahdhīb*, 4:148–149.
21. Cf. Ibn al-Mubārak, *Kitāb al-jihād*, 35, #54–56.
22. Ibid., 95–96, #196.
23. See chapter 5, note 36.
24. For whom, see, for example, *GAS*, 1:284–285. Abū 'l-Aswad's *maghāzī* work survives in fragmentary form in Ibn Ḥajar's *Iṣāba*, and he is generally regarded as a *thiqa*.
25. Ibn al-Mubārak, *Kitāb al-jihād*, 97, #199.
26. Ibid., 99, #205.
27. Ibid., 40, #68.
28. Ibid., #69.
29. Ibid., 66, #129.
30. Ibid., 96, #198.
31. See *GAS*, 1:522.
32. Ibn Abī 'Āṣim, *Kitāb al-jihād*, ed. Abū 'Abd al-Raḥmān (Damascus, 1989), 1:152, #14.
33. 'Aṭā' b. Yazīd al-Laythī was generally regarded as a *thiqa*; see Ibn Ḥajar, *Tahdhīb*, 4:133–134.
34. Ibn Abī 'Āṣim, *Kitāb al-jihād*, 1:191, #35; the editor's list of the occurrence of this *ḥadīth* in other compilations is on the same page. Variants of this *ḥadīth* are given in ibid., 1:192, #36–37.
35. He is Aḥmad b. 'Abd al-Wahhāb b. Najda al-Ḥawṭī Abū 'Abd Allāh al-Shāmī in the sources; cf. Ibn Ḥajar, *Tahdhīb*, 1:105.
36. See our previous discussion of him in chapter 5.
37. Ibn Abī 'Āṣim, *Kitāb al-jihād*, 1:133, #5. Other variants of this *ḥadīth* are recorded in ibid., 1:134–136.
38. Cf. Ibn Ḥajar, *Tahdhīb*, 6:295–296. His full name is given as Abū Bakr b. 'Abd Allāh b. Abī Maryam al-Ghassānī al-Shāmī.
39. Ibn Abī 'Āṣim, *Kitāb al-jihād*, 1:153. A variant of this *ḥadīth* is listed in ibid., 1:155 with a different *isnād*.
40. See the entry on him in Ibn Ḥajar, *Tahdhīb*, 4:237–238. 'Alī b. Yazīd b. Abī Ziyād al-Alhānī was from Damascus and related reports from Makḥūl the Syrian besides al-Qāsim.

41. See Ibn Ḥajar, *Tahdhīb*, 4:500–501.
42. Ibn Abī ʿĀṣim, *Kitāb al-jihād*, 1:182, #29. This is a widely attested *ḥadīth*, included by ʿAbd al-Razzaq in his early *Muṣannaf*, by al-Bukhārī in his *Saḥīḥ*, and by al-Nasāʾī in his *Sunan* under *jihād*, among others.
43. Ibid., 1:183, #30 and #31, respectively. The editor notes that both *isnāds* are rather problematic.
44. Ibid., 1:240–241, #69.
45. Cf. Ibn Ḥajar, *Tahdhīb*, 2:549–550.
46. He was one of the *ahl al-ṣuffa* who settled in Ḥimṣ, known by the *kunya* of Abū Najīḥ; see Ibn Ḥajar, *Tahdhīb*, 4:109.
47. Ibn Abī ʿĀṣim, *Kitāb al-jihād*, 2:680, #296. Two variants with different *isnāds* are given in ibid., 2:681, #297; 2:684, #298.
48. Ibid., 2:689–690, #303.
49. See the editor's discussion in ibid., 2:690.
50. Variants of such hortatory reports with different *isnāds* are given in ibid., 2:692, #304; 2:700, #309; 2:704, #312; 2:706, #314; 2:709, #317; such reports testify to the promotion of what we may call statist *jihād* ideology starting in the Umayyad period and continuing into subsequent periods. Khalid Yahya Blankinship emphasizes this in his *The End of the Jihad State: The Reign of Hishām Ibn ʿAbd al-Malik and the Collapse of the Umayyads* (New York, 1994), esp. 11–19. Blankinship, however, overstates this position when he traces the pedigree of the Umayyad *jihād* ideology back to the Qurʾān and the Prophet's time, leading him to remark that "In general, the impression of the *jihād* that one gets from the Qurʾān and the *ḥadīth* is of a highly motivated mass ideology directed toward a single goal" (ibid., 15)—thereby anachronistically reading back into key Qurʾanic verses that deal with fighting the genesis of later Umayyad state ideology. Such views, however, are fairly standard in modern historical studies produced by rigorous scholars; Hugh Kennedy, for example, already discerns "an ideology of conquest" during Muḥammad's lifetime in his highly readable *The Great Arab Conquests*, 51; as do Carole Hillenbrand in *The Crusades: Islamic Perspectives* (New York, 2000), 92–97; Rudolph Peters, *Jihad in Classical and Modern Islam* (Princeton, 1996), 3; Donner in *The Early Islamic Conquests*, 87–90, and more recently in his *Muhammad and the Believers*, 87–89. It is understandable why these views predominate in the literature; Muslim historians themselves from at least al-Ṭabarī onward have presented the early conquests as religiously motivated, and many Muslim jurists from al-Shāfiʿī onward have held that offensive military *jihād* against non-Muslims to spread at least Islamic rule is mandated by religious texts. In less responsible hands, this perspective can deteriorate into unprincipled invective—see, for example, Paul Fregosi, *Jihad in the West: Muslim Conquests from the 7th to the 21st centuries* (Amherst, NY, 1998)—and lead to a rather skewed and monolithic account of Islamic political history; cf. Efraim Karsh, *Islamic Imperialism: A History* (New Haven, CT, 2006).
51. Ibn Abī ʿĀṣim, *Kitāb al-jihād*, 2:693, #305.

52. Ibid., 2:694.
53. Cf. Ibn Ḥajar, *Tahdhīb*, 4:347–348.
54. Ibn Abī ʿĀṣim, *Jihād*, 2:697, #307.
55. For this discussion, see ibid., 2:697.
56. Ibid., 2:498–499.
57. Ibn Ḥajar gives his name as Zayd b. al-Ḥabāb b. al-Rayyān; see his *Tahdhīb*, 2:240–241, where he is identified as a Kufan transmitter with a mixed reputation.
58. For this discussion, see Ibn Abī ʿĀṣim, *Jihād*, 2:496–497.
59. See *GAS*, 1:32. For Saʿīd b. Jubayr, who had been a student of Ibn ʿAbbās and ʿAbd Allāh b. ʿUmar, see ibid., 1:28–29.
60. It is important to note here that there was no single Umayyad army as such, but a number of different armies at different times, as Hugh Kennedy points out. The Syrian army, the *ahl al-shām*, was the most important, but there were also the armies of Basra, Kufa, and Khorasan, which retained their separate identities. Around 80/700, there were probably about 300,000 fighting men (*muqātila*) in these combined armies; see Kennedy, *Armies of the Caliphs*, 18–21.
61. Ibn Abī ʿĀṣim, *Jihād*, 2:501.
62. The editor points out that this *ḥadīth* is found in less well-known collections like al-Ṭabarānī's *al-Muʿjam al-kabīr* and al-Ḥākim's *al-Mustadrak*; ibid.
63. Ibn Abī ʿĀṣim, *Jihād*, 2:576; also recorded in ibid., 1:223.
64. As noted by the editor in ibid., 1:222.
65. Ibid., 2:566.
66. See editor's discussion of this *ḥadīth* in ibid., 2:566–567.
67. Ibid., 1:139.
68. See editor's copious attestation in ibid., 1:139–140.
69. Ibid., 1:280.
70. Cf. Ibn Ḥajar, *Tahdhīb*, 2:10–12.
71. Ibid., 2:125–126.
72. See the brief entry on him in *EI*², 3:694. The comment there that "none of his works seems to have survived" will now have to be revised.
73. Muḥammad b. ʿAbd Allāh b. Abī Zamanīn, *Kitāb qudwat al-ghāzī*, ed. ʿĀʾisha al-Sulaymānī (Beirut, 1989), 141–142, #7.
74. Ibid., 140, #4.
75. Ibid., 144, #9. A variant of this *ḥadīth* occurs in ibid., 144–145, #11.
76. See Ibn Ḥajar, *Tahdhīb*, 4:131–132.
77. Ibn Abī Zamanīn, *Qudwat al-ghāzī*, 164, #42.
78. See editor's note, ibid., n. 2.
79. Ibid., 247, and n. 2.
80. See Frank P. Trombley, "The Arabs in Anatolia and the Islamic Law of War (*fiqh al-jihād*) Seventh–Tenth Centuries," *Al-Masāq* 16 (2004):151–61.
81. The rise of a sophisticated system of *ḥadīth* criticism and standardized *ḥadīth* collections and the overall institutionalization of learning did not lead to a closed

canon of *ḥadīth*, so to speak. As Stephen Humphreys has remarked, "There came to be a stable core, defined by the *Ṣaḥīḥayn* or (more fuzzily) by the Six Books, but outside these limits the corpus of *ḥadīth* in circulation seems to have been remarkably plastic"; see his "Borrowed Lives: The Reproduction of Texts in Islamic Cultures," in *Text and Context in Islamic Societies*, ed. Irene A. Bierman (Reading, PA, 2004), 73.

82. Ibn Abī Zamanīn, *Qudwat al-ghāzī*, 223.
83. Al-Balādhurī, *Futūḥ*, 189; Theophanes, 422; cited by Michael Bonner, *Aristocratic Violence*, 58, n. 94.
84. Ibn Abī Zamanīn, *Qudwat al-ghāzī*, 224–225, #93.
85. See Ibn Ḥajar, *Tahdhīb*, 1:226.
86. Ibn Abī Zamanīn, *Qudwat al-ghāzī*, 1:402–404.
87. For the editor's useful assessment of these narrators, see ibid., 224.
88. Ibid., 227–228, #96.
89. See our previous discussion of him in chapter 5, 232.
90. Muḥammad b. Muslim b. 'Ubayd Allāh b. 'Abd Allāh b. Shihāb al-Zuhrī, the famous Medinan traditionist and historian, is said to have been the first to use *isnād*s in his *ḥadīth*s and the first to record *ḥadīth*s at the behest of 'Umar b. 'Abd al-'Azīz. He was very close to several other Umayyad rulers from the time of 'Abd al-Malik b. Marwān to Hishām, officiating at different periods as *qāḍī*, tax collector, and police chief. His *ḥadīth* dictation sessions were attended by Umayyad officials, such as Shu'ayb b. Dīnār, who is said to have learned about 1,700 of al-Zuhrī's reports, and by Ibn Abī Ḥamza al-Ḥimṣī (d. 162/778–779), a *mawlā* of the Umayyads and a scribe of Hiṣḥām. Al-Zuhrī reportedly accused Iraqi scholars of tampering with his *ḥadīth*s and adding to them—details that raise concerns about the reliable transmission of his reports; cf. *GAS*, 1:280–283; art. "al-Zuhrī," *EI*², 11:565–566. For more details, see M. Lecker, "Biographical notes on Ibn Shihāb al-Zuhrī," *Journal of Semitic Studies* 41 (1996): 21–63; for his *fiqh*, see H. Motzki, *Der Fiqh des Zuhri: die Quellenproblematik*, in *Der Islam* 48 (1991):1–44.
91. See the editor's useful discussion of the reliability of these transmitters in Ibn Abī Zamanīn, *Qudwat al-ghāzī*, 228–229, nn. 4–6.
92. Ibid., 226–227, #95.
93. See editor's comments in ibid, 152, n. 1.
94. For an account of some of the discussions centered on the identity of the *qurrā*, see the art. "Ḳurrā'," *EI*², 5:499.
95. See my article, "Excellences of the Qur'an," 1–24.
96. Ibn Abī Zamanīn, *Qudwat al-ghāzī*, 225–226.
97. Ibid., 225, n. 3.
98. Ibid., 225–226, n. 4.
99. Ibid., 231–232, #100.
100. Ibid., 232–233, #101.

101. See the editor's comments, ibid., 232, n. 4.; also Lucas, *Constructive Critics,* 293.
102. Ibn Abī Zamanīn, *Qudwat al-ghāzī,* 228–229.
103. 'Abd al-Quddūs' reputation is better than those of the other two; he was generally regarded as *ṣadūq* ("truthful"); cf. Ibn Ḥajar, *Tahdhīb,* 3:457.
104. Earlier reports emanating from the Umayyad period could be put to effective use in the 'Abbasid period, when war against Byzantium also became one of the main concerns of the 'Abbasid state, starting with the reign of al-Mahdi (158–169/775–785) and peaking during the reign of Hārūn al-Rashīd (170–193/786–809). Michael Bonner describes Hārūn al-Rashīd as the first "Ghāzī-Caliph" because of his frequent campaigns against Byzantium, the motives for which have been interpreted variously by different historians; see this discussion in his *Aristocratic Violence,* 99–106; also id., "Some Observations," 30–31. For accounts of these early 'Abbasid skirmishes with the Byzantines, see, for example, C. Edmund Bosworth, "Byzantium and Syrian Frontier in the early 'Abbasid Period," in *Proceedings of the Fifth International Conference on the History of Bilād al-Shām, Amman 1410/1990,* ed. M. A. al-Bakhit and R. Schick (Amman, 1991).
105. See the art. "al-Sulamī," *EI*[2], 9:182.
106. 'Izz al-Dīn 'Abd al-'Azīz b. 'Abd al-Salām al-Sulamī, *Aḥkām al-jihād wa-faḍā'ilihi,* ed. 'Iyāḍ Khālid al-Ṭābba' (Beirut, 1996), 18.
107. Ibid., 27.
108. Previously discussed in chapter 3.
109. Al-Sulamī, *Aḥkām al-jihād,* 28–29.
110. Ibid., 30.
111. Ibid., 30–60, for the full range of these reports.
112. Ibid., 46–47.
113. Ibid., 61.
114. Ibid., 61–63.
115. Ibid., 65.
116. Ibid., 66.
117. Ibid., 67.
118. Ibid., 69.
119. Ibid., 60–61.
120. For a useful overview of his life and works, see the art. "Ibn Kathīr," *EI*[2], 3:817.
121. Ibn Kathīr, *Kitāb al-ijtihād fī ṭalab al-jihād,* ed. 'Abd Allāh 'Abd al-Raḥīm 'Asilan (Riyadh, 1985), 61.
122. Ibid., 68.
123. Ibid., 69. For other *ḥadīths* and reports, see further ibid., 69–72.
124. Ibid., 73 ff.
125. Ibid., 77.
126. Ibid., 82.

127. Ibid., 83 ff.
128. Ibid., 89–90.
129. Ibid., 96–98.
130. Ahmad b. Ibrāhīm Ibn Naḥḥās, *Mashāri' al-ashwāq ilā maṣāri' al-'ushshāq wa-muthīr al-gharām ilā dār al-salām* (Beirut, 2002), 1:79–82. For an extensive literary analysis of this work, see Maher Jarrar, "*Maṣāri' al-'ushshāq*: dirāsa fī aḥādīth al-jihād wa-'l-ḥūr al-'ayn: nash'atuhā wa-bunyatuhā al-ḥikā'iyya wa-waẓā'ifuhā," *al-Abḥāth* 41 (1993):27–121.
131. Ibn Naḥḥās, *Mashāri' al-ashwāq*, 1:82–98.
132. Ibid., 1:98–99.
133. Ibid., 1:101.
134. Ibid., 1:134–137.
135. Ibid., 1:138–140.
136. Ibid., 1:141–151.
137. Ibid. 1:204 ff.
138. Ibid., 1:204–205.
139. Ibid., 1:244.
140. Ibid., 1:270 ff.
141. Ibid., 1:303 ff.
142. Ibid., 1:357.
143. Ibid., 1:452–460.
144. Ibid., 1:465 ff.
145. Ibid., 1:494–501.
146. Ibid., 1:434–436.
147. Ibid., 1:504.
148. Ibid., 1:526.
149. Ibid., 1:526–528.
150. See Ibn Ḥajar, *Tahdhīb*, 4:509.
151. Ibn Naḥḥās, *Mashāri' al-ashwāq*, 2:657.
152. Ibid., 2:658.
153. Ibid., 2:1019 ff.
154. Ibid., 2:1224.
155. Ibid., 2:1022 ff.
156. Ibid., 2:1081.
157. Ibid., 2:1083–1086.
158. Ibid., 2:1086–1089.

CHAPTER 7

1. For discussions of the practice of this attribute during the Jāhiliyya, see H. Ringgren, "The Concept of Ṣabr in the pre-Islamic Poetry and in the Qur'an," in *Islamic Culture* 26/1 (1952):75–90; Izutsu, *Ethico-Religious Concepts*, 101–104.
2. Muqātil, *Tafsīr*, 3:672.

3. Hūd b. Muḥakkam, *Tafsīr*, 4:34.
4. The verse states in Arabic: *wa-man ʿamila ṣāliḥan min dhakar aw unthā wa-huwa muʾmin fa-ʾūlāʾika yadkhulūn al-janna yurzaqūn fīhā bi-ghayr ḥisāb.*
5. Al-ʿAyyāshī, *al-Mustadrak*, 3:149.
6. As quoted by al-Ṭabarī, *Jāmiʿ*, 10:622.
7. Ibid.; cf. al-Suddī, *Tafsīr*, 417.
8. Al-Wāḥidī, *Wasīṭ*, 3:574.
9. Al-Zamakhsharī, *Tafsīr*, 5:294.
10. Ibid.
11. Al-Rāzī, *Tafsīr*, 9:430–431.
12. Ibid., 9:431.
13. Al-Qurṭubī, *Jāmiʿ*, 15:211.
14. Ibid., 15:211–212.
15. Ibid., 15:212.
16. Although the sixteenth chapter (al-Naḥl) on the whole is deemed a late Meccan revelation.
17. Hūd b. Muḥakkam, *Tafsīr*, 2:391.
18. Muqātil, *Tafsīr*, 2:489.
19. Al-Qummi, *Tafsīr*, 1:393.
20. Al-Ṭabarī, *Jāmiʿ*, 7:653.
21. Ibid.
22. Ibid., 7:653–654.
23. Al-Wāḥidī, *Wasīṭ*, 3:87.
24. Al-Zamakhsharī, *Kashshāf*, 3:477.
25. Al-Rāzī, *Tafsīr*, 7:277.
26. Al-Qurṭubī, *Jāmiʿ*, 10:170–171.
27. The third chapter is generally dated to the third or fourth year after the *hijra*.
28. Muqātil, *Tafsīr*, 1:304.
29. Hūd b. Muḥakkam, *Tafsīr*, 1:317–318.
30. Al-Ṭabarī, *Jāmiʿ*, 3:452–453.
31. Ibid.
32. Al-Wāḥidī, *Wasīṭ*, 1:498.
33. Al-Zamkhsharī, *Kashshāf*, 1:634.
34. Al-Rāzī, *Tafsīr*, 3:375.
35. This is most certainly Abū ʿAmr al-Furātī from the fifth/eleventh century, whose *tafsīr* was used by al-Thaʿlabī; cf. van Ess, *Theologie*, 3: 91–92.
36. Al-Rāzī, *Tafsīr*, 3:375.
37. Al-Qurṭubī, *Jāmiʿ*, 4:216–217.
38. The *faḍāʾil* literature was prolific in the medieval period. Works of praise were composed about many meritorious activities and religious duties, in addition to prominent people and places. For a brief introduction to this genre, see Afsaruddin, *Excellence and Precedence*, 26–35, and references cited therein.

39. Cf. art. "Ibn Abī 'l-Dunyā," *EI*[2], 3:684.
40. See Ibn Abī 'l-Dunyā, *Al-Ṣabr wa-'l-thawāb 'alayhi* (Beirut, 1997), 24.
41. Ḥawshab b. Muslim al-Thaqafī was a close companion of al-Ḥasan al-Baṣrī and transmitted reports from him; cf. Ibn Ḥajar, *Tahdhīb*, 2:43.
42. Ibn Abī 'l-Dunyā, *Ṣabr*, 26.
43. Ibid., 86.
44. For whom, see Ibn Ḥajar, *Tahdhīb*, 5:126–127, generally regarded as a *thiqa*. Ibn Ḥibbān described him as "one of the pietists (*min ahl al-'ibāda*), [characterized by] virtue, religiosity, and generosity."
45. Ibn Abī 'l-Dunyā, *Ṣabr*, 87. The literary genre known as *al-Faraj ba'd al-shidda* emphasizes this point.
46. The debate over political and social quietism versus sociopolitical activism/engagement is rather encoded in the debates over free will versus predetermination, as has already been suggested by others: for example, Montgomery Watt, *Free Will and Predestination in Early Islam* (London, 1948); and the more recent article by Richard M. Frank, "Two Islamic Views of Human Agency," in *Classical Islamic Theology: The Ash'arites*, ed. Dimitri Gutas (Aldershot, UK, 2008).
47. Ibn Abī 'l-Dunyā, *Ṣabr*, 59. A variant from Sa'īd b. 'Abd al-'Azīz is given in ibid., 64.
48. Ibid., 61.
49. Ibid., 17.
50. Ibid., 23. As the editor of this work points out (note 2), in some versions of this *ḥadīth*, *ahl al-ṣabr* is replaced by *ahl al-faḍl*. The text is considered *gharīb*, and the *isnād* weak because of the presence of the Kufan Muḥammad b. 'Ubayd Allāh al-Fazārī (d. 155/771), who is generally described as untrustworthy in his transmissions; cf. Ibn Ḥajar, *Tahdhīb*, 5:193–194.
51. Ibn Abī 'l-Dunyā, *Ṣabr*, 116.
52. Ibid., 84–85.
53. Reports such as this belie Reuven Firestone's statement to the effect that there is virtually no evidence of dissenting traditions challenging the predominantly militaristic interpretation of *jihād* (and thus of martyrdom) by the third/ninth century; see his *Jihād*, 100.
54. This is very likely 'Abd al-Malik b. Ḥabīb al-Azdī (d. 123/740), also known as Abū 'Imrān al-Jūnī, a scholar from Basra who was generally regarded as a *thiqa*; cf. Ibn Ḥajar, *Tahdhīb*, 3:468.
55. Ibn Abī 'l-Dunyā, *Ṣabr*, 85.
56. Ibid., 51.
57. See Wensinck, *Concordance*, 2:165.
58. His real name was Lāḥiq b. Ḥumayd al-Baṣrī..
59. 'Abd al-Razzāq, *Muṣannaf*, 5:175.
60. Ibn Abī 'l-Dunyā, *Ṣabr*, 31.
61. For a comprehensive study of al-Ghazālī's life and thought, see the recent reprint of the still useful study by Montgomery Watt, *The Faith and Practice of al-Ghazālī* (Oxford, UK, 2000); cf. also the art. "Ghazālī," *EI*[2], 2:1038.

62. Al-Ghazālī, *Iḥyā' 'ulūm al-dīn*, ed. 'Abd Allāh al-Khālidī (Beirut, n.d.), 4:84. We are only focusing on the attribute of *ṣabr* in our discussion here.
63. Ibid.
64. As the editor of the *Iḥyā'* helpfully points out, this *ḥadīth* is recorded by Abū Nu'aym and al-Khaṭīb al-Baghdādī, among others, on the authority of Ibn Mas'ūd.
65. Al-Ghazālī, *Iḥyā'*, 4:84–85.
66. Ibid., 4:86.
67. Ibid.
68. Ibid.
69. Ibid., 4:87.
70. Ibid., 4:94–95. As the editor points out, this *ḥadīth* related by Ibn 'Abbās is recorded by Aḥmad b. Ḥanbal and al-Tirmidhī.
71. Ibid., 4:98.
72. Variants of this report occur in earlier *ḥadīth* compilations. According to the editor al-Khālidī, al-Bukhārī records the following *ḥadīth* from 'Abd Allāh b. 'Umar: "The Muslim is one from whose tongue and hand [other] Muslims are safe, and the Emigrant is one who has emigrated from what God has forbidden." Variants are given by Ibn Māja and Abū Dā'ūd. Aḥmad b. Ḥanbal records a *ḥadīth* from Fuḍāla b. 'Ubayda in which the Prophet says, "The striver (*al-mujāhid*) is the one who fights his self for [the sake of] God or speaks [the truth] concerning God the Exalted." A variant is given by al-Tirmidhī; see editor's notes in ibid.
73. Al-Ghazālī, *Iḥyā'*, 4:100.
74. Al-Ghazālī refers to Jesus throughout the *Iḥyā'* and in his other mystical writings, which influenced later Sufis like Jalāl al-Dīn al-Rūmī; see this discussion in S. M. Zwemer, "Jesus Christ in the Ihya of al-Ghazali," *The Muslim World* 7 (1917): 144–158.
75. Al-Ghazālī, *Iḥyā'*, 4:100.
76. In his work on Shāfi'ī jurisprudence, *al-Wajīz fī fiqh al-imām al-shāfi'ī*, al-Ghazālī discusses the military *jihād* as one of the duties of the ruler.
77. Cf. *EI*^{2}, 3:821.
78. Ibn Qayyim al-Jawziyya, *'Uddat al-ṣābirīn wa-dhakhīrat al-shākirīn*, ed. Muḥammad 'Alī Quṭb (Beirut, n.d.), 14.
79. Ibid., 25–26.
80. Ibid., 14–15.
81. Ibid., 16.
82. Ibid., 28–29.
83. Ibid., 24.
84. Ibid., 30.
85. Ibid., 30–31.
86. Ibid., 66
87. Ibid., 66–80.

88. Cf. Ibn Ḥajar, *Tahdhīb*, 5:575–576. An example of Ibn Mihrān's piety is included in this entry; he is said to have completed seventeen thousand *rak'as* of prayer in a mere seventeen days.
89. Ibn Qayyim, *'Uddat al-ṣābirīn*, 80–84.
90. Quoted by Ibn Ḥajar, *Tahdhīb*, 5:438.
91. The term derives from Michel Foucault, "Technologies of the Self," in his *Ethics: Subjectivity and Truth*, ed. Paul Rabinow, trans. Robert Hurley et al. (New York, 1997), 223–251. The impetus for adopting this term here was provided by discussions with Wael Hallaq.

CHAPTER 8

1. Cf. Peters, *Jihad in Classical and Modern Islam*, 6–7; 103 ff.; and his *Islam and Colonialism: The Doctrine of Jihad in Modern History* (The Hague, 1979). Temporally, this excludes Muḥammad b. 'Abd al-Wahhāb (d. 1206/1792), the founder of Wahhābism, whose name and movement often become imbricated in militant discourses. However, militant groups today typically cite the tracts of Ibn Taymiyya and Sayyid Quṭb rather than those of Ibn 'Abd al-Wahhāb as sources of inspiration for their radical ideologies. They also tend to be highly critical of the Saudi government, as will be evident in our following discussion.
2. For the definitive study of *baghy* in Islamic law, see Khaled Abou el Fadl, *Rebellion and Violence in Islamic Law* (Cambridge, UK, 2001).
3. For a lucid discussion of various juridical perspectives on *ḥirāba*, see Sherman Jackson, "Domestic Terrorism in the Islamic Legal Tradition," *The Muslim World* 91 (2001):293–310.
4. The classic study of Ḥasan al-Bannā and the Ikhwān remains Richard P. Mitchell's *The Society of the Muslim Brothers* (New York, 1993). See also Ibrahim Abu Rabi, *Intellectual Origins of Islamic Resurgence in the Modern Arab World* (Albany, NY, 1990), 62–91.
5. Ḥasan al-Bannā, "Risālat al-jihād," in *al-Jihād fī sabīl allāh* (Cairo, 1977), 63–64. An English translation of this work exists: Ḥasan al-Bannā, "*On Jihād*," in *Five Tracts of Ḥasan al-Bannā*, trans. Charles Wendell (Berkeley, CA, 1978). I am only referring to the Arabic original.
6. Al-Bannā, "Risālat al-jihād," 64.
7. Ibid., 64–69.
8. Ibid., 69–79.
9. Ibid., 77.
10. Ibid., 79. This title is obviously a variant of *Mashāri' al-ashwāq ilā maṣāri' al-'ushshāq* by Ibn al-Naḥḥās, previously discussed in chapter 6.
11. Ibid., 80–84.
12. Ibid., 83.
13. He was a student of al-Ḥasan al-Baṣrī and described as a Ṣūfī *shaykh* and preacher; cf. al-Dhahabī, *Mīzān al-i'tidāl fī naqd al-rijāl*, ed. 'Alī Muḥammad Mu'awwaḍ and 'Ādil Aḥmad 'Abd al-Mawjūd (Beirut, 1995), 4:424–425, #5293.

14. Al-Bannā, "Risālat al-jihād," 84.
15. Ibid., 85. Compare this to the view of Augustine, who believed, as part of his just war doctrine, that Christians could lawfully engage in war until there was no one left to resist, a situation that would conduce to peace; see Augustine, *City of God*, bk XV, Chapter Four. As Johannes Pedersen points out in his discussion of war and peace in ancient Israel, "In the olden time peace is not in itself the opposite of war.... Peace consists in complete harmony between friends and victory in the war against enemies...; see his *Israel: Its Life and Culture* (Oxford, 1940), 1:311.
16. Al-Bannā, "Risālat al-jihād," 86–87.
17. Ibid., 87–88.
18. Ibid., 89–90.
19. Ibid., 90.
20. Ibid., 91.
21. For further details, see Charles J. Adams, "Mawdudi and the Islamic State," in *Voices of Resurgent Islam*, ed. John Esposito (Oxford, UK, 1983), 99–133; Seyyed Vali Nasr, *Mawdudi and the Making of Islamic Revivalism* (New York: Oxford University Press, 1996), 9–46; and more recently, Roy Jackson, *Mawlana Mawdudi and Political Islam: Authority and the Islamic State* (New York, 2011).
22. S. Abul A'la Maududi, *Jihad in Islam* (Salimiah, KW, 1977).
23. Maududi, *Jihad*, 5.
24. Ibid., 7.
25. Ibid., 5. See also Mawdudi, *Towards Understanding the Qur'an*, trans. and ed. by Zafar Ishaq Ansari (Leicester, UK, 1988), 1:169, n. 234, where in exegesis of Qur'ān 2:218, he describes *jihād* as having a wider connotation than *qitāl*.
26. Maududi, *Jihad*, 7.
27. Ibid.
28. Ibid., 27.
29. Ibid.
30. Ibid., 6–7.
31. Ibid., 13.
32. Ibid., 10.
33. Ibid., 16.
34. Ibid., 17.
35. Ibid., 23.
36. Ibid., 5. In another work, Mawdudi avers that Muslim refusal or inability to accept this revolutionary charge has ushered in a new era of *Jāhiliyya*, which signifies everything that antedated Islam and is therefore morally worthless in his evaluation; see his *al-Islam wa al-Jahiliyya* ("Islam and the Age of Ignorance") (Beirut, 1980), *passim*.
37. Mawdudi, *Jihad*, 25–26.
38. For further analysis of Mawdudi's views on *jihād* and their influence on contemporary militants in South Asia, see Ayesha Jalal, *Partisans of Allah: Jihad in South Asia* (Cambridge, MA, 2008), 242–301. See also Nasr, *Mawdudi*, 74, where the

author notes that Mawdudi's views on *jihād* softened over the years so that he came to regard military action as a last resort to be undertaken when victory was likely.

39. For a comparative study of Quṭb and Mawdudi, see Leonard Binder, *Islamic Liberalism: A Critique of Development Ideologies* (Chicago, 1988), 170–205.
40. See further Yvonne Haddad, "Sayyid Quṭb: Ideologue of Islamic Revival," in *Voices of Resurgent Islam*, ed. John L. Esposito (New York, 1983), 67–98; Ibrahim Abu Rabi, *Intellectual Origins*, 92–165; Ahmad S. Moussalli, *Radical Islamic Fundamentalism: The Ideological and Political Discourse of Sayyid Quṭb* (Beirut, 1992); John Esposito, *Unholy War: Terror in the Name of Islam* (New York, 2002), 55–64; and more recently John Calvert, *Sayyid Quṭb and the Origins of Radical Islamism* (New York, 2010).
41. Sayyid Quṭb, *Ma'ālim fī 'l-ṭarīq* (Beirut, 1982), 65–66.
42. Ibid., 66–67.
43. Ibid., 71.
44. Ibid., 67; also 85.
45. Ibid., 72–73. For a discussion of Quṭb's understanding of *Jāhiliyya*, which has permeated contemporary hard-line Islamist discourses, see William Shepard, "Sayyed Quṭb's Doctrine of *Jāhiliyya*," *International Journal of Middle East Studies* 35 (2003): 521–545; and Sayed Khatab, *The Political Thought of Sayyid Quṭb: The Theory of Jahiliyya* (Oxford and New York, 2006). See also Yousef Choueiri, *Islamic Fundamentalism* (London, 1990), 140–157, where he points out that Quṭb in his own writings admitted to being influenced by the thinking of Alexis Carrel, the French surgeon and biologist with fascist proclivities who won the Nobel prize for medicine in 1912, and whose writings had been translated into Arabic. Choueiri describes Qutb's conception of *jāhiliyya* as being derived from Carrel's own diagnosis of modern Western society as a relapse into "barbarism" (*la barbarie*). Qutb's notion of a revolutionary vanguard (*ṭalī'a*) may also be traced back to Carrel's conception of "a new elite that would restore humanity to the right path…"; cf. Calvert, *Sayyid Qutb*, 334; Vanessa Martin, *Creating an Islamic State: Khomeini and the Making of a New Iran* (London, 2000), 134. The maverick nature of Qutb's political writings, essentially divorced from the classical Islamic tradition despite his Islamicizing rhetoric, has been further highlighted by Carl Brown, who has remarked, "It cannot be stressed too often just how much Qutb's hardline interpretation departs from the main current of Islamic political thought throughout the centuries"; see his *Religion and State: The Muslim Approach to Politics* (New York, 2000), 156–157.
46. Qutb, *Ma'ālim*, 73–74.
47. Ibid., 89–90.
48. Ibid., 84.
49. Walter Wink has insightfully dealt with redemptive violence within the Christian tradition; see his *The Powers that Be: Theology for a New Millenium* (New York, 1999), esp. 37–62.

50. I am relying on the translation of *al-Farīḍa al-ghā'iba* by Johannes J. G. Jansen in his *The Neglected Duty: The Creed of Sadat's Assassins and Islamic Resurgence in the Middle East* (London, 1986), 160–161; the original Arabic was not available to me.
51. Ibid., 195–197.
52. Ibid., 167–176.
53. Ibid., 163.
54. Ibid., 199–200.
55. Ibid., 192–193. This doctrine of fighting the "near enemy" is ostensibly derived from Qur'an 9:123, which states, "O those who believe—fight those among the unbelievers who are near to you, and let them find hardness in you, and know that God is with those who keep their duty to Him."
56. Jansen, *Neglected Duty*, 185–187.
57. Ibid., 188–190.
58. Ibid., 200–201.
59. Ibid., 216–220. The report attributed to Abū Bakr in which he famously proscribes attacking different groups of civilians, forbids the burning of fruit-bearing trees, and the unnecessary killing of animals, is routinely listed in legal manuals and *siyar* works; see, for example, Mālik b. Anas, *al-Muwaṭṭa'*, ed. Bashshār 'Awad Ma'rūf and Maḥmūd Muḥammad Khalīl (Beirut, 1993), 1: 356–357, #918. Some later jurists attempted to circumvent this absolute proscription by listing exceptions that they considered justified in specific circumstances; for this discussion, see, for example, al-Māwardī, *al-Ḥāwī al-kabīr fī fiqh madhhab al-imām al-shāfi'ī raḍī allāhu 'anhu wa-huwa sharḥ mukhtaṣar al-muzānī*, eds. 'Alī Muḥammad Mu'awwaḍ and 'Ādil Aḥmad 'Abd al-Mawjūd (Beirut, 1994), 14:185–186.
60. Jansen, *Neglected Duty*, 222–225. This is somewhat ironic, considering the fact that some pre-modern jurists were of the opinion that Muslim soldiers should refrain from cutting down trees, etc., in enemy land precisely out of considerations of material gain! See, for example, al-Sarakhsī, *Kitāb al-mabsūṭ*, ed. Muḥammad Ḥasan Muḥammad Ḥasan Ismā'īl al-Shāfi'ī (Beirut, n.d.), 10:37–38.
61. Cf. *Princeton Readings in Islamic Thought: Texts and Contexts from al-Bannā to Bin Laden*, ed. Roxanne L. Euben and Muhammad Qasim Zaman (Princeton, NJ, 2009), 155–162.
62. *Jihād al-nafs aw al-jihād al-akbar*, with an introduction by Hasan Hanafi (Cairo, 1980?).
63. Ibid., 35.
64. See Martin, *Creating an Islamic State*, 105–107, where she describes Khomeini as "third-worldist," "populist," and "Islamist anti-imperialist."
65. Khomeini, *Jihād al-nafs*, 37.
66. Ibid., 90.
67. In his other writings, Khomeini also criticized the British imperialists of three hundred years ago who sought to control Iran, followed by Americans and others, who were "the new imperialists." See, for example, *Islam and Revolution:*

Writings and Declarations of Imam Khomeini, trans. Hamid Algar (Berkeley, CA, 1981), 139.

68. *Islam and Revolution*, 385.
69. Ibid., 148–149.
70. These differences are further developed in his treatise titled *Jang va jihād* (Tehran, 1982).
71. For a study of Qur'anic terms, like *ṭāghūt*, put to new political use by Khomeini, see Saskia Maria Gieling, *Religion and War in Revolutionary Iran* (London, 1999), 74 ff.
72. *Messages to the World: The Statements of Osama Bin Laden*, ed. Bruce Lawrence and trans. James Howarth (London and New York, 2005), 24 ff.
73. See FBIS Report: Compilation of Usama Bin Ladin Statements 1994-January 2004, 14; available at www.fas.org/irp/world/para/ubl-fbis.pdf; last accessed on 11/21/2012.
74. *Messages to the World*, 25.
75. For example, ibid., 93.
76. Ibid., 107.
77. John Kelsay, *Arguing the Just War in Islam* (Cambridge, MA, 2007), 149.
78. For the brief version of this provocative thesis, see Samuel P. Huntington "The Clash of Civilizations?" *Foreign Affairs* 72 (1993): 22–49.
79. Faisal Devji, *Landscapes of the Jihad: Militancy, Morality, Modernity* (Ithaca, NY, 2005), 76.
80. For a comprehensive and insightful account of the rise of al-Qā'ida, see Fawaz A. Gerges, *The Far Enemy: Why Jihad Went Global* (Cambridge, UK, and New York, 2009); for its decline, see id., *The Rise and Fall of al-Qaeda* (Oxford, UK, 2011).
81. Posted on the website http://www.al-hesbah.org; last accessed July 24, 2010. I am grateful to my former student Christopher Anzalone for bringing this essay to my attention.
82. Al-Lībī, *al-Nathr al-jawāhir*, 1.
83. Ibid., 2.
84. Ibid., 13–14.
85. Ibid., 14–15.
86. Ibid., 15.
87. Ibid., 16.
88. Ibid.
89. Ibid., 5–6.
90. Ibid., 6–7. See also the online tract by Abū Baṣīr al-Tartūsī, *al-Jihād wa 'l-siyāsa al-shar'iyya*, available online at www.abubaseer.bizland.com, 37 ff,. where he describes rising up against the "tyrants of the government, unbelief, and apostasy" as a mandatory duty for believers.
91. For a recent exploration of various facets of al-Qaraḍāwī's thought and writings, see Bettina Gräf and Jakob Skovgaard-Petersen, *Global Mufti: The Phenomenon of Yusuf al-Qaradawi* (London, 2009).

92. Yūsuf al-Qaraḍāwī, *Fiqh al-jihād* (Cairo, 2009), 1:52.
93. Ibid., 1:52–54.
94. Ibid., 1:54.
95. Ibid., 1:54–55.
96. He was an important *muḥaddith* and jurist from Kufa and was part of the overall Kufan pietist opposition to the Umayyads; cf. *EI*^{2}, 3:938; van Ess, *Theologie*, 2:286; Cook, *Commanding Right*, 45.
97. Al-Qaraḍāwī, *Fiqh al-jihād*, 1:63.
98. Ibid., 1:64.
99. Ibid.
100. Ibid., 64–65.
101. These chapters have the following titles in the Qur'ān: al-Baqara, al-Anfāl, al-Mu'minīn, al-Ra'd, al-Furqān, al-Dhāriyāt, and al-Insān.
102. Al-Qaraḍāwī, *Fiqh al-jihād*, 1:69.
103. Ibid., 1:70–72.
104. Ibid., 1:73–79.
105. Ibid., 1:79–81. The classical legal theory of *jihād* and its connection to the state and its administrative policies is recognized by al-Qaraḍāwī and further expounded upon in ibid., 1:81–87.
106. Ibid., 1:228. It should be noted that al-Qaraḍāwī wrote a separate, short treatise on the importance of *ṣabr* in the Qur'ān; the title is *al-Ṣabr fī 'l-qur'ān* (Cairo, 1977).
107. Al-Qaraḍāwī, *Fiqh al-jihād*, 1:239.
108. Ibid., 1:240.
109. Ibid., 1:240–243.
110. Ibid., 1:244.
111. Ibid., 1:245.
112. Ibid., 1:245–246.
113. Ibid., 1:255–266.
114. Robert Baer, "The making of a suicide bomber," *The Sunday Times*, Sept. 3, 2006.
115. See also the influential study by Robert Pape, *Dying to Win: The Strategic Logic of Suicide Terrorism* (New York, 2005), 14, where he points out that the historical antecedents of suicide terrorism go back much further in time to the two militant Jewish groups, the Zealots and the Sicarii from the first Christian century, who intended to liberate Judea from Roman occupation.
116. Neil L. Whitehead and Nasser Abufarha, "Suicide, Violence, and Cultural Conceptions of Violence in Palestine," *Social Research* 75 (summer 2008):395–416.
117. Cf. Bernard K. Freamon, "Martyrdom, Suicide, and the Islamic Law of War: A Short Legal History," *Fordham International Law Journal* 27/1 (2003):355–369, where he convincingly points to strong militant Shī'ī influence on contemporary militant Sunnī rationales for martyrdom operations. See further Talal Asad who explores the contested motivations behind suicide terrorism in his *On Suicide Bombing* (New York, 2007), esp. 39–64.

118. Accessed at www.abubaseer.bizland.com on May 11, 2010. Once again, I am grateful to Christopher Anzalone for alerting me to this tract.
119. Abū Baṣīr, *Maḥādhīr*, 1.
120. Ibid., 2–3.
121. Ibid., 3.
122. Ibid., 3–4.
123. Ibid., 4–5.
124. Ibid., 6.
125. Takrūrī, *al-'Amaliyyāt al-istishhādiyya fī 'l-mizān al-fiqhī* (Damascus, 2003), 49–51; also Cook, *Martyrdom*, 150. See also Pape, *Dying to Win*, esp. 38–60, in which he points to primarily political, rather than religious, motivation on the part of suicide bombers, especially under conditions of military occupation, as in the Palestinian occupied territories.
126. Al-Qaraḍāwī et al, *Shubuhāt ḥawla al-'amaliyyat al-istishhādiyya* (Miknas, Morocco, 2002), 6–8; cited in *Princeton Readings in Islamist Thought*, 227–228; see also Kelsay, *Arguing the Just War*, 140–143. Similar views have been expressed by the prominent ethicist James P. Sterba; see, for example, his "Terrorism and International Justice," in *Terrorism and International Justice*, ed. James P. Sterba (Oxford, UK, 2003), 206–228. The unprecedented ethical and moral conundrum presented by Palestinian suicide bombings in the face of continuing violent Israeli occupation is further sensitively explored by Richard Falk in his article, "Azmi Bishara, the Right of Resistance, and the Palestinian Ordeal," *Journal of Palestine Studies* 31 (2002):19–33.
127. Al-Maqdisī, *This is our 'Aqīdah*, second edition, available at www.archive.org, last accessed on May 31, 2010, 13.
128. Ibid.
129. Ibid., 18–19.
130. Emile Durkheim recognized the altruistic nature of suicide carried out for the sake of the good of the larger community in his *Suicide: A Study in Sociology* (New York, 1951), 217–240; cf. also Pape, *Dying to Win*, 171–198. Asad remarks tellingly, "For what needs to be identified here is not simply the willingness to die or to kill but what one makes of death – one's own and that of others;" *On Suicide Bombing*, 95.

CHAPTER 9

1. See the art. "'Abduh, Muḥammad," in EI^3, online (last accessed July 23, 2011). For a monograph-length study, see Mark Sedgwick, *Muhammad Abduh* (Oxford, UK, 2009).
2. Muḥammad Rashīd Riḍā, *Tafsīr al-Qur'ān al-karīm al-mashhūr bi-tafsīr al-manār* (Beirut, 1999), 2:169–170; henceforth referred to in brief as *Tafsīr al-manār*. For a study of this work, see M. A. Zaki Badawi, *The Reformers of Egypt* (London, 1978), chapter 2, 35–95.

3. This sharp rejoinder is clearly directed at a number of Orientalist scholars and Christian missionaries of his day who were prone to making such statements. 'Abduh's interpretation of these views is shared by the later modernist exegete Muhammad Asad, for example, who stresses that Qur'ān 2:190 and the subsequent verses "lay down unequivocally that only self-defence (in the widest sense of the word) makes war permissible for Muslim;" see his *The Message of the Qur'ān*, 51, n. 167. See also our earlier discussion of these verses in chapter 2.
4. Riḍā, *Tafsīr al-manār*, 2:170–171. Qur'ān 29:2 states, "Do the people reckon that they will be left alone after saying that they have believed and that they will not be put to the test?"
5. Ibid., 2:171.
6. Ibid., 2:171–172. Similar views are expressed by the Lebanese Imāmī *marja'* Muḥammad Ḥusayn Faḍl Allāh (d. 2010); in regard to Qur'ān 2:193 in particular, he comments that the verse is not concerned with the cessation of unbelief, but with wrongdoing and aggression (*al-ẓulm wa-'l-'udwān*); see his *Tafsīr min waḥy al-qur'ān* (Beirut, 1998), 4:74–83.
7. Riḍā, *Tafsīr al-manār*, 10:161–162.
8. This verse states, "You will find the closest in affection to those who believe are those who say we are Christians."
9. Riḍā, *Tafsīr al-manār*, 10:162–163.
10. Ibid., 10:171–175.
11. Ibid., 10:257–279.
12. Ibid., 10:279.
13. For example, Emile Tyan states that "The notion [sc. *jihād*] stems from the fundamental principle of the universality of Islam: this religion, along with the temporal power which it implies, ought to embrace the whole universe, if necessary by force"; see art. "Djihād," *EI*[2], 2:538. Such views can be found already in early Christian apologetic literature, such as the *Kitāb al-Burhān* of 'Ammār al-Baṣrī from the third/ninth century; see the discussion of this work by Sydney Griffith, 'Ammār al-Baṣrī's *Kitāb al-Burhān*: Christian *Kalām* in the First Abbasid Century," *Le Muséon* 96 (1983):164–165. After September 11, 2001, some of these views have mutated into extremist statements of wholesale denunciation of Islam itself and its alleged exclusive penchant for violence.
14. Many of these points are also made strenuously by other modern Muslim scholars, such as Abū Zahra, *al-'Alaqāt al-dawliyya fī 'l-islām* (Cairo, 1964), 47:52; Sobhi Mahmassani, "The Principles of International Law in the Light of Islamic Doctrine," *Recueil des Cours* 117 (1966):249–279; Tawfiq Wahba, *Al-Ḥarb fī 'l-islām wa fī 'l-ijtimā' al-dawlī al-mu'āṣir* (Cairo, 1973), 21 ff.; Wahba al-Zuḥaylī, *Āthār al-ḥarb fī 'l-fiqh al-islāmī: dirāsa muqārana* (Damascus, 1982), 503; al-Ghunaymī, *Qānūn al-salām fī 'l-islām* (Alexandria, 1988), 129 ff.; and Hilmi M. Zawati, *Is Jihād a Just War? War, Peace, and Human Rights under Islamic and Public International Law* (Lewiston, NY, 2001), esp. 38–39.

15. Riḍā, *Tafsīr al-manār*, 10:280.
16. Ibid., 10:282–284.
17. Jansen, *The Neglected Duty*, 54–55.
18. Published by Dār Thābit in Cairo, 1984.
19. Al-Bannā, *al-Farīḍa*, 7–8.
20. For a discussion of this work, see Sherman Jackson, *On the Boundaries of Theological Tolerance in Islam: Abū Ḥāmid al-Ghazālī's* Fayṣal al-Tafriqa Bayna al-Islām wa al-Zandaqa (Oxford, UK, 2002).
21. Al-Bannā, *al-Farīḍa*, 23–27.
22. Ibid., 28.
23. This is described in some detail in ibid., 28–30.
24. Ibid., 30–33.
25. Ibid., 35–37.
26. Ibid., 53.
27. Ibid.
28. Ibid., 54–57.
29. Ibid., 58.
30. Ibid., 60–61.
31. Ibid., 62–69.
32. Similar views are expressed by Abū Zahra, "Naẓariyyat al-ḥarb fī 'l-islām," *al-Majalla al-miṣriyya li 'l-qānūn al-dawlī* (1958), 33; and Wahba al-Zuḥaylī, *Āthār al-ḥarb*, 192–196.
33. Al-Bannā, *al-Farīḍa*, 69 ff.
34. Ibid., 89.
35. For more details, see Andreas Christmann, "Islamic Scholar and Religious Leader: Shaikh Muhammad Sa'id Ramadan al-Buti," in *Islam and Modernity*, ed. John Cooper et al. (London and New York, 1998), 57–81.
36. Muḥammad Sa'īd Ramaḍān al-Būṭī, *al-Jihād fī 'l-islām* (Damascus, 1993), 19–20.
37. Ibid., 20–21.
38. Ibid., 21–22.
39. Ibid., 23–24.
40. Ibid., 26.
41. Ibid., 26–27.
42. Ibid., 27; see also 42–46 for an explication of *da'wā* and its importance.
43. Ibid., 46–47.
44. Ibid., 48–52.
45. Ibid., 52–53.
46. Ibid., 52–54.
47. Ibid., 54–57.
48. Ibid., 58–61.
49. Ibid., 62–63.

50. Ibid., 63–73, for al-Būṭī's fairly lengthy critique of Islamists. The rest of al-Būṭī's book offers further details or mere repetitions of these main points that we have discussed so far and that need not concern us here.
51. Ibid., 197.
52. Ibid., 232.
53. Ibid., 237.
54. Ibid., 83 ff.
55. Ibid., 227 ff.
56. Ibid., 242.
57. 'Alī Jum'a, *al-Jihād fī 'l-islām* (Cairo, 2005).
58. Ibid., 3–4.
59. Ibid., 4–5.
60. Ibid.
61. Ibid., 9–12.
62. Ibid., 13–15.
63. Ibid., 14.
64. Ibid., 15.
65. Ibid., 22.
66. Ibid., 22–24.
67. Ibid., 35–41.
68. Ibid., 45–70.
69. Ibid., 70–71.
70. Ibid., 77.
71. For an insightful study of Abdul Ghaffar Khan's movement, see Robert C. Johansen, "Radical Islam and Nonviolence: A Case Study of Religious Empowerment and Constraint among Pashtuns," *Journal of Peace Research* 34 (1997):53–71. For a monograph-length study, see Eknath Easwaran, *A Man to Match His Mountains: Badshah Khan Nonviolent Soldier of Islam* (Petaluma, CA, 1984).
72. Translated by Munzer A. Absi and H Hilwani (Damascus, 2002) from the original Arabic. This and other works by Sa'īd on the theme of nonviolence in Arabic, as well as the works of Fethullah Gülen in Turkish, belie the crudely polemical remark made by Cook in his *Understanding Jihad*, 165–166, that "Today it is certain that no Muslim, writing in a non-Western language (such as Arabic, Persian, Urdu) would ever make claims that jihad is primarily nonviolent or has been superseded by the spiritual jihad." He then goes on to give gratuitous offense by stating that only Western and Muslim apologists resort to such efforts "to present Islam in the most innocuous manner possible."
73. Translation in Sa'īd, *Non-Violence*, 27. See further Sa'īd's *Madhhab ibn Ādam al-awwal* (Damascus, 1966); and *Kun ka-ibn Ādam* (Beirut, 1997).
74. Sa'īd, *Non-Violence*, 35.
75. Ibid., 34.
76. Ibid., 37.

77. Ibid., 28–29.
78. Ibid., 78.
79. Ibid., 37–57.
80. Ibid., 62.
81. Ibid., 74.
82. Ibid., 77–79.
83. Ibid., 111.
84. Ibid., 114.
85. Ibid., 124–25.
86. Cf. the article by Irfan A. Omar, "Islam and the Other: the Ideal Vision of Mawlana Wahiduddin Khan," *Journal of Ecumenical Studies* 36 (1999):423–439.
87. Published in New Delhi, 2002.
88. Khan, *True Jihad*, 13–16.
89. Ibid., 16–23.
90. Ibid., 25.
91. Ibid., 26.
92. Ibid., 27.
93. Ibid., 23–38.
94. Ibid., 39.
95. Ibid., 39–40.
96. Ibid.
97. Ibid., 42–43.
98. Ibid., 44–45.
99. Ibid., 46–48. For the importance of *ṣabr* as a basic principle of nonviolence and peacebuilding, see also Mohammed Abu-Nimer, *Nonviolence and Peace Building in Islam: Theory and Practice* (Gainesville, 2003), 71–73.
100. Khan, *True Jihad*, 49–52.
101. Ibid., 53–58.
102. Ibid., 86.
103. Ibid., 90–91.
104. Ibid., 93–94.
105. Ibid., 101.
106. Ibid., 105.
107. Ibid., 105–108.
108. For an appraisal of the Gülen movement as it relates to official Turkish secularism, see M. Hakan Yavuz and John L. Esposito, *Turkish Islam and the Secular State: the Gülen Movement* (Syracuse, NY, 2003). For an account of its peacebuilding activities, see *Islam and Peacebuilding: Gülen Movement Initiatives*, ed. John Esposito and Ihsan Yilmaz (New York, 2010).
109. M. Fethullah Gülen, *Toward a Global Civilization of Love & Tolerance* (Somerset, NJ, 2004), 171.
110. Ibid.

111. Ibid.
112. M. Fethullah Gülen, *Key Concepts in the Practice of Sufism* (Fairfax, VA, 1999), 100.
113. Ibid., 102.
114. Ibid.
115. Ibid., 103.
116. Ibid., 100.
117. Reprinted in Gülen, *Toward a Global Civilization*, 179–183.
118. For the importance of forgiveness in the ethics of nonviolence and peacebuilding, see also Abu-Nimer, *Nonviolence*, 67–69.
119. Gülen, *Toward a Global Civilization*, 182.
120. Ibid., 178.
121. From the recording, "The Verdicts of the Scholars concerning Assassinations and Bombings," found on the website www.IslamAgainstExtremism.com, last accessed on November 25, 2011. The translation has been slightly modified to make it more comprehensible.
122. Shaykh Ibn Bāz, *Kayfa nu'ālij wāqi'anā al-alīm*, p. 119, as quoted in *The Saudi Gazette*, at www.saudigazette.com.sa, last accessed on November 25, 2011.*123 Al-Sharq al-Awsaṭ*, April 21, 2001.
124. Muḥammad Ṭāhir-ul-Qadrī, *Fatwa on Suicide Bombings & Terrorism*, 2010, available online at www.minhaj.org, last accessed on June 1, 2010.
125. Ibid., 35–36.
126. Ibid., 38.
127. Ibid., 42.
128. Ibid., 44.
129. Ibid., 45.
130. Ibid., 48; translation as given by Qadrī.
131. Ibid., 51.
132. Ibid.
133. Ibid., 52.

CONCLUSION

1. In this context, it is useful to bring up Ronald Bainton's definition of "holy war" in relation to the Crusades as one that was "fought under the auspices of the church or some inspired religious leader, not on behalf of justice conceived in terms of life and property, but on behalf of an ideal, the Christian faith"; see his *Christian Attitudes toward War and Peace* (Nashville, TN, 1986), 14.
2. Albrecht Noth has insightfully observed that the concept of a "holy war" was lacking at the outset of the conquests, although later the concept of what he terms a "holy struggle" would emerge; see his *Heiliger Krieg und Heiliger Kampf in Islam und Christentum* (Bonn, 1966), 41–42; 87–88; 139–148.
3. Cf. Afsaruddin, *Excellence and Precedence*, passim.

Selected Bibliography

PRIMARY SOURCES

'Abd al-Razzāq al-Ṣan'ānī. *Al-Muṣannaf*. Ed. Ayman Naṣr al-Dīn al-Azharī. Beirut, 2000.

______. *Tafsīr 'Abd al-Razzāq*. Ed. Maḥmūd Muḥammad 'Abduh. Beirut, 1999.

Abū Dā'ūd al-Sijistānī. *Ṣaḥīḥ Sunan Abī Dā'ūd*. Ed. Muḥammad Nāṣir al-Dīn al-Albānī. Riyadh, 1989.

Abū 'Ubayd al-Qāsim b. Sallām. *Abū 'Ubayd al-Qāsim b. Sallām's* K. al-nāsikh wa-l-mansūkh. Ed. John Burton. Cambridge, UK, 1987.

Al-'Ayyashī, Muḥammad b. Mas'ūd. *Tafsīr*. Ed. Qism al-dirāsāt al-islāmiyya; Mu'assasat al-ba'tha. Qum, 1320.

Al-Balādhurī, Aḥmad b. Yaḥyā. *Futūḥ al-buldān*. Ed. M. J. de Goeje. Leiden, 1866, repr. Leiden, 1968.

Al-Bukhārī, Muḥammad b.Ismā'īl. *Ṣaḥīḥ*. Ed. Qāsim al-Shammā'ī al-Rifā'ī. Beirut, n.d.

Al-Dhahabī, Shams al-Dīn. *Mīzān al-i'tidāl fī naqd al-rijāl*. Ed. 'Alī Muḥammad Mu'awwaḍ and 'Ādil Aḥmad 'Abd al-Mawjūd. Beirut, 1995.

Furāt b. Ibrāhīm, *Tafsīr Furāt al-Kūfī*. Ed. Muḥammad al-Kāẓim. Beirut, 1992.

Al-Ghazālī, Abū Ḥāmid Muḥammad. *Iḥyā' 'ulūm al-dīn*. Ed. 'Abd Allāh al-Khālidī. Beirut, n.d.

Hūd b. Muḥakkam al-Huwwārī. *Tafsīr kitāb allāh al- 'azīz*. Ed. Balḥāj b. Sa'īd Sharīfī. Beirut, 1990.

Ibn Abī 'Āṣim, Aḥmad b. 'Amr. *Kitāb al-jihād*. Ed. Abū 'Abd al-Raḥmān. Damascus, 1989.

Ibn Abī 'l-Dunyā , 'Abd Allāh b. Muḥammad, *Al-Ṣabr wa-'l-thawāb 'alayhi*. Beirut, 1997.

Ibn Abī Shayba, 'Abd Allāh b. Muḥammad. *Al-Kitāb al-muṣannaf fī 'l-aḥādīth wa-'l-āthār*. Ed. Muḥammad 'Abd al-Salām Shāhīn. Beirut, 1995.

Ibn Abī Zamanīn, Muḥammad b. 'Abd Allāh. *Kitāb qudwat al-ghāzī*. Ed. 'Ā'isha al-Sulaymānī. Beirut, 1989.

Ibn 'Asākir, 'Alī b. al-Ḥasan. *Ta'rīkh madīnat dimashq*. Beirut, 1995.

Ibn Ḥajar al-'Asqalānī. *Tahdhīb al-tahdhīb*. Ed. Khalīl Ma'mūn Shīḥā et al. Beirut, 1996.

Ibn Hishām, 'Abd al-Malik. *Al-Sīra al-nabawiyya*. Ed. Suhayl Zakkār. Beirut, 1992.

Ibn al-Jawzī, 'Abd al-Raḥmān. *Kitāb al-ḍu'afā' wa-'l-matrūkīn*. Ed. Abū 'l-Fidā' 'Abd Allāh al-Qāḍī. Beirut, 1986.

Ibn Kathīr, Ismā' īl b. 'Umar. *Kitāb al-ijtihād fī ṭalab al-jihād*. Ed. 'Abd Allāh 'Abd al-Raḥīm 'Asilan. Riyadh, 1405/1985.

______. *Tafsīr*. Beirut, 1990.

Ibn Māja, Muḥammad b. Yazīd. *Al-Sunan*. Ed. Muḥammad Nāsir al-Dīn al-Albānī. Riyadh, 1998.

Ibn al-Mubārak, 'Abd Allāh. *Kitāb al-jihād*. Beirut, 1988.

Ibn al-Naḥḥās, Aḥmad b. Ibrāhīm. *Mashāri' al-ashwāq ilā maṣāri' al 'ushshāq wa-muthīr al-gharām ilā dār al-salām*. Beirut, 2002.

Ibn Qayyim al-Jawziyya. *'Uddat al-ṣābirīn wa-dhakhīrat al-shākirīn*. Ed. Muḥammad 'Alī Quṭb. Beirut, n.d.

Ibn Sa'd, Muḥammad. *Al-Ṭabaqāt al-kubrā*. Beirut, 1998.

Ibn Taymiyya, Taqī al-Dīn. *Qā'ida mukhtaṣara fī qitāl al-kuffār wa-muhādanatihim wa-taḥrīm qatlihim li-mujarrad kufrihim*. Ed. 'Abd al- 'Azīz b. 'Abd Allāh b. Ibrāhīm. Riyadh, 2004.

Ibn Wahb, 'Abd Allāh. *Al-Ǧāmi': tafsīr al-Qur'ān*. Ed. Miklos Muranyi. Wiesbaden, Germany, 1993.

Al-Jāḥiẓ, 'Amr b. Baḥr. *Risālat al-'uthmāniyya*. Ed. 'Abd al-Salām Hārūn. Cairo, 1955.

Mālik b. Anas. *Al-Muwaṭṭa'*. Ed. Bashshār 'Awad Ma'rūf and Maḥmūd Muḥammad Khalīl. Beirut, 1993.

Mujāhid b. Jabr. *Tafsīr Mujāhid*. Ed. Abū Muḥammad al-Asyūṭī. Beirut, 2005.

Muqātil b. Sulaymān. *Tafsīr Muqātil b. Sulaymān*. Ed. 'Abd Allāh Maḥmūd Shiḥāta. Beirut, 2002.

Muslim b. Ḥajjāj. *Ṣaḥīḥ*. Beirut, 1995.

Al-Nasafī, Abū 'l-Mu'īn. *Ǧihād*. Ms. Bibliothèque Nationale de France. Arabe, 4589.

Al-Nasā'ī, Abū 'Abd al-Raḥmān. *Ṣaḥīḥ Sunan al-Nasā'ī*. Ed. Nāṣir al-Dīn al-Albānī. Beirut, 1988.

Al-Qummī, 'Alī b. Ibrāhīm. *Tafsīr Qummī*. Beirut, 1991.

Al-Qurṭubī, Muḥammad. *Al-Jāmi' li-aḥkām al-qur'ān*. Beirut, 2001.

Al-Rāzī, Fakhr al-Dīn. *Al-Tafsīr al-kabīr*. Beirut, 1999.

Riḍā, Muḥammad Rashīd. *Tafsīr al-Qur'ān al-karīm al-mashhūr bi-tafsīr al-manār*. Beirut, 1999.

Al-Sulamī, Abū 'Abd al-Raḥmān. *Ziyādāt ḥaqā'iq al-tafsīr*. Ed. Gerhard Böwering. Beirut, 1995.

Al-Ṭabarī, Muḥammad b. Jarīr. *Jāmi' al-bayān fī tafsīr al-qur'ān*. Beirut, 1997.

Al-Tirmidhī, Abū ʿĪsā. *Al-Jāmiʿ al-Ṣaḥīḥ*. Ed. Kamāl Yūsuf al-Ḥūt. Beirut, n.d.

Al-Wāḥidī, ʿAlī b. Aḥmad. *Al-Wasīṭ fī tafsīr al-qur'ān al-majīd*. Ed. ʿĀdil Aḥmad ʿAbd al-Mawjūd et al. Beirut, 1994.

Al-Zamakhsharī, Maḥmūd b. ʿUmar. *Al-Kashshāf ʿan haqā'iq ghawāmiḍ al-tanzīl wa-ʿuyūn al-aqāwīl fī wujūh al-ta'wīl*. Ed. ʿĀdil Aḥmad ʿAbd al-Mawjūd and ʿAlī Muḥammad Muʿawwaḍ. Riyadh, 1998.

SECONDARY WORKS

Abou El Fadl, Khaled. *Rebellion and Violence in Islamic Law*. Cambridge, UK, 2001.

Abu-Nimer, Mohammed. *Nonviolence and Peace Building in Islam: Theory and Practice* Gainesville, 2003.

Abu Rabi, Ibrahim. *Intellectual Origins of Islamic Resurgence in the Modern Arab World*. Albany, NY, 1990.

Abū Zahra. *Al- ʿAlaqāt al-dawliyya fī 'l-islām*. Cairo, 1964.

Adams, Charles J. "Mawdudi and the Islamic State," in *Voices of Resurgent Islam*. Ed. John Esposito. Oxford, UK, 1983.

Afsaruddin, Asma. *Excellence and Precedence: Medieval Islamic Discourse on Legitimate Leadership*. Leiden, 2002.

______. "The Excellences of the Qur'an: Textual Sacrality and the Organization of Early Islamic Society," *Journal of the American Oriental Society 122* (2002):1–24.

Asad, Muhammad. *The Message of the Qur'ān*. Bristol, UK, 2003.

Asad, Talal. *On Suicide Bombing*. New York, 2007.

Al-Bannā, Ḥasan. "Risālat al-jihād," in *al-Jihād fī sabīl allāh*. Cairo, 1977.

Blankinship, Khalid Yahya. *The End of the Jihâd State: The Reign of Hishām Ibn ʿAbd al-Malik and the Collapse of the Umayyads*. New York, 1994.

Bonner, Michael. "Some Observations concerning the Early Development of Jihad on the Arab-Byzantine Frontier," *Studia Islamica* 75 (1992):5–31.

______. *Aristocratic Violence and Holy War: Studies in the Jihad and the Arab-Byzantine Frontier*. New Haven, CT, 1996.

______. *Jihad in Islamic History*. Princeton, NJ, 2006.

Bosworth, C. Edmund . "Byzantium and Syrian Frontier in the early ʿAbbasid Period," in *Proceedings of the Fifth International Conference on the History of Bilād al-Shām, Amman 1410/1990*. Ed. M. A. al-Bakhit and R. Schick. Amman, 1991.

Brooks, E. W. "Byzantines and Arabs in the time of the early ʿAbbasids," *English Historical Review 15* (1900):728–747 and *16* (1901):84–92

Al-Būṭī, Muḥammad Saʿīd Ramaḍān. *Al-Jihād fī 'l-islām*. Damascus, 1993.

Calvert, John. *Sayyid Quṭb and the Origins of Radical Islamism*. New York, 2010.

Choueiri, Yousef. *Islamic Fundamentalism*. London, 1990.

Christmann, Andreas. "Islamic Scholar and Religious Leader: Shaikh Muhammad Saʿid Ramadan al-Buti," in *Islam and Modernity*. Ed. John Cooper et al. London and New York, 1998.

Cook, David. *Martyrdom in Islam*. Cambridge, UK, 2007.

Cook, Michael. *Commanding Right and Forbidding Wrong in Islamic Thought.* Cambridge, UK, 2000.

Al-Dawoody, Ahmed. *The Islamic Law of War: Justifications and Regulations.* New York, 2011.

Devji, Faisal. *Landscapes of the Jihad: Militancy, Morality, Modernity.* Ithaca, NY, 2005.

Donner, Fred McGraw. *The Early Islamic Conquests.* Princeton, NJ, 1981.

______. *Muhammad and the Believers: At the Origins of Islam.* Cambridge, MA, 2010

Encyclopaedia of Islam. New edition. Ed. C. E. Bosworth et al. Leiden, 1980–1997.

Encyclopaedia of Islam. Third edition. Ed. Gudrun Krämer et al. Leiden, 2007–.(also available online).

Encyclopaedia of the Qur'ān. Ed. Jane Dammen McAuliffe. Leiden, 2001–2006.

Gerges, Fawaz A. *The Rise and Fall of al-Qaeda.* Oxford, UK, 2011.

Gülen, M. Fetullah. *Key Concepts in the Practice of Sufism.* Fairfax, VA, 1999.

______. *Toward a Global Civilization of Love & Tolerance.* Somerset, NJ, 2004.

Hillenbrand, Carole. *The Crusades: Islamic Perspectives.* New York, 2000.

Izutsu, Toshihiko. *Ethico-Religious Concepts in the Qur'ān.* Montreal and Kingston, 2002.

Jackson, Roy. *Mawlana Mawdudi and Political Islam: Authority and the Islamic State.* New York, 2011.

Jansen, Johannes J. G. *The Neglected Duty: The Creed of Sadat's Assassins and Islamic Resurgence in the Middle East.* London, 1986.

Jum'a, 'Alī. *Al-Jihād fī 'l-islām.* Cairo, 2005.

Kelsay, John. *Arguing the Just War in Islam.* Cambridge, MA, 2007.

Kennedy, Hugh. *The Armies of the Caliphs.* London and New York, 2001.

______. *The Great Arab Conquests: How the Spread of Islam Changed the World We Live In.* Philadelphia, 2007.

Khadduri, Majid. *War and Peace in the Law of Islam.* Baltimore, MD, 1955.

______. *The Islamic Law of Nations: Shaybānī's* Siyar. Baltimore, MD, 1966.

Khan, Wahiduddin. *The True Jihad: The Concept of Peace, Tolerance and Non-Violence.* New Delhi, 2002.

Khomeini, Ruhollah. *Islam and Revolution: Writings and Declarations of Imam Khomeini.* Trans. Hamid Algar. Berkeley, CA, 1981.

______. *Jihād al-nafs aw al-jihād al-akbar.* Introduction by Hasan Hanafi. Cairo, 1980(?).

Lucas, Scott C. *Constructive Critics,* Ḥadīth *Literature, and the Articulation of Sunnī Islam.* Leiden, 2004.

Al-Maqdisī, Abū Muḥammad 'Āṣim. *This is our 'Aqīdah.* Second edition. Available at www.archive.org. Last accessed on May 31, 2010

Martin, Vanessa. *Creating an Islamic State: Khomeini and the Making of a New Iran.* London, 2000.

Maududi, S. Abul A'la. *Jihad in Islam.* Salimiah, KW, 1977.

_______. *Towards Understanding the Qur'an*. Trans. and ed. Zafar Ishaq Ansari. Leicester, UK, 1988.

Messages to the World: The Statements of Osama Bin Laden. Ed. Bruce Lawrence and trans. James Howarth. London and New York, 2005.

Morabia, Alfred. *Le Ǧihâd dans l'Islam médiéval: Le "combat sacré" des origines au XIIe siècle*. Paris, 1993.

Mottahedeh, Roy, and Ridwan al-Sayyid, "The Idea of the Jihad in Islam before the Crusades," in *The Crusades from the Perspective of Byzantium and the Muslim World*. Ed. Angeliki E. Laiou and Roy Parviz Mottahedeh. Washington, DC, 2001.

Nasr, Seyyed Vali. *Mawdudi and the Making of Islamic Revivalism*. New York, 1996.

Pape, Robert A. *Dying to Win: The Strategic Logic of Suicide Terrorism*. New York, 2005.

Peters, Rudolph. *Jihad in Classical and Modern Islam*. First edition. Princeton, NJ, 1996.

Princeton Readings in Islamic Thought: Texts and Contexts from al-Bannā to Bin Laden. Ed. Roxanne L. Euben and Muhammad Qasim Zaman. Princeton, NJ, 2009.

Al-Qaraḍāwī, Yūsuf. *Fiqh al-jihād*. Cairo, 2009.

Quṭb, Sayyid. *Ma'ālim fī 'l-ṭarīq*. Beirut, 1982.

Saleh, Walid. "The last of the Nishapuri School of *Tafsīr*: al-Wāḥidī (d. 486/1076) and His Significance in the History of Qur'anic Exegesis," *Journal of the American Oriental Society* 126 (2006): 223–244.

Sa'īd, Jawdat. *Non-Violence: The Basis of Settling Disputes in Islam*. Trans. Munzer A. Absi and H Hilwani. Damascus, 2002.

Sezgin, Fuat. *Geschichte des arabischen Schrifttums*. Leiden, 1967–1984.

Shaltūt, Maḥmūd. *Tafsīr al-qur'ān al-karīm: al-ajzā' al-'ashara al-ūlā*. Beirut, 1983,

Sizgorich, Thomas. *Violence and Belief in Late Antiquity: Militant Devotion in Christianity and Islam*. Philadelphia, PA, 2009.

Ṭāhir-ul-Qadrī, Muḥammad. *Fatwa on Suicide Bombings & Terrorism*, 2010. Available online at www.minhaj.org.

Al-Tartūsī, Abū Baṣīr. *Al-Jihād wa 'l-siyāsa al-shar'īyya*. Available online at www.abubaseer.bizland.com.

Van Ess, Josef. *Theologie und Gesellschaft im 2. Und 3. Jahrhundert Hidschra*. Berlin and New York, 1991.

Wahba, Tawfīq. *Al-Ḥarb fī 'l-islām wa fī 'l-ijtimā' al-dawlī al-mu'āṣir*. Cairo, 1973.

Wensinck, A. J. "The oriental doctrine of the martyrs," in *Semietische Studiën uit de nalatenschap*. Leiden, 1941.

_______. *Concordance et indices de la traditions musulmane*. Leiden, 1988.

Al-Zuḥaylī, Wahba. *Āthār al-ḥarb fī 'l-fiqh al-islāmī: dirāsa muqārana*. Damascus, 1982.

Index

Index of Qur'anic Verses